Revised Ninth Edition

Flea Market Trader

Edited by
Sharon & Bob Huxford

COLLECTOR BOOKS
A Division of Schroeder Publishing Co., Inc.

The current values in this book should be used only as a guide. They are not intended to set prices, which vary from one section of the country to another. Auction prices as well as dealer prices vary greatly and are affected by condition as well as demand. Neither the Editors nor the Publisher assumes responsibility for any losses that might be incurred as a result of consulting this guide.

Searching For A Publisher?

We are always looking for knowledgeable people considered to be experts within their fields. If you feel that there is a real need for a book on your collectible subject and have a large comprehensive collection, contact us.

COLLECTOR BOOKS
P.O. Box 3009
Paducah, Kentucky 42002-3009

COVER INFORMATION

Heavenly Blue Wedding paper dolls, uncut, M, $9.00; Carlton Rocket Bubble Gum Dispenser, 22" tall, $225.00; Squibb's Bouquet Talcum tin, 6", $6.00; Amber glass bead necklace, 16" long, $8.00; Wooden alphabet blocks, 1¼", $1.00 each; Postcards, pansy & parrot hello, $4.00 each; 6" head vase, lady w/fan, $48.50; Tumbling Blocks quilt, made in 1965 w/1950s material, $450.00; Cuckoo wall pocket, $12.00; Bird house wall pocket, $12.00; Cat planter, pottery, 9" tall, $15.00; Musical light-up church, plastic, plays 'Silent Night,' $35.00; Ruby juice glass, 3¼" tall, $8.00; Ruby stemmed glass, 5½" tall, $12.50.

Additional copies of this book may be ordered from:

COLLECTOR BOOKS
P. O. Box 3009
Paducah, Kentucky 42002-3009

@ $12.95. Add $2.00 for postage and handling.

Copyright: Schroeder Publishing Company, Inc., 1994

Printed by IMAGE GRAPHICS, INC., Paducah, Kentucky

INTRODUCTION

The Flea Market Trader is a unique price guide, geared specifically for the convenience of the flea market shopper. Several categories have been included that are not often found in general price guides, while others on antiques not usually seen at flea markets have been omitted. The new categories will serve to introduce you to collectibles that are currently coming on, the best and often the only source for which is the market place. As all of us who religiously pursue the circuits are aware, flea markets are the most exciting places in the world to shop; but unless you're well-informed on current values those 'really great' buys remain on the table. Like most pursuits in life, preparation has its own rewards; and it is our intention to provide you with the basic tool of education and awareness toward that end. But please bear in mind that the prices in this guide are meant to indicate only general values. Many factors determine actual selling prices; values vary from one region to another, dealers pay various wholesale prices for their wares, and your bargaining skill is important too.

We have organized our listings into general categories for easy use; if you have trouble locating an item, refer to the index. Unless another condition code is present in the description line, the values we have suggested reflect prices of items in mint condition. NM stands for minimal damage, VG indicates that the item will bring 40% to 60% of its mint price, and EX should be somewhere between the two. Glassware is assumed clear unless a color is noted. Only generally accepted abbreviations have been used.

This is our first full-color edition; we hope you enjoy the photos. We would like to take this opportunity to thank each author, dealer, and auction house who allowed us to use their photographs.

The Editors

3

PHOTO CREDITS

Advertising Playing Cards, An Identification & Value Guide, Everett Grist.

American Trade Catalogs, Don Fredgant.

An Illustrated Value Guide to Cookie Jars, Ermagene Westfall.

Antique Brass, Identification & Values, Mary Frank Gaston.

Bedroom & Bathroom Glassware of the Depression Years, Margaret & Kenn Whitmyer.

Black Collectibles Sold in America, P.J. Gibbs.

Blue & White Stoneware, Kathryn McNerney.

Blue Willow, Identification & Value Guide, Mary Frank Gaston.

Character Toys & Collectibles, First & Second Series, David Longest.

Children's Glass Dishes, China & Furniture, Doris Anderson Lechler.

Christmas Collectibles, Margaret & Kenn Whitmyer.

Collectible Glassware From the 40s, 50s & 60s, Gene Florence.

Collectible Male Action Figures, Paris & Susan Manos.

Collecting Royal Haeger, Lee Garmon & Doris Frizell.

Collector's Encyclopedia of California Pottery, Jack Chipman.

Collector's Encyclopedia of Fiesta, Sharon & Bob Huxford.

Collector's Encyclopedia of Fry Glass, H.C. Fry Glass Society.

Collector's Encyclopedia of Geisha Girl Porcelain, Elyce Litts.

Collector's Encyclopedia of Hall China, Margaret & Kenn Whitmyer.

Collector's Encyclopedia of McCoy Pottery, Sharon & Bob Huxford.

Collector's Encyclopedia of Occupied Japan Collectibles, Third Series, Gene Florence.

Collector's Guide to Antique Radios, Marty & Sue Bunis.

Collector's Guide to Art Deco, Mary Frank Gaston.

Collector's Guide to Country Baskets, Don & Carol Raycraft.

Collector's Guide to Country Store Antiques, Don & Carol Raycraft.

Collector's Guide to TootsieToys, David E. Richter.

Covered Animal Dishes, Everett Grist.

Elegant Glassware of the Depression Era, Gene Florence.

Goldstein's Coca-Cola Collectibles, published by Collector Books.

Guide to Collecting Cookbooks, Colonel Bob Allen.

Head Vases, Identification & Values, Kathleen Cole.

Liddle Kiddles Dolls & Accessories, Tamela Storm & Debra Van Dyke.

Modern Collector's Dolls, Fifth Series, Pat Smith.

Modern Toys, American Toys 1930–1980, Linda Baker.

Phoenix Bird China, Debra Hadley.

Pocket Guide to Depression Glass, Gene Florence.

Salt & Pepper Shakers, Second Edition, Helen Guarnaccia.

Shoes of Glass, Libby Yalom.

Standard Encyclopedia of Carnival Glass, Bill Edwards.

Stern's Guide to Disney Collectibles, Michael Stern.

Toys, Antiques & Collectibles, David Longest.

50 Years of Fashion Jewelry, Lillian Baker.

ABC Plates

Popular in the 1800s as well as the early years of this century, plates with the ABCs in their borders encouraged children toward learning their letters even during meal time. They were made from a variety of materials, but examples in earthenware with a colorfully-printed central motif are most collectible, especially those dealing with sports, transportation, or a famous person, place, or thing.

Crusoe Rescues Harry, Staffordshire, 7", $110.00.

Bowl, ceramic, girl & boy playing doctor, scalloped, 8½" **70.00**
Mug, ceramic, Jack in the Corner, embossed alphabet, Staffordshire **165.00**
Mug, glass, twig handle **75.00**
Plate, ceramic, blind girl, multicolored transfer, 5¾", EX .**125.00**
Plate, ceramic, boys crossing stile, Staffordshire **80.00**
Plate, ceramic, cats in cherry tree, black transfer, 6", EX ..**145.00**
Plate, ceramic, clock face, brown transfer, RN #1752, 8" ..**45.00**
Plate, ceramic, dandies riding bucking horses, Staffordshire, 7⅛" **145.00**

Plate, ceramic, dog chasing bird, black transfer, Staffordshire, 7⅝" **60.00**
Plate, ceramic, Miss Muffet, blue transfer, England **75.00**
Plate, ceramic, organ grinder, Staffordshire, 8¼" **40.00**
Plate, ceramic, Rule of Three, Staffordshire, 8" **195.00**
Plate, ceramic, seal hunters, Elsmore, 7" **150.00**
Plate, ceramic, Sioux Indian Chief, brown transfer, 7⅜" **130.00**
Plate, glass, ducks w/ducklings, 6" **50.00**
Plate, glass, elephant w/howdah & riders, 6" **70.00**
Plate, glass, bouquet of flowers w/bow **50.00**
Plate, glass, Garfield, 6" **95.00**
Plate, tin, cat w/yarn, 4" **35.00**
Plate, tin, girl on swing, 6¼" .**65.00**
Plate, tin, Hey Diddle Diddle, 8" **85.00**
Plate, tin, Mary Had a Little Lamb, 8" **125.00**

Abingdon Pottery

Produced in Abingdon, Illinois, from 1934 to 1950, this company made vases, cookie jars, utility ware, and lamps. Our advisors for Abington cookie jars, Fred and Joyce Roerig, are listed in the Directory under South Carolina. See also Cookie Jars.

Ashtray, #615, chick **15.00**
Bookends, #441, horse's head, pr **50.00**
Bowl, #383, sunflower, sm ...**35.00**
Bowl, #546, Streamliner, lg ..**20.00**
Candle holder, #384, sunflower, pr **35.00**
Cornucopia, #569, low **25.00**
Creamer & sugar bowl, #681/682, Daisy **27.59**

Figurine, #571, goose, white, 5" **25.00**
Figurine, #657, swordfish, decorated **45.00**
Figurine, #661, swan, 3¾" ...**35.00**
Flowerpot, #151 ....**18.00**
Jardiniere, P-7, 6" **24.00**
Planter, #668, daffodil **20.00**
String holder, #712, mouse ..**72.50**
Vase, #101, Alpha Classic **20.00**
Vase, #593, bow knot, medium blue, 9" **25.00**

Vase, blue with trumpet neck and handles, 10", $35.00.

Wall pocket, #508, shell **40.00**
Wall pocket, #711, carriage lamp, 10" **50.00**

Advertising Collectibles

Since the late 1800s competition among manufacturers of retail products has produced multitudes of containers, signs, trays, and novelty items, each bearing a catchy slogan, colorful lithograph or some other type of ploy, all flagrantly intent upon catching the eye of the potential customer. In their day some were more successful than others, but now it's the advertising material itself rather than the product that rings up the big sales – from avid collectors and flea market shoppers, not the product's consumers! Condition plays a vital role in evaluating advertising collectibles. Our estimates are for items in at least near mint condition, unless another condition code is present in the description. Try to be very objective when you assess wear and damage.

See also Breweriana; Coca-Cola; Keen Kutter; Labels; Maytag; Planters Peanuts; Winchester. Refer to *Huxford's Collectible Advertising* (Collector Books) and *Back Bar Breweriana, A Guide to Advertising Beer Statues and Beer Shelf Signs,* by George J. Baley (L-W Book Sales) for more information.

Ad Cards

When color lithography became commonplace, it impacted Victorian Americans in much the same way as color TV did kids of more modern times. Grocers and dry-good merchants used cards printed with beautiful children, animals, and birds, while farm machinery dealers seem to have preferred those that depicted examples of their equipment. All were avidly collected by children and adults alike and often pasted in scrapbooks or saved in a shoe box. Now they're being collected by many who find them just as attractive today. Though rare, the most expensive cards are very early examples from before 1850, Currier and Ives prints, those signed by Prang, mechanicals, metamorphics, hold-to-lights, and cards relative to certain very popular brand name products. Some of the more valuable are listed here, but most can be bought for less than $5.00. Remember, condition is of the utmost importance.

Ad card, Acme Soap Powder, boy and girl by lake, 4½x3", $6.50.

Ayer's Hair Vigor, girl w/extra-long hair, EX **20.00**
Buckeye Forge Pumps, Black man & flaming house, EX **30.00**
Buffalo Scale Company, scarce, 7x4⅝", VG **75.00**
Centuar Liniment, Jumbo Feeds Baby Castoria, w/PT Barnum quote, EX **15.00**
Chase & Sanborn, Columbia Exposition, die-cut openings, EX **46.00**
Chase & Sanborn, Souvenir Montreal Winter Carnival, 1885, VG **7.00**
Clark's ONT Spool Cotton, metamorphic, EX **20.00**

Congress Bitters, view of Capitol, EX **14.00**
DD Knapp Watchmaker, vignette of Elgin watch, EX **85.00**
Dr Miller's Magnetic Balm, boy, hold-to-light, VG **12.50**
Edison Phonograph, seated boy w/table model, EX **35.00**
Erie & Western RR, Time & Erie Wait for No Man, EX **55.00**
Ferry & Co Sweet Peas, colorful, EX **12.00**
French Laundry Soap, die-cut frog, EX **16.00**
Grandpa's Wonder Soap, bearded man & children, VG **10.00**
Heckler's Buckwheat, die-cut stand-up baby in highchair, 1893, EX **20.00**
JW Stoddard & Co, Tiger Rake, EX **35.00**
Kineo Stoves & Ranges, ice skating scene, EX **20.00**
McLaughlin's XXXX Coffee, The Smythy, forge scene, EX .**25.00**
Metropolitan Life Insurance Co, cat w/goldfish, NM **18.00**
Nestles' Milk Food, Little Miss Muffet, EX **15.00**
Philadelphia Centennial, Pork Packers, 1876, VG **15.00**
Pike's Toothache Drops, office scene, EX **48.00**
Schubert Piano, woman plays piano, mechanical **85.00**
Sunflower Baking Powder, die-cut of girl's face framed by sunflower, EX **38.00**
Superior, Improved Fertilizer Drill No 3, horse-drawn, VG ..**15.00**
Universal Clothes Wringer, Black lady, metamorphic, EX ..**22.00**
US Mail Steamer Uncle Sam, timetable, 1907, EX **20.00**
Van Houten's Cocoa, Early Visitors, 3 dogs & girl in bed, EX ..**32.00**
Washburn Crosby Co Merchant Millers, Gold Medal Flour, VG **6.00**

XXXX Coffee, boy & girl cutouts,
EX **6.00**

Banks

Burgermeister Beer, tin can,
paper label depicts Burgie
Man, EX **11.00**
Cincy Stoves, cast iron w/blue
porcelain, 4", EX **45.00**
Colonel Sanders, vinyl figural,
light wear, 1965, 13" **40.00**
Coors Beer, aluminum can **5.00**

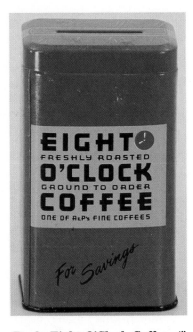

**Bank, Eight O'Clock Coffee, 4",
EX, $9.00.**

Esso, glass block, Watch Your
Savings Grow..., ca 1940-50s,
5x5" **70.00**
Gillies Coffee, tin, ring handle on
round lid, wire bail, 5x5" dia,
G **50.00**
Hoadley's Gum, tin can, multicol-
ored, lettering on top rim,
11", VG **200.00**

JS Fry & Sons Candy, pictorial &
figural, Montreal Canada,
4x5x3", VG **150.00**
Lennie Lenox, painted composition figure, decal on chest,
'49, 7½" **235.00**
Log Cabin Syrup, glass cabin
shape, EX **32.00**
Magic Chef, vinyl chef figure, head
is removable, 7½", EX **40.00**
Marathon, glass pig, The Ohio Oil
Co, ca 1940-50s, 3¼" **75.00**
Metz Beer, ceramic barrel shape,
embossed letters, EX **22.00**
Olympia Beer, tin can, horseshoe,
EX **10.00**
Phillip's 66, glass block, Phill Up
w/Phillip's..., ca 1940-50s,
5x5" **75.00**
Sinclair, tin gas pump shape,
green & cream, 1940-50s,
minor wear, 4" **45.00**
Sunoco, tin, gas pump shape,
blue, red & yellow, 1940-50s,
4", EX **35.00**
Tootsie Roll, dispenses candy, A
Tootsie a Day Puts a Penny
Away **60.00**

Calendars

Atlanta Life Insurance Co, Black
scenes, complete, 1955 ..**38.00**
Atlantic Steel Co, wartime scenes,
1943 ....**20.00**
Bemis Bag Co, pictures game
birds, complete, 1902 ..**225.00**
Brookshire Insurance Co, com-
plete, 1901 ....**35.00**
Clark's Spool Thread, complete,
1889 ....**40.00**
Grapette Soda, 1949, M **25.00**
Hood's Milk, 1933, NM **85.00**
Hood's Sarsaparilla, Victorian
children, 1900 ....**65.00**
Ivory Soap, complete & unused,
1890 ....**125.00**
Little Fairies Bath Powder, lady
w/baby, 1917, 9x10" **18.50**

Pepsi-Cola, complete, 1947 ..**55.00**
Royal Crown Cola, 1956 ....**40.00**
Scott's Emulsion, 1888 ....**65.00**
Squirt, tin border, 1948, 16x22",
    EX **28.00**
Winchester Repeating Arms, hunt
    scene, complete, 1899 ..**625.00**

Calendar, Dot Food Store, 1954,
16x10", VG, $12.50.

Clocks

Alka Seltzer, tablet shape, M ..**75.00**
Aunt Jemima, pictures a waffle,
    EX **30.00**
Canada Dry, light-up, EX **60.00**
Cat's Paw Shoes, reverse-painted
    glass, light-up, M **225.00**
Four Roses Whiskey, 1940s, work-
    ing, EX **75.00**
Monarch Foods, light-up, lion
    head, Telechron, EX **125.00**
NuGrape, pictures a bottle of soda,
    EX **135.00**
Pearl Beer, neon, Bottle of Pearl
    Lager Please, EX **395.00**
Purina, light-up, reverse-painted
    glass, M **155.00**

Tetley Tea, EX **145.00**
Winchester, pictures Rough Rider,
    EX **100.00**

Dolls

Though some of the older
dolls are expensive, most advertising dolls are within the reach of
the beginning collector; many
may be purchased for under
$25.00. Refer to *Advertising Dolls*
by Joleen Robison and Kay Sellers (Collector Books) for more
information.

Blue Ribbon Malt Extract, Lena,
    uncut printed cloth, 1930, 14",
    EX **175.00**
Bradford House Restaurants,
    Bucky Bradford, vinyl,
    squeaks, 7½" **10.00**

Doll, Campbell's Kids,
Bicentennial boy, vinyl, hat
missing, 10", $25.00.

Chuck E Cheese Pizza, Chuck E
    Cheese w/telescope, plush,
    12", G **18.00**

Coast-to-Coast Hardware, Elfy,
inflatable, 20" **15.00**
Fresca, March Hare, plush, 1970,
28" **25.00**
General Mills, Boo Berry, vinyl,
1975, 7½" **20.00**
Joy Detergent, inflatable, EX .**20.00**
Keebler Co, Keebler Elf, vinyl,
1974, 6½" **10.00**
Kellogg's, Dandy Duck, cloth,
1935, 12", G- **40.00**
Kellogg's, Tony Tiger, cloth, 1973,
14", G **9.00**
Kitty Pan Litter, Glamour Kitty,
firm vinyl wearing cloth cape,
7½" **30.00**
McDonald's, Hamburglar, 1972,
17" **15.00**
Mennen Shaving Lotion, replica
of bottle, 10" **12.00**
Michelin Tire Man, inflatable,
25", NM **10.00**
Munsingwear, penguin, vinyl,
EX **20.00**
Nabisco, Mr Salty, printed cloth,
11", G **10.00**

Door Push Plates

Door push plates were generally used on old screen doors of
general stores in a convenient
spot where you would reach out to
'push' or 'pull' the door open. They
carried a message to remind you
to buy manufacturers' particular
products. Many of the early (and
the most desirable) push plates
were made of porcelain, but other
varieties were made of tin as well
as celluloid. Average size of most
push plates is 4" x 7" (although
size may vary). Prices quoted are
for push plates in very good to
excellent condition; rarity is also
considered. For further information we recommend contacting
Edward Foley, who is listed in the
Directory under Pennsylvania.

**Push plates, Majors Cement,
$110.00; Red Rose Tea,
$175.00.**

American Seal Paint, porcelain,
EX **75.00**
Barmann's, porcelain **200.00**
Canada Dry Ginger Ale, tin ..**40.00**
Chesterfield Cigarettes, porcelain,
EX **125.00**
Copenhagen, tin **40.00**
Crisco, porcelain **150.00**
Dr Caldwell's Syrup Pepsin,
porcelain **85.00**
Fleischmann's Yeast, porcelain,
EX **75.00**
Foley Honey & Tar Liniment,
porcelain **75.00**
Foley Kidney Pills, porcelain ..**75.00**
Golden Bridge Root Beer, tin ..**45.00**
Hires Root Beer, tin **65.00**
King Cole Coffee (King's face),
porcelain **225.00**
King Cole Coffee & Tea (plain),
porcelain **70.00**
Normand's Special Loaf, celluloid,
EX **40.00**
Old Gold Cigarettes, tin **45.00**
Polar Bear Tobacco, porcelain,
EX **250.00**
Polarine Motor Car Oil &
Greases, porcelain **300.00**
Portage Tires, porcelain **185.00**
Rex Tobacco, porcelain **145.00**
Salada Tea, porcelain **100.00**
Slipknot Rubber Heels, tin ...**30.00**

Spencerian Steel Pens, porcelain, EX **135.00**
Stagg Tobacco, porcelain **185.00**
Star Naptha Washing Soda, porcelain **125.00**
Sweetheart Products, porcelain, EX **125.00**
Tetley Tea, porcelain **95.00**

Lunch Boxes

During the first quarter of this century, products (such as tea, coffee, or tobacco) were sometimes sold in tins that were designed to have a second use — as lunch boxes.

Lunch box, Mayo's Cut Plug Tobacco, 8" long, VG, $65.00.

Arm & Hammer Baking Soda, tin, yellow, slip lid, double handles, EX **220.00**
Bagley's Burley Boy Tobacco, tin, hinged lid, wire handle, VG+ **500.00**
Comet Cut Plug Tobacco, tin, paper label, 5x8x5", G- **225.00**
Crow-Mo Smoker's Tobacco, crowing rooster on box, 4x7x5", G **250.00**
Dan Patch Cut Plug Tobacco, man on surrey, 4x7x5", G **90.00**
Dixie Queen Smoking Tobacco, lady's portrait & lettering, EX **160.00**

Educator Cakelets, pictures Peter Rabbit & others, 3x6x4", EX **170.00**
Fashion Cut Plug Tobacco, depicts well-dressed couple, 4x8x5", G- **125.00**
Gail & Ax Navy Tobacco, sailor on silver background, 5x8x5", G **75.00**
Lorillard's Redicut Tobacco, pictures hands w/product **175.00**
Mayo's Tobacco, collapsible, 4x8x5", EX **250.00**
Plow Boy Tobacco, product name, wire & wood bail, G **55.00**
Tiger Chewing Tobacco, red & black wicker design, 6x8x7", G **40.00**
Union Blend Tobacco, leaf inset on green background, 4x7x5", G- **150.00**
Winner Cut Plug Tobacco, racing cars, 4x8x5", EX **140.00**
Yellow Daisy Long Cut Tobacco, 2 crossed yellow daisies, G- **400.00**

Match Holders

Acorn Stoves & Ranges, acorn figural, tin, 6x5", EX+ **425.00**
Allyn & Blanchard Co, man in turban, die-cut tin, yellow & black, VG+ **200.00**
Ballard's Obelisk Flour, tin, rare, EX **325.00**
Black Cat Polish, Shoes & Stoves, tin, rare, 6x4", G **150.00**
Bliss Native Herbs, pictures the capital building, VG+ .**200.00**
Ellwood Steel Fences, pictures a fence w/white lettering, tin VG **60.00**
EO Weber Lumber, black & silver lettering, tin, 5x5", VG+..**110.00**
Ideal Leather Polish, pictures product, tin, 6x4", VG+ **325.00**
International Harvester, tin, 5x3", VG **180.00**

Merry War Lye, washtub shape w/washerwoman, tin, 6x4", VG **210.00**

Milwaukee Binders & Mowers, gold lettering on brown background, VG+ **100.00**

Old Judson Whiskey, rain-soaked father, tin, 7x2x1", G ..**125.00**

Othello Ranges, stove on white background, tin, 5x3", VG **100.00**

Shippensburg Working Garmets, tin, EX **150.00**

Solarine Metal Polish, pictures product, tin **100.00**

Wrigley's Juicy Fruit, tin, rectangular, EX **240.00**

Pin-Back Buttons

Literally millions of these have been made, and obviously many have little or no collector value. But the older ones with advertising relating to a popular type of product — beer, automobilia, and farm machinery, for example — can be pricey! Our listings describe some of the better, more desirable buttons; most you'll find will be worth much less.

Badger, farm machine encircled by lettering, round **39.00**

Bucher & Gibbs Plow Co, 2 gents & plow encircled by lettering, round **49.00**

Buick, early roadster, Simplicity, Durability, Power **26.00**

Buster Brown Shoes, Buster Brown & Tige, Radio Club, round **42.00**

Crescent Creamery Co, crescent moon, round **35.00**

E-Z Shoes, boy in landscape, I Wear E-Z Shoes, round ..**20.00**

Ford, Ford Drive on the diagonal, 1937 1938... above & below, oval **20.00**

Ford V8, America's Choice for '34, close-up of car grill, round **79.00**

Happy Farmer Tractor Co, farmer's portrait encircled by lettering **29.00**

Jacob Schmit Brewing Co, St Paul, star logo in center, round **30.00**

MacArthur-Zollers Motor Co, pictures roadster, gold on blue, round **21.00**

Old Dutch, The Good Beer, depicts couple, Krantz Brewing Co, round **28.00**

Peters Cartridges, pictures cartridge, Experts Use..., round **30.00**

Pontiac, early logo, red & white, rectangular **28.00**

Willy's Overland Co, Overland on the diagonal, oval **30.00**

Playing Cards

Birdseye Cool Whip, logo w/floral design on black background, NM **3.50**

Chocolate Cream Coffee, gold on blue w/gold & white border, NM **4.00**

Gatorade, red logo w/white border, MN **5.00**

Gerber, Gerber baby in white circle on red background **6.50**

Johnnie Walker Black Label Scotch, yellow logo on black background **5.00**

Keebler Zesta Saltines, cracker box covers surface **10.00**

Kellogg's, Tony the Tiger eating cereal, lettering above, 1978-80 ....**5.00**

Kemply Ice Cream Co, dish of ice cream, geometric border ..**5.00**

Kool Milds, depicts cigarette package, M **8.00**

Marlboro Cigarettes, logo right side up & upside down, M **9.00**

Pepsi-Cola, red, white & blue logo & repeated lettering on white background **7.50**

Phoenix Coffee, red can on white ground w/red & yellow border, NM **10.00**

Pillsbury Plus, Oats 'n Brown Sugar Cake Mix box covers surface **10.00**

Royal Crown Cola, RC logo on white background **5.00**

Winston Cigarettes, cowboy on bronco, M **20.00**

Pocket Mirrors

Pocket mirror, Bell's Mocha & Java, 2", EX, $20.00.

Angelus Marshmallows, cherub w/horn, oval, 2¾", EX **55.00**

Cascarets Candy Cathartic, Best for the Bowels, 2⅛" dia, VG ..**55.00**

Denver Dry Goods Co, Front Door of the West, 2" dia, EX ..**65.00**

Dowagiac Drills & Seeders, ...Are the Leaders, 2" dia, EX ...**90.00**

Dr Swett's Root Beer, pictures bottle, 3" dia, VG **130.00**

Gillette Safety Razor, 1909 calendar, 2¼" dia, EX **100.00**

Great Majestic, The Modern Range, 2⅛" dia **100.00**

Ice Cream Dairy Co, Springfield IL, EX **45.00**

Kingan's Sausage Lard, Always the Best, 2¼" dia, EX **6.00**

Mathie Red Ribbon Beer, For Purity, Quality, oval, 2¾", VG **45.00**

MJ Theisen Wholesale Lumber, red & white on black background, 3" dia **14.00**

Morton's Salt, Pouring Can, 4" dia **25.00**

Old Reliable Coffee, dock worker, 2" dia, NM **40.00**

Peters Classic Shoes, 2¼" dia, EX **60.00**

Ponciana Chewing Gum, pictures pack of gum, oval, 2¾", EX **100.00**

Red Seal Lye, pictures product, 1¾" dia, EX **40.00**

Studebaker Vehicle Works, shows railroad tracks, oval, 2¾", VG **20.00**

Valley Forge Special, Adam Scheidt Brewing Co, oval, 2¾", EX **40.00**

Welch's Grape Juice, Absolutely Pure, oval, 2¾", VG+ **45.00**

Signs

A&P, paper, pictures Ben Franklin drinking tea, 1884, VG **35.00**

Arbuckles Coffee, embossed tin, Pure, Wholesome, self-framed, EX **325.00**

Canada Dry, tin, w/embossed shield **35.00**

Cavalier Cigarettes, tin, 11x19", EX **30.00**

Dad's Root Beer, cardboard, shows Elizabeth Montgomery, 1960, M **35.00**

DeLaval Separator, porcelain, 12x16", M **95.00**

Grapette, cardboard, pictures Grapette girl, EX **95.00**

Grizzly Gasoline, tin, Watch Your Miles, tombstone form ..**625.00**

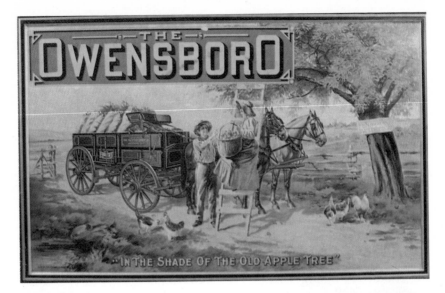

Sign, The Ownesboro, Hickman Ebbert Co., tin litho, 24x36", EX, $2,200.00.

Horseshoe Tobacco, cardboard, Chew Horseshoe 10 Cents, framed, EX **175.00**

King Midas Flour, pictures little girl, 1920s, 13x38" **285.00**

Moxie, tin, 1958, 10x28" **150.00**

Nichol Cola, tin, bottle cap design, 14½x14½" **58.00**

Orange Crush, tin, bottle cap shape, 1950s, 19", EX **55.00**

Pepo Worm Syrup, embossed tin, 25¢ at Druggists, self-framed, EX **225.00**

Quaker State Racing Oil, tin, double-sided, horizontal, EX .**75.00**

Royal Crown Cola, tin, bottle shape, 1936, 58" **150.00**

Texaco, keyhole shape, 1939, EX **160.00**

Thermometers

Arbuckles Coffee, tin litho, black on red, white & yellow, 19", VG **40.00**

Baker's Hygrade Ice Cream, painted & stenciled wood, 14", VG+ **40.00**

Camels, embossed tin litho, yellow & white on red, 13½", EX **10.00**

Cobbs Creek Whisky (sic), Drink-O-Meter, tin litho, 39", G+ **25.00**

Drink Moxie, painted & stenciled tin, white lettering on red, 25½", G **90.00**

Fatima Cigarettes, porcelainized steel, 27", G **25.00**

Happy Jim Tobacco, painted & stenciled tin, blue & red on white, 17" **15.00**

Ital-Ama Tomato Paste, painted & stenciled wood, product on blue, 15" **25.00**

K&B Best Flour, stenciled wood, red, yellow & blue on white, 10½" **15.00**

Natures Remedy, porcelain, white lettering & product on blue, 27", G **25.00**

Nesbitt's California Orange, painted & stenciled tin, 27", VG **80.00**

Orange-Crush, glass face, round, 12" dia, EX+ **55.00**

Orange-Crush, tin bottle shape, 29", EX **45.00**

Royal 400 Gasoline, painted & stenciled wood, red, green & white, 21" **170.00**

Thermo Anti-Freeze, stenciled tin in wood frame, 72", VG+ .**90.00**

William's Shaving Soap, painted & stenciled wood, black on yellow, 24" **80.00**

Tin Containers

Ammen's Powder, paper label, G **10.00**

Arco Coffee, key-wind lid, 1-lb, NM **45.00**

Around the World Motor Oil, screw lid, ca 1925-45, 2-gal, 12x9", EX **100.00**

Atlantic Motor Oil, ca 1935-45, 1-qt, 4" dia, VG **75.00**

Autocrat Coffee, paper label, 1-lb, 5x4" dia, VG **20.00**

Azurea Talc, rare, NM **150.00**

Bagley's Old Colony Mixture Tobacco, pocket tin, 5x3", EX **70.00**

Battleship Coffee, 9" dia **28.00**

Bickmore Gall Salve, shows old work horse **9.00**

Dr Nebb's Talcum, shaker top, EX **65.00**

Dream Girl Talcum, shaker top, EX **43.00**

Drum Major Marshmallows, slip lid, 5x11" dia, EX **45.00**

Dutch Master's Cigars, canister, 5¼x5½" **12.00**

Edgeworth Tobacco, pocket tin, flat, 3¼x2¼x⅝", NM **9.00**

Ex-Cel-Cis Talcum, G **15.00**

Flaroma Coffee, 1-lb, 6x4" dia, VG+ **55.00**

Floressence Violette Talc, Art Nouveau, G **15.00**

Freshpak Coffee, 1-lb **40.00**

Granger Tobacco, canister, 14-oz, 6x4¾" dia, EX **22.50**

Half & Half Tobacco, canister, key-wind, unopened, 7-oz, 4x4¼", EX **8.00**

Imperial Peanuts, 10-lb, 10x8", G **150.00**

Invader Motor Oil, ca 1950, 1-qt, NM **15.00**

Kemp Golden Glow Peanuts, slip lid, 10-lb, 10x8" dia **45.00**

Kentucky Club Tobacco, pocket tin, G **15.00**

La Korina Talcum, shaker top, EX **18.00**

Manhattan Cocktail Tobacco, pocket tin, flat, 4½x3¼x1", G **22.00**

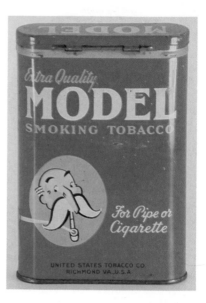

Tin container, Model Smoking Tobacco, 4½", VG, $15.00.

Mohican Pure Cream Cheese, press lid & bail, 30-lb ..**130.00**

Mona Motor Oil, ca 1915, ½-gal, 6x8x4", NM **250.00**

Noonan's Cleansing Cream, sample, 1930s, 2" dia, EX **25.00**

PCW Cough Drops, slip lid, rectangular **45.00**

Peanuts, Elephant Salted, 10-lb, 11x8" dia, G 100.00
Providence Salad Oil, sm screw top, 10", EX 70.00
Towle's Log Cabin Syrup, log cabin shape, EX+ 55.00
Union Leader Tobacco, pocket tin, 4¼x3", EX 6.00
Victory-V Lozenges, 1x5x3", VG+ 45.00
Whiz Cup Grease, wire handle, 1910, 5-lb, 5x7" dia 160.00
Y-B Cigars, slip lid, 6x6x4", EX 95.00

Tip Trays

Tip tray, Fairy Soap, EX, $55.00.

Baby Ruth Gum, glass, M ..185.00
Dot Cigars, glass, NM 125.00
Dr Pepper, tin, Black child eating watermelon, 3", M 275.00
Lily Beverage, tin, Rock Island Brewing Co, 6½x4½", M ..95.00
Old Angus Whiskey, tin, EX ..30.00
Pepsi-Cola, tin, roses on black background, M 10.00
Prudential Insurance, tin, oval, 2½x3½" 25.00
Rockford Watches, tin, pictures young lady, 3x5" 115.00
Smith Bros Typewriters, tin, shows typewriter & horses, M 250.00

Tehuagen Mineral Water, tin ..20.00
Wrigley's Soap, tin, pictures a cat, NM 175.00

Trays

Fairy Soap, tin, oval, Have You a Little Fairy..., 14", NM ..80.00
Franklin Brewery, tin, tavern scene, Wilkes-Barre PA, NM ...125.00
Hershey's Kisses, tin, NM ...24.00
Jamestown Ice Cream, tin, ca 1930 ....55.00
Miller Beer, tin, girl on crescent moon, round, NM 65.00
Paul Luithle's Bakery, tin, lady w/flowers, 1911, EX 150.00
Standard Brewing Co, paper label on wood-grain background, NM 125.00
Superior Beer, tin, pictures Indian maiden 50.00
Union Pacific Tea Co, tin, child in center, 8" 55.00
Walter Brewing Co, brass, pictures brewery, NM 275.00

Miscellaneous

A&P, measuring spoon, tin 7.50
Arm & Hammer, booklet, A Friend in Need, 1923, 32 pages, VG 4.50
Blue Valley Butter, blotter, 1934, EX 7.50
Bromo Seltzer, spoon, long handle, marked Cures Headache, ca 1920s 22.50
Bull Durham Tobacco, bag, cloth, black & gold paper label, VG 16.50
Campbell's Tomato Soup, thermal mug, M 7.50
Emerson Piano Co, glass paperweight, w/horse, wagon & trolley, EX 35.00
Excelsior Stove Works, egg separator, stamped tin, ca 1910, NM 20.00

Firestone, bottle opener/spoon-stirrer combination, iron ..**2.50**

Frigidaire, tape measure, celluloid, EX **30.00**

Gooch's Flour, pot scraper, metal, EX **85.00**

Green River Whiskey, bottle opener/corkscrew combination, cast metal **20.00**

Hartford Fire Insurance, bookends, bronze, ca 1935, EX, pr ...**95.00**

Hoover Vacuum, tape measure, EX **28.50**

Ivory Soap, booklet, Unusual Uses of Ivory Soap, 1916, EX ..**35.00**

Kentucky Club, shot glass, lg etched lettering, EX **16.00**

Kleenex, paper doll, Little Lulu, 1950, EX **15.00**

Malleable Range, biscuit cutter, metal, 1½" **7.50**

Medford Lager Beer, bottle opener, dachshund figural, nickeled iron **45.00**

Moller's Cod Liver Oil, bookmark, metal, fish figural, EX **6.50**

Monarch Stoves, cooking spoon, NM **22.50**

Red Goose Shoes, figure, chalk, 12", EX **125.00**

Robin Hood Flour, cookie cutter, Maid Marian figural, tin..**12.50**

Royal Crown Cola, lighter, bottle shape, 2½", M **15.00**

Rumford Baking Powder, measuring cup, stamped tin, 1-cup ...**20.00**

Silver Top Chewing Gum, box, pictures boy w/his top, 1880, NM **165.00**

Star Soap, booklet, Little Red Riding Hood, ca 1880s, EX ..**20.00**

Stone Malt Co, bottle opener, double-ended, flat steel, 7½" ..**4.50**

Swans Down Cake Flour, measuring cup, spun aluminum, 1-cup **15.00**

Swift & Co, key chain, enamel, EX **12.00**

Truth Bread, bread box, tin, hinged door, George Washington, EX **225.00**

Tums, fan, ca 1920s, EX **10.00**

Uneeda, letter opener, NM ..**65.00**

Welch's Grape Juice, corkscrew, Westfield NY, M **48.00**

Western Queen Flour, apron, NM **30.00**

Wrigley's Spearmint Gum, match cover, yellow & brown, green arrow, M **5.50**

Sewing kit, Lipton Tea, Made in West Germany, 4x5", $8.00.

Flour sifter, Pendleton Feed & Fuel, 2-cup, $22.50.

Airline Memorabilia

Collectors now seek nearly every item used by or made for commercial (i.e., non-military) airlines. The primary focus of interest are items actually used on the planes such as dishes, glassware, silver serving pieces and flatware, wings and badges worn by the crew, playing cards, and junior wings given to passengers. Timetables and large travel agency plane models are examples of advertising items which are also widely collected. Pre-war items are the most desirable, and items from before 1930 are quite rare. For further information we recommend contacting Mr. Dick Wallin, who is listed in the Directory under Illinois.

Aeroflot, cup & saucer, china, gold logo/blue trim, Soviet-made, 1970s **35.00**

Air Afrique, tumbler, 3¾" **4.00**

Air France, coffee mug, glass, marked Houston-Paris 747 Non-Stop, 1970s **5.00**

Air Mauritius, salt & pepper shakers, china, w/bird, 1980s, pr, minimum **15.00**

American, cup, Syracuse China, Airlite, 1940s **35.00**

American, doll, stewardess, vinyl, 1967, 12" **10.00**

American, fork, Flagship, 1930s-40s **25.00**

American, knife, Flagship, 1930s-40s **35.00**

American, menu, Coach, red & blue patchwork quilt cover, 1970s **2.50**

American, plate, Syracuse China, Airlite, 1940s **125.00**

American, spoon, Flagship, 1930s-40s **20.00**

Brandiff International, playing cards, BI logo, M in original package **5.00**

Delta, coffee cup, china, logo on side, pedestal base **4.00**

Delta, frizbee, plastic **2.50**

Eastern, tumbler, frosted, Golden Falcon Electra, 1950s ...**20.00**

Eastern, tumbler, Golden Falcon in blue ribbon, 1950s **20.00**

Eastern, tumbler, name in ribbon, ca 1940s, 4¾" **20.00**

Eastern, tumbler, Silver Falcon, bird & globe, 1950s **20.00**

Eastern, tumbler, Uncle Sam hat, red bird, 1950s **20.00**

Frontier, coffee cup, china, FAL on bottom **3.00**

Tumblers from Eastern Airlines, $20.00 ea.

Frontier, goblet, wine; logo on side **7.00**
Iberia, seat pocket folder, complete, 1970s **4.00**
Luftansa, flight map, Europe to N America, early 1960s ...**2.50**
Luftansa, menu, First Class, Khartoum-Cairo-Frankfort, dated 1985 ....**4.00**
National, dish, Jackson China, ivory w/gold border, 6" dia **10.00**
National, doll, stewardess, vinyl, 1973, on card, 11½" **5.00**
North Central, junior wings, metal, 1960s **65.00**
Northeast, junior wings, metal, V-shape, 1950s **150.00**
Olympic, menu, wine list w/fuzzy red & gold cover, 1970s ...**5.00**
Pan American, cup & saucer, demitasse; Noritake, Presidential, 1960s **35.00**
Pan American, menu, First Class, dated 1987 ....**3.00**
Pan American, playing cards, African picture, M in plastic wrapper **5.00**
Royal Jordanian, salt & pepper shakers, china, logo, 1980s, pr, minimum value **15.00**
Scandanavian Airlines System, glass, SAS on side, 2" **5.00**
TAT, playing cards, Rail-Air Coast to Coast, 1929 ....**200.00**
TWA, booklet, Ambassador Service, illustrated, lg format, ca 1970s **4.50**
TWA, booklet, International Air Route, dated 1960 ....**3.00**
TWA, cap badge, gold, circular w/red letters, 1960-80s ..**45.00**
TWA, cup & saucer, china, name in star on red sash, Japan, 1970s-80s **10.00**
TWA, cup & saucer, china, name in star on red sash, Rosenthal, 1960s **15.00**
TWA, drink stirrer, figural handle represents a country, any.. **.50**

TWA, jigsaw puzzle, scene w/Connie plane, 1950s **35.00**
United, bowl, Syracuse China, Swirl pattern, gold trim, 1960s **35.00**
United, cup & saucer, Syracuse China, Swirl pattern, gold trim, 1960s **75.00**
United, menu, First Class, The Red Carpet, 1970s **3.50**
United, plate, Syracuse China, Swirl pattern w/gold trim, 1960s, sm **15.00**
Virgin, salt & pepper shakers, china, 1980s, pr, minimum price **15.00**
Western, pitcher, 1926 in shield on side, 1980s, sm **4.00**
Western, plate, Fiesta, red, white & blue, Block of Portugal, 1960s **30.00**

Akro Agate

This company operated in Clarksburg, West Virginia, from 1914 to 1951, manufacturing marbles, novelties, and children's dishes, for which they are best known. Though some were made in clear solid colors, their most popular, easy-to-identify lines were produced in a swirling opaque type of glass similar to that which was used in the production of their marbles. Their trademark was a flying eagle clutching marbles in his claws. Refer to *The Collector's Encyclopedia of Children's Dishes* by Margaret and Kenn Whitmyer (Collector Books) for more information.

Chiquita, creamer, clear, 1½" .**19.50**
Chiquita, creamer, transparent cobalt, 1½" **15.00**
Chiquita, cup, baked-on colors, · 1½" **7.00**

Chiquita, teapot, green opaque, w/lid, 3" **15.00**

Chiquita, 12-pc boxed set, opaque colors other than green **135.00**

Concentric Rib, creamer, opaque other than green or white, 1¼" **16.00**

Concentric Rib, cup, opaque green or white, 1¼" **6.00**

Concentric Rib, plate, opaque other than green or white, 3¼" **8.00**

Concentric Rib, teapot, opaque green or white, w/lid, 3⅜" **13.00**

Concentric Rib, 10-pc boxed set, opaque other than green or white **80.00**

Concentric Ring, cereal bowl, transparent cobalt, lg, 3⅜" **35.00**

Concentric Ring, creamer, marbleized blue, lg, 1⅜" **45.00**

Concentric Ring, cup, opaque yellow or lavender, lg, 1⅜" ...**30.00**

Concentric Ring, cup, solid opaque colors, sm, 1¼"...**11.00**

Concentric Ring, plate, marbleized blue, sm, 3¼" **23.00**

Concentric Ring, saucer, solid opaque colors, sm, 2¾" **4.50**

Concentric Ring, sugar bowl, marbleized blue, w/lid, lg, 1⅞" **60.00**

Concentric Ring, teapot, solid opaque colors, w/lid, lg, 3¾" **42.00**

Interior Panel, cereal bowl, pink or green luster, lg, 3⅜" **25.00**

Interior Panel, creamer, lemonade & oxblood, lg, 1⅜" **35.00**

Interior Panel, cup, marbleized blue & white, sm, 1¼" **24.00**

Interior Panel, cup, marbleized green & white, lg, 1⅜" **18.00**

Interior Panel, cup, pink luster, sm, 1¼" **13.00**

Interior Panel, plate, azure blue or yellow, sm, 3¾" **11.00**

Interior Panel, plate, marbleized blue & white, lg, 4¼" **17.50**

Interior Panel, plate, marbleized red & white, sm, 3¾" **13.00**

Octagonal, sm; pumpkin cup, $22.00; yellow saucer, $4.00; green plate, $5.00.

Interior Panel, saucer, marbleized green & white, lg, 3⅛" **7.50**

Interior Panel, sugar bowl, marbleized green & white, sm, 1¼" **22.00**

Interior Panel, sugar bowl, transparent green or topaz, sm, 1¼" **20.00**

Interior Panel, tumbler, transparent green or topaz, sm, 2" **9.00**

JP, cereal bowl, baked-on colors, 3¾" **11.00**

JP, cup, transparent green, 1½" **18.00**

JP, plate, baked-on colors, 4¼" **6.00**

JP, sugar bowl, transparent red or brown, w/lid, 1½" **50.00**

Miss America, creamer, white, 1¼" **45.00**

Miss America, cup, forest green or marbleized orange & white, 1⅝" **45.00**

Miss America, sugar bowl, white w/decal, w/lid, 2" **70.00**

Octagonal, plate, green, white or dark blue, lg, 4¼" **4.50**

Octagonal, sugar bowl, dark blue, w/lid, closed handle, 1½" ...**14.00**

Octagonal, teapot, beige, w/lid, closed handle, 3⅝" **28.00**

Octagonal, 17-pc boxed set, green, white or dark blue, lg **95.00**

Raised Daisy, cup, green, 1¾" .**18.00**

Raised Daisy, teapot, blue, w/lid, 2⅜" **75.00**

Raised Daisy, teapot, blue, no lid, 2⅜" **35.00**

Raised Daisy, tumbler, yellow, 2" **25.00**

Stacked Disc, pitcher, opaque green or white, 2⅞" **13.00**

Stacked Disc, teapot, opaque other than green or white, w/lid, 3⅜" **15.00**

Stacked Disc, tumbler, opaque green or white, 2" **7.00**

Stacked Disc, tumbler, pumpkin, 2" **22.00**

Stacked Disc & Interior Panel, cereal bowl, transparent cobalt, 3⅜" **28.50**

Stacked Disc & Interior Panel, cup, solid opaque colors, 1¼" ..**12.50**

Stacked Disc & Interior Panel, plate, marbleized blue, 4¾" **22.00**

Stippled Band, pitcher, transparent amber, 2⅞" **20.00**

Stippled Band, sugar bowl, transparent green, w/lid, 1⅞" ..**24.00**

Stippled Band, teapot, transparent green, w/lid, 3⅜" **18.50**

Stippled Band, tumbler, transparent amber, 1¾" **10.00**

Aladdin Lamps

Aladdin lamps have always been the most popular kerosene lamps around; they've been made since 1908 by the Mantle Lamp Company of America in over eighteen models and more than one hundred styles. During the 1930s to the 1950s, this company was a leading manufacturer of electric lamps as well. Many of the electrics are collectible; however, not everyone knows this, so many electric Aladdins turn up in shops, flea markets, and yard sales. The company is known today as Aladdin Industries Inc. of Nashville, Tennessee, and still makes kerosene mantle lamps in a wide variety of styles. Refer to *Aladdin—The Magic Name in Lamps; Aladdin Electric Lamps;* and *A Collector's Manual and Price Guide.* All are written by our advisor, J.W. Courter, who is listed in the Directory under Illinois.

#2080, electric, bridge lamp, NM **160.00**

#3505, electric, floor lamp, EX **145.00**

#3978, electric, floor lamp, w/night light, NM **225.00**
#4886C, electric, floor lamp, florescent, EX **150.00**
A-4181, kerosene, Designer Marble, Model #23, M **85.00**
B-100, kerosene, Corinthian, clear, NM **70.00**
B-139, kerosene, table lamp, Model C, aluminum, NM **28.00**
B-23000, Caboose Lamp, Model #23, aluminum, complete, M..**48.00**
B-28, kerosene, Simplicity, rose, NM **95.00**
B-75, kerosene, Tall Lincoln Drape, Alacite, M **140.00**
B-81, kerosene, Beehive, green crystal, EX **85.00**
BL-1983, kerosene, student lamp replica, Model #23, brass, NM **450.00**

G-312 Alacite electric table lamp, 1949. Base, $30.00; shade, $50.00; bride and groom finial, $200.00.

BW-2404, kerosene, wood wall sconce, NM **90.00**
G-192, electric, table lamp, Alacite, NM **50.00**
G-24, electric, Cupid, Alacite, M **85.00**
G-31, electric, boudoir lamp, Alacite, EX **30.00**
G-33, electric, boudoir lamp, Moonstone, EX **40.00**
G-353, electric, pin-up wall lamp, Alacite, EX **45.00**
G-375, electric, Dancing Ladies Urn, Alacite, EX **525.00**
G-69, electric, table lamp, Moonstone, EX **80.00**
Model #12, kerosene, table lamp, nickel, NM **75.00**
Model #6, kerosene, table lamp, nickel, EX **85.00**
New 76, kerosene, Short Lincoln Drape, cobalt, M **95.00**
New 76, kerosene, Short Lincoln Drape, ruby, NM **90.00**
P-416, electric, table lamp, ceramic, EX **30.00**
W-346, electric, table lamp, oak wood, NM **35.00**

Aluminum

From the late 1930s until early in the 1950s, kitchenwares and household items were crafted from aluminum, usually with relief-molded fruit or flowers on a hammered background. Today many find that these diversified items make an interesting collection. Especially desirable are those examples marked with the manufacturer's backstamp or the designer's signature.

You've probably also begun to see the anodized (colored) aluminum pitchers, tumblers, sherbet holders, etc., that were popular in the late fifties, early sixties.

All of a sudden, they're everywhere, and with a wide range in asking prices. Tumblers in good condition with very little wear seem to be about $10.00 and up for a set of six; the pitchers are common and shouldn't be worth much more than the price of six tumblers.

Our advisor for this category is Danny Woodard, author of *Hammered Aluminum, Hand Wrought Collectibles* (watch for Book II), and publisher of *The Aluminist*, a newsletter printed six times a year. Her address is in the Directory under Texas.

Basket, lily in the center, signed Roger Kent, #429, 5x7", $15.00.

Basket, plain w/twisted double handle, Buenilum, 9" dia **15.00**
Bowl, fruit & flowers, rolled handles, Cromwell, 12" **24.00**
Bowl, fruit & leaf, heavy, Everlast, 10" **18.00**
Bowl, grapes, Hammerkraft, 11½" **7.00**
Bread tray, pine cones, scalloped edge, Everlast, oval, 12¾" **23.00**
Butter dish, Kent, ¼-lb **12.00**
Candy dish, mums, flower shaped knob, 3-part, Continental, #756, 7" **15.00**
Casserole, Buenilum, hammered, w/lid **12.50**

Casserole holder, hammered, footed, w/lid, Rodney Kent, #407 ....**21.00**
Dish, grapes, ruffled edge, handled, Hammerkraft, 7½"..**8.00**
Dish, raspberries, Farberware, 15" **14.00**
Ice bucket, hammered, w/lid, double-walled, Canterbury Arts, 8" **45.00**
Lazy Susan, tulips, glass insert, Rodney Kent, #413, 18" ..**15.00**
Napkin holder, hammered, footed, Rodney Kent **15.00**
Pitcher, hammered, looped ice guard, Cromwell, 2-qt ...**29.00**
Salt & pepper shakers, hammered, pr **14.00**
Silent butler, tulip, Rodney Kent, #439 ....**18.00**
Tray, daisies, Farber & Shlevin, #1772, 11x17" **20.00**
Tray, fruit & flowers, Keystone Paisley, round, 16½" **14.00**
Tray, tidbit; dogwood, looped handle, Designed Aluminum, round, 7" **8.00**

Animal Dishes with Covers

Popular novelties for part of this century as well as the last, figural animal dishes were made by many well-known glasshouses in milk glass, slag, colored opaque, or clear glass. These are preferred by today's collectors, though the English earthenware versions are highly collectible in their own right. Many on the market today are reproductions. Beware. Refer to *Covered Animal Dishes* by Everett Grist (Collector Books) for more information.

Bambi, powder jar, carnival, Jeannette Glass, ca 1950s **22.00**

Bird on round basket, milk glass, unmarked Vallerysthal reproduction **25.00**

Bird w/berry on basketweave base, any color, Wright ..**25.00**

Bird w/berry on split-rib base, any color, Degenhart **25.00**

Bull's head, mustard jar, purple slag, Smith, no ladle **35.00**

Chick & eggs, round compote base, milk glass, Westmoreland **95.00**

Chick emerging from horizontal egg, milk glass, unmarked **95.00**

Dog on wide ribbed base, amber, Westmoreland **65.00**

Dolphin, chocolate, sawtooth rim, St Clair reproduction **65.00**

Dolphin, clear or colored, sawtooth rim, Kemple reproduction **45.00**

Donkey, powder jar, pink, attributed to Jeannette Glass **15.00**

Duck, soap dish, carnival w/painted bill **15.00**

Duck, swimming, blue, Vallerysthal, 5¾" **100.00**

Elephant, standing, transparent pink, unmarked, 9" long ..**65.00**

Fox, ribbed lid, lacy base, milk glass, Imperial **65.00**

Hand & dove, lacy square base, milk glass, Westmoreland **65.00**

Hen on lacy base, opaque blue head, Atterbury, $225.00.

Hen, milk glass, Fenton, 8" ..**150.00**

Hen, milk glass, Vallerysthal, 1" **35.00**

Hen on basketweave base, amberina, attributed to LG Wright ...**25.00**

Hen on basketweave base, frosted, Challinor Taylor **75.00**

Hen on basketweave base, milk glass, unmarked, 5⅝" long **35.00**

Hen on basketweave base, milk glass w/red trim, Westmoreland, 3" **10.00**

Hen on cattail base, milk glass, unmarked, 5½" **65.00**

Hen w/chicks on base, clear, Flaccus **155.00**

Horse shoe, butter dish, clear, unmarked **45.00**

Lady, powder jar, clear w/paint inside, unmarked **25.00**

Lion, ribbed lid, ribbed base, milk glass, Westmoreland **65.00**

Lion on picket base, blue, Westmoreland **145.00**

Lion on scroll base, milk glass, unmarked, 5½" long **75.00**

Lovebirds, powder jar, clear, attributed to Westmoreland **15.00**

Milady, powder jar, marigold carnival **45.00**

Mother eagle, milk glass, Westmoreland **75.00**

Poodle, powder jar, carnival, Jeannette Glass, ca 1950s **22.00**

Quail on scroll base, milk glass, unmarked **65.00**

Rabbit, full figure, milk glass, Imperial **65.00**

Rabbit on basketweave base, clear, attributed to Atterbury, 8" base **55.00**

Rat on lg egg, transparent pink, Vallerysthal **225.00**

Robin on pedestal base, milk glass, unmarked recent reproduction **15.00**

Rooster, ribbed lid, lacy base, purple slag, Imperial **55.00**

Rooster, standing, clear w/red, attributed to LE Smith ..**55.00**
Rooster on diamond basketweave base, blue, Westmoreland Specialty **125.00**
Swan, closed neck, on diamond basketweave, milk glass, Westmoreland **75.00**
Swan, complete figural, clear, unmarked **45.00**
Turkey, milk glass, Imperial, sm **45.00**
Turtle, complete figural, amber, unmarked **100.00**

Appliances

Old electric appliances are collected for nostalgic reasons as well as for their unique appearance and engineering. Especially interesting are early irons, fans, vacuum cleaners, and toasters. Examples with Art Deco styling often bring high prices at today's auctions and flea markets.

Beaters: Challenge, custard glass bottom, $25.00; Kenmore, $25.00.

Churn, Duraglas, 2-gal glass base w/screw-on motor top, 1947, 22" **75.00**
Coffee urn, Universal, Landers, Frary & Clark, 1910-20s, 11" **45.00**

Coffeepot, Edison General Electric Hotpoint, chrome **30.00**
Coffeepot, Forman Bros, football form w/tan handles & spigot, 1950s **25.00**
Corn popper, Dominion Electric, straight-sided metal w/lid, 1930s **40.00**
Doughnut maker, Wallace Ray Co, hinged oval w/7 convex rings, ca 1968 ....**22.50**
Drink mixer, Arnold Sanitary Mixer #12, nickel plated **65.00**
Egg cooker, Hankscraft Co #599, red ceramic w/chrome lid, ca 1930s **40.00**
Fan, oscillating, Diehl Mfg Co, cage type on cast iron base, 1930s **40.00**
Hot dog cooker, Lightning Wiener Cooker, metal w/pottery insert, 1930s **30.00**
Iron, Coleman Instant Lite, ca 1910, 11", w/brass & wood primer, 7" **125.00**
Iron, Frary & Clark #E-909, nickel plated, 106-114 volts, 7" **40.00**
Iron, Hotpoint Model R, Edison Electric Appliance Co, 6½" **25.00**
Mixer, Sears Powermaster DeLuxe, w/detachable base, 1930s **65.00**
Percolator urn, Robeson Rochester Corp, #E639, 1930s, 15" **45.00**
Teakettle, Simplex, Art Nouveau-styled stand, ca 1915 ....**75.00**
Teakettle, Speedmaster, chrome-plated metal w/element handle, 1930s **45.00**
Teapot, American Electric Heater Co, Detroit MI, 1904 .....**30.00**
Toaster, Dominion #1109, flip-down doors **35.00**
Toaster, Merit-Made, chrome w/Bakelite handles, 1-slice, 1940s **40.00**

Toaster, The Handy Hot, green-painted sheet metal, ca 1930s **25.00**

Vacuum cleaner, Lewyt, Brooklyn NY, w/disposable bag, ca 1950s **60.00**

Waffle iron, Westchester Automatic, chrome w/enamel, ca 1938, 12" dia **120.00**

Art Deco

The Art Deco movement began at the Paris International Exposition in 1925 and lasted into the 1950s. Styles of apparel, furniture, jewelry, cars, and architecture were influenced by its cubist forms and sweeping, aerodynamic curves. Sleek greyhounds and female nudes (less voluptuous than Art Nouveau nudes), shooting stars and lightning bolts, exotic woods and lush fabrics — all were elements of the Art Deco era. Today's fashions, especially in home furnishings, reflect the movement; and collectors delight in acquiring authentic examples to recreate the posh Art Deco environment. Refer to *A Collector's Guide to Art Deco* by Mary Frank Gaston (Collector Books) for more information.

Ashtray, ceramic, marked Snufferette, National Porcelain Co, 4" dia **35.00**

Belt buckle, enameled metal w/gold trim, German **20.00**

Belt buckle, square tortoise shell, beveled edges, plain, lg ...**15.00**

Cigarette box, semicircular red & black plastic, 5x5½" **55.00**

Cigarette holder, black plastic, 6" **20.00**

Crumber set, crescent form, chrome w/celluloid trim, Chase **75.00**

Cup & saucer, Tricorn pattern, ceramic, Salem China Co ..**20.00**

Dress clip, blue rhinestones w/turquoise beads **35.00**

Flower frog, nude holding crescent-formed drape, ceramic, German, 7" **60.00**

Garters, pink & white beads w/butterfly wing design, pr **40.00**

Hairbrush, tortoise shell plastic, stepped design **18.00**

Jewel box, red & black painted brass w/geometric-cut lid, 8x5" **70.00**

Newspaper holder, cut-out boy & Paper, copper-finished metal, 11¼" **45.00**

Powder box, chrome w/Bakelite & ebony hearts on lid, marked Chase **65.00**

Powder box, Jeannette Glass, Windsor Diamond pattern, 1938, 3½" dia **20.00**

Purse, lg white plastic beads link to form pentagons **35.00**

Sconce, painted metal, frosted glass shade w/pink-painted interior **50.00**

Silent butler, lute form, chrome w/Bakelite handle, Chase, 11½" **60.00**

Sugar bowl, lustreware w/zigzag design, Japan, w/lid, 5¼" ..**35.00**

Temperature gauge, plastic, marked Taylor Humidiguide, 3½" square **30.00**

Watch pendant, black & green enamel w/sterling trim, Borel, 1¼" **275.00**

Autographs

Autographs of famous people from every walk of life are of interest to students of philography, as it is referred to by those who enjoy this hobby. Values hinge on many things—rarity of the signature and content of the signed material are major considerations. Autographs of sports figures or entertainers often sell at $10.00 to $15.00 for small signed photos. Beware of forgeries. If you are unsure, ask established dealers to help you.

Aaron, Hank; signature on 3x5" card **15.00**

Alda, Alan; inscribed signature on 8x10" photo **10.00**

Baker, Howard; US Senator, signature on newswire message, 1981 ....**15.00**

Bardot, Brigitte; signature on card **8.00**

Berle, Milton; signature on 8x10" color photo in tuxedo **12.00**

Bernhardt, Sarah; signature on 5-word note in French, dated, 1913 ....**80.00**

Blanc, Mel; inscribed & signed 8x10" color photo w/cartoon friends **75.00**

Brooks, Mel; signature on 11x14" lobby card for Blazing Saddles, 1974 ....**15.00**

Cohan, George M; signature on note, 1934 ....**90.00**

Connery, Sean; signature on lined card **20.00**

Cruise, Tom; in-person signature on 8x10" photo from Risky Business **45.00**

Danson, Ted; in-person signature on 8x10" waist length photo **38.00**

Domino, Fats; signature on photo of Fats playing the piano **20.00**

Dreyfus, Richard; signature on 8x10" photo from The Goodbye Girl **15.00**

Dulles, John Foster; Secretary of State, signature on 8x10" photo **50.00**

Feinstein, Dianne; signature on typed letter, 1980 ....**12.00**

Fields, Sally; signature on 11x14" lobby card for Norma Rae, 1979 ....**13.00**

Ford, Edsel; son of Henry, signature on 3x5" card **60.00**

Frazier, Joe; signature on 8x10" photo holding WBC belt ..**6.00**

Greely, AW; Arctic explorer, signature on 5x5" typed letter, 1913 ....**25.00**

Henley, Don; singer, signature on 8x10" color bust-length photo **35.00**

Henson, Jim; signature on 8x10" half-length photo **150.00**

Hoffa, James; bold signature on 4x5" card **135.00**

Cancelled check signed by Ty Cobb, 1956, $300.00.

Iacocca, Lee; signature on early 8x10" black & white portrait photo **40.00**

Iswald, Steve; astronaut, signed letter, NASA stationery ..**45.00**

Kennedy, Ted; in-person signature on paper **20.00**

King, Stephen; signature on flyleaf of book titled Cujo, 1981 ....**100.00**

Landon, Michael; signature on 8x10" photo as Little Joe ..**60.00**

Linkletter, Art; signature on postcard, 1963 ....**10.00**

Loy, Myrna; inscribed signature on 8x10" photo, 1940s ...**10.00**

Matthau, Walter; signature on 8x10" color photo from Charlie Varrick **8.00**

Mondale, Walter; signature on typed letter, 1982 ....**30.00**

Monroe, Vaughn; bandleader, inscribed signed photo ..**25.00**

O'Conner, Sandra Day; signature on 5x8" magazine photo w/biography **30.00**

O'Hara, Maureen; inscribed signature on 3x5" vintage arcade card **8.00**

Pacino, Al; signature on 11x14" lobby card for Dog Day Afternoon, 1975 ....**30.00**

Price, Vincent; signature on 11x14" lobby card for Diary of a Madman **18.00**

Rayburn, Sam; Speaker of the House, 1955-61, signed 3x5" card **10.00**

Robbins, Marty; signature on 8x10" photo taken from vintage tour book **40.00**

Rockwell, Norman; signature on 5x7" magazine picture ..**150.00**

Russell, Jane; signature on 8x10" color photo, in evening gown, 1950s **18.00**

Schulz, Charles M; cartoonist, signed 3x5" card w/envelope, 1968 ....**95.00**

Shannon, Del; musician, signature on 4x5" card **45.00**

Shepherd, Cybill; signature on 8x10" photo **20.00**

Smith, Jaclyn; inscribed signature on 8x10" photo **10.00**

Statler Brothers, signatures of all 4 members on color photo ..**20.00**

Swanson, Gloria; inscribed signature on paper **30.00**

Tierney, Gene; signature on 8x10" photo from Rings on Her Fingers **15.00**

Tunney, Gene; boxer, signature on 3x5" **45.00**

Unitas, Johnny; inscribed signature on 5x7" promotional photo **10.00**

Urich, Robert; signature on 8x10" photo from Spencer for Hire **8.00**

Walton, Sam; inscribed signature on 3½x5" color photo **70.00**

Welch, Raquel; signature on 8x10" photo, 1960s **15.00**

Williams, Billy Dee; signature on 8x10" color photo from Star Wars **30.00**

Williams, Robin; signature on 8x10" photo as Mork from Ork **20.00**

Wilson, Edith Bolling; First Lady, signature on card **70.00**

Automobilia

Many are fascinated with vintage automobiles, but to own one of those 'classy chassis' is a luxury not all can afford! So instead they enjoy collecting related memorabilia such as advertising, owners' manuals, horns, emblems, and hood ornaments. The decade of the 1930s produced the items that are most in demand today, but the fifties models have their own band of devoted fans as well. Usually made of porcelain on cast iron, first-year license plates in hard-to-find excellent condition may bring as much as $200.00 for the pair. If you're especially interested in chauffeur and other transportation badges, Edward H. Miles has prepared a publication on their history and values. He is listed in the Directory under New York. See also License Plates.

Sign, porcelain, 30" wide, EX, $1,300.00.

Ashtray, Victor Gaskets, metal, green w/embossed gaskets, 3¾" dia **20.00**
Badge, Motor Wheel Corp employee's, red, green & white...............................**25.00**
Badge, New York City Hack, 1935-1936, each **25.00**
Badge, New York City Hack, 1937-43, each **20.00**
Badge, New York City Hack, 1947-52, each **25.00**
Badge, New York State, 1924-28, each **10.00**
Badge, taxi driver; Albany, NY, 1957 ....**10.00**
Bank, Chrysler Corp, Mr Fleet, painted plastic, 1973, 10" ..**5.00**
Book, instruction; Ford, radiator repairs, 1919, 54 pages ..**35.00**
Booklet, Ford, 1964, 16 pages, 8x10" **6.00**

Booklet, Kaiser, black & white, Please Read Our Mail, 1948, 8 pages **5.00**
Booklet, Mercury, black & white, 1956, 12 pages, 9x8", NM ..**8.00**
Brochure, Ford Thunderbird, 1973, 16 pages, EX **7.50**
Bud vase, carnival glass, w/bracket **85.00**
Catalog, Austin Healey Sprite MKIII sports convertible, color, 12 pages **10.00**
Catalog, Buick, color illustrations, 1949, 20 pages, 9x9" **60.00**
Catalog, Corvair, color illustrations, 1960, 8 pages, 10x7" **6.00**
Catalog, Harry Alter Co, car parts, 1928, 104 pages, 6x9" **22.50**
Catalog, Studebaker, color illustrations, 1950, 8 pages, 5x17", EX **10.00**
Cigarette lighter, under-dash clamp-on w/pull cord, EX **35.00**
Compass, Taylor Navigator, self-illuminated, swivel mount, original box **35.00**
Compass, Union 76, suction-cup mount **12.00**
Cup & saucer, bone china w/early car, Crown Staffordshire, England **20.00**
Flashlight, key chain; Buick in block letters, eagle w/spread wings **12.00**
Folder, Chevrolet, souvenir from Chicago World's Fair **15.00**
Folder, Desoto, color illustrations, 1950, 28x20" **7.00**
Folder, Ford, 4-cylinder, 1932, 18x22", VG **20.00**
Foldout, Oldsmobile, 1950, unfolded: 30x24", EX **10.00**
Hat visor, Chevrolet, blue & white cardboard, 20-years Sales Leadership **5.00**
Hub cap, Willys-Knight, WK logo, 7¾" dia, set of 5, NM ...**125.00**
Lapel pin, Edsel, white 'E' on green enamel, ½" dia **45.00**

Lapel pin, Willys Overland Football Club, 4-color enamel **45.00**

License, driver's; Syracuse NY, 1923 ....**20.00**

License, driver's; Syracuse NY, 1933 ....**15.00**

License, hack; Lynbrook NY, 1967 ....**10.00**

License, public vehicle; Buffalo NY, 1926 ....**25.00**

License, taxi; Hempstead NY, 1965 ....**10.00**

Manual, owner's; for 1951 De Soto, illustrated, 52-page, 5½x8½" **20.00**

Mug, frosted glass, Indy winner Troy Ruttman, 1952 ......**25.00**

Pencil clip, red, white & blue w/Hupmobile logo **25.00**

Pin, Ford Good Drivers League, steering wheel, 1940, blue & white **40.00**

Pocketknife, Cadillac, shield logo, 2-blade, by Shrade **60.00**

Radiator ornament, Corning frosted glass, lady's face w/flowing hair **265.00**

Screwdriver, Chevrolet Sales & Service, bow tie logo, metal handle **25.00**

Shop manual, Chrysler, some color, 1941, 279 pages ...**30.00**

Sign, Pontiac, die-cut embossed cardboard w/logo, 12½" dia, EX **10.00**

Spark intensifier, Sur-Fry, mounts to top of coil or distributor cap **12.50**

Steering wheel spinner knob, Santay Deluxe, red plastic, NM in box **25.00**

Tape measure, Royal Packard, St Paul-Minneapolis, blue & yellow, EX **50.00**

Tire ashtray, BF Goodrich Lifesaver Radial HR70-15, clear glass insert **20.00**

Tire ashtray, Firestone Deluxe 600-16, Made in England **35.00**

Tire ashtray, Firestone Giant Steel Radial, w/glass insert **35.00**

Tire ashtray, US Royal Master Air Ride, US Rubber embossed on insert **35.00**

Tire gauge, brass, marked Scovill Mfg **40.00**

Tire gauge, Michelin ad on silvered brass, ca 1909, 3½x¾" dia **30.00**

Toy truck, Esso Petro Pump Series #18 Foden Dumper Lorry, gas pump box **65.00**

Autumn Leaf

Autumn Leaf dinnerware was a product of the Hall China Company, who produced this extensive line from 1933 until 1978 for exclusive distribution by the Jewell Tea Company. The Libbey Glass Company made coordinating pitchers, tumblers and stemware. Metal, cloth, plastic, and paper items were also available. Today, though very rare pieces are expensive and a challenge to acquire, new collectors may easily reassemble an attractive, usable set at a reasonable price. Hall has produced special club pieces (for the NALCC) as well as some limited editions for an Ohio company, but these are well marked and easily identified as such. Refer to *The Collector's Encyclopedia of Hall China* by Margaret and Kenn Whitmyer (Collector Books) for more information.

Baker, French, 2-pt **75.00**

Ball jug, #3 ....**28.00**

Bean pot, 2-handle **135.00**

Bowl, cream soup **18.00**

Bowl, divided, oval **80.00**

Bowl, Radiance, 6" **9.50**

Bowl, Radiance, 7½" **12.00**	Sugar bowl, w/lid, Rayed **18.50**
Bowl, salad **12.50**	Sugar bowl, w/lid, ruffled-D ..**12.50**
Bowl, 9" dia **80.00**	Teapot, Rayed **40.00**
Butter dish, ¼-lb **150.00**	Teapot, 1970s, Newport **125.00**
Cake plate **12.50**	Tidbit tray, 2-tier **35.00**
Cake stand, metal base **150.00**	Tumbler, Brockway, 16-oz **20.00**
Canister, sugar, 8¼" **24.00**	Tumbler, frosted, 5½" **12.50**
Canister, tea, 4" **18.00**	Tumbler, Libbey, 15-oz **50.00**
Casserole, Glasbake, shallow .**20.00**	Warmer, no decal **28.00**
Casserole, round, 2-qt **24.00**	
Coaster, 3" dia **4.50**	
Coffeepot, Rayed, 9-cup **32.50**	
Cookie jar, Rayed **120.00**	
Creamer, Rayed **15.00**	
Creamer, ruffled-D **8.50**	
Cup, ruffled-D **6.00**	
Custard, Radiance **4.50**	
Drip jar **16.50**	
Gravy boat, w/underplate **16.50**	
Hot pad, tin back, 7¼" **10.00**	
Jug, Rayed, 2½-pt **12.50**	
Marmalade **55.00**	
Mixing bowl, 2-qt **60.00**	
Mug, Irish coffee **90.00**	
Plate, 10" **12.50**	
Platter, oval, 9" **16.00**	
Sauce dish, Douglas **130.00**	
Saucepan, 2-qt **100.00**	
Saucer, ruffled-D **1.50**	
Sherbet, Libbey, 6½-oz **50.00**	

Avon

Originally founded in 1886 under the title California Perfume Company, the firm became officially known as Avon Products Inc. in 1939. Among collectors they are best known, not for their cosmetics and colognes, but for their imaginative packaging and figural bottles. Avon offers something for almost everyone such as cross-collectibles including Fostoria, Wedgwood, commemorative plates, Ceramarte steins, and hundreds of other quality items. Also sought are product samples, awards, magazine ads, jewelry, and catalogs. Their Cape Cod glassware has been sold in vast quantities since the seventies and is becoming a common sight at flea markets and antique malls. Our advisor for Avon is Tammy Rodrick, who is listed in the Directory under Illinois.

1941, Perfection Food Coloring, 4 in metal box, each bottle or box **18.00**
1941, Perfection Food Coloring Set, each bottle w/lid **25.00**
1953, Quartet, After Shave, Deodorant, 2 Shaving Creams, each pc **2.20**
1953, Quartet Set, 4-pc: After Shave, Deodorant, 2 Shaving Creams **65.00**

Percolator, all china, $225.00.

1958, Wishing Set, Cologne, Creme & Lotion Sachets, each pc **2.50**

1958, Wishing Set, 3-pc: Cologne, Creme & Lotion Sachets, MIP **50.00**

1962-65, Liberty Bell plate, blue & white, rep award **30.00**

1962-65, Men's Spicy Talc, white metal tin w/red letters, $10.00 to **12.00**

1970, Ruby Red bud vase, glass stopper **5.00**

1972, Delft Blue pitcher & bowl, $8.50 to **10.00**

1972, Hobnail decanter, white glass, $5.00 to **7.00**

1973, Betsy Ross plate, produced by Enoch Wedgwood, 9", $15.00 to **20.00**

1973, Christmas plate, Christmas on the Farm, Wedgwood, $75.00 to **80.00**

1974-78, King Chessman **5.00**

1976, Independence Hall plate, blue & white, rep award **30.00**

1976-77, George Washington candle holder, Fostoria, $12.50 to **15.00**

1976-77, Martha Washington candle holder, Fostoria, $12.50 to **15.00**

1976-77, Mt Vernon sauce pitcher, blue, Fostoria, $12.50 to ..**15.00**

1977, Anniversary Keepsake Powder tin, Avon & date on bottom, $4.00 to **5.00**

1977, Cape Cod wine decanter, ruby red glass **15.00**

1978, Victoriana pitcher & bowl, blue slag, $13.50 to **15.00**

1981, Nativity Collection, Holy Family, white ceramic, $45.00 to **50.00**

1982, Emerald Accent, green clear, tray, decanter, 2 tumblers, $45.00 to **50.00**

1983, Townhouse Canisters, set of 4, rep award **100.00**

Azalea China

Manufactured by the Noritake Company from 1916 until the mid-thirties, Azalea dinnerware was given away as premiums to club members and home agents of the Larkin Company, a door-to-door agency who sold soap and other household products. Over the years seventy chinaware items were offered as well as six pieces of matching hand-painted crystal. Early pieces were signed with the blue 'rising sun' Nippon trademark, followed by the Noritake M-in-wreath mark. Later the ware was marked Noritake, Azalea, Hand Painted, Japan.

Berry sugar shaker and creamer, #122, $160.00.

Bowl, salad; #12, 10" dia **42.50**

Bowl, vegetable; #172, oval, 9¼" **58.00**

Bowl, vegetable; open, #101, oval, 10½" **60.00**

Butter tub, w/insert, #54 .....**48.00**

Cake plate, #10, 9¾" **39.50**

Casserole, regular, #16 ......**125.00**

Cup & saucer, bouillon; #124 ...**24.50**

Jam jar, #125 ....**155.00**

Plate, bread & butter; #8, 6½" ..**10.00**

Platter, #17, 14" **60.00**

Relish dish, #194, 7⅛" **85.00**

Relish dish, divided, #171 ....**58.00**

Salt & pepper shakers, bulbous,
#89, pr **30.00**
Spoon holder, #189 ....**115.00**
Sugar bowl & creamer, regular,
#7, set **45.00**
Tray, celery or roll; #99, 12"..**55.00**

Banks

After the Depression, everyone was aware that saving 'for a rainy day' would help during bad times. Children of the '40s, '50s, and '60s were given piggy banks in forms of favorite characters to reinforce the idea of saving. They were made to realize that by saving money they could buy that expensive bicycle or a toy they were particulary longing for. Many of the banks from this era were ceramic, and today these banks are popular again. They were made not only by American companies such as McCoy, American Bisque, Cardinal, Shawnee, Cleminson, etc.; but many were imported from Japan and may bear the mark or label of Napco, Enesco, and Lefton. Our advisor for Ceramic Banks is Carol Silagyi, who is listed in the Directory under New Jersey.

The most popular (and expensive) type of older bank with today's collectors are the mechanicals, so called because of the antics they perform when a coin is deposited. Over three hundred models were produced between the Civil War period up to the first World War. On some, arms wave, legs kick, or mouths open to swallow up the coin – amusing nonsense intended by the inventor to encourage and reward thriftiness.

The registering bank may have one or more slots and, as the name implies, tallies the amount of money it contains as each coin is deposited.

Many old banks have been reproduced – beware! Condition is important; look for good original paint and parts. Some of the banks listed here are identified by D for Davidson, M for Moore, and N for Norman, oft-used standard reference books. Our advisor for still, registering, and mechanical banks is Charlie Reynolds; he is listed in the Directory under Virginia.

Popeye with pipe, American Bisque, $260.00; organ grinder monkey, Regal China (I Miller), $65.00; Herbert Lion, Lefton, H-13384, $35.00.

Ceramic Figurals

Betty Boop, Vandor **48.00**
Cat w/garbage pail, marked Feed
   the Kitty on lid, Japan ..**12.00**
Dog w/garbage pail, marked Scrap
   Money on lid, Japan **12.00**
Garfield, Enesco **18.00**
Hubert Lion, Lefton, H-13384..**35.00**
Humpty Dumpty, head vase type,
   Rubens Originals **35.00**
Kilban Cat, w/red sneakers,
   Japan **30.00**
Little Orphan Annie & Sandy..**38.00**
Miss Piggy **18.00**
Organ grinder monkey, Regal
   China (I Miller) **65.00**
Pay telephone, Japan **25.00**
Pig, w/1950s 'hep sayings' (Cool
   Man, See Ya Later Alligator,
   etc) **28.00**
Pig bride & groom turnabout,
   Thames (Japan) **22.00**
Popeye, Vandor **75.00**
Popeye, American Bisque ..**260.00**
St Bernard w/liquor barrel,
   McCoy **25.00**

Mechanical Banks

Always Did 'Spise a Mule, N-
   2940B, yellow, Stevens,
   NM **2,700.00**
Beehive, D-32, Northside Build-
   ing Loan, painted cast iron,
   6¾", VG **250.00**
Bulldog (standing), D-69, painted cast
   iron, worn paint, 3½" **400.00**
Devil (2-faced), painted cast iron,
   4¼", VG **600.00**
Eagle & Eaglets, D-165, painted
   cast iron, Stevens, no trap, 8",
   EX **715.00**
Feed the Goose, N-2400D, bronze,
   Pat 1927, EX **450.00**
Frog (on rock), D-203, painted
   cast iron, Kilgore, minor
   wear, 2¾" **700.00**

Humpty Dumpty, D-248, painted
   cast iron, 7½", G **275.00**
Jennings Trick Money Box, N-3440,
   painted cast iron, NM ..**600.00**
Magic Safe, N-3740A, painted
   cast iron, Germany, ca 1930,
   EX **550.00**
Minstrel Bank, N-2020A, w/verse,
   Germany, Pat '02, EX ..**850.00**
Monkey & Parrot, N-3950,
   painted cast iron, attributed
   to Selheimer & Straus,
   M **800.00**
Mosque Patterns, N-4010, brass
   roof, Judd, ca 1875, M ..**700.00**
Owl, D-375, painted cast iron, yellow
   eyes, head turns, 7", G ...**300.00**
Rooster, D-419, painted cast iron,
   Kyser & Rex, 6½", EX ..**550.00**
Tammany, D-455, painted cast
   iron, 5¾", EX **125.00**

Registering Banks

**Franklin Life Insurance, Steel
Products Corp., patented March
31, 1942, 4" dia, $20.00.**

Bed Post 5¢ Register, M-1305,
   EX **70.00**
Beehive 10¢, M-681, nickel-plated
   cast iron, 5¼", NM **440.00**
Bucket 1¢ register, cast iron,
   Japan, 2¾" **90.00**
Commonwealth Three Coin...,
   cash register, painted tin,
   5x4", EX **50.00**

Dopey 10¢ Register, Disney, 1938, EX **60.00**

Five Coin Security Bank, ca 1918, 7", EX **90.00**

Jr Cash, M-930, worn nickel-plated cast iron, light rust, 4¼" **50.00**

Keep 'Em Sailing, 10¢, battleship litho on tin, 1930s, 2½", EX **150.00**

New York World's Fair 1¢ register, M-1566, tin, M on card ..**55.00**

Popeye 10¢ register, NM **65.00**

Spinning Wheel, 2 scenes on tin, square, 4½", EX **25.00**

Trunk, Phoenix 10¢ register, M-947, nickel-plated cast iron, 5", EX **95.00**

Still Banks

Billy Bounce, M-14, painted cast iron, Wing, 4¾", EX **650.00**

Bird on Stump, M-644, cast iron, gold, 4¾", VG **175.00**

Boston Bull Terrier, M-421, painted cast iron, 5¼", VG **90.00**

Camel, M-768, cast iron, 4¾", EX **200.00**

Captain Kidd, M-38, painted cast iron, 5⅝", G **250.00**

Donkey, cast iron with paint traces, $85.00.

Cat, W-248, cast iron w/paint traces, seated **195.00**

Dutch Boy, M-180, painted cast iron, minor wear, 5¼" **75.00**

Fido, 417, cast iron, assorted colors, Hubley, 1914, 5", VG **145.00**

Fido on Pillow, M-443, cast iron, Hubley, repainted, 4" ..**125.00**

General Eisenhower (bust), M-133, pot metal w/bronze paint, 5½", VG **68.00**

Horse (Beauty), M-532, cast iron, assorted colors, ca 1932, 4½", G **100.00**

House, M-922, 2-story, painted cast iron, green & silver, 4⅛", EX **110.00**

Labrador Retriever, M-412, cast iron, black w/gold collar, 4½", EX **375.00**

Metropolitan, M-904, painted cast iron, broken lock, 5⅞", G **185.00**

Mulligan (policeman), M-177, painted cast iron, 5¾", VG **200.00**

Professor Pug Frog, M-311, cast iron, assorted colors, 3¼", EX **245.00**

Quilted Lion, M-758, cast iron, worn gold paint, 5" **245.00**

Seal on Rock, M-732, cast iron, gold or black, 3½", EX ..**450.00**

State Bank, M-1085, cast iron, bronzed, 3⅛", VG **175.00**

Terrier, white metal, trap missing, 5½", VG **100.00**

Treasure Chest, M-928, cast iron, red, 2", VG **195.00**

Underwood Typewriter, M-1272, painted white metal, 1⅜", VG **95.00**

Washington Monument, M-1048, painted cast iron, gold, 6⅛", EX **125.00**

White City Safe #10, M-913, painted cast iron, 4⅝", EX **200.00**

Barbed Wire

The collecting of antique barbed wires began in earnest about twenty-five years ago and today has grown into a national and international hobby. At the present time there are twelve State and Regional Collectors Associations and one National Society. See the Clubs and Newsletters section for relevant information.

Beginning with production of the first wire in 1868 and continuing into the early 1890s, many inventors vied for their share of a booming market that saw nearly every conceivable pattern introduced. In all, over 1,200 wires and variations were designed. It is these wires that today's collectors buy, sell, and trade at shows and conventions throughout the United States and via the mail. As in most other hobbies, scarcity and uniqueness go hand in hand in determining value.

Many museums across the country are finally recognizing antique barbed wires as the true historical items they are. More than the Winchester '73 and the windmill, barbed wire changed the once wide-open ranges of the Old West into civilized communities with established property lines.

Our advisor, John Mantz, is listed in the Directory under California. See the Clubs and Newsletters section for the address of the American Barbed Wire Collectors Society. Please note that prices are for wires made in the 19th century that are 18" in length. Pricing information is from *The Barbed Wire Collector*.

Allis's Buckthorn, 1881 .... **.25**
Brinkerhoff's XIT Ranch Wire, 1879, custom order **50.00**
Bronson's Link Wire, 1877 ...**15.00**
Burnell's Parallel, 1877 ....**3.00**
Dodge & Washburn's Bread Loaf Line, 1882 ....**25.00**
Dodge's Rowel Wire, 1881, very rare **300.00**
Ellwood's Ribbon Wire, 1874, hard to find **250.00**
Ford's Link & Coil, 1885 ......**12.00**
Freese's Link & Bar Diamond Wire, 1888, extremely rare **350.00**
Glidden's Three Line RR Wire, 1874, One Line Square ..**10.00**
Glidden's UPPR Wire, 1874, custom order .... **.50**
Glidden's Winner, 1874 (pattern for most modern wires) .... **.10**
Guilleaume's Two Line, 1893..**50.00**
Haish's Walking Cane, 1875 ..**3.00**
Havenhill's Y-Barb, 1878 ....**1.00**
Hearst's Ranch, Copper Horse Wire, 1920(?) **10.00**
Hodge's Spur Rowel, 1887 .....**5.00**
Judson's Notched Ribbon, 1871 ....**200.00**
Kelly's Diamond Point, 1868 ... **.25**
Kelly's Pin Wire, 1868 ....**150.00**
Kelly's Single Line, 1868 .....**70.00**
Merrill's Buffalo Wire, 1876, very heavy **2.00**

Hodge 10-Point Spur Rowel, Pat. Aug. 2, 1887, 18" length, $5.00.

Rose's Wooden Rail, 1873, very
rare, per inch **20.00**
Stubbe's Large Plate, 1883 ....**2.00**
Wilke's Double Staple Wire,
1879 ....**3.00**

Barware

Gleaming with sophistication
and style, vintage cocktail shakers are skyrocketing in value as
the hot new collectible of the '90s.
Young trend-setters are using this
swank and practical objet d'art to
serve their pre-dinner drinks.
Form and function never had a
better mix. The latest acquisition
from America's classic Art Deco
past is occasion enough for a
party and a round of martinis.

In the 1920s it was prohibition that brought the cocktail
hour and cocktail parties into the
home. Today the high cost of dining out along with a more
informed social awareness about
alcohol consumption brings at-
home cocktail parties back into
fashion. Released across the country from after a half century of
imprisonment in attics and china
closets, these glass and chrome
shaker sets have been recalled to
life—recalled to hear the clank of
ice cubes and to again become the
symbol of elegance.

For further information we
recommend our advisors, Arlene
Lederman (listed in the Directory
under New York) and Stephen
Visakay (listed in the Directory
under New Jersey).

Book, Savoy Cocktail Book, Crad-
dock, London, 1930 .....**150.00**
Cigarette dispenser, Black bartender, France, 6½x6" ..**700.00**

**Sailboat, cocktail shaker, 11",
$38.00; ice bowl, 4½" diameter,
$28.00; tumbler, 4¾", $12.50.**

Cocktail set, cobalt w/silver overlay, 1920s, 11" shaker+8 3⅝"
cups **350.00**
Cocktail set, Doric, chrome, 6
cups w/plastic feet on 12"
tray, Chase **160.00**
Cocktail shaker, bell form, nickeled
brass, wood handle, 11" ..**45.00**
Cocktail shaker, bell form, stainless steel, wood handle,
1900s, 11" **50.00**
Cocktail shaker, bowling pin form,
chrome w/wood top, late '30s,
56-oz **50.00**
Cocktail shaker, chrome, plastic
handle, generic type, w/tray
& cups **50.00**
Cocktail shaker, chrome, red plastic handle, generic type,
1930s **42.50**
Cocktail shaker, cobalt glass,
horse & rider decor, Hazel
Atlas, 10" **48.00**
Cocktail shaker, cranberry
flashed & cut, silverplated
top, 10½" **150.00**
Cocktail shaker, dumbbell form,
cobalt, silver trim, 1930s, +6
glasses **400.00**

Cocktail shaker, Empire, chrome & Catalin, Revere, 1937, 12⅛x3" **325.00**
Cocktail shaker, Gaiety, Deco style, Chase, 11½x3¾" ..**50.00**
Cocktail shaker, glass, horse's head top, Heisey, 3-pc **200.00**
Cocktail shaker, glass, plain top, Heisey, 3-pc **40.00**
Cocktail shaker, glass, pressed diamonds, plastic top, 1928, 12½" **40.00**
Cocktail shaker, glass, rooster's head top, Heisey, 3-pc ...**70.00**
Cocktail shaker, glass w/pink elephants, Hazel Atlas, 10" ..**42.50**
Cocktail shaker, Hammertone, black handle, Krome Kraft, 2½-qt, 15" **65.00**
Cocktail shaker, hourglass form, glass & chrome, Maxwell Phillip, 9x5" **75.00**
Cocktail shaker, Kensington, skyscraper form, aluminum, 13x3½" dia **95.00**
Cocktail shaker, Krome Kraft, chrome, plastic handle & knobs, '30s **40.00**
Cocktail shaker, lady's leg, high-heel shoe, WV Specialty, 1937, 15" **450.00**
Cocktail shaker, milk can shape, Reed & Barton silverplate, 10¼" **70.00**
Cocktail shaker, nickel silver, Expressware, 1-gal, 18½" ..**95.00**
Cocktail shaker, onyx glass w/ silkscreened recipes, chrome top, 1-qt **165.00**
Cocktail shaker, penguin form, chrome, 11x4" dia **350.00**
Cocktail shaker, penguin form, silverplate, marked Napier, 12x4¼" **1,100.00**
Cocktail shaker, Precision Cooler, aluminum, 11¼x4¼" **70.00**
Cocktail shaker, Ritz, chrome & plastic, glass inserts, 1930s **65.00**

Cocktail shaker, ruby glass w/white silkscreened recipes, 10½" **42.50**
Cocktail shaker, ruby w/silver hunt scene, chrome top, 1930s, 1-qt **165.00**
Cocktail shaker, ruby w/silver roosters, silverplated top, 1-qt **165.00**
Cocktail shaker, school bell form, stainless steel, 11" **55.00**
Corkscrew, waiter w/wine bottle, molded wood composition, '30s, 8" **40.00**
Drink mixer, glass jar w/tin lid, spiral tin whipper, Pat 1915, 16" **25.00**
Drink stirrer, Spoonmat, stainless steel, telescoping, 11¾" .**15.00**
Gyroscopic rack, chrome, 20", 8½" dia rings, +4 glasses ...**200.00**
Gyroscopic rack, 20", w/4¼" dia rings, +4 glasses **115.00**
Ice bucket, aluminum w/embossed penguins, wood handle, West Bend, 1944 ....**32.50**
Ice bucket, apple form, anodized aluminum, red or blue, Italy, 1950s **30.00**
Ice bucket, chrome plate on copper, Keystone Wear, 1930s, +tray **85.00**
Jigger, top hat shape, marked Chase, ca 1935, 1½-oz, +4 swizzle sticks **30.00**
Seltzer dispenser, marked Soda King Syphon...Norman Bel Geddes, 9½" **150.00**
Tray, 'Here's How!,' 4 cartoon flappers, cocktail recipes, J Held Jr **100.00**

Baseball Cards

The first baseball cards were issued in the late 1800s by cigarette and tobacco companies who packed them with their products to promote sales. The practice was revived for a few years just before WWI and again just in time to be curtailed by the Depression. From 1933 until the onset of WWII and from early in the 1950s to the present, chewing gum companies produced sports cards, the most popular of which are put out by Bowman and Topps. The colored photo cards from the thirties are the most treasured, and one of a baseball great or Hall of Famer is the most valued in any particular issue. Condition is of utmost importance. A card that is worth $50.00 in near-mint condition may be worth only half of that amount if rated excellent. One that has been obviously handled, the corners frayed and rounded, a little soiled, or with a slight crease or fading may drop to only $5.00. Refer to *Gene Florence's Standard Baseball Card Price Guide* (Collector Books) for up-to-date information on values.

Bowman, Bob Avila, 1952, NM, $15.00.

Bowman, #102, Ricco Brogna, 1989, EX/NM .... .35

Bowman, #105, Bob Dillinger, 1950, VG 4.50

Bowman, #115, Marquis Grissom, 1990, EX/NM .... .35

Bowman, #138, Ted Wilks, 1952, VG **3.75**

Bowman, #14, Curt Simmons, 1949, EX/NM **26.00**

Bowman, #141, Joe Garagiola, 1954, VG **11.25**

Bowman, #156, Al Zarilla, 1949, EX/NM **75.00**

Bowman, #16, Bob Friend, 1953, EX/NM **35.00**

Bowman, #184, Willie Mayes, 1955, EX/NM **225.00**

Bowman, #202, Cliff Chambers, 1950, EX/NM **18.00**

Bowman, #213, George Kell, 1955, VG **5.50**

Bowman, #2136, Ray Coleman, 1951, EX/NM **14.00**

Bowman, #220, Ken Griffey Jr, 1989, EX/NM **5.00**

Bowman, #225, Nolan Ryan, 1989, EX/NM .... .50

Bowman, #225, Paul Richards, 1955, EX/NM **17.00**

Bowman, #266, John Smoltz, 1989, EX/NM .... .50

Bowman, #268, Steve Avery, 1989, EX/NM **1.50**

Bowman, #32, Wade Boggs, 1989, EX/NM .... .25

Bowman, #38, Whitey Lockman, 1952, VG **3.75**

Bowman, #454, Sandy Alomar, 1989, EX/NM .... .35

Bowman, #54, Billy Pierce, 1952, VG **5.50**

Bowman, #58, Frank Thomas, 1955, VG **2.50**

Bowman, #7, Gil Hodges, 1951, VG **20.00**

Bowman, #73, Willard Marshall, 1950, VG **4.50**

Bowman, #82, Joe Astroth, 1953, VG **7.50**

Bowman, #88, Steve Bilko, 1955, EX/NM **7.00**

Bowman, #95, Luke Easter, 1952, VG **3.75**

Donruss, #0, Johnny Bench, 1984, EX/NM **10.00**

Donruss, #111, Steve Carlton, 1984, EX/NM **3.00**

Donruss, #119, Rickey Henderson, 1981, VG **4.50**

Donruss, #131, Roberto, Alomar, 1991, EX/NM **75**

Donruss, #14, Bo Jackson, 1987, EX/NM **3.50**

Donruss, #156, Jeff Reardon, 1981, EX/NM **6.00**

Donruss, #183, Mike Schmidt, 1984, EX/NM **15.00**

Donruss, #188, Phil Niekro, 1984, EX/NM **1.00**

Donruss, #19, Hal Morris, 1992, EX/NM **3.50**

Donruss, #193, Jesse Barfield, 1984, EX/NM **40**

Donruss, #222, Bret Saberhagen, 1985, EX/NM **7.00**

Donruss, #240, Jim Presley, 1985, EX/NM **1.00**

Donruss, #249, Ben McDonald, 1990, EX/NM **4.00**

Donruss, #3, Barry Larkin, 1991, EX/NM **6.00**

Donruss, #30, Bobby Bonilla, 1986, EX/NM **6.00**

Donruss, #30, Ron Darling, 1984, EX/NM **3.00**

Donruss, #31, Jim Abbott, 1990, EX/NM **2.50**

Donruss, #4, Julio Franco, 1992, EX/NM **2.50**

Donruss, #4, Mike Greenwell, 1987, EX/NM **2.00**

Donruss, #435, Ivan Calderon, 1986, EX/NM **1.50**

Donruss, #44, Sid Fernandez, 1984, EX/NM **3.00**

Donruss, #481, Steve Avery, 1990, EX/NM **20.00**

Donruss, #483, Randy Johnson, 1990, EX/NM **75**

Donruss, #5, Ellis Burks, 1987, EX/NM **2.00**

Donruss, #5, Willie Banks, 1991, EX/NM **3.00**

Donruss, #54, George (Jorge) Bell, 1982, EX/NM **6.50**

Donruss, #586, Wade Boggs, 1983, VG **6.00**

Donruss, #593, Kirk Gibson, 1984, EX/NM **1.00**

Donruss, #8, Len Dykstra, 1991, EX/NM **5.00**

Donruss, #83, Andy Van Slyke, 1984, EX/NM **7.00**

Fleer, #102, Pete Rose, 1984 update card, EX/NM **20.00**

Fleer, #106, Tom Seaver, 1984 update card, VG **6.25**

Fleer, #258, Wes Chamberlain, 1991, EX/NM **1.25**

Fleer, #286, Kirby Puckett, 1985, EX/NM **35.00**

Fleer, #349, Roger Clemens, 1988, EX/NM **1.00**

Fleer, #407, Jack McDowell, 1988, EX/NM **1.50**

Fleer, #48, Ozzie Guillen, 1985, EX/NM **2.00**

Fleer, #520, Reggie Jackson, 1984, EX/NM **2.50**

Fleer, #574, Rickey Henderson, 1981, EX/NM **15.00**

Fleer, #58, Carlton Fisk, 1984, EX/NM **2.00**

Fleer, #640, Johnny Bench, 1984, EX/NM **2.50**

Fleer, #644, Gene Walter, 1986, EX/NM **3.50**

Fleer, #646, Paul O'Neill, 1986, EX/NM **5.00**

Fleer, #82, Dwight Gooden, 1985, VG **3.00**

Fleer, #85, Frank Thomas, 1991, VG **1.50**

Score, #1, Wade Boggs, EX/NM **1.50**

Score, #606, Kevin Maas, 1990, EX/NM **75**

Score, #647, Ron Gant, 1988, EX/NM **2.50**

Score, #672, Chuck Knoblauch, 1990, EX/NM 2.00

Score, #88, Jim Abbott, 1989, EX/NM 1.00

Sportflics, #158, Randy Asadoor, 1987, EX/NM 1.50

Sportflics, #224, Ramon Martinez, 1989, EX/NM 75

Sportflics, #6, Will Clark, 1986, EX/NM 6.00

Sportflics, #93, Kirby Puckett, 1986, EX/NM 2.50

Topps, Roy Campanella, 1952, NM, $1,000.00.

Topps, #1, Bob Friend, 1964, VG 5.00

Topps, #100, Hank Aaron, 1969, EX/NM 60.00

Topps, #138, Minnie Minosa, 1957, VG 3.00

Topps, #139, Dalton Jones, 1967, EX/NM 1.60

Topps, #140, Lou Gehrig, 1962, VG 5.00

Topps, #147, Ernie Banks, 1959, EX/NM 12.00

Topps, #159, Charlie Dees, 1964, EX/NM 1.80

Topps, #251, Billy Herman, 1965, EX/NM 3.00

Topps, #257, Bobby Avila, 1952, VG 11.25

Topps, #26, Chico Carrasquel, 1951, VG 10.00

Topps, #265, Chuck Diering, 1952, EX/NM 45.00

Topps, #274, Ralph Branca, 1952, VG 22.50

Topps, #290, Jerry Lumpe, 1960, EX/NM 3.00

Topps, #295, Phil Caverretta, 1952, VG 15.00

Topps, #3, George Crowe, 1953, VG 6.25

Topps, #36, Johnny Groth, 1953, EX/NM 15.00

Topps, #371, Marty Keough, 1958, EX/NM 4.00

Topps, #375, Ron Fairly, 1962, EX/NM 4.00

Topps, #384, Dick Hughes, 1967, EX/NM 2.00

Topps, #386, Ed Bailey, 1959, VG 2.50

Topps, #4, Del Ennis, 1951, VG 6.25

Topps, #422, Hobie Landrith, 1959, EX/NM 4.00

Topps, #430, Tony Kubek, 1962, VG 2.00

Topps, #480, Roy Campanella, 1961, EX/NM 35.00

Topps, #488, Jerry Adair, 1963, EX/NM 10.00

Topps, #508, Steve Hargan, 1966, EX/NM 6.00

Topps, #535, Marv Breeding, 1960, VG 2.75

Topps, #557, Bob Anderson, 1962, VG 5.00

Topps, #583, Ray Barker, 1967, EX/NM 18.00

Topps, #592, Joe Bonikowski, 1962, VG 12.50

Topps, #596, Bernie Allen, 1962, VG 15.00

Topps, #620, Jose Canesco, 1987, EX/NM 3.00

Topps, #625, Lou Brock, 1971, VG 7.00

Topps, #90, Jim Nash, 1967, EX/NM **1.60**
Topps, #93, Steve Bilko, 1955, EX/NM **9.00**

Bauer

The Bauer Company moved from Kentucky to California in 1909, producing crocks, gardenware, and vases until after the Depression when they introduced their first line of dinnerware. From 1932 until the early 1960s, they successfully marketed several lines of solid-color wares that are today very collectible. Some of their most popular lines are Ring, Plain Ware, and Monterey Moderne.

Baking dish, Ring, yellow, jade green or light blue, w/lid, 4" **20.00**
Bowl, batter; Ring, black, 1-qt **175.00**
Bowl, fruit; Al Fresco, speckled, green or gray, 5" **5.00**
Bowl, fruit; Monterey Moderne, all colors but black, 4¼" **12.50**
Bowl, ramekin; La Linda, burgundy or dark brown **10.00**
Bowl, vegetable; Al Fresco, coffee brown, 9¼" **18.00**

Butter dish, Ring, dark blue or burgundy, oblong **125.00**
Candlestick, Monterey, all colors but white **40.00**
Canister, grease; Al Fresco, coffee brown or Dubonnet **12.00**
Chop plate, Monterey, all colors but white, 13" **45.00**
Coffee server, Monterey, white, 8-cup **45.00**
Cup, jumbo coffee; La Linda, light brown, pink or ivory **24.00**
Cup & saucer, Al Fresco, coffee brown or Dubonnet **12.00**
Custard cup, La Lina, burgundy or dark brown **8.00**
Gravy boat, Al Fresco, coffee brown or Dubonnet **12.50**
Gravy bowl, Monterey Moderne, all colors but black **30.00**
Mug, plain, black, 8-oz **65.00**
Pitcher, La Linda, green, yellow or turquoise, w/ice lip, 2-qt ..**45.00**
Pitcher, plain, all colors but black, 1-qt **50.00**
Plate, El Chico, any, 7½" **15.00**
Plate, El Chico, any, 9" **25.00**
Plate, Monterey, white, 9" ...**20.00**
Platter, plain, all colors but black, oval, 12" **25.00**
Sherbet, Ring, orange-red, dark blue or burgundy **40.00**
Soup plate, La Linda, green, yellow or turquoise, 7" **22.00**

Teapot, Gloss Pastel Kitchenware, 1940s, 8-cup, $70.00.

Soup plate, Ring, yellow, jade
green or turquoise, 7½"..**45.00**
Sugar bowl, Al Fresco, speckled,
green or gray, w/lid **10.00**
Teapot, La Linda, light brown, ivory
or olive green, 6-cup **35.00**
Teapot, Ring, yellow, light blue or
red-brown, 2-cup **65.00**
Tumbler, La Linda, green, yellow
or turquoise, 8-oz **12.00**
Tumbler, Ring, black, no handle,
6-oz **45.00**

The Beatles

Beatles memorabilia is
becoming increasingly popular
with those who grew up in the
'60s. Almost any item that could
be produced with their pictures or
logos were manufactured and sold
by the thousands in department
stores. Some have such a high
collector value that they have
been reproduced, beware! Refer to
*The Beatles: A Reference and
Value Guide* by Michael Stern,
Barbara Crawford, and Hollis
Lamon (Collector Books) for more
information.

Apron, paper-like fiber, records,
faces & music, black on
white, NEMS **375.00**
Balloons, group pictured on each,
United Industries, M in
package **60.00**
Bank, plastic, 1964, NM **40.00**
Beach hat, The Beatles & portraits
in black on white crown, red
band **120.00**
Belt buckle, black & white pic-
ture, brass-like trim, rectangular, EX **125.00**
Binder, 2- or 3-ring, Beatles &
facsimile signatures on yel-
low, VG **110.00**

Book, A Hard Day's Night, paper-
back, 1964, EX **10.00**
Bowl, porcelain, EX **70.00**
Bracelet, portrait on each of 4
white disks, gold-tone chain,
Randall **225.00**
Calendar, John & Yoko, LP
promo, spiral bound, 1970,
M **15.00**
Cartoon dolls, inflatable, 15", set
of 4, M **165.00**
Cel, Policeman (from Yellow Sub-
marine) **400.00**
Change purse, satin, photo of
John playing guitar, 1970s,
M **15.00**
Cigar band, face of Beatle, from
Jamaica, EX **90.00**
Clothes hanger, bust of Beatle,
Henderson-Haggard, 16",
each **100.00**
Doll, Paul, rubber, Remco, 5",
VG **55.00**

**Fan, cardboard on wooden stick,
EX, $35.00.**

Halloween costume, John Lennon, 1960s, MIB **325.00**

Handkerchief, excerpts from hit songs, 4 stars & The Beatles, VG **200.00**

Hatbox, vinyl, black & white portraits, fascimile signatures, Air-Flite **550.00**

Headband, Love the Beatles, EX **125.00**

Magazine, All About the Beatles, #1 issue, 1964, EX **25.00**

Magazine, Beatle Song Magazine, Summer 1964, VG **6.00**

Magazine, Beatles Whole True Story, 1966, EX **20.00**

Model kit, Paul McCartney, Revell, 1964, assembled, NM **75.00**

Nodder dolls, plastic, unlicensed, 5", 4 for **20.00**

Note pad, M **50.00**

Pillow, waist-up portraits, Lennon w/guitar, 3-color on white, EX **175.00**

Pillow, waist-up portraits, 3-color on white, Nordic House, EX **150.00**

Pin, drum & guitar shape w/The Beatles lettered between, M **150.00**

Postcard, Yellow Submarine, EX **65.00**

Poster, John Lennon, Alan Aldridge, signed, limited edition, 1981, M **115.00**

Poster, John Lennon, psychedelic image, Look Magazine, 31x22" **25.00**

Poster, Paul McCartney, Wings Over America, 1975, 28x19", M **65.00**

Poster, Ringo Star, dove in hand, Look Magazine, 31x22" **25.00**

Poster, Yellow Submarine, 3-sheet, 1968, EX **600.00**

Record album, Something New, Capitol #2108, stereo, M ..**25.00**

Ring, flasher type, M **15.00**

Scarf, portraits & facsimile signatures, 1964, 26", EX **150.00**

Sweatshirt, black on white, 1960s, NM **140.00**

Tour book program, ca 1964, 12x12", M **18.00**

Tray, 4 color 'snapshots' on white, Worcester Ware, square ..**60.00**

Tumbler, insulated plastic, lips, full-length Beatles w/instruments, M **125.00**

Tumblers, fired-on 1-color portrait & music symbols, complete set of 4 ....**425.00**

Bedroom & Bathroom Glassware

During the lean years of the 'Great Depression,' American glassware companies produced vast amounts of inexpensive wares for bed and bathroom in an all-out effort to remain solvent. Their products were made in a wide array of colors and shapes. Many remain to the present and continue today to attract the attention of veteran collectors as well as the transient flea market shopper. For more information consult *Bedroom and Bathroom Glassware of the Depression Years* by Margaret and Kenn Whitmyer (Collector Books).

Atomizer, Cambridge, ivory, 8 panels w/black outlines, 4¼" **50.00**

Atomizer, Fenton, Horizontal Rib pattern, blue opalescent ..**25.00**

Atomizer, Fenton, Swirled Feather pattern, satin blue, frosted lid **90.00**

Barber bottle, Fenton, Hanging Hearts pattern, custard, 1953 ....**75.00**

Cologne bottle, Imperial, Twisted Optic pattern, amber **55.00**

Compact, Cambridge, ivory w/ enameled iris decoration..**95.00**

Compact, Fostoria, blue fan shape, fleur-de-lis finial **40.00**

Doorknob, crystal, cut design, oval **55.00**

Doorknob, topaz, cut center ..**95.00**

Guest set, Cambridge #489, amber, etched hunt scene, 4-pc .**120.00**

Guest set, Fenton #401, topaz, 2-pc **25.00**

Hair receiver, Tiffin, frosted topaz **35.00**

Jar, cold cream; Dubarry-Richard Hudnut label, pink, footed, 4½" **22.50**

Jar, cold cream; Fenton, Coin Dot, cranberry opalescent, crystal lid **40.00**

Jar, cold cream; New Martinsville, embossed crystal, w/green lid **12.00**

Lamp, Oriental Girl, fired-on blue **50.00**

Lamp, Victorian Lady, frosted pink, metal base & shade **80.00**

Boudoir lamp, Southern Bell, crystal with fired-on pink, 9½", $50.00.

Manicure set, marked EW Inc, Chicago, frosted green, heart shape **70.00**

Mirror, Imperial, Candlewick pattern, crystal, 4¼" dia **75.00**

Night light, covered wagon, frosted crystal **135.00**

Perfume bottle, Cambridge, emerald, beehive stopper **45.00**

Perfume bottle, Cambridge #575, emerald **55.00**

Perfume bottle, Fostoria #2322, ebony, gold trim **85.00**

Perfume bottle, New Martinsville, frosted green, 8-sided ...**50.00**

Perfume bottle, Paden City #502-5, crystal, 4½" **25.00**

Perfume bottle, US Glass, crystal, black stopper **50.00**

Pin tray, Baccarat, yellow, oval **60.00**

Pin tray, Heisey, Winged Scroll pattern, emerald **40.00**

Powder jar, Akro Agate, vertical ribbing, opaque white ...**35.00**

Powder jar, Art Deco, pleated fan form, cobalt **85.00**

Powder jar, crystal, elephant finial, 6¾" dia **30.00**

Powder jar, Fenton Wave Crest, powder blue, cased **95.00**

Powder jar, Fostoria #2276, amber, etched Vesper design ...**100.00**

Powder jar, Jeannette Glass Co, transparent pink, elephant finial **25.00**

Powder jar, Rose Blossom, frosted pink **45.00**

Puff box, Akro Agate, Colonial Lady, opaque pink, 3½" dia **50.00**

Puff box, Cambridge, Wetherford pattern, amber **25.00**

Puff box, Fostoria #2338, blue, wheel-cut decor, flat lid, 4" dia **25.00**

Puff box, Heisey, clear base, enameled top **40.00**

Puff box, Imperial, Swirl pattern, pink, fan-shaped stopper..**25.00**

Puff box, LE Smith, pink, disk-shaped stopper **30.00**

Puff box, Liberty Glass Co, American Pioneer pattern, pink, 4" dia **70.00**

Puff box, Paden City, amber, 4" dia **20.00**

Ring holder, Cambridge, primrose pink **40.00**

Soap dish, frosted pink, nude figural, 4x6" **40.00**

Torchiere lamp, US Glass, frosted crystal, black top & base..**135.00**

Towel bar, pink, twisted, clip holders **30.00**

Tray, Fenton #957, amber, fan shape **15.00**

Trinket box, Heisey, Winged Scroll pattern, crystal **30.00**

Vanity set, Fenton #3986, Hobnail pattern, blue opalescent **80.00**

Bells

The earliest bells were probably connected with religion, since they have been traced to superstitions such as are evident in graves over 3,000 years old. Their purpose was to protect the dead, animals and humans alike, from evil spirits. As time passed, bells became more closely associated with Christianity, so we find them mentioned in the Bible. For further information we recommend our advisor (author of several books) Dorothy Malone Anthony, who is listed in the Directory under Kansas. See also Clubs and Newsletters.

Brass, Child Crusader figural handle, Hemony, old, 6½" ..**135.00**

Brass, Dutch twins, marked China, old, 3" **35.00**

Brass, Napoleon figural handle, old, 4" **40.00**

Brass, school bell, heavy, w/wood handle, 6½" **40.00**

Brass, tap bell, w/ornate iron base, 5" **35.00**

Bronze, Ballantyne 1981, Robin Hood figural handle, 6½" **235.00**

Bronze, evangelist altar bell, 4" **25.00**

Bronze, worn by Civil War mule, 3¾" **50.00**

Copper, cow bell, old, 6" **12.00**

Custard glass, souvenir, Kansas Sod House, 6½" **95.00**

Cut glass, tear-drop handle, Irish **50.00**

Glass, Columbian World's Fair, 1893, Chicago, 5" **125.00**

Glass, gold wash, Hungarian, old, 6½" **80.00**

Goebel, glass w/chimney sweep china handle, 6¼" **40.00**

Hammersley 1971 annual, 6"..**30.00**

Metal, draped female, upraised arms hold twirler bell, 8"..**85.00**

Little Red Riding Hood, china figural, 4½", $25.00.

46

Pairpoint, teal glass, wedding type, 12" **130.00**

Pressed carnival glass, diamond-daisy design, 6" **350.00**

Quimper, fish head, 4¼" **65.00**

Shaft bells, 3 on metal frame w/wood mount **35.00**

Spaghetti porcelain, Italian, round strands, 2¾" **15.00**

Wedgwood NY 1979, blue Jasper, 3" **25.00**

Big Little Books

Probably everyone who is now forty to sixty years of age owned a few Big Little Books as a child. Today these thick hand-sized adventures bring prices from $10.00 to $75.00 and upwards. The first was published in 1933 by Whitman Publishing Company. Dick Tracy was the featured character. Kids of the early fifties preferred the format of the comic book, and Big Little Books were gradually phased out. Stories about super heroes and Disney characters bring the highest prices, especially those with an early copyright.

Andy Panda & the Mad Dog Mystery, Whitman #1431, 1947, NM **40.00**

Andy Panda & the Pirate Ghosts, Whitman #1459, 1949, EX........................**22.50**

Andy Panda's Vacation, Whitman #1485, 1946, EX **30.00**

Blondie & Dagwood in Hot Water, Whitman #1410, 1946, NM **40.00**

Blondie & Dagwood/Everybody's Happy, Whitman #1438, 1948, EX **40.00**

Blondie in No Dull Moments, Whitman #1450, 1948, EX..**55.00**

Buck Jones in the Roaring West, Whitman #1174, 1935, VG **26.00**

Bugs Bunny & the Pirate Loot, Whitman #1403, 1947, EX **30.00**

Captain Midnight and the Moon Woman, 1942, G, $25.00.

Chandu the Magician, Saalfield #1093, 1935, VG **20.00**

Don Winslow & the Giant Girl Spy, Whitman, 1946, EX **35.00**

Donald Duck Gets Fed Up, Whitman #1462, 1938, VG ...**50.00**

Dr Doom & the Ghost Submarine, Whitman #1460A, 1939, VG **25.00**

G-Man in Action, Saalfield #1173, 1940, NM **48.00**

Ghost Avenger Strikes, Whitman #1462A, 1943, EX **48.00**

Invisible Scarlet O'Neil vs King of the Slums, Whitman #1406, 1946, EX **40.00**

Jack Swift & His Rocket Ship, Whitman #1102, 1934, VG **30.00**

Jim Starr of the Border Patrol, Whitman #1428B, 1937, VG **15.00**

Gunsmoke, Whitman, 1958, EX, $25.00.

Lassie's Adventure in Alaska, 1967, VG **2.50**

Little Orphan Annie & the Ghost Gang, Whitman #1154, 1935, VG **35.00**

Mandrake the Magician, Whitman #1167, 1935, VG **32.50**

Marge's Little Lulu, Alvin & Tubby, Whitman #1429, 1947, EX **65.00**

Mickey Mouse & the Seven Ghosts, Whitman #1475, 1940, EX **75.00**

Peggy Brown & the Secret Treasure, Whitman #1423, 1947, EX **35.00**

Popeye & the Jeep, Whitman #1405C, 1937, EX **60.00**

Red Barry, Undercover Man; Whitman #1426A, 1939, VG ..**22.50**

Red Ryder & the Western Border Guns, Whitman #1450C, 1942, EX **40.00**

Return of Tarzan, Whitman #1102A, 1936, EX **32.50**

Skeezix Goes to War, Whitman #1414, 1944, EX **35.00**

Skeezix in Africa, Whitman #112A, 1934, EX **50.00**

Smilin' Jack & the Jungle Pipe Line, Whitman #1419, 1947, EX **50.00**

Tailspin Tommy & the Hooded Flyer, Whitman #1423D, 1937, EX **50.00**

Tailspin Tommy & the Sky Bandits, Whitman #1494, 1938, EX **37.50**

Tarzan & the Jewels of Opar, Whitman #1495A, 1940, EX **50.00**

Terry & the Pirates in the Mountain Stronghold, Whitman 1499A, 1941, G **16.00**

Terry & War in the Jungle, Whitman #1420, 1946, EX **35.00**

Tom & Jerry Meet Mr Fingers, Whitman #2006, 1967, M..**5.00**

Tom Mix & the Hoard of Montezuma, Whitman, #1462, 1937, EX **45.00**

Tom Swift & His Giant Telescope, Whitman #1495C, 1939, EX **50.00**

Two-Gun Montana, Whitman #1104, 1936, EX **32.50**

Uncle Wiggily's Adventures, Whitman #1405, 1946, EX **40.00**

Will Rogers, Saalfield #1096, 1935, VG **32.50**

Woody Woodpecker & the Sinister Signal, Whitman #2028, 1969, EX **7.50**

Wyatt Earp, Whitman #1644, 1958, EX **10.00**

Zane Grey's Tex Thorne Comes Out of the West, Whitman #1440A, 1937, NM **45.00**

Black Americana

This is a wide and varied field of collector interest. Advertising, toys, banks, sheet music, kitchenware items, movie items, and even the fine arts are areas that offer Black Americana buffs many opportunities to add to their collections. Caution! Because some pieces have become so valuable, reproductions abound. Watch for lots of new ceramic items, less detailed in both the modeling and the painting. One of our advisors for this category is Judy Posner, who is listed in the Directory under Pennsylvania. Refer to these books for more information: *Black Collectibles Sold in America* by P.J. Gibbs, and *Black Dolls, An Identification and Value Guide, 1820-1991*, by Myla Perkins (Collector Books).

Chalkware group, Universal Statuary Corp., Chicago, ca 1974, 7½", $40.00.

Advertising print, Chesapeake & Ohio, Black porter, ca '30s, 20x19" **125.00**
Advertising tin, Luter's Lard, bail handle, 4-lb, 6x6", EX ..**125.00**
Ashtray, Mammy's Shanty Restaurant, glass, ca '40s, M **80.00**
Blocks, Sambo & Tiger, '40s, graduated in size, stacking set of 5 ....**125.00**
Blotter, Green River Whiskey, late 1800s-early 1900s **45.00**

Book, Booker T Washington, memorial edition, FE Drinker, 1915 ....**28.00**
Book, Kentucky Yarns, paperback, by Opie Meade, ca 1912, EX **30.00**
Book, Little Brown Koko, Blanch Seale Hunt, 1940, 10¾x7¾", EX **55.00**
Book, Little Watermelon Pete..., Rand McNally, 1927, 6¾x5½", EX **18.00**
Book, Twin Kids, Inez Hogan, hard cover, 1938, 6x8" ...**75.00**
Box, Plantation Flavor Creole Pralines, cardboard, ca 1930s, EX **60.00**
Button, Aunt Jemima Breakfast Club, full color, M **15.00**
Candle holder, Black genie figural, Brayton Pottery, ca 1940s, 5¼" **75.00**
Cigar display box, Cochran's Sampler, ca 1940s, 2¼x15½x6¾", EX **125.00**
Cigarette holder & ashtray, musician in center, ceramic, 3¾x3" dia **80.00**
Cookie jar, chef wearing black & white striped pants, ceramic, 9½" **115.00**
Cookie jar, Mammy figural, red & white plastic, F&F, '30s-40s, 12" **300.00**
Coupon, features Aunt Jemima Rag Doll Family, color litho, '20s, NM **65.00**
Creamer, full-figure Black man, individual, pottery, 2¾", M **65.00**
Creamer & sugar bowl, attached figurals, plastic, F&F, '30s-40s **150.00**
Cruet set, 4 Black family ceramic figurals on metal rack, 1930-40 ....**75.00**
Dinner bell, praying Black girl, ceramic, '40s, EX **70.00**
Drinking glass, features Black jazz band, 4", M **25.00**

Figurine, Angel of Africa, Art Gift Corporation, ca 1958 .....**75.00**

Figurine, souvenir, watermelon boy on cotton bale, bisque, boxed, EX **55.00**

Figurines, sitting boy & girl, he plays harmonica, ceramic, 3", pr **60.00**

Folio, Hazel Scott Boogie-Woogie Piano Transcriptions, '30s, EX **30.00**

Game, Game of Black Sambo, Sam'l-Gabriel & Sons, NY, ca 1920, 13x18" **100.00**

Game, Hit Me Hard, Klesfeld Works, Germany, ca 1920, 11½x9" **70.00**

Magazine, Jet, Inside the March on Washington, Sept 1963 ....**9.00**

Matches, Dinah's Shack, Palo Alto, CA, features Dinah, M ...**25.00**

Measuring tape, Mammy figural, celluloid, '30s, EX **150.00**

Note pad, hanging Mammy figure, '30s, 8¼", EX **125.00**

Syrup pitcher, F&F, 5½", $70.00.

Oil & vinegar set, Mammy & Chef, ceramic, 5¼", EX **115.00**

Pancake mold, Aunt Jemima premium, metal, 8½" dia **75.00**

Paper doll, Stymie from Our Gang, '30s, framed, 10½x9", EX **70.00**

Paper plate, Aunt Jemima's Restaurant, ca 1940s, 9" dia, M **49.00**

Pin, Black 'flapper' girl, Bakelite, '30s, 2¼" **85.00**

Pin, Black lady in striped turban & gold earrings, gold-tone metal **39.00**

Placemat, The Story of Aunt Jemima, dated 1955, 13¾x9¾" **25.00**

Planter, Black girl stands next to ear-of-corn planter, EX ..**60.00**

Plate, I'll Be Down To Get You in a Taxi Honey, 6" dia, M **50.00**

Postcard, Black child w/watermelon, The World Is So Full..., 1913 ....**15.00**

Postcard, Thanksgiving Joys, embossed color litho, early 1900s, EX **29.00**

Potholder, features Mammy in polka dots, 6¼x6½" **45.00**

Recipe booklet, Aunt Jemima Cake Mix Miracles, '40s, 6½x4½" **45.00**

Record, The Blue-Tail Fly, 78 rpm, cardboard sleeve, 1953 ..**28.00**

Salt & pepper shakers, Aunt Jemima & Uncle Moses, plastic, F&F, 5" **55.00**

Salt & pepper shakers, Black Salty & Peppy, wood, 4", EX **30.00**

Salt & pepper shakers, kissing natives, ceramic, 3" **40.00**

Salt & pepper shakers, Mammy carries baskets hanging from yoke, 4½" **70.00**

Salt & pepper shakers, Mammy in red & white dress, chalkware, 2½" **90.00**

Sewing caddy, pickaninny's braids hold 5 spools of thread, wood, '30s **90.00**

Sheet music, That Dixie Rag, Victor Moulton, ca 1890-1910, 14x10" **15.00**

Sign, Hy-Beaute Hair Dressings, cardboard, easel back, 1949, 14x10" **55.00**

Tin container, Roreen Ointment & Brightner, '30s, unused, 2" dia **28.00**

Trade card, Spring, Spring, Gentle Spring, black & white, 1800s, EX **20.00**

Wall pocket, woman in turban & earrings, ceramic, '40s, 6⅛", EX **90.00**

Black Cats

This line of fancy felines was marketed mainly by the Shafford Company, although black cat lovers accept similarly modeled, shiny glazed kitties of other importing firms into their collections as well. Some of the more plentiful items maybe purchased for $15.00 to $35.00, while the Shafford cigarette lighter and the six-piece spice set in a wooden rack usually sell for more than $125.00. These values and the ones that follow are for items in mint paint, a very important consideration in determining a fair market price. Shafford items are often minus their white whiskers and eyebrows, and this type of loss should be reflected in your evaluation. An item in poor paint may be worth even less than half of given estimates.

Ashtray, head form, open mouth, green eyes **18.00**

Cigarette lighter, sm cat standing by lamp w/shade, book as base **50.00**

Creamer & sugar bowl, heads are shakers, yellow eyes, gold whiskers, Regal **50.00**

Creamer & sugar bowl, squatting sugar, upright creamer, Shafford **40.00**

Cruet, very slender, gold collar & tie, tail handle **12.00**

Cruets, oil & vinegar, he has 'O' eyes, she has 'V' eyes, Shafford, pr **50.00**

Decanter, red polka dots, green eyes, head removes, 9", +6 shots **25.00**

Egg cup, footed, green eyes, Shafford **25.00**

Mug, face embossed on side, cat handle, Shafford, 3½" ...**30.00**

Planter, upright cat, green eyes, Shafford **30.00**

Salt & pepper shakers, seated, 1 has head tilted, green eyes, 5", pr **40.00**

Salt & pepper shakers, seated, 1 has head tilted, Shafford, 3¾", pr **25.00**

Shot tumbler, embossed cat face, green eyes **20.00**

Spice rack, wireware face w/ green marble eyes, 4 hanging shakers **150.00**

Teapot, marked Japan, 4½", $35.00.

Stacking tea set, 'mamma' pot, 'kitty' creamer & sugar, yellow eyes **50.00**
Teapot, ball-shaped body, green eyes, Shafford, 5¾" **45.00**
Teapot, panther-type face, squinty eyes, gold trim, 5" **20.00**
Utensil (fork, spoon, or strainer), wood handle, green eyes, Shafford, each **50.00**
Wall pocket, flattened 'teapot' cat, Shafford, rare **75.00**

Blair Ceramics

American dinnerware has been a popular type of collectible for several years, and the uniquely styled lines of Blair Ceramics, who operated in Ozark, Missouri, for a few years from the mid-forties until the early fifties are especially appealing, though not often seen except in the midwest. Gay Plaid, recognized by its squared-off shapes and brush-stroke design (in lime, brown, and dark green on white), is the one you'll find most often. Several other lines were made as well. You'll be able to recognize them easily enough, since most pieces (except for the smaller items) are marked.

Bowl, cereal; Rick Rack **12.00**
Bowl, serving; Bird, rectangular w/tab handles, divided ..**30.00**
Casserole, Plaid or Gay Plaid, handles, w/lid **30.00**
Coffee server, Bamboo, twist handle **35.00**
Creamer, Plaid or Gay Plaid ..**15.00**
Cruet, Bird, loop handle **25.00**
Cup, Autumn Leaf **10.00**
Cup, Plaid or Gay Plaid **10.00**
Cup & saucer, Bamboo **20.00**
Cup & saucer, Plaid or Gay Plaid, twist handle **12.00**

Mug, Plaid or Gay Plaid, barrel form **18.00**
Nut dish, Autumn Leaf **8.00**
Pitcher, water; Plaid or Gay Plaid, leaf as ice lip **38.00**
Plate, Bamboo, square, 8" **8.00**
Plate, Bird, 6" **15.00**
Plate, dinner; Bamboo **12.00**
Plate, dinner; Bird **15.00**
Plate, dinner; Plaid **12.00**
Plate, Plaid or Gay Plaid, 6"...**5.00**
Plate, serving; Yellow Plaid, rectangular, divided **25.00**
Salt & pepper shakers, Plaid or Gay Plaid, pr **12.00**
Sugar bowl, Bamboo, w/lid ..**15.00**
Sugar bowl, Plaid or Gay Plaid, w/lid **15.00**
Tumbler, Plaid or Gay Plaid, tapered sides **12.00**

Blue and White Stoneware

Collectors who appreciate the 'country look' especially enjoy decorating their homes with this attractive utility ware that was made by many American potteries from around the turn of the century until the mid-thirties. Examples with good mold lines and strong color fetch the highest prices. Condition is important, but bear in mind that this ware was used daily in busy households, and signs of normal wear are to be expected. Refer to *Blue and White Stoneware* by Kathryn McNerney (Collector Books) for more information.

Bowl, berry; Diffused Blue, 4½" **55.00**
Bowl, berry/cereal; Pale Blue Band, 4" **55.00**
Bowl, mixing; Flying Bird, 7½", VG **110.00**

Bowl, mixing; Wildflower, stencil design w/blue rim, 7" **80.00**
Butter crock, Butterfly, original lid & bail, 6½" **175.00**
Butter crock, Dragonfly & Flower, lid & bail missing, sm crack, 5" **110.00**
Butter crock, Grapes & Leaves, double ring around rim, 3x5½" **175.00**
Creamer, Spongeware, 3¾" ..**95.00**
Crock, berry; Fluted, 4" **95.00**
Cup, Bowtie, w/bird transfer, 3½" **95.00**
Cup, custard; Fishscale, 2½" ..**75.00**
Cup, measuring; Spearpoint & Flower Panels, 6" **115.00**
Jar, Wesson Oil, rounded bottom, marked For Making Things To Eat, 5" **125.00**
Match holder, duck figural, 5" ..**95.00**
Mug, Basketweave & Flower, bulbous bottom w/rolled rim, 5" **125.00**
Pie plate, pale blue, X in center, 9", minimum price **145.00**
Pitcher, American Beauty Rose, 10" **275.00**
Pitcher, Apricot, 8" **165.00**
Pitcher, Basketweave & Flower, 9" **225.00**
Pitcher, Blue Band, 8" **95.00**

Pitcher, Swan, 8", $285.00.

Pitcher, Bluebird, 9x7" **250.00**
Pitcher, Cattails, 7½" **150.00**
Pitcher, Cherry Cluster & Basketweave, 10" **175.00**
Pitcher, Dutch Landscape, 6¼" **175.00**
Pitcher, Indian Boy & Girl, 6" **300.00**
Pitcher, Leaping Deer, 8½" ..**165.00**
Pitcher, Rose on Trellis **165.00**
Pitcher, Simplicity, 9" **75.00**
Roaster, Diffused Blue, applied handles, flat finial, oval, 9x19" **225.00**
Spittoon, Spongeware, w/brass top, 10½x4" **245.00**
Toothpick holder, swan figural, 4" **75.00**
Tumbler, Diffused Blue, 6" ...**75.00**

Blue Ridge

Some of the most attractive American dinnerware made in the 20th century is Blue Ridge, produced by Southern Potteries of Erwin, Tennessee, from the late 1930s until 1956. More than four hundred patterns were hand painted on eight basic shapes. The Quimper-like peasant-decorated line is one of the most treasured and is valued at double the values listed below. For the very simple lines, subtract about 20%, and add 20% for more elaborate patterns. Refer to *Blue Ridge Dinnerware, Revised Third Edition,* by Betty and Bill Newbound (Collector Books) for more information.

Ashtray, w/cigarette rest **16.50**
Bonbon, divided; china, center handle, artist signed, rare **80.00**
Bowl, salad; 10½" **42.00**
Bowl, vegetable; divided, oval, 9" **22.00**
Bowl, vegetable; 8" dia **15.00**

Butter dish **40.00**
Cake tray, Maple Leaf pattern,
   china, artist signed, rare ..**45.00**
Coffeepot **90.00**
Cup & saucer, jumbo **35.00**
Egg cup, double **25.00**
Jug, batter; w/lid **65.00**
Pitcher, Spiral shape **60.00**
Plate, cake; 10½" **28.00**
Plate, child's **28.00**
Plate, dinner; 10" **12.50**
Plate, dinner; 9½" **10.00**
Plate, pie; 7" **8.50**
Platter, 12½" **14.00**
Powder box, china, artist signed,
   round, w/lid **100.00**
Ramekin, w/lid, 7½" **30.00**
Relish, china, artist signed, T-
   handle, rare **40.00**
Salad spoon **25.00**
Shakers, Blossom Top, pr **32.00**
Shakers, Chickens, pr **85.00**

**Range shakers, 4½", $40.00 for
the pair.**

Sugar bowl, demitasse; china,
   artist signed, rare **35.00**
Tea tile, round or square, 6" ..**30.00**
Teapot, ball shape **48.00**
Teapot, Colonial shape **85.00**
Tidbit, 3-tier **25.00**
Tumbler, juice; glass **9.50**
Vase, china, artist signed, rare,
   5½" dia **65.00**
Vase, handled **70.00**
Wall sconce **62.00**

Bookends

Made popular after the invention of the linotype, bookends of every type and material were produced in forms such as ships, animals, people, etc., and many today find they make an interesting and diverse collection.

Amish couple seated, cast iron,
   4½", pr **35.00**
Blacksmith, bronze-plated iron,
   gilt traces, pr **32.00**
Buddha, cast metal w/bronze finish, 7¾", pr **65.00**
End of Trail, bronzed metal, dated
   1930, pr **42.00**
German shepherd, brass, pr ..**58.00**
Horse, bronze over plaster, 8x8",
   pr **65.00**
Horse, Frankart, pr **110.00**
Mayflower, #381, pr **65.00**
Nude on rearing horse, glass, 6",
   pr **65.00**
Owl, cast iron, 5¼", pr **40.00**
Parrots, copper clad, heavy,
   6½x6¼", pr **55.00**
Spanish man serenades lady at
   window, cast iron, 1920s, 5½",
   pr **55.00**
Terrier, Frankart, pr **125.00**
Terrier, seated, gilt-painted iron,
   pr **22.50**

Bookmarks

Bookmarks have been around as long as books themselves, yet only recently has bookmark collecting been growing in popularity. Most collectors like modern ones as well as the antique; there is so much available that a person could establish a collection in a short time and on a limited budget. Many of the modern bookmarks from publishers and advertisers are free. Bookmarks are found in almost any material, brass, plastic, and paper to antique silk, silver, and celluloid (the latter three the hardest to come by and therefore the most highly prized). The old paper ones are still plentiful and modestly priced. Dated commemorative bookmarks, old or new, are the most popular with collectors. Our advisor for bookmarks is Joan L. Huegel, who is listed in the Directory under Pennsylvania. See also Clubs and Newsletters.

Advertising, Hoyt's, 4½", $12.00.

Aluminum, Boston, Old South Church souvenir, heart form w/silk cord **4.00**

Cardboard, colorful floral w/1903 calendar on back, no advertising **2.00**

Cardboard, Compliments of Paris Fashion Co, 1910 catalog ad on back **2.00**

Celluloid, Carnation canned milk, carnation at top w/page flap, 4" **6.00**

Chrome, George Washington Bicentennial, George in profile, 1932 ....**4.50**

Chrome, souvenir Empire State Building, shield at top, '30s, 4½" **4.00**

Chrome, souvenir of Washington DC, shield at top, ca 1935, 4½" **4.00**

Laminated, wild flowers, souvenir of Alaska & Yukon, 1981..**1.00**

Leather, Jimmy Carter Library/ Museum, gold letters on blue, new **2.00**

Leather, MI Parents & Teachers Congress Convention, white & blue, 1939 ....**1.25**

Metal, NY World's Fair, 1939, 4½", w/attached silk cord **6.00**

Metal, souvenir, arrowhead form, clip type, 1930-40, 3" **2.25**

Paper, Book-Mark for the Arts, by Hendrick VanLoon, 1930s, thin **10.00**

Paper, bus figural, colorful, plugs book, new .... **.50**

Photo, Kirk Douglas figural, black & white, plugs book Ragman's Son **1.50**

Photo, Shelley Winters figural, black & white, plugs book Shelley **1.50**

Plastic, elephant at top & at one side, early, 5" **5.00**

Silk, Home Sweet Home, J Chester Mfg, NJ, woven, ca 1880-90, 11x2½" **30.00**

Silk, Memorial Day 1910, patriotic colors on ribbon **5.00**

Bottle Openers

Figural bottle openers are figures designed for the sole purpose of removing a bottle cap. To qualify as an example, the cap lifter must be part of the figure itself. Among the major producers of openers of this type were Wilton Products; John Wright, Inc.; L & L Favors; and Gadzik Sales. These and advertising openers are very collectible. Our advisor for this category is Charlie Reynolds; he is listed in the Directory under Virginia. The FBOC (Figural Bottle Opener Collectors) are listed under Clubs and Newsletters.

Clown, painted cast iron, 4", EX, $87.00.

Dachshund, brass 30.00
Dachsund, nickeled iron, Medford
   Lager Beer 45.00
Drunk embracing cactus, painted
   cast iron 100.00
Elephant, seated upright, cast
   iron w/multicolored paint, 5",
   EX 25.00
Iroquois Indian, aluminum,
   EX 20.00
Lobster, red painted cast iron,
   John Wright Inc, 1960s,
   3½x2¼" 30.00
Nude, up-stretched arms, white
   metal, Herbert Specialty,
   1970s, 4½" 27.50

Nude w/arms stretched above
   head, cast brass & steel,
   4" **30.00**
Parrot, Deco style, w/corkscrew,
   chrome **15.00**
Parrot on perch, cast iron w/mul-
   ticolored paint, 5" **40.00**
Pelican, beak is opener, cast iron
   w/EX paint **50.00**
Pointer, left paw up, cast iron
   w/worn multicolored paint,
   4½" **40.00**
Sailor, cast iron, marked Wright,
   EX **40.00**
Steer head, Cubist form, cast iron
   w/bronzed finish, 1920-30s,
   7" **40.00**
4-Eyed man, cast iron, marked
   Wright, EX **55.00**

Bottles

Bottles have been used as containers for commercial products since the late 1800s. Specimens from as early as 1845 may be occasionally found today (a rough pontil indicates this early production date). Some of the most collectible are bitters bottles, used for 'medicine' that was mostly alcohol, a ploy to avoid paying the stiff tax levied on liquor sales. Spirit flasks from the 1800s were blown in the mold and often conveyed a historic, political, or symbolic message. Even bottles from the 1900s are collectible, especially beer or pop bottles and commercial containers from defunct bottlers. Refer to *Bottle Pricing Guide, Third Revised Edition,* by Hugh Cleveland (Collector Books) for more information.

A-1 Sauce & Co, aqua, 7½" **5.00**
Absorbine, Springfield MA,
   amber, 7½" **6.00**

**Brandell & Smith Co.,
Philadelphia, PA, figural
candy bottle, ca 1910,
10½", $35.00.**

Acme Brewing Co, aqua, 9¼"..**8.00**
Ayer's Cherry Pectoral Lowell,
aqua, rectangular, 7½" **3.00**
Bender's Bitters, med aqua blue,
10½" **60.00**
Bromo-Seltzer, cobalt, M1 in circle
on bottom, round, machine
made, 5" **2.00**
Brown's Iron Tonic, aqua, rectangular, 10" **12.00**
Bull Dog Brand Liquid Glue,
aqua, 3½" **4.00**
Buxton's Rheumatic Cure, aqua,
8½" **10.00**
Carter's Ink, aqua, #11 on bottom,
2½" **6.00**
Cod Liver Oil, amber, screw top,
square, machine made, 6" ..**4.00**
Colgate & Co Perfumers,
amethyst, 3¾" **5.00**
Compound Calisaya Bitters,
amber, square, tapered top,
9½" **18.00**

Crab Apple Cream, clear, rectan-
gular, 5" **2.00**
De Kuyper Gin, dark amber,
w/label, 10½" **30.00**
Delavan's Whooping Cough Rem-
edy, aqua, 6¼" **4.00**
Diamond Ink Co, Milwaukee,
amethyst, Patented Dec 1st,
No 622, 1⅝" **5.00**
Down's Vegetable Balsamic Elixir,
aqua, cylindrical, 7½" ...**10.00**
Dr Parker's Cough Cure, aqua,
ring top, 6" **10.00**
East Indian Corn Plant, clear,
rectangular, 2" **3.00**
Eli Lilly & Co Poison, amber,
2" **10.00**
ER Durkee & Co Salad Dressing,
clear, 8" **2.00**
Eureka Hair Restorative, aqua,
7" **10.00**
Friedman Keiler & Co, Distillers
& Wholesale Liquor, amber,
12" **10.00**
Gold Medal Quality Hydrogen
Peroxide, amber, 8" **4.00**
Gordon's Dry Gin, aqua, 1-qt,
9" **8.00**
Granger Bitters, clear, flask form
w/label, 8" **22.50**
Gun Oil, clear, rectangular
w/sunken embossed panel,
4¾" **4.00**
H Van Emden Posthorn Gin,
amethyst, M in circle on bot-
tom, 10⅝" **12.00**
Hire's Household Extract, Philadel-
phia PA, blue, 4½" **10.00**
Hire's Improved Root Beer Maker,
aqua, 4½" **4.00**
HJ Heinz Catsup, amethyst,
7¾" **5.00**
Holton's Electric Oil, clear, cylindrical w/square collar, 3¼" **6.00**
Imperial Cement, clear, 3" **2.00**
Lash's Kidney & Liver Cure,
amber, 9" **30.00**
Lippman's Liver Pills, aqua,
2¼" **4.00**

Listerine, Lambert Pharmacal Co, clear, embossed lettering at shoulder **4.00**

Lyman Co Druggists, clear, 5" **2.00**

Madison Original Ale, amber, star on bottom, 7" **15.00**

Magic Mosquito Bite Cure & Insect Exterminator, aqua, 8" **20.00**

McCormick & Co Extracts & Spices & Etc, clear, 5¼" ...**4.00**

Melvin & Badger Apothecaries, cobalt, 6-sided, 6¾" **12.00**

Mrs ME Converse's Sure Cure for Epilepsy, clear, ring top, 6¾" **8.00**

Orange Bitters, light green, 6-point star w/3 dots on base, 11¾" **10.00**

Pepper sauce, amethyst, 6" **6.00**

Pike's Peak Old Rye, aqua, 1-pt **50.00**

Poison, amber, square w/raised ridges, 4½" **4.00**

Poison, blue, rectangular w/raised ridges, 4" **10.00**

Quaker Maid Whiskey, clear, 3½" **20.00**

Queen Olives, clear, 5½" **10.00**

Raven Gloss Shoe Dressing, green, 5" **6.00**

Red Snapper Sauce, amethyst, 7¾" **3.00**

Salter's Eye Lotion, aqua, rectangular, 4½" **4.00**

SF Gaslight Co Ammonia, aqua, 8" **3.00**

Snuff, amber, w/label, #16 on bottom, beveled corners, 4x2¼x1" **6.00**

Sperm Sewing Machine Oil, clear, 5½" **4.00**

Tillman's Extract, aqua, 7" **2.00**

Well's Neuralgia Cure, clear, rectangular, 6¾" **10.00**

White Rye, amethyst, w/label, 11¾" **6.00**

Dairy

The storage and distribution of fluid milk in glass bottles became commonplace around the turn of the century. They were replaced by paper and plastic containers in the mid-1950s. Perhaps 5% of all US dairies are still using some glass, and glass bottles are still widely used in Mexico and some Canadian provinces.

Milk-packaging and distribution plants hauled trailer loads of glass bottles to dumping grounds during the conversion to the throw-away cartons that are now in general use. Because of this practice, milk bottles and jars are scarce today. Most collectors search for bottles from home-town dairies; some have completed a fifty-state collection in the three popular sizes.

Bottles from 1900 to 1920 had the name of the dairy, town, and state embossed in the glass. Nearly all of the bottles produced after this period had the copy painted and then pyro-glazed onto the surface of the bottle. This enabled the dairyman to use colors, pictures of his dairy farm or cows on the bottles. Collectors have been fortunate that there have been no serious attempts at this point to reproduce a particularly rare bottle! For further information we recommend contacting Mr. O.B. Lund, who is listed in the directory under Arizona.

AJ Dorr Dairy, Watertown NY, painted, tall, 1-pt **8.00**

Barlow Dairy, Sugar Grove PA, painted, square, ½-pt **4.00**

Best Ice Cream Co, juice type, embossed & painted, ca 1935, 1-qt **8.50**

Borden's, painted label, w/Elsie the Cow, amber, square, ca 1950, 1-qt **12.00**

Buy Burn Boost, Anthracite Coal, pyro colors, 1945, ½-pt ..**15.00**

Chevy Chase Dairy, Washington DC, embossed, 1945, 1-qt **12.50**

Cloverleaf, Stockton CA, ribbed cream top, painted, ½-pt ..**18.00**

Dairylee Milk, Our New Baby Top Bottle, painted, square, 9½", $90.00.

Deerfoot Farm, embossed, pear form w/screw lid, ca 1900, 1-pt **30.00**

Diamond Farms, Salem NH, painted, 10-oz **7.00**

Howell & Demarest Farm Dairies, embossed, wire bail, ca 1900, ½-pt **30.00**

Indian Hill, Greenville ME, painted, 1-qt **12.50**

Johns Hopkins Hospital, embossed, ca 1940, 1-qt **17.50**

Jordan's Dairy, Hobbs NM, pyro color, ca 1945, 1-qt **17.50**

Lake View Dairy, Ithaca NY, painted, cream top, ca 1940, 1-pt **12.50**

Land-O-Sun, Phoenix AZ, painted, ca 1950s, ½-gal **20.00**

Lone Oak Dairy, coffee creamer, embossed, ca 1930, 2-oz ..**10.00**

Magnolia Dairy, Houston TX, embossed, ca 1930, ½-pt ..**8.00**

Meadow Brook, Clarksville NY, painted, square, 1-qt **7.50**

Pine State Dairy, Bangor ME, painted, green, square, 1-qt **75.00**

Protect the Children, Golden Jersey Milk, pyro colors, ca 1937, 1-qt **15.00**

Purity Maid Products Co Dairy Creamer, painted, ¾-oz ..**16.00**

Reehl's Dairy, Grand Ledge MI, amber, painted, square, 1-qt **10.00**

Reynold's Dairy, painted, w/cow, square, 1-qt **7.50**

Rojeck's Delicious Sour Cream, painted, wide mouth **10.00**

Rosebud Creamery, painted, square, ca 1940s-50s, ¾-oz **7.50**

Shade's Dairy, Santa Fe NM, pyro colors, ca 1940, 1-qt **17.50**

Shadow Lawn Dairy, East Providence RI, painted, tall, 1-pt **15.00**

Silver State Dairy, Denver CO, pyro colors, 1950s, 1-qt..**28.00**

State Tech Dairy, Alfred NY, embossed, ca 1945, ½-pt..**12.50**

Sun Glo, embossed, amber, square, ca 1950, 2-qt **6.00**

Thatcher Farms, Milton MA, cream top, painted, square, 1-qt **17.50**

University of Georgia, pyro colors, ca 1950, ½-pt **12.50**

University of Tennessee, Knoxville TN, embossed, ca 1945, 1-qt **12.50**

Whiting Milk Co, Boston, embossed, ca 1920, ½-pt ..**6.00**

Wilson Goat Farm, San Bernadino CA, pyro colors, ca 1950, 1-qt **30.00**

Zenda Farms Golden Guernsey, Clayton NY, pyro colors, ¼-pt **22.50**

Soda Bottles With Applied Color Labels

This is an area of bottle collecting that has recently shown strong and sustained growth. Market prices have been climbing steadily. Refer to *The Official Guide to Collecting Applied Color Label Soda Bottles* by Thomas Marsh for more information. Mr. Marsh is listed in the Directory under Ohio.

Clear quarts: Rose Valley, $8.00; Saturn, $20.00.

A-Treat Premium Beverages, clear, 7-oz **6.00**

Acme Club Beverage Co, green, 1-qt **20.00**

Alert, green, 6-oz **10.00**

Alkalaris Club Soda, clear, 7-oz **15.00**

Barney's Club Beverage, green, 7-oz **6.00**

Batchelor's Beverages, clear, 8-oz **6.00**

Bob's Cola Good for Thirst, clear, 7-oz **6.00**

Bortner's Pale Dry Ginger Ale, green, 1-qt **6.00**

Buckeye Sparkling Beverages, green, 7-oz **10.00**

Bull Dog Ginger Beer, green, 8-oz **30.00**

Canada Dry Ginger Ale, green, 7-oz **6.00**

Carousel Pop Shoppe, clear, 12-oz **10.00**

Chero, clear, 6-oz **6.00**

Cloverdale Pale Dry Gingerale, green, 7-oz **8.00**

Cotton Club Beverages, clear, 12-oz **15.00**

Dad's Big Jr Root Beer, amber, 7-oz **15.00**

Double Eagle Bottling Co, clear, 1-qt **8.00**

Dr Up, Youngstown OH, green, 7-oz **10.00**

Fizz, Low in Calories, green, 12-oz **8.00**

Glen Hazel, Super Charged Mixer, green, 7-oz **8.00**

Grilli's Club Soda, clear, 1-qt ..**8.00**

Hazel Club Sparkling Beverage, Hazelton PA, clear, 7-oz ..**6.00**

Liberty Beverage, green, 7-oz **20.00**

Mason's Root Beer, amber, 1-qt **15.00**

Padgett Beverage, clear, 10-oz ..**6.00**

Pepsi-Cola Fountain Syrup, clear, 12-oz **20.00**

Scot, Dog Gone Good Drink, clear, 7-oz **15.00**

Seher's Old English Ginger Beer, amber, 7-oz **8.00**

Snow-Cap Beverage Co, Easthampton MA, green, 1-qt ..**8.00**

Sun-Drop Lemonade, clear, 12-oz **6.00**

Sunny Kid Beverages, Buffalo NY, clear, 7-oz **8.00**

Supreme Beverage Co, Cleveland OH, clear, 1-qt **8.00**

Turner's Club Soda, 7-oz **6.00**

VD Korker Lemon Soda Blender, green, 7-oz **8.00**

White Rock Quinine Water, clear, 7-oz **10.00**

Yaky's Beverages, clear, 7-oz ..**6.00**

Boxes

Ranging from tiny porcelain examples with fine hand painted designs to large, more primitive ones made for storage, old boxes can be found in boundless varieties. Those that are handmade and hand decorated often are looked upon as fine examples of 'folk art,' and some of the better ones may command prices in the thousands of dollars. But even the small boxes decorated with wood-burning or built from less than the finest woods are appreciated by collectors who may choose to decorate with them or simply put them to the use for which they were originally intended.

Bentwood, copper tacks, old patina, oval, 4" **85.00**

Bentwood, varnished, 9¾x15½", EX **175.00**

Candle, pine, square nails, EX patina, 3½x12¼x4¼" ...**125.00**

Document, leather covered, brass fittings, 1820s, 8x12x6" ..**55.00**

Egg, pine, tin bands, wire loop hinges, 14½x14½x13" **75.00**

Handkerchief, burntwood, brass fittings, square, 1910, 6" **15.00**

Mahogany, dovetailed, brass bail & lock, 9½" **75.00**

Salt, pine, mustard paint, hinged lid, 1800s, 10x7x7" **85.00**

Spice, bentwood, tin edging, stenciled labels, +8 tins **65.00**

Walnut, cross-hatching w/carved anchor, sliding lid, dovetailed, 5" **65.00**

Workman's, soft pine, ca 1900, refinished, 12x26x14" ..**165.00**

Boyd Crystal Art Glass

Since it was established in 1978, this small glasshouse located in Cambridge, Ohio, has bought molds from other companies as they went out of business, and they have designed many of their own as well. They may produce several limited runs of a particular shape in a number of the lovely colors of glass they themselves formulate, none of which are ever reissued. Of course, all of the glass is handmade, and each piece is marked with their 'B-in-diamond' logo. Most of the pieces we've listed are those you're more apt to find at flea markets, but there are also a few of the more expensive examples included to let you know that some are worth a great deal more. Our advisor for this category is Joyce Pringle who is listed in the Directory under Texas.

Beaded Oval Toothpick, Impatient incised w/grain pattern..**22.50**

Beaded Oval Toothpick, Royalty Slag **6.00**

Bird Salt, Buckeye **6.00**

Bird Salt, Royalty **15.00**

Brian Bunny, Mandarin, 2" ...**6.00**

Bunny Salt, Classic Black Carnival **8.00**

Bunny Salt, Heather Gray **7.00**

Bunny Salt, Thistlebloom **25.00**

Candy Dish, Rubina **15.00**

Chick Salt, Cardinal Red Carnival **8.00**

Chick Salt, Cobalt Carnival ..**17.50**
Chick Salt, Nile Green **6.00**
Child's Mug, Mahogany **9.00**
Colonial Drape Toothpick, Cardinal Red **7.00**
Debby Duck, Mardi Gras **5.00**
Duck Salt, Cobalt Carnival ...**7.00**
Duck Salt, Lime Carnival **8.00**
Elephant Head Toothpick, Apricot **25.00**
Elephant Head Toothpick, Green Whisper **15.00**
Elephant Head Toothpick, Willow Blue **12.50**
Elizabeth, Buckeye, 2" **8.00**
Elizabeth, Classic Black, 2" ...**8.00**
Elizabeth, Lime Carnival **25.00**
Forget-Me-Not Toothpick, Columbus Blue (short run color) ..**8.00**
Forget-Me-Not Toothpick, Elizabeth Slag #1 ....**20.00**
Forget-Me-Not Toothpick, Vaseline **8.00**
Freddie the Clown, Cobalt Carnival **10.00**
Gypsy Pot Toothpick, Pecan Slag **6.00**
Gypsy Pot Toothpick, Russet Green **18.00**
Hand, Primrose **4.50**
Hand, Purple Variant **5.00**
Hand, Ruby **25.00**
Heart Toothpick, Crown Tuscan, light pink **8.00**
Heart Toothpick, Frosty Blue..**18.00**
Joey Horse, Flame **25.00**
Joey Horse, Snow **15.00**
Kitten on a Pillow, Frosty Blue **15.00**
Kitten on a Pillow, Pink Champagne **22.50**
Lamb Salt, Crown Tuscan Carnival **7.00**
Lamb Salt, Windsor Blue **7.00**
Little Joe the Horse, Jadite ...**5.50**
Little Luck the Unicorn, Cobalt Carnival **10.00**
Little Luck the Unicorn, Indian Orange **5.00**

Little Luck the Unicorn, Patriot White (hand painted) **13.50**
Louise, Furr Green **12.00**
Louise, Ice Blue **60.00**
Louise, Persimmon **12.00**
Mini-vase, Smoke **6.00**
Mini-vase, Sunburst **30.00**
Miss Cotton (kitten), Heather Gray **7.00**
Owl Bell, Pocono Blue **10.00**
Owl Bell, Snow **10.00**
Patrick Bear, Enchantment ..**22.50**
Patrick Bear, Sunglow Carnival **7.50**
Pooch, Mahogany **8.00**
Pooch, Root Beer **15.00**
Tractor, Nile Green **10.00**
Tuck Car, Cobalt Carnival....**12.50**
Tuck Car, Grape Parfait **12.50**
Tuck Car, Primrose (yellow) ..**10.00**
Zak Elephant, Flame **45.00**
Zak Elephant, Mulberry Mist ..**60.00**
Zak Elephant, Zak Boyd Slag **15.00**

Brass

Brass, a non-rusting alloy of copper and zinc, was used as far back in civilization as the first century A.D. Items most often found today are from the 19th century, although even 20th-century examples are collectible due to the simple fact that most are now obsolete. Even decorative brass from the 1950s has collector value. Refer to *Antique Brass and Copper* by Mary Frank Gaston (Collector Books) for more information.

Ashtray, cast hand-held type, ca 1920s, 1x2" dia **15.00**
Candelabrum, Art Deco, 5-light, embossed floral design, 1930s, 16" **75.00**
Car horn, trumpet form, missing rubber pump, 12" **30.00**

Ashtray, 1950s, $25.00.

Chisel, Beryl Co #108, 7½" ..**60.00**
Coal tongs, 10½" **50.00**
Curtain tie-backs, pineapple
    design, sm, pr **20.00**
Curtain tie-backs, scroll design,
    pr **55.00**
Doorknob, ring design **30.00**
Fork, toasting type, w/figural cat
    on handle, 20" **40.00**
Handle, pull type, embossed
    design on back plate **15.00**
Lamp, clamp-on; marked Adjusto-
    Light, Farberware, Pat
    1914 ....**75.00**
Mail box, envelope style, lion's
    head w/ring, 1950s **40.00**
Planter, Art Deco, Egyptian's head
    in relief, ca 1920s, 4½" ...**45.00**
Playing card case, marked
    Smoleroff Kard Pack, ca
    1920s, 3½x2⅜" **25.00**

Scale, Chatillon, hanging tube
    type **40.00**
Scale, Lander's Improved Spring
    Balance, hanging, 23"..**125.00**
Shoe mold, 11x9" **30.00**
Test tube holder, 8" **10.00**
Tray, Art Nouveau design in
    relief, pierced handles,
    9x14" **100.00**
Trouble light, 8" **30.00**
Wall sconce, electrified candle
    form w/acanthus leaf cup,
    1920s, 11" **80.00**
Washboard, advertising, ca
    1910 ....**50.00**

Brayton Laguna

Located in Laguna Beach,
California, this small pottery is
especially noted for their amusing
Disney figurines and their children's series which were made
from the 1930s to the early 1950s.
Refer to *The Collector's Encyclopedia of California Pottery* by
Jack Chipman (Collector Books)
for more information.

Candle holder, seated Blackamoor
    figure **50.00**
Cookie jar, Gingham Dog,
    unmarked **195.00**

Mexican man, 9", $80.00; mule, 10" long, $50.00.

Cookie jar, Lady, marked ...**200.00**
Figurine, Dutch boy & girl, pr ..**90.00**
Figurine, girl knitting sock ..**32.00**
Figurine, peacock 17" **85.00**
Flower holder, Sally **30.00**
Planter, baby w/pillow **35.00**
Planter, lady w/shawl, 8" **35.00**
Planter, Mandy **45.00**
Toothpick holder, Gingham Dog
    figural **75.00**
Wall vase, Blackamoor, 23" ..**125.00**

Bread Plates

Bread Plates were very popular during the last part of the
1800s. They were produced by
various companies, many of whom
sold their wares at the 1876
Philadelphia Centennial Exposition. Though they were also made
in earthenware and metal, the
most popular with collectors are
the glass plates with embossed
designs that convey a historical,
political, or symbolic message.

Golden Rule, 11", $32.00.

Balky Mule **85.00**
Baltimore Pear, handles **28.00**
Canadian Seal **45.00**
Columbia, L-54 ....**115.00**
Cupid & Venus, 10½" dia **45.00**
Dewdrop w/Sheaf of Wheat, Give
    Us This Day..., 10" **50.00**

Egyptian, Cleopatra center, 13"
    long **50.00**
Flaming Sword, L-209 ....**95.00**
Give Us This Day, sheaf of wheat,
    round **75.00**
Ionia **25.00**
Kansas, plain center **30.00**
Liberty Bell, 10" dia **40.00**
Lion **100.00**
Lord's Supper, goofus, L-235 ..**35.00**
Nelly Bly, 11" **200.00**
Niagara Falls, L-489 ....**95.00**
Peabody, L-272 ....**45.00**
Pope Leo XIII, milk glass **50.00**
Retriever, milk glass **80.00**
Shell & Tassel, oval **55.00**
Texas Centennial, Alamo in cen-
    ter **85.00**
Washington Centennial 1876,
    frosted, L-27 ....**130.00**
Wheat & Barley, milk glass ..**60.00**
Wildflower, square **28.00**

Breweriana

Beer can collectors and
antique advertising buffs as well
enjoy looking for beer-related
memorabilia such as tap knobs,
beer trays, coasters, signs, and
the like. While the smaller items
of a more recent vintage are quite
affordable, signs and trays from
defunct breweries often bring
three-digit prices. Condition is
important in evaluating early
advertising items of any type.

Bottle, Blatz, Milwaukee, olive,
    9¼" **4.00**
Bottle, Kansas City Breweries Co,
    amber, crown top, 9" **4.00**
Bottle, Reno Brewing, Reno
    NV, amber, tapered top,
    10¾" **8.00**
Bottle, York Brewing Co, em-
    bossed eagle & logo, crown
    top, 12-oz, EX **10.00**

Bottle opener, Ballantine's, metal, logo forms end, EX **5.00**

Calendar, Pabst Extract, pictures an Indian, 1905, NM ...**140.00**

Can, Fuhrmann & Schmidt, red, white & gold, cone top, 12-oz, VG **75.00**

Clock, Olympia Light, electric, M **35.00**

Cookbook, Schmidt & Sons Brewing Co, Dainty Home Lunches, G **7.50**

Corkscrew, Anheuser Busch, nickel-plated brass, bottle shape, 23", EX **35.00**

Crate, for bottles, Schlitz, dated 5-33, logos on sides, 18¼x12x10" **40.00**

Decanter, Hamm's, bear holding label, 1972, 10¾", M **85.00**

Foam scraper, Rheingold, celluloid, M **24.50**

Foam scraper, Stegmaier, celluloid, 8½x1", VG **18.50**

Letterhead, FC Miller Pittsburgh Bottling house, ca 1885 ...**2.00**

Plate, Fred Krug Brewery, 50th Anniversary, 9¾", M ...**100.00**

Shakers, Miller Beer, bottle shape, miniature, EX, pr **10.00**

Sign, Blatz, light-up, ca 1950s, VG **45.00**

Sign, Ruppert's, reverse-painted glass, 1908, NM **225.00**

Stein, Budweiser, pewter, w/lid, in original box, 7½" **95.00**

Stein, made for Coors employees, 1988, 7¼", M **95.00**

Tip tray, Indianapolis Brewing Co, tin, 5" dia **40.00**

Tray, Blatz, tin, pictures man pouring from bottle, 1933 .....**60.00**

Tray, Budweiser, tin, pictures long-neck bottle, 1940s-50s, NM **60.00**

Tray, Duquesne Pilsner, prince w/glass, 11¾" dia, EX ..**20.00**

Tray, Hohenadel Brewery, table scene, oval, ca 1935-43, G **130.00**

Tumbler, Bartholomy Rochester, enamel on crystal, logo, 4x2" dia, EX **22.50**

Left: Beer can, Fort Pitt Special, cone top, 12-oz., VG, $30.00.
Right: Tumbler, Falstaff, 5½", $5.00.

Brownies

The Brownie characters (The London Bobby, The Bellhop, Uncle Sam, and others) were strange little creatures with potbellies and long spindle legs who emerged in the night to do wondrous deeds for children to delight in discovering the next morning. They were the progeny of Palmer Cox, who in 1883 introduced them to the world in the poem called *The Brownies Ride*. Books, toys, napkin rings, and advertising items are just a few of the treasures available to today's Brownie collectors. Our advisor for this category is Faye Pisello, who is listed in the Directory under New York.

Book, Bomba the Merry Old King, 1903, EX **30.00**
Book, Brownie Town, Palmer Cox illustrated, EX **200.00**
Book, Brownies in Fairyland, Century Co **35.00**
Book, Jolly Chinee, 1903, VG ..**35.00**
Book, Monk's Victory, 1911, EX **25.00**
Bottle, soda; embossed Brownies, M **30.00**

Box, Log Cabin Brownies, cabin form, National Biscuit Co, 1920s **125.00**
Comic sheet, 1907, lg, EX **25.00**
Crayons, in wood container showing Brownies, EX **55.00**
Cup & saucer set, china **75.00**
Game, Auto Race, lithographed tin board **40.00**
Game, Jump-Up, in original box, EX **50.00**
Plate, china, lobster chasing Brownies **35.00**
Sign, Howell's Root Beer, embossed tin, EX **150.00**
Stickpin, Brownie policeman..**20.00**
Tin container, Brownie Ointment, 1924, MIB **40.00**

Bubble Bath Containers

Figural bubble bath containers were popular in the 1960s and have become highly collectible today for various reasons. They are colorful, cute, and were made in a vast range of character figurals. The Colgate-Palmolive Company produced the widest variety called Soakies. Purex's Bubble

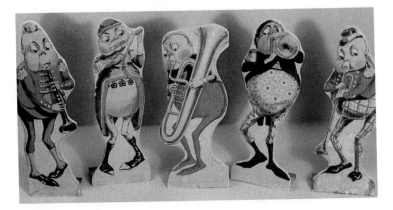

Wooden band figures, unmarked, ca 1900, each 8", set of five in excellent condition, $95.00.

Club characters were also popular. Most Soaky bottles came with detachable heads made of brittle plastic which cracked easily. Purex bottles were made of a softer plastic but lost their paint easier. Condition affects price considerably. The following prices are for containers in excellent to near-mint condition; all are Soaky bottles unless stated. Our advisor is Rick Rowe, Jr., who is listed in the Directory under Wisconsin.

Augie Doggie, Purex, hard vinyl, 1950s, 10", EX **35.00**
Baloo, Soaky, ca 1967, EX **25.00**
Bugs Bunny slip-over, M **20.00**
Bullwinkle, EX **24.00**
Casper, vinyl w/hard plastic head, 10", M **25.00**
Cinderella, Soaky, movable arms, 1960s, 10½", M **28.00**
Deputy Dawg, yellow & brown, 1966, 10", NM **20.00**
Dick Tracy, NM **30.00**
Felix the Cat, red, M **25.00**

Fred Flintstone, Purex, NM **20.00**
Let's Go Mets, ball player figural, 10½", NM **65.00**
Mighty Mouse, 1965, lg, M ..**25.00**
Mousketeer, painted vinyl girl w/mouse-ears hat, 1960s, 9½", EX **20.00**
Mr Jinks w/Pixie & Dixie, NM **22.00**
Pebbles, M **20.00**
Popeye, Woolfoam Corp, ca 1967, EX **45.00**
Porky the Pig, NM **18.00**
Ricochet Rabbit, movable arm, M **50.00**
Smokey Bear, sm, NM **25.00**
Superman, Avon, 1978, NM ..**15.00**
Sylvester the Cat, NM **15.00**
Tennessee Tuxedo, Colgate-Palmolive, hard vinyl, 1965, 10", EX **25.00**
Theodore (chipmunk), M **20.00**
Touche Turtle, Purex, 1960s, 10½", EX **40.00**
Tweety, Soaky, 8¼", EX **30.00**
Wendy, Soaky, 10½", EX **25.00**

Left: Bozo the Clown, Soaky, 9½", $20.00. Right: Pinocchio, Soaky, 9¾", $25.00.

Cake Toppers

Cake toppers began to appear around the 1880s, made almost exclusively of sugar. During the 1900s, toppers (bride and groom figures) were carved from wood and placed on plaster bases. A few single-mold toppers made from poured lead or bisque porcelain also appeared around the same time. From the 1920s to the 1950s, bisque porcelain was extremely popular. Celluloid Kewpie-types made a brief appearance around the 1940-50 era as did those made of a chalk (plaster of Paris) substance. A very few china pieces made a brief appearance.

From the 1950s well into the 1970s, plastics were used nearly exclusively. Toppers took on an assembly-line appearance with no specific attention to detail or fashion. Some bisque porcelain figures can be found in the more expensive toppers, and grooms in military dress began to appear. From the 1980s to the present, elegant and elaborate toppers have remained very popular and collectible keepsakes — especially those from some of the finest china and porcelain houses, i.e., Royal Doulton, Goebel, Lladro, etc. Our advisor is Jeannie Greenfield, who is listed in the Directory under Pennsylvania.

Brides and Grooms

Bisque, Black couple waltzing, marked Lefton China, 1980s, 3" **20.00**
Bisque, cutie couple, jointed, crepe paper tux, Japan, 1930s, 3" **40.00**
Bisque, Marine (or Army, etc) uniform, Wilton, 1960s, 4½"..**25.00**

Bride and groom from Japan, 1930-40, 4½", $40.00 for the pair.

Bisque, marked A196 & A197, incised Japan, 4½" **40.00**
Bisque, painted, cloth clothes, 1940s, 4" **35.00**
Bisque, single mold, bride w/head band, marked Japan, 1920s, 3½" **25.00**
Bisque, single mold, bride w/head band, unmarked, 1920s, 3½" **25.00**
Celluloid, Kewpies, painted-on clothes, Japan, 1940s, fragile, 2½" **35.00**
Chalk type, single mold, incised ACA on base, 1930s, 3½" ..**25.00**
China, single mold, net veil & dress, unmarked, 1950s-60s, 6"...**30.00**
German, she holds rosary w/cross, he wears tails & spats, '20s, 1½" **20.00**
Lead, single mold, painted-on clothes w/cloth flowers, 1900-20, 5" **60.00**
Plaster, black, pink & white paint w/pearlized headdress, 1948, 5" **10.00**
Plastic, single mold, double-breasted jacket, unmarked, 1950s, 4" **15.00**

Wood, on plaster base inscribed Good Luck, cloth flowers, 1890s, 8" **75.00**

Cambridge

Organized in 1901 in Cambridge, Ohio, the Cambridge Glass Co. initially manufactured clear glass dinnerware and accessory pieces. In the 1920s they began to concentrate on color and soon became recognized as the largest producers of this type of glassware in the world. The company used various marks, the most common of which is the 'C in triangle.' They closed in 1958. Refer to *Colors in Cambridge Glass* by the National Cambridge Society and *Elegant Glassware of the Depression Era* by Gene Florence for more information. Cambridge's animals are featured in *Glass Animals of the Depression Era* by Lee Garmon and Dick Spencer. (All are published by Collector Books.)

Apple Blossom, crystal; creamer, footed **12.50**
Apple Blossom, pink or green; shakers, pr **90.00**
Apple Blossom, yellow or amber; sugar bowl, footed **16.00**
Candlelight, crystal; plate, dinner; #3900/24, 10½" **65.00**
Candlelight, crystal; tumbler, iced tea; #3111, footed, 12-oz ..**25.00**
Caprice, blue or pink; bowl, salad; #57, 4-footed, 10" **100.00**
Caprice, blue or pink; stem, cocktail; #3, 3½-oz **50.00**
Caprice, crystal; #300, 12-oz ..**20.00**
Caprice, crystal; mayonnaise, #106, 8", 3-pc set **40.00**
Chantilly, crystal; cake plate, tab handled, 13½" **32.50**
Chantilly, crystal; candlestick, 2-light, fleur-de-lis, 6" **32.50**
Cleo, blue; platter, 12" **150.00**
Cleo, pink, green, yellow, or amber; bowl, 8½" **40.00**
Decagon, pastels; bowl, cereal; flat rim, 6" **10.00**
Decagon, pastels; plate, dinner; 9½" **20.00**
Decagon, red or blue; cup **10.00**

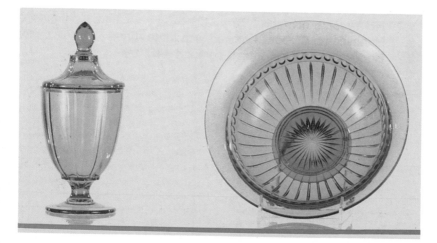

Candy dish, Plainware, light cobalt, ½-pound, $45.00; bowl, light cobalt, 9½", $37.00.

Diane, crystal; comport, blown, 5⅜" **35.00**
Diane, crystal; shakers, pr ...**28.00**
Elaine, crystal; bowl, flared, 4-footed, 12" **35.00**
Elaine, crystal; tumbler, juice; #3500, footed, 5-oz **17.00**
Figurine, blue jay, peg base ..**125.00**
Figurine, Buddha, amber, 6"..**225.00**
Figurine, heron, 9" **75.00**
Figurine, scottie, bookend ...**75.00**
Figurine, sea gull, flower frog ..**50.00**
Gloria, crystal; bowl, cereal; round, 6" **12.00**
Gloria, crystal; plate, bread & butter; square **6.00**
Gloria, green, pink, or yellow; candlestick, 6", each **32.50**
Gloria, green, pink, or yellow; plate, 8½" **14.00**
Imperial Hunt Scene, colors; tumbler, #3085, footed, 2½" **30.00**
Imperial Hunt Scene, crystal; creamer, footed **45.00**
Mt Vernon, amber or crystal; bowl, fruit; #6, 5¼" **10.00**
Mt Vernon, amber or crystal; comport, #34, 6" **15.00**
Mt Vernon, amber or crystal; shakers, #28, pr **22.50**
Portia, crystal; bowl, relish; 2-part, 7" **16.00**
Portia, crystal; stem, claret; #3126, 4½-oz **35.00**
Rosalie, amber; platter, 12" ..**35.00**
Rosalie, blue, pink, or green; bowl, 11½" **65.00**
Rose Point, crystal; creamer, #137, flat **110.00**
Rose Point, crystal; cup **30.00**
Rose Point, crystal; sugar bowl, #137, flat **105.00**
Valencia, crystal; ice pail, #1402/52 ....**55.00**
Valencia, crystal; sugar basket, #3500/13 ....**75.00**
Wildflower, crystal; bud vase, #1528, 10" **30.00**

Wildflower, crystal; cake plate, #3900/35, 2-handled, 13½" ..**32.50**
Wildflower, crystal; comport, #3121, blown, 5⅜" **40.00**

Cameras

Box, folding, novelty, and newer 35mm cameras are often found at flea markets. Most models are too common or too cheaply constructed to be collectible, valuable, or usable; some are. Whether for a collection or for resale, look for these types of cameras: box cameras with colored coverings and those with an Art Deco design on the front; folding cameras that use 120 film; novelty cameras with advertising, especially if mint in the box; and mint-condition 35mm cameras, especially those with extra lenses and cases. Caution: many camera models look alike; McKeown's *Price Guide to Antique and Classic Cameras* (8th edition) describes over 8,000 cameras; identify with care. Prices here reflect average retail values. For further information we recommend our advisor, Steve Gabany, listed in the Directory under Indiana.

Colored-cover & Art Deco box camera, Bear Photo Special ..**75.00**
Colored-cover & Art Deco box camera, Coronet Consul **20.00**
Colored-cover & Art Deco box camera, Coronet Eclair Lux ..**30.00**
Colored-cover & Art Deco box camera, Kodak Beau Brownie **70.00**
Colored-cover & Art Deco box camera, Kodak Brownie Flash IV **20.00**
Colored-cover & Art Deco box camera, Kodak Six-16 .....**5.00**

Eastman Brownie #2A, EX, $65.00; NM in box, $125.00.

Colored-cover & Art Deco box camera, Kodak Six-20 Brownie Junior **5.00**

Folding 120 camera, Agfa Billy-Clack **25.00**

Folding 120 camera, Balda Baldax **40.00**

Folding 120 camera, Conley Junior **20.00**

Folding 120 camera, Kodak Autographic Junior No 1 ......**10.00**

Folding 120 camera, Kodak Hawkette Camera No 2 ..**60.00**

Novelty camera, Child Guidance Mick-a-Matic **40.00**

Novelty camera, Eiko Can Cameras (7-Up, Coke, Budweiser, etc), each **50.00**

Novelty camera, Eiko Populat, car tire form **25.00**

35mm camera, Aires, 35-V ...**80.00**

35mm camera, Argus C-3 ......**5.00**

35mm camera, Argus Golden Shield **50.00**

35mm camera, Bolsey C **70.00**

35mm camera, Canon Canon-flex **75.00**

35mm camera, case, from $15 up to **25.00**

35mm camera, extra lens, from $20 up to **40.00**

35mm camera, Kodak Retina Reflex, all models, each **100.00**

35mm camera, Kodak Signet 35 ....**20.00**

35mm camera, Kodak 35 Camera **15.00**

Candlewick

Candlewick was one of the all-time best-selling lines of The Imperial Glass Company of Bellaire, Ohio. It was produced from 1936 until the company closed in 1982. More than 741 items were made over the years; and though many are still easy to find today, some (such as the desk calendar, the chip and dip set, and the dresser set) are a challenge to collect. Candlewick is easily identified by the beaded stems, handles, and rims characteristic of the tufted needlework of our pioneer women for which it was named.

Ashtray, #400/19, 2¾" dia **8.00**

Ashtray, heart, #400/172, 4½" **9.00**

Basket, w/handle, #400/40/0, 7" **27.50**

Bowl, fruit; #400/1F, 5" **12.00**

Bowl, relish; #400/60, 7" **25.00**

Bowl, round, #400/10F, 9" **40.00**

Cake stand, high foot, #400/103D, 11" **65.00**

Candle holder, heart shape, #400/40HC, 5" **40.00**

Candle holder, rolled edge, #400/79R, 3½" **10.50**

Candy box, #400/59, 5½" dia ..**42.50**

Cigarette holder, beaded foot, #400/44, 3" **40.00**

Compote, 4-bead stem, #400/45, 5½" **22.00**

Creamer, beaded handle, #400/30, 6-oz **7.50**

Ice tub, #400/63, 5½"x8" **80.00**

Marmalade set, beaded foot, w/lid & spoon, #400/1989, 3-pc **40.00**

Party set, oval plate w/indent for cup, #400/98, 2-pc **30.00**

Pitcher, plain, 40-oz **40.00**

Plate, bread & butter; #400/1D, 6" **8.00**

Plate, salad; #400/5D, 8" **9.00**

Punch ladle, #400/91 ....**22.50**

Salt spoon, #400/616, 3" **9.00**

Saucer, demi; #400/77AD **5.00**

Shakers, beaded foot, straight side, chrome top, #400/247, pr ..**16.00**

Stem, cocktail; #400/190 ......**18.00**

Sugar bowl, beaded handle, #400/30, 6-oz **6.50**

Tid bit server, 2-tier, cupped, #400/2701 ....**45.00**

Tray, celery; oval, w/2 handles, #400/105, 13½" **30.00**

Tray, upturned handles, #400/42E, 5½" **18.00**

Tumbler, iced tea; #400/18, 12-oz **40.00**

Vase, rolled rim, beaded handle, #400/87R, 7" **35.00**

Candy Containers

From 1876 until about 1960, figural glass candy containers of every shape and description have been manufactured for the use of candy companies who filled them with tiny colored candy beads. When the candy was gone, kids used the containers as banks or toys. While many are common, some (such as Charlie Chaplin by L. E. Smith, Barney Google by the Barrel, Felix on the Pedestal, or

Creamer and sugar bowl on tray, $35.00.

the Rabbit Family) are hard to find and command prices in the $450.00 to $3,000.00 range. Numbers refer to *The Compleat American Glass Candy Container Handbook* by Adele Bowden. Our advisor for this category is Doug Dezso, who is listed in the Directory under New Jersey. For the figural papier-mache candy containers, see Christmas; Halloween; etc.

Fire Engine, Large Boiler; #380, $85.00.

Airplane, Army Bomber 15-P-7, #6 ....**50.00**
Airplane, Spirit of Goodwill, #8 ....**100.00**
Amos & Andy in Car, #21 ..**500.00**
Automobile, Electric Runabout; open top, #47 ....**70.00**
Automobile, limousine, West Bros Co, tin wheels, #43 ......**100.00**
Automobile, Miniature Streamlined; #33 ....**25.00**
Barney Google & Ball on Tub, #72 ....**225.00**
Boat, Battleship on Waves, #96 ....**150.00**
Boat, Submarine F-6, #101 ..**500.00**
Bus, Country Club, #117 ...**400.00**
Bus, Greyhound, w/tin wheels, #113 ....**200.00**
Cannon, 2-Wheel Mount #1, #123 ....**275.00**
Cash Register, #135 ....**300.00**

Charlie Chaplin, by Borgfeldt, #137 ....**75.00**
Chick, Baby Standing; #145 ..**70.00**
Chick in Shell Auto, #144 ..**275.00**
Chicken, on nest, #149 ....**15.00**
Clock, octagon, #163 ....**150.00**
Dog by Barrel, #190 ....**135.00**
Duck w/Large Bill, #199 ....**100.00**
Felix, next to bank, #211 ...**450.00**
Fire Engine, ladder truck w/tin wheels, #216 ....**150.00**
Gun, Kolt, #285 ....**100.00**
Jeep, #350 ....**20.00**
Liberty Bell, w/hanger, #85 ..**35.00**
Locomotive, lithographed closure, #496 ....**100.00**
Locomotive, Single Window #888; #481 ....**35.00**
Owl, #566 ....**100.00**
Pumpkin-Head Witch, #494 .**500.00**
Rabbit Running on Log **175.00**
Rabbit Wearing Hat (or Mr Rabbit), #610 ....**975.00**
Rabbits, Mother & Daughter; #605 ....**975.00**
Santa Claus Leaving Chimney, #673 ....**100.00**

Stop and Go, #317, lever missing, 4½", $250.00.

Santa Claus w/Plastic Head,
   #674 ....**55.00**
Spark Plug, #699 ....**75.00**
Telephone, West Bros Co, 1907,
   #735 ....**75.00**
Uncle Sam's Hat, #303 ....**50.00**
Watch, w/fob, #823 ....**225.00**
Windmill, Dutch, #843 ....**40.00**

Cardinal China Company

Not a manufacturer of china-ware as the name might suggest, the Cardial China Company was instead a distributer with retail outlets and showrooms in several states. They used their own marks on the cookie jars, kitchen-wares, and novelty items they sold from the late 1940s through the '50s. They also went under the name of Carteret China Company, and some of their merchandise carried this mark as well.

Spoon holder, #1 Measure Boy, $18.50.

Cookie jar, castle, yellow & brown
   door & windows, pink roof,
   #307 ....**75.00**

Cookie jar, garage, Free Parking...
   over door, #306 ....**75.00**
Cookie jar, pig, Go Ahead Make a
   Pig of Yourself **85.00**
Cookie jar, telephone, white
   w/black ringer & mouthpiece,
   #311 ....**60.00**
Salt & pepper shakers, heads of
   Chinese man & lady, pr ..**22.00**
Scissors holder, chick on
   nest **25.00**
Spoon rest, double sunflower ..**10.00**
Spoon rest, single sunflower ..**6.00**
String holder, chicken figural ..**25.00**

Carnival Chalkware

Chalkware statues of Kewpies, glamour girls, assorted dogs and horses were given to winners of carnival games from about 1910 until the 1950s. Today's collectors especially value those represent-ing well-known personalities such as Disney characters and comic book heroes. Refer to *The Carnival Chalk Prize* by Tom Morris for more information. Mr. Morris is in the Directory under Oregon.

Cat & the goldfish bowl, glass
   bowl, unmarked, ca 1930-40,
   9½" **55.00**
Circus Horse, rearing, ca 1930-40,
   16" **90.00**
Dog, sitting in chair, unmarked,
   ca 1930-40, 5½" **18.00**
Dog bookends, unmarked, ca
   1935-40, 6½", pr **30.00**
Elephant, bank, marked El
   Segundo Novelty Co 1955,
   12½" **35.00**
Good Time Willie (William Pow-
   ell), in suit & top hat, 1939 &
   1949, 9" **50.00**
Indian Chief, standing, arms
   folded, unmarked, ca 1930-
   45, 19" **40.00**

Flapper girl, flesh tone, 13½", M, $150.00.

King Kong, ca 1930-40, 13¼" ..**35.00**
Lighthouse, lamp, unmarked, ca 1935-45, 15½" **60.00**
Little Cowboy, standing w/hat in hand, unmarked, ca 1940, 8½" **18.00**
Little Red Riding Hood, marked Connie Mamat, ca 1930-40, 14" **35.00**
Mae West, copyrighted as May Doll, 1936, 10½" **65.00**
Mexican figure on base, marked Pancho, flat-backed, ca 1940s, 11½" **30.00**
Ming Toy, flapper girl on marked base, Jenkins, 1924, 13"...**85.00**
Papa, inscribed Call Me Papa, ca 1935-45, 14" **15.00**

Scottish Lass, w/bagpipes, no marks, ca 1940-50, 15" **20.00**
Sergeant Bilko, bank, ca 1945-50, 12" **35.00**
Snow White, JY Jenkins, flat-backed, 1938, 13½" **75.00**
Sweater Girl, wearing a tam, no marks, ca 1930-40, 11½" ..**25.00**
Winner, horses head in horseshoe, #60, flat-backed, ca 1940-50, 10" **20.00**

Carnival Glass

From about 1905 until the late 1920s, carnival glass was manufactured by several major American glass houses in hundreds of designs and patterns. Its characteristic iridescent lustre was the result of coating the pressed glassware with a sodium solution before the final firing. Marigold, blue, green, and purple are the most common colors, though pastels were also used. Because it was mass-produced at reasonable prices, much of it was given away at carnivals. As a result, it came to be known as carnival glass. Refer to *The Standard Encyclopedia of Carnival Glass* by Bill Edwards (Collector Books) for more information.

Acanthus, bowl, marigold, Imperial, 8" **65.00**
Acorn, bowl, green, Fenton, 8½" **80.00**
Acorn Burrs, tumbler, amethyst, Northwood **85.00**
Apple Blossoms, bowl, marigold, Dugan, 7½" **30.00**
Apple Tree, tumbler, blue, Fenton **52.00**
Arcs, compote, amethyst, Imperial **50.00**
Asters, bowl, marigold, 6" **58.00**

Autumn Acorns, bowl, marigold, Fenton, 8¾" 37.00

Aztec, sugar bowl, marigold, McKee 200.00

Ball & Swirl, mug, marigold ..90.00

Balloons, cake plate, marigold, Imperial 60.00

Banded Diamonds, bowl, amethyst, Crystal, 5" 65.00

Banded Grape, tumbler, blue, Fenton 45.00

Banded Panels, sugar bowl, amethyst, open, Crystal 45.00

Beaded Acanthus, milk pitcher, marigold, Imperial 75.00

Beaded Bull's Eye, vase, amethyst, Imperial, 14" 40.00

Beaded Hearts, bowl, amethyst or green, Northwood 60.00

Beaded Shell, butter dish, marigold, w/lid, Dugan 120.00

Beaded Stars, bowl, marigold, Fenton 35.00

Beaded Swirl, sugar bowl, marigold, English 40.00

Bells & Beads, bowl, green, Dugan, 7½" 50.00

Big Basketweave, vase, peach opalescent, Dugan, 14" ..80.00

Birds & Cherries, compote, amethyst, green, or blue, Fenton 60.00

Blackberry, bowl, marigold, footed, Northwood, 9" 47.00

Blackberry Wreath, bowl, marigold, Millersburg, 9" 65.00

Blossoms & Band, bowl, marigold, Imperial, 5" 20.00

Broken Arches, punch cup, amethyst, Imperial 30.00

Bull's Eye & Leaves, bowl, amethyst or green, Northwood, 8½" 50.00

Butterfly & Berry, butter dish, marigold, w/lid, Fenton ..130.00

Cane, compote, marigold, Imperial 70.00

Captive Rose, plate, blue, Fenton, 7" 95.00

Cathedral, bowl, marigold, Sweden, 10" 40.00

Chatham, candlesticks, marigold, US Glass, pr 75.00

Checkers, plate, marigold, 7"..50.00

Cherry, sugar bowl, amethyst, Millersburg 200.00

Cherry & Cable, bowl, marigold, Northwood, scarce, 9" ...95.00

Cherry Circles, bonbon, blue, Fenton 55.00

Cosmos & Canes, spooner, marigold 95.00

Crackle, plate, amethyst or green, Imperial 45.00

Dahlia, butter dish, amethyst, Dugan 150.00

Daisy & Plum, compote, green, Northwood 65.00

Dandelion, tumbler, green, Northwood 65.00

Diamond & Sunburst, decanter, green, Imperial 150.00

Diamond Point Columns, vase, marigold, Imperial 30.00

Diamonds, pitcher, amethyst, Millersburg 285.00

Dogwood Sprays, compote, peach opalescent, Dugan 160.00

Double Dolphins, cake plate, pastel, center handle, Fenton 70.00

Drapery, candy dish, green, Northwood 75.00

Dugan Fan, gravy boat, amethyst, footed, Dugan 60.00

Enamelled Grape, tumbler, blue, Northwood 40.00

English Button Band, creamer or sugar, marigold 38.00

Engraved Grapes, juice glass, marigold, Fenton 20.00

Estate, bud vase, marigold, Westmoreland, 6" 40.00

Fanciful, plate, pastel, Dugan, 9" 260.00

Fantail, bowl, pastel, footed, Fenton, 5" 90.00

Fashion, punch bowl & base, amethyst, Imperial 165.00

Fentonia, fruit bowl, blue, 10" **90.00**

Fentonia Fruit, bowl, marigold, footed, Fenton, 6" **45.00**

Field Thistle, spooner, marigold, US Glass, rare **70.00**

Fine Cut Rings, jam jar, marigold, w/lid, English **50.00**

Floral & Wheat, compote, amethyst, US Glass **45.00**

Flute, bowl, marigold, Millersburg, 5" **20.00**

Flute & Cane, milk pitcher, marigold, Imperial **120.00**

Frosted Block, rose bowl, marigold, Imperial **45.00**

Fruit & Flowers, plate, pastel, Northwood, 7" **230.00**

Garden Mums, bowl, green, Northwood, 10" **80.00**

Golden Honeycomb, creamer or sugar bowl, marigold, Imperial **32.00**

Graceful, vase, blue, Northwood **80.00**

Grape, fruit bowl, green, Imperial, 8¾" **48.00**

Grape & Gothic Arches, bowl, green, Northwood, 5" **45.00**

Greek Key, tumbler, green, Northwood, rare **210.00**

Heart & Vine, plate, green, Fenton, 9" **200.00**

Hobstar, fruit bowl, amethyst, w/base, Imperial **50.00**

Holly, goblet, pastel, Fenton ..**58.00**

Holly Sprig, bonbon, marigold, plain, Millersburg **55.00**

Imperial #5, bowl, marigold, 8" **40.00**

Intaglio Daisy, bowl, marigold, English, 4½" **26.00**

Inverted Feather, compote, marigold, Cambridge ..**100.00**

Iris, compote, green, Fenton ..**58.00**

Jeweled Heart, bowl, peach opalescent, Dugan, 5" ...**65.00**

Jewels, creamer or sugar bowl, amethyst, Imperial **70.00**

Kittens, cereal bowl, blue, Fenton, scarce **165.00**

Lacy Dewdrop, creamer or sugar, pastel, Westmoreland ...**90.00**

Lattice & Daisy, tumbler, amethyst, Dugan **55.00**

Leaf & Beads, candy dish, green, footed, Dugan **52.00**

Lotus & Grape, plate, marigold, Fenton, 9½" **175.00**

Lustre Flute, hat, green, Northwood **45.00**

Maple Leaf, pitcher, blue, Dugan **300.00**

Mayflower, compote, open, amethyst **50.00**

Mitered Diamond & Pleats, bowl, blue, shallow, English, 8½" **40.00**

Mitered Diamonds and Pleats, sauce bowl, marigold, 4½", $25.00.

Moonprint, banana boat, marigold, English, rare **135.00**

Nippon, bowl, blue, Northwood, 8½" **60.00**

Octagon, goblet, pastel, Imperial **80.00**

Open Rose, plate, green, Imperial, 9" **185.00**

Orange Tree, powder jar, blue, w/lid, Fenton **87.00**

Oval & Round, plate, amethyst, Imperial, 10" **70.00**

Palm Beach, butter dish, marigold, US Glass **120.00**

Pansy, dresser tray, amethyst, Imperial **90.00**

Peacock Tail and Daisy (Fenton), bowl, marigold, rare, $1,000.00.

Peacock, ice cream bowl, amethyst, Millersburg, 5" **80.00**
Peacock & Urn, compote, blue, Fenton **42.00**
Persian Garden, berry bowl, amethyst, Dugan, 5" **58.00**
Persian Medallion, bonbon, green, Fenton **52.00**
Pineapple, butter dish, marigold, English **85.00**
Premium, candlesticks, amethyst, Imperial, pr **95.00**
Quartered Block, creamer or sugar bowl, marigold **50.00**
Ranger, breakfast set, marigold, Mexican, 2-pc **160.00**
Rose Garden, bowl, blue, Sweden, 8¾" **60.00**
Ruffled Rib, vase, marigold, 14" **60.00**
Sailboats, compote, marigold, Fenton **37.00**
Six Petals, bowl, peach opalescent, Dugan, 8½" **90.00**
Smooth Rays, compote, green, Northwood-Dugan **52.00**
Soda Gold, candlestick, marigold, Imperial, 3½", each **32.00**
Star Medallion, celery tray, pastel, Imperial **50.00**
Studs, tray, marigold, Imperial, lg **60.00**

Thistle & Thorn, nut bowl, marigold, English **70.00**
Tiger Lily, tumbler, green, Imperial **38.00**
Tree of Life, perfumer, marigold, w/lid, Imperial **40.00**
Two Flowers, bowl, amethyst, flat, Fenton, 8" **120.00**
Vineyard, pitcher, marigold, Dugan **90.00**
Vintage, plate, marigold, ruffled, Fenton, 11" **180.00**
Waffle Block, shakers, marigold, Imperial, pr **75.00**
Weeping Cherry, bowl, amethyst, flat base, Dugan **75.00**
Whirling Star, compote, green, Imperial **62.00**
Windmill, pickle dish, green, Imperial **45.00**
Wreathed Cherry, bowl, amethyst, oval, Dugan, 10½" **135.00**
Zippered Heart, bowl, marigold, 5" **37.00**

Catalogs

Vintage catalogs are a fine source of reference for collectors as well as being quite collectible in their own right. While some collectors specialize in trying to accumulate a particular company's catalogs in sequence, others prefer to look for those specializing in only one area of interest — knives, lighting fixtures, or farm machinery, for instance. Original catalogs are often hard to find, and several companies' earlier editions have been reprinted.

Aldens, Spring & Summer, general merchandise, 1964 ....**30.00**
Allied Radio, Christmas Book, electronics, 80 pages, 1963 ....**25.00**

Arcor Creative Handicrafts, American Reedcraft Corp, 50 pages, 1924 ....**9.00**

Atlas Modern Shop Machines, 72 pages, 1941 ....**12.00**

Atlas Woodworking Tools, Kalamazoo, Michigan, 42 pages, 1950 ....**9.00**

Buckbee Co, Rockford IL, seeds, plants & tools, 113 pages, 1897 ....**15.00**

Burgess Seed & Nursery, Galesburg MI, 1932 ....**12.00**

Ethan Allen Furniture, 388 pages, 1971 ....**25.00**

Gateway Sporting Goods, 68 pages, 1957 ....**10.00**

Globe Machinery & Supplies, #50, 1424 pages, 1949 ....**75.00**

H&I Fishing Tackle, Utica NY, 74 pages, 1957 ....**20.00**

Hurd Shoes, Fall, 54 pages, 1916 ....**35.00**

Jason Weiler & Sons, 66th Year, jewelery, gifts, 50 pages, 1937 ....**18.00**

JC Penney, general merchandise, 1973 ....**30.00**

John Wanamaker, Spring & Summer, general merchandise, 176 pages, 1906 ....**90.00**

Lane Bryant, Fall & Winter, women's specialty, 108 pages, 1956 ....**20.00**

Marshall Fields Co, jewelry, silverware patterns, 1931 ......**35.00**

Milton Bradley, games & books, 60 pages, 1971 ....**40.00**

Montgomery Ward, Power-Kraft Tools, 60 pages, 1954 ....**10.00**

National Magic Co, #7, magic supplies & novelties, 350 pages, 1947 ....**50.00**

Nieman Marcus, 1982 ....**20.00**

Nokes & Nicolai, musical equipment, 96 pages, 1910 ....**60.00**

Olson Rug Co, 38 pages, 1942..**35.00**

Rawson's Seed Co, 92 pages, 1894 ....**25.00**

RCA Victor, Bluebird Records, 612 pages, 1940 ....**40.00**

Sears Roebuck & Co, Camera Book, 40 pages, 1940 ....**25.00**

Sears Roebuck & Co, Craftsman Power Tools, 44 pages, 1938 ....**9.00**

Sears Roebuck & Co, Grocery Store, 66 pages, 1920 ....**10.00**

Sears Roebuck & Co, woodworking machinery, 1925 ....**4.00**

Slack Manufacturing Co, Il, #236, novelties, ca 1930 ....**25.00**

Southern Furniture Co, #50, furniture & appliances, 244 pages, 1950 ....**45.00**

Speigel, 1956 ....**90.00**

Speyer Brothers Drapery, Hardware & Fittings, 36 pages, 1892 ....**9.00**

Stanley Rule & Level Co, New Britian CT, 66 pages, 1892 ..**8.00**

Troy Laundry Machinery Co, Troy NY, 142 pages, 1902 ....**21.00**

Union Furniture & Novelty Co, Warren PA, #7, ca 1920s, 16 pages **18.00**

Walker-Turner, machinery, 40 pages, 1935 ....**10.00**

Wallmann Manufacturing Co, service station equipment, 36 pages, 1910 ....**8.50**

Webber Tackle Co, Stevens Point, WI, 73 pages, 1959 ....**18.00**

Winchester-Western Sporting Arms & Ammunition, 24 pages, 1963 ....**35.00**

York Supply Co, auto supply & garage equipment, 447 pages, 1920 ....**26.00**

Ceramic Arts Studio

Whether you're a collector of American pottery or not, chances are you'll like the distinctive styling of the figurines, salt and pepper shakers, and other novelty items made by the Ceramic Arts Studio of Madison, Wisconsin, from about 1938 until about 1952. This is a popular area of collecting, and a trip to any good flea market will usually produce one or several good buys of their shelf sitters or wall-hanging pairs. They're easily spotted, once you've seen a few examples; but if you're not sure, check for the trademark: the name of the company and its location.

Drummer girl, 4½", $35.00.

Bank, Paisley Pig, 3" **75.00**
Candle holder, Hear No Evil, angel, 5" **32.00**
Figurine, accordion boy, 5" ...**48.00**
Figurine, bride & groom, 4¾" & 5" **65.00**
Figurine, dachshund, 3½".....**22.00**
Figurine, Elsie elephant, 5" **45.00**
Figurine, fox, modern, 3" **45.00**
Figurine, Hans & Katinka (chubby), 6½" & 6¼", pr **60.00**
Figurine, Harry & Lillibeth, 6½", pr **65.00**
Figurine, Poncho & Pepita, 4½", pr **60.00**
Figurine, Winter Willy, 4" **35.00**

Figurine, Woody, sitting, 3¼"..**55.00**
Jug, Diana the Huntress, 3" ..**28.00**
Lamp, Zor on base **95.00**
Planter, head, Bonnie, 7" **48.00**
Planter, seashell, 3" **32.00**
Plaque, fish, striped mother & baby **55.00**
Plaque, Jack Be Nimble, 5" ..**45.00**
Plaque, mermaid, 6" **60.00**
Plaque, Zor & Zorina, 9", pr ..**70.00**
Salt & pepper shakers, Chinese boy & girl, 4¼" & 4", pr **25.00**
Salt & pepper shakers, Chirp & Twirp, 4", pr **45.00**
Salt & pepper shakers, kissing bunnies, 4" & 2½" **32.00**
Shelf sitter, banjo girl, 4" **38.00**
Shelf sitter, Dutch boy & girl, 4½", pr **40.00**
Shelf sitter, Greg & Grace, 6", pr **75.00**
Shelf sitter, mother collie, 5"..**25.00**
Shelf sitter, Nip & Tuck, 4¼" & 4", pr **38.00**
Shelf sitter, Tuffy the cat, white, 5¼" **45.00**
Vase, bird motif, round, 2" ...**18.00**
Vase, modern, square, 2" **22.00**

Cereal Boxes

When buying real estate, they say 'location, location, location.' When cereal box collecting its 'character, character, character.' Look for Batman, Quisp, Superman or Ninja Turtles — the so-called 'Grain Gods' emblazoned across the box. Dull adult and health cereals such as Special K or shredded wheat, unless they have an exciting offer, aren't worth picking up (too boring). Stick to the cavity-blasting presweets aimed at kids, like The Jetsons, Froot Loops, or Trix. You can hunt down the moldy FrostyOs and Quake from childhood in old stores and pantries or collect the new stuff at your supermarket. Your local cereal aisle – the grain ghetto – is chock full of future bluechips, so squeeze the moment! The big question is: once you've gotten your flaky treasures home, how do you save the box? If you live where pests (bugs or mice) aren't a problem, display or store the box unopened. Otherwise, eat its contents, then pull out the bottom flaps and flatten the package along the fold lines. If you don't want to flatten the box, empty it by gently pulling out the bottom flaps and removing the bag. Be sure to save the prize inside, called an inpack, if it has one; they're potentially valuable too. Prices are for cereal boxes that are full or folded flat, in mint condition. For further information, Scott Bruce, Mr. Cereal Box, is listed in the Directory under Massachusetts. See also Clubs and Newsletters.

1910, Corn Flakes w/baseball game, Kellogg's **750.00**
1935, Dizzy Dean Grape Nuts, Post **350.00**
1937, Wheaties w/Joe DiMaggio back panel **1,500.00**
1960, Sugar Crisp w/mug & bowl offer, Post **75.00**
1960, Wheat Honeys w/Indian War medal, Nabisco **75.00**
1962, Huckleberry Hound All Stars, Kellogg's **450.00**
1966, Quake w/Quake's miner helmet offer, Quaker Oats ..**750.00**
1968, All Pro w/Roger Maris, Ralston **750.00**
1969, Clackers w/Dick Dastardly cars, General Mills **225.00**
1969, TEAM Flakes w/baseball player mini-posters, Nabisco **350.00**

1970, Corn Flakes w/Willie Mays (3-D card offer), Kellogg's ...**300.00**
1970, Puffa Puffa Rice w/Monkees rings **450.00**
1972, Quisp w/Quisp bank offer, Quaker Oats **400.00**
1974, Jellephants, Nabisco ..**100.00**
1974, Normans, Nabisco **150.00**

Kellogg's Rice Krispies 75th Anniversary package, dated February 23, 1982, 13-oz., $12.00.

1985, Wheaties w/Pete Rose, General Mills **50.00**
1992, Urkelos, Ralston **12.00**
1992, World Federation Wrestling Stars, Ralston **15.00**
1993, Nolan Ryan Corn Flakes, Kellogg's **7.00**
1993, Wheaties w/Larry Bird, General Mills **25.00**

Character and Promotional Glassware

Once routinely given away by fast food restaurants and soft drink companies, these glasses have become very collectible; and though they're being snapped up by avid collectors everywhere, you'll still find there are bargains to be had. The more expensive are those with Disney or Walter Lantz cartoon characters, super-heroes, sports greats, or personalities from Star Trek or the old movies. We've also listed mugs and pitchers. For more information refer to *The Collector's Guide to Cartoon and Promotional Drinking Glasses* by John Hervey (L-W Book Sales).

A&W, mug, 3" **8.00**
A&W Great Root Bear, pitcher **28.00**
Action Series, 1977, McDonald's, 6¼", any **6.00**
Adventure Series, 1980, McDonald's, each **3.50**
Apollo 11, red, white & blue w/astronaut, short **4.50**
Battlestar Galactica, 1979, Universal Studios, w/1 character, any **6.50**
BC Ice Age, Arby's, any **10.00**
BC Ice Age, frosted juice pitcher, Arby's **10.00**
Bernard (character from movie), mouse w/lantern, 1977, Pepsi **14.50**
Breakfast Brigade, milk glass mug, ca 1976, McDonald's **2.00**
Brutus, tall indented base, 1975, Coca-Cola **3.00**
Camp Snoopy, 1983, McDonald's, 6", any **3.00**
Care Bears, Funshine, Grumpy & Tenderheart, 1983, Pizza Hut, any **2.50**
Charlie Brown, Rats! Why Is Having Fun Always So Much Work? **3.00**
Chipmunks, marked Bagdesarian, 1985, Hardee's, any **5.00**
Coca-Cola logo on stained glass design, inset bottom, straight sides **2.50**

Currier & Ives, Arby's, some dated 1981, some undated, any scene **4.00**
Denver Broncos, 1977, Dr Pepper, 5⅝", any **5.00**
Dinosaurs, 1989, Welch's, any ..**2.00**
Endangered Species, indented base, '78, Burger King, 5⅝", each **7.00**
ET, I'll Be Right Here, indented base, 1982 ....**12.00**
ET Collector's Series, flared top, 1982, Pizza Hut, 6", each **2.00**
Fantasia, Mickey as sorcerer & 1940 below, short mug w/handle **4.50**
Flintstone Kids, round bottom, 1986, Pizza Hut, 6", each **2.00**
Flintstones, Fred in His Sports Car, 1962, Welch's **8.50**
Flintstones, Going to the Drive-In, 1964 ....**13.50**
Garfield, Are We Having Fun Yet, 1978, McDonald's, any **7.50**
Garfield mug, I'm Not One..., 1978, McDonald's **2.50**
Garfield's I've Never Met a Dinner, mug, McDonald's, 3½" **4.00**
Gone for the Morning, ceramic mug, ca 1985, McDonald's **3.00**
Good Morning, Arches w/sun, ca 1975, McDonald's **2.00**
Goonies in Organ Chamber ...**5.00**
Great Muppet Caper, Great Gonzo (or any other), 1981, McDonald's, each **2.00**
Great Root Bear, logo on sweater, indented base, A&W Root Beer **7.50**
Happy Days, Pizza Hut & Dr Pepper, any character **16.00**
Holly Hobbie, Twelve Days of Christmas, 1979, American Greetings, Coke **2.50**
Holly Hobbie Christmas, 1977, American Greeting, any ..**2.50**
Keebler Soft Batch Cookie premium, Ernest, You Don't Bite..., 1984 ....**12.50**

Laurel & Hardy, Take 3, indented base, 1979, Arby's **10.00**

Masters of the Universe, indented base, 1983, any character ..**6.50**

McDonald's Big Mac, straight sides, indented base **5.00**

McDonald's Mayor McCheese, straight sides, thick base ..**16.50**

Mickey's Christmas Carol, flared rim, 1982, Coca-Cola, any **14.50**

Mickey's Christmas Carol, 1982, Coca-Cola, any **16.00**

Monopoly, 1985, Arby's, any from series **5.00**

Movie Stars, smoke-colored glass, 1979, Arby's, 5⅝", each ...**5.00**

Pack Man mug, Gobble Ghosts, 1980 ....**4.00**

Patriots of American Revolution, 1976, Coca-Cola, any **5.00**

Popeye Kolect-A-Set, Olive Oyl, 1975, Pizza Hut, 5⅝" **5.00**

Presidents & Patriots Bicentennial, 1976, Burger King, any **8.50**

Return of Jedi, indented base, 1983, Burger King, 5⅝", each **5.00**

Return of the Jedi, 1983, Burger King & Coca-Cola, any in the series **2.00**

Rise & Shine, ceramic mug, 1989, Hardee's **2.00**

Santa in chair, elves at his feet, 1960, Coca-Cola **3.00**

Saturday Evening Post, Rockwell, straight sides, indented base, any **3.50**

Saturday Evening Post Santa, Rockwell, curved-in base, any **3.50**

Search for Spock, Star Trek III; 1984, Burger King, 5⅝", each **5.00**

Smurf, round bottom, 1982, Hardee's, 6" **2.00**

Smurfs, Grouchy, I Hate Music, curved-in base, 1982 ....**3.00**

Snoopy, The Peoples Choice, curved-in base, Dolly Madison **3.00**

Star Trek, Taco Bell, each **5.00**

Star Trek, 1976, Dr Pepper, any character **25.00**

Star Wars, indented base, 1977, Burger King & Coke, any character **16.00**

Sunday Funnies, Brenda Star, indented base **13.50**

Super Heroes, 1978, Pepsi, any character **10.00**

Supergirl, Moon Series, slightly flared sides, NPP, 1976, Pepsi **12.50**

Superman the Movie, straight sides, indented base, 1978, Pepsi, any **9.00**

The Chipmunks, Alvin, round bottom, 1985, Hardee's, 6" ...**4.00**

The Goonies, indented base, 1985, Godfather's Series, 5⅝", each **5.00**

The Great Muppet Caper, 1981, McDonald's, 5¾", any **3.00**

Thought Factory, heavy base, 1982, Arby's, 4⅝", any **4.00**

Tony the Tiger (or any from series), Kellogg's premium, 1977, each **14.00**

Twelve Days of Christmas, curved-in bottom, Pepsi, 16-oz, any **4.50**

Whataburger, pitcher **15.00**

Character Collectibles

One of the most popular areas of collecting today and one with the most available memorabilia is the field of character collectibles. Flea markets usually yield some of the more common examples – toys, books, lunch boxes, children's dishes, and sheet music are for the most part quite readily found. Trade papers are also an excellent source. Often you will find even the rare and hard-to-find listed for sale. Disney characters, television personalities, and western and comic book heroes are among the most sought after.

One of our advisors for this category is Judy Posner, who is listed in the Directory under Pennsylvania. Refer to *Cartoon Friends of the Baby Boom Era* by Bill Bruegman, see the Directory under Ohio.

Only fictional characters are listed here. See also Cereal Boxes; Character and Promotional Drinking Glasses; Character Clocks and Watches; Cookie Jars; Fast Foods; Games; View-Master Reels and Packets; Western Heroes; Wizard of Oz.

Addams Family, card game, Milton Bradley, EX in box **35.00**
Addams Family, cartoon board game, Milton Bradley, 1974, EX **30.00**
Addams Family, colorforms, 1965, NM in original box **120.00**
Addams Family, flashlight w/ cereal box, 1991 ....**6.00**
Addams Family, game, Milton Bradley, 1973, NM **70.00**
Addams Family, puzzle, Family Mystery, jigsaw, 1964, EX in box **40.00**
Addams Family, Thing, hand in lithographed box, NM ...**10.00**
Alvin & Chipmunks, Christmas stocking, vinyl, 1963, 14", NM **12.50**
Alvin & Chipmunks, harmonica, Alvin's official, plastic, 5x5½", M **12.50**
Alvin & Chipmunks, magic slate, Saalfield, 1962, 12x8", NM **7.50**
Alvin & Chipmunks, mug, Alvin walking down a lane, heavy glass, '59, M **7.50**

Alvin & Chipmunks, tattoo wrapper, Alvin on front, Fleer, 1966, M **25.00**
Atom Ant, coloring book, hardback, Watkins-Strathmore, 1965, 8x10", EX **8.50**
Barney Google, book, Saalfield, 1935, EX **40.00**
Barney Google, doll, stuffed, ca 1920s or '30s, 12", EX ..**100.00**
Barney Google, salt & pepper shakers, 1940s, 3", EX, pr **45.00**
Batman, battery tester, M on original card **8.50**
Batman, belt, c 1966, Morris Belt Co, EX on original card ..**20.00**
Batman, board game, Batman vs the Joker, Hasbro, 1965, complete, NM **35.00**
Batman, bread bag, 1966, unused, M **20.00**
Batman, charm bracelet, all characters, 1966, M **35.00**
Batman, coffee mug, ceramic, 1950s, M **15.00**
Batman, figure & parachute, CDC, 1966, unused, M on original card **35.00**
Batman, hand puppet, Ideal, 1966, M **60.00**
Batman, lamp, Vanity Fair, 1977, EX **45.00**
Batman, ring, plastic w/embossed bat, NM **4.50**
Batman & Robin, bookends, plaster, 1960, M, pr **75.00**
Batman & Robin, talking clock, 1960s, EX **30.00**
Beany & Cecil, bath mit, in window display box, Roclar 1962, MIB **40.00**
Beany & Cecil, Colorforms cartoon kit, 1962, in box, NM **50.00**
Beany & Cecil, coloring book, Whitman, 1953, NM **30.00**
Beetle Bailey, nodder, composition, 7", EX **45.00**
Ben Casey, notebook, 1962, EX **12.50**

Betty Boop

Betty Boop was developed by the Fleischer Studios in 1930. All in all, there were about one hundred black and white cartoons produced during the decade of the thirties. Very few of these cels remain today. Many of the cartoons were copied and colored in the sixties, and many of these cels are still available. Hoards of related items were marketed in the thirties, and many other products became available over the next forty years. During the eighties, still others were marketed. One of the leading companies in this resurgence of popularity was Vandor; they came out with dozens of different ceramic items. Another innovative company is Bright Ideas of San Francisco; they feature items ranging from playing cards to Christmas tree light sets. King Features still owns the copyright, and all items should carry the appropriate labeling. Our advisor for Betty Boop is Leo A. Mallette, who is listed in the Directory under California.

Betty Boop string holder, chalkware, ca 1925, 10" wide, M, $150.00.

Ashtray, Betty & Bimbo figural, china, 1930s, EX **75.00**
Belt buckle, celluloid, M **45.00**
Big Little Book, VG **150.00**
Candy dish, figure on heart, Vandor, 1983, 3¾", M **25.00**
Doll blanket, c Max Fleisher Studio, 1930s, NM **70.00**
Figurine, bisque, Japan, 1930s, 3", VG **125.00**
Handkerchief, 1930s, 9" square, EX **40.00**
Pin, Betty & Bimbo, silverplated, 1930s, G **100.00**
Playing cards, 1930s, VG **75.00**
Rub-on decals, 1930s, 2 cards, M **25.00**
Sheet music, Poor Cinderella, 1934, EX **45.00**
Tea set, china, 1930s **300.00**
Wall pocket, w/Bimbo, lusterware, 1930s, 5½", NM **100.00**

Beverly Hillbillies, card game, Milton Bradley, 1960s, MIB **15.00**
Bionic Woman, doll, vinyl, Kenner, 1974, 12", EX **20.00**
Blondie, figure, wood composition, marked KFS, 1944, 5", EX **30.00**
Blondie, paint book, Whitman, ca 1945, 11x8½", EX **20.00**
Blondie & Dagwood, doll stroller, lithographed metal, 1950s, NM **55.00**
Bonzo, figure, bisque, 1930s, 3", NM **40.00**
Bonzo, postcard, British, 1930s, EX **20.00**
Bozo the Clown, decal, 1950s, M in package **10.00**
Bozo the Clown, nodder, Bayard, 1950s, EX **50.00**
Bozo the Clown, radio, 1960s, EX in box **30.00**
Bozo the Clown, yo-yo, 1950s, EX **7.50**

Brady Bunch, paper dolls, M..**20.00**

Buck Rogers, doll, Mego, 1979, 12", MIB **35.00**

Buck Rogers, shaker maker, Ideal, 1980, M **25.00**

Buck Rogers, View-Master set, cartoon version, 1979, complete, M **10.00**

Bugs Bunny, Better Little Book, Bugs...& His Pals, Whitman, 1945, EX **20.00**

Bugs Bunny, lamp, Bugs Bunny in chair, 1970, EX **30.00**

Bugs Bunny, planter, ceramic, ca 1950s, M **35.00**

Bugs Bunny, soap, 1930s, MIB .**45.00**

Bugs Bunny, squeeze toy, 1930s, 8", NM **60.00**

Bugs Bunny, tricycle, pull toy, wood & paper litho, Brice, 11", M **75.00**

Bullwinkle, bulletin board **35.00**

Bullwinkle, bumper sticker, Bullwinkle for President, 1972, M **22.50**

Bullwinkle, coloring book, Whitman, 1971, M **20.00**

Bullwinkle & Rocky, mug, 1960s, EX **20.00**

California Raisins

In the Fall of 1986, the California Raisins made their first commercials for television. In 1987 the PVC figurines were introduced. Initially there were four: a singer, two conga dancers, and a saxophone player. At this time Hardee's, the fast food restaurant, issued similar but smaller figures. Later that same year, Blue Surfboard (Horizontal), and three Bendees (which are about 5½" tall with flat pancake-style bodies) were issued for retail sale.

In 1988 twenty-one Raisins were made for sale in retail stores

and in some cases used for promotional efforts in grocery stores: Blue Surfboard (vertical), Red Guitar, Lady Dancer, Blue/Green Sunglasses, Guy Winking, Candy Cane, Santa Raisin, Bass Player, Drummer, Tambourine Lady (there were two styles), Lady Valentine, Male Valentine, Boy Singer, Girl Singer, Hip Guitar Player, Sax Player with Beret, and four Graduates. The Graduates are identical in design to the original four characters released in 1987 but stand on yellow pedestals and are attired with blue graduation caps and yellow tassels. Bass Player and the Drummer were initially distributed in grocery stores along with an application to join the California Raisin Fan Club located in Fresno, California. That same year, Hardee's issued six more: Blue Guitar, Trumpet Player, Roller Skater, Skateboard, Boom Box, and Yellow Surfboard. As was true with the 1987 line, the Hardee's characters were generally smaller than those produced for retail sales.

Eight more made their debut in 1989: Male in Beach Chair, Green Grunks with Surfboard, Hula Skirt, Girl Sitting on Sand, Piano Player, 'AC,' Mom, and Michael Raisin. That year the Raisins starred in two movies: *Meet the Raisins* and *The California Raisins – Sold Out*, and were joined in figurine production by five movie characters (their fruit and vegetable friends): Rudy Bagaman, Lick Broccoli, Banana White, Leonard Limabean, and Cecil Thyme.

The latest release of Raisins came in 1991 when Hardee's issued four more Raisins: Anita

Break, Alotta Style, Buster, and Benny. All Raisins issued for retail sales and promotions in 1987 and 1988, including Hardee's issues for those years, are dated with the year of production (usually on the bottom of one foot). Of those Raisins released for retail sale in 1989, only the Beach Scene characters are dated, and they are actually dated 1988. Hardee's Raisins, issued in 1991, are also undated.

In the last two years, California Raisins have become extremely popular collectible items and are quickly sold at flea markets and toy shows. On Friday, November 22, 1991, the California Raisins were enshrined in the Smithsonian Institution to the tune of *I Heard It Through the Grapevine*. Our advisor, Larry De Angelo, is listed in the Directory under Virginia.

Bendee, conga dancer, blue or orange shoes, each 8.00
Bendee, lead singer, eyes closed, w/microphone 10.00
Calrab, 'Mom' Lulu Arborman ..35.00
Calrab, AC, red shoes, hand in 'low five' position 35.00
Calrab, bass player 7.00
Calrab, blue tennis shoes & glasses 6.00
Calrab, boy singer, eyes open, w/microphone 6.00
Calrab, Candy Cane Raisin ...5.00
Calrab, conga dancer, blue or orange shoes, each 4.00
Calrab, drummer 10.00
Calrab, girl singer, w/yellow heels & microphone 6.00
Calrab, girl sitting on sand, green shoes 5.00
Calrab, girl, grass hula skirt ..5.00
Calrab, guitar player, red guitar & blue shoes 6.00

Calrab, guy winking, pink tennis shoes 6.00
Calrab, hip guitar player, 'Jimi Hendrix' headband 15.00
Calrab, lady dancer, hot pink shoes 5.00
Calrab, lady w/tambourine, 2 versions, each 5.00
Calrab, lead singer, eyes closed, w/microphone 4.00
Calrab, man w/orange sunglasses in beach chair 5.00
Calrab, Michael Raisin 25.00
Calrab, piano player, 'Red' ...20.00
Calrab, sandals & green trunks w/surfboard 5.00
Calrab, Santa Raisin 5.00
Calrab, saxaphone player 6.00
Calrab, surfboarder, horizontal or vertical, each 8.00
Calrab, The Graduate, any of 4 styles, each 20.00
Calrab, Valentine Be Mine, in pink heels 5.00
Calrab, Valentine I'm Yours, red shoes 5.00
Claymation Friend, Banana White 5.00
Claymation Friend, Cecil Thyme 20.00
Claymation Friend, Leonard Limabean 20.00
Claymation Friend, Lick Broccoli 5.00
Claymation Friend, Rudy Bagaman 5.00
Hardee's, Allota Style, w/boom box & pink boots 5.00
Hardee's, Anita Break, w/shopping bags 2.00
Hardee's, Benny, w/bowling ball & bag 5.00
Hardee's, Buster, black & yellow shoes, skateboard 5.00
Hardee's, conga dancer, blue or orange shoes, each 2.00
Hardee's, guitar player, blue guitar, orange shoes 2.00
Hardee's, lead singer w/mike..2.00

Hardee's, roller skater or skate-boarder, each 2.00
Hardee's, saxophone player ...2.00
Hardee's, surfboarder, red shoes, sunglasses 2.00
Hardee's, trumpet player 2.00
Hardee's, yellow shoes & sun-glasses, w/boom box 2.00

Captain America, coloring book, Whitman, 1966, M 15.00
Captain Kangaroo, finger-paint set, 1956, EX 20.00
Captain Kangaroo, record, EX 10.00
Captain Kangaroo, school tablet, 1950s, EX 5.50
Captain Marvel, booklet, Fawcett, 1940s, sm, EX 16.50
Captain Marvel, club membership button, 1947 ....80.00
Captain Marvel, magic flute, M on illustrated card 50.00
Captain Marvel, tie clip, Fawcett Publication, 1946, M on card 25.00
Captain Midnight, cup, Ovaltine premium, plastic, 4", EX ..20.00
Captain Midnight, premium, Code-O-Graph magnifier/decoder, 1945, EX 55.00
Casper the Ghost, doll, Mattel, pull-string voice, 1960s, M 30.00
Casper the Ghost, record, 1962, M 10.00
Charlie Tuna, figure, vinyl, Prod-uct People, 1970, MIB ...45.00
Charlie Tuna, lamp, plaster, 1960s, original shade, EX 45.00
Charlie Tuna, wristwatch, ca 1960, EX 30.00
Creature From the Black Lagoon, 3-D glasses, EX 30.00
Dagwood, figure, wood composi-tion, marked KFS, 1944, 5", M 30.00
Daisy Mae, key chain, sliding puz-zle type, ca 1950, EX 20.00

Dennis the Menace, finger-paint set, Pressman, 1960s, com-plete, M 50.00
Dennis the Menace, gloves, western-type fringe, 1960s, EX 20.00
Dennis the Menace, hand puppet, cloth & vinyl, 1950s, EX ..10.00

Dick Tracy

The most famous master detective of them all, Dick Tracy stood for law and order. Whether up against Boris Arson or the Spider Gang, he somehow always came out on top, teaching his young followers in no uncertain terms that 'Crime Does Not Pay.' Many companies parlayed his persona through hundreds of items for retail sales; and radio premiums such as badges, but-tons, secret code books, and rings were free just for 'sending in.' In 1990 with the release of the movie, a new round of potential collectibles appeared. Our advisor is Larry Doucet, who is listed in the Directory under New York. He offers free appraisals to anyone who will send a long SASE and detailed descriptions or a photo-graph.

Badge, Quaker Secret Service Patrol premium, girl's ...50.00
Badge, Quaker Secret Service Patrol premium, member's, brass 30.00
Badge, Quaker Secret Service Patrol, Sergeant's 75.00
Big Little Book, Dick Tracy & the Mad Killer 30.00
Big Little Book, Dick Tracy & the Spider Gang 40.00
Big Little Book, Dick Tracy Encounters Facey 20.00
Big Little Book, Dick Tracy Returns 40.00

Dick Tracy pop-up book, Pleasure Books, Incorporated, dated 1935, 9½x8", NM, $75.00.

Book, Ace Detective, Whitman, 1942, w/dust jacket **25.00**
Camera, Seymour Sales Co, early 1950s **40.00**
Caramel card, #121-144, each ..**1.00**
Caramel card, #97-120, each..**3.00**
Christmas tree bulb, 1940s ..**75.00**
Colorforms, cartoon kit, 1962 ..**50.00**
Coloring book, Saalfield Publishing, 1946 ....**40.00**
Game, Master Detective, Sel Right, 1967 ....**75.00**
Game, Sunday Funnies, Ideal, 1972 ....**50.00**
Hand puppet, Ideal, 1961 ....**40.00**
Jumbo Movie Style Viewer, Acme, early 1960s, M on card ..**75.00**
Little Golden Book, 1962 .....**20.00**
Lunch box, Aladdin, 1967 ..**100.00**
Model kit, Aurora, '68, MIB ..**200.00**
Official 2-Way Electronic Wrist Radio, Remco, 1950s **100.00**
Paint set, Sparkle Paint, Kenner, 1963 ....**75.00**
Pin-back button, Quaker Secret Service Patrol premium, member's **25.00**
Puzzle, Bank Holdup, Jaymar, 1961 ....**25.00**

Puzzle, Crime Does Not Pay Club, Jaymar, late 1940s **50.00**
Rack toys, Larami Corp, early 1970s, M on card, each ..**25.00**
Salt & pepper shakers, Dick & Junior, ceramic, late 1930s, pr **50.00**
Secret code book, Quaker Secret Service Patrol premium ..**50.00**
Toy, Copmobile, plastic, Ideal, 1961, 24" **90.00**
Toy, Squad Car, #1, Marx, tin friction or wind-up, 1950s ..**150.00**

Elmer Fudd, figure, American Pottery, 1940s, 6½", NM **75.00**
Elmer Fudd, Fire Chief pull toy, wood, 1950s, EX **60.00**
Elmer Fudd, pistol/flashlight, EX **15.00**
Elmer Fudd, wristwatch, Sheraton, 1972, original package, M **85.00**

Elsie the Cow

Elsie has been representing the Borden company since the late 1930s, and even though she 'retired' in the late fifties. She's been brought back again, and you'll often see her in special promotions. Her husband was Elmer (of Elmer's Glue), and their babies were Beulah, Beauregard and a late-in-life set of twins, Lobelia and Larabee. Grown-up kids who remember Elsie as part of their childhood now collect the salt and pepper shakers, recipe booklets, store figures, and other items made in her likeness or on which she appears.

Booklet, Magic Recipes, Borden's, 1942, 22 pages **15.00**
Container, cheese product, glass w/lithographed tin lid, 3x4½", EX **65.00**

Elsie the Cow ice cream dish, M, $35.00.

Cookie jar, M **45.00**
Doll, Elsie, 1950s, EX **145.00**
Funbook, 1950s, EX **10.00**
Lamp, ceramic, M **65.00**
Mug, marked Juvenile Ware, Universal Cambridge, EX ...**65.00**
Pin-back button, yellow & red on white, 1" **10.00**
Playing cards, MIB **75.00**
Premium catalog, Borden's, 1955, 39 pages, 6x5", EX **25.00**
Salt & peppers, Baby Beulah & Beauregard, ceramic, pr, EX **65.00**
Toy baby bottle, decals on plastic, Borden's, ca 1956, M on card **65.00**
Tumbler, glass, Elsie logo on white, 1940s, EX **12.50**

ET, alarm clock, Nelsonic, MIB **25.00**
ET, pop-up spaceship, M **14.50**
Fat Albert, doll, vinyl, 1970s, M **10.00**
Felix the Cat, ashtray, ceramic, unmarked, 1930s, 4", EX **40.00**
Felix the Cat, Dandy Candy game, ca 1957, MIB **35.00**

Felix the Cat, pencil case, paper label on top, 1950s, EX **25.00**
Felix the Cat, yarn holder, NM **25.00**
Flash Gordon, kite, NM **65.00**
Flash Gordon, paint book, Whitman, 1936, 96 pages, 14x11", EX **40.00**
Flash Gordon, pencil box, Eagle Pencil Co, 1951, M **40.00**
Flash Gordon, puzzle, #4221-1, Milton Bradley, 1951, 12x9", EX **20.00**

Flintstones

Anyone alive today knows that Fred, Wilma, Barney, Betty, Pebbles, and Bamm Bamm lived in Bedrock, had a dinosaur for a pet, and preferred bowling over any other sport. The invention of Hanna-Barbera who introduced them all in 1959, they met with immediate, sustaining success and to date literally thousands of items have been sold such as games, playing cards, pin-back buttons, cookie jar, puzzles, toys, dolls, T-shirts, etc., so today's collectors can build a large and varied collection of Flintstones memorabilia with ease.

Ashtray, figural, Arrow Houseware Products, 1961, 6x8" **58.00**
Bank, Dino figural, ceramic, 1960s, EX **15.00**
Book, The Rubbles in Problem Present, Whitman, 1965, EX **5.00**
Bubble pipe, Bamm Bamm figural, Transogram, 1963, M **25.00**
Camera, 1960s, M **15.00**
Card game, 1961, MIB **16.50**
Checkers, Empire, 1961, NM in box **35.00**
Colorforms, 1972, NM **17.50**

Coloring book, Whitman, 1965, 8x11½", 192 pages, EX ..**25.00**

Doll, Barney Rubble, Knickerbocker, 1960, NM **65.00**

Figure, Barney Rubble, vinyl, 1960s, 10", EX **12.50**

Figure, Fred, vinyl, 1960, 12", EX **15.00**

Flashlight, Fred, 1976, M **7.50**

Game, Animal Rummy, Ed-U-Cards, 1960, NM **12.50**

Game, Brake Ball, Whitman, 1962, EX **75.00**

Game, Stoneage, Transogram, 1961, NM **45.00**

Hand puppet, Bamm Bamm, Ideal, 1960s, EX **30.00**

Lunch box, hard plastic, new ..**25.00**

Paper cup, Happy Birthday, 1960s, set of 10, M in package **17.50**

Paper dolls, Pebbles & Bamm Bamm, Whitman, 1965, M **45.00**

Pillow, Fred, 1970s, M **14.50**

Pressbook, A Man Called Flintstone, 1966, 10 pages, NM **17.50**

Pull toy, Fred, Fisher-Price, 1960s, M **65.00**

Puppet, Dino, plush, Kohner, 1963, NM **25.00**

Puppet, Fred, hard plastic, Kohner Bros, 1960s, 4", EX **27.50**

Record, Flip Fables, Hanna Barbara Records, 1965, LP, NM **15.00**

Squeak toy, Barney, vinyl, 1960, M **15.00**

Squeak toy, Dino, vinyl, 1960, 12", EX **7.50**

Squeak toy, Fred figure, rubber, Knickerbocker, ca 1960 ..**60.00**

Thermometer, Bamm Bamm figure, MIB **20.00**

Yo-Yo decoder, 1972, MIB **14.50**

Flying Nun, board game, Milton Bradley, 1968, NM **50.00**

Flying Nun, doll, Hasbro, 12", MIB **85.00**

Flying Nun, paper dolls, Saalfield, 1969, complete, M **45.00**

Green Hornet, Better Little Book, The Green Hornet Strikes, EX **12.00**

Green Hornet, mug, milk glass, 1966, M **10.00**

Green Hornet, pin-back button, 1966, M **20.00**

Green Hornet, ring, plastic w/hornet in center, 1966, unused, M ..**7.50**

Green Hornet, spoon, embossed figure on handle, 1966, EX **16.50**

Gumby, Dot-to-Dot book, Whitman, 1968, 8x11", M **15.00**

Gumby, hand puppet, Lakeside, 1965, EX **12.50**

Gumby, sunglasses, M on original card **18.50**

Gumby, Super-Flex figure, Lakeside, 1965, M on original 6x9" card **45.00**

Howdy Doody, bank, ceramic figural, 1950s, 9", EX **345.00**

Howdy Doody, breakfast set, child's, 1950s, 3-pc, EX ..**45.00**

Howdy Doody, Christmas card, 1950s, M **10.00**

Howdy Doody, cup, ceramic, 1950s, EX **15.00**

Howdy Doody, earmuffs, plastic faces w/wool-like fur, 1950s, EX **15.00**

Howdy Doody, mug, red plastic decorated w/portrait decal, 1950s, NM **65.00**

Howdy Doody, night light, Howdy riding pig, 1987, MIB **7.50**

Howdy Doody, paint-by-number set, National Broadcasting, 1976, NM **20.00**

Howdy Doody, umbrella, plastic, 1950s, 18" long, EX **30.00**

Huckleberry Hound, camera, Sun Pix, 1964, MIB **25.00**

Huckleberry Hound, charm bracelet, child's, various figures, 1959, M **10.00**

Huckleberry Hound, official club picture, 1960s, EX **7.50**

Huckleberry Hound, squeeze toy, Dell, 1960s, M **10.00**

Huckleberry Hound, Tiddlywinks game, 1959, MIB **25.00**

Incredible Hulk, paint set, 1981, complete, M **5.00**

Incredible Hulk, puzzle, Whitman, 1982, circular, complete, MIB **10.00**

James Bond, action figure, scuba attire, 1960s, EX **30.00**

James Bond, board game, Milton Bradley, 1964, NM **30.00**

James Bond, gum card wrapper, 1965, NM **48.00**

James Bond, pillowcase, 1960s, EX **15.00**

Jetsons, bank, Elroy in bed, 1985, MIB **16.00**

Jetsons, book, Great Pizza Hunt, Wonder Books, 1976, EX ..**8.00**

Jetsons, figure, wind-up, Marx, 1950s, 4", EX **60.00**

Jetsons, game, Fun Pad, Milton Bradley, 1963, EX **75.00**

Jetsons, game, Out of This World, Transogram, 1963, NM **140.00**

Jetsons, game, Race Through Space, Milton Bradley, 1985, M **15.00**

Jetsons, Whitman, 1962, 70-pc, EX **35.00**

Joe Palooka, figure, wood jointed, 1940s, 4", NM **70.00**

Joe Palooka, wristwatch, 1940s, VG **75.00**

Li'l Abner, bank, ceramic, 1975, 7½" **45.00**

Li'l Abner, canoe, wind-up, Ideal, 1950s, EX **50.00**

Li'l Abner, Halloween costume, 1950s, NM in box **55.00**

Li'l Abner, mug, ceramic, profile on side, 1968, NM **12.00**

Li'l Abner, plate, china, Capp Enterprises, 1968, M **20.00**

Li'l Abner & Daisy Mae, bookends, painted plaster, 9" & 6", NM, pr **85.00**

Little Lulu, bean bag doll, ca 1940s, 10", NM **75.00**

Little Lulu, store display for Kleenex, 10", NM **40.00**

Little Lulu, valentine, 1950s, EX **18.50**

Little Orphan Annie, Big Little Book, Annie & Chizzler, EX **20.00**

Little Orphan Annie, coloring book, McLoughlin, 1930s, M **45.00**

Little Orphan Annie, mug, Ovaltine premium, Beetleware, 3", EX **20.00**

Little Orphan Annie, napkin ring, metal, 1933 World's Fair, EX **30.00**

Little Orphan Annie, nodder, bisque, German, 3½", M ..**95.00**

Little Orphan Annie, pull toy, painted wood, Trixitoy, 13" long, NM **100.00**

Little Orphan Annie, Rummy cards, Whitman, 1935, complete, M **40.00**

Little Orphan Annie, tea set, ceramic, Germany, 12-pc, M **150.00**

Mighty Mouse, coloring book, early 1950s, EX **15.00**

Mighty Mouse, doll, Rushton, ca 1950, 16", NM **125.00**

Mighty Mouse, squeeze toy, M **20.00**

Mighty Mouse, wallet, Laramie, 1978, M **8.00**

Mr Jinx, push-button puppet, plastic, jointed, Kohner, 1965, M **20.00**

Mr Magoo, advertising doll, GE promotion, 1960s, 12", EX **40.00**

Mr Magoo, bank, pink, plastic, 16", EX **30.00**

Mr Magoo, glass tumbler, child's, ca 1960, M **10.00**

Mr Magoo, playing cards, double pack in plastic casing, 1960s, NM **15.00**

Munsters, card game, Milton Bradley, 1960, MIB **10.00**

Munsters, colorforms, 1965, complete, EX **60.00**

Munsters, flasher ring, Lily w/name, 1965, EX **17.50**

Munsters, game, Milton Bradley, 1966, EX **42.50**

Munsters, lunch box, metal ..**65.00**

Munsters, paper dolls, Whitman, 1966, complete, M **15.00**

Munsters, talking puppet, Herman, Mattel, 1964, EX ..**15.00**

Olive Oyl, figure, jointed wood, 1930s, 4", NM **80.00**

Olive Oyl, ponytail holder, 1950s, EX **10.00**

Olive Oyl, premium, Kellogg's Pep pin, EX **15.00**

Pappy Yokum, drinking glass, dated 1949, 5", M **20.00**

Peanuts

First introduced in 1950, the *Peanuts* comic strip has become the world's most widely read cartoon. It appears daily in about 2,200 newspapers. From that funny cartoon about kids (that readers of every age could easily relate to) has sprung an entertainment arsenal featuring movies, books, Broadway shows, toys, theme parks, etc. And surely as the day follows the night, there comes a bountiful harvest of *Peanuts* collectibles. If you want to collect, you should know that authenticity is important. To be authentic, the United Features Syndicate logo and copyright date must appear somewhere on the item. In most cases the copyright date simply indicates the date that the character and his pose as depicted on the item first appeared in the comic strip. Refer to *The Official Price Guide to Peanuts Collectibles* by Freddi Margolian (our advisor) and Andrea Podey. Ms. Margolian is listed in the Directory under New York. See also Clubs and Newsletters.

Avon Bubble Bath gel, green rubber Lionus, suctions to wall, '68, MIB **35.00**

Bank, Schroeder in catcher's mask, papier-mache, '73, Determined, rare **65.00**

Bank, sitting Snoopy, glass, Anchor Hocking, embossed United Features **30.00**

Bank, Snoopy on doghouse, marked Bank of America, Determined, MIB **55.00**

Bank, Snoopy on doghouse, marked Bank of America, Determined, no box **35.00**

Bank, Snoopy on doghouse, no mark, Bank of America, Determined, MIB **45.00**

Bank, Snoopy sitting on gray elephant, papier-mache **50.00**

Banner, All Systems Go, Astronaut Snoopy, 1970, Determined Productions **20.00**

Bobblehead, Snoopy as Santa, 1976, Determined Productions ..**25.00**

Bookends, Flying Ace Snoopy, ceramic, Butterfly, 1979, MIB **50.00**

Card game, Snooping Around, orange box, Snoopy as Sherlock, Hallmark **22.00**

Card game, Woodstock holds red flowers on green box, Hallmark, '70s **15.00**

Dish, Snoopy lying on back on lid, ceramic, 1977, Determined, 7½x4" **150.00**

Figurescene, Even My Anxieties..., papier-mache, '72, Determined, MIB **65.00**

Figurescene, How Can We Lose, 5-figure group, '72, Determined, 5½" **150.00**

Lunch box, Schroeder at piano +5 others, vinyl, +thermos, King Seeley **175.00**

Musical, Schroeder at piano, I Could Have Danced, wall mount, Anri, 8" **200.00**

Musical, Try To Remember, Lucy & Charlie at psychiatrist booth, 9" **275.00**

Peanuts baseball w/4 characters, more on box, official, '67, Wilson, MIB **125.00**

Poster, Support the Olympics, paper, 1971, Springbok, sold by Hallmark **20.00**

Punching bag, Charlie Brown, I Need All Friends..., Determined, 34", MIB **50.00**

Push puppet, cowboy Snoopy, push bottom to activate, Ideal, $20 to (MIB) **40.00**

Rag doll, Lucy, #1411-8, 1976, Ideal, $15 up to (MIB) ...**50.00**

Snap-Tite toy, Snoopy in yellow plane on box, 'Curse You...,' 1975, MIB **125.00**

Talking Bus, Happiness Is Annual Outing, '67, Chein, $300 to (MIB) **500.00**

Toy, Snoopy the Critic, microphone activates 2 characters, 1977, Aviva **175.00**

Pee Wee Herman, colorforms, MIB **7.50**

Pee Wee Herman, doll, talking, 17", MIB **35.00**

Pee Wee Herman, kite, M in package **8.50**

Pee Wee Herman, yo-yo, M **4.50**

Perry Winkle, bookmark, 1940s, EX **10.00**

Pink Panther, costume, Ben Cooper, 1974, MIB **30.00**

Pink Panther, wind-up, w/cymbal, 1970s, MIB **25.00**

Pixie & Dixie, dolls, Knickerbocker, 1960, 12", NM, pr **40.00**

Popeye, cookie jar, ceramic, 1950s, 10", EX **65.00**

Popeye, jigsaw puzzle, Jaymar, 1945, 22x13½", EX **20.00**

Popeye, napkin ring, yellow Bakelite w/decal, EX **40.00**

Popeye, Pez dispenser, 1960s, NM **40.00**

Popeye Spinach can, pop-up head, metal and plastic, 6", $20.00.

Popeye, punching bag, inflatable, 1950s, MIB **35.00**

Popeye, ramp-walking figure, composition, 1930s, EX..**70.00**

Popeye, song book, Famous Music, 1936, EX **30.00**

Popeye, squeeze toy, soft vinyl, Rempel, ca 1950s, M **45.00**

Porky Pig, bank, china, ca 1950s, 8", M **40.00**

Porky Pig, figure, glazed china, 1940s, 5", EX **40.00**

Porky Pig, planter, ceramic, 1940s, M **22.00**

Scooby Doo, gumball machine, M **15.00**

Scooby Doo, squeeze toy, 1970s, M **5.00**

Sergeant Snorkel, nodder, ceramic, 1960s, M **95.00**

Six Million Dollar Man, doll, vinyl, Kenner, 1973, 13", EX ...**18.50**

Smitty, bookmark, 1940s, 3", EX **7.50**

Smokey Bear, activity book, 1962, M **7.50**

Smokey Bear, ashtray, ceramic, Japan, 1960s, EX **30.00**

Smokey Bear, badge, lapel; 1960s, EX **6.50**

Smokey Bear, doll, w/shovel, NM **12.00**

Smurfs

A creation of Pierro 'Peyo' Culliford, the little blue Smurfs that we have all come to love have found their way to the collectibles market of today. There is a large number of items currently available at reasonable prices, though some, such as metal lunch boxes, cereal premiums and boxes, and promotional items and displays, are beginning to attract special interest. Because the Smurfs' 'birthplace' was in Belgium, many items are Euopean in nature. The values listed here are for items in mint condition. Those seeking further information may contact the Smurf Collectors' Club, listed in our Clubs and Newsletters section.

Alarm clock, Bradley, 2-bell wind-up, MIB **22.00**

Calendar, licensed product only, 1965 ....**30.00**

Cereal box, European, minimum value **12.50**

Christmas ornament, PVC, 2", minimum value **6.00**

Colorforms, Shrinky Dinks, Papa Smurfs, MIB **3.00**

Crib mobile, Danara, MIB ...**17.00**

Doll, lg baby Smurf, Hasbro, MIB **25.00**

Figurine, porcelain, Happy Birthday Series **18.00**

Figurine, PVC, Argentina, 2", minimum value **10.00**

Figurine, PVC, marked Brazil, 2", minimum value **5.00**

Figurine, Schleich, 2", minimum value **6.00**

Fire truck, Ertl, die-cast **5.00**

Lunch box, metal **100.00**

Musical carousel, Illco, MIB ..**40.00**

Poster, national promotion, 1978 ....**25.00**

Puzzle, Smurfette ice skater, Playskool, EX **8.00**

Radio & headset, AM, Power-Tronic, MIB **10.00**

Smurf cottage, Schleich, lg, MIB **25.00**

Tomi Pocketeers, England ...**11.00**

Wristwatch, battery operated, EX **17.00**

Wristwatch, Timex **65.00**

Spider Man, hand puppet, Ideal, 1966, EX **55.00**

Spider Man, model kit, Aurora, 1966, assembled, NM **80.00**

Spider Man, pillow, plastic, inflatable, Mass Art, 1968, M ..**25.00**

Spider Man, View-Master, 1977, M in package **5.00**

Superman, coloring book, Saalfield, 1941, EX **58.00**

Superman, comic book, #21, dated March-April 1943, M **55.00**

Superman, horseshoe set, 1940s, unused in EX box **145.00**

Superman, premium, Kellogg's Pep pin, EX **8.50**

Superman, spoon, silverplated, 1930s, M **15.00**

Sylvester the Cat, hand puppet, ca 1950, EX **15.00**
Tarzan, Better Little Book, ...& the Golden Lion, 1943, EX ...**20.00**
Tom & Jerry, figures, plaster, ca 1940, M, pr **35.00**
Tom & Jerry, hand puppet, cloth & vinyl, 1952, EX **25.00**
Tweety Bird, doll, Dakin, 1969, 7½", NM- **32.00**
Underdog, Halloween costume, 1969-73, NM in box **35.00**
Wile E Coyote, doll, Dakin, w/tag, 1968, 12", EX **18.00**
Wile E Coyote, finger puppet, Dakin, 1970s, M in package **20.00**
Wonder Woman, roller skates, Larami, 1977, NM in box ..**30.00**
Wonder Woman, valentine, 1940s, EX **12.50**
Woody Woodpecker, kazoo, Rice Krispies premium, EX ..**12.50**
Woody Woodpecker, planter, china, Walter Lantz, 1960s, M..**30.00**
Woody Woodpecker, slippers, infant's, 1957, NM **22.50**
Woody Woodpecker, View-Master, 1950, NM **15.00**
Yogi Bear, cake plate, musical, Artcraft, 1962, MIB **25.00**
Yogi Bear, camera, 1960s, EX..**20.00**
Yogi Bear, colorforms, 1963, EX in box **30.00**
Yogi Bear, inflatable ring toy, 1963, MIB **28.00**
Yogi Bear, postcard, multicolored, 1963, M **8.00**
Yogi Bear, yo-yo, VG **5.00**
Yosemite Sam, hand puppet, toothpaste premium, M **12.00**

Character Clocks and Watches

Since the 1930s kids have enjoyed watches whose dials depicted their favorite cartoon character, western hero, or movie and TV personality. They're relatively scarce today (since they often met with abuse at the hand of their young owners) and as a result can be rather expensive to collect. The boxes they came in are even more hard to find and are often tagged with prices about equal to that of the watch they contained. Condition is of the utmost importance when evaluating a watch or clock such as these – watch for rust, fading, scratches, or other signs of wear that will sharply decrease their values. Refer to *Comic Character Clocks and Watches* by Howard S. Brenner (Books Americana) for more information.

Bambi, watch, Ingersoll (US Time), Birthday Series, 1949, EX ..**75.00**
Bugs Bunny, clock, Ingraham, square, 1951, EX **90.00**
Bugs Bunny, watch, Warner Bros, for Rexall Drug Stores, 1951, EX **75.00**
Captain Marvel (Deluxe), watch, Fawcett, 1948, EX **60.00**
Cinderella, watch, US Time, 1950, M **50.00**
Dale Evans, watch, Ingraham, expansion or leather band, 1951, MIB **150.00**
Davy Crockett, electric clock, Haddon, 1954, rare, M **175.00**
Davy Crockett, watch, Bradley, 1956, M **65.00**
Dick Tracy, watch, New Haven, pistol moves back & forth, 1951, EX **90.00**
Dizzy Dean, pocket watch, New Haven, 1935, EX **90.00**
Donald Duck, pocket watch, Ingersoll, Mickey decal on back, 1939, EX **240.00**
Donald Duck, watch, Ingersoll (US Time), 1947, EX **75.00**

Gene Autry, watch, Wilane, 1948, EX **75.00**
Howdy Doody, watch, Ingraham, 1954, scarce, M **100.00**
Jeff Arnold (English cowboy), pocket watch, Ingersoll LTD, EX **165.00**
Joe Palooka, watch, New Haven, 1947, EX **90.00**
Li'l Abner, watch, New Haven, Movin' Mule, 1947, EX ..**60.00**
Lone Ranger, lapel watch, New Haven, 1939, EX **120.00**
Mickey Mouse, alarm clock, Bradley, oversized pocket watch, 1979, MIB **35.00**
Mickey Mouse, alarm clock, Ingersoll (US Time), round on base, 1947, M **125.00**

Mickey Mouse alarm clock, Bayard, France, 1970s issue, M, $175.00.

Minnie Mouse, watch, US Time, 1958, EX **30.00**
Orphan Annie, watch, New Haven, 1948, EX **60.00**
Pinocchio, alarm clock, Bayard, made in France, 1964, MIB **100.00**
Popeye, pocket watch, New Haven, 1935, EX **180.00**
Robin Hood, watch, Viking, 1938, M **100.00**

Roy Rogers, watch, Ingraham, Roy on rearing Trigger, 1951, EX **45.00**
Snow White, watch, US Time, 1950, M **40.00**
Superman, watch, New Haven, 1948, EX **105.00**
Tom Corbett, watch, Ingraham, 1951, EX **30.00**
Woody Woodpecker, alarm clock, Columbia Time, round on base, 1950, M **125.00**
Zorro, watch, US Time, 1957, EX **15.00**

Children's Books

Books were popular gifts for children in the latter 1800s; many were beautifully illustrated, some by notable artists such as Frances Brundage and Maxfield Parrish. From this century tales of Tarzan by Burroughs are very collectible. Our advisor for Rand McNally Elf Books and Wonder Books is Steve Santi, who is listed in the Directory under California. See also Little Golden Books.

A Child's Book of Prayers, Random House, 1941, w/dust jacket, VG **20.00**
A Day No Pigs Would Die, Knopf, 1972, 1st edition, w/dust jacket, EX **22.00**
Adventures of Three Little Cottontails, Donohue, 1922, 54 pages, VG........................**35.00**
An Explorer for an Aunt, Follett, 1960, 1st US edition w/dust jacket **8.50**
Anno's Counting Book, Crowell, 1977, 1st US edition, w/dust jacket, VG **28.00**
Arthur's Christmas Cookies, Harper Row, 1972, 1st edition **15.00**

At the Back of the North Wind, McKay, 1919, 342 pages, 1st edition, G **60.00**

Babar's Mystery, Random House, 1978, 1st edition, unpaged, VG **15.00**

Baby's Own ABC Book, McLoughlin, 1899, 12 linen pages, VG **45.00**

Ballet for Drina, Vanguard, 1958, 1st edition, w/dust jacket, VG **10.00**

Beverly Gray on a Treasure Hunt, Grosset & Dunlap, 1938, dust jacket **7.00**

Birds, Saalfield, 1943, FB Peat illustrations, w/dust jacket, NM **30.00**

Black Stallion Mystery, Random House, 1957, 1st edition, w/dust jacket **16.00**

Black Stallion Revolts, Random House, 1953, 1st edition, dust jacket **25.00**

Bobbsey Twins in Volcano Land, Grosset & Dunlap, 1961, dust jacket, VG **12.00**

Bomba the Jungle Boy in the Abandoned City, Grosset & Dunlap, 1927, VG **12.50**

Borrowers Aloft, Harcourt Brace & World, 1st US edition, w/dust jacket **35.00**

Bouncing Betsey, Macmillan, 1936, 1st edition, w/dust jacket, VG **48.00**

Boys' Stories From Dickens, Winston, 1929, Clara Burd illustrations **15.00**

Bunnie Bear, Saalfield, 1936, unpaged, pictorial cloth binding, G **15.00**

Bunnie Cottontail, McLoughlin, 1945, unpaged, w/dust jacket, 7½x9" **15.00**

Campfire Girls at Sunrise Hill, Winston, 1913, w/dust jacket, VG **10.00**

Cherry Ames, Rest Home Nurse; Grosset & Dunlap, 1954, picture cover **6.50**

Contented Little Pussy Cat, Platt & Munk, 1929, w/dust jacket, EX **25.00**

Dainty Darling's ABC, Gabriel, 1911, unpaged, picture wrappers, VG **15.00**

Dick & Jane, We Come & Go; Scott Foresman, 1946, 6x8", VG..................................**20.00**

Dick & Jane, We Work & Play; Scott Foresman, 1946, unpaged, VG **20.00**

Dick & Jane & Our New Friends, Scott Foresman, 1946, 191 pages, VG **35.00**

Dwindling Party, Random House, 1982, pop-up, Gorey illustrations, VG **30.00**

Eddie Elephant, Donohue, 1921, Johnny Gruelle illustrations, unpaged, VG **35.00**

Five Little Peppers Midway, Lothrop, Lee & Shepherd, 1893, green cloth **15.00**

Friendly Bear, Doubleday, 1957, 1st edition, w/dust jacket, VG **20.00**

Frisky Squirrel's Story, AL Burt, 1906, 69 pages, 7½x5", VG **12.00**

Fun With Dick & Jane, Scott Foresman, 1946, 159 pages, NM **60.00**

Fun With Dick & Jane, Scott Foresman, 1946, 159 pages, 6x8", G **30.00**

Funny Little Book, Donohue, ca '17, Gruelle illustrations, dust jacket **35.00**

Grandville's Animals, Thames & Hudson, 1981, 1st edition, dust jacket **20.00**

Happy Hollisters at Lizard Cover, Doubleday, 1957, 1st edition, VG **7.00**

Hardy Boys & the Phantom Fighter, Grosset & Dunlap, 1947, dust jacket **8.00**

Isabell & the Enchanted Fish, Artcraft, ca 1950, pop-up, unpaged, VG **17.50**

Kiki Is an Actress, Doubleday, 1958, 1st edition, w/dust jacket, VG **32.00**

Koko's Circus, Animated Book Co, 1942, pop-up, picture cover, VG **30.00**

Little Black Sambo, Rand McMally & Co., 1934, VG, $25.00.

Little Black Sambo, Saalfield, ca 1940, 10 pages, picture wrapers, VG **55.00**

Little Brown Koko Has Fun, American Colortype, 1945, 2nd edition, VG **55.00**

Little Kitten That Would Not Wash Its Face, Samuel Gabriel, 1922, G **10.00**

Little Lame Prince, Whitman, 1937, 4th printing, 128 pages, 7x9", EX **18.00**

Little Lulu on Parade, David McKay, 1941, w/color dust jacket, NM **40.00**

Lone Ranger Rides North, Grosset & Dunlap, 1946, w/dust jacket, VG **17.50**

Meadow-Brook Girls Across Country, Saalfield, 1913, w/dust jacket, VG **6.50**

Mickey Never Fails, DC Heath, Disney illustrations, G ..**25.00**

Miss Bianca & the Bridesmaid, Little Brown, 1972, 1st edition, VG **32.00**

Motor Maids in Fair Japan, Hurst, 1913, VG **8.50**

Nonsense ABCs, Rand McNally, 1918, Bye-Lo Series, 1st edition, VG **40.00**

Now We Are Six, Dutton, 1927, 1st US edition, EH Shepherd illustrations **62.00**

Paddington's Garden, Random House, 1973, 1st US edition, 32 pages, VG **12.00**

Penny Parker & Ghost Beyond the Gate, Cupples Leon, 1943, dust jacket **25.00**

Polly French & the Surprising Stranger, Whitman, 1956, picture cover **5.00**

Pollyanna's Castle in Mexico, Grosset & Dunlap, 1934, dust jacket, VG **8.00**

Pollyanna's Jewels, Page, '25, 1st edition, picture cover, VG ...**25.00**

Pony Rider Boys in the Ozarks, Altemus, 1910, w/dust jacket, VG **15.00**

Pop-Up Book of Gnomes, Abrams, 1979, 8x11", VG **15.00**

Puppy Who Learned, Messner, 1944, unpaged, 9x8½", w/dust jacket **10.00**

Puss 'n Boots, McLoughlin, Cinderella Series, R Andre illustrations, VG **35.00**

Rum Tum Tummy, Saalfield, 1936, picture cover, VG **38.00**

Ruth, Winston, 1938, Petershams illustrations, w/dust jacket, VG **20.00**

Snow White & Seven Dwarfs, Platt & Munk, Merry-Go-Round edition, 1980s **10.00**

Story of Roland, Scribner Illustrated Classic, 1930, 347 pages, VG **35.00**

Susanna & Sue, Houghton Mifflin, 1909, Wyeth illustrations, 225 pages **60.00**

Three Musketeers, Rand McNally, 1923, Windermeer Series, 547 pages, VG **17.50**

Tom Swift & His Flying Lab, Grosset & Dunlap, 1954, picture cover, VG **8.00**

Two Children & Three Storks, EP Dutton, 1931, w/dust jacket, VG **18.00**

Uncle Remus, His Songs & His Sayings; Appleton, 1932, 265 pages, VG **35.00**

Uncle Wiggly & the Pirates, Whitman, 1940, Lang Campbell illustrations **25.00**

Wilderness Champion, Lippincott, 1944, 1st edition, w/dust jacket, VG **15.00**

Wind in the Willows, World, 1960, Tasha Tudor illustrations, dust jacket **17.50**

Wizard of Oz, Saalfield, 1944, pop-up, spiral-bound picture cover, G **35.00**

Wonderful Performing Monkeys, McLoughlin, 1904, 16 pages, VG **95.00**

Rand McNally Elf Books

Bartholomew, The Beaver; #471, 1952, M **5.00**

Children That Lived in a Shoe, The; #8616, 1951, M **3.00**

Daniel the Cocker Spaniel, #505, 1955, M **4.00**

Elves & the Shoemaker, The; #8682, 1959, M **2.00**

Five Little Bears, #498, 1955, M **5.00**

Happy Holidays, #482, 1953, M **5.00**

House That Jack Built, The; #8312, 1959, M **2.00**

Little Lost Angel, #483, 1953, M **6.00**

Noah's Ark, #461, 1952, M **5.00**

Pillowtime Tales, #552, 1956, M **5.00**

Rip Van Winkle, #8383, 1961, M **3.00**

Sergeant Preston & the Yukon King, #500, 1955, M **15.00**

Superliner United States, the World's Fastest Liner; #474, 1953, M **15.00**

Tubby Turtle, #8321, 1959, M ..**3.00**

Zippy the Chimp, #487, 1953, M **8.00**

Wonder Books

Alice in Wonderland, #574, 1951, M **10.00**

Alvin's Lost Voice, #824, 1963, M **10.00**

Baby Elephant, The; #541, 1950, M **5.00**

Blondie's Family Cookie, Alexander, & Dog, Elmer; #666, 1954, M **10.00**

Cats Who Stayed for Dinner; The; #556, 1951, M **5.00**

Fixit Man, The; #756, 1952, M ..**4.00**

How Peter Cottontail Got His Name, #668, 1957, M **4.00**

Kewtee Bear's Christmas, #867, 1965, M **6.00**

Make-Believe Parade, The; #520, 1949, M **15.00**

Mr Bear Squash-You-All-Flat, #523, 1950, M **25.00**

Once Upon a Time (the Cow in the Silo), #700, 1950, M ..**5.00**

Puppy Who Found a Boy, The; #561, 1951, M **5.00**

Romper Room Do Bee Book of Manners, The; #763, 1950, M **5.00**

What Happened to Piggy?, #629, M **5.00**

Wonder Book of Clowns, The; #638, 1955, M **4.00**

Children's Dishes

In the late 1900s, glass companies introduced sets of small-scaled pressed glass dinnerware, many in the same patterns as their regular lines, others designed specifically for the little folks. Many were of clear glass, but milk glass, opalescent glass, and colors were also used. Not to be outdone, English ceramic firms as well as American potteries made both tea sets and fully accessorized dinnerware sets decorated with decals of nursery rhymes, animals, or characters from children's stories. Though popularly collected for some time, your favorite flea market may still yield some very nice examples of both types. Refer to *The Collector's Encyclopedia of Children's Dishes* by Margaret and Kenn Whitmyer (Collector Books) for more information.

Baby dish, North Pole Discovered by Pooh, Bavaria Germany, 8" **45.00**

Tea set, gold lustre with floral decoration, Japan, MIB, $40.00.

Chamber set, pink luster, gold trim, England **50.00**

Gravy boat, Flow Blue Dogwood, Minton **57.00**

Ice bucket, tan luster, floral decor, octagonal, w/lid, Japan ..**21.00**

Mug, barnyard scene, Royal Windsor, England **18.00**

Mug, Dutch girl, Roseville ...**55.00**

Mug, Little Bo Peep, Shenango China **19.00**

Plate, Betsy McCall's Friends, handles hold fork & spoon **28.00**

Plate, Children at Play, Knowles China Co, 6⅞" **12.00**

Plate, Sunbonnet Babies, ABC, 6¼" **27.00**

Platter, Bluebird, KT&K China, 7¾" **19.00**

Rolling pin, Blue Onion Kitchenware, Germany **300.00**

Rolling pin, boy w/pink rabbit, 9" **112.00**

Stein, dancing children, Bavaria **17.00**

Sugar bowl, elephant figural, tan luster, w/lid, Japan **18.00**

Sugar bowl, Silhouette Children, Victoria Czechoslovakia, w/lid **9.00**

Teapot, Chinaman figural, gold trim, w/lid, Japan **60.00**

Teapot, Gaudy Ironstone, w/lid, England **150.00**

Teapot, Mary Had a Little Lamb, w/lid, Staffordshire **33.00**

Pattern Glass

Acorn, creamer **105.00**

Acorn, spooner, frosted **187.00**

Arched Panel, tumbler **7.00**

Austrian No 200, spooner **97.00**

Bead & Scroll, spooner **65.00**

Beaded Swirl, butter dish **50.00**

Block, creamer, blue **175.00**

Bucket, creamer **55.00**

Button Panel No 44, sugar bowl, w/lid **80.00**

Whirligig No. 15101 (U.S. Glass Co.), spooner, 2¼", $20.00; butter dish, 2½", $27.00; creamer, 2¼", $16.00; punch cup (watch for reproductions), 1¼", $7.00.

Buzz Saw No 2697, creamer ..**24.00**
Chimo, sugar bowl, w/lid **80.00**
Colonial No 2630, spooner ...**20.00**
Dewdrop, sugar bowl, w/lid ..**90.00**
Drum, mug, 2" **37.00**
Dutch Boudoir, pitcher, blue milk
    glass **122.00**
Fine Cut Star & Fan, sugar bowl,
    w/lid **27.00**
Flattened Diamond & Sunburst,
    punch set, bowl + 7 cups ..**65.00**
Grapevine w/Ovals, mug, amber,
    blue or yellow **27.00**
Horizontal Threads, sugar bowl,
    w/lid **60.00**
Nursery Rhyme, creamer **50.00**
Pattee Cross, tumbler **13.00**
Sandwich Ivy, creamer **75.00**
Sawtooth, creamer **31.00**
Stippled Raindrop & Dewdrop,
    creamer **57.00**
Twist, creamer, frosted **52.00**
Twist No 137, butter dish, blue
    opalescent **180.00**
Wee Branches, spooner **80.00**
Whirligig No 15101, butter
    dish **27.00**

Christmas

No other holiday season is celebrated to the extravagant extent as Christmas, and vintage decorations provide a warmth and charm that none from today can match. Ornaments from before 1870 were imported from Dresden, Germany – usually made of cardboard and sparkled with tinsel trim. Later, blown glass ornaments were made there in literally thousands of shapes such as fruits and vegetables, clowns, Santas, angels, and animals. Kugles, heavy glass balls (though you'll sometimes find fruit and vegetable forms as well) were made from about 1820 to late in the century in sizes from very small up to 14". Early Santa figures are treasured, especially those in robes other than red. Figural bulbs from the '20s and '30s are popular, those that are character related in particular. Refer to *Christmas Collectibles, Second Edition*, by Margaret and Kenn Whitmyer (Collector Books) for more information.

Book, Jolly Santa Claus, Charles
    E Graham & Co **25.00**
Book, Santa's Circus, White
    Plains Greeting Card Co,
    1952 ....**10.00**
Book, Visions of St Nick in
    Action, Philips Publisher Inc,
    1950 ....**8.00**
Bulb, bear, sitting, pink-painted
    milk glass, NM **50.00**
Bulb, clown's head, paper insula-
    tor, Germany, 3" **165.00**

Bulb, cottage, multicolored paint on milk glass, 2½", EX ..**12.50**
Bulb, Jack & Jill, 1940s-50s..**245.00**
Bulb, snowman, pink, Japan, 1930s-50s, 1½" long **20.00**
Candle holder, brass, made to hang on tree, marked Germany, 1920s, 2" **35.00**
Candle holder, farm scene, enameled, spring-type clip, 1900s, 2½" **50.00**
Candy container, baby in shoe, cloth over cardboard, 4" ..**30.00**
Candy container, Santa face, cardboard, 4" dia **5.00**
Candy container, snowman, mica-covered cardboard, marked Germany, 9" **45.00**
Candy container, tin, shows Santa landing on roof in airplane, oval **22.00**
Die-cut, Santa head, in original sheet, 6" **10.00**
Die-cut, Santa holding tree & bag, gold coat, 4" **8.50**
Figure, bisque snow baby on wooden sled, Germany, 3¼" long ..**85.00**

Figure, Santa pulled by horse, bisque, Germany, 2¾" long **55.00**
Garland, glass beads w/colored center bands, 1950s, 110" long **20.00**
Greeting card, die-cut snowman, Best Christmas Wishes, 1940s-50s **8.00**
Lamp, Santa figural, glass, 1920s-30s, 8" **85.00**
Lights, Mazda lamps, Zelda, early 1920s, in original box ..**125.00**
Magazine ad, Whitman's Candy, 1934 ....**3.50**
Nativity set, plaster & wood, 14-pc, complete **55.00**

Rudolph night light with light-up nose, E.M.C. Art, 12" long, $45.00.

Ornament, birdcage, metal, 2½" **25.00**
Ornament, butterfly, spun glass wings, 2½" long, 4" wingspan **100.00**
Ornament, candy cane, chenille, 12" long **8.50**
Ornament, doll face, glass, painted face & eyes, 1930s-40s, 1¼" **120.00**
Ornament, elephant on ball, glass, 1920s-30s, 2¼" **45.00**
Ornament, icicle, glass, 1950s, 14" **25.00**
Ornament, Italian military figural, glass, 1950s-70s, 6" **30.00**
Ornament, mandolin, scraps, tinsel & cardboard, 9" long..**36.00**

Santa Claus lamp with bubble light, 1950s, 8", $30.00.

Ornament, pear, pressed cotton, 3½" **20.00**
Ornament, red grape cluster, glass, 1950s, 3½" **10.00**
Ornament, rocking horse, coated cardboard, 2½" **12.50**
Ornament, Santa on ball, wire-wrapped, 7" **25.00**
Ornament, snowman, cotton on cardboard cylinder, 6" ...**50.00**
Ornament, snowman, glass w/ frosted body, 1950s, 3½"..**20.00**
Postcard, embossed poodle delivering gifts, A Merry Christmas **9.50**
Postcard, Santa arriving in automobile, Peaceful Christmas **8.00**
Postcard, 3 snow babies on sled, May Happiness..., NM ..**14.00**
Print, His First Christmas, family gathering around tree ...**60.00**
Print, little girl w/puppies, 18x22" **55.00**
Santa, cardboard w/plastic face, cotton suit, Japan, 1950s-60s, 11" **14.00**
Santa, w/drum, battery operated, Cragston, 1950s, 12" **85.00**
Santa bank/music box, plastic, 1960-80s, 12" **35.00**

Trade card, Star Soap, Santa filling stockings, early 1900s, 7x5" **16.00**
Trade card, Woolson Spice Co, Santa & children, early 1900s, 7x4½" **14.50**
Tree, aluminum, silver, 1960s, 18" **18.00**
Tree, bottle-brush type, snow-covered, red base, 10" **16.50**
Tree fence, red & green wood, single gate closure, 4-sided 18" square **40.00**
Tree stand, metal, 8 series lamps w/add-on plug, Noma, 3-footed **35.00**
Tree-top light, star-shape, Noma, 1920s-30s **25.00**

Cigarette Lighters

Pocket lighters were invented sometime after 1908 and were at their peak from about 1925 to the 1930s. Dunhill, Zippo, Colibri, Ronson, Dupont, and Evans are some manufacturers. An early Dunhill Unique model if found in its original box would be valued at hundreds of dollars. Quality

Chenille wreaths, large, original box, $15.00; small, $8.00.

metal and metal-plated lighters were made until sometime in the 1960s. About that time disposable lighters never needing a flint were introduced, causing a decline in sales of figurals, novelties, and high-quality lighters.

What makes a good lighter? – novelty of design, type of mechanism (flint and fuel, flint and gas, battery, etc.), and manufacturer (and whether or not the company is still in business). Most of the lighters listed here are from the 1930s. Sizes listed are approximate. For further pricing information and an illustrated catalog, we recommend contacting our advisor, Jack Seiderman, who is listed in the Directory under Florida.

ASR, gold-plated dagger w/green marble on handle, USA, 10", VG **17.50**

Aurora, chrome-plated square flashlight form, battery, Japan, 2", EX **15.00**

Beattie, Jet Lighter, nickel plate, square w/rounded corners, 2", VG **22.50**

Candlestick, silver plate, detailed stem, street lamp top, 10", VG **45.00**

Clark, lift arm, 18k Gold Electro Plated, July 27, 1926, USA, 2", EX **65.00**

Dunhill, Bumper or Tankard, chrome plate figural, England, 3", M **250.00**

Dunhill, Rollagas, silver plate, fine barley design, Swiss, 2¼", VG **55.00**

Dunhill, Rollagas Longboy, silver plate, square Tartan pattern, 5", EX **175.00**

Dunhill, Rollalite, gold plate, heavy rib design, England, 2½", VG **65.00**

Evans, Baron Liter-Case, nickel plate w/black stripes, w/original bag, MIB **55.00**

Evans, Imperial, nickel plate under worn gold plate, T under crown, VG **17.50**

Evans (surmised), black cat w/lamp, blue metal shade, Japan, 5⅝" **85.00**

Fumalux, FL400, flashlight/lighter, chrome plate, Germany, ca '63, EX **15.00**

Galter, The Giant, chrome plate, black cloth on body, 2¼x3⅞", VG **15.00**

German, bottle form, enameled metal, advertising souvenir, 2⅛", VG **17.50**

Golden Wheel, sm lift arm, gold plate, Coquette, USA, ca 1930, MIB **50.00**

Imco, Triplex Super 6700, nickel plate w/green decor, Austria, 2½" **17.50**

Kaschie/Kay-Ess, chrome plate, table type, Germany, ca 1947, 3½", M **35.00**

KW, Original, nickel plate, separate fuel reservoir, Germany, '50, VG **25.00**

Lektrolite, Glopoint, gold tube w/black plastic ends, ca 1945, 3", VG **15.00**

Lucky Key, chrome-plated figural, unmarked, 1½", M **17.50**

Mylflam, nickel plate, band decor, table type, Germany, ca '48, 3", VG **27.50**

Mylflam, nickel plate w/silver band, table type, Germany, 2½", EX **22.50**

Parker, chrome plate, vertical stripe design, table type, USA, 3", EX **55.00**

Polo, silver plate, oval w/rib foot, table model, England, 2½", M ..**50.00**

Reliance, MIOJ, nickel plate, striped, table type, Japan, 4", VG **45.00**

Ritepoint, MC310 Liter, chrome & red Lucite reservoir, USA, w/bag, MIB **25.00**

Ronson, Banjo, chrome plate 1918 replica, England, ca 1986, w/bag, MIB **125.00**

Ronson, cast bronze bulldog, AMW, early, 6" long, original striker, VG **275.00**

Ronson, De-Light, chrome plate, WH on stripes, 1¾", new screws, VG **27.50**

Ronson, De-Light, nickel plate, Art Metal Works USA, ca 1928, 2", VG **45.00**

Ronson, Decanter, silver plate figural, footed, USA, 4⅞", EX **25.00**

Ronson, Diana, silver plate, leaf, stripes, ribbed foot, USA, 2", VG **22.50**

Ronson, Gloria, silver plate, bulbous w/ribbed foot, USA, 3⅝", VG **45.00**

Ronson, Mastercase, tortise enamel & chrome on black, USA, 4¼", EX **45.00**

Ronson pocket lighter, tortoise shell with chrome trim, $50.00.

Ronson, Penciliter, rhodium plate pen/lighter, USA, 5⅝", MIB **95.00**

Ronson, striker, copper-plated seated Lincoln figural, 5¼",VG **150.00**

Ronson, Touch-Tip, chrome plate w/black enamel on stepped base, 4", EX **125.00**

Rowenta, nickel plate, advertising, Der Spiegel, Germany, 4", EX **27.50**

Scripto, Vu-Lighter, chrome, olive plastic & smoke Lucite, 2½", EX **12.50**

Sterling Silver 950, Japan scenes, Zippo insides, Japan, '50s, 2", EX **45.00**

Thorens, ashtray & lighter set, Orlik china w/gold plate, Swiss, 2-pc **95.00**

Thorens, Portor, gold plate, white marble barrel base, Swiss, 4", EX **75.00**

Thorens, Portor, nickel plate, green marble base, Swiss, 3⅝", VG **55.00**

TWC, Roxy, floral nickel plate w/wind screen, Germany, ca 1938, 2", VG **22.50**

Wifeu, Tiki, gold plate w/tan leather, map of France, Austria, 2", MIB **45.00**

Wifeu, Tiki, nickel-plated ball, ivory enamel on base, Austria, 3", EX **35.00**

Zippo, Barcroft, brushed chrome, advertising, stepped base, 3⅝", EX **40.00**

Zippo, Barcroft, brushed chrome, plain w/stepped base, USA, 3⅝", VG **30.00**

Zippo, Lady Bradford, rhodium plate, made only in 1951, 4", VG **45.00**

Zippo, Regular Military, chrome plate, tank & missiles, 1991, 2", MIB **27.50**

Zippo, Regular Military, Lockheed AEW Radar..., brushed chrome, 2", EX **35.00**
Zippo, Regular Military, USS Philippine Sea, brushed chrome, 1957, 2" **27.50**
1000 Zunder, nickel plate, advertising, Germany, 1¾", worn, VG **12.50**

Cleminson

Hand-decorated Cleminson ware is only one type of the California-made novelty pottery that collectors have recently taken an interest in. Though nearly always marked, these items have a style that you'll quickly become acquainted with, and their distinctive glaze colors will be easy to spot. It was produced from the early 1940s until 1963.

Canister, cherries on tree branch, tea size **25.00**
Cookie jar, potbellied stove ..**75.00**
Egg cup, man w/mustache ...**15.00**
Hair receiver, girl w/hands folded, 2-pc **25.00**
Match holder, red long johns ..**27.50**
Pitcher, Gala Gray, 7" **22.50**
Plaque, Let's Pay Off the Mortgage **12.00**

Plaque, 7¼x8½", $15.00.

Plate, crowing rooster in center, sun's rays at edge, 9½" **9.00**
Spoon rest, leaf form **12.50**
String holder, heart form, You'll Always Have a Pull **35.00**
Sugar shaker, girl figural, ca 1950s **35.00**
Tray, sandwich; Deco fruit, center handle, marked **25.00**
Wall pocket, coffeepot **12.00**

Clocks

Quartz-movement clocks are very common; few have any collectible value. Wooden and black iron mantle clocks are the most valuable and are most likely to be found at flea markets. Tambour clocks, called 'camel-back' or 'humped-back,' are newer and were made from around 1915 until today. Rectangular clocks, longer than they are tall, are older and date from about 1880 to 1920; these are often black, mostly flat-topped, made of iron or with a wood case. Seth Thomas, Ansonia, Sessions, Gilbert, and Ingraham prevail. Look for clocks with labels. Retail customers want good-looking, working clocks. Repairs can cost from $50 to over $100. Figure an additional cleaning cost (average about $75) into the price. Reproductions abound. Older clocks have spiral gongs or bells; newer ones use brass chime rods. Ehrhardt's *Official Price Guide to Antique Clocks*, 3rd edition, is a good reference. For further information we recommend The Clock Doctor (Steve Gabany, our advisor), listed in the Directory under Indiana. See also Advertising.

Ansonia, Chester, rectangular case **150.00**

Ansonia, Grenada, rectangular case **150.00**

Ansonia, Savoy, rectangular case **80.00**

Clock Wise Inc, frying pan, cast iron, battery operated, early 1980s, 6" **10.00**

Emig Products, painted frying pan w/white letters, 1960s, 12" **15.00**

English, Delft china plate w/Dutch scene **40.00**

General Electric, battery, china plate, florals & numerals, '60s, 10" **15.00**

German, frying pan w/knife & fork hands, sheet metal, ca 1910 ....**100.00**

Gilbert Clock Co, shelf, oak case w/brass works, key wound, 1890s **285.00**

Ingraham, Grinnell, tambour style **50.00**

Ingraham, Hammond, tambour style **45.00**

Ingraham, Sage, tambour style **40.00**

New Haven, Garfield, tambour style **30.00**

New Haven, Tambour No 1 ..**75.00**

Red Wing, Aunt Jemima, works not marked **100.00**

Sessions, electric, frying pan, stamped tin, ca 1920s ...**40.00**

Sessions, electric, teapot, painted stamped metal, ca 1940, 7x8½" **15.00**

Seth Thomas, Adnaw, rectangular case **110.00**

Seth Thomas, Hull, rectangular case **135.00**

Seth Thomas, Pelham, rectangular case **110.00**

Seth Thomas, Ridune, tambour style **115.00**

Seth Thomas, Tambour #18 ..**100.00**

Seth Thomas, Tambour #2 ..**100.00**

Seth Thomas, Tambour #9 ..**110.00**

Seth Thomas, Trent **100.00**

Seth Thomas, Trent, tambour style **100.00**

Seth Thomas, Wanda, rectangular case **125.00**

Spartus, electric, avocado green plastic hutch, 1960s, 12"..**12.00**

Waterbury, Allen, rectangular case **140.00**

Waterbury, Croyden, tambour style **115.00**

Waterbury, Glouster **145.00**

Waterbury, Groyden **115.00**

Waterbury, Riva, rectangular case **140.00**

Waterbury, Salerad, rectangular case **125.00**

Waterbury, Stanhope **125.00**

Novelty

Pendulette wall clocks were made by Lux, Keebler, Westclox, and Columbia Time Clock companies. These small, wind-up, novelty clocks were often animated. Lux Manufacturing Co., the major producer of the clocks, was formed

Vanity clock, plastic base with blue glass frame, marked Teletron, $125.00.

in 1912 and reached peak production of 3,000 clocks per day in 1930. Clocks were made of pressed wood, porcelain, metal, and (by the late 1950s) plastics. Another company, Mastercrafter Novelty Clocks, first obtained a patent to produce their novelty animated clocks in the late 1940s. These clocks are made of plastic and are electric powered. Prices of novelty clocks vary according to condition, rarity, and location of purchase. For further information we recommend contacting Carole Kaifer, who is listed in the Directory under North Carolina.

Lux, alarm, woman working moving spinning wheel, ca 1950s **65.00**

Lux Pendulette, Beer Barrel Drinkers, non-animated, from $250, up to **275.00**

Lux Pendulette, Bluebird, animated, from $25 up to ...**30.00**

Lux Pendulette, Bobbing Bird, animated, from $20 up to **25.00**

Lux Pendulette, Boy Scout, non-animated, from $300 up to **350.00**

Lux Pendulette, Cat, animated eyes, from $150 up to ..**175.00**

Lux Pendulette, Checkered Borders, from $75 up to **125.00**

Lux Pendulette, Cocker Spaniel, animated, from $250 up to **275.00**

Lux Pendulette, Country Scene, non-animated, from $325 up to **350.00**

Lux Pendulette, Enchanted Forest, animated, from $100 up to **125.00**

Lux Pendulette, Hungry Dog, animated, from $225 up to ..**265.00**

Lux Pendulette, Hunting Scene, non-animated, from $65 up to **85.00**

Lux Pendulette, Kiddy Clock, non-animated, from $250 up to **275.00**

Lux Pendulette, Love Birds, animated, from $100 up to ..**125.00**

Lux Pendulette, Playful Scottie, animated, from $200 up to **250.00**

Lux Pendulette, Rudolph, animated, from $95 up to ..**115.00**

Lux Pendulette, Sailor, animated, from $100 up to **125.00**

Lux Pendulette, Small Dove, non-animated, from $30 up to ..**35.00**

Lux Pendulette, US Capitol, non-animated, from $300 up to **325.00**

Lux Pendulette, Woody Woodpecker, animated, from $250 up to **275.00**

Mastercrafter, Boy & Girl on Swing, animated, from $50 up to **75.00**

Mastercrafter, Church w/Bell Ringer, animated, from $35 up to **45.00**

Mastercrafter, Fireplace, animated, from $25 up to ...**35.00**

Mastercrafter, Girl on Swing, animated, from $50 up to ...**65.00**

Mastercrafter, Waterfall, animated, from $25 up to ...**35.00**

Clothes Sprinkler Bottles

From the time we had irons, clothes were sprinkled with water before ironing for the best results. During the 1930s through the 1950s when the steam iron became a home staple, some of us merely took sprinkler tops and stuck them into bottles to accomplish this task, while the more imaginative enjoyed the bottles made in figural shapes and bought the ones they particularly liked. The most popular, of course, were the Chinese men marked 'Sprinkle Plenty.' Some bottles were made by American Bisque, Cleminson of California, and other famous figural pottery makers. Many were made in Japan for the export market. Note that all of the Chinese men listed here are inscribed 'Sprinkle Plenty.' Our advisor for this category is Carol Silagyi, who is listed in the Directory under New Jersey.

Matilda, Pfaltzgraff, from $75.00 to $85.00; Chinaman, $30.00; cat with marble eyes, American Bisque, $75.00.

Black Mammy, white dress w/pink trim, from $100 up to **175.00**
Chinaman, pink & green, Sprinkle Plenty, Cleminson, from $30 up to **35.00**
Chinaman, red flowers w/black trim, Sprinkle Plenty, from $40 up to **45.00**
Chinaman, yellow & green, Sprinkle Plenty, Cardinal, from $20 up to **30.00**
Chinaman w/iron in left hand, Japan, from $60 up to ...**70.00**
Elephant, gray w/pink blush highlights, from $40 up to **45.00**

Elephant w/4-leaf clovers, from $35 up to **40.00**
Iron, w/1950s scene of woman ironing, from $30 up to..**40.00**
Iron w/ivy trim, from $20 up to **25.00**
Mandarian, flowing pink robe, from $70 up to **75.00**
Siamese cat, from $50 up to ..**60.00**
Sprinkle Maid, yellow or red plastic, each, from $10 up to **15.00**
Victorian lady w/purse, from $100 up to **125.00**

Coca-Cola

Since it was established in 1891, the Coca-Cola Company has issued a wide and varied scope of advertising memorabilia, creating what may well be the most popular field of specific product-related collectibles on today's market. Probably their best-known item is the rectangular Coke tray, issued since 1910. Many sell for several hundred dollars each. Before 1910 trays were round or oval. The 1904 tray featuring Lillian Nordica is valued at $2,350.00 in excellent condition. Most Coca-Cola buffs prefer to limit their collections to items made before 1970. Refer to *Goldstein's Coca-Cola Collectibles* by Sheldon Goldstein (Collector Books) for more information. Beware of reproductions!

Banner, Santa w/dog, When friends drop in..., 20x11" **20.00**
Blotter, cardboard, 3 girls at the fountain, 1944, 4x8", NM..................................**6.00**
Book cover, Coke bottle & button logo w/safety ABCs, EX ..**12.00**
Bottle, straight-sided, amber ..**35.00**
Bottle, 1986 Hardees, 30 cases made **50.00**

Bottle carrier, red, white & yellow, cardboard, 1960s, 10-oz **7.00**

Bottle carrier, yellow w/red, wood, 1940s, 4½x8" **60.00**

Bottle opener, bottle shape, 1950s, EX+ **10.00**

Bottle opener, metal spoon, Greenwood MS, 1930s ..**45.00**

Calendar, couple at table, complete, 1969 ....**35.00**

Calendar, paper, complete, 1958, EX **85.00**

Can, 1984 Olympics, Gymnastics **3.00**

Chalkboard, Coke Is It!, metal, 28x20" **13.00**

Channel card, cardboard, mountains & glass of Coke, 1960s, 7x24", NM **30.00**

Clock, plastic, depicts Betty, 1974, working **50.00**

Coaster, cardboard, Sprite boy & bottle, octagonal, 4" dia, M **5.00**

Cooler, vinyl, Drink Coca-Cola, 11x9x6", VG+ **25.00**

Coupon, boy in grass, 1927 ....**8.00**

Cuff links, red celluloid, 1920s, pr **75.00**

Doll, Gretchen, 1949, EX **35.00**

Fan, cardboard on wood stick, 1956, 12x8", NM **28.00**

Fan pull, double-sided Santa form, 1957 ....**13.00**

Handerchief, Kit Carson on red, cotton **65.00**

Lighter, bottle form, M **14.00**

Magazine advertisement, girl in buggy, 1906, EX **23.00**

Matchbook, Refresh Yourself..., 1930s **15.00**

Mechanical pencil, bottle-shaped metal clip, 1940s, MIB ..**20.00**

Message pad cube, formed as case of Coke, 1983, 4x6" **5.00**

Miniature case, yellow w/24 green bottles, 1960s **10.00**

Mobile, double-sided w/red disk, 1950s, 19" dia **150.00**

Money clip, brass w/red plastic logo, 1949, EX **22.00**

Needle case, cardboard, woman enjoying Coke, 1924, NM, 3x2" **60.00**

Notebook, spiral-bound, 1987 Coca-Cola advertising schedule **8.00**

Pencil sharpener, 1960s **8.00**

Placemats, Around the World/ scenes, 1950s, set of 4 .....**10.00**

Playing cards, Coke Has It!, 1980s **8.00**

Playing cards, lady w/tray of Cokes, 1963, MIB **45.00**

Playing cards, stewardess, 1943, NM **95.00**

Postcard, Bobby Allison Coca-Cola race, 1973 ....**4.00**

Rain hat, Coke Adds Life to... Rainy Days, 1970s **3.00**

Service pin, green & black metal, 25-years, 1", M **125.00**

Sign, 1950s, 11x28", NM, $135.00.

Shot glass, Season's Greetings, 1978 ....**3.00**

Sign, cardboard, Sweetheart Special, easel-back, 1974, 24x18", NM **15.00**

Sign, die-cut bottle, tin, 1950s, 16½x5" **125.00**

Sign, die-cut ribbon, Sign of Good Taste, metal, 1960s, 6½x45½", NM **95.00**

Sign, metal, Coke Adds Life..., 1970s, 35x17" **30.00**

Sign for rack, metal, Take Home a Carton, 1940s, 12" dia ..**95.00**

Thermometer, gold bottle form, 1956, 9x2", M **45.00**

Toy top, plastic, Coke Adds Life...Fun Times, 1970s ..**3.00**

Tray, white on red plastic, Enjoy Coca-Cola, 1970s, 7½x14" ..**10.00**

Tray, woman sitting pretty, 1938, 13x11", VG **65.00**

Trolley sign, Santa w/Coke & children, fold marks **140.00**

Wallet, brown leather, 1920s, 9x4", MN **50.00**

Writing tablet, Pure As Sunlight, 1930s **12.00**

Comic Books

The 'Golden Age' is a term referring to the period from 1930 until 1950, during which today's most-prized comic books were published. First editions or those that feature the first appearance of a popular character are the most valuable and may bring prices of several hundred dollars – some even more. The original Batman comic, issued in the spring of 1940, is today worth $8,000.00 in fine condition. Most early comics, however, are valued at less than $5.00 up $30.00. Remember – rarity, age, condition, and quality of the art work are factors to consider when determining value. Because of the hundreds of thousands of comic books that have been printed, if you find yourself wanting collect them, you should buy a comprehensive price guide such as Overstreet's.

The Many Ghosts of Doctor Graves, #25, EX, $1.00.

Bullwinkle & Rocky, #9, Marvel, NM **1.25**

Camp Candy, #6, Marvel, EX ...**.75**

Captain Marvel Presents the Terrible Five, #5, MF Enterprises, NM **7.50**

Chuck Norris, #3, Marvel, VG ..**.50**

Fright Night, #22, Now Comics, EX **1.00**

Frosty the Snowman, #359, Dell, VG **7.50**

Frosty the Snowman, #359, VG **7.50**

Get Smart, #8, Don Adams photo cover, Dell, VG **7.00**

Ghost Manor, #32, Charlton, EX **2.75**
GI Joe Special Missions, #28, Marvel, NM **3.25**
Godzilla, #24, Marvel, VG **1.00**
Hawk & Dove, #28, DC Comics, NM **1.75**
Heathcliff's Funhouse, #10, Star Comics, EX .... **.75**
I Dream of Jeannie, #2, Barbara Eden photo cover, Dell, VG **6.50**
Johnny Quest, #31, Comico, NM **4.00**
Land of the Giants, #5, Gold Key, VG **3.75**
Leave It to Beaver, #912, Dell, VG **16.50**
Little Lizzie, #5, Marvel, VG ..**3.00**
Marines in Battle, #25, Atlas, VG **3.00**
My Love Story, #9, Atlas, EX ..**4.75**
New Archie, #22, Archie Enterprises, NM **1.25**
Night Nurse, #4, Marvel, VG .. **.50**
Outlaws of the West, #11, Charlton, VG **4.50**

Outlaw and El Diablo, All-Star Western, NM, $3.50.

Partridge Family, #21, Charlton, EX **3.75**
Power Pachyderms, #1, Marvel, EX .... **.75**
Roger Rabbit's Toontown, #5, Disney, VG .... **.50**
Rootie Kazootie, #415, Dell, VG **7.50**
Smurfs, #3, Marvel, NM **1.00**
Spy Thrillers, #4, Atlas, VG ..**3.50**
Tale of Two Cities, #7, Classic Comics, VG **3.00**
Top Cat, #20, Charlton, EX ...**2.75**
Uncle Scrooge Adventures, #21, Gladstone, EX **1.25**
Underdog, #10, Charlton, NM **12.50**
Vampire Tales, #11, Marvel, EX **1.00**
Werewolf by Night, #43, Marvel, NM **2.75**

Compacts

Prior to World War I, compacts were frowned upon. It was not until after the war when women became liberated and entered the work force that the use of cosmetics became acceptable. A compact became a necessity as a portable container for cosmetics and usually contained a puff and mirror. Compacts were made in many different styles, shapes, and motifs as well as every type of natural and man-made material. The fine jewelry houses made compacts in all of the precious metals — some studded with precious stones. The most sought-after compacts today are those in an Art Deco style or made of plastic, figurals, and any that incorporate gadgets. Compacts that are combined with other accessories are also very desirable. Refer to *Ladies' Compacts of the 19th and 20th*

Centuries (Wallace-Homestead Book Co.) by our advisor, Roselyn Gerson, for more information; she is listed in the Directory under New York. Another good reference is *The Collector's Encyclopedia of Compacts, Carryalls, and Face Powder Boxes* by Laura M. Mueller. See also Clubs and Newsletters.

Beaded, multicolor floral on white, square, minimum value **75.00**

Daniel, courting scene in plastic dome on gold, oblong, minimum value **60.00**

EA Bliss, compact/bracelet, etched floral w/cutouts, minimum value **150.00**

Enamel, blue & white on gold w/cabachon stones, chain, minimum value **100.00**

Enamel, blue on silver w/marcasite flower, oblong, minimum value **60.00**

Round gold-tone case with filigree lid set with colored stones, attached rouge case, $75.00 to $100.00.

Enamel, red on gold bolster form, miniature, minimum value **25.00**

Enamel, vanity case, blue Art Deco design, square, minimum value **60.00**

Flato, open umbrella on lid, fitted black faille case, minimum value **100.00**

Fuller, plastic, horseshoe form, comb in lid, sm, minimum value **40.00**

Harriet Hubbard Ayer, vanity case, gold-tone, oblong, minimum value **60.00**

Leather, gold-tooled fleur-de-lis, navy horseshoe form, minimum value **60.00**

Majestic, copper basketweave design, sm, minimum value **30.00**

Marine Corps, insignia on sterling, finger ring chain, minimum value **200.00**

Miref, gold watchcase form, engine turned, w/ring, minimum value **80.00**

Plastic, yellow w/green cloisonne lid, octagonal, minimum value **40.00**

Square, sailor & copper steering wheel on gold-tone lid, minimum value **80.00**

Terri, silhouettes on blue metal, plastic base, square, minimum value **30.00**

Vanity case, basketweave on horseshoe form, finger ring, minimum value **60.00**

Volupte, floral & stones w/strapwork design, square, minimum value **40.00**

Cookbooks

Advertising cookbooks, those by well-known personalities, and figural diecuts are among the more readily available examples on today's market. Cookbooks written prior to 1874 are the most valuable; they often sell for $200.00 and up. Refer to *A Guide to Cookbook Collecting* by Colonel Bob Allen and *The Price Guide to Cookbooks and Recipe Leaflets* by Linda Dickinson for more information. (Both books are published by Collector Books.)

Aunt Jenny's Favorite Recipes, Spry advertising, 7x6", $6.00.

Ann Pillsbury's $200,000 Prize Winning Cookbook, 1952, 144 pages **15.00**
BBQs & Picnics, Better Homes & Gardens, 61 pages, 1963..**10.00**
Better Ways w/Gel Cookery, Knox, 1952, 27 pages **60.00**
Betty Crocker's Dinner for Two Cookbook, 1964, hard-bound, 156 pages **8.00**
Betty Crocker's Hostess Cookbook, 1967, 168 pages ...**10.00**
Betty Crocker's Picture Cookbook, 1956, hard-bound, 446 pages **10.00**
California Cooks, 1970, hard-bound, 166 pages **8.00**

Calumet Book of Oven Triumphs, 1934, 32 pages **6.00**
Ceresota Cookbook, ca 1880s, 42 pages **28.00**
Cheese Cookbook, Kraft, 1942, hard-bound, 63 pages ...**18.00**
Cooking Hints & Tested Recipes, Crisco, 1937, 32 pages ..**10.00**
Cooking the Modern Way, Planters, 1948, 38 pages **6.00**
Cooking the Sportsman Harvest, 144 pages **6.00**
Cuto Cookbook, Volume 1, 1961, hard-bound, 123 pages **7.00**
Davis Baking Powder Recipes, 1922, 48 pages **12.00**
Foods Actually Bake Better This Way, Pyrex, 1929, 30 pages **12.00**
Ford Treasury of Favorite Recipes, Volume 3, 1959, 252 pages **10.00**
Franklin Sugar Candy Book, ca 1920s, 16 pages **18.00**
Good Housekeeping's Book of Ice Creams & Cool Drinks, 1958, 67 pages **4.00**
Good Things To Eat, Arm & Hammer, 1938, 15 pages **10.00**
Heinz Salad Book, ca 1930s, 99 pages, 8¾x6" **7.00**
Hood's Cookbook Number Three, ca late 1800s, 32 pages..**12.00**
How To Bake by the Ration Book, General Foods, 1943, 23 pages, 8x4" **6.00**
Keep on the Sunny Side of Life, Kellogg Co, 1933, 32 pages **8.00**
Modern Family Cookbook, 1943, hard-bound, 906 pages **25.00**
New Cake Secrets, Swans Down, 1931, 48 pages, 7x4½" **5.00**
New Coconut Treasure Book, General Foods, 1934, 38 pages, 6⅝x5" **8.00**
Presto Cooker Recipe Book, 1947, 127 pages **7.00**

Proven Recipes Showing the Uses of the Three Great Products From Corn; Argo, Karo, and Mazola advertising on back, 6½x5", $8.00.

Quaker Cereal Products & How To Use Them, 1927, 56 pages **10.00**

Salad Book, Better Homes & Gardens, 1958, 158 pages ...**12.00**

Shefford Cheese Recipes, 1928, 31 pages **7.50**

Short Cut to Better Jams & Jellies, Certo, 1941, 32 pages **3.00**

Sixty Ways To Serve Ham, Armour, ca 1920s, 26 pages **8.00**

Success in Seasoning, Lea & Perkins, 1936, 48 pages ..**10.00**

Sunsweet Prune Recipes, 1939, 40 pages **7.00**

Watkins Cookbook, 1938, hardbound, metal spiral binding, 285 pages **15.00**

What Mrs Dewey Did with the New Jell-O!, 1933, 23 pages **8.00**

Woman's Day Collector's Cookbook, 1960, soft cover, 320 pages **6.00**

Your Health Cookbook, Jack Lalanne, 1954, hard-bound, 239 pages **9.00**

Cookie Jars

The Nelson McCoy Pottery Co., Robinson Ransbottom Pottery Co., and the American Bisque Pottery Co., are three of the largest producers of cookie jars in the country. Many firms made them to a lesser extent. Today cookie jars are one of the most popular of modern collectibles. Figural jars are the most common (and the most valuable), made in an endless variety of subjects. Early jars from the 1920s and '30s were often decorated in 'cold paint' over the glaze. This type of color is easily removed – take care that you use very gentle cleaning methods. A damp cloth and a light touch is the safest approach.

For further information we recommend *The Collector's Encyclopedia of McCoy Pottery* by Sharon and Bob Huxford, *The Collector's Encyclopedia of Cookie Jars* by Joyce and Fred Roerig, *An Illustrated Value Guide to Cookie Jars* by Ermagene Westfall (all published by Collector Books) and *McCoy Cookie Jars From the First to the Last* by Harold Nichols (self-published).

Alice in Wonderland, Japan ..**125.00**

Alpo Dog, Disco **50.00**

Apple, McCoy, 1950-64 ....**50.00**

Baby Pig, Regal **300.00**

Ballerina, Metlox **105.00**

Baseball, Vandor **50.00**

Beanpot, embossed snowflake design, Shawnee USA, minimum value **50.00**

Beau Bear, Metlox **50.00**

Betsy Ross, Enesco, M **210.00**

Big Bird Chef, California Originals **78.00**

Bo Peep, Abingdon #694 ....**240.00**

Bobby Baker, McCoy, ivory w/red & black details, 1974-75 ....**55.00**

Bust of Santa, Carol Gifford, gold trim **210.00**

Cat on Beehive, American Bisque **55.00**

Cat w/Hat, Tawain **30.00**

Chick, American Bisque, blue & white **55.00**

Chicken, Fapco **40.00**

Christmas Tree, McCoy, 1959, minimum value **550.00**

Churn Boy, Regal **200.00**

Cinderella Pumpkin, Brush..**165.00**

Clown Bust, McCoy...............**75.00**

Cookie Kettle, American Bisque **50.00**

Cookie Monster, Newcor **42.50**

Cookie Safe, McCoy, marked USA on leg, 1962-63 ....**65.00**

Cow & Calf, Wisecarver **90.00**

Daisy, Abingdon #677 ....**45.00**

Davy Crockett, Brush, no gold trim **200.00**

Dog on Pillow, American Bisque **150.00**

Donkey w/Cart, Brush #33, gray **350.00**

Drum Major, Shawnee USA, minimum value **150.00**

Dutch Boy, McCoy, 1945 ......**45.00**

Dutch Boy, Shawnee, blue pants, no gold **80.00**

Dutch Girl, Red Wing, blue ..**105.00**

Dutch Girl, Shawnee, cold paint, minimum value **50.00**

Elephant, McCoy, 1943 ......**130.00**

Elephant w/Split Trunk, McCoy, 1943 ....**325.00**

Elf School House, California Originals **60.00**

Engine, McCoy, black w/red & yellow trim, 1963-64 ....**140.00**

Ernie, California Originals ..**50.00**

Fat Boy, Abington **240.00**

Formal Pig, Brush, yellow hat & coat **285.00**

Fruit Basket, Shawnee #84, minimum **125.00**

Graduate Owl, Dorrane of California **65.00**

Graduate Owl, Japan, green ..**15.00**

Cat, American Bisque, $70.00.

Dutch Boy, Pottery Guild, $80.00.

117

Granny, Brush, plain skirt ..**360.00**
Granny, McCoy, USA, 1972-73 ....**80.00**
Gray Squirrel on Pine Cone, Metlox **78.00**
Hen on Basket, Brush **160.00**
Hen on Nest, McCoy, USA, 1959 ....**85.00**
Hi Diddle Diddle, Robinson Ransbottom, gold trim **235.00**
Hillbilly Bear, McCoy, early 1940s, minimum **900.00**
Hippo, Abingdon #549, w/decoration, 1942 ....**225.00**
Hobby Horse, Abingdon **185.00**
Howdy Doody, Vandor **275.00**
Human Bean, Enesco **60.00**
Humpty Dumpty, Abingdon ..**250.00**
Humpty Dumpty, Brush, w/beanie & bow tie **235.00**
Humpty Dumpty, Clay Art ..**70.00**
Jack-in-the-Box, Abingdon ..**250.00**
Jack-in-the-Box, American Bisque **60.00**
Jukebox, silver, 'cookie' songs ..**95.00**
Kittens on Ball of Yarn, McCoy, 1954-55 ....**110.00**
Lamb Head w/Hat, Metlox ..**70.00**
Lamb on Basketweave, McCoy, 1956-57 ....**55.00**
Lantern, Brush **55.00**
Little Chef, Shawnee USA, minimum value **80.00**
Little Girl, Abingdon #693 ...**60.00**
Little Girl, Brush **285.00**
Little Miss Muffet, Abingdon **200.00**
Little Miss Muffet, Abingdon #622 ....**200.00**
Little Red Riding Hood, Pottery Guild **95.00**
Love Birds (or Kissing Penguins), McCoy, 1945 ....**80.00**
Lunch Box, Dorrane of California, blue **50.00**
Mammy w/Churn & Boy, Wisecarver **185.00**
McNutt's Red Chicken Coupe, Dept 56 ....**85.00**

Mickey & Pluto, Walt Disney, 1980 ....**105.00**
Midnight Snack, Clay Art **40.00**
Modern Pineapple, McCoy, unmarked, green, 1970 ....**50.00**
Mona Lisa, Vandor **50.00**
Money Sack, Abingdon **70.00**
Mother Goose, Abingdon **295.00**
Mr Peanut, MIB **32.50**
Mrs Pots, Treasure Craft, Walt Disney **50.00**
Muggsy, Shawnee, marked Pat Muggsy USA, gold w/decals, minimum value **450.00**
Nite Owl, Brush **95.00**
Nun, Deforest of California ..**300.00**
Old Clock, Brush **185.00**
Old Shoe, Brush **85.00**
Owl, Shawnee, marked USA, minimum **225.00**
Ozark Hillbilly, Morton Potteries **55.00**
Panda, Brush **210.00**
Pantry Parade Yellow Tomato, gold handle **62.50**
Picnic Basket, McCoy, USA, 1962-63 ....**70.00**
Pillsbury Doughboy **70.00**
Pine Cone, Dorrane of California **34.00**
Pineapple, Abingdon #664 ...**60.00**
Pink Elephant, Shawnee #60, minimum value **80.00**
Pumpkin, Abingdon #674 ...**310.00**
Red Apple, Metlox, lg **65.00**
Rio Rita, Fitz & Floyd, Black face **125.00**
Rocking Chair, Dalmations; McCoy, 1962 ....**350.00**
Rooster, McCoy, 1955-57 ......**95.00**
Sack of Cookies, American Bisque **60.00**
Sheriff Pig, Robinson Ransbottom, yellow or green hat **95.00**
Sitting Elephant, Shawnee, marked USA, minimum..**75.00**
Sitting Hippo, Brush **465.00**
Smiley the Pig, Shawnee, w/clover buds, marked **100.00**

Snoopy on Doghouse, McCoy, $225.00.

Spaceship, Friendship; McCoy, unmarked, black w/red & white, 1962-63 ....**165.00**

Squirrel on Log, Brush, gray ..**80.00**

Squirrel w/Top Hat, Brush, green coat **220.00**

Strawberry, Metlox **85.00**

Stylized Siamese, Brush **460.00**

Teapot, McCoy, 1971 ....**45.00**

Telephone, Sierra Vista **60.00**

Tepee, McCoy, w/straight top, 1957-59 ....**235.00**

Three Bears, Abingdon #696 ..**90.00**

Thumper, Walt Disney **150.00**

Train, Sierra Vista **65.00**

Treasure Chest, Brush **160.00**

Uncle Sam's Hat, McCoy, marked USA, 1973 ....**210.00**

Wedding Jar, McCoy, white w/gold trim, 1961 ....**90.00**

Wigwam, Abingdon #665, minimum value **300.00**

Windmill, #678, Abingdon ..**185.00**

Windmill, McCoy, 1961 ......**100.00**

Winnie the Pig, Shawnee, blue or green collar, marked USA, minimum value **175.00**

Winnie the Pig, Shawnee, marked Pat Winnie USA, clover bud, gold trim **400.00**

Winnie the Pooh Hunny Pot, California Originals, #907 ..**105.00**

Wishing Well, McCoy **40.00**

Witch, Abingdon #692, minimum value **350.00**

Woodsy Owl, McCoy, USA, 1973-74 ....**200.00**

Yarn Doll, American Bisque, light green & yellow **75.00**

Coors

Though they made a line of commercial artware as well, the Coors Pottery is best represented at today's flea markets and dinnerware shows by their popular dinnerware line, Rosebud. Rosebud was made in solid colors accented only by small contrasting floral elements; the line is extensive and includes kitchen and baking ware as well as table settings.

Rosebud plate, 9", $15.00.

Baker, Rosebud, 4¾" dia **12.50**

Bowl, mixing; Rosebud, handles, 3 ½-cup **15.00**

Cake knife, Rosebud, 10" **22.50**

Casserole, Rosebud, straight sides, 2-pt **20.00**

Casserole, Rosebud, w/lid, 14-cup **38.00**

Jar, utility; Rosebud, 2½-pt ..**25.00**
Plate, Rosebud, 7" **7.50**
Salt & pepper shakers, Rosebud,
2½", pr **24.00**
Saucer, Rosebud, 5½" **6.00**
Tumbler, Rosebud, w/handle, 8½-
oz **25.00**

Miscellaneous

Bank, clown **100.00**
Mug, Colorado State Fair,
1934 ....**45.00**
Mug, lion decal **18.00**
Shaker, bottle form **15.00**
Shaker, keg form **15.00**
Vase, leaves & berries, bulbous,
6½" **35.00**

**Vase, bulbous urn form with
handles, 7½", $45.00.**

Copper

Early copper items are popular
with those who enjoy primitives,
and occasionally fine examples
can still be found at flea markets.
Check construction to help you
determine the age of your piece.
Dovetailed joints indicate 18th-
century work; handmade seamed
items are usually from the 19th
century. Teakettles and small
stills are especially collectible.
Most of what we've listed here is
mid-century and beyond – the
type of things you're most likely
to encounter. Refer to *Antique
Brass and Copper* by Mary Frank
Gaston (Collector Books) for more
information.

Ashtray, cowboy hat form, commemorative of 1926 Dallas
Cotton Palace **10.00**
Funnel, ring hanger, 6x6" **35.00**
Jar, Art Deco, ringed design
w/footed base & knob finial,
1920s, 5" **45.00**
Letter opener, advertising,
marked Lone Star Bag & Bag-
ging Co, 12" **25.00**
Match holder, cowboy boot figural,
4" **25.00**
Plaque, chrysanthemums in high
relief, ca 1940, 8½x12" ..**50.00**
Teakettle, Majestic, wood & iron
handle, 10" dia **70.00**
Teakettle, wide flat handle
w/rolled edges, ca 1920s, 10"
dia **65.00**
Tip tray, hammered, 5x7¼" ..**15.00**
Tray, restaurant; embossed
Jamie's on border, ca 1950s,
12" dia **35.00**

Corkscrews

Webster's dictionary defines a
corkscrew as an instrument consisting of a metal screw or helix
with a sharp point and a traverse
handle whose use is to draw corks
from bottles. In early times this
task was done by using the worm

end of a flintlock gun rod. The history of corkscrews dates back to the mid-1600s, when wine makers concluded that the best-aged wine should be stored in smaller containers, either stoneware or glass. Since plugs left unsealed were often damaged by rodents, corks were cut off flush with the bottle top and sealed with wax or a metal cover. Numerous models with handles of wood, ivory, bone, porcelain, silver, etc., have been patented through the years. Our advisor for this category is Paul P. Luchsinger; he is listed in the Directory under New York.

Red devil, painted cast iron, 3½", $35.00.

Advertising, Carter's Ink, Pat 1894, folding type, sm **15.00**
Advertising, Listerine, tin, folding type, 1900s-1920s **12.00**
Advertising, Welch's Grape Juice, lithographed metal **18.00**
Alligator-form horn handle w/steel worm, American, 20th century **135.00**
Anheuser Busch, nickel-plated bottle form, w/brass plate, dated 1897 ....**50.00**
Cat figural, brass & steel, 1900s, 3¾" **55.00**

Clown head, molded plastic, 4½" **75.00**
Diamant JP Paris, Archimedean screw, steel, ca 1900 ....**150.00**
Edie Patent, Pat 1890, cast metal bar type w/screw clamps, 1890 ....**80.00**
Elephant head, ivory handle w/glass eyes, sterling ferrule, 8" **65.00**
Gilchrist, puller type, nicked iron, marked Yankee, 1900s ..**35.00**
Godinger, Bacchus head, cast brass, double-lever type, ca 1983 ....**30.00**
Lady's legs, folding type, plated metal w/enamel trim, German, 5½" **45.00**
Sailing ship, cast brass, ca 1950s **35.00**
Syroco, figural waiter w/bottle, molded wood composition, 8" **55.00**
T-type, cigar form handle w/nickeled shaft, Pat 1898 ......**25.00**
The Club **120.00**
The Utility, English, 1800s ..**100.00**
Viking ship, nickel-plated cast iron, 3½x4¼" **35.00**
World's Fair, figural key, 1939 ..**22.00**

Cracker Jack

The name Cracker Jack was first used in 1896. The trademark as well as the slogan 'The more you eat, the more you want' were registered at that time. Prizes first appeared in Cracker Jack boxes in 1912. Prior to then, prizes or gifts could be sent for through catalogs. In 1910 coupons that could be redeemed for many gifts were inserted in the boxes.

The Cracker Jack boy and his dog, Bingo, came on the scene in 1916 and have remained one of the world's most well-known trademarks. Prizes themselves came in a variety of materials, from paper and tin to pot metal and plastic. The beauty of Cracker Jack prizes is that they depict what was happening in the world at the time they were made. All items listed are marked Cracker Jack. For further information we recommend our advisor, Phil Helley, listed in the Directory under Wisconsin.

Air Corps wings, pot metal ..**125.00**
Bank, tin litho, What? **450.00**
Bottle opener, metal, 2 types, each **95.00**
Cart, tin w/wood handle **65.00**
Clicker, tin **75.00**
Fortune wheel, paper **75.00**
Mirror, celluloid, round, 2 styles, each **115.00**
Pencil **30.00**
Pencil clip, celluloid, round ..**250.00**
Pin-back button, pictures Victorian women, celluloid ..**100.00**
Postcard, Cracker Jack stand at fair, real photo **45.00**
Postcard, any 1 of 16 different styles **28.00**
Radio, tin, Tune In **165.00**
Spinner, Big League Baseball at Home, paper **135.00**
Spinner, pencil-tip, card board **145.00**
Train engine, #512, tin **155.00**

Credit Cards

Credit items predate the 20th century and have been made from various types of materials. Celluloid tokens and paper cards were among the earliest, followed by paper and metal plates with holders, metal tokens, and, finally, plastic cards. They have been issued by merchants, oil companies, the travel and entertainment industries, and banks, to name the most common. Credit card collecting is one of the fastest growing hobbies today. By their very nature, credit cards and charge tokens were usually deliberately destroyed, making older credit items fiercely sought after. Our advisor, Walt Thompson, is listed in the Directory under Washington. See also Clubs and Newsletters for information concerning a relevant publication.

American Express Gold Card, expired 1985 ....**48.50**
American Express Violet Card, expired 1969 ....**72.50**
Arizona State Bank, expired 1988 ....**6.50**
AT&T Telephone Credit Card, expired 1992 ....**7.00**
AT&T Telephone Credit Card, paper, expired 1968 ....**12.50**

Top, tin, 1933, 1½", EX, $40.00; watch, tin, 1½", G, $12.00 (NM, $65.00).

Bell Systems Card, paper, expired
1962 ....**20.00**
Canadian Gulf Oil, expired
1973 ....**17.00**
Canadian Tire, expired 1985..**5.00**
Citibank Credit Card, expired
1989 ....**3.00**
Diners Club Booklet, expired
1957 ....**85.00**
Diners Club Booklet, expired
3/1954 ....**280.00**
First Federal Saving Bank,
expired 1992 ....**4.00**
L Bamberger Co, celluloid ..**227.50**
Macy's Depositor Account, paper,
damaged **27.00**
Mobil Socony, expired 1958 ..**45.00**
Phillips Oil Co, expired 1972 ..**8.00**
Skelly Oil Co, lady's card, expired
1974 ....**18.00**
Trans Texas Airways, paper ..**27.50**
Wolf Dessaur Co, celluloid ..**227.50**

**Sunoco, Sun Oil Co.,
expired 1972, $8.00.**

Czechoslovakian Collectibles

Items marked Czechoslovakia
are popular modern collectibles.
Pottery, glassware, jewelry, etc.,
were produced there in abundance. Refer to *Czechoslovakian
Glass and Collectibles* by Dale
and Diane Barta and Helen M.
Rose (Collector Books) for more
information.

Ceramics

Ashtray, white w/dark blue
anchor, white rope design,
4x2" **35.00**
Basket, light orange lusterware
finish, 5" **40.00**
Basket, purple lusterware finish,
3¼" **35.00**
Bowl, Peasant Art Pottery, blue-
green w/oval floral design,
2½" **60.00**
Creamer, Erphila Art, white
w/orange flowers & green
vines, 4¼" **45.00**
Creamer, pearl lusterware, cat
handle, black rim, 4½" ..**35.00**
Creamer, seated cow, white w/rust
spots, black handle, 4¾"..**40.00**
Figurine, white w/high-gloss glaze,
gold highlights, 5¼" **45.00**
Pitcher, Erphila Art Pottery, bird
design, cream w/red & black,
5¾" **90.00**

**Powder box, ceramic, Deco geo-
metrics, artist signed, marked,
$60.00.**

Sugar bowl, cream shading to yellow, black rim & handles,
w/lid, 4" **35.00**
Tumbler, Peasant Art Pottery,
black w/floral decor around
top, 4¼" **55.00**
Wall pocket, orange & white spiral
seashell w/bird, 5⅛" **50.00**

Glass

Atomizer, cased, bright orange w/gold trim, 3" **70.00**

Basket, cased, red w/applied jet rim & handle, 6½" **80.00**

Bowl, cased, black w/orange interior, 6¼" **95.00**

Bowl, cased, white ruffled edge w/ maroon rim, 6" **130.00**

Bowl, cobalt, silver design & rim, 3¼" **65.00**

Candlestick, cased, mottled colors, 3" **55.00**

Candlestick, cased, varicolored, 8½" **80.00**

Candy dish, cased, cream w/mottled colors, w/lid, 7½" **85.00**

Candy dish, mottled, applied black 4-footed pedestal base, w/lid, 8" **130.00**

Cuspidor, ladies'; cased, mottled colors, 4" **165.00**

Decanter, clear w/painted green stripes, 9" **55.00**

Mustard pot, cased knob, orange w/black design, 4½" **85.00**

Perfume, black opaque base w/jeweled decoration, black stopper, 3" **85.00**

Puff box, cased, red w/black & white enameling, 3½" ...**95.00**

Salt & pepper shakers, crystal w/red porcelain duck head tops, 2", pr **45.00**

Toothpick holder, cased, orange w/black & green design, 2¼" **35.00**

Tumbler, clear w/green base overlay, cobalt threading, 5" **65.00**

Vase, amber cased, mottled colors, 3½" **55.00**

Vase, cased, light blue, applied crystal handles, ruffled edge, 7⅞" **95.00**

Vase, cased, orange w/applied flowers, ruffle top, 7½" ..**90.00**

Vase, cased, red w/applied serpentine, jet rim, 8¼" **95.00**

Vase, cased, varicolored, applied 3-footed pedestal base, 7¼"..**72.00**

Vase, cased, varicolored w/applied blue handles, 8⅜" **95.00**

Vase, cased, yellow w/applied jet rim, 8¼" **80.00**

Vase, green ridged top w/mottled overlay bottom, 9" **55.00**

Decanters

The James Beam Distilling Company produced its first ceramic whiskey decanter in 1953 and remained the only major producer of these decanters throughout the decade. By the late 1960s, other companies such as Ezra Brooks, Lionstone, and Cyrus Noble were also becoming involved in their production. Today these fancy liquor containers are attracting many collectors. Our advisors for decanters are Judy and Art Turner of Homestead Collectibles, who are listed in the Directory under Pennsylvania.

1969 Camaro Pace Car, $50.00.

Beam, Automotive Series, Bass Boat **19.00**

Beam, Casino Series, Binion's Horseshoe **7.00**

Beam, Casino Series, Circus Circus Clown **39.00**

Beam, Centennial Series, Chicago Fire **15.00**

Beam, Centennial Series, Hawaii's 200th **15.00**

Beam, Centennial Series, Statue of Liberty, 1985 ....**24.00**
Beam, Club Series, Blue Hen ..**15.00**
Beam, Club Series, Five Seasons Club **10.00**
Beam, Club Series, Milwaukee Stein **25.00**
Beam, Customer Series, Delco Battery **25.00**
Beam, Ducks Unlimited Series, #14, Gadwalls, 1988 ......**24.00**
Beam, Elks National Foundation **10.00**
Beam, Executive Series, Blue Cherub, 1960 ....**60.00**
Beam, Executive Series, Fantasia, 1971 ....**9.00**
Beam, Foreign Series, Fiji Islands **5.00**
Beam, People Series. Buffalo Bill **15.00**
Beam, Political Series, New York Donkey, 1976 ....**10.00**

Prospector, panning for gold, 1970, $9.00.

Beam, Regal China Series, Hemisfair **9.00**
Beam, Regal China Series, New Hampshire Eagle **20.00**
Beam, Regal China Series, Tombstone **5.00**
Beam, Sports Series, Bowling Pin **10.00**
Beam, Sports Series, Chicago Cubs **35.00**
Beam, State Series, Delaware ..**5.00**
Beam, Trophy Series, Horse, black, 1967 ....**10.00**
Beam, Trophy Series, Panda Bear **20.00**
Brooks, Automotive Series, Corvette Mako Shark, 1962 ....**15.00**
Brooks, Automotive Series, Mustang Pace Car **25.00**
Brooks, Bareknuckle Fighter ..**25.00**
Brooks, Cigar Store Indian **5.00**
Brooks, Laurel **20.00**
Brooks, Man of War **15.00**
Famous Firsts, Automotive Series, Ferrari, yellow ..**30.00**
Famous Firsts, Hurdy Gurdy ..**15.00**
Famous Firsts, Transportation Series, Spirit of St Louis, mini **65.00**
Grenadier, Nancy Hart **25.00**
Hoffman, Alabama Crimson ..**10.00**
Hoffman, Automotive Series, Distillery Truck **65.00**
Hoffman, Buffalo Man **25.00**
Hoffman, Mr Lucky Bartender **30.00**
Hoffman, Political Elephant ..**15.00**
Lewis & Clark, Mr Troll Series, Grandmother **15.00**
Lionstone, Automotive Series, Stutz, mini **15.00**
Lionstone, Bartender **24.00**
Lionstone, Cavalry Scout **10.00**
Lionstone, Hunter w/Black Lab **35.00**
Lionstone, Johnny Unitas ...**95.00**
McCormick, Automotive Series, Packard Hood Ornament ..**35.00**
McCormick, Clown #5 ....**25.00**

McCormick, Elvis Designer #1, mini **65.00**

McCormick, Elvis, Graceland **125.00**

McCormick, World's Greatest Fan **15.00**

Michter, Ice Wagon **15.00**

Mike Wayne, John Wayne Portrait **25.00**

Mount Hope, Fireman & Soldier, mini **15.00**

Neiman, Baseball **12.00**

Old Bardstown, Foster Brooks **15.00**

Old Commonwealth, Coal Miner #5, Coal Shooter **25.00**

Old Commonwealth, Fireman #2, Nozzleman **65.00**

Old Crow, Chess Piece **8.00**

Old Fitzgerald, Nebraska Football, 1972 ....**30.00**

Pacesetter, Transportation Series, Tractor, Massey Ferguson **75.00**

Ski Country, Animal Series, African Lions **60.00**

Ski Country, Animal Series, Raccoon, mini **45.00**

Ski Country, Banded Waterfowl Series, Bufflehead **85.00**

Ski Country, Bird Series, Gila Woodpecker, mini **40.00**

Ski Country, Christmas Series, Bob Cratchit **65.00**

Ski Country, Circus Series, Circus Elephant, mini **44.00**

Ski Country, Circus Series, PT Barnum **55.00**

Ski Country, Customer Specialties Series, Caveman **30.00**

Ski Country, Domestic Animal Series, Labrador w/Pheasant, mini **40.00**

Ski Country, Fish Series, Brown Trout, mini **29.00**

Ski Country, Game Bird Series, Sage Grouse **95.00**

Ski Country, Horned & Antlered Series, White-Tail Deer ..**150.00**

Ski Country, Indian Series, End of the Trail, mini **150.00**

Ski Country, Rodeo Series, Wyoming Bronco, mini ..**44.00**

Ski Country, Waterfowl Series, Canadian Goose, 1973 ..**135.00**

Wild Turkey, #11, Turkey & Falcon **85.00**

Wild Turkey, #7, Turkey & Fox, mini **25.00**

Wild Turkey, Flying Turkey, 1973 ....**40.00**

Wild Turkey, Lore Series, #3 ..**35.00**

Wild Turkey, Striding Turkey, 1976 ....**15.00**

Degenhart

The 'D' in heart trademark indicates the product of the Crystal Art Glass factory, which operated in Cambridge, Ohio, from 1947 until the mid-1970s. It was owned by John and Elizabeth Degenhart who developed more than 145 distinctive colors to use in making their toothpick holders, figurines, bells, and other novelties. See also Glass Shoes.

Beaded Oval Toothpick, Fawn **22.50**

Beaded Oval Toothpick, Vaseline **18.00**

Bell, Blue Fire, dated 1776-1976 ....**10.00**

Bell, Red Carnival, dated 1776-1976 ....**30.00**

Bird Salt & Pepper, Nile Green **35.00**

Bird Salt w/Cherry, Lavender Marble **30.00**

Bird Salt w/Cherry, Sapphire **12.00**

Bird Toothpick (Museum), Opalescent **18.00**

Bow Slipper, Blue Marble Slag **25.00**

Bow Slipper, Rose Marie **15.00**

Buzz Saw Wine (Sunburst), Light Custard **30.00**

Chick, Cobalt, 2" **25.00**

Chick, Heliotrope, no mark, 2" **50.00**

Colonial Drape Toothpick, Amethyst **17.50**

Daisy & Button Salt, Amethyst **15.00**

Daisy & Button Toothpick, Amethyst **17.50**

Daisy & Button Toothpick, Light Amberina **27.50**

Forget-Me-Not Toothpick, Lavender **20.00**

Gypsy Pot Toothpick, Amethyst **15.00**

Hand, Clear Peach **8.00**

Hand, Crown Tuscan **18.00**

Heart & Lyre Cup Plate, Cobalt, no mark **15.00**

Heart & Lyre Cup Plate, Crown Tuscan **25.00**

Heart Box, Baby Green **30.00**

Heart Box, Baby Pink **30.00**

Heart Box, Blue Jay **25.00**

Heart Box, Vaseline **22.50**

Hen Covered Dish, Crystal, 3" ..**20.00**

High Boot, Crystal **20.00**

Hobo Shoe, Crown Tuscan ...**20.00**

Kat Slipper, Bloody Mary **50.00**

Miniature Pitcher, Chocolate Cream **20.00**

Miniature Slipper (Museum), Amberina **25.00**

Owl, Amberina **50.00**

Owl, Fog Opaque **50.00**

Owl, Red Carnival **150.00**

Owl (Museum), Buttercup ...**50.00**

Pooch, Buttercup Slag **40.00**

Pooch, Green Opal Slag **25.00**

Pooch, Grey Marble **15.00**

Pooch, Ivory **20.00**

Pooch, Sapphire **15.00**

Pottie Salt, Honey **10.00**

Pottie Salt, Nile Green **17.50**

Priscilla Doll, Daffodil **90.00**

Seal of Ohio Cup Plate, Opalescent **12.50**

Skate Shoe, Cobalt Carnival ..**40.00**

Texas Boot, Baby Green **20.00**

Texas Boot, Sapphire **16.00**

Turkey, Amethyst, 5" **50.00**

Depression Glass

Depression Glass, named for the era when it sold through dime stores or was given away as premiums, can be found in such varied colors as amber, green, pink, blue, red, yellow, white, and crystal. Mass-produced by many different companies in hundreds of patterns, Depression Glass is one of the most sought-after collectibles in the United States today. Refer to *The Pocket Guide to Depression Glass* by Gene Florence (Collector Books). See also Bedroom and Bathroom Glassware; Fire-King; Fry Oven Glassware; Glass Knives; Jadite.

Pooch, Green Opalescent, $20.00.

Adam, bowl, dessert; pink or green, 4¾" **12.50**

Adam, pitcher, green, 32-oz,
8" **37.50**
Adam, plate, dinner; pink, square,
9" **20.00**
Adam, sugar bowl, green **16.00**
American Pioneer, bowl, console;
green, 10¾" **55.00**
American Pioneer, candlesticks,
crystal, 6½", pr **57.50**
American Pioneer, creamer,
green, 3½" **20.00**
American Pioneer, plate, green,
handled, 11½" **17.00**
American Pioneer, sugar bowl,
crystal, 3½" **17.50**

**American Sweetheart 2-tier
tidbit tray, red, $175.00.**

American Sweetheart, bowl,
cereal; pink, 6" **11.50**
American Sweetheart, plate,
salver; monax, 12" **11.00**
American Sweetheart, sherbet,
monax, footed, 4¼" **15.00**
Anniversary, cake plate, crystal,
12½" **5.50**
Anniversary, pickle dish, pink,
9" **9.00**
Anniversary, plate, dinner; irides-
cent, 9" **5.75**
Aunt Polly, bowl, berry; blue,
4¾" **12.00**
Aunt Polly, creamer, irides-
cent **25.00**
Aunt Polly, tumbler, blue, 8-oz,
3⅝" **22.50**

Aurora, bowl, cereal; crystal,
5⅜" **5.00**
Aurora, cup, green **7.50**
Aurora, plate, cobalt, 6½" **8.00**
Aurora, tumbler, pink, 10-oz,
4¾" **16.00**
Avocado, bowl, relish; green,
footed, 6" **23.00**
Avocado, plate, luncheon; green,
8¼" **17.00**
Avocado, sugar bowl, pink,
footed **27.50**
Beaded Block, bowl, amber,
square, 5½" **7.00**
Beaded Block, jelly, green,
stemmed, 4½" **9.00**
Beaded Block, pitcher, pint jug;
pink, 5¼" **90.00**
Block Optic, butter dish, green,
3x5" **45.00**
Block Optic, plate, dinner; yellow,
9" **35.00**
Block Optic, tumbler, pink, footed,
10-oz, 6" **22.00**
Bowknot, bowl, berry; green,
4½" **12.00**
Bowknot, plate, salad; green, 7" ..**9.00**
Bubble, bowl, fruit; crystal,
4½" **3.50**
Bubble, plate, dinner; forest
green, 9⅜" **12.50**
Bubble, platter, blue, 12" **14.00**
Bubble, tumbler, water; Royal
Ruby, 9-oz **8.00**
Cameo, bowl, cereal; crystal,
5½" **6.00**
Cameo, bowl, cream soup; green,
4¾" **55.00**
Cameo, cake plate, pink, flat,
10½" **115.00**
Cameo, candy jar, yellow, w/lid,
4" **65.00**
Cameo, cup, crystal **5.00**
Cameo, plate, dinner; pink,
9½" **60.00**
Cameo, plate, sherbet; yellow,
6" **3.00**
Cherry Blossom, bowl, berry;
pink, 4¾" **12.00**

Cherry Blossom, platter, pink or green, 13" **50.00**

Cherry Blossom, sugar bowl, green **13.00**

Cherry Blossom, tray, sandwich; delphite, 10½" **16.00**

Cherryberry, bowl, salad; crystal or iridescent, 6½" **15.00**

Cherryberry, plate, salad; pink or green, 7½" **12.00**

Christmas Candy, creamer, crystal **8.00**

Christmas Candy, plate, luncheon; teal, 8¼" **15.00**

Circle, pitcher, pink or green, 60-oz **27.50**

Circle, tumbler, water; pink or green, 8-oz, 4" **9.00**

Cloverleaf, bowl, dessert; pink, 4" **10.00**

Cloverleaf, plate, sherbet; green, 6" **4.00**

Cloverleaf, sugar, green, footed, 3⅝" **14.00**

Colonial, bowl, vegetable; pink, oval, 10" **25.00**

Colonial, goblet, claret; 4-oz, 5¼" **23.00**

Colonial, shakers, crystal, pr ..**50.00**

Colonial, tumbler, water; red, 9-oz, 4" **95.00**

Colonial Block, candy jar, pink or green, w/lid **32.50**

Colonial Block, creamer, white ..**6.00**

Colonial Fluted, bowl, cereal; green, 6" **7.50**

Colonial Fluted, plate, luncheon; 8" **4.00**

Columbia, bowl, salad; crystal, 8½" **14.00**

Columbia, plate, bread & butter; pink, 6" **10.00**

Coronation, bowl, berry; pink, 4¼" **4.00**

Coronation, cup, red **5.00**

Coronation, plate, luncheon; 8½" **30.00**

Cube, candy jar, pink, w/lid, 6½" **25.00**

Cube, shakers, pink or green, pr **30.00**

Cube, tumbler, green, 9-oz, 4" ..**55.00**

Cupid, bowl, fruit; footed, 9¼" **135.00**

Daisy, bowl, cereal; green, 6"..**11.00**

Daisy, platter, amber or red, 10¾" **12.50**

Diamond Quilted, bowl, cereal; pink or green, 5" **6.00**

Diamond Quilted, plate, luncheon; pink or green, 8" ..**5.00**

Diamond Quilted, sugar bowl, blue or black **14.00**

Diana, bowl, salad; crystal; 9" ..**5.00**

Diana, cup, pink **11.00**

Diana, tumbler, amber, 9-oz, 4⅛" **23.00**

Dogwood, cake plate, pink, solid foot, 13" **75.00**

Dogwood, cup, green **22.00**

Dogwood, plate, salver; monax or cremax, 12" **15.00**

Doric, butter dish, pink **60.00**

Doric, candy dish, delphite, 3-part **5.00**

Doric, tray, green, w/handles, 10" **12.00**

Doric & Pansy, bowl, berry; green, 4½" **12.00**

Doric & Pansy, plate, sherbet; pink or crystal, 6" **7.00**

English Hobnail, bowl, cream soup; amber **14.00**

English Hobnail, celery dish, cobalt, 9" **20.00**

English Hobnail, grapefruit, pink, flange rim, 6½" **16.00**

English Hobnail, plate, pie; turquoise, 7¼" **5.00**

English Hobnail, tumbler, green, footed, 12½-oz **22.00**

Floragold, bowl, deep salad; iridescent, 9½" **32.50**

Floragold, sherbet, iridescent, low footed **12.00**

Floral, butter dish, pink **75.00**

Floral, plate, salad; green, 8" ..**9.00**

Floral, sherbet, delphite **77.50**

Floral & Diamond Band, compote, pink, 5½" **13.00**

Floral & Diamond Band, tumbler, water; green, 4" **20.00**

Florentine No 1, bowl, berry; blue, 5" **15.00**

Florentine No 1, cup, crystal or green **8.00**

Florentine No 1, plate, dinner; yellow, 10" **19.00**

Florentine No 1, tumbler, pink, ribbed, 9-oz, 4" **18.00**

Florentine No 2, bowl, crystal or green, 5½" **27.50**

Florentine No 2, coaster, pink, 3¼" dia **14.00**

Florentine No 2, comport, blue, ruffled, 3½" **50.00**

Florentine No 2, sugar bowl, yellow **9.00**

Forest Green, pitcher, round, 86-oz **25.00**

Forest Green, tumbler, iced tea; 13-oz **7.00**

Fortune, bowl, dessert; pink or crystal, 4½" **4.00**

Fortune, tumbler, juice; pink or crystal, 5-oz, 3½" **6.00**

Fruits, pitcher, green, flat, 7" ..**50.00**

Fruits, tumbler, juice; pink, 3½" **12.00**

Georgian, butter dish, green ..**65.00**

Georgian, hot plate, crystal, 5" center design **20.00**

Harp, cake stand, crystal, 9"..**20.00**

Harp, saucer, crystal **3.50**

Heritage, bowl, berry; crystal, 5" **7.00**

Heritage, plate, sandwich; crystal, 12" **11.50**

Hex Optic, bowl, mixing; pink or green, 7¼" **11.00**

Hex Optic, platter, pink or green, round, 11" **11.00**

Hobnail, bowl, cereal; crystal, 5½" **3.50**

Hobnail, plate, luncheon; pink, 8½" **3.00**

Holiday, butter dish, pink **32.50**

Holiday, pitcher, milk; crystal, 16-oz, 4¾" **15.00**

Holiday, tumbler, iridescent, footed, 5-oz, 4" **10.00**

Homespun, bowl, pink or crystal, closed handles, 4½" **6.00**

Homespun, plate, dinner; pink or crystal, 9¼" **14.00**

Homespun, tumbler, pink or crystal, footed, 15-oz, 6⅜" **22.50**

Horseshoe, bowl, cereal; green, 6½" **19.00**

Horseshoe, plate, luncheon; green, 9⅜" **11.00**

Horseshoe, tumbler, yellow, footed, 9-oz **17.00**

Indiana Custard, bowl, berry; French ivory, 5½" **7.50**

Indiana Custard, plate, dinner; French ivory, 9¾" **18.00**

Iris, butter dish, iridescent ..**37.50**

Iris, plate, dinner; crystal, 9"..**45.00**

Iris, vase, pink or green, 9" ..**95.00**

Jubilee, bowl, fruit; yellow, handled, 9" **95.00**

Jubilee, plate, salad; pink, 7" ..**20.00**

Jubilee, tray, cake; yellow, 2-handled, 11" **40.00**

Lace Edge, bowl, cereal or cream soup; pink, 6⅜" **15.00**

Lace Edge, platter, pink, 5-part, 12¾" **24.00**

Lace Edge, tumbler, pink, flat, 9-oz, 4½" **13.00**

Laced Edge, bowl, fruit; opalescent, 4½" **25.00**

Laced Edge, mayonnaise, opalescent, 3-pc **115.00**

Laced Edge, plate, dinner; opalescent, 10" **50.00**

Lake Como, bowl, vegetable; white, 9¾" **30.00**

Lake Como, plate, salad; white, 7¼" **14.00**

Lake Como, shakers, white, pr **35.00**

Laurel, bowl, berry; white opal or jade, 9" **16.00**

Laurel, saucer, Poudre Blue ..**6.00**

Laurel, sugar bowl, French ivory, short **9.00**

Lincoln Inn, bowl, fruit; cobalt or red, 5" **11.00**

Lincoln Inn, comport, amber .**14.00**

Lincoln Inn, tumbler, cobalt or red, 5-oz **24.00**

Lorain, bowl, cereal; yellow, 6" ..**50.00**

Lorain, plate, dinner; crystal or green, 10¼" **32.00**

Lorain, tumbler, yellow, footed, 9-oz, 4¾" **25.00**

Madrid, bowl, salad; amber, 8" ..**12.00**

Madrid, pitcher, pink, square, 60-oz, 8" **35.00**

Madrid, platter, green, oval, 11½" **14.00**

Madrid, tumbler, blue, 12-oz, 5½" **35.00**

Manhattan, bowl, sauce; crystal, handled, 4½" **8.00**

Manhattan, pitcher, crystal, 24-oz **27.50**

Manhattan, shakers, pink, square, 2", pr **40.00**

Mayfair, bowl, cereal; pink, 5½" **19.00**

Mayfair candy dish, blue, $225.00.

Mayfair, cake plate, blue, footed, 10" **50.00**

Mayfair, plate, luncheon; green, 8½" **115.00**

Miss America, bowl, cereal; crystal, 6¼" **8.00**

Miss America, cake plate, pink, footed, 12" **35.00**

Miss America, plate, salad; green, 8½" **9.00**

Moderntone, bowl, cream soup; cobalt, 4¾" **17.00**

Moderntone, plate, dinner; amethyst, 8⅞" **10.00**

Moderntone, platter, cobalt, oval, 12" **50.00**

Moondrops, bowl, soup; cobalt or red, 6¾" **70.00**

Moondrops, creamer, amber, 3¾" **9.00**

Moondrops, plate, dinner; pink, 9½" **15.00**

Moondrops, tumbler, crystal, 12-oz, 5⅛" **13.00**

Moonstone, bowl, opalescent, cloverleaf shape **12.00**

Moonstone, creamer, opalescent **7.00**

Moonstone, sugar bowl, opalescent, footed **7.00**

Mt Pleasant, bowl, fruit; pink or green, footed, square, 9¼" **17.50**

Mt Pleasant, cake plate, black, amethyst, or cobalt, 10½" **35.00**

Mt Pleasant, saucer, black, amethyst, or cobalt **4.00**

New Century, bowl, berry; green or crystal, 8" **15.00**

New Century, plate, dinner; green or crystal, 10" **14.00**

New Century, tumbler, pink, cobalt, or amethyst, 5-oz, 3½" **11.00**

Newport, bowl, cereal; cobalt, 5¼" **28.00**

Newport, shakers, cobalt, pr ..**42.50**

Newport, sugar bowl, amethyst **12.00**

Nora Bird, candy dish, pink, w/lid, 3-part, 6½" **85.00**

Nora Bird, cup, pink or green ..**47.00**

Nora Bird, sugar bowl, pink or green, pointed handles, 5" **37.50**

Normandie, creamer, amber, footed **7.00**

Normandie, plate, luncheon; pink, 9¼" **12.00**

Normandie, saucer, iridescent ..**2.00**

Old Cafe, bowl, cereal; red, 5½" ..**9.00**

Old Cafe, pitcher, pink, 36-oz, 6" **60.00**

Old Cafe, tumbler, water; pink, 4" **10.00**

Old English, egg cup, crystal ..**7.50**

Ovide, candy dish, black, w/lid **40.00**

Ovide, shakers, green, pr **25.00**

Oyster & Pearl, candle holder, red, 3½", pr **40.00**

Oyster & Pearl, plate, sandwich; red, 13½" **35.00**

Parrot, bowl, berry; green, 5" ..**18.00**

Parrot, bowl, vegetable; amber, oval, 10" **55.00**

Patrician, bowl, cream soup; pink, 4¾" **16.00**

Patrician, cookie jar, amber ..**80.00**

Patrician, sugar bowl, amber ..**7.50**

Patrick, bowl, fruit; yellow, handled, 9" **40.00**

Patrick, plate, salad; yellow, 7½" **10.00**

Petalware, bowl, berry; pink, 9" **12.50**

Petalware, plate, salver; monax, 12" **17.50**

Petalware, sherbet, monax, low, footed, 4½" **17.50**

Primo, bowl, yellow or green, 7¾" **18.00**

Primo, plate, grill; yellow or green, 10" **8.50**

Princess, bowl, cereal; topaz, 5" **26.00**

Princess, relish, pink, divided, 7½" **20.00**

Princess, tumbler, iced tea; green, 13-oz, 5¼" **32.00**

Pyramid, bowl, berry; crystal, 4¾" **10.00**

Pyramid, creamer, pink **22.00**

Pyramid, sugar bowl, green ..**22.00**

Pyramid, tumbler, yellow, footed, 11-oz **65.00**

Queen Mary, bowl, cereal; pink, 6" **20.00**

Queen Mary, celery or relish dish, crystal, 5x10" **8.00**

Queen Mary, plate, dinner; pink, 9¾" **35.00**

Radiance, cup, amber **11.00**

Radiance, mayonnaise, ice blue or red, 3-pc **50.00**

Raindrops, bowl, fruit; green, 4½" **4.50**

Raindrops, plate, luncheon; green, 8" **5.00**

Raindrops, sugar bowl, green ..**6.00**

Raindrops, tumbler, green, 2-oz, 2⅛" **4.00**

Ribbon, bowl, cereal; green, 5" **13.50**

Ribbon, plate, luncheon; black, 8" **12.00**

Ring, bowl, soup; crystal, 7" ...**8.00**

Ring, goblet, green, 9-oz, 7¼" ..**13.50**

Ring, plate, sandwich; crystal, 11¾" **6.00**

Rock Crystal, relish dish, crystal, 2-part, 11½" **28.00**

Rock Crystal, tumbler, juice; red, 5-oz **50.00**

Rose Cameo, bowl, berry; green, 4½" **7.50**

Rose Cameo, plate, salad; green, 7" **7.50**

Rosemary, bowl, berry; amber, 5" **5.00**

Rosemary, saucer, green **3.50**

Rosemary, tumbler, pink, 9-oz, 4¼" **40.00**

Roulette, bowl, fruit; crystal, 9" **9.00**

Roulette, plate, sandwich; pink or green, 12" **10.00**

Round Robin, creamer, iridescent, footed **6.00**

Round Robin, sugar bowl, green **5.50**

Roxana, bowl, white, 4½" **12.00**

Roxana, plate, sherbet; 6" **4.00**

Royal Lace, bowl, cream soup; crystal, 4¾" **9.50**

Royal Lace, cup, pink **11.00**

Royal Lace, plate, dinner; green, 9⅞" **20.00**

Royal Lace, tumbler, blue, 12-oz, 5⅜" **60.00**

Royal Ruby, bowl, cereal; Old Cafe, 5½" **9.00**

Royal Ruby, candle holder, Queen Mary, 4½", pr **30.00**

Royal Ruby, plate, luncheon; Coronation, 8½" **6.50**

S Pattern, plate, luncheon; crystal, 8¼" **4.00**

S Pattern, saucer, yellow, amber, or crystal w/trims **2.00**

Sandwich (Hocking), bowl, Desert Gold, scalloped, 5¼" **6.00**

Sandwich (Hocking), bowl, salad; crystal, 7" **6.50**

Sandwich (Hocking), creamer, pink **20.00**

Sandwich (Hocking), plate, dinner; crystal, 9" **15.00**

Sandwich (Indiana), bowl, pink, 6" **3.50**

Sandwich (Indiana), pitcher, red, 68-oz **125.00**

Sandwich (Indiana), sugar bowl, amber, lg, open **8.50**

Sharon, bowl, vegetable; amber, oval, 9½" **14.00**

Sharon, plate, bread & butter; pink, 6" **5.00**

Sharon, sugar bowl, green ...**11.00**

Ships, pitcher, blue w/white decoration, ice lip, 86-oz **40.00**

Ships, tumbler, water; blue w/ white decoration, 9-oz, 4⅝" **9.50**

Sierra, bowl, cereal; pink, 5½" ..**9.50**

Sierra, plate, dinner; green, 9" **16.00**

Sierra, sugar bowl, pink **15.00**

Spiral, bowl, berry; green, 8" ..**11.00**

Spiral, plate, luncheon; green, 8" **3.00**

Starlight, bowl, salad; crystal or white, 11½" **16.00**

Starlight, plate, sandwich; pink, 13" **13.00**

Royal Lace, butter dish, green, $375.00.

Strawberry, butter dish, pink or green **140.00**

Strawberry, plate, salad; crystal or iridescent, 7½" **8.00**

Sunflower, cake plate, pink or green, 3-footed, 10" **12.00**

Sunflower, saucer, pink **6.00**

Swirl, bowl, cereal; pink, 5½" ..**8.50**

Swirl, plate, dinner, delphite or pink, 9¼" **10.00**

Swirl, plate, dinner; ultramarine, 9¼" **13.00**

Tea Room, cup, pink or green ..**45.00**

Tea Room, shakers, green, pr ..**50.00**

Thistle, bowl, cereal; pink, 5½" **18.00**

Thistle, plate, grill; green, 10¼" **18.00**

Thumbprint, bowl, berry; green, 4¾" **3.00**

Thumbprint, sugar bowl, green, footed **11.50**

Twisted Optic, bowl, cereal; all colors, 5" **4.50**

Twisted Optic, plate, sandwich; all colors, 8" **3.00**

US Swirl, bowl, berry; green, 4⅜" **5.00**

US Swirl, pitcher, pink or green, 48-oz, 8" **40.00**

US Swirl, tumbler, pink, 12-oz, 4⅜" **12.00**

Vernon, cup, green **14.00**

Vernon, plate, sandwich; crystal, 11½" **11.00**

Vernon, sugar bowl, yellow ...**21.00**

Victory, bowl, flat soup; amber, pink, or green, 8½" **15.00**

Victory, plate, bread & butter; blue or black, 6" **12.00**

Vitrock, bowl, fruit; white, 6" ..**5.00**

Vitrock, plate, dinner; white, 10" **6.00**

Waterford, cup, crystal **6.00**

Waterford, cup, pink **12.00**

Waterford, shakers, crystal, 2 styles **8.00**

Windsor, bowl, cream soup; crystal, 5" **5.00**

Windsor, butter dish, pink, 2 styles **45.00**

Windsor, sugar bowl, green ..**25.00**

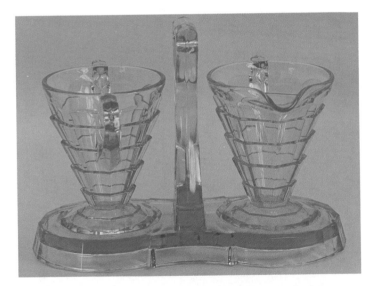

Tea Room, creamer and sugar bowl on tray, pink, $60.00.

Dionne Quintuplets

Scores of dolls, toys, books, and other types of memorabilia made to promote these famous quints are very collectible today. These five tiny girls were born in Canada in 1934, the first quintuplets ever delivered who survived for more than a few days after birth. King George V made them his wards and built them a private nursery near their parents' home where they remained until they were ten years old. The quints were used to promote products, appeared on countless magazine covers, and were otherwise commercialized, whereby, of course, they earned enormous sums of money for their once-poor parents. Today only three survive.

Book, We're Two Years Old, Whitman, 1936, G **12.00**
Calendar, Five Little Sweethearts, 1939, full pad, 16x11", NM **30.00**
Cereal bowl, stainless steel, names at rim, 6" dia **25.00**
Dish, New Home of Quints, gold trim, 5½" dia **25.00**
Doll, Dr Defoe, Madame Alexander, composition, 14" ...**250.00**
Doll, Marie, Madame Alexander, wrist tag, 12", EX **225.00**
Picture album, Dell, 1936, original price 10¢ **35.00**
Trade card, Puretest Cod Liver Oil, 1936, rare, VG **80.00**
Watch, paper & cardboard, elastic band, Japan **17.50**

Disney Collectibles

Though there are lots of collectors for this facet of character-related memorabilia and the early examples are now fairly hard to find and expensive, items from the '50s to the present can easily be found on your flea market outings, and their prices are often very reasonable. For more information we recommend *The Col-*

Calendar, 1938, 7x10¼", $30.00.

lector's Encyclopedia of Disneyana by Michael Stern and David Longest, *Stern's Guide to Disney Collectibles, First and Second Series,* and Longest's *Toys, Antique and Collectible.* Our advisor for this category is Judy Posner who is listed in the Directory under Pennsylvania.

Alice in Wonderland, ceramic figure sold w/watches, 1950s, 5½" **45.00**
Alice in Wonderland, marionette, composition, EX in original box **165.00**
Alice in Wonderland, purse, Alice, rabbit, rocking horse fly, 6x6", M.....................................**55.00**
Alice in Wonderland, trinket, Alice & flowers on lid, gold trim................................**65.00**
Babes in Toyland, sentry soldier w/gun, Marx, 1961, MIB..**35.00**

Cinderella watch stand, figural plastic, 5¼", $12.00.

Baby Thumper, figurine, standing, Evan Shaw, 1940s, paper label, 3", M **85.00**
Baby Weems, figurine, Vernon Kilns, M........................**525.00**
Bambi, pencil sharpener, Bakelite figural, M........................**95.00**
Bambi pitcher, child size, American Pottery, 1940s, M ..**175.00**
Bambi, soap figural, full color, 1940s, EX **35.00**
Cleo, valentine, mechanical, 1940s, M...............................**30.00**
Disneykins, display, 34 characters, Marx, MIB **450.00**
Disneyland, guide, Summer, 1974, EX **18.00**
Disneyland, sunglasses on Mickey Mouse mask card, 1960s, M...............................**30.00**
Donald Duck, figurine, reclining, Shaw Pottery, EX.........**165.00**
Donald Duck, pencil sharpener, celluloid, long-bill Donald, 1930s, EX **325.00**
Donald Duck & Ludwig Von Drake, salt & pepper shakers, figural, 1950s..............................**125.00**
Donald's nephew, figurine, baseball player, Shaw Pottery, 2⅞", NM........................**95.00**
Dopey, figurine, Leeds Pottery, rare, 6½" **85.00**
Fantasia, book, Ave Maria, hardcover, dust jacket worn, book M.....................................**95.00**
Fifer Pig & Practical Pig, salt & pepper shakers, ceramic, 1930s, pr.........................**75.00**
Figaro, salt & pepper shakers, pink, National Porcelain, 1940s, pr.......................**85.00**
Geppeto, figure, wood composition, Multi-Products, 5¾" ......**85.00.**
Goofy, twistable figure, Marx, EX..............................**45.00**
Grumpy, pin, wood composition, Multi-Products, 1938, M **45.00**

Halloween costume, Collegeville Costumes, Donald Duck, original price $1.98, EX in box, $30.00.

Ludwig Von Drake, bank, musicial figural, Dan Brechner, 1961, 6", NM **195.00**

Mickey & Minnie Mouse, tankard, embossed images, Behind Every..., Enesco **55.00**

Mickey Mouse, All Wood Mitt & Muffler Ensemble, Migson, 1940s, MIB **125.00**

Mickey Mouse Birthday Party Doll, 50th birthday, Remco, 1978, MIB.......................**95.00**

Mickey Mouse, brush, red, black & silver graphics, ©WDE...**45.00**

Mickey Mouse, Christmas ornament, glass, bust of Mickey on ball, 1940...................**75.00**

Mickey Mouse, Christmas ornament, glass, full figure, 1940s, M....................................**95.00**

Mickey Mouse, dinner bell, figural, Cavalier Silverplate, MIB..................................**95.00**

Mickey Mouse, fire engine, Sun Rubber, 1940s, NM **85.00**

Mickey Mouse, metal figure, Allied Toys, 1933, 2½", M w/ package...........................**95.00**

Mickey Mouse, picture cubes, W Germany, 1970s, M in carrying case box...........................**45.00**

Mickey Mouse, pin-back button, Buy Cote's Master Loaf, © WDE................................**85.00**

Mickey Mouse, plate, 50th Birthday, limited edition, Schmid, MIB................................**125.00**

Mickey Mouse, toy, Fun on Wheels, Marx, MIB **35.00**

Mickey Mouse & Donald Duck on seesaw snow dome, EX ..**60.00**

Mickey Mouse & Friends, lollipop jar, Dan Brechner paper label, 8", EX............................**150.00**

Mickey Mouse & Pluto, bisque figure, Mickey riding Pluto, 1930s, EX **145.00**

Minnie Mouse, rag doll, Dean, 1930s, 8½", EX original ..**695.00**

Mousketeers, girl's western playsuit, 1950s, in original box **110.00**

Pinocchio, snow dome, plastic, 1970s, EX **95.00**

Pluto, metal figure, Allied Toys, 1933, 2½", M w/envelope ..**95.00**

Pluto, night light, pottery, house is shade, WDP, 1960s...**125.00**

Pluto, salt & pepper shakers, Leeds Pottery, pr, EX.....**35.00**

Sleeping Beauty, book, Castle, full color, Disneyland, 1957, M.....**75.00**

Sleeping Beauty, book, Tell a Tale, Whitman, 1959, EX.......**22.00**

Sleeping Beauty, Colorforms Dress Designer, 1959, MIB.....**110.00**

Sleeping Beauty, game, Parker Bros, 1958, EX in box **45.00**

Sleeping Beauty, stamp book, 1950s, EX.....**50.00**

Snow White, bank, Wishing & Saving..., Enesco label, 1960s, 5¼x5".....**125.00**

Snow White & Seven Dwarfs, book, Whitman, #925, ca 1938, WDE, EX.....**55.00**

Tinkerbell, brooch, sterling, Disneyland souvenir, 1950s, M.....**75.00**

Tweedle-Dee, figurine, Shaw Pottery, 1950s, M.....**275.00**

Winnie the Pooh, figurine, Enesco, 1964, 5¼", EX.....**65.00**

Dollhouse Furnishings

Collecting antique dollhouses and building new ones is a popular hobby with many today, and all who collect these houses delight in furnishing them right down to the vase on the table and the scarf on the piano! Flea markets are a good source of dollhouse furnishings, especially those from the 1940s through the '60s made by Strombecker, Tootsietoy, Renwal, or the Petite Princess line by Ideal.

Bathinet, Renwal.....**10.00**

Bed, pink w/silver tracings, Renwall, 5¼".....**10.00**

Bed, twin size, brown w/molded ivory bedspread, Renwal ..**6.00**

Blanket chest, lid opens, Strombecker.....**9.50**

Bookcase, Tinietoy.....**75.00**

Chair, barrel shape, turquoise w/hand painting, Renwall ..**8.00**

Chair, blue satin, Petite Princess.....**8.50**

Vanity and stool, Petite Princess, MIB, $28.00.

Chair, Chippendale style, navy, Tinietoy **40.00**

Chair, dining; brown & white, Renwal, set of 4 ....**12.50**

Chair, wing style, white brocade w/ flowers, Petite Princess ..**15.00**

Chaise lounge, Petite Princess, NM **12.50**

Chest of drawers, block front, 4 drawers open, Marx **8.00**

End table, 'marble' top, Petite Princess **3.50**

Fireplace, clock & lamps on mantel, Miner Industries, Hong Kong **11.50**

Fireplace, Little Hostess **12.50**

Footstool, flocked tan, Strombecker **5.00**

Grandfather clock, w/door, Little Hostess **12.00**

Piano, baby grand; closed keyboard, Strombecker **12.00**

Radio, brown, floor style, Renwal **4.50**

Secretary desk, all doors & drawers open, Marx **25.00**

Sideboard, serpentine front, 4 drawers & 4 doors (all open), Marx, M **8.00**

Table, bedside; Strombecker ..**10.00**

Table, kitchen; ivory, Renwal **7.50**

Table, 6 straight legs, Strombecker **12.50**

Tub, pink w/blue faucets, Renwal **7.00**

Dolls

Doll collecting is no doubt one of the most popular fields today. Antique as well as modern dolls are treasured, and limited edition or artist's dolls often bring prices in excess of several hundred dollars. Investment potential is considered excellent in all areas. Dolls have been made from many materials. Early to middle 19th-century dolls were carved of wood, poured in wax, and molded in bisque or china. Primitive cloth dolls were sewn at home for the enjoyment of little girls when fancier dolls were unavailable. In this century from 1925 to about 1945, composition was used. Made of a mixture of sawdust, clay, fiber, and a binding agent, it was tough and durable. Modern dolls are usually made of vinyl or molded plastic.

Learn to check your intended purchases for damage which could jeopardize your investment. Bisque dolls may have breaks, hairlines, or eye chips; composition dolls may sometimes become crazed or cracked. Watch for ink or crayon marks on vinyl dolls. Original clothing is important, although on bisque dolls replacement costumes are acceptable as long as they are appropriately styled.

In the listings, unless noted otherwise, values are for mint or mint-in-box dolls in these categories: Annalee, Hasbro, Horseman, Ideal, and Mattel. Played-with, soiled dolls are worth from 50% to 75% less, depending on condition. Authority Pat Smith has written many wonderful books on the subject: *Patricia Smith's Doll Values, Antique to Modern; Modern Collector's Dolls* (five in the series) and *Vogue Ginny Dolls, Through the Years With Ginny.* (All are published by Collector Books.) See also Advertising, Dolls; Liddle Kiddles; Strawberry Shortcake.

Annalee

Annalee Davis Thorndike

made her first commercially sold dolls in the late 1950s. They're characterized by their painted felt faces and the meticulous workmanship involved in their manufacture. Most are made entirely of felt, though Santas and rabbits may have flannel bodies. All are constructed around a wire framework that allows them to be positioned in imaginative poses. The average doll may increase in value more than ten times its original price, depending on rarity, appeal, and condition. Refer to *Teddy Bears, Annalee's, and Steiff Animals* by Margaret Fox Mandel (Collector Books). Values are for dolls in mint condition.

Tennis Boy Mouse, 1972, 7", $75.00.

Aerobic Dancer, redhead in nylon leotard, 1984, 10" **150.00**

Baby Bear w/Bee on Nose, blue sunsuit, felt pads, 1985-86, 10" **200.00**

Bear w/Sled, felt mittens, knit scarf, 1986, 10" **30.00**

Bowling Mouse, yellow shirt, blue pants, 1984, 7" **75.00**

Boy Frog, paper-type tag, 1980, 18" **150.00**

Bunny w/Box & Daisies, white w/red ears & scarf, 1972, 7" ...**125.00**

Cheerleader Mouse, plastic megaphone, yarn pompon, 7" ..**200.00**

Cowboy & Cowgirl Mouse, he wears fur chaps, both have lariet, 7", pr **300.00**

Cupid, white felt wings, plastic quiver w/arrows, 1984, 7" **125.00**

Fishing Boy, red hair, burlap hat, wooden pole w/vinyl frog, 1983, 7" **300.00**

Gingerbread Boy, red shirt, rick-rack-trimmed jacket, 1984, 10" **150.00**

Gnome, white beard, pointed hat, 1978, 12" **300.00**

Indian Boy, feather in headband, bow & arrow, 1987, 7" ..**150.00**

Kitten w/Yarn & Basket, 1987, 10" **50.00**

Mrs Santa w/Cardholder Skirt, wire in hem, 18" **200.00**

Santa Fox w/Bag, fur-trimmed red felt jacket, 1981, 18" **400.00**

Scarecrow, 1984, 10" **325.00**

Skateboard Mouse, on green board w/wooden wheels, 7" **300.00**

Skunk w/Snowball, felt hat & boots, 1982, 12" **225.00**

Valentine Bear, Be My Honey Bear on shirt, 1985-86, 18" **175.00**

Wee-Ski, white felt suit, tinsel scarf, on skis, 1960, 7" ..**350.00**

Workshop Elf, plastic tool, 1980s, 10" **75.00**

Arranbee

Arranbee, Littlest Angel, plastic/vinyl, rooted hair, 10½" ..**165.00**

Baby Donna, plastic, latex & cloth, 1949, redressed, 17" **45.00**

Debu-Teen, cloth & composition, brown wig, sleep eyes, redressed, 18" **245.00**

Judy, plastic, blond wig in braids, blue sleep eyes, redressed, 19" **500.00**

Nancy, composition, molded & painted hair & eyes, redressed, 12" **185.00**

Nanette, hard plastic, mohair wig, sleep eyes, all original, 17" **295.00**

Peachy, brown plastic, molded hair, open hands, redressed, 10" **25.00**

Susan, stuffed vinyl, brown wig, blue sleep eyes, toddler legs, 15", M **65.00**

Taffy, hard plastic, caracul hair, sleep eyes, redressed, 17" **285.00**

Barbie and Friends

Barbie has undergone some minor makeovers since 1959 – the first one had just white irises but no eye color. Today they're almost impossible to find, but if you can find one in mint condition, she's worth about $1,500.00 – $1,000.00 more if the original box is with her. Refer to *The World of Barbie Dolls* and *The Wonder of Barbie, 1976 to 1986,* by Paris, Susan, and Carol Manos. Sibyl De Wein and Joan Ashabraner have written *The Collector's Encyclopedia of Barbie Dolls and Collectibles*; and *Barbie Fashion, Vol I, 1959 to 1967,* by Sarah Sink Eames is also an excellent reference. (All are published by Collector Books.)

Barbie, Ballerina on Tour, 1976, limited edition, MIB ...**100.00**

Barbie, Bubble Cut, 1962, red swimsuit, MIB **200.00**

Barbie, Busy Talking, 1972, blond hair, bibbed pants, G **50.00**

Barbie, Fashion Queen, 1963, gold & white swimsuit, G **35.00**

Barbie, Twist 'N Turn, 1967, salmon bikini & net cover-up, MIB **200.00**

Barbie, Walk Lively, 1972, red shirt & pants, MIB **100.00**

Barbie Color 'N Curl set, molded head & 2 wigs, M **325.00**

Barbie Goin' Camping set, 1973-75, M **50.00**

Barbie Going Boating set, 1973-76, M **75.00**

Barbie Olympic Ski Village, 1975, M **45.00**

Barbie Sport Plane, 1964, M **300.00**

Barbie Sun 'N Fun Buggie, 1971-72, M **100.00**

Christie, Twist 'N Turn, 1970, pink & yellow swimsuit, MIB **125.00**

Fashion Queen Barbie & Friends gift set, 1964, M **400.00**

Fashion Queen Barbie & Ken Trousseau gift set, 1964, M **500.00**

Francie, Quick Curl, 1973, long yellow dress, MIB **85.00**

Barbie Doll Case, cardboard, 1963, VG, $10.00.

Ken, Bendable Legs, 1965, red trunks & blue jacket, G ..**100.00**
Ken, Live Action on Stage, 1971, MIB **150.00**
Live Action PJ, red & purple mini dress, 11", EX **65.00**
Midge, Straight Legs, 1963, 2-pc multicolored swimsuit, MIB **400.00**
PJ, Live Action, '71, MIB ...**100.00**
Singing Chatty, plastic & vinyl, pull string for singing, 1964, 17" **35.00**

Betsy McCall

The tiny 8" Betsy McCall was manufactured by the American Character Doll Company from 1957 until 1962. She was made from fine quality hard plastic with a bisque-like finish and had hand-painted features. Betsy came with four hair colors — tosca, blond, red, and brown. She has blue sleep eyes, molded lashes, a winsome smile, and a fully jointed body with bendable knees. On her back is an identification circle which reads ©McCall Corp. The basic doll could be purchased for $2.25 and wore a sheer chemise, white taffeta panties, nylon socks and Maryjane-style shoes.

There were two different materials used for tiny Betsy's hair. The first was a soft mohair sewn onto mesh. Later the rubber scullcap was rooted with saran which was more suitable for washing and combing.

Betsy McCall had an extensive wardrobe with nearly one hundred outfits, each of which could be purchased separately. They were made from wonderful fabrics such as velvet, felt, taffeta, and even real mink fur. Each

ensemble came with the appropriate footware and was priced under $3.00. Since none of Betsy's clothing is tagged, it is often difficult to identify other than by its square snap closures (although these were used by other companies as well).

Betsy McCall is a highly collectible doll today but is still fairly easy to find at doll shows. The prices remain reasonable for this beautiful clothes horse and her many accessories. For more information we recommend our advisor, Marci Van Ausdall, who is listed in the Directory under California.

Betsy McCall Fashion Designer Studio **225.00**
Doll, nude, EX **75.00**
Doll, w/pink tissue & pamphlet, MIB, from $175 up to ..**200.00**
Doll, w/red ballerina outfit, EX **125.00**
First year skating outfit, complete **45.00**
Pamphlet, original **15.00**
Paper doll sheet, from McCall magazine, each **2.50**
Pony Pals outfit, w/scarf **30.00**
Pretty Pak case, empty **15.00**
Sun 'n Sand outfit, M **35.00**

Cameo

Baby Mine, vinyl, sleep eyes, all original, 20" **185.00**
Kewpie, hard plastic, sleep eyes, redressed, 1952, 16" **350.00**
Kewpie Doll Beanbag, vinyl & cloth, marked & tagged, 10", M **45.00**
Miss Peep, vinyl, w/hinged hips & shoulders, redressed, 18" **60.00**
Plum, latex & vinyl, 2 squeakers, all original, 24" **90.00**

Scootles, vinyl, marked & numbered on head, MIB, minimum value 185.00

Celebrities

Dolls that represent movie or TV personalities, fictional characters, or famous sports figures are very popular collectibles and can usually be found for well under $100.00. Mego, Horsman, Ideal, and Mattel are among the largest producers.

Angela Lansbury, Horseman, 1971, 6½", M 25.00
Billy the Kid, Durham, 1975, MIB 32.00
Black Knight, Mego, 1975-76, MIB 175.00
Captain America, Mego, 1975, MIB 150.00
Captain Patch, Mego, all original, 8" 65.00
Charlie Chaplin, cloth w/walking mechanism, Kenner, 1973, 14", EX 45.00
Cher, swimsuit, Mego, 1976, 12", photo on box, M 85.00
Cheryl Ladd, Mattel, 1970s, 12", MIB 35.00
CHIPS officer, John, Mego, 1970s, M on card 15.00
Diana Ross, Mego, 1977, 12¼", MIB 80.00
Dorothy Hamill, w/skating rink, Ideal, 1970s, MIB 40.00
Indiana Jones, Kenner, 12", MIB 175.00
Ivanhoe, Mego, 1975, MIB ..125.00
Jimmy Osmond, Mattel, 1978, 10", rare, MIB 95.00
Jimmy Walker (JJ of Good Times), 1975, MIB 45.00
Joe Namath, plastic & vinyl, all original, Mego, 7½" 85.00
John F Kennedy, Kamar, 1960s, VG 150.00

Michael Jackson doll in 'Thriller' outfit, 1984, MIB, $32.00.

Lieutenant Uhura, Mego, all original, 8" 30.00
Little John, Mego, 1974, MIB ..95.00
Madonna as Breathless Mahoney, Playmate, 1990, 14", MIB ..45.00
Mae West, F&B, 1982, 19", M in NM box 150.00
Mohammad Ali the Champ, Mego, 1976, 9½", M on card ...110.00
Sarah Brown (International Velvet), Kenner, 1978, 11", MIB 125.00
Shaun Cassidy of Hardy Boys, Kenner, 1970s, 12", MIB 45.00
Sir Lancelot, Mego, all original, 1974, 8" 50.00
Sitting Bull, Mego, all original, 1973, 8" 30.00
Six Million Dollar Man, Kenner, 1970s, 12", EX in box 35.00
Sonny Bono, Mego, 1976, MIB 85.00

Suzanne Somers, Mego, 1970s, 12", MIB **45.00**

Toni Tennille, Mego, 1970s, 12", MIB **35.00**

Wonder Woman, Mego, all original, 1973, 8" **15.00**

Eegee

Chubby Schoolgirl, jointed knees, sleep eyes, 1957, 10½", M ..**10.00**

Kid Sister, plastic, rooted hair, freckles, 9¼", M **10.00**

Lizabeth, composition, sleep eyes, 4 teeth, 1939, M, minimum value **145.00**

Mary Kay, plastic, open mouth/nurser, redressed, 1971, 10½", M **4.00**

Miss Charming, Shirley Temple lookalike, composition, 19", M, minimum value **265.00**

Play Pen Pal, vinyl, jointed hips, redressed, 1956, 10½" **5.00**

Playpen Baby, plastic, rooted hair, nurser hole in mouth, 1968, 14", M **5.00**

Effanbee

Ann Shirley, composition, marked w/name, original, 15" **250.00**

Babyette, cloth & composition, all original, 12" **300.00**

Brother, composition & cloth, yarn hair, all original, 12" **165.00**

Candy Kid, all composition, black, redressed, 12" **275.00**

Composition, painted eyes, molded hair, original, '30s, 9" ..**165.00**

Currier & Ives collection, 1978-80, each **70.00**

Fluffy, vinyl, 10" **40.00**

Girl, composition, open mouth, 4 teeth, sm breasts, redressed, 18" **185.00**

Grumpy, composition & cloth, straight legs, redressed, 1912-39, 12" **245.00**

Honey Walker, hard plastic, original ball gown, 19" **185.00**

Little Lady, composition, original majorette clothes, 1940, 14" **265.00**

Little Lady, composition & cloth, painted eyes, original clothes, 27" **600.00**

Mary Ann, composition & cloth, marked w/name, original clothes, 18" **350.00**

Patricia, composition, original clothes, 14" **385.00**

Precious Baby, Limited Edition Club, all original, 1975 ..**125.00**

Prince Charming, hard plastic, original clothes, 16" **450.00**

Regal Heirloom Collection, 1976-78, each **100.00**

Sugar Plum, cloth & vinyl, original clothes, 1964, 18" **40.00**

Susie Sunshine, all original, 18" **75.00**

Sweetie Pie, composition & cloth, redressed, 14" **65.00**

Twinkie, vinyl (thin), original clothes, 1980, 16" **40.00**

Hasbro

Adam, plastic & vinyl, molded hair, snapping knees, 1971, 9" **18.00**

Bonnie Breck, plastic & vinyl, rooted hair, 1972, 9" **30.00**

Daisy Darling, vinyl, plastic flowers, all original, 1968, 3" **10.00**

Dolly Darling, Wednesday, rooted hair, 1965, 4¼" **10.00**

Jamie (date for Dolly Darling), molded hair, 1965, 5" **10.00**

Leggy Jill, vinyl, rooted blond hair, all original, 1972, 10" **20.00**

Music, World of Love series, plastic & vinyl, 1971, 9" **15.00**

That Kid, plastic & vinyl, battery operated, redressed, 1967, 21" **85.00**

Hasbro Asleep Baby, marked 1894/J Turner, on head: Real Baby/H-23/1985, 21", $50.00.

Horsman

Cleo Pipsqueak, plastic & vinyl, rooted hair, redressed, 1967, 13" **20.00**

Floppy, dimples, foam body & legs, rooted hair, 1965, 18" **20.00**

Girl, plastic & vinyl, marked Ogigi on head, Pat Pend on back, 15" **25.00**

Loonie Lite, vinyl w/red eyes & nose, battery operated, 1968, 4" **10.00**

Pippi Longstocking, vinyl & cloth, freckles, 1972, 18" **40.00**

Teensie Baby, plastic & vinyl, painted eyes, 1964, 12" ...**6.00**

Twin Tot, plastic & vinyl, nurser, baby legs, 1963, 11" **9.00**

Yvonne, plastic & vinyl, key-wind music box, redressed, 1961, 12" **9.00**

Ideal

Baby Belly Button, plastic & vinyl, rooted hair, redressed, 1970, 9" **15.00**

Baby Betsy Wetsy, vinyl, open mouth/nurser, 1964, 9" ..**10.00**

Baby June, vinyl 1-pc body, open hands, 1956, 15" **60.00**

Betsy Wetsy, hard plastic & vinyl, tear ducts, 1955, 13" **75.00**

Cinnamon, w/hairdoodler, 1973, 12", NM in box **45.00**

Goody Two Shoes, plastic & vinyl, battery-operated walker, 1965, 18" **85.00**

Magic Skin Baby, latex & vinyl, rooted brown hair, 1948, 15" **15.00**

Penny Playpal, plastic & vinyl, posable head, 1959, 32" **185.00**

Plassie, plastic head, composition limbs, cloth body, 17½" ..**45.00**

Tiny Kissey, plastic & vinyl, press arms together for kiss, 1962, 16" **65.00**

Toni, hard plastic, sleep eyes, redressed, 1949, 15", minimum value **250.00**

Ideal Toni, sleep eyes, glued-on nylon wig, hard plastic, marked P-90 on back, original, 14", M, $250.00.

Velvet, vinyl & plastic, 'grow' hair
feature, 1969, 16" **60.00**

Knickerbocker

Donald Duck, composition, jointed
legs, 1936, 8½", EX **40.00**
Donald Duck, stuffed fabric, all
original, 1938, 17", EX ..**325.00**
Multi-Face, cloth & vinyl topsy
turvy, painted features, 1962,
12" **6.00**
Snow White, composition, glued-
on wig, bent right arm, 1939,
15" **225.00**
Woody Woodpecker, stuffed cloth,
1960s, 16", EX **45.00**

Mattel

Baby First Step, plastic & vinyl,
battery-operated walker,
1964, 18" **40.00**
Baby Secret, vinyl w/foam body,
Chatty ring on hip, 1965,
18" **25.00**
Baby Tenderlove, dublon foam,
open mouth/nurser, 1969,
15" **12.00**
Buffie, vinyl, rooted hair, holds
3½" Mrs Beasley doll, 1967,
10" **50.00**
Casper the Ghost, plastic & cloth,
pull-string talker, 16" **30.00**
Dancerina, plastic & vinyl, battery
operated, 1968, 24" **65.00**
Rock Flower Heather, has record,
1970, M in worn box **25.00**
Shogun Warrior Raydeen, 1970s,
23", VG in box **45.00**
Skipper & her Swing-A-Rounder
Gym set, 1972, M **250.00**
Tearful Baby Tender Love, 1972,
17", EX in box **25.00**

Remco

Baby Stroll-a-Long, plastic & vinyl,
battery operated, 15", M ..**20.00**

Mattel Saucy, rotate arms to make expressions change and eyes move, 16", $85.00; Black: $140.00.

Heidi That Grows Up, vinyl, 2
wigs, waist extends, 1966,
from 6 to 7" **8.00**
Linda Lee, vinyl & cloth, painted
eyes, sewn-on shoes, 1970,
10" **30.00**
Mimi, battery operated, sings,
19", M **37.50**
Snugglebun, plastic & vinyl,
rooted hair, redressed, 1965,
16" **15.00**
Tumbling Tomboy, 16", M **15.00**

Shirley Temple

Bisque, Japan, 7½" **265.00**
Composition, flirty eyes, cotton
dress, all original, 1934,
15" **675.00**
Vinyl, dressed as Captain Jan-
uary, 1958, 12" **200.00**
Vinyl, dressed as Little Red Riding
Hood, original, '50s, 15" ..**265.00**
Vinyl, dressed as Little Stowaway,
Ideal, 1982, 8" **45.00**

Vinyl, flirty eyes, all original, 1952, 15", M **265.00**

Vinyl, velveteen dress, replaced shoes, 1959, 12" **165.00**

Terri Lee

Baby Linda, vinyl, molded & painted hair, painted black eyes, 1951, 9" **150.00**

Little Debbi Eve, plastic & vinyl, rooted hair, 1963, 16" **6.00**

Terri Lee, hard plastic, painted features, 1950, 18" **185.00**

Walking Tiny Jerry Lee, hard plastic, caracul hair, 1950, 10" **195.00**

Uneeda

Baby Dollikins, vinyl, jointed body, 1958, 20" **45.00**

Baby Peewee, plastic & vinyl, painted features, 1966, 3" ..**5.00**

Bathtub Baby, plastic & vinyl, rooted hair, 1969, 16" **8.00**

Blue Fairy, plastic & vinyl, white hair, redressed, '60, 10" **35.00**

Coquette, plastic & vinyl, rooted hair, sleep eyes, '63, 16" ...**15.00**

Dollikins, plastic & vinyl, jointed limbs, 1957, 19" **40.00**

Miss Debteen, plastic & vinyl, plastic eyelids, redressed, 1962, 23" **9.00**

Needa Tottles, plastic & vinyl, rooted hair, 1964, 19" **5.00**

Pri-Thilla, vinyl, bent left arm, toddler legs, 1961, 12" ...**25.00**

Purty, vinyl, squeeze stomach & eyes squirt, head turns, 1961, 15" **25.00**

Tiny Trix, vinyl w/bean bag body, painted eyes, 1970, 7" **5.00**

Door Knockers

Though many of the door knockers you'll see on the market today are of the painted cast iron variety (similar in design to doorstop figures), they're also found in brass and other metals. Most are modeled as people, animals, and birds; baskets of flowers are common.

Basket of flowers, cast iron, original paint **65.00**

Betty Boop, cast iron, M paint, reproduction **22.50**

Cat w/arched back, brass **55.00**

Devil's head, brass, old **60.00**

Kissing couple w/roses, brass, 5½" **50.00**

Monkey, brass **35.00**

Oliver Twist, brass **22.50**

Parrot, cast iron, EX original paint **75.00**

Sea horse & shell, brass, EX..**80.00**

Woodpecker, tree backplate, cast iron, EX paint **60.00**

Doorstops

Doorstops, once called door porters, were popular from the Civil War period until after 1930. They were used to prop the doors open during the hot summer months so that the cooler air could circulate. Though some were made of brass, wood, and chalk, cast iron was by far the most preferred material, usually molded in amusing figurals – dogs, flower baskets, frogs, etc. Hubley was one of the largest producers. Refer to *Doorstops, Identification and Values,* by Jeanne Bertoia (Collector Books) for more information. Beware of reproductions!

Cape Cod Cottage, Hubley, 5½", VG **225.00**

Cat, Sculptured Metal Studios, flat casting, 13", EX **325.00**

Cottage w/Fence, National Foundry, flat, 5¾", EX **215.00**

Daisy Bowl, Hubley, flat casting, 7½", EX **165.00**

El Capitan, full-figure hollow casting, 7¾", VG **285.00**

French Girl, Hubley, flat casting, 9¾", G **165.00**

Fruit Bowl, Hubley #456, flat casting, 6⅞", EX **165.00**

Game Cock, full-figure solid casting, 7", EX **395.00**

German Shepherd, Hubley, full-figure hollow casting, 9¼", VG **185.00**

Girl by Wall, Albany Foundry, full-figure solid casting, 5¼", G **225.00**

Girl w/ Lg Bonnet, flat casting, 8" **295.00**

Halloween Cat, Greenblatt Studio, flat casting, 9¼", EX **325.00**

Lobster, flat casting, 12½", EX **375.00**

Old Fashioned Lady, Hubley, flat casting, G **225.00**

Peacock, flat casting, 5⅝", EX **385.00**

Persian Cat, Hubley, full-figure hollow casting, 8½", EX **175.00**

Pheasant, Hubley, signed Fred Everett, flat casting, 8½", EX **425.00**

Poppies & Corn, Hubley #265, flat casting, 7¼", VG **155.00**

Poppies & Snapdragons, Hubley, flat casting, 7½", EX ...**165.00**

Spanish Girl, Hubley, flat casting, G, 9" **165.00**

Springer Spaniel, flat casting, 6¾", EX **155.00**

Windmill, National Foundries, flat casting, 6¾", VG ...**175.00**

Woman w/Fan, flat casting, 9½", G **185.00**

Yawning Child, full-figure hollow casting, 9", EX **365.00**

Duncan and Miller

From the turn of the century until 1955, The Duncan and Miller Glass Company of Newark, Ohio, manufactured pressed glass dinnerware, glass animals, and opalescent vases in many different patterns and colors. Add 50% to values given below for etched designs.

Canterbury, amber; berry bowl, 5" **11.00**

Canterbury, amber; goblet ...**14.00**

Canterbury, amber; plate, 8" ..**8.00**

Canterbury, chartreuse; goblet, water **14.00**

Canterbury, color; relish, divided, 2-part **20.00**

Canterbury, crystal; cigarette box, silver lid **40.00**

Canterbury, crystal; creamer & sugar bowl **24.00**

Canterbury, crystal; goblet ..**10.00**

Rose Basket, Hubley, 11x8", $125.00.

Canterbury, crystal; plate, serving; 12" **35.00**

Canterbury, crystal; sherbet ..**8.50**

Caribbean, color; bowl, fluted sides, 2 handles, 3¾x5"...**30.00**

Caribbean, color; salt & pepper shakers, metal tops, 5", pr **75.00**

Caribbean, color; salt cellar ...**15.00**

Caribbean, color; tumbler, iced tea; footed, 11-oz, 6½" ...**40.00**

Caribbean, crystal; candy dish, w/lid, 4x7" **35.00**

Caribbean, crystal; wine **21.00**

Caribbean, crystal; relish, 2-part, 6" dia **10.00**

Caribbean, crystal; tray, 12¾" dia **17.50**

Fine Rib, color; pitcher, lg **85.00**

Fine Rib, color; tumbler, iced tea, flat **18.00**

Fine Rib, tumbler, juice **14.00**

First Love, crystal; bowl, scalloped, oval, 13" **75.00**

First Love, crystal; candle holder, 4½" **25.00**

First Love, crystal; candy dish, 3-part **32.00**

First Love, crystal; champagne goblet **25.00**

First Love, crystal; cocktail goblet **24.00**

First Love, crystal; cornucopia vase, 8" **85.00**

First Love, crystal; creamer & sugar bowl, lg **45.00**

First Love, crystal; goblet, 7" ..**27.00**

First Love, crystal; plate, #111, 13" **65.00**

First Love, crystal; plate, 2 handles, 11" **50.00**

First Love, crystal; vase, #115, 5" **30.00**

First Love, crystal; vase, urn; 2 handles, 7" **70.00**

Hobnail, blue opalescent; candy dish, 1-lb, 9½" **65.00**

Hobnail, crystal; decanter lamp, electric, 10" **35.00**

Hobnail, crystal; mug, cobalt handle, 3¾" **15.00**

Hobnail, crystal; plate, dinner; 8½" **15.00**

Hobnail, pink opalescent; tumbler, iced tea; flat **30.00**

Indian Tree, relish, 2-part, handled, 6" **20.00**

Language of Flowers, crystal; bowl, 11½" **35.00**

Language of Flowers, crystal; candlesticks, 3", pr **35.00**

Mardi Gras, crystal; cake plate, footed, 10" **75.00**

Mardi Gras, crystal; creamer, individual **25.00**

Murano, milk glass; bowl, oval, 10x7" **17.00**

Murano, pink opalescent; bowl, crimped, 11½" **85.00**

Sandwich, crystal; bonbon, heart shape, ring handle, 5" ...**15.00**

Sandwich, crystal; bowl, fruit; crimped, footed, 11½" **50.00**

Sandwich, crystal; bowl, salted almond; 2½" **12.50**

Sandwich, crystal; butter dish, w/lid, ¼-lb **40.00**

Sandwich, crystal; cigarette holder, footed, 3" **27.50**

Sandwich, crystal; coaster, 4½" dia **5.00**

Sandwich, crystal; cocktail **6.50**

Sandwich, crystal; creamer & sugar bowl **16.00**

Sandwich Lazy Susan with turntable, $95.00.

Sandwich, crystal; goblet, 9-oz **8.00**

Sandwich, crystal; hostess plate, 16" **62.00**

Sandwich, crystal; plate, dinner; 8" **10.00**

Sandwich, crystal; salt & pepper shakers, glass tops, 2½", pr **25.00**

Sandwich, crystal; sugar shaker, metal top, 13-oz **75.00**

Sandwich, crystal; tumbler, flat, 5" **9.00**

Sanibel, blue opalescent; relish, 2-part, 8¾" **35.00**

Sanibel, color; nappy, 6½" **20.00**

Sanibel, pink opalescent; celery, 9" **45.00**

Ships, amber; plate, 8" **16.00**

Ships, green; plate, 8" **18.00**

Spiral Flutes, color; bowl, bouillon; 3¾" **15.00**

Spiral Flutes, color; bowl, nappy; 11" **30.00**

Spiral Flutes, color; compote, 4⅛" **15.00**

Spiral Flutes, color; cup & saucer **15.00**

Spiral Flutes, color; platter, oval, 11" **32.50**

Spiral Flutes, crystal; bowl, nappy, 8" **15.00**

Starlight, cocktail, #D8 ....**20.00**

Sylvan, crystal; plate, 7¼" **7.50**

Tear Drop, crystal; candy dish, heart shape, 7½" **22.00**

Tear Drop, crystal; cheese & cracker set, 2-pc **42.50**

Tear Drop, crystal; plate, torte; rolled edge, 16" **37.50**

Teardrop, crystal; ashtray, individual **5.00**

Teardrop, crystal; bowl, divided, 6" **6.00**

Teardrop, crystal; bowl, oval, 6" long **7.00**

Teardrop, crystal; bowl, salad; 12" **35.00**

Teardrop, crystal; bowl, salad;

9" **27.00**

Teardrop, crystal; claret, 5½"..**16.00**

Teardrop, crystal; comport, 2 handles, 6" **12.00**

Teardrop, crystal; creamer & sugar bowl, 6-oz **12.00**

Teardrop, crystal; goblet, champagne; 5" **7.00**

Teardrop, crystal; ice bucket, footed **30.00**

Teardrop, crystal; marmalade, w/ lid **37.00**

Teardrop, crystal; nappy, 2 handles, 6½" **8.00**

Teardrop, crystal; nut dish, 2-part, handled, 6" **11.00**

Teardrop, crystal; pitcher, lg **95.00**

Teardrop, crystal; plate, canape; 6¼" **10.00**

Teardrop, crystal; plate, 6½" ..**3.00**

Teardrop, crystal; plate, 7½" ..**4.00**

Teardrop, crystal; relish, 3-part, oval, 12" **25.00**

Teardrop, crystal; saucer, demitasse; 4½" **7.00**

Teardrop, crystal; tumbler, footed, 12-oz, 5¼" **11.00**

Teardrop, crystal; tumbler, flat, 5¾" **14.00**

Teardrop, crystal; wine goblet, #5301, 4¾" **20.00**

Terrace, cobalt; plate w/handles, 5"....................................**35.00**

Terrace, color; ashtray, square, sm **28.00**

Terrace, color; cup & saucer ..**65.00**

Terrace, color; tumbler, juice; flat **32.00**

Touraine, crystal; goblet, water ..**8.00**

Willow, crystal; sherbet or champagne, 4¾" **14.00**

Egg Cups

For generations Europeans and Americans ate their eggs from an egg cup. A soft-boiled egg was put in the cup and the shell gently tapped so that the top third could be removed and the egg consumed. Some egg cups were double-ended; the end that was not in use became the base. The smaller end was for a boiled egg that was eaten from the shell and the larger for eggs (either poached or boiled) that were to be eaten by 'toast dunkers,' a perfectly acceptable social practice at this time.

Today's collectors find ceramic figural egg cups make very interesting collectibles. The majority are shaped like chickens (hens and roosters), ducks, and birds; those in the shapes of other animals, people, or characters are highly prized. Our advisor for this category is Carol Silagyi, who is listed in the Directory under New Jersey.

Chick pulling a cart, Japanese mark, 2", $6.00.

Chicken, English **10.00**
Chicken, Keele St Pottery, English **12.00**
Cottage Ware, square base, unmarked, English **14.00**
Elephant, English **15.00**
Girl w/egg (separate salt shaker), unmarked **15.00**
Humpty Dumpty, Japan **16.00**
Lady, hat ashtray, Japan **12.00**
Man, hat salt shaker, Japan ..**12.00**
Miss Cutie Pie, yellow, blue or pink, Napco, each **10.00**

Woman, w/hat pepper shaker, Japan **12.00**

Egg Timers

Figural egg timers were produced primarily during the 1930s and 1940s and were made mainly in Japan or Germany; some are marked accordingly. Figures can range from maidens to animals and from clowns to bellboys – the variety is almost limitless. Many figurals no longer have the timer piece (sand tube), but they are still easily recognizable by a hole that goes through a back portion of the figure or the stub of a hand or arm. This is where the egg-timer tube was once inserted. These sand tubes were made of thin glass and easily broken. Figurals generally range in size from 3" to 5". Almost all are made of ceramic (china or bisque) and are either painted in one solid color or in detail.

Listings below are for egg timers with their tubes present and intact. Our advisor is Jeannie Greenfield; she is listed in the Directory under Pennsylvania.

Amish woman w/churn, painted cast metal, John Wright Inc, ca '60s, 2x3" **20.00**
Bellboy holds phone, timer at side, Japan, 3" **15.00**
Black chef, sitting, timer in right hand, Germany, 3" **35.00**
Goebel, double, chef & lady baker, #E240, incised crown mark, 1935-49 ....**65.00**
Goebel, double, Friar Tuck, #E96, 1960-63, 3½" **50.00**
Goebel, double, rabbits, 1 is green, 1 is blue, #E229, 1972-79, 3¾" **55.00**

Goebel, double chicks, #E230, 1972-1979, 2¼", $40.00.

Goebel, single, chimney sweep, #81501, 1972, 3½" **45.00**
Goebel, single, Friar Tuck, #E104, 1959, 3½" **40.00**
Parlor maid, talking on phone, timer at side, Japan, 3" ..**12.00**
Swami, red jacket, green turban, timer in right hand, Germany, 3" **20.00**

Elvis Presley

The King of Rock and Roll, the greatest entertainer of all time (and not many would disagree with that), Elvis remains just as popular today as he was at the height of his career. In just the past few months, values for Elvis collectibles have skyrocketed. The early items marked 'Elvis Presley Enterprises' bearing a 1956 or 1957 date are the most valuable. Paper goods such as magazines, menus from Las Vegas hotels, ticket stubs, etc., make up a large part of any Elvis collection, and are much less expensive. His records were sold in abundance, so unless you find an original Sun label (some are worth $500.00), a colored vinyl or a promotional cut, or EPs and LPs in wonderful condition, don't pay much! The picture sleeves are usually worth much more than the record itself!

Our advisor is Rosalind Cranor, author of *Elvis Collectibles* and *Best of Elvis Collectibles* (Overmountain Press); see the Directory under Virginia for ordering information.

Ashtray/coaster, black & white, 1956, 3½" dia, NM **300.00**
Ballpoint pen, souvenir from Las Vegas, EX **35.00**
Banner, paper, from Las Vegas Hilton **120.00**
Billfold, EP Enterprises, 1956, EX **500.00**
Booklet, A Legendary Performer, EX **12.00**
Booklet, Memories of Elvis ..**10.00**
Bracelet, dog tag style, '60s ..**20.00**
Bracelet, silver, w/6 figural charms **210.00**
Bubble gum cards, #1-46, Ask Elvis series, 1956, each **10.00**
Bust, plastic, 4½" **50.00**
Candy cards, Holland, mid to late '50s, 1¾x2¾" **14.00**
Catalog, Elvis' Christmas Special, 1967 ....**60.00**
Catalog, RCA Victor Records, full color, 1967, 3½x7" **20.00**
Christmas ornament, Blue Hawaii, paper **37.50**
Doll, white outfit, guitar, & microphone, 1984, 12", MIB **70.00**
Fan club button, 'I Like Elvis & His RCA Records,' pink & black **80.00**
Fan club publication, Elvis World, #1, March 1969 ....**20.00**
Guitar, Love Me Tender, 4 or 6-string, Emenee, w/original case, EX **1,500.00**

Lobby card, GI Blues, full color, 11x14" **20.00**
Lobby card, Harum Scarum ..**35.00**
Lobby card, King Creole **25.00**
Lobby card, Wild in the Country, full color, 11x14" **20.00**
Magazine, Confidential, 1957..**20.00**
Magazine, Green Valley Record Store 1978, bound-in record, EX **15.00**
Magazine, Look, May 4, 1971 ..**20.00**
Magazine, Modern Teen, July 1960 ....**20.00**

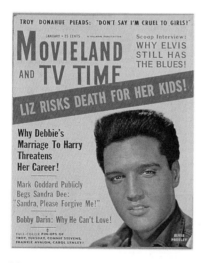

Magazine, Movieland and TV Time, January 1961, EX, $20.00.

Magazine, Movieland, February 1957 ....**25.00**
Magazine, People, January 13, 1975 ....**15.00**
Magazine, Photoplay, November, 1974 ....**10.00**
Magazine, TV Star Parade, July 1958 ....**25.00**
Menu, used at International Hotel in Las Vegas, 1970 ....**95.00**
Menu, used at Sahara Tahoe Hotel, record shape, 1973 ....**30.00**
Mug, glass, GI Blues **225.00**

Paperback, Wild in the Country, EX **25.00**
Patch, iron-on, red & white heart-shape **40.00**
Photograph, Moss Photo Service, full color, 8x10" **30.00**
Pin-back button, I Like Elvis, celluloid, 1956, 3½", NM ...**45.00**
Pocket calendar, RCA 1963 ..**60.00**
Pocket mirror, concert souvenir, 3⅜" dia **20.00**
Postcard, Easter Greetings, full color, 1967, 3½x5½" **15.00**
Postcard, Seasons Greetings, full color, 1966 ....**40.00**
Poster, color, All Stars Shows ..**40.00**
Poster, Fun in Acapulco, 1-sheet, EX **60.00**
Poster, Kid Galahad, 1-sheet ..**75.00**
Poster, King Creole, 27x41"..**275.00**
Poster, Kissin' Cousins, 27x41", EX **60.00**
Poster, Love Me Tender, light cardboard, 30x40" **800.00**
Poster, Loving You, 3-sheet ..**300.00**
Poster, point-of-sale; Give Elvis for Christmas, RCA 1959 ...**45.00**
Poster, RCA promotion, black & white, 17x22" **85.00**
Poster, Speedway, 1-sheet **45.00**
Poster, Stay Away Joe, 3-sheet **80.00**
Pressbook, Charro! **25.00**
Pressbook, Fun in Acapulco ..**30.00**
Pressbook, Paradise Hawaiian Style **28.00**
Ring, clear crystal cabochon, 18k gold-plated, 1956 ....**85.00**
Ring, metal, w/picture of Elvis Presley, England **18.00**
Sewing kit **55.00**
Sheet music, A House That Has Everything **15.00**
Sheet music, All Shook Up ..**35.00**
Sheet music, His Latest Flame, NM **20.00**
Sheet music, I Want To Be Free, illustrated cover, 1957 ..**20.00**
Sheet music, Jailhouse Rock ..**30.00**

Sheet music, They Remind Me
Too Much of You **15.00**
Still, GI Blues, black & white,
8x10" **8.00**
Still, Jailhouse Rock, black &
white glossy, 1957, 8x10",
EX **20.00**
Sweater clip, dog tag, no card,
early **160.00**
Trailer, Jailhouse Rock **125.00**
TV Guide, Elvis on cover, Sept
8-14, 1956, M **125.00**
Window card, Girl Happy **30.00**
Window card, Kid Galahad ..**40.00**
Window card, King Creole ..**150.00**

Ertl Banks

Fred Ertl, Sr., who was
already in the toy business, produced his first bank in 1981 – a
promotional item for the postal
service, the 1913 Model T #9647.
Thousands of other models have
followed. Some were made in
limited quantities, and these are
usually the ones that appreciate
the most rapidly. Those with oil
or beverage company labels are
favored. Be sure to preserve the
boxes they come in, since only
the boxes carry stock numbers.
Our advisors for this category
are Art and Judy Turner (Homestead Collectibles), who are listed
in the Directory under Pennsylvania.

Ace Hardware, 1918 Ford,
1989 ....**35.00**
Allis-Chalmers, 1926 Mack,
1984 ....**29.00**
Amoco Motor Club, 1931 Hawk/
Wrecker, 1992 ....**29.00**
Amoco 100th Anniversary, 1917
Ford, 1989 ....**30.00**
Anheuser Busch, 1926 Mack,
1989 ....**49.00**
Armor All, 1905 Ford, 1991 ..**32.00**

Atlanta Falcons, 1913 Ford,
1984 ....**35.00**
Bell System, 1913 Ford,
1982 ....**35.00**
Ben Franklin, 1932 Ford,
1987 ....**13.00**
Campbells Pork & Beans, 1918
Ford, 1987 ....**65.00**
Castrol Oil GTX, 1913 Ford,
1991 ....**24.00**
Cincinnati Bengals, 1913 Ford,
1984 ....**30.00**
Citgo, 1913 Ford, 1990 ....**54.00**
Co-Op (farm store), 1913 Ford,
1985 ....**29.00**
Dairy Queen, 1926 Firetruck,
1991 ....**27.00**
Diamond Salt, 1913 Ford,
1987 ....**55.00**
Diamond Walnuts, 1931 Hawk-
eye, 1991 ....**19.00**
Dominos Pizza, 1950 Chevy,
1991 ....**32.00**
Fanny Farmer, 1913 Ford,
1983 ....**35.00**
Forbes Magazine, 1950 Chevy,
1991 ....**29.00**
Gulf Oil, 1926 Tanker, 1990 ..**45.00**
Gulf Oil, 1932 Ford, 1991 ....**32.00**
Heartbeat of America, 1950
Chevy, white, 1988 ....**35.00**
Heinz 57, 1913 Ford, 1982 ...**75.00**
Hemmings Motor News, 1923
Chevy, 1992 ....**27.00**
Hershey Cocoa, 1905 Ford,
1989 ....**65.00**
Hires Root Beer, 1918 Ford,
1991 ....**29.00**
IGA, 1932 Ford, 1985 ....**45.00**
IGA, 1950 Chevy, 1989 ....**20.00**
Jack Daniels, 1918 Ford,
1989 ....**55.00**
JC Penney, 1926 Mack, '89 ..**30.00**
JI Case, 1913 Ford, 1990 .....**17.00**
John Deere, 1950 Chevy,
1989 ....**22.00**
Kraft, 1917 Ford, 1989 ....**35.00**
Lea & Perrins Steak Sauce, 1913
Ford, 1991 ....**25.00**

Lion Coffee, 1913 Ford, 1988.................................**49.00**
Lonestar Beer, 1918 Ford, 1991............................**45.00**
Marshall Fields, 1913 Ford, 1983............................**39.00**
Meijer Foods, 1913 Ford, 1985............................**23.00**
Michigan Sesquicentennial, 1913 Ford, 1987.....................**35.00**
National Van Lines, 1913 Ford, 1986............................**59.00**
Neilson Ice Cream, 1913 Ford, 1984............................**18.00**
Old Milwaukee Beer, 1950 Chevy, 1991............................**27.00**
Pennzoil, 1931 Hawk, 1992..**21.00**
Philadelphia Cream Cheese, 1913 Ford, 1988.....................**40.00**
Quaker State Oil, 1926 Mack, 1991............................**25.00**
Radio Shack, 1931 Hawkeye, 1991............................**29.00**
RC Cola, 1917 Ford, 1988....**35.00**
Safeguard Soap, 1950 Chevy, 1991............................**17.00**
Sears, 1913 Ford, 1984........**35.00**
Shell Oil Company, 1920 International, 1991....................**49.00**
Skelly Oil Company, 1931 International Tanker, 1992...**40.00**
Southwest Airlines, 1931 Hawkeye, 1992.........................**26.00**
Toymaster, 1913 Ford, 1984..**29.00**
Tractor Supply Company, 1932 Ford, 1984.....................**55.00**
True Value Hardware #6, 1905 Ford, 1987.....................**25.00**
United Hardware, 1917 Ford, 1991............................**17.00**
United Van Lines, 1917 Ford, 1988............................**28.00**
Walgreen Drug Store, 1913 Ford, 1991............................**23.00**
Wheelers, 1913 Ford, 1982..**35.00**
Winn Dixie, 1918 Ford, 1987.................................**25.00**
Yelton Trucking Company, 1913 Ford, 1986....................**25.00**

Fast Food Collectibles

Everyone is familiar with the kiddie meals offered by fast-food resturants, but perhaps you didn't realize that the toys tucked inside are quickly becoming some of the hottest new fun collectibles on today's market. Played-with items are plentiful at garage sales for nearly nothing, but it's best if they're still mint in the original package they came out in. The ones to concentrate on are Barbies, the old familiar Disney characters, and those that tie in with the big blockbuster kids' movies. Collectors look for the boxes the meals came in, too, and even the display signs that the restaurants promote each series with are valuable. The toys don't have to be old to be collectible. Though there are exceptions, loose figures are worth only about half as much as one still sealed. Our advisors and authors of a book on McDonald's® premiums are Joyce and Terry Losonsky, who are listed in the Directory under Maryland. See also Character and Promotional Drinking Glasses.

Figurines

Action Figures, Kid Vid, Burger King.................................**3.00**
Adventures of Ronald, Birdie, McDonald's, hard rubber, 1981, 2".............................**4.00**
Alf Tales, Little Red Riding Alf, Wendy's............................**3.00**
All Dogs Go to Heaven, Car Face, Wendy's............................**3.00**
Alvin & the Chipmunks, Theodore as disk jockey, McDonald's, 1990.................................**5.00**
Astrosniks, Drill, McDonald's, in package.........................**12.50**

Astrosniks, Robo Robot, McDonald's, molded plastic, 1983 ....**8.00**

Bambi, Thumper, McDonald's, 1988 ....**3.00**

Barbie/Hot Wheels, Barbie in Concert, McDonald's, w/paper scene, 1990 ....**12.50**

Barbie/Hot Wheels, Lights & Lace Barbie, McDonald's, 1991..**3.00**

Batman, Catwoman cat coupe, McDonald's, 1992 ....**2.00**

Beach Bunnies, girl on skates, Hardee's **2.00**

Beauty & the Beast, Belle, Burger King, yellow, M in package **10.00**

Berenstain Bears, Papa w/wheelbarrow, McDonald's, flocked head, 1987 ....**3.00**

Big Boy, baseball player, Frisch's, 3", M in package **5.00**

Captain Planet Flip Over Star Cruisers, Verminous Skumm, Burger King **3.00**

Carnival, Birdie on Swing, McDonald's, plastic, 1991 ....**4.00**

Fender Bender 500 Races, red & green car, Hardee's **3.00**

Fish Car, Long John Silver, any color, each **2.00**

Flintstone Rock n' Rollers, Betty, Denney's, M in package ..**4.00**

Flintstone Vehicles, Pebbles, Denney's **3.00**

Fry Benders, Roadie the Bicycler, McDonald's, bendable plastic, 1990 ....**4.00**

Funny Fry Friends, Sweet Cuddles, McDonald's, w/bonnet & bottle, 1989 ....**2.50**

Going Places, Hot Wheels, McDonald's, 1983, 14 different in series, each **4.00**

Halloween Hideaway, ghost in bag, Hardee's, M in package **3.00**

Jetsons, Elroy in orange spaceship, Wendy's **4.00**

Jungle Book, Baloo, McDonald's, marked Disney China, windup, 1989 ....**4.00**

Little Mermaid, Ursula, McDonald's, suction cup, 1989 ....**5.00**

Little Miss, Miss Sunshine, Arby's, yellow w/red bows **2.00**

Looney Car Tunes, Sylvester Catillac, Arby's **2.00**

Mac Tonight, Mac on scooter, McDonald's, 1988 ....**3.50**

Marvel Super Heroes, Spider Man, Hardee's, M in package **4.00**

Matchbox Miniflexies, Baja Buggy, McDonald's, soft rubber, 1979 ....**1.00**

McDonaldland Moveables, Ronald, McDonald's, painted rubber, 1988, 4" **6.00**

Muppet Babies, Baby Gonzo on airplane, McDonald's, 1990 ..**3.00**

Burger King, Tricky Treaters, 1989, Zelda Zoom Broom, Frankie Steen, and Gourdy Goblin, $3.00 each (loose.)

Muppet Babies, Fozzie on horse, McDonald's, 1987 ....**3.00**

Noid, Magician, Dominos, M in package **5.00**

Old West, Indian, McDonald's, hard rubber, 1981 ....**7.50**

Potato Heads, Slugger, Wendy's **3.00**

Raggedy Ann & Andy, Camel w/teeter totter, McDonald's, 1989 ....**6.00**

Runaway Robots, Skull, McDonald's, blue plastic, 1988 ...**6.50**

Safari Adventure, Safari Monkey, McDonald's, rubber, 1980..**1.00**

Sea World, Dolly Dolphin, McDonald's, 1988, 2½" **7.00**

Simpsons, Homer w/skunk, Burger King **4.00**

Space Theme, Space Aliens, Insectman, McDonald's, orange, 1979 ....**1.00**

Super Mario 3 Nintendo, Koopa Paratrooper Hops, McDonald's, 1990 ....**2.50**

Surfin' Smurfs, Papa w/surfboard, Hardee's, red **3.00**

Tail Spin, Sea Duck, McDonald's, 1990 ....**1.50**

Tiny Toon, U-E Gogo Dodo in bathtub, McDonald's, soft rubber, 1990 ....**3.00**

Undersea Happy Meal, alligator, McDonald's, marked Diener, 1980 ....**1.00**

101 Dalmations, Pogo the Dog, McDonald's, 1990 ....**3.00**

Miscellaneous

Bag, Arby's, Barbar in Kenya, 1991 ....**2.00**

Ball, Alvin's Chipmunk Adventure, Burger King, rubber, 1½" **3.00**

Boat, rubber band motor boat, Hamburglar, McDonald's, 1981 ....**10.00**

Book, My Little Book of Trains, Golden Books Classics **2.00**

Book, Poky Little Puppy, McDonald's, 1982 ....**5.00**

Book, Tom & Jerry's Party, McDonald's, 1982 ....**5.00**

Box, Long John Silvers, Treasure Chest, 1990 ....**1.00**

Box, McDonald's Happy Meal, Olympic Sports I, Boats Afloat, 1984 ....**3.00**

Box, McDonald's Happy Meal, Star Trek, Klingons, 1979 .....**16.50**

Box, Wendy's, Yogi Bear & Friends, 1990 ....**2.00**

Bracelet, Star Trek, McDonald's, 1979 ....**15.00**

Button, Be Safe Safe Kids, McDonalds, 1985, 3" **1.50**

Button, I Love McDonald's, white, red & black, 1989, 1½" dia **1.50**

Denney's, Stone Age Cruisers, any character, $3.00 each (loose).

Calendar, Ronald McDonald's Coloring Calendar, McDonald's, 1977 ....**10.00**

Christmas stocking, Fievel on ball, McDonald's, 1986 ....**5.00**

Comb, Grimace, McDonald's, 1980 ....**1.00**

Comic book, Shoney Bear & Friends, Shoney's, 1991 ..**1.00**

Cup, Crayon Squeeze Bottle, McDonald's, crayon-shaped plastic, 1992 ....**3.00**

Cup, Dukes of Hazzard, McDonald's, white plastic, 1982, 16-oz, each **5.00**

Detective kit, Ronald McDonald, 1982, 4-pc **8.00**

Doll, Fluffer, Taco Bell, stuffed plush **3.00**

Doll, Hamburglar, stuffed, McDonald's, 1972 ....**20.00**

Doll, Marvelous Magical Burger King, 13", EX **8.00**

Doll, Shoney Bear, Shoney's, stuffed plush **3.00**

Dolls, Shirt Tales, Digger, Hardee's, stuffed plush ...**3.00**

Finger puppet, Babar's World Tour, Queen Celeste, Arby's, pink **3.00**

Frisbee, Ronald McDonald flyer, blue script letters, 1980 ..**1.50**

Furskins, Farrell, Wendy's, stuffed plush, plaid shirt & blue jeans **5.00**

Hat, USA Olympic, cloth, McDonald's, 1984 ....**3.50**

ID bracelet, Big Mac, McDonald's, w/alphabet sticker sheet, 1979 ....**5.00**

Iron-on transfer, Star Trek, Spock, McDonald's, 1979, each .**12.50**

Jump rope, Michael Jordan Fitness Fun, McDonald's, 1992 ....**2.00**

Lego helicopter building set, McDonald's, 1984, 19-pc, M in package **7.00**

License plate for bicycle, metal, McDonald's, 1975 ....**5.50**

Magazine, Burger King, Kids' Club Adventures, any dated 1990, each **1.00**

Magazine, McDonaldland Fun Times, McDonald's, 1988, each **4.00**

McDonaldland Dough, Ronald mold w/modeling clay, McDonald's, 1990 ....**3.50**

Ornament, Little Mermaid, Flounder or Sebastian, McDonald's, 1989 ....**2.50**

Ornament, Norman Rockwell, McDonald's, brass, 1983 ..**6.00**

Ornament, Rudolph, McDonald's, stuffed plush, 1985, 3½" ..**5.00**

Ornament, Tiny Tim w/stand, McDonald's, Lucite, 1979 ..**7.00**

Paint book, Adventure on Volcano Island, Long John Silver ..**2.00**

Paint-by-number set, Cosmic Crayola, McDonald's, 1987, complete **3.00**

Pencil, Ghostbusters, w/case, McDonald's, 1987 ....**2.50**

Pencil case, Ron & Birdie, McDonald's, clear vinyl, 1984 ....**4.00**

Placemat, Flintstones, Bedrock Derby, Denney's **3.00**

Plate, Ronald McDonald Was Watering May Flowers, McDonald's, 1977, 7" **6.50**

Poster, Beauty & the Beast, Burger King, 30x40" **20.00**

Poster, Play Scrabble, McDonald's, cardboard, 17x60", M **10.00**

Puzzle, Captain Crook w/Big Mac, McDonald's, 1978, 12-pc **8.50**

Puzzle, Guess Who Makes the Biggest Splash, McDonald's, 1984 ....**12.50**

Ring, Star Trek, Captain Kirk, McDonald's, 1979 ....**10.50**

Straw, Captain Crook, McDonald's, blue plastic, 1978 ....**9.00**

Straw holder, Thundercats, Burger King **4.00**

Toothbrush, Fry Guy in shower, McDonald's, green plastic, 1985 ....**3.00**

Tote bag, French Fry, plastic lined & insulated, McDonald's **4.50**

Toy, World Wild Life, Koala bear, Wendy's, stuffed plush.....**4.00**

Watch, Duck Tales, McDonald's, w/ secret compartment, 1987..**3.00**

Watch, Big Mac, McDonald's, secret compartment, 1970s..........**2.00**

Fenton

The Fenton glass company, organized in 1906 in Martin's Ferry, Ohio, is noted for their fine art glass. Over 130 patterns of carnival glass were made in their earlier years (see Carnival Glass), but even items from the past 25 years of production (Hobnail, Burmese, and the various colored 'crest' lines) have collector value.

Aqua Crest, basket, w/handle, #1923, 10" **70.00**

Aqua Crest, vase, triangular, #36, 4" **25.00**

Beaded Melon, basket, blue opalescent, #711, 1949-51 ....**60.00**

Beaded Melon, vase, rose opalescent, #711, 8" **48.00**

Block & Star, jam set, milk glass, #5603 ....**30.00**

Chinese Yellow, mixing bowl, ca 1933 ....**32.00**

Coin Dot, bowl, honeysuckle opalescent, #203, 1948-49, 6" ...**45.00**

Coin Dot, pitcher, cranberry opalescent, #1924, 4" **38.00**

Coin Dot, tumbler, cranberry opalescent, #1447, 12-oz ..**25.00**

Diamond Optic, bowl, blue, rolled edge, #1502 ....**30.00**

Diamond Optic, salt & pepper shakers, amber, pr **45.00**

Emerald Crest, flowerpot, attached saucer, #401, 4½" **45.00**

Georgian, cup, amber, #1611 ..**12.50**

Gold Crest, tulip vase, 5½" ..**20.00**

Hobnail, candlestick, cranberry opalescent, #3870, each ..**75.00**

Hobnail, jug, lime opalescent, handled, 6" **70.00**

Hobnail, mayonnaise, blue opalescent, 3-pc set **60.00**

Hobnail, salt & pepper shakers, cranberry opalescent, pr ..**90.00**

Jade Green, compote, 6x6½" ..**40.00**

Lincoln Inn, creamer, cobalt ..**37.50**

Lincoln Inn, finger bowl, red ..**30.00**

Lincoln Inn, water tumbler, red, footed, 9-oz **24.00**

Peach Crest, basket, 7" **55.00**

Peach Crest, vase, #186, 8" ..**37.00**

Rib Optic, creamer & sugar bowl, green opalescent, #1604 ..**85.00**

Rose Crest, plate, 12" **37.00**

San Toy, bowl, etched, #349, 8½" **40.00**

Sheffield, bowl, French opal, crimped, #1800, 12" **38.00**

Silver Crest, basket, 7" **30.00**

Silver Crest, cake plate, low footed, 11" **45.00**

Silver Crest, mayonnaise, #7203, 3-pc set **35.00**

Swan, bonbon, green, #5 ....**20.00**

Fiesta

Since it was discontinued by Homer Laughlin in 1973, Fiesta has become one of the most popular collectibles on the market. Values have continued to climb until some of the more hard to find items now sell for several hundred dollars each. In 1986 HLC re-introduced a line of new Fiesta that buyers should be aware of. To date these colors have been used: cobalt (darker than the original), rose (a strong pink), black, white, apricot (very pale), yellow (a light creamy tone), turquoise, (country) blue, and seamist (a light mint green). When old molds were used, the mark will be the same. The ink stamp differs from the old – all the letters are upper case.

'Original colors' in the listings indicate values for three four of the original six colors – light green, turquoise, and yellow. Refer to *The Collector's Encyclopedia of Fiesta* by Sharon and Bob Huxford (Collector Books) for more information.

Ashtray, original colors **37.50**
Bowl, cream soup; '50s colors ..**55.00**
Bowl, cream soup; red, cobalt, or ivory **45.00**
Bowl, footed salad; original colors **190.00**
Bowl, fruit; '50s colors, 4¾" ..**26.00**
Bowl, individual salad; medium green, 7½" **72.00**
Bowl, nappy; original colors, 8½" **28.00**
Bowl, nappy; red, cobalt, or ivory, 9½" **45.00**
Candle holders, bulbous; original colors, pr **65.00**
Casserole, original colors ...**100.00**
Coffeepot, original colors ...**130.00**
Compote, sweets; original colors **45.00**
Compote, sweets; red, cobalt, or ivory **60.00**
Creamer, '50s colors **25.00**
Creamer, medium green **45.00**
Cup, demitasse; original colors **45.00**
Egg cup, '50s colors **120.00**
Egg cup, original colors **40.00**
Mixing bowl, #1, original colors ..**85.00**
Mixing bowl, #2, red, cobalt, or ivory **75.00**
Mixing bowl, #3, red, cobalt, or ivory **80.00**

Mixing bowl, #6, original colors **120.00**
Mug, Tom & Jerry; ivory w/gold letters **50.00**
Mustard, original colors **120.00**
Pitcher, disk water; original colors **75.00**
Pitcher, ice; original colors ...**75.00**
Pitcher, jug, 2-pint, '50s colors **90.00**
Plate, '50s colors, 9" **18.00**
Plate, calendar; 1954 or 1955, 10" **30.00**
Plate, chop; medium green, 13" **100.00**
Plate, chop; original colors, 15" **30.00**
Plate, compartment; original colors, 10½" **28.00**
Plate, deep; '50s colors **40.00**
Plate, medium green, 10" **75.00**
Plate, red, cobalt, or ivory, 10" ..**32.00**
Platter, medium green **80.00**
Sauce boat, original colors ...**32.00**
Saucer, medium green **7.00**
Shakers, original colors, pr ..**15.00**
Sugar bowl, individual; yellow **75.00**
Teacup, '50s colors **30.00**
Teacup, medium green **45.00**
Tray, relish, mixed colors, no red **185.00**
Tray, utility; original colors ..**28.00**
Tumbler, juice; red, cobalt, or ivory **32.00**

Medium teapot, rose, $175.00.

160

Tumbler, water; original colors **40.00**
Vase, bud; original colors **45.00**

Finch, Kay

From 1939 until 1963, Kay Finch and her husband, Braden, operated a small pottery in Corona Del Mar, California, where they produced figurines of animals, birds, and exotic couples as well as some dinnerware. Most items are marked. Refer to *The Collector's Encyclopedia of California Pottery* by Jack Chipman (Collector Books) for more information.

Pair of circus monkeys, ca 1947, 4", $85.00.

Bank, panda figural, 9" **60.00**
Bank, pig, floral decor, 10" ...**80.00**
Cookie jar, Pup, multicolor, 12¾" **200.00**
Figurine, choir boy, 7¾" **45.00**
Figurine, elephant, 5" **75.00**
Figurine, Hannibal the angry cat, 10¼" **150.00**
Figurine, Hoot the owl, 9" **95.00**
Figurine, lamb, 2¼" **35.00**
Figurine, peasant girl, 5½" ..**30.00**
Figurine, Pete the penguin, 7½" **80.00**
Figurine, squirrel, sm **45.00**
Flower bowl, low, 12" **55.00**

Salt & pepper shakers, turkey, brown w/gold & red, 3¼x3¾", pr **25.00**
Vase, footed, incised marks, 9" **45.00**

Fire Fighting Collectibles

Firefighting squads from the early 19th century were made up of volunteers; their only pay was reward money donated by the homeowner whose property they had saved. By 1860 cities began to organize municipal fire departments. Much pomp and ceremony was displayed by the brigade during parade festivities. Fancy belts, silver trumpets, and brightly colored jackets were the uniform of the day. Today these are treasured by collectors who also search for fire marks, posters, photographs of engines and water wagons, and equipment of all types.

Axe, pick head, wooden handle, 6-lb **24.00**
Badge, department name & number on silver-tone metal ..**25.00**
Bell, Simpson Electric, Canton MA, 110 volts, 10" dia ...**85.00**
Book, Fires & Firefighters, JV Morris, 394 pages, EX ...**25.00**
Bucket, galvanized, red, round bottom, EX **20.00**
Bucket, leather, original green paint, w/handle, EX **225.00**
Buckle, belt; San Francisco Fire Brigade, CA, brass, VG ..**50.00**
Button, Brooklyn Fire Department, brass, embossed lady w/axe, 1" dia **32.50**
Clamp, hose; Peerless, all metal **60.00**

Extinguisher, Badgers, painted label, pony size **70.00**
Extinguisher, Liberty, tin, dry chemicals, EX **30.00**
Gong, Fire Gong Rope Fire Escape Co, electromechanical, cast iron, 8" **65.00**
Grenade, Harden's Star, blue, round, empty **75.00**
Grenade, Red Comet, MIB ..**25.00**
Helmet, black aluminum w/leather front, Cairns **120.00**
Helmet, fiberglass, leather front-piece, EX **35.00**
Helmet, leather, low front w/front-piece, Cairns, NM **160.00**
Helmet, low front, tin, Senator **45.00**
Kit, Shur-Strop, metal case w/ 6 grenades, EX **115.00**
Lantern, Dietz, tin, mill type w/wire cage **40.00**
Lantern, Dietz King, brass, marked Dietz, Pat 07 ..**235.00**
Nozzle, AJ Morse, brass, 20" **25.00**
Nozzle, Akron Brass, foam, aluminum w/cord covering, EX **75.00**

Nozzle, brass, w/Ashworth shut-off, 26", EX **70.00**
Nozzle, Imperial, Akron Brass, 11" **40.00**
Nozzle, Samuel Eastman, leather handles, 16", EX **150.00**
Punch, paper tape register; Gamewell, brass, w/key, EX **140.00**
Rattle, alarm; single reed, 11" **50.00**
Reel, paper tape take-up; Gamewell, brass, VG **150.00**
Ribbon, convention; common variety, post-1900 ....**12.50**
Trumpet, brass, quality reproduction, 21" **85.00**
Wrench, combination spanner, Boston Coupling Co, 9½" **10.00**

Fire-King Glass

From the 1930s to the '60s, Anchor Hocking produced a line called Fire-King; various patterns and colors were used in its manufacture. Collectors are just begin-

Oven Glass hot plate in custard, 10¼" wide, $17.50.

ning to reassemble sets, so prices are relatively low, except for some of the jadite pieces that are especially popular. (Jadite is listed in its own category.) Refer to *Collectible Glassware of the '40s, '50s, and '60s* by Gene Florence (Collector Books) for more information. See also Peach Lustre Glassware.

Alice, cup, white w/red rim **5.50**
Anniversary Rose, creamer ...**4.50**
Anniversary Rose, plate, salad; 7⅜" **3.50**
Blue & Gold Floral, cup, white w/wheat & floral decal, 8-oz **3.25**
Blue & Gold Floral, sugar bowl, white w/wheat & floral decal, open **5.50**
Blue Mosaic, plate, salad; white w/mosaic decal, 7⅜" **3.25**
Bubble, plate, dinner; milk white, 9¼" **6.00**
Bubble, sugar bowl, crystal, open, footed **5.50**
Charm, bowl, dessert; ruby red **7.00**
Charm, saucer, forest green ...**3.25**
Fleurette, plate, bread & butter; 6¼" **2.00**
Game Birds, bowl, vegetable; 8¼" **11.00**
Golden Anniversary, creamer, white w/gold trim **5.50**
Golden Anniversary, egg plate, white w/gold trim **8.00**
Golden Shell, bowl, soup; white w/gold scalloped rim, 6⅜" ..**5.00**
Golden Shell, saucer, white w/gold scalloped rim, 5¾" **2.00**
Gray Laurel, bowl, dessert; gray w/laurel leaf band, 4⅞" **4.00**
Gray Laurel, cup, gray w/laurel leaf band, 8-oz **3.50**
Hand-Painted Anchorwhite, bowl, custard; 6-oz **3.25**
Hand-Painted Anchorwhite, bowl, mixing; Colonial, 6" **5.50**

Harvest, platter, white w/grain sheaths, oval, 9x12" **6.00**
Homestead, bowl, soup; white w/scroll design, 6⅝" **5.00**
Homestead, plate, salad; white w/scroll design, 7⅜" **3.00**
Honeysuckle, plate, bread & butter; white w/floral, 6¼" ...**2.50**
Honeysuckle, saucer, white w/floral decal, 5¾" **1.25**
Ivory, mug, no design, 8-oz **4.00**
Ivory, plate, dinner; no design, 9½" **6.50**
Ivory Laurel, sugar bowl, ivory w/laurel leaf band, footed, open **4.25**
Meadow Green, casserole, white w/floral, w/lid, 1-qt **4.50**
Meadow Green, platter, white w/floral, 9x12" **6.00**
Meadow Green, saucer, white w/floral, 5¾" **1.50**
Primrose, cup, snack set; white w/floral decal, 5-oz **2.00**
Primrose, plate, snack set; white w/floral decal, 6x11" **4.00**
Primrose Ovenware, casserole, white w/floral decal, w/lid, 2-qt **7.00**
Royal Lustre, creamer, ribbed w/scalloped edge **4.25**
Royal Lustre, cup, ribbed w/scalloped edge, 8-oz **2.25**
Sunrise, bowl, dessert; white swirl design w/red rim **4.00**
Sunrise, cup, white swirl design w/red rim, 8-oz **3.50**

Tulips mixing bowl, large, $15.00.

Swirl, bowl, cereal; ivory, 5⅞" ..**5.00**
Swirl, plate, dinner; blue,
9½" **7.00**
Swirl, platter, white, 9x12"...**11.00**
Swirl, saucer, pink, 5¾" **2.25**
Turquoise Blue, egg plate, gold
rim **16.00**
Turquoise Blue, plate, dinner;
9" **7.25**
Wheat, bowl, vegetable; white
w/wheat decal, 8¼" **6.50**
Wheat, cup, white w/wheat decal,
8-oz **3.50**
Wheat, utility dish, white w/
wheat decal, 8x12½" **6.50**

Fishing Collectibles

Very much in evidence at flea
markets these days, old fishing
gear is becoming popular with collectors. Because the hobby is
newly established, there are some
very good buys to be found. Early
20th-century plugs were almost
entirely carved from wood,
sprayed with several layers of
enamel, and finished off with
glass eyes. Molded plastics were
of a later origin. Some of the more
collectible manufacturers are
James Heddon, Shakespeare,
Rhodes, and Pfluger.

Catalog, Creek Chub, 1945 ..**45.00**
Catalog, Heddon, 1952 ....**25.00**
Catalog, Paw Paw, 1947 ......**25.00**
Fly rod, Heddon Black Beauty,
bamboo, 9-ft **75.00**
Fly rod, South Bend, bamboo,
9-ft **25.00**
Live bait can, curved, 1900 ..**15.00**
Lure, Al Foss Oriental Wiggler,
plastic, glass eyes **12.00**
Lure, Clark Water Scout, 1946,
2¼", NM **25.00**
Lure, Creek Chub Champ Spoon,
metal, painted eyes **22.00**
Lure, Creek Chub Jointed Pike,
1950, 5" **40.00**
Lure, Creek Chub Striper Pikie,
1950, 6" **30.00**
Lure, Deltoa Barracuda, 4" ..**15.00**
Lure, Foss Wigler #3, 1917, in
box **40.00**
Lure, Heddon Baby Vamp, 1931,
3½" **25.00**
Lure, Heddon Sam-Spoon #2160,
metal, no eyes **25.00**
Lure, Heddon Surface Minnow, 300
series, wood, glass eyes ..**20.00**
Lure, Heddon Tiny Runt, 1955,
1⅞" **10.00**
Lure, Jamison Twin Spinner
Bucktail, 1932 ....**20.00**
Lure, Millsite Paddle Bug, 1937,
2" **15.00**
Lure, Millsite Wig Wag, 1946,
3" **15.00**

Lure, South Bend Fish Oreno, NM in original box, $25.00.

164

Lure, Pal O Mine Jr, 1928, 3¼" **20.00**
Lure, Paw Paw Pikie, 1946, 3¼" **15.00**
Lure, Shakespeare Grumpy, wood, carved eyes **5.00**
Lure, Skipjack, 1958, 2½" **10.00**
Lure, Snook Pike Creek Chub, 4¼" **85.00**
Lure, South Bend Babe Oreno, w/feather tail, 2¾" **25.00**
Lure, South Bend Bass Oreno, 1915, 3¼" **25.00**
Lure, South Bend Sun Spot, 1941, 2½" **20.00**
Reel, Horton #3, non level-wind **90.00**
Reel, Langely Plug Cast, level-wind **12.00**
Reel, Meisselbach, Tripart, non-levelwind **25.00**
Reel, Ocean City Sea Girt, non-levelwind **15.00**
Reel, Pflueger Skilcast #1953, 1926, M **50.00**
Reel, Pflueger Taxie #3138, levelwind, w/braided copper line **20.00**
Reel, Shakespeare Marhoff #1964-HE, jeweled, level-wind **12.50**
Reel, South Bend Perfectoreno #750, levelwind **16.50**
Tackle box, Heddon, metal, 3-tray **20.00**

Florence Ceramics

Produced in California during the 1940s and '50s, these lovely figurines of beautiful ladies and handsome men have become items of much collector interest. Boxes, lamps, planters, and plaques were also made. Values are based on size, rarity, and intricacy of design. Refer to *The Collector's Encyclopedia of California Pottery* by Jack Chipman (Collector Books) for more information.

Abigail, 8¼" **95.00**
Annabel, 8½" **145.00**
Ballerina, 7½" **85.00**
Choir boy, black & white robe, 6" **55.00**

Cynthia, lace and fur trim, 22k gold accents, 9¼", $175.00.

Delia, 8" **95.00**
Delores **100.00**
Diane, 7¾" **120.00**
Douglas, 8¼" **85.00**
Irene, 6" **45.00**
Jeanie **115.00**
Jennifer, 8½" **130.00**
Jim, blue coat, leans on pedestal, 6¼" **85.00**
Joy **45.00**
June, planter **40.00**
Lillian, gold trim, 8" **110.00**
Lisa, rose, 6" **90.00**
Madelyn **135.00**
Marcie **70.00**
Martin, 10½" **125.00**

Matilda, gray w/green trim, 8¼" **75.00**

Patsy, planter, 6" **65.00**

Rebecca, seated, 7½" **100.00**

Rhett, fancy, 9" **100.00**

Vivian, green dress, holds umbrella, 9¾" **140.00**

Yvonne, plain **85.00**

Fostoria

Fostoria has been called the largest producers of handmade glassware in the world. One of their most famous lines was their American pattern, which was introduced in 1915 and continued in production until the plant closed in 1986. (Beware, the market is now flooded with reproductions. Know your dealer.) They also produced lamps and figures of animals and birds.

American, crystal; bowl, footed, 8" **57.50**

American, crystal; cologne bottle, w/stopper, 6-oz, 5¾" **70.00**

American, crystal; creamer, 9½" **11.00**

Baroque, blue; candlestick, 5½", pr **80.00**

Baroque, blue; plate, 14" **37.50**

Baroque, crystal; bowl, cereal; 6" **20.00**

Baroque, crystal; salt & pepper shakers, pr **45.00**

Baroque, yellow; mayonnaise, w/liner, 5½" **37.50**

Baroque, yellow; tumbler, juice; 5-oz, 3¾" **25.00**

Century, crystal; bowl, fruit; 5" **13.00**

Century, crystal; butter dish, w/lid, ¼-lb **30.00**

Century, crystal; plate, salad; 7½" **7.50**

Century, crystal; tray, muffin; handled, 9½" **25.00**

Chintz, crystal; bowl, cream soup; #2496 ....**37.50**

Chintz, crystal; candlestick, #6023, double **35.00**

Chintz, crystal; sauce boat, #2496, oval **67.50**

Chintz, crystal; tray, #2375, center handle, 11" **37.50**

American footed bowl with handles, 8", $85.00.

Coin Glass, amber; urn, #1372/829, w/lid, footed, 12¾" **80.00**

Coin Glass, amber; vase, #1372/799, footed, 8" **22.00**

Coin Glass, blue; lamp, coach; #1372/320, oil, 13½" **175.00**

Coin Glass, blue; shakers, #1372/652, w/chrome tops, 3¼", pr **45.00**

Coin Glass, crystal; creamer, #1372/680 ....**10.00**

Coin Glass, crystal; nappy, #1372/495, 4½" **18.00**

Coin Glass, crystal; plate, #1372/550, 8" **20.00**

Coin Glass, crystal; stem, wine; #1372/26, 5-oz, 4" **30.00**

Coin Glass, green; candy jar, #1372/347, w/lid, 6¼" **75.00**

Coin Glass, green; cigarette urn, #1372/381, footed, 3⅜" ..**50.00**

Coin Glass, green; sugar bowl, #1372/673, w/lid **60.00**

Coin Glass, olive; bowl, #1372/189, oval, 9" **30.00**

Coin glass, olive; candle holder, #1372/326, 8", pr **50.00**

Coin Glass, ruby; ashtray, #1372/123, 5" **22.50**

Coin Glass, ruby; bowl, #1372/179, 8" dia **45.00**

Colony, crystal; bowl, celery; 11½" **30.00**

Colony, crystal; plate, luncheon; 8" **10.00**

Fairfax, amber; plate, dinner; 10¼" **17.00**

Fairfax, green; sugar pail **28.00**

Fairfax, rose, blue, or orchid; candlestick, 3" **12.50**

Figurine, chanticleer, 10¼" ..**200.00**

Figurine, colt, kicking **185.00**

Figurine, deer, standing **40.00**

Figurine, donkey **250.00**

Figurine, elephant, lg **350.00**

Figurine, frog **35.00**

Figurine, hen **360.00**

Figurine, mermaid, 11½" ...**115.00**

Figurine, mother duck **25.00**

Figurine, plug horse **110.00**

Figurine, seal **60.00**

Figurine, sparrow **80.00**

Figurine, wood duck **550.00**

June, crystal; bowl, 10" **30.00**

June, crystal; plate, bread & butter; 6" **4.50**

June, rose or blue; candlestick, 5" **45.00**

June, rose or blue; saucer **7.50**

June, topaz; cup, demitasse ..**40.00**

June, topaz; platter, 12" **60.00**

Kashmir, blue; stem, wine; 2½" **40.00**

Kashmir, blue; sugar bowl ...**20.00**

Kashmir, yellow or green; cake plate, 10" **35.00**

Kashmir, yellow; cup **15.00**

Navarre, crystal; creamer, #2440, footed, 4¼" **20.00**

Navarre, crystal; cup **17.50**

Navarre, crystal; salt & pepper shakers, #2364, flat, 3¼", pr **55.00**

Romance, crystal; bowl, baked apple; #2364, 6" **15.00**

Romance, crystal; ice tub, #4132, 4¾" **57.50**

Romance, crystal; plate, sandwich; #2364, 11¼" **35.00**

Rose, crystal; ashtray, 3" **37.50**

Rose, crystal; bowl, mint; footed, 5½" **35.00**

Royal, amber or green; bowl, cereal; #2350, 6½" **15.00**

Royal, amber or green; celery, #2350, 11" **25.00**

Royal, amber or green; cup, #2350, flat **12.00**

Royal, amber or green; tumbler, #869, flat, 5-oz **22.50**

Seville, amber; bowl, footed, 10" **35.00**

Seville, amber; stem, cocktail; #870 ....**15.00**

Seville, green; cup, demitasse; #2350 ....**30.00**

Seville, green; tumbler, #5084, footed, 5-oz **15.00**

Trojan, rose; creamer, #2375, footed **22.50**
Trojan, rose; plate, salad; #2375, 7½" **9.00**
Trojan, topaz; ashtray, #2350, lg **40.00**
Trojan, topaz; saucer, #2375 ..**5.00**
Versailles, blue; sugar bowl, #2375½, footed **20.00**
Versailles, pink or green; celery, #2375, 11½" **35.00**
Versailles, yellow; bowl, baker; #2375, 9" **55.00**
Versailles, yellow; tumbler, #5098, footed, 5-oz, 4½" **22.00**
Vesper, amber; egg cup **35.00**
Vesper, amber; stem, water; #5093 ....**17.00**
Vesper, blue; plate, bread & butter; #2350, 6" **12.00**
Vesper, blue; tumbler, #5100, footed, 9-oz **30.00**
Vesper, green; ice bucket **60.00**
Vesper, green; platter, #2350, 12" **40.00**

Fountain Pens

Fountain pens have been manufactured commercially since the 1880s. Today's collectors value those made by well-known companies such as Waterman, Parker, and Sheaffer's, or those made of gold or set with jewels. Various types of pumping mechanisms were employed. The Pen Fancier's Club (See Clubs and Newsletters in the Directory) publishes a monthly magazine with loads of good information on this area of collecting; we recommend it highly.

Condition is extremely important in assessing value. Look for pens with all parts still intact and working, no ink staining or corrosion, and if repaired, make sure the correct replacement parts have been used. Our values reflect pens in this condition. Any defects greatly reduce their worth.

Chilton, marbleized jade, gold-filled trim, touchdown filler, 1929 ....**180.00**
Conklin, black, gold-filled trim, lever filler, 1934 ....**100.00**
Conklin Endura, marbleized gold, gold-filled trim, lever filler, 1930 ....**100.00**
Eversharp Doric, green-lined/ gold-filled trim, twist filler, 1933 ....**35.00**
Eversharp Doric Gold Seal, Kashmir Green, lever filler, 1931 ....**75.00**
Eversharp Skyline, maroon, gold-filled cap/trim, lever filler, 1942 ....**20.00**
Eversharp Skyline, royal blue, gold-filled cap, lever filler, 1945 ....**20.00**
Gold Bond No 4, marbleized coral, gold-filled trim, lever filler, 1930 ....**90.00**
Mont Blanc Masterpiece 12, black, gold-filled trim, twist filler, 1960 ....**225.00**
Mont Blanc No 24, black, gold-filled trim, twist filler, 1962 ....**200.00**
Mont Blanc 3-42G, black, gold-filled trim, twist filler, 1958 ....**170.00**
Parker Demi-Vacumatic, brown, gold-filled trim, 1940 ....**20.00**
Parker Duofold Jr, black, gold-filled trim, 1930 ....**120.00**
Parker Duofold Sr, red, gold-filled trim, button filler, 1925 ....**295.00**
Parker Parkette DeLuxe, red pearl/gold-filled trim, lever filler, 1935 ....**20.00**
Parker Vacumatic, black, gold-filled trim, 1946 ....**70.00**

Parker Vacumatic, gold pearl, gold-filled trim, 1935 ..**165.00**

Parker VS, Lustraloy cap, gray barrel, 1947 ....**35.00**

Parker 51, Lustraloy cap, black barrel, vacumatic filler, 1950 ....**15.00**

Parker 61, Lustraloy cap, blue, capillary filler, 1960 ......**80.00**

Sheaffer, black, gold-filled trim, lever filler, 1935 ....**20.00**

Sheaffer Craftsman #350, blue, gold-filled trim, lever filler, 1946 ....**25.00**

Sheaffer Imperial White Dot, black, touchdown filler, 1960 ....**25.00**

Sheaffer Jr, red-streaked pearl/ nickel-plated trim, lever filler, 1934 ....**50.00**

Sheaffer Lifetime White Dot, ebonized pearl, lever filler, 1934 ....**75.00**

Sheaffer Saratoga Snorkel, burgundy, touchdown filler, 1954 ....**25.00**

Sheaffer Statesman Feather Touch, burgundy, touchdown filler, 1949 ....**25.00**

Sheaffer White Dot, green, chromium cap, touchdown filler, 1950 ....**30.00**

Wahl, black chased hard rubber, roller clip, 1920 ....**45.00**

Wahl, gold-filled metal, wave design, lever filler, 1925 ..**45.00**

Wahl-Eversharp, jade green, roller clip, lever filler, 1930 .....**50.00**

Wahl-Eversharp Gold Seal, rosewood hard rubber, lever filler, 1928 ....**65.00**

Wahl-Eversharp Ladies Doric, Kashmir Green, lever filler, 1932 ....**30.00**

Wahl-Eversharp Miniature, blue pearl, gold-filled trim, 1931 ....**20.00**

Waterman, black, chrome-plated trim, lever filler, 1943 ...**15.00**

Waterman, red, transparent ends, gold-filled trim, lever filler, 1941 ....**150.00**

Waterman #0552, gold-filled filigree cap/barrel, lever filler, 1927 ....**125.00**

Waterman #3, silver & brown agate, lever filler, 1937 ..**20.00**

Waterman #32, blue & tan, nickel-plated trim, lever filler, 1930 ....**25.00**

Waterman #32A, red & silver, nickel-plated trim, lever filler, 1938.............................**20.00**

Waterman #4521/2V, sterling barrel/cap, lever filler, 1923 ....**40.00**

Waterman #54, black chased hard rubber, lever filler, 1915 ..**35.00**

Waterman Commando, black, gold-filled trim, lever filler, 1943 ....**20.00**

Waterman Taperite, black, gold-filled trim, lever filler, 1948 ....**80.00**

Waterman Thorobred, marbleized blue & red, lever filler, 1935 ....**50.00**

Franciscan

Dinnerware has been made by Gladding McBean and Company from 1934 until the present day. Their earlier lines have long been popular collectibles, especially Coronado (Swirl) which was made in more than sixty shapes and fifteen solid colors; and Apple, the ivory line with the red apple on the branch whose design was purchased from the Weller Pottery. Today collectors are becoming very interested in their later, embossed patterns as well. During the 1930s the ware was marked with a large 'F' in a double-walled square; a two-line mark was used in the 1940s, and after 1947 a circular mark identified their product.

Apple, ashtray, individual ...**12.00**
Apple, egg cup **18.00**
Apple, tumbler, 5⅛*" **22.00**
Coronado, bowl, cereal **12.00**
Coronado, candlesticks, pr ...**28.00**
Coronado, casserole, w/lid ...**28.00**
Coronado, chop plate, 14" **35.00**
Coronado, coffeepot, demitasse...............................**50.00**
Coronado, cup & saucer, demitasse **22.00**
Coronado, plate, 8½" **12.00**
Desert Rose, bowl, soup; flat ..**18.00**
Desert Rose, sugar bowl, open, sm **30.00**
El Patio, bowl, fruit **12.00**
El Patio, creamer **10.00**
El Patio, plate, 8½" **12.00**
El Patio, sherbet **10.00**
Forget-Me-Not, mug, lg **22.00**
Forget-Me-Not, plate, 6½" ...**10.00**
Fresh Fruit, bowl, vegetable; sm **15.00**
Fresh Fruit, pitcher, 1-pt **30.00**
Ivy, bowl, 8¼" **40.00**

Ivy, egg cup **18.00**
Ivy, relish, 3-part, 11" **45.00**
Meadow Rose, bowl, batter ..**50.00**
Meadow Rose, pitcher, lg **65.00**
Meadow Rose, plate, 8½" **18.00**
October, cup & saucer, jumbo ..**35.00**
October, platter, 12½" **35.00**
Strawberry, plate, 9½" **20.00**
Strawberry, salt & pepper, tall, pr **35.00**

Frankoma

Since 1933 the Frankoma Pottery Company has been producing dinnerware, novelty items, vases, etc. In 1965 they became the first American company to produce a line of collector plates. The body of the ware prior to 1954 was a honey tan color. A brick red clay was used from then on, and this and the colors of the glazes help determine the period of production. Refer to *Frankoma Treasures* by Phillis and Tom Bess, who are listed in the Directory under Oklahoma.

Coronado, teapot, 5¾", $40.00.

Ashtray, Cocker Spaniel, Desert Gold, Ada clay, unmarked, 3" **50.00**
Billiken, any color **75.00**
Bookends, Dreamer Girl, green, pr **275.00**
Bowl, Lazybones, 9" **8.00**
Candle holder, Oral Roberts ..**8.00**
Carafe, w/lid, all colors **20.00**
Donkey Mug, 1975, Autumn Yellow **25.00**
Jug, Golda's Corn, brown, dated 1951 ....**20.00**
Plaque, Indian, 3¾" **10.00**
Plate, Wagon Wheel, 9" **8.00**
Plate, Wildlife, Buffalo **50.00**
Salt & pepper shakers, Snail, Desert Gold, Ada clay, #558-H, pr **10.00**
Sculpture, cowboy boot, marked Frankoma Pottery **15.00**
Sculpture, greyhound, 6 petals on back of base, 1983 reproduction, 14" **15.00**
Tray, oval, #36, 12" **25.00**

Vase, stylized duck, cactus plant incised on back, ca 1930s, 6½x5½", $25.00.

Vase, Cactus, Red Bud **40.00**
Vase, collector; V-13, black & Terra Cotta, 1981, 13" ...**40.00**
Wall pocket, boot, Robin Egg Blue, #133, 6½" **7.50**

Fruit Jars

Some of the earliest glass jars used for food preservation were blown, and corks were used for seals. During the 19th century, hundreds of manufacturers designed over 4,000 styles of fruit jars. Lids were held in place either by a wax seal, wire bail, or the later screw-on band. Jars were usually made in aqua or clear, though other colors were also used. Amber jars are popular with collectors, milk glass jars are rare, and cobalt and black glass jars often bring $3,000.00 and up if they can be found! Condition, age, scarcity and unusual features are also to be considered when evaluating old fruit jars.

ABGM Co, wax sealer, aqua, 1-qt **35.00**
Acme, on shield w/stars & stripes, clear, 1-qt **1.00**
Atlas EZ Seal, aqua, 48-oz ...**15.00**
Atlas Mason, clear, ½-pt **3.00**
Atlas Mason Improved Pat'd, aqua, 1-pt **8.00**
Atlas Strong Shoulder Mason, aqua, 1-qt **1.00**
Atlas Strong Shoulder Mason, green, 1-qt **23.00**
Atlas Whole Fruit, clear, 1-pt ..**2.00**
Ball Eclipse, clear, 1-qt **5.00**
Ball Ideal, blue, ½-gal **5.00**
Ball Mason, light olive green, 1-qt **22.00**
Ball Perfect Mason, blue, square, 1-qt **10.00**
Ball Sanitary Sure Seal, blue, 1-qt **8.00**
CL Fancy Jar, 1-pt **22.50**
Clark's Peerless, in circle, 1-pt .**7.00**
Conserve Jar, clear, 1-pt **7.00**
Crown Emblem, aqua, ½-gal ..**7.00**
Empire, in stippled cross, clear, 1-pt **5.00**

Globe (embossed on side), Pat May 25, 1886 (embossed on lid), amber, 1-qt, $60.00.

Putnam Glass Works, Zanesville OH, aqua, 1-qt **32.50**
Root Mason, aqua, 1-qt **6.00**
Schram Automatic Sealer, in script, aqua, 1-pt **15.00**
Security, in triangles, clear, 1-pt **5.00**
Silion, in circle, aqua, 1-qt ...**12.00**
Stevens TN, Pat'd July 27 1875, aqua, 1-qt **72.50**
Tight Seal, in circle, Pat'd July 1908, blue, 1-qt **5.00**
Trade Mark Lightning, aqua, 1-qt **2.00**
Wears, on banner below crown, clear, 1-pt **14.00**
4 Seasons Mason, clear, 1-pt ..**3.00**

Furniture

Golden oak continues to be a favorite of furniture collectors; Victorian, Country, and Mission Oak are also popular, and flea markets are a good source for all these styles. After the industrial revolution, mail-order furniture companies began to favor the lighter weight oak over the massive rosewood and walnut pieces, simply because shipping oak was less costly. This type of furniture retained its popularity throughout several decades of the 20th century. Mission was a style developed during the Arts and Crafts movement of the late 1900s. It was squarely built of heavy oak, with extremely simple lines. Two of its leading designers were Elbert Hubbard and Gustav Stickley. Country furniture is simply styled, usually handmade, and generally primitive in nature. Recently, good examples have been featured in magazine articles on home decorating.

Refer to these books for more

Excelsior Improved, aqua, 1-qt **48.00**
Genuine Boyd's Mason, aqua, ½-gal **6.00**
Hazel HA Preserve Jar, clear, 1-pt **5.00**
Hazel Preserve Jar, ½-pt **38.00**
Hero over Cross, aqua, 1-qt..**48.00**
Kerr Self Sealing, clear, ½-pt ..**2.00**
Lamb Mason, clear, 1-qt **2.00**
LCG Co, wax sealer, aqua, ½-gal **22.50**
Leotric, in circle, aqua, 1-pt ...**4.00**
Mason's E Patent Nov 30th 1858, aqua, 1-qt **24.00**
Mason's Patent, clear, 1-qt **3.00**
Mason's X Patent Nov 30th 1858, aqua, 1-qt **28.00**
New Gem, clear, 1-qt **4.00**
Ohio Quality Mason, clear, 1-qt.......................................**9.00**
Pacific Mason, clear, 1-qt **20.00**
Pansy, panelled, clear, 1-qt ...**198.00**

information: *Furniture of the Depression Era* and *The Collector's Encyclopedia of American Furniture, Volumes I and II,* by Harriet and Robert Swedberg; *Antique Oak Furniture, An Illustrated Value Guide,* by Conover Hill; *American Oak Furniture* and *Victorian Furniture, Our American Heritage,* by Kathryn McNerney. (All are published by Collector Books.)

Oak lady's desk with swell drawers, applied carvings, early 1900s, 55", $850.00.

Bench, pine, primitive, weathered brown finish, cut-out legs, 61" long **150.00**

Cabinet, single file; oak, brass fittings, early 1900s, 53x18x 29" **475.00**

Candlestand, maple, turned column, replaced 18" top ..**200.00**

Cedar chest, waterfall style, veneers, 1940s, 22x19x47" **235.00**

Chair, arm; ladderback, 5 arched slats, new splint seat, refinished **175.00**

Chair, arm; quarter-sawn oak, S-curve back, tall finials, bentwood arms **195.00**

Chair, child's, oak, Mission style, saddle seat **45.00**

Chair, desk; splat back, pressed cane seat, cabriole legs, 1920s, 37" **65.00**

Chair, dining; oak, elaborate embossed back, 13 spindle rails, EX **275.00**

Chair, dining; oak, pressed wing pattern, restored cane seat **125.00**

Chair, side; Duncan Phyfe style, mahogany stain, 1940s, 33" set of 4 ....**225.00**

Chair, side; ladderback, 3-slat back, turned finials, worn rush seat **85.00**

Chair, side; mahogany, Hepplewhite, serpentine seat front, repaired **200.00**

Chair, side; oak, pressed back, cane seat, Windsor-type spindles, 44" **150.00**

Chair, side; oak, slat back, upholstered seat, 1920s, 37", set of 5 ....**325.00**

Dresser, oak, 3-drawer, 1920s, 32x18x40" **225.00**

Footstool, pine, worn green paint, primitive, 18" long **75.00**

Hall mirror, oak, plain, rectangular, 1920s, 32x21" **175.00**

High chair/go cart combination, maple, Heywood-Wakefield, 1950s, 41" **135.00**

Ice box, oak, 3-door, brass hardware, 1920s, 39x18x35" ..**395.00**

Magazine rack, painted metal, 1930s, 13x8x13" **18.00**

Pedestal, quarter-sawn oak, grotesque head, early 1900s, 33x12x12" **150.00**

Piano stool, oak, lg center post & 4 legs, claw & glass ball feet **125.00**

Rack, drying; poplar & pine, 3
mortised bars, primitive,
32x40", VG **95.00**
Rocker, oak, pressed back, cane
seat, turned spindles, 1920s,
36" **65.00**
Rocker, sewing; oak, 3-slat back,
upholstered seat **200.00**
Rocker, Windsor, high-back, 5-
spindle, refinished **450.00**
Sewing stand, Priscilla style,
mahogany, 1920s, 25x13x
12" **50.00**
Smoking stand, onyx & metal,
1940s, 28x13x13" **135.00**
Smoking stand, painted wood,
1930s, 28x12x12" **58.00**
Table, end; hard rock maple,
Heywood-Wakefield, 1950s,
22x30x21" **95.00**
Table, end; mahogany, oval w/
mirror top, ca 1940, 23x16x
20" **145.00**
Table, gaming; oak, scooped
troughs for chips, early
1900s, 29x36x36" **125.00**

**Oak cloverleaf table, early 1900s,
31x22", $135.00.**

Table, 3-tier; mahogany, tripod
base, 1940s, 42" **68.00**
Telephone stand, walnut veneer &
stain, upholstered seat,
31x27x18" **165.00**

Gambling Collectibles

By collecting gambling memorabilia, you can immerse yourself
in gambling and still have the
odds in your favor. Prices have
risen steadily and future interest
looks auspicious as countless
hard-pressed government units
look to legalized gambling as a
painless revenue source.

In evaluating these items,
add a premium for: (1) equipment
rigged for cheating, (2) items
bearing the name of an old-time
gambling saloon or manufacturer,
particularly of the American West
(e.g., Will & Finck, San Francisco;
Mason, Denver; Mason, San Francisco), as signed and named pieces
are worth at least 50% more than
unsigned ones; (3) items typically
found in American gambling halls
of the middle and late 19th century (parlor game items of whist,
bezique, cribbage, bridge, pinochle,
etc., are not as valuable as those of
faro, poker, craps, roulette, etc.);
and (4) gambling supply catalogs
which are dated and have many
large, colorful pages and good
graphics.

Not listed here but of interest
to many gambling collectors are
myriad objects with gambling/
playing card motifs: paintings and
lithographs, ceramics, jewelry and
charms, postcards, match safes,
cigarette lighters, casino artifacts
(ashtrays, swizzle sticks, etc.),
souvenir spoons, tobacco tins,
cigar box labels, song sheets,

board games, etc. Values given here are for items in fine condition. Our advisor for this category is Robert Eisenstadt, who is listed in the Directory under New York.

Book, Fools of Fortune by John Philip Quinn, 1890, EX ..**150.00**
Book, Foster's Practical Poker by RF Foster, 1905, EX **100.00**
Book, Official Rules of Card Games, Hoyle, US Playing Card Co, annual **15.00**
Box, combination game; early 1900s, from $25 up to ..**150.00**
Card press, wooden box w/loose boards & threaded wooden dowel **75.00**
Card shuffler/dealer, automatic, 1940s, 5x5x5", common..**20.00**
Catalog, Blue Book, KC Card Co, 50+ pages, 1930s-60s, any, from $20 to **50.00**
Catalog, Club & Casino Equipment, HC Evans & Co, 1935, 64 pages, EX **150.00**
Chip, bone, plain, solid color, set of 100 ....**15.00**
Chip, bone w/design or color border, 1mm thick, set of 100 ......**35.00**
Chip, bone w/engraving, 2-3mm thick, set of 100 ....**75.00**
Chip, Catalin or marbleized Bakelite, red, yellow & green, set of 100 ....**25.00**
Chip, clay, embossed, inlaid or engraved, each, from $1 up to..**3.00**
Chip, clay, plain, solid color, set of 100 ....**5.00**
Chip, clay or metal, w/casino name, minimum value **3.00**
Chip, clay w/molded design, set of 100 ....**15.00**
Chip, clay w/painted engraving, set of 100 ....**25.00**
Chip, clay w/white plastic inlay, set of 100 ....**20.00**
Chip, dealer; clay w/goat head, each **50.00**

Chip, dealer; clay w/jackpot cup in relief, each **50.00**
Chip, plastic, wood or rubber, no design, set of 100 ....**5.00**
Chip, scrimshawed ivory, marked 5 or 25, each **25.00**
Chip, scrimshawed ivory w/concentric circle design **10.00**
Chip, scrimshawed ivory w/quatro or floral design, each **20.00**
Chip rack, marbleized Bakelite, ice block type, 3x4x7", +200 chips **125.00**
Chip rack, marbleized Bakelite, ice block type, 3x4x7", no chips **75.00**
Chip rack, wood chest w/lid & pull-out rack, no chips, minimum value **35.00**
Chip rack, wood Lazy Susan (carousel) type, cover, no chips ..**10.00**
Counter, mother-of-pearl, etched, eliptical, 1½", 1mm thick ..**3.00**
Counter, mother-of-pearl, relief carving, 2½", 3mm thick ..**35.00**
Dice, ivory, ⅝", pr **55.00**
Dice, poker; celluloid, card symbols on sides, set of 5 ....**10.00**
Dice cage, felt-lined cardboard, thin wire & metal **25.00**
Dice cage, hide drums, heavy chrome, 9x14" **300.00**
Dice cage, hide drums, heavy metal & Catalin, 5x10" **100.00**
Dice cup, ivory **100.00**
Dice cup, leather **15.00**
Faro dealing box, metal, open top, spring for cards, minimum value **200.00**
Faro layout, cloth attached to wood board, 40x16x1", minimum value **300.00**
Holdout, cuff link w/clip, metal, Jewell, Pat 1899, 2½" **20.00**
Keno goose, polished walnut bowl between posts, 13x24" ..**500.00**
Playing cards, faro; poker size w/square edges, set of 52, minimum **50.00**

Roulette wheel, brown Bakelite wheel & bowl, 9" **25.00**

Roulette wheel, toy; plastic & cardboard, 1930s, 4" **15.00**

Roulette wheel, 10" wood bowl w/ wheel & simple design ..**90.00**

Roulette wheel, 24" wood bowl w/elaborate inlays & veneer, chrome trim **600.00**

Wheel of fortune, crude carnival type, from $25 up to **65.00**

Games

The ideal collectible game seems to be one that combines playability (i.e., good strategy, interaction, surprise, etc.) with interesting graphics and unique components. Especially sought-after are the very old games from the 19th and early 20th centuries as well as those relating to early or popular TV shows and movies. As always, value depends on rarity and condition of the box and playing pieces. Our games advisor is Phil McEntee, who is listed in the Directory under Pennsylvania. See also Character Collectibles.

ABC Monday Night Football, Aurora, 1972, VG **15.00**

Annie Oakley, Milton Bradley, 1960, complete, VG **25.00**

Art Linkletter's House Party, Whitman, 1968, M in EX box ..**15.00**

Assembly Line, Selchow & Righter, 1953, EX **20.00**

Atomic Submarine, Hasbro, 1950s, missing ship, G **30.00**

Banana Splits, spinner game, Hasboro, 1969, MIB **50.00**

Battlestar Galactica, Parker Bros, 1978, NM in box **10.00**

Beat the Clock, Milton Bradley, 2nd edition, 1969, complete, G **25.00**

Beverly Hillbillies Card Game, Milton Bradley, 1963, complete, VG **25.00**

Boake Carter's Star Reporter, Parker Brothers, 1930, complete, G/VG **45.00**

Boom or Bust, Parker Brothers, 1951, G **15.00**

Bozo the Clown Circus Game, Transogram, 1960, 8x16" box, NM **20.00**

Bullwinkle Hide 'n Seek, Milton Bradley, 1961, NM in EX box **55.00**

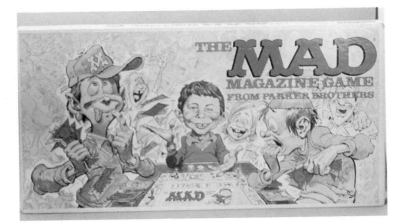

Mad Magazine Game, #124, Parker Bros., 1979, NM, $12.00.

Casper the Friendly Ghost Fun Box, Saalfield, 1960, complete, VG **28.00**

Chaos, Amsco, 1965, never used, M **18.00**

Charlie McCarthy Game of Topper, Whitman, 1938, NM **65.00**

Chasing Charlie, Charlie Chalpin, Spears Games of England, EX **45.00**

Cherry Ames' Nursing Game, Parker Bros, 1959, EX in VG box **38.00**

Dragnet, Transogram, 1955, complete, G **30.00**

Dukes of Hazzard, Ideal, 1981, missing roadblock, VG ..**18.00**

Eye Guess, Milton Bradley, 3rd edition, 1966, VG **15.00**

Family Ties, Applestreet, 1986, sealed, M **12.00**

Felix the Cat's Down on the Farm, Built-rite, 1952, never used, MIB **50.00**

Godfather Game, Family Games, 1971, EX in box **10.00**

Huckleberry Hound Western Game, board type, 1959, MIB **35.00**

Hulk Smash-Up Action, Ideal, 1979, sealed, M **30.00**

Hungry Henry, Ideal, 1969, EX in VG box **10.00**

Jetsons Out of This World, Transogram, 1962, VG **50.00**

Korg 70,000 BC, Milton Bradley, 1974, MIB **25.00**

Li'l Abner, board game, 1969, Parker Bros, MIB **45.00**

Lie Detector, Mattel, 1960, EX in G box **8.00**

Little House on the Prairie, Parker Brothers, 1978, complete, EX **25.00**

Lucy Show, Transogram, 1962, EX in box **175.00**

Magilla Gorilla, board game, Ideal, 1964, MIB **85.00**

Major Matt Mason Space Exploration, Mattel, 1967, EX in G box **35.00**

Movie-Land Keeno, Wilder Mfg Co, 1929, 7¼x9½", EX **75.00**

Mr Magoo Visits the Zoo, Lowell, 1961, complete, VG **70.00**

Mystic Skull, voodoo game, Ideal, EX **48.00**

Name That Tune, Milton Bradley, 1957, complete, VG **35.00**

Nancy & Sluggo, board game, 1944, MIB **200.00**

National Velvet, Lori Martin as Velvet, NM in box **32.00**

NBC TV News w/Chet Huntley, Dadan, 1962, VG **50.00**

Official New York World's Fair Game, Milton Bradley, 1961, EX **25.00**

Password, Milton Bradley, volume 10, 1970, complete, VG ...**5.00**

Patty Duke, Milton Bradley, 1963, EX **22.00**

Pigskin, Tom Hamilton's Football Game, Parker Brothers, 1935, G/VG **45.00**

Pin the Nose on Pinocchio, Parker Brothers, 1939, complete, VG in G box **45.00**

Pit, Parker Brothers, 1950s, complete, G- **12.00**

Planet of the Apes, Milton Bradley, 1974, EX **18.00**

Police Surgeon, American Publishing, 1972, VG **12.00**

Rin Tin Tin, Transogram, 1956, EX **25.00**

Roger Maris Action Baseball, Pressman, 1962, EX in VG box **45.00**

Roll-O-Fax, Dr George Crane, 1940s, EX **80.00**

Rook, Parker Brothers, 1943, complete, G- **10.00**

Sandlot Slugger, Milton Bradley, 1968, EX **45.00**

See New York, Transogram, 1963, MIB **32.00**

Snow White and the Seven Dwarfs, Milton Bradley, 1938, EX, $60.00.

Shindig, Remco, 1965, complete, EX in box **35.00**

Sinking of the Titanic, Ideal, 1976, complete, VG **20.00**

Six Million Dollar Man, Parker Brothers, 1975, VG **15.00**

Steve Canyon, board game, 1959, Lowell, M in 10x20" box ..**65.00**

Stock Market, Whitman, 1963, NM in EX box **12.00**

Superboy, Hasbro, 1965, G ..**15.00**

The A-Team, Parker Brothers, 1984, complete, EX **10.00**

The Great Escape, Ideal, 1967, EX in VG box **20.00**

Three Chipmunks Big Record, Hasboro, 1960, NM **35.00**

To Tell the Truth, Lowell, 1960s, complete **20.00**

Walt Disney's Peter Pan, Transogram, 1953, VG **50.00**

Wheel of Fortune, Pressman, 1985, complete, EX **12.00**

Who Can Beat Nixon, Harrison-Blaine, 1971, EX in box ..**45.00**

Yertle the Turtle, Dr Seuss, Revell, 1959, MIB **100.00**

You Don't Say, Milton Bradley, 1963, complete, EX **20.00**

77 Sunset Strip, Lowell, 1960, complete, G **30.00**

Gas Globes and Panels

Globes that once crowned gasoline pumps are today being collected as a unique form of advertising memorabilia. There are basically four types: plastic frames with glass inserts from the 1940s and '50s; glass frames with glass inserts from the '30s and '40s; metal frames with glass inserts from the '20s and '30s; and one-piece glass globes (no inserts) with the oil company name etched, raised, or enameled onto the face from 1914 to 1931. There are variations.

American, glass frame, glass inserts, 1926-40s **250.00**

Atlantic White Flash, metal frame, glass inserts, 1915-30s, 16½" **350.00**

Champlin, plastic body, glass inserts, 1931-50s **125.00**

Diamond, 1-pc glass **650.00**

DX Ethyl, plastic body, glass inserts, 1931-50s **150.00**

Gulf, glass frame, glass inserts, 1926-40s **225.00**

Marathon, red metal body, milk glass globe with orange runner, 15", EX, $950.00.

Happy Gas, metal frame, glass inserts, 1915-30s, 16½" ..**350.00**

Mobil Gas, glass frame, glass inserts, 1926-40s **300.00**

Red Crown Ethyl, metal frame, glass inserts, 1915-30s ..**425.00**

Republic, 3-sided 1-pc glass, 1914-31 ....**750.00**

Shamrock, plastic oval body, glass inserts, 1931-50s **150.00**

Shell, 1-pc round etched glass, 1914-31 ....**450.00**

Sinclair, 1-pc etched milk glass, 1914-31 ....**750.00**

Sinclair Dino, glass frame, white inserts, 1926-40s, EX ..**175.00**

Spartan, glass frame, glass inserts, 1926-40s **300.00**

Spur, plastic body, glass inserts, 1931-50s **125.00**

Texaco, 1-pc milk glass w/embossed letters, brass collar, 1914-31 ....**700.00**

Texaco Sky Chief, plastic body, glass inserts, 1931-50s ..**150.00**

Tydol, metal frame, glass inserts, 1915-30s, 16½" **350.00**

Wood River, plastic body, glass inserts, 1931-50s **125.00**

Geisha Girl China

More than sixty-five different patterns of tea services were exported from Japan around the turn of the century, each depicting geishas going about the everyday activities of Japanese life. Mt. Fudji is often featured in the background. The generic term for these sets is 'Geisha Girl China.' Refer to *The Collector's Encyclopedia of Geisha Girl China* by Elyce Litts (Collector Books).

Bowl, berry; Plum Blossom Branch, red-orange w/gold, individual **12.00**

Bowl, Cherry Blossoms, red-orange edge, 7½" **35.00**

Bowl, dessert; Court Lady, cobalt blue, dot background, 3 reserves **7.00**

Bowl, Feather Fan, pierced handles, red-orange w/gold lacing & dots **25.00**

Butter pat, Flower Gathering C, red **8.00**

Butter pat, Geisha Face, 2 geisha w/flowers, gold border **5.00**

Cake platter, Boat Festival, pale cobalt blue, 11" **30.00**

Chocolate pot, Basket A, conical body, dark apple green w/gold, 6½" **45.00**

Chocolate pot, Recital on an Ikebana B, swirl ribbed, apple green, 7" **50.00**

Creamer, Fan Dance A, scalloped, red-orange w/gold line ..**15.00**

Cup, nut; Lady in Rickshaw B, footed, red w/gold trim, individual **5.00**

Cup & saucer, Bamboo Trellis, scalloped, cobalt, gold line on handle **20.00**

Cup & saucer, cocoa; Garden Bench P, scalloped, cobalt blue w/gold **18.00**

Cup & saucer, demitasse; Boy's Processional, red-orange w/gold **15.00**

Cup & saucer, demitasse; Daikoku, ribbed, red & green floral border **28.00**

Cup & saucer, demitasse; Samurai Dance, red & gold **15.00**

Cup & saucer, tea; Battledore, 2" interior cherry blossom border **20.00**

Cup & saucer, tea; Cat & Crab, red w/gold buds **30.00**

Cup & saucer, tea; Child Reaching for Butterfly, red-orange, gold buds **12.00**

Cup & saucer, tea; Drum A, blue green w/gold, 2 reserves ..**28.00**

Cup & saucer, tea; Garden Bench B, red w/gold buds **10.00**

Cup & saucer, tea; Leaving the Teahouse, cobalt blue w/ gold **8.00**

Dish, mint; Gardening, 4-lobed, cobalt blue w/gold **12.50**

Dish, sauce; Gift Processional, red w/gold buds **9.00**

Egg cup, Cherry Blossom Ikebana, cobalt blue **10.00**

Hair receiver, Battledore, dark apple green w/gold **35.00**

Hair receiver, Fan Silhouette of Hoo Bird, wavy cobalt w/red & gold **32.00**

Hatpin holder, Garden Bench D, mint green, 4¼" **35.00**

Mustard pot, Bamboo Trellis, scalloped, blue **25.00**

Perfume bottle, Meeting A, red-orange, stenciled, stopper missing **15.00**

Plate, Boy w/Scythe, cobalt blue w/gold, 6" **10.00**

Plate, Oni Dance A, swirl fluted, scalloped, red w/gold lacing, 7¼" **18.00**

Plate, To the Teahouse, swirl fluted, scalloped, cobalt blue, 6" **10.00**

Roll tray, Bird Cage, red-orange w/gold lines **35.00**

Salt & pepper shakers, Black Parasol, red-orange **10.00**

Salt & pepper shakers, Visiting the Baby, blue & gold, individual, pr **20.00**

Sauce dish, Baskets of Mums A, 4-lobed, cut-out handle, green w/gold **8.00**

Saucer, tea; Inside the Teahouse, red-orange w/gold buds ...**5.00**

Sugar bowl, Lantern A, red w/ gold, lg **20.00**

Toy teapot, geishas on bridge, $15.00.

Toothpick holder, Child Reaching for Butterfly, red **10.00**

Toothpick holder, Duck Watching B, apple green w/gold lacing below, 4" **25.00**

Trinket box, Rokkasen, red-orange **22.00**

Vase, bud; Carp A: Watching the Carp; red-orange neck, gold lacing **18.00**

Glass Knives

Glass fruit and cake knives, which are generally between 7½" and 9¼" long, were made in the United States from about 1920 to 1950. Distribution was at its greatest in the late 1930s and early 1940s. Glass butter knives, which are about 5" to 6½", were made in Czechoslovakia. Colors of the fruit and cake knives generally follow Depression Glass dinnerware: crystal, light blue, light green, pink, and more rarely amber, forest green, and white (opal). The range of butter knife colors is even broader, including bicolors with crystal. Glass knives are frequently found with hand-painted decorations. Many were engraved with a name and occasionally with a greeting. Original boxes are frequently found along with a paper insert extolling the virtues of the knife and describing its care. As long as the original knife shape is maintained and the tip is not damaged, glass knives with nicked or reground blades are acceptable to collectors. Our advisor, Adrienne Escoe, is listed in the Directory under California. See also Clubs and Newsletters.

Aer-Flo (Grid), forest green, 7½" **200.00**
Block, pink, painted decoration, 8¼" **28.00**
Butter, crystal & amber **23.00**
Butter, red & crystal, 6¼" **25.00**
Candlewick, crystal, 8½" ...**325.00**

Cryst-o-lite, crystal, 3 pinwheels, 8½" **8.00**
Dagger, crystal, 9¼" **75.00**
Dur-x 3 Leaf, crystal, 9¼", w/ original box **10.00**
Dur-x 5 Leaf, blue, 9⅜" **18.00**
JCW, crystal, 9¼" **25.00**
Plain handle, green, 9" **25.00**
Plain handle, pink, 9" **22.00**
Rose Spray, crystal, 8½", w/original box **16.00**
Rose Spray, green, 8½" **65.00**
Steel-ite, pink, 8½" **65.00**
Stonex, amber, 8½" **110.00**
Thumbguard, crystal, painted flowers, 9¼", MIB **25.00**
Vitex (3 Star), pink, 9¼", w/original box **17.00**

Glass Shoes

While many glass shoes were made simply as whimseys, you'll also find thimble holders, perfumes, inkwells, salts, candy containers, and bottles made to resemble shoes of many types. Our advisor for this category is Libby Yalom, author of *Shoes of Glass*; see the Directory under Maryland for information on how to order her book. See also Degenhart.

Crysto Lite, clear, in original box, $12.00.

Bottle, right shoe w/patch & lg toe showing through, Pat Apld For **100.00**

Bottle, roller skate w/6 wheels, marked Depose, registry mark on ankle **75.00**

Bow on front w/long streamers, #3 in circle on sole, marked Gillinder **35.00**

Daisy & Button, amber, 12 eyelets, clear heel, Duncan, w/advertising **45.00**

Daisy & Button, bow slipper, 8 laces, front half of sole is ribbed **37.00**

Daisy & Button, crystal, on rectangle tray, Pat 1886, Bryce, 4x5½" **120.00**

Daisy & Button, gold, open front, no eyelets, mesh sole, clear heel, 6 ....**42.00**

Daisy & Button boot on oval pedestal w/scalloped edge, buttons on left **75.00**

Daisy & Button on sides of sandal, plain flat heel, 4½" long ..**38.00**

Daisy & Button skate, 15 eyelets each side front panel, 3¼x5" **60.00**

Finecut, laced up to bottom of finely stippled 'V,' diamond mesh sole **40.00**

Finecut high-button left shoe bottle holder, vaseline, B&H on base, 6" **48.00**

Blue Finecut skate, 1880s, 3x4", $50.00.

Finecut roller skate, amber, 12 eyelets, solid above laces, 3¾x6" **75.00**

Finecut roller skate, blue, no laces, 3x4" **50.00**

Frosted Burmese, ruffled edge, ca 1960s, Italy, 2½x6⅜" **80.00**

Frosted shoe w/lg bow & streamers, ca 1890, 2¾x5" **45.00**

Millefiori, blue, white & gold, crystal heel, rolled edge, 2¼x6" **60.00**

Spatter glass, crystal leaf & rigaree, 3x5¾" **100.00**

Vertical ribs sides & back, horizontals on front, peacock head mark **49.00**

Gone With the Wind

Because it is the second bestselling book and the second most-awarded movie in history, *Gone With the Wind* fans have a wide variety of memorabilia from which to choose. The May 1936 first edition book with dust jacket sells for as much as $2,000 (depending on condition). And movie memorabilia from the original 1939 release is available as well as items from the re-releases of 1942, 1943, 1947, 1954, 1961, 1968, 1974, 1980 and the 50th anniversary showing in Atlanta in December of 1989. Our advisor, Patrick McCarver, has written a very informative book, *Gone With the Wind Collector's Guide*. See Tennessee in the Directory for more information.

Advertising, Southern Comfort w/Scarlett placard, w/trivia quiz, ca 1958 ....**10.00**

Book, Charleston, Alexandra Ripley, Avon, 1982, 1st print **10.00**

Book, GWTW, Macmillan, Book Club Edition, 1964, w/dust jacket **15.00**

Book, GWTW, Perma Books, Sept 1958, 2nd print **45.00**

Book, Selznick, Bob Thomas, Pocketbook Edition, August 1972 ....**10.00**

Book, Vivien Leigh, Simon Schuster, 1977, w/picture dust jacket **20.00**

Booklet, Margaret Mitchell & Her Novel, Macmillan, 1936..**400.00**

Cigarette card, GWTW, Vivien Leigh & Leslie Howard, 2⅝x1⅜" **25.00**

Figurine, Ashley or Tara, Avon, 1985, each **35.00**

Figurine, Rhett & Scarlett dancing, Avon, 1985 ....**50.00**

Set of eight lobby cards, each 11x14", EX, $3,300.00.

Magazine, Screen Guide, Vivien Leigh cover, April 1941..**70.00**

Magazine ad, Life, Scarlett nail polish, 1940 ....**25.00**

Newspaper magazine, Atlanta Journal, Margaret Mitchell Memorial Issue **25.00**

Paint book, Merrill Publishing, ca 1940, 30-pages **125.00**

Plate, Burning of Atlanta, Knowles, 8" **30.00**

Plate, Clark, Collectors Originals, 10" **45.00**

Poster, Academy of Motion Pictures..., 1983, 1-sheet **25.00**

Poster, MGM, pastel colors, 1961, 22x28" **150.00**

Press book, GWTW, Civil War Centennial re-release, 1961 ..**45.00**

Press book, GWTW, 1st re-release, Jan 1941 ....**400.00**

Press book, GWTW, 1954 .....**75.00**

Record, GWTW, Ferrante & Teicher, 45 rpm, United Artists **25.00**

Record, GWTW, MGM SIE-10ST, Civil War Centennial issue, 1961, LP **25.00**

Record, GWTW, original picture score, Warner Bros, WS-1322, LP **20.00**

Record, GWTW, RCA Victor, 1954, 10", w/album cover **75.00**

Record, Tara Theme, Buddy Morrow & Orchestra, 45 rpm **25.00**

Song sheet, GWTW, Magidson & Wrubel, Bourne Music Publishers **45.00**

Stamp sheet, 100 Margaret Mitchell 1¢, issued 1986 ..**1.50**

Toy watch, Rhett & Scarlett photo, Occupied Japan ..**25.00**

Graniteware

A collectible very much in demand by those who enjoy the 'country' look in antiques, graniteware (also called enameled ware) comes in a variety of colors, and color is one of the most important considerations when it comes to evaluation. Purple, brown, or green swirl pieces are generally higher than gray, white, or blue, though blues and blue-swirled examples are popular. Decorated pieces are unusual, as are salesman's samples and miniatures; and these also bring top prices. For more information refer to *The Collector's Encyclopedia of Granite Ware, Colors, Shapes, and Values, Vols I and II,* by Helen Greguire (Collector Books).

Bowl, dough or salad; blue & white fine mottle, white interior, G+ **70.00**

Bowls, nesting; 1 each red, green, yellow, blue, black trim, 4-pc, M **125.00**

Bread box, white, black trim & lettering, vented lid, round, tall, G+ **125.00**

Bucket, deep red & white fine mottle, w/matching lid, wood bail, G+ **255.00**

Colander, blue & white inside & out, black handles & trim, lg, NM **45.00**

Creamer, light blue, white interior, straight sides, NM **125.00**

Cuspidor, gray medium mottle, seamed, M **115.00**

Cuspidor, hotel; blue & white mottle, white interior, black trim, 2-pc **310.00**

Dishpan, red & white lg swirl, black trim, 1960s, NM ..**75.00**

Double boiler, white w/cobalt handles & trim, M **75.00**

Dustpan, light gray mottle, riveted handle, ridged bottom, G+ **145.00**

Foot tub, cobalt & white lg swirl, black trim, oval, G+ **195.00**

Grater, solid cobalt, lg, G ...**130.00**

Grater, white w/light blue trim, G+ **135.00**

Iron, child's electric; light blue, lg wood handle, Gold Seal, M **135.00**

Kettle, gray lg mottle, wire bail w/ wood handle, sm, M **85.00**

Ladle, soup; blue & white swirl, white interior, black handle, G+ **60.00**

Milk can, gray lg mottle, wood bail, handled lid, short, G+ **80.00**

Milk can, gray mottle, wire bail, seamed, G+ **70.00**

Miner's dinner bucket, black & white swirl, wood bail, tin lid, round **285.00**

Child's plate, iris swirl, 4", EX, $135.00; measure, blue and white mottle, 3¼", VG, $150.00.

Pan, baking; cobalt & white, white interior, side handle, oblong, G+ **125.00**

Pan, baking; light blue & white lg swirl, handles, G+ **85.00**

Pan, bread; gray lg mottle, oval, NM **145.00**

Pan, bread; solid blue w/white interior, ring hanger, oblong, G+ **60.00**

Pan, ladyfinger; light & dark gray fine mottle, NM **265.00**

Pan, muffin; dark gray lg mottle, 9-cup **50.00**

Pan, muffin; gray mottle, cups riveted & crimped over wire frame, G+ **175.00**

Pan, stove; gray lg mottle, deep oblong, G+ **30.00**

Pie plate, brown & gray lg mottle inside & out, NM **55.00**

Pitcher & bowl, red, black handle & trim, no lip, squatty style, G+ **200.00**

Pitcher & bowl, white w/cobalt trim, sm, rare, M **110.00**

Salt box, white w/dark blue trim & lettering, wood lid, Germany, G+ **110.00**

Saucepan, blue & white swirl, black handle & trim, Berlin style, G+ **165.00**

Saucepan, charcoal & white lg mottle, w/handle & lid ..**135.00**

Scoop, grocer's; gray lg mottle, tubular handle, rolled edge, G+ **135.00**

Scoop, thumb; white w/cobalt handle, NM **115.00**

Sink strainer, gray mottle, rolled edge, square, NM **55.00**

Skimmer, cobalt & white lg mottle, perforated, flat, G+ **95.00**

Soap dish, bathtub; gray mottle, perforated bottom, rolled hanger, G+ **185.00**

Soap dish, hanging; cobalt & white medium swirl, G+ **145.00**

Spatula, white w/dark red handle, perforated, keyhole shape, G+ **55.00**

Spatula or turner, gray mottle, perforated, shield shape, G+ **75.00**

Spoon, blue & white lg mottle, black handle, G+ **60.00**

Spoon, ice cream; gray & white mottle, cast iron base, wood handle, G+ **115.00**

Tea steeper, gray mottle, NM ..**75.00**

Teakettle, red & white lg mottle, black handle & trim, 1960s, M **145.00**

Teakettle, yellow w/black handle & trim, rare color, G+ ...**75.00**

Toothbrush holder, white w/light blue veining, perforated lid, G+ **65.00**

Water pail, blue & white swirl, white interior, wood bail, sm, M **185.00**

Griswold

During the latter part of the 19th century, the Griswold company began to manufacture the finest cast iron kitchenware items available at that time. Soon after they became established, they introduced a line of lightweight, cast aluminum ware that revolutionized the industry. The company enjoyed many prosperous years until its closing in the late 1950s. Look for these marks: Seldon Griswold, Griswold Mfg. Co., and Erie. Refer to *Griswold Cast Collectibles* by Bill and Denise Harned for more information.

Ashtray, pattern #770, square skillet form, 1936-50s, 3½" **22.00**

Barbeque grill, 3-legged kettle base, bail, 1922-57, 12¼" dia **95.00**

Broiler, pattern #875, round grid-iron form, 1891-1954, 10½" dia **105.00**

Cake mold, rabbit form, 1938-57, 11x10" **225.00**

Dutch oven, #8, glass lid, cast handles w/bail holes, 40s-50s, 4x9" **45.00**

Griddle, #7, without bail, 1915, 7¼x16½" **45.00**

Griddle, #8, pattern #745, w/ bail, diamond mark, 9¼x 19" **80.00**

Griddle, skillet; #110, pattern #203, 1915-39, 1x12" dia **85.00**

Heat regulator, pattern #300, ?-1957, 7⅜" dia **185.00**

Hot plate, electric, #101, 1-burner, 1925-30s, 5¼x8¼" square................................**35.00**

Hot plate, gas, #501, 1-burner, 1915-30s, 5¼x10" square **85.00**

Kettle, pattern #918, flat bottom handles, 1880-1909, 8-qt .**95.00**

Kettle, table service; #00, pattern #100, 3-legged, bail, 2x4" ..**30.00**

Mailbox, wire paper rack, sheet metal back, 1940-57, 12x6x 3" **45.00**

Pan, Danish cake or egg poacher; #32, pattern #962, 1935-57, 9" dia **47.00**

Pan, Gem; #8, pattern #951, 1900-40s, 11 cakes, 11x8" **85.00**

Pan, meatloaf; pattern #877, handles on side, 1928-40s, 5½x 10x2¾" **45.00**

Pan, Swedish pancake or Plett; #34, pattern #2930A, 1925-57, 10" dia **38.00**

Pan, Vienna roll; #6, 1900-30s, 6 loaves, 6½x12x1¼" **85.00**

Roaster, #3, pattern #643/lid #644, porcelain interior, 1924-57, 4-qt **85.00**

Skillet, #5, hammered, hinged lid, 1942, 1¾x7½" **45.00**

Skillet, egg; pattern #53/126/1090, 1940-57, square, 4¾" **22.00**

Skillet, fish; #15, pattern #1013/ lid #1013C, 1938-57, oval, 10x15" **97.00**

Skillet, hotel; #20, oval w/handles, no lid, 1938-57 ....**130.00**

Skillet, 3-in-1; pattern #666, 1934-51, square, 1x9" **35.00**

Skillet, 3-in-1; #8, pattern #1008, 1930-39, 2¼x9" dia **65.00**

Tobacco or plug cutter, #3 Tri-umph, marked Griswold, 1883-20s **150.00**

Trivet, coffeepot; 5-legged, 5" dia **65.00**

Waffle iron, #12, pattern #2608, coil handles, 1922-40s, 9x4" pans **110.00**

Waffle iron, regular; #7, coil handle, top bail, 1922-30, 6¾" pans **65.00**

Wax ladle, side pour spout, 1880-1930s, 8" **27.00**

Yankee bowl, #4, pattern #786, 6 ½-qt, 5¾x10⅝" **70.00**

Hall

Most famous for their extensive lines of teapots and colorful dinnerwares, the Hall China Company still operates in East Liverpool, Ohio, where they were established in 1903. Refer to *The Collector's Encyclopedia of Hall China* by Margaret and Kenn Whitmeyer (Collector Books) for more information. For listings of Hall's most popular dinnerware line, see Autumn Leaf.

Arlington, cup **4.00**

Arlington, plate, 10" **5.00**

Blue Bouquet, bowl, fruit; 5½" ..**4.00**

Blue Bouquet, platter, 13¼" ..**18.00**

Blue Bouquet, salt & pepper shakers, teardrop, pr **16.00**

Cameo Rose, gravy boat, w/under-plate **22.00**

Cameo Rose soup bowl, $9.00.

**Orange Poppy pretzel jar, 7",
$85.00.**

Cameo Rose, salt & pepper shakers, pr **16.00**
Crocus, bowl, cereal; 6" **11.00**
Crocus, custard **8.00**
Crocus, plate, 9" **15.00**
Crocus, tidbit, 3-tier **40.00**
Flamingo, sugar bowl, Viking, w/lid **22.00**
Flamingo, syrup, Five Band ..**45.00**
Floral Lattice, casserole, #99, oval **30.00**
Floral Lattice, cookie jar, Five Band **65.00**
Heather Rose, flared, 6¾" **8.00**
Heather Rose, plate, 10" **5.50**
Heather Rose, sugar bowl **10.00**
Meadow Flower, ball jug, #3 ..**45.00**
Meadow Flower, salt & pepper shakers, w/handles, pr ..**32.00**
Monticello, bowl, fruit; 5¼" **2.50**
Monticello, cup & saucer **5.50**
Morning-Glory, bowl, Thick Rim, 8½" **16.00**
Morning-Glory, casserole, Thick Rim, w/lid **22.00**
Mums, bowl, salad; 9" **12.00**
Mums, platter, oval, 11¼" **14.00**
Orange Poppy, cake plate **12.00**
Orange Poppy, canister set, metal, 4-pc **40.00**
Orange Poppy, leftover, loop handle **34.00**

Pastel Morning-Glory, bowl, soup; flat, 8½" **10.00**
Pastel Morning-Glory, plate, dinner; 10" **11.00**
Red Poppy, bowl, cereal; 6" **7.00**
Red Poppy, coffee dispenser, all metal **20.00**
Red Poppy, drip jar, Radiance, w/lid **16.00**
Red Poppy, pie baker **18.00**
Red Poppy, sifter, metal **18.00**
Richmond/Brown-Eyed Susan, plate, 10" **5.00**
Richmond/Brown-Eyed Susan, platter, oval, 15½" **16.00**
Rose Parade, bowl, salad; 9" ..**25.00**
Rose Parade, custard, straight-sided **10.00**
Rose White, casserole, w/lid, tab handles **18.00**
Rose White, drip jar, w/lid, tab handles **14.00**
Royal Rose, bowl, Thick Rim, 7½" **12.00**
Serenade, cup **4.50**
Serenade, platter, 13¼" **14.00**
Serenade, teapot, New York ..**35.00**
Shaggy Tulip, casserole, Radiance **28.00**
Shaggy Tulip, shirred egg dish ..**20.00**
Silhouette, bowl, cereal; 6" **7.00**
Silhouette, tray, metal, oval ..**28.00**

Silhouette coffeepot, Medallion shape, 9", $65.00.

original price. Values are given for examples mint in their original boxes with the price tabs or strips still intact. Deduct about 20% when no box is present. Refer to *The Ornament Collector's Price Guide, Hallmark's Ornaments and Merry Miniatures*, by our advisor, Rosie Wells, for more information. She is listed in the Directory under Illinois. See also Clubs and Newsletters.

Springtime, cake plate **12.00**
Springtime, sugar bowl, Modern, w/lid **9.00**
Stonewall, drip jar, open **22.00**
Teapot, Airflow, turquoise or canary, 8-cup **30.00**
Teapot, Aladdin, cobalt w/gold decoration, oval opening **50.00**
Teapot, Manhattan, red **45.00**
Teapot, New York, black, gold label decoration, 10-cup **32.00**
Teapot, Philadelphia, rose, 10-cup **40.00**
Tulip, baker, French fluted ..**17.00**
Tulip, custard **4.50**
Tulip, gravy boat **20.00**
Wild Poppy, baker, oval **18.00**
Wild Poppy, creamer, New York **20.00**
Wildfire, bowl, oval **14.00**
Wildfire, casserole, Thick Rim..**22.00**
Wildfire, plate, 10" **8.00**
Yellow Rose, bowl, fruit; 5½" ..**3.50**
Yellow Rose, coffeepot, Waverly **30.00**
Yellow Rose, cup & saucer **7.00**

Acorn Inn, #QX424-3, 1986 ..**25.00**
Baby Redbird, #QX410-1, 1988 ....**12.00**
Beary Special, #QX455-7, 1987 ....**17.00**
Betsey Clark, #QX168-1, 1975, set of 4 ....**45.00**
Chickadees, #QX204-1, 1976 ..**35.00**
Children in the Shoe, #QX490-5, 1985 ....**37.50**
Christmas Teddy, #QX404-2, 1981 ....**16.00**
Currier & Ives, #QX130-2, 1977 ....**45.00**
Dad-To-Be, #QX491-3, 1990 ..**16.00**
Goin' South, #QX410-5, 1989 ..**22.00**
Heavenly Harmony, #QX465-9, 1987 ....**25.00**

Hallmark

Since 1973 the Hallmark Company has made Christmas ornaments, several of which are today worth many times their

Victorian Dollhouse, 1984, MIB, $115.00.

Here Comes Santa, #QX432-4, 1984 ....**60.00**
Holiday Puppy, #QX412-7, 1983 ....**27.50**
Jingle Bell Clown, #QX477-4, 1988 ....**20.00**
Little Drummers, #QX511-6, 1986 ....**30.00**
Nativity, #QX253-6, 1978 ....**35.00**
Porcelain Bear, #QX442-6, 1990 ....**16.00**
Rocking Horse, #QX340-7, 1979 ....**15.00**
Rudolph the Red-Nosed Reindeer, #QLX725-2, 1989 ....**40.00**
Santa's Hot Tub, #QX426-3, 1986 ....**30.00**
Star Swing, #QX421-5, 1981 ..**35.00**
Tin Soldier, #QX483-6, 1982 ..**30.00**
Two Peas in a Pod, #QX492-6, 1990 ....**22.00**

Halloween

Halloween items are fast becoming the most popular holiday-related collectibles among today's collectors. Although originally linked to pagan rituals and superstitions, Halloween has long since evolved into a fun-filled event; and the masks, noisemakers, and jack-o'-lanterns of earlier years are great fun to look for.

Candy container, black cat, plastic w/face on back, 1950s, 3" **12.50**
Candy container, black cat w/ horn, papier-mache, Germany, 7" **28.00**
Candy container, boot, orange papier-mache, Halloween face, Germany, 3" **55.00**
Candy container, caldron, orange papier-mache pot, green handles, 2" **38.00**

Pressed cardboard pumpkin head, Occupied Japan, $40.00.

Candy container, pumpkin man atop jack-o'-lantern, hard plastic, 5" **18.00**
Candy container, witch's head, papier-mache, Made in Germany, 6" **18.00**
Costume, Atom Ant, Ben Cooper, 1965, NM in box **25.00**
Costume, Birdman, Ben Cooper, 1967, EX in box **15.00**
Costume, Cecil (of Beany & Cecil), Ben Cooper, 1961, NM in box **50.00**
Costume, Impossibles, mask & 1-pc bodysuit, Ben Cooper, 1967, MIB **45.00**
Costume, Steve Canyon, mask & bodysuit, Halco, 1959, MIB **45.00**
Crepe paper, designs on orange, M in original package ...**25.00**
Decoration, crepe paper & chenille witch w/plastic face, 2" ..**25.00**
Decoration, die-cut black cat, jointed, 6" **10.00**
Decoration, die-cut cat sitting on nose of man-in-the-moon, 14" **35.00**
Decoration, die-cut owl perched on branch, 20" **35.00**
Decoration, die-cut skeleton, jointed, 60" **35.00**

Decoration, die-cut witch riding honeycomb spaceship, 18" EX **24.00**
Decoration, embossed cardboard, black cat, jointed, 1920s, 7x 8" **12.50**
Decoration, embossed die-cut bat encircled by man in moon, 5" dia **45.00**
Decoration, stand-up ghost in graveyard, 8", EX **20.00**
Decoration, stand-up scarecrow & moon, 8", EX **20.00**
Decoration, stand-up scarecrow w/honeycomb cornstalk, 10", EX **20.00**
Decoration, stand-up winking black cat on orange base, cardboard, 12" **15.00**
Lantern, clowns & witches, orange cardboard, bail handle, 7" **45.00**
Mask, cat face w/honeycomb hat, 14", EX **22.00**
Party hat, witch style, black & orange, Germany, 1930s, 12x11½", NM **17.50**
Tambourine, orange w/black cat, tin litho **25.00**

Harker

One of the oldest potteries in the East Liverpool, Ohio, area, the Harker company produced many lines of dinnerware through the late 1920s until it closed around 1970. Refer to *A Collector's Guide to Harker Pottery* by Neva W. Colbert (Collector Books) for more information.

Ashtray, Dainty Flower **5.00**
Batter jug, Dainty Flower ...**28.00**
Bean pot, Deco Dahlia, individual **8.00**
Bowl, Mallow, 7½" **8.00**
Bowl, Pansy, 6" **6.00**

Bowl, Petit Point Rose, 6" **8.00**
Bowl, Petit Point Rose, 7½" ..**18.00**
Bowl, utility; Lisa, medium ..**20.00**
Bowl, utility; Petit Point Rose, 11½" **25.00**
Bowl, vegetable; Colonial Lady, oval **15.00**
Butter dish, Wood Song **8.00**
Cake lifter, Monterey **18.00**
Casserole, individual; Petit Point Rose **4.00**
Casserole, Monterey, w/lid ...**36.00**
Coffeepot, Mallow **30.00**
Creamer, Rose Spray **12.00**
Creamer & sugar bowl, Ivy ..**20.00**
Cup, Spring Time **5.00**
Cup & saucer, Cameo, Shell Shape **10.00**
Custard, individual; Autumn Leaf **20.00**
Custard, individual; English ..**5.00**
Custard, individual; Mallow, set of 4 in wire basket **40.00**
Custard cup, Mallow **10.00**
Custard cup, Modern Tulip ..**10.00**
Custard cup, Red Apple **10.00**
Drip jar, Cameo.....................**18.00**
Fork, Petit Point Rose **20.00**
Fork & spoon, Red Apple **20.00**
Jug, Cameo, w/lid, 1-cup **16.00**
Pie baker, Deco Dahlia **25.00**
Pie baker, Ivy **25.00**

Cameo plate, 8½", $3.50.

Pie pan, Petit Point Rose **20.00**
Pie plate, Carv-Kraft White
    Rose **12.00**
Pitcher, Blue Blossoms **18.00**
Pitcher, Boyce **35.00**
Plate, Brim, w/cup indent **8.00**
Plate, Cameo, Shell Shape, 9" ..**10.00**
Plate, Colonial Lady, 6" **8.00**
Plate, dinner; Amy **8.00**
Plate, Ivy, 8" **8.00**
Plate, Modern Tulip, 6" **5.00**
Plate, Red Apple, 9" **10.00**
Plate, Rose Spray, 9" **8.00**
Plate, salad; Rose Spray, 7"
    square **4.00**
Platter, Amy **25.00**
Platter, Cherry Blossom **8.00**
Platter, Deco Dahlia, 11" **5.00**
Salt & pepper shakers, Pansy,
    pr **27.50**
Saucer, Basket **3.00**
Saucer, Cherry Trim **3.00**
Server, Ruffled Tulip **18.00**
Serving tray, Ruffled Tulip, 11¾"
    dia **25.00**
Shaker, pepper; Carv-Kraft White
    Rose **10.00**
Stack set, Amy, w/lid **35.00**
Sugar bowl, Amy **8.00**
Teacup & saucer, Wood Song .**10.00**
Teapot, Amy, w/lid **35.00**
Teapot, Cameo **27.00**
Teapot, Red Apple, Zephyr ..**30.00**
Tidbit tray, Spring Time, 1-tier ..**66.00**
Trivet, Petit Point Rose, octago-
    nal **10.00**

Harlequin

Made by the Homer Laughlin
China Company who also produced
the popular Fiesta, Harlequin was
a lightweight dinnerware line
made in several solid glaze colors.
It was introduced in 1938 and
was marketed mainly through
Woolworth stores. During the
early forties, the company made a
line of Harlequin animals: a fish,
lamb, cat, duck, penguin, and
donkey. Values designated 'low' in
the listings that follow are for
turquoise and yellow. 'High' values
are for maroon, gray, medium
green, spruce green, chartreuse,
dark green, rose, mauve blue,
red, and light green. Refer to *The
Collector's Encyclopedia of Fiesta*
by Sharon and Bob Huxford (Collector Books) for more information.

Animals, standard colors, any ..**75.00**
Ashtray, regular; high **47.50**
Ashtray, regular; low **32.00**
Bowl, '30s oatmeal; high **17.00**
Bowl, '36s oatmeal; low **11.50**
Bowl, '36s; high **26.50**
Bowl, '36s; low **17.00**
Bowl, cream soup; high **20.00**
Bowl, cream soup; low **16.00**
Bowl, fruit; high, 5½" **9.00**
Bowl, fruit; low, 5½" **6.00**
Bowl, individual salad; high ..**26.50**
Bowl, individual salad; low ..**17.00**
Bowl, nappy; high, 9" **26.50**
Bowl, nappy; low, 9" **16.50**
Bowl, oval baker, high **25.00**
Bowl, oval baker, low **18.00**
Butter dish, ½-lb, high **90.00**
Butter dish, ½-lb, low **75.00**
Candle holders, high, pr **195.00**
Candle holders, low, pr **162.50**
Casserole, w/lid, high **95.00**
Casserole, w/lid, low **58.00**
Creamer, high lip, any color ..**72.00**
Creamer, individual; high **17.00**
Creamer, individual; low **12.50**
Creamer, novelty, high **23.00**
Creamer, novelty, low **16.00**
Creamer, regular, high **13.50**
Creamer, regular, low **8.00**
Cup, demitasse; high **46.00**
Cup, demitasse; low **27.50**
Cup, lg, any color **92.00**
Cup, tea; high **9.50**
Cup, tea; low **7.50**
Egg cup, double, high **20.00**

Egg cup, double, low **14.00**
Gravy boat, high **23.00**
Gravy boat, low **16.00**
Marmalade, any color **125.00**
Nut dish, basketweave, any
   color **8.00**
Pitcher, service water; high..**55.00**
Pitcher, service water; low ...**37.50**
Pitcher, 22-oz jug, high **46.00**
Pitcher, 22-oz jug, low **26.00**
Plate, deep; high **20.00**
Plate, deep; low **15.00**
Plate, 10", high **24.00**
Plate, 10", low **14.00**
Plate, 9", high **12.00**
Plate, 9", low **7.00**
Platter, 11", high **17.50**
Platter, 11", low **12.00**
Platter, 13", high **25.00**
Platter, 13", low **16.50**
Salt & peppers, pr, high **16.50**
Salt & peppers, pr, low **13.00**
Saucer/ashtray, high **47.00**
Saucer/ashtray, ivory **65.00**
Saucer/ashtray, low **42.50**
Sugar bowl, w/lid, high **17.00**
Sugar bowl, w/lid, low **12.00**
Syrup, any color **200.00**
Teapot, high **88.00**

Teapot, low **58.00**
Tray, relish; mixed colors ...**200.00**
Tumbler, high **40.00**
Tumbler, low **30.00**

Hatpin Holders

Made from many materials, hatpin holders are most often encountered in china decorated by hand painting or floral decals. Glass hatpin holders are rare, especially those of slag or carnival glass. Refer to *Hatpin and Hatpin Holders* by Lillian Baker (Collector Books) for more information.

Bavaria, black floral on white,
   heavy silver overlay top &
   bottom, 5" **125.00**
Bisque, white w/2 olive green
   cameos & pink raised flowers,
   5½" **165.00**
Bisque, 4-sided pink & white
   Egyptian motif, ca 1909,
   5¼" **155.00**
Brass, w/pincushion, pin tray, &
   ring holder **140.00**

Pitcher, high, $55.00, low $37.50; tumblers, high, 40.00, low, $30.00.

English china, souvenir, Isle of Man **45.00**

Germany, china w/multicolored roses in high relief **60.00**

Rosenthal, hand-painted Art Nouveau floral, heavy gold overlay, 4¾" **150.00**

Royal Doulton, hand-painted hunt scene of man on horse, 1902-22, 5" **225.00**

Unmarked porcelain, souvenir, transfer portrait of George V, 4½" **95.00**

Willow Art, souvenir, red transfer design inscribed Jerusalem, 5½" **110.00**

Hatpins

Hatpins range in length from about 4" to as long as 12", depending upon the fashion of the day. The longer type was required to secure the large bonnets that were in style from 1890 to 1914. Many beautiful examples exist – some with genuine or manufactured stones, some in silver or brass with relief-molded Art Nouveau motifs, others of hand-painted porcelains, and 'nodder' types.

Large amethyst stone in center, three more on sides with rhinestones, 11" pin, $135.00.

Celluloid, Deco pleated fan shape, 3" on 4¼" pin **65.00**

Emerald glass head, round, ¾" on 8" pin **55.00**

Enamel on copper, Nouveau floral figural, 1" on 9½" brass pin **55.00**

Enamel on sterling, green & white Nouveau floral design, 12" pin **55.00**

Glass, red foil ball w/peacock eye atop, ⅝" on 6⅜" pin **85.00**

Gold-tone horn butterfly w/99 colored rhinestones, 3" on 9½" pin **95.00**

Japanese carved bone globe in open-weave design, ¾" on 10" pin **85.00**

Japanese cloisonne, red floral on blue, spherical, 1¼" on 12" pin **125.00**

Plastic, Deco beaded flame design, 3¼" on 4½" brass pin **45.00**

Plastic, Deco papyrus leaf, 2x2" on 4½" pin **65.00**

Plastic, Deco ram's horn w/ antique finish, 2¼x2½" on 4" pin **75.00**

Porcelain, maiden & butterfly transfer on button mount, 1" on 8" pin **125.00**

Pressed horn butterfly w/peacock eye & rhinestones, 3" on 9" pin **110.00**

Satsuma, porcelain, geshia girl design, gold trim, spherical, 1" on 8" pin **150.00**

Silver foil flattened glass globe w/peacock eyes, ½" on 8" pin **45.00**

Silver-toned plastic circlet, 2" on 4¾" brass pin **45.00**

Head Vases

Many of them Japanese imports, head vases were made primarily for the florist trade.

They were styled as children, teenagers, clowns, and famous people. There are heads of religious figures, Blacks, Orientals, and even some animals. One of the most common types are ladies wearing pearl earrings and necklaces. Refer to *Head Vases, Identification and Value Guide,* by Kathleen Cole (Collector Books) for more information.

Baby in blue ruffled bonnet, EO Brody #A987, 6½" **47.50**
Blond, asymetrical hairdo, closed eyes w/lashes, Velco #10759, 5½" **37.50**
Blond, curly hairdo, hand to ear, pearls, Relpo #2055, 6" ..**47.50**
Blond, fancy hairdo, black glove w/fan to chin, earrings, Inarco, 5" **42.50**
Blond, looks left, painted eyelashes, green dress, no mark, 6" **27.50**
Blond, looks right, bouffant hairdo, pearl jewelry, Napco #C7313, 4½" **37.50**
Blond, ponytail to left, earrings, halter dress, Inarco, 7½" ..**67.50**

Boy, 7¾", $35.00.

Blond, scarf tied around hat & under her chin, Relpo #1783, 7½" **65.00**
Blond, smooth hairdo, telephone, Inarco #E3548, 5½" **32.50**
Blond, w/bangs, pink headscarf, Relpo #K1615, 5½" **32.50**
Blond, white rose in hair, white collar, pearls, Rubens #497/M, 6½" **17.50**
Blond girl, pigtails, pearl earrings, Rubens #4135, 6" **37.50**
Blond girl, shoulder-length hairdo w/black headband, Relpo #K1931, 8½" **95.00**
Blond in hat, both hands at chin, pearls & earrings, Rubens #495, 6" **42.50**
Blond in pink hat & collar, earrings, Nancy Pew #2260, 7" **57.50**
Blond w/black-gloved hand to chin, pearls & earrings, Lefton, 6" **42.50**
Chinese lady w/white headdress & fan, gold lashes, 4¾" ..**37.50**
Clown, red curly hair, blue hat, ruffle, Inarco #E6730, 5½" **32.50**
Girl, flip hairstyle, pink bow atop, pearl jewelry, long eyelashes, 7½" **75.00**
Girl, hand to wide flowered hat that matches her dress, Lefton, 6" **42.50**
Girl graduate, blond, white mortarboar, Napco #C4072G, 6" **42.50**
Girl in ponytail mounted on flower-like wire hanger, VCAGCO, 4½" **47.50**
Girl wall pocket, red & white plaid dress, marked Jean, 7"...**42.50**
Lady, black & white bow on gray hat, lashes, Napco #C3959A, 5½" **47.50**
Lady, chin up, eyes w/lashes closed, pearls & earrings, 5½" **37.50**
Lady, hand to throat, eyelashes, pearls, Inarco #E2104, 7"..**42.50**

194

**Lady with long eyelashes, 6",
$32.50.**

Lady, white hat & collar, pearls,
eyelashes, Inarco #E3969/S,
4½" **32.50**

Lady in green hat w/white flowers, red & white scarf, Napco,
6" **42.50**

Lady in very wide pink hat, eyes
closed/chin down to right,
#214, 6" **42.50**

Lady in wide-brimmed hat blows
kiss, pearls, Napco #C3307C,
5½" **42.50**

Lady w/white hair, eyes w/eye-
lashes closed, pearl jewelry,
5½" **37.50**

Little blond girl in lg hat,
waving, Reliable Glass-
ware, 6" **32.50**

Little blond w/pigtails, umbrella
overhead, 4¼" **52.50**

Little boy clown, tuft of red hair,
blue hat & bow, 4½" **32.50**

Little girl holds white kitten to
shoulder, Enesco, 5½" ...**42.50**

Madonna holds Child in cupped
hands, Napcoware #R77075,
5" **32.50**

Praying child, Inarco #E778,
Cleve Ohio, 1962, 5" **27.50**

Snow White, bird on shoulder, red
hairbow, WDP, 5½" **225.00**

Heisey

The Heisey glassware com-
pany operated in Ohio from 1896
until 1957, producing many fine
dinnerware lines, many of which
were made in lovely colors and
etched with intricate floral motifs.
They also made animal and bird
figures, some of which sell today
for more than $500.00 each. They
signed their ware with an H in a
diamond mark or with a paper
label. Refer to *The Collector's
Encyclopedia of Heisey Glass,
1925-1938*, by Neila Bredehoft
(Collector Books) for more information.

Animal, Clydesdale, crystal,
frosted, or amber, 1942-48,
7½x7" **400.00**

Animal, fish bowl, crystal, solid
base, 1941-46, 9½x8½"..**450.00**

Animal, fish candlesticks, crystal,
open mouth, 1941-48, 5x4",
pr **350.00**

Animal, giraffe, crystal, frosted,
or amber, 1942-52, 10¾x
3" **240.00**

Animal, plug horse, crystal,
frosted, amber, or cobalt,
1941-46, 4" **135.00**

Animal, rabbit paperweight, crystal or frosted, 1941-46, 2¾x
3¾" **150.00**

Bird, fighting rooster, crystal or
frosted, 1940-46, 8x6"..**200.00**

Bird, goose, wings up, crystal or
frosted, 1942-53, 7x8"..**110.00**

Bird, mallard, wings down, crystal or frosted, 1947-55, 4½x
4½" **325.00**

Bird, ringneck pheasant, crystal or
frosted, 1942-53, 5x12"..**140.00**

Bird, rooster vase, crystal or frosted, 1939-48, 6¼x6" ..**85.00**

Bird, sparrow, crystal or frosted, 1942-45, 2¼x4" **100.00**

Bird, stylized, light blue, 5" ..**125.00**

Charter Oak, crystal; plate, salad; #1246, Acorn & Leaves, 6" ..**8.00**

Charter Oak, pink; tumbler, flat, #3362, 12-oz **17.50**

Chintz, crystal; bowl, jelly; footed, 2-handled, 6" **15.00**

Chintz, crystal; comport, cheese; #2496, 3¼" **22.50**

Crystolite, crystal; bowl, dessert or nappy; 4½" **8.00**

Crystolite, crystal; salad dressing set, 3-pc **38.00**

Empress, alexandrite; bowl, nut; dolphin footed, individual ..**125.00**

Empress, green; cup **40.00**

Greek Key, crystal; pitcher, 1-qt **85.00**

Greek Key, crystal; sherbet, flared rim, footed, 4½-oz **12.50**

Ipswich, cobalt; plate, square, 8" **40.00**

Ipswich, crystal; finger bowl, w/underplate **20.00**

Lariat, crystal; bottle, oil; oval, 6-oz **65.00**

Lariat, crystal; cheese dish, w/lid, 8" **50.00**

Lodestar, dawn; bowl, mayonnaise; 5" **55.00**

Lodestar, dawn; creamer, w/handle **85.00**

Lodestar, dawn; sugar bowl ..**50.00**

Minuet, crystal; candlestick, 1-light, #112 ....**25.00**

Minuet, crystal; vase, urn shape, #5012, 6" **65.00**

New Era, crystal; celery tray, 13" **30.00**

New Era, crystal; relish dish, 3-part, 13" **25.00**

Octagon, amber; dessert dish, #500 ....**50.00**

Octagon, green; plate, sandwich; center handle, 10½" **45.00**

Old Colony, crystal; bowl, jelly; 2-handled, footed, 6" **15.00**

Old Colony, yellow; saucer, square **10.00**

Old Sandwich, green; stem, sherbet; 4-oz **18.00**

Old Sandwich, pink; ashtray, individual **35.00**

Orchid, crystal; butter dish, w/lid, Cabochon, ¼-lb **300.00**

Orchid, crystal; dinner bell, #5022 or #5025 ....**125.00**

Plantation, crystal; candle block, 1-light **85.00**

Plantation, crystal; mayonnaise, w/liner, 5¼" **45.00**

Plantation, butter dish, ¼-lb., $85.00; pitcher with ice lip, $300.00; syrup pitcher, 4¾", $75.00.

Pleat & Panel, green; marmalade, 4¾" **25.00**

Pleat & Panel, pink; bowl, grapefruit or cereal; 6½" **12.50**

Provincial, crystal; bowl, nut or jelly; 2-handled, 5" **12.00**

Provincial, green; plate, luncheon; 8" **50.00**

Ridgeleigh, crystal; cigarette box, w/lid, oval **55.00**

Ridgeleigh, crystal; plate, square, 7" **12.00**

Rose, crystal; celery tray, Waverly, 12" **55.00**

Rose, crystal; stem, cordial; #5072, 1-oz **145.00**

Saturn, crystal; salt & pepper shakers, pr **45.00**
Saturn, green; bowl, baked apple **65.00**
Twist, amber; bonbon **30.00**
Twist, pink; creamer, zigzag handles, footed **30.00**
Victorian, crystal; tumbler, old-fashioned; 8-oz **30.00**
Waverly, crystal; comport, jelly; 6½" **35.00**
Waverly, crystal; honey dish, footed, 6½" **22.00**
Yeoman, amber; bowl, baker; 9" **55.00**
Yeoman, pink; stem, soda; 5-oz ..**8.00**

Homer Laughlin

Founded in 1871, the Homer Laughlin China Company continues today to be a leader in producing quality tablewares. Some of their earlier lines were produced in large quantity and are well marked with the company name or HLC logo; collectors find them fun to use as well as to collect, since none are as yet very expensive. Refer to *The Collector's Encyclopedia of Homer Laughlin China* by Joanne Jasper and *The Collector's Encyclopedia of Fiesta* by Sharon and Bob Huxford (both published by Collector Books). *Homer Laughlin China, An Identification Guide,* is another good reference; it is written by our advisor, Darlene Nossaman, who is in the Directory under Texas. See also Fiesta; Harlequin; Riviera.

Cavalier Shape (available in Berkshire, Crinoline, Jade Rose, and Turquoise Melody)

Bowl, cereal; 5½", from $5.00 up to **7.00**

Bowl, fruit; 5", from $3.00 up to ..**5.00**
Bowl, rim soup; 8", from $5.00 up to **7.00**
Bowl, vegetable; round, 8½", from $8.00 up to **10.00**
Casserole, w/lid, from $20.00 up to **25.00**
Creamer, from $6.00 up to **8.00**
Cup, AD; from $6.00 up to **8.00**
Pickle dish, from $10.00 up to ..**12.00**
Plate, pie; 7", from $3.00 up to ..**5.00**
Platter, oval, 13", from $10.00 up to **12.00**
Salt & pepper shakers, pr, from $8.00 up to **10.00**
Sauce boat, from $6.00 up to ..**8.00**
Sauce boat stand, from $8.00 up to **10.00**
Saucer, AD; from $3.00 up to ..**5.00**
Saucer, from $2.00 up to **3.00**
Sugar bowl, w/lid, from $6.00 up to **8.00**
Teacup, from $3.00 up to **5.00**
Teapot, from $30.00 up to **35.00**

Georgian Eggshell Shape (available in Belmont, Chateau, Greenbriar, and Cashmere)

Bowl, fruit; 5", from $5.00 up to ..**7.00**
Bowl, lug soup; from $10.00 up to **12.00**
Bowl, rim soup; from $8.00 up to **10.00**
Bowl, vegetable; oval or round, from $12.00 up to **15.00**
Casserole, w/lid, from $30.00 up to **35.00**
Chop plate, 14", from $18.00 up to **20.00**
Creamer, from $10.00 up to ..**12.00**
Pickle dish, from $12.00 up to **15.00**
Plate, bread & butter; 6", from $4.00 up to **6.00**
Plate, dinner; 10", from $8.00 up to **10.00**
Salt & pepper shakers, pr, from $16.00 up to **20.00**

Sauce boat, from $12.00 up to ..**15.00**
Sauce boat faststand, from $15.00
up to **18.00**
Sugar bowl, w/lid, from $10.00 up
to **12.00**
Teacup, from $6.00 up to **8.00**
Teapot, from $35.00 up to **40.00**

Rhythm Shape (available in Allegro, Daybreak, Rybaiyat, and Something Blue)

Bowl, cereal/soup; 5½", from $3.00
up to **5.00**
Bowl, coupe soup; 8", from $4.00
up to **6.00**
Bowl, vegetable; round, 8¼", from
$8.00 up to **10.00**
Casserole, w/lid, from $20.00 up
to **25.00**
Creamer, from $6.00 up to **8.00**
Jug, water; 2-qt, from $18.00 up
to **20.00**
Plate, luncheon; 9", from $4.00 up
to **6.00**
Platter, oval, 15½", from $12.00
up to **15.00**
Salt & pepper shakers, from $8.00
up to **10.00**
Sauce boat, from $6.00 up to ..**8.00**
Sauce boat stand/pickle dish, 9",
from $8.00 up to **10.00**
Snack plate, divided, from $15.00
up to **18.00**
Sugar bowl, w/lid, from $6.00 up
to **8.00**
Teacup, from $3.00 up to **5.00**
Teapot, from $25.00 up to **30.00**
Tidbit tray, 3-tier, from $15.00 up
to **18.00**

Swing Shape (available in Blue Flax, Chinese Three, Moss Rose, and Pate Sur Pate)

Bowl, cream soup; from $10.00 up
to **12.00**
Bowl, soup; 8", from $6.00 up
to **8.00**

Bowl, vegetable; oval, from $10.00
up to **12.00**
Butter dish, round, from $20.00
up to **25.00**
Casserole, w/lid, from $25.00 up
to **30.00**
Cream soup liner, from $6.00 up
to **8.00**
Creamer, from $5.00 up to **8.00**
Cup, AD; from $5.00 up to **8.00**
Egg cup, from $10.00 up to ..**12.00**
Muffin cover, from $25.00 up
to **30.00**
Plate, dinner; 10", from $6.00 up
to **8.00**
Plate, pie; 7", from $4.00 up to ..**6.00**
Platter, 13", from $14.00 up
to.....................................**16.00**
Salt & pepper shakers, pr, from
$12.00 up to **16.00**
Saucer, AD; from $3.00 up to ..**5.00**
Saucer, from $2.00 up to **3.00**
Sugar bowl, w/lid, from $5.00 up
to **8.00**
Teacup, from $4.00 up to **5.00**
Teapot, from $30.00 up to **35.00**

Virginia Rose Shape (available in Original, Louise, Gold Circle, and Tulip Basket)

Bowl, fruit; 4", from $4.00 up
to **6.00**
Bowl, soup; from $8.00 up to ..**10.00**
Bowl, vegetable; oval or round,
from $10.00 up to **12.00**
Butter dish, oblong, from $60.00
up to **65.00**
Casserole, w/lid, from $30.00 up
to **35.00**
Creamer, from $10.00 up to..**15.00**
Cup, AD; from $8.00 up to ...**10.00**
Egg cup, from $12.00 up to ..**15.00**
Pepper shaker, KK shape, from
$12.00 up to **15.00**
Plate, bread & butter; 6", from
$4.00 up to **6.00**
Platter, oval, 15", from $18.00 up
to **20.00**

Salt & pepper shakers, pr, from $12.00 up to **15.00**
Sauce boat, faststand, from $12.00 up to **15.00**
Sauce boat, from $10.00 up to .**12.00**
Sugar bowl, w/lid, from $12.00 up to **15.00**
Teacup, from $5.00 up to **7.00**
Teapot, from $45.00 up to **50.00**

Yellowstone Shape (available in Caledonia, Dresden Rose, Fruit Decorated, and Garden Bouquet)

Baker, 7", from $6.00 up to **8.00**
Bowl, '36s,' from $8.00 up to ..**10.00**
Bowl, fruit; 4", from $4.00 up to ..**6.00**
Bowl, soup; 7", from $5.00 up to **6.00**
Bowl, vegetable; 8" or 9", from $10.00 up to **12.00**
Butter dish, round, from $20.00 up to **25.00**
Casserole, w/lid, from $25.00 up to **30.00**
Coffee cup, from $3.00 up to ..**4.00**
Creamer, from $5.00 up to **7.00**
Cup, AD; from $6.00 up to **8.00**
Jug, '24s,' from $25.00 up to ..**30.00**

Pickle dish, from $10.00 up to ..**12.00**
Plate, dinner; 10", from $6.00 up to **8.00**
Platter, 10", from $8.00 up to ..**10.00**
Sauce boat, faststand, from $10.00 up to **12.00**
Sauce boat, from $8.00 up to ..**10.00**
Saucer, AD; from $3.00 up to ..**5.00**
Saucer (coffee), from $2.00 up to **3.00**
Saucer (tea), from $2.00 up to ..**3.00**
Sugar bowl, w/lid, from $5.00 up to **7.00**
Syrup jug, from $25.00 up to ..**30.00**
Teacup, from $3.00 up to **4.00**
Teapot, from $35.00 up to **40.00**

Hull

Established in Zanesville, Ohio, in 1905, Hull manufactured stoneware, florist ware, art pottery, and tile until about 1935, when they began to produce the lines of pastel matt-glazed artware which are today very collectible. The pottery was destroyed by flood and fire in 1950. The factory was rebuilt and equipped

Wells shape with orange floral, platter, 13", $12.00; casserole, $45.00; underplate, 8", $20.00.

with the most modern machinery which they soon discovered was not geared to duplicate the matt glazes. As a result, new lines – Parchment and Pine, and Ebb Tide, for example – were introduced in a glossy finish. During the forties and into the fifties, their kitchenware and novelty lines were very successful. Refer to *Robert's Ultimate Encyclopedia of Hull Pottery* and *The Companion Guide,* both by Brenda Roberts (Walsworth Publishing), for more information.

Athena, cornucopia, #608, green, 8½" **35.00**
Athena, window box, #605, lilac, flared **25.00**
Blue Band, bowl, #19, 5½" **30.00**
Bow-Knot, ewer, B1 ....**100.00**
Bow-Knot, sugar bowl, B22 ..**95.00**
Bow-Knot, vase, B7 ....**150.00**
Butterfly, ashtray, B3, 7" **35.00**
Butterfly, vase, B14, 10½x6" ..**70.00**
Capri, bonbon, #C47C, sea green, w/lid **40.00**
Capri, candy dish, coral, C62C, w/lid, 8½" **45.00**

Capri, pitcher, C87, sea green, 12" **90.00**
Cinderella Blossom, pitcher, #29, 16-oz **38.00**
Cinderella Blossom, salt & pepper shakers, #25, pr **40.00**
Debonair, cookie jar, #0-8 ....**65.00**
Essentials, bowl, E1, 7" **30.00**
Essentials, casserole, E13, w/lid, 6½" **25.00**
Fantasy, candle holders, #78, 6½", pr **28.00**
Fantasy, compote, #79C, footed, brass knob on lid, 8x7" ..**30.00**
Iris, candle holder, #411 ....**55.00**
Iris, vase, #404, 4¾" **50.00**
Jubilee, jardiniere, #426, panelled, 8" dia **25.00**
Jubilee, vase, #103, Egyptian style, 12" **35.00**
Mardi Gras, bowl, #421A, 10¼" dia **35.00**

Mirror Brown

Ashtray, #563, 8" dia **12.50**
Bean pot, #510, w/lid, 2-qt **18.50**
Bowl, vegetable; #542, divided, 10¾x7¼" **16.50**
Butter dish, #561, w/lid **14.00**

Mirror Brown, spoon rest, $18.00 and salt and pepper shakers, $6.00 for the pair.

Casserole, #548, oval, w/lid, 2-qt, 10x7¼" **18.00**
Chip & dip leaf, 15x10½" **18.00**
Coffeepot, #522, 8-cup **25.00**
Cookie jar, #523, embossed, 94-oz **30.00**
Creamer, #518, 8-oz **8.50**
Custard cup, #576, 6-oz **2.00**
Gravy boat & underplate, #511/512 ....**20.00**
Jam jar, #551, w/lid, 12-oz **10.00**
Jug, #525, 2-pt **18.50**
Mug, #502, 9-oz **2.50**
Plate, dinner; #500, 10¼" **4.00**
Plate, salad; #501, 6½" **2.50**
Salt & pepper shakers, #587/588, mushroom shape, 3¾", pr ..**5.00**
Teapot, #549, 5-cup **20.00**

Regal, vase, #302, square top, 5⅗" **12.00**
Sueno, jardiniere, #106/33, 5"..**70.00**
Sueno, vase, #920/33, 9" **95.00**
Sun-Glow, jug, #52, 1½-pt **30.00**
Sun-Glow, wall pocket, #80, cup & saucer shape **50.00**

Parchment and Pine, cornucopia vase, 12", $100.00.

Wildflower, cornucopia, W7 ..**65.00**
Wildflower, vase, W9 ....**100.00**
Woodland Hi-Gloss, jardiniere, W7 ....**60.00**
Woodland Two-Tone, cornucopia, W2 ....**35.00**
Zane Grey, bowl, #420, 11⅛" ..**65.00**
Zane Grey, jug, #440, 2½-pt ..**85.00**

Imperial Glass

The Imperial Glass Company became a well-known fixture in the glassmaking business in 1910, due to the large quantities of carnival glass they produced. During the next decade they employed the lustre process in the manufacture of another successful product, Imperial Jewels, today called stretch glass. In 1958 Imperial bought the old Heisey and Cambridge molds and reproduced some of their original lines; Imperial marked these items with the 'I' superimposed over a 'G' logo. For information on Imperial's glass animals, refer to *Glass Animals of the Depression Era* by Lee Garmon and Dick Spencer (Collector Books). Ms. Garmon is listed in the Directory under Illinois.

Animal, balking colt, Heisey mold, 3½x3½" **185.00**
Animal, bull, signed **1,300.00**
Animal, donkey **250.00**
Animal, elephant bookend **65.00**
Animal, fish, horizontal, rare ..**125.00**
Animal, piglet, sitting or standing, each **75.00**
Animal, plug horse **110.00**
Animal, plug horse, amber ..**600.00**
Animal, polar bear, frosted ..**60.00**
Animal, rabbit paperweight ..**135.00**
Animal, sea horse bookend ..**115.00**
Ashtray, Cathay Crystal, butterfly, #5006 ....**25.00**

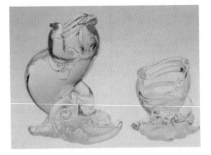

Fish candlestick, sunshine yellow, 1982, made for HCA, marked IG, 5", $45.00; fish match holder, sunshine yellow, made for HCA, marked IG, 3", $20.00.

Basket, caramel slag satin ..**35.00**
Bowl, Doeskin, swan, milk glass, 8" **35.00**
Cake stand, Vintage Grape, milk glass, glossy **40.00**
Creamer & sugar bowl, Cape Cod, #160/30 ....**17.50**
Cruet, purple slag satin **36.00**
Decanter, Peachblow **150.00**
Figurine, cygnet, ruby, marked D&HCA, 2½" **25.00**
Figurine, duck, sitting, caramel slag, 1969-78, 4½" **45.00**
Figurine, elephant, meadow green carnival, limited edition of 750, 4" **95.00**
Figurine, horse, head forward, frosted crystal, 1982, 8½" ..**75.00**
Figurine, mallard, wings up, caramel slag, 1969-78, 7" **35.00**
Figurine, rabbit paperweight, milk glass, 1977, 2¾" **25.00**
Figurine, tiger paperweight, jade, 1980, 8" long **85.00**
Ming jar, Cathay Crystal **80.00**
Mug, Storybook, milk glass, glossy **23.00**
Mustard, Cape Cod, #160/156, w/lid & spoon, 3-pc **17.50**
Oyster cocktail, Cape Cod **8.00**
Plate, Monticello, square, 12" ..**18.00**
Plate, Traditional Blue, 8" ...**10.00**

Salt & pepper shakers, Cape Cod, #160/109, square, pr **18.00**
Spoon rest coaster, Cape Cod, #160/76 ....**6.00**
Tumbler, Bambu, 14-oz **5.00**
Tumbler, Big Shot Series, red, 16-oz **15.00**
Vase, daffodil design, milk glass, glossy, 6" **10.00**

Imperial Porcelain

From 1947 through 1960, the Imperial Porcelain Company of Zanesville, Ohio, produced a line of figurines, trays, bottles, etc., called Blue Ridge Mountain Boys, designed by Paul Webb. It is for this series that they are best known, although they also produced others: the Al Capp Dogpatch series and American Folklore Miniatures, a line of twenty-three animals measuring one inch or less.

Planter, man with jug and snake, $65.00.

American Folklore Miniatures, cow, 1¾" **35.00**
American Folklore Miniatures, hound dogs **35.00**
American Folklore Miniatures, sow **30.00**
Ashtray, hillbilly & skunk, #103 ....**75.00**

Ashtray, 2 men by tree stump, for pipes, #92 ....**125.00**
Decanter, Ma leaning over stump, w/baby & skunk, #104 ..**95.00**
Decanter, man leaning against tree trunk, #101, 5" **90.00**
Figurine, man sitting, 3½" ...**95.00**
Hot pad, Dutch boy w/tulips, round, not Paul Webb ...**30.00**
Jug, Willie & snake, #101 ....**75.00**
Pitcher, lemonade **200.00**
Planter, man drinking from jug, sitting by washtub, #81 ..**75.00**
Planter, man w/chicken on knee, washtub, #105 ....**110.00**
Shakers, Ma & Old Doc, pr **95.00**

Insulators

After the telegraph was invented in 1844, insulators were used to attach the transmission wires to the poles. With the coming of the telephone, their usefullness increased, and it is estimated that over 3,000 types were developed. Collectors today value some of them very highly – the threadless type, for example, often bring prices of several hundred dollars. Color, rarity, and age are all important factors to consider when evaluating insulators. Our advisor is Mike Bruner, who is listed in the Directory under Michigan.

Brookfield, aqua, smooth base ..**3.00**
Brookfield No 20, forest green ..**8.00**
Canadian Pacific RY, light blue **4.00**
Diamond, straw, smooth base ..**8.00**
Diamond/Bar, ice blue, sharp drip points **4.00**
Gayner/No 36-190, aqua, sharp drip points **5.00**
HC Co/Petticoat, aqua, smooth base **6.00**

Hemingray D-990, aqua **2.50**
Hemingray TS, clear or light green **2.00**
Hemingray 109, amber **10.00**
Hemingray 109, Made in USA, clear **7.00**
Hemingray 17, clear, unopened case of 50 ....**30.00**
Hemingray 19, blue or aqua ..**1.50**
Hemingray 40, green w/light amber streaking **5.00**
Hemingray 43, Made in USA, aqua **4.00**
Hemingray 60, Made in USA, light green **5.00**
Hemingray 62, flashed amber ..**25.00**
Hemingray 680, ice green, smooth base **20.00**
Hemingray 9, aqua, flare skirt ..**10.00**
Kerr TW, clear **2.00**
Kimble 830, light green **5.00**
McLaughlin/No 19, light blue, smooth base **6.00**
Surge, clear **3.00**
W Brookfield, 45 Cliff St, aqua, 1 date **5.00**
W Brookfield, 55 Fulton, snowy ice blue, 3 dates **4.00**

Ironstone

There are many types of decorated ironstone available today, but the most sought-after is the simple white dinnerware sometimes decorated in relief with fruit, grains, foliage, ribbing and scallops. It was made by many English potters from the last quarter of the 18th century until well into the 1900s. Most collectors prefer pieces that are well marked, though some of the smaller, very interesting items seldom are. Watch for the 'Red Cliff' mark; these are mid-20th century reproductions. Though they're of high quality and collectible in their own right, don't pay 'antique' prices for them.

Baker, Diamond Thumbprint, Gelson Bros Hanley, 5x7" **60.00**

Bowl, soup; Mocho, T&R Boote, 8⅝" **18.00**

Chamber pot, Panelled Thistle, Bridgwood & Clark **45.00**

Coffeepot, Lily, Burgess **195.00**

Compote, New York, unmarked, round, 9½" **195.00**

Cookie plate, Cherry Scroll, T&R Boote **45.00**

Creamer, Wheat & Clover, Turner & Tompkinson, 7⅜" **85.00**

Cup & saucer, Wheat, W&E Corn, MM **35.00**

Dish, relish; Wheat, J&G Meakin **25.00**

Dish, sauce; Sharon Arch, Davenport, 4" **20.00**

Dish, vegetable; Star Flower, JW Pankhurst & Co **85.00**

Gravy boat, Sydenham, unmarked **85.00**

Mug, Ceres, unmarked, 3⅛x3⅝" dia **75.00**

Pitcher, Ceres, Turner, Goddard & Co, 8¾" **150.00**

Pitcher, Olympic, Elsmore & Forster, 9⅜" **95.00**

Pitcher, President, Edwards, 8⅝" **150.00**

Plate, Athenia, W Adams, 9"..**18.00**

Plate, Laurel, unmarked, 5" ..**12.50**

Plate, Mocho, T&R Boote, 7"..**6.00**

Plate, Rolling Star, James Edwards, 9½" **25.00**

Plate, Sharon Arch, Davenport, 10½" **30.00**

Plate, Sydenham, T&R Boote, 7½" **12.00**

Platter, Ribbed Raspberry, J&G Meakin, 12x9⅛" **38.00**

Platter, Sharon Arch, Wedgwood, 16½" **45.00**

Soap dish, Fig Cousin, Davenport, scarce **75.00**

Toothbrush holder, Columbia, unmarked, 4⅞" **95.00**

Tureen, sauce; Cable & Ring, Bridgwood & Son, w/ladle & underplate **125.00**

Tureen, sauce; Sevres, Edwards, w/underplate **95.00**

Tureen, stew; Wrapped Sydenham, John Maddock, 8x8¾"..**195.00**

Wash bowl, Leaf & Crossed Ribbon, Livesley Powell & Co **65.00**

Wash bowl & pitcher, Scalloped Decagon, Davenport ...**295.00**

Wash pitcher, Forget-Me-Not, Wood, Rathbone & Co, 12" **120.00**

Waste bowl, Lily of the Valley, Anthony Shaw, 3x4¾" **38.00**

Teapot, Ceres, 11", $165.00.

Jadite Glassware

Many of today's kitchenware collectors have found the lovely green jadite glassware just as attractive today as it was to the homemakers of the forties through the mid-sixties. It was produced by the tons by several companies; Anchor Hocking and McKee were two of the larger producers, for both home and restaurant use. It was inexpensive then, and even today with all the collector demand, prices are still very reasonable. Refer to *Glassware of the '40s, '50s, and '60s* by Gene Florence (Collector Books) for more information.

Compote, ribbed, Fire-King, 3¼x6", $15.00.

Dinnerware

Bowl, cereal; Shell, Fire-King, 1964-late 1970s, 6⅜" **3.50**

Bowl, dessert; Jane Ray, Fire-King, 1945-63, 4⅞" **3.00**

Bowl, fruit; Restaurant Ware, Fire-King, 1950-53, 4¾" ..**3.00**

Bowl, Restaurant Ware, Fire-King, 15-oz, 5⅝" **9.00**

Bowl, salad; Charm, Fire-King, 1940-54, 7⅜" **7.50**

Bowl, vegetable; Jane Ray, Fire-King, 1945-63, 8¼" **8.00**

Creamer, Charm, Fire-King, 1950-54 ....**5.50**

Creamer, Shell, Fire-King, 1964-late 1970s, footed **5.00**

Creamer, Swirl, Fire-King **7.50**

Cup, Alice, Fire-King, '40s **2.50**

Cup & saucer, Charm, Fire-King, 1950-54 ....**3.75**

Cup & saucer, demitasse; Jane Ray, Fire-King, 1945-63 ....**20.00**

Cup & saucer, Jane Ray, Fire-King, 1945-63 ....**3.00**

Cup & saucer, Restaurant Ware, Fire-King, 1950-53 ....**6.50**

Plate, Alice, Fire-King, early 1940s, 9½" **12.50**

Plate, dinner; Restaurant Ware, Fire-King, 9" **7.50**

Plate, dinner; Shell, Fire-King, 1964-late 1970s, 10" **4.50**

Plate, luncheon; Restaurant Ware, Fire-King, 1950-53, 8" **3.50**

Plate, Restaurant Ware, Fire-King, 1950-53, 5-compartment, 9⅝" **12.50**

Plate, salad; Restaurant Ware, Fire-King, 1950-53 ....**2.50**

Plate, soup; Jane Ray, Fire-King, 1945-63, 7⅝" **6.00**

Platter, Charm, Fire-King, 1950-54, 11x8" **10.00**

Platter, Shell, Fire-King, 1964-late 1970s, 9½x13" **10.00**

Saucer, Alice, Fire-King, early 1940s **1.00**

Saucer, Jane Ray, Fire-King ..**1.50**

Sugar bowl, Jane Ray, Fire-King, 1945-63, w/lid **8.00**

Miscellaneous

Batter bowl, marked Fire-King, minimum value **12.00**

Bowl, Jeannette Glass, horizontal rib desi⋯ 5½" **12.00**

Bowl, Jeannette Glass, vertical ribs, 9¾" **18.00**

Bowl, serving; Bubble, Fire-King, 8½" **7.50**

Butter dish, Jeannette Glass, embossed Butter in lid, 1-lb, 2-pc **35.00**

Candy dish, Fire-King, scalloped bowl w/foot, 6" **8.00**

Canister, Jeannette Glass, black letters on square form, 48-oz, 5½" **40.00**

Cup, dessert; Leaf & Blossom, Fire-King, ca 1950, 4¾" ..**4.00**

Cup, measuring; McKee Glass, 2-spout **145.00**

Dish, refrigerator; Jeannette Glass, w/floral embossed lid, 5x5" **20.00**
Dish, refrigerator; Jeannette Glass, 4x4" **12.50**
Egg cup, McKee Glass **12.00**
Match holder, Jeannette Glass, rounded rim & foot **12.00**
Novelty, dish, Fire-King, maple leaf form, 6⅝" **3.25**
Novelty, skillet, Fire-King, 1-spout, 6¼" **18.00**
Pitcher, measuring; McKee, graduated, w/handle, 4-cup ..**30.00**
Pitcher, reamer; Jeannette Glass, light green, 2-cup **20.00**
Reamer, McKee Glass, sm ...**20.00**
Trinket box, Fire-King, relief rose on lid, 3½x4½" **22.50**
Tumbler, water; Jeannette Glass, 12-oz **12.00**
Vase, Fire-King, Deco-style rings, 5" **5.50**

Bud vase, tree trunk with applied birds, 7", $25.00.

Japanese Lusterware

Imported from Japan during the 1920s, novelty tableware items, vases, ashtrays, etc., often in blue, tan, and mother-of-pearl lustre glazes were sold through five-and-dime stores or given as premiums for selling magazine subscriptions. You'll find several nice examples at nearly any large flea market you attend this summer, and they may be purchased at very reasonable prices.

Ash receiver, figural pelican w/open mouth, wings held wide, 2½" **12.00**
Ashtray, 3 Little Pigs, Walt Disney, #573, ca 1930s, 3¼x 4¼" **145.00**
Egg cup, Donald Duck, diving pose, marked WDP/Japan, ca 1940, 2½" **165.00**

Figurine, sleeping cat, allover gold lustre w/gold neck tie, 5" long **20.00**
Planter, Fifer Pig, 4", NM **65.00**
Shakers & mustard jar, See No Evil Monkeys, orange & blue, w/spoon **35.00**
Teapot, 3 Little Pigs, gold on white ground, 1930s, w/lid, EX **22.50**
Tray, figural clown sits on fanned-out hand of playing cards, 1½x4" **15.00**
Tumble-up, elephant-form pitcher, allover gold lustre, lg **50.00**
Wall pocket, bird w/flowers, marked Made in Japan, 5", EX **12.50**
Wall pocket, Mickey Mouse & Minnie w/toys, '30s, NM **135.00**

Jasco Bells

Jasco bells are little people figurals that have a theme – Christmas, nursery rhymes, working girls, etc. These were made from the mid-1970s until about 1980 and may be marked Jasco-Taiwan or Made in Taiwan inside the bell base. An imprinted mark or small gold paste stamp may also be found, and dates are imprinted inside the bell's base.

Gold paper, bell-shaped tags tied with a gold cord around the figure's neck may carry the name Merri-Belles, Adorabelles T.M., Cutie Belle T.M., or Strawberry Patches. These tags are also marked Jasco and are dated. All Jasco bells have two holes at the back of the figure (midway down the back) where the clacker is attached with gold cord or string. Another identifying feature is a sprig of holly or a small animal (usually a dog or cat) that is usually found at the base or back of the figure. Our advisor is Jeannie Greenfield, who is listed in the Directory under Pennsylvania.

Angel, holly in hair, colored gown, 4½"-5", from $1.00 up to ..**5.00**
Choir boy w/slingshot in pocket, 4½"-5", from $1.00 up to ..**5.00**

Cinderella (maid), w/broom & slipper, 4½"-5", from $1.00 up to **5.00**
Girl w/broom, 4½"-5", from $1.00 up to **5.00**
Girl w/mixing bowl, 4½"-5", from $1.00 up to **5.00**
Girl w/teakettle, 4½"-5", from $1.00 up to **5.00**
Jack Be Nimble, red nightclothes, 4½"-5", from $1.00 up to ..**5.00**
Shepherd boy, striped coat, staff & lamb, 4½"-5", from $1.00 up to **5.00**

Jewelry

Today, anyone interested in buying gems will soon find out that the antique stones are the best values. Not only are prices from one-third to one-half less than on comparable new jewelry, but the craftsmanship and styling of modern-day pieces are lacking in comparison. Costume jewelry from all periods is popular, especially Art Nouveau and Art Deco examples. Signed pieces are par-

Bells, from $1.00 to $5.00 each.

ticularly good, such as those by Miriam Haskell, Georg Jensen, David Anderson, and other well-known artists.

Plastic jewelry (Catalin or Bakelite, celluloid, and Lucite, in particular) from the '20s to the '50s is extremely collectible, and some of the better pieces have become very expensive. Refer to *Fifty Years of Collectible Fashion Jewelry* by Lillian Baker (Collector Books) for more information.

Bracelet, Beau, linked etched & engraved leaves, 1940 ....**45.00**
Bracelet, Emmons, Coins of the Realm, overlapping gold disks, 1970 ....**60.00**
Bracelet, Emmons, Rustic Beauty, antiqued gold-tone replica, 1950 ....**30.00**
Bracelet, Emmons, Scimitar, faux gems & pearl spacers **20.00**
Bracelet, Jewel Art, linked sterling chain w/engraved heart drop, 1940 ....**60.00**
Bracelet, Sarah Coventry, Harvest Wheat, antique gold-tone, 1950 ....**30.00**
Bracelet, Trifari, rhinestones & faux ruby in enamelled rhodium, 1945 ....**95.00**
Brooch, Castlecliff, pink baroque pearl in gold coral design, 1960 ....**55.00**
Brooch, Danecraft, sterling repouse & openwork grape & leaf, 1950 ....**60.00**

Brooch, Kramer, rhinestones & Aurora Borealis stones in filigree, 1960 ....**60.00**
Brooch, Mimi, rhinestones in ribbon design, 1960 ....**40.00**
Brooch, Tortolani, pearls in crown, 1970 ....**40.00**
Brooch, Trifari, cabachon faux gems & rhinestones in crown, 1960 ....**80.00**
Comb, side; stones in celluloid, Victorian, ca 1890, sm **35.00**
Cuff links, Avon, enamelled antique autos on gilt brass, 1970 ....**15.00**
Cuff links & tie tac, die-stamped Indian head penny, electroplate, 1960 ....**20.00**
Cuff studs, fleur-de-lis center in mother-of-pearl horseshoe, 1950 ....**30.00**
Dress clip, Eisenberg, rhinestones in gold-wash sterling, 1930-40 ....**100.00**
Earrings, Castlecliff, cast-pierced rhodium, 1950-60 ....**80.00**
Earrings, Charel, foiled & faceted Aurora Borealis, 1950 ...**15.00**
Earrings, folded silver mesh drops, ca 1940 ....**75.00**
Earrings, Hattie Carnegie, pave-set rhinestones in rhodium, 1945 ....**85.00**
Earrings, Hollycraft, pastel stones in goldtone metal, 1960 ..**30.00**
Earrings, Mosell, hand-painted gold shell, 1960 ....**30.00**
Earrings, Mosell, hand-painted gold electroplate shell ...**30.00**

Bracelet, red Czechoslovakian crystals and rhinestones, gold wash, $90.00.

Necklace and earrings, plastic beads, marked Hobe on clasp, $30.00 for the set.

Earrings, Napier, gold electroplate twisted rope design, 1950 ....**15.00**

Earrings, Nettie Rosenstein, pave-set rhinestones in rose, 1960 ....**40.00**

Earrings, polished agate in sterling, marked Pat Sterling, 1940 ....**55.00**

Earrings, Renoir, Art Moderne design, copper, 1950-55 ..**25.00**

Earrings, Siam, silver, 1950 ..**25.00**

Earrings, Trifari, cabachons & pave-set rhinestones in gold, 1960 ....**80.00**

Earrings, Trifari, rhinestones & enamelled rhodium cluster, 1945 ....**50.00**

Earrings, Weiss, Austrian faux gems in japanned setting, 1950-60 ....**75.00**

Hat ornament, child's, jeweled chicks w/bar between, ca 1924-45 ....**20.00**

Hatpin, 2 faux pearls separated by jeweled ring, screw end, ca 1924-45 ....**17.50**

Necklace, Danecraft, cast sterling in floral design, 1940 ....**55.00**

Necklace, Trifari, pave set rhinestones & faux sapphire drops, 1950 ....**175.00**

Necklace & earrings, Trifari, white beads & filigree leaves, 1955-60 ....**50.00**

Pin, Assessocraft, gold electroplate Maltese cross, 1940 ....**15.00**

Pin, Beau, sterling Art Moderne cat, 1950 ....**30.00**

Pin, Boucher, Blackamoor, enamel & faux gems on gold, 1960 ..**85.00**

Pin, Boucher, cultured pearl & rhinestones, gold electroplate, 1960 ....**40.00**

Pin, Boucher, enamelled gold angelfish, 1955 ....**50.00**

Pin, Cadoro, gold-tone double bow, 1955 ....**15.00**

Pin, Coro, emamelled peacock, gold electroplate, 1950 ..**65.00**

Pin, Danecraft, sterling repousse leaf, 1940 ....**50.00**

Pin, Danecraft, sterling shamrock w/ring (can be used as charm), 1950s **40.00**

Pin, Emmons, Glamour-Puss, Art Moderne cat, green stone eyes, 1967 ....**17.50**

Pin, Emmons, Lambkin, enamelled oxidized brass, 1960 ......**12.50**

Pin, Emmons, Rainbow Star, Aurora Borealis stones & pearls on gold, 1950 ......**27.50**

Pin, Hollycraft, faux gems in Christmas tree, 1955-65 .**30.00**

Pin, Jeanne, heavy cast, burnished gold acorn & leaf, 1950-60 ....**40.00**

Pin, Park Lane, 2-tone Florentine prancing horse, 1950-60 ..**30.00**

Pin, large amber glass stones studded with round crystals, $35.00.

Pin, Polcini, enamelled gold clown, movable limbs, 1950 ......**75.00**

Pin, scarf; Assessocraft, gold electroplate lion head w/ring, 1955-65 ....**75.00**

Pin, scarf; Emmons, rhodium tassles, screw-tip, 1950 .**30.00**

Pin, scarf; Trifari, gold feather, 1960 ....**12.50**

Pin, scatter; Emmons, Scarecrow, gold-tone & pearl, tassle limbs, 1960 ....**27.50**

Pin, scatter; enamelled mouse on ice skates, marked JJ, 1960...............................**15.00**

Pin, scatter; Gerry's, enamelled gold fox, 1960 ....**15.00**

Pin, scatter; hand-cast gold cat, gem accents, marked BSK, 1960 ....**30.00**

Pin, scatter; Manolf, gold lion w/gem eyes, 1960 ....**30.00**

Pin, scatter; Trifari, gold bird w/glass eye, 1960 ....**17.50**

Pin, Schiaparelli, pink rhinestone & faux pearl flower design, 1935 ....**45.00**

Pin, Trifari, basket design, baguette rhinestones & pear topazes, 1960 ....**40.00**

Pin, Trifari, dragonfly, enamelled metal, 1960 ....**40.00**

Pin, Trifari, white enamelled gold flower w/glass bead center, 1955-60 ....**30.00**

Pin, Weiss, faux rubies in electroplated gold heart, 1950 ..**35.00**

Pin, Weiss, multicolor stones in Christmas tree, 1960 ....**30.00**

Pin & earrings, Emmons, Blue Bud, faceted glass in rhodium, 1970 ....**27.50**

Pin & earrings, Sarah Coventry, Snowflake, smoke glass & rhodium, 1960 ....**60.00**

Ring, Hopi Indian, turquoise & silver, plain, ca 1950 .....**85.00**

Plastic

Bracelet, bangle; geometric carving, narrow **28.00**

Bracelet, bangle; rhinestones set in deep carving **80.00**

Bracelet, bangle; scratch carved, narrow **18.00**

Bracelet, bangle; no carving, narrow **6.00**

Bracelet, bangle; no carving, wide **10.00**

Bracelet, bangle; 4-color (or more) stripes **125.00**

Bracelet, bangle; 6 inlaid polka dots, narrow **180.00**

Bracelet, clamper; inlaid geometric designs **150.00**

Bracelet, clamper; w/inlaid rhinestones **40.00**

Buckle, latch type, 1-color, uncarved **5.00**

Buckle, slide type, 1-color, no carving **4.00**

Dress clip, floral carving **20.00**

Earrings, lg drop style, pr **10.00**

Earrings, novelty, figural, animal, or vegetable; pr **35.00**

Hair pin, French paste in Art Moderne design celluloid, ca 1930 ....**15.00**

Hatpin, faceted bead, ca 1930-40, 4½" **25.00**
Necklace, carved red & amber beads, 18" **65.00**
Necklace, uncarved green beads, 20" **40.00**
Pin, animal, resin wash w/glass eye, sm **75.00**
Pin, animal or vegetable, 1-color, lg **80.00**
Pin, animal or vegetable, 1-color, sm **60.00**
Pin, carved floral, sm **32.00**
Pin, geometric design w/danglers, 1-color **45.00**
Pin, multicolor Art Deco design, sm **40.00**
Pin, novelty or patriotic figural, 1-color, sm **65.00**
Ring, inlaid Art Deco stripe design, 2-color **45.00**
Ring, no carving, 1-color **15.00**
Ring, no carving, 2-color **25.00**

Keen Kutter

Watch for items marked Keen Kutter, a brand name used before the mid-1930s by E.C. Simmons Hardware Company. Not only are their products (household items, tools of all types, knives, etc.) collectible, but so are the advertising materials they distributed.

Bottle, oil; glass w/paper label, #K114 ....**65.00**
Calipers, outside; #K46 ....**40.00**
Carpenter pencil, #K107 ....**7.00**
Clippers, hair; #K543, w/original box **35.00**
Emery cloth, per sheet **8.00**
Flint paper, #KF2 ....**10.00**
Glass cutter, w/original box .**40.00**
Hammer, brick; 5½" head **55.00**
Hatchet, guage; #S20 ....**20.00**
Knife, linoleum; #K64 ....**18.00**
Kraut cutter, 8" blade, 26" ...**75.00**

Mallet, #KK306 ....**22.50**
Nail puller, 18" **40.00**
Plane, smooth; #KK35, 9", wood bottom & handle **45.00**
Pliers, slim nose; #KK25 .....**22.50**
Plumb bob, hexagonal, 8-oz ..**45.00**
Punch, revolving; #KK44 .....**22.50**
Rachet, utility; rigid **55.00**
Razor, straight; #K15, black handle w/logo **35.00**
Razor, straight; Celebrated, ½" blade, black handle **25.00**
Rule, zigzag; #KK506, 72" ...**27.50**
Saw, butcher; #K15, 20" blade .**40.00**
Saw, compass; 14" **20.00**
Saw, metal cutting; #K106, 15 teeth per inch **85.00**
Screwdriver, #K50, 8" blade ..**17.50**
Sharpening stone, sm **10.00**
Spatula, metal **15.00**
Tack claws, #KK5 ....**15.00**
Vise, bench; #KK500 ....**45.00**
Wrecking bar, carpenter's, goose neck, 18" **15.00**
Wrench, #K1000, ½ & ⁷/₁₆ **20.00**
Wrench, adjustable; #K6 ......**25.00**

Kentucky Derby Glasses

Kentucky Derby glasses are the official souvenir glasses sold filled with mint juleps on Derby Day. The first glass (1938), picturing a black horse within a black and white rose garland and the Churchill Downs stadium in the background, is said to have either been given away as a souvenir or used for drinks among the elite at the Downs. This glass, the 1939, and two glasses said to have been used in 1940 are worth thousands and are nearly impossible to find at any price.

Preakness glasses beginning in 1973 and Belmont glasses

beginning in 1976 are also becoming increasingly popular with collectors. Most dealers suggest buying the most expensive glasses first, as their values appreciate rather rapidly.

Bar Derby glasses, as they are called by dealers and collectors, are glasses making reference to the Derby in some way but were sold in bars, other retail stores, or possibly as souvenirs — they were not the official glasses sold at the track. Our advisor, Betty Hornback, is listed in the Directory under Kentucky.

1959-60, ea	**60.00**
1961	**85.00**
1962	**60.00**
1963-64, ea	**40.00**
1965-66, ea	**40.00**
1967-68, ea	**38.00**
1969	**32.00**
1970	**45.00**

1975, $8.00.

1971-72, ea	**28.00**
1973	**30.00**
1974, mistake	**14.00**
1974, regular	**12.00**
1976	**12.00**
1976, plastic	**10.00**
1977	**7.50**
1978-79, ea	**9.00**
1980	**15.00**
1981	**8.00**
1982	**6.00**
1983	**7.00**
1984-85, ea	**6.00**
1986	**7.00**
1986 ('85 copy)	**15.00**
1987-89, ea	**5.00**
1990-91, ea	**3.50**

Souvenir Glasses From Other Racing Events

Belmont, 1976	**60.00**
Belmont, 1977	**325.00**
Belmont, 1978	**125.00**
Belmont, 1979	**60.00**
Belmont, 1980	**125.00**
Belmont, 1981	**325.00**
Belmont, 1982	**300.00**
Belmont, 1983	**300.00**
Belmont, 1984	**150.00**
Belmont, 1985	**90.00**
Belmont, 1986	**55.00**
Belmont, 1987	**30.00**
Belmont, 1988	**30.00**
Belmont, 1989	**25.00**
Belmont, 1990	**10.00**
Belmont, 1991	**8.00**
Belmont, 1992	**6.00**
Belmont, 1993	**5.00**
Breeder's Cup, 1988	**10.00**
Breeder's Cup, 1989	**25.00**
Breeder's Cup, 1990	**12.00**
Derby Festival, 1984	**10.00**
Derby Festival, 1987	**8.00**
Derby Festival, 1988	**7.00**
Derby Festival, 1989	**6.00**
Derby Festival, 1990	**5.00**
Derby Festival, 1991	**4.00**
Derby Festival, 1992	**3.00**

Jim Beam, 1983 ....**32.00**
Jim Beam, 1984 ....**15.00**
Jim Beam, 1985 ....**20.00**
Jim Beam, 1986 ....**15.00**
Jim Beam, 1987 ....**8.00**
Jim Beam, 1988 ....**7.00**
Jim Beam, 1989, 1990, or 1991,
    ea **6.00**
Jim Beam, 1992 or 1993, ea ..**5.00**
Preakness, 1973 ....**325.00**
Preakness, 1974 ....**150.00**
Preakness, 1975 ....**75.00**
Preakness, 1976 ....**50.00**
Preakness, 1977 ....**50.00**
Preakness, 1978 ....**60.00**
Preakness, 1979 ....**55.00**
Preakness, 1980 ....**55.00**
Preakness, 1981 ....**50.00**
Preakness, 1982 ....**50.00**
Preakness, 1983 ....**47.00**
Preakness, 1984 ....**40.00**
Preakness, 1985 ....**25.00**
Preakness, 1986 ....**30.00**
Preakness, 1987 ....**25.00**
Preakness, 1988 ....**22.00**
Preakness, 1989 ....**20.00**
Preakness, 1990 ....**10.00**
Preakness, 1991 ....**8.00**
Preakness, 1992 ....**6.00**
Preakness, 1993 ....**5.00**

King's Crown

This is a pattern that's been around since the late 1800s, but what you're most apt to see on today's market is the later issues. Though Tiffin made it early, our values are for the glassware they produced from the forties through the sixties and the line made by Indiana Glass in the seventies. It was primarily made in crystal with ruby or cranberry flashing, but some pieces (from Indiana Glass) were made with gold and platinum flashing as well. Tiffin's tumblers are flared while Indiana's

are not, and because the latter are much later and more easily found, they're worth only about half as much as Tiffin's. Refer to *Collectible Glassware from the '40s, '50s, and '60s* by Gene Florence (Collector Books) for more information.

Footed fruit compote, 7x9¾", $25.00.

Ashtray, square, 5¼" **10.00**
Bowl, cone; 11¼" **40.00**
Bowl, finger; 4" **15.00**
Bowl, flower floater; 12½" **35.00**
Bowl, salad; 9¼" **45.00**
Cake salver, footed, 12½" **60.00**
Candy box, w/lid, flat, 6" **32.00**
Cheese stand **15.00**
Compote, sm, flat **15.00**
Pitcher **100.00**
Plate, dinner; 10" **30.00**
Plate, salad; 7⅜" **12.00**
Punch set, footed, 15-pc **300.00**
Stem, wine, 2-oz **7.50**
Vase, bud; 9" **25.00**

Kitchen Collectibles

From the early patented apple peelers, cherry pitters, and food choppers to the gadgets of the twenties through the forties, many collectors find special appeal in kitchen tools. Refer to

Kitchen Antiques, 1790-1940, by Kathyrn McNerney (Collector Books) for more information.

Apple corer, tin w/wooden handle, Boye Needle Co, Patent 1916 ....**10.00**

Apple corer/parer, Dandy, tin & wood, non-mechanical, Patent 1913 ....**15.00**

Bean stringer/slicer, steel blade, marked Bean-X, Orange NJ, 6½" **10.00**

Bowl, mixing; Western Stoneware, salt glazed, 10" dia **55.00**

Bread knife, carbon steel & wood, American Cutlery, Victoria, 14¾" **15.00**

Bread knife, carbon steel w/iron loop handle, Comet, Patent Nov 1890 ....**17.50**

Bread machine, cast iron, Cyrus Chambers Jr...Machine Co, 1900s, 16" **90.00**

Cake mixer/cream whip, tin, Rumford, Patent 1908 ..**15.00**

Cake pan, stamped tin, Py-O-My, 9½" **18.00**

Cake turner, nickeled steel, Kitchen Kumfort Trowel, ca 1915, 10" **10.00**

Cake whip, stainless steel, painted wood handle, LA & J Mfg, 1930s, 13" **10.00**

Can opener, metal, For Karo Cans Only, Patent 1935 ....**10.00**

Can opener, nickeled & tempered steel, wood handle, marked A&J, 8½" **15.00**

Can opener, steel w/wood handle, marked Sure Cut, 1904 ..**15.00**

Can opener, tan & brown marbelized Catalin handle **7.50**

Cheese slicer, plated hacksaw form w/wires, ca 1920-49, 6⅝" **3.00**

Cherry pitter, cast iron, Cherry Stoner No 17, #2884, Patent 1903, 12" **38.00**

Cherry pitter, cast iron, Home Cherry Stoner, Patent 1917, 10½" **35.00**

Clothes dryer, wooden, folding umbrella type, ca 1905 ..**25.00**

Clothespin bag, made from Purina chicken feed sack, ca 1920s-40s **15.00**

Corn stick pan, molded glass, 6 ear, Miracle Maize, 12x7" **25.00**

Cream separator, tin w/wooden legs, Marvel, ca 1900s ...**25.00**

Cream whip, Andirock **22.00**

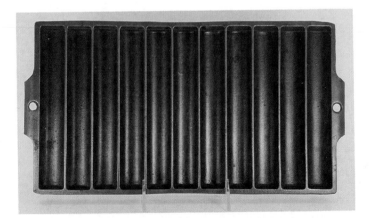

Wagner Ware cornstick pan, 5¾x13", $40.00.

214

Cutter, doughnut; tin, wide arched handle, ca 1900s, 2½" dia **12.00**

Egg separator, aluminum w/2 slots in shallow cup, advertising, 3¾" **12.00**

Egg slicer, cast aluminum, hinged top, Bloomfield Industries, ca 1935 ....**12.00**

Egg whip, tinned wire, twisted handle, 8" **27.00**

Eggbeater, nickeled metal, 8 wings w/painted knobs, Androck, 1930s, 7" **25.00**

Eggbeater, nickled steel, No 75 Super Center Drive, Ekco, 1930, EX **25.00**

Flour sifter, scoop-shaped tin w/side handle, Shift-Chine, ca 1931 ....**12.00**

Flour sifter, tin, yellow wood handle, KWIK, 5-cup **15.00**

Food mill, cast iron, Eveready #55, screw clamps, 8" **22.50**

Food mill, cast iron, Rollman Food Chopper #12, screw clamps **12.50**

Fork, olive; rod w/2 tines, Just the Tool for Small Bottles, 8" ..**3.00**

Fork, stainless steel, painted green wood handle, ca 1930s, 14½" **8.00**

French fry cutter, stamped tin, Maid of Honor, ca 1920s-30s **5.00**

Fruit baller, metal shaft, red wood handle, 1940s, 7¾" **4.00**

Grater, revolving drum type, tin, screw clamp, marked BME #620, 1930s **15.00**

Grater, wood & tin, marked Favorite, 12½x3" **18.00**

Ice cream scoop, nickeled brass, wood handle, Hamilton Beach #60, 1930s **25.00**

Ice crusher, Dazey **10.00**

Ironing board, wooden, height adjusts, folding type, 1920s, 30" long **50.00**

Juicer, orange; aluminum w/ reamer inside, crank top, Knapps, 1930 ....**10.00**

Ladle, cream; stamped tin, dated 1924 ....**8.00**

Lemon squeezer, maple, hinged, w/porcelain insert, 8½" ..**40.00**

Meat grinder, tinned cast iron, Enterprise #5, screw clamp, ca 1910 ....**20.00**

Meat tenderizer, carved wood roller w/wire handle, 12" **20.00**

Milk skimmer, stamped perforated tin w/crimped & turned rim, 6" **15.00**

Milk strainer, bowl w/brass wire-cloth bottom, Central Stamping, 9" dia **12.50**

Mixer jar, glass w/wire dasher, Robert's Lightning Mixer, 8" **30.00**

Egg beater, Turbine, ca 1930, 9½", $20.00.

215

Nutmeg grater, nickeled cast iron, w/wood knob on crank, ca 1910 ....**80.00**

Nutmeg grater, stamped & punched tin, coffin type, 6½x2½" **25.00**

Pan, lady finger; stamped tin, Kreamer, Brooklyn NY ..**20.00**

Pan, muffin; tin, 6 fluted cups in solid frame, EKCO **8.00**

Pan, pastry; tin w/scalloped sides, 3" dia **5.00**

Pan, pastry; tin w/scalloped sides, 4" dia **8.00**

Pastry blender, heavy nickeled iron w/wood handle, 9¼" **12.00**

Pastry blender, steel w/6 wires, red plastic handle, ca 1930s, 6x4" **12.00**

Pastry blender, wire, steel & wood, Androck, Pat'd 1929, 5¼x4" **7.50**

Pea sheller, painted sheet metal, crank handle, Homes, ca 1910, 5¼" **42.50**

Pie crimper, green Catalin handle, Vaughn's, 1920s **17.50**

Pie pan, tin, flared sides, embossed Manning, 7¾" dia **10.00**

Pie server, tinned metal w/green painted wood handle, Rumford, 1910s **8.00**

Pineapple corer/peeler, tinned metal, ca 1930s, 5" **18.00**

Pineapple eye clip, nickeled steel, trigger action, Patterson's, 1905 ....**5.00**

Pineapple eye snips, painted cast iron, WH Collins, ca 1928, 5⅝" **8.00**

Potato masher, flat steel disk w/wood handle, Hercules, ca 1904 ....**12.50**

Potato masher, Kilbourne Mfg, twisted wire, wood handle, ca 1908 ....**22.50**

Raisin seeder, cast iron, table clamps, EZY...Scald the Raisins, 5" **40.00**

Raisin seeder, cast iron, wire & rubber, screw clamps, 1890s **20.00**

Rice ball, tin & wire w/locking handle, 1930, 5¼" **12.50**

Rice baller, aluminum **10.00**

Ricer, plated tin, hinged cast iron handle, ca 1925, 10¾" ...**18.00**

Ricer, tin & zinc-plated iron, painted red wood handle, ca 1930s **13.00**

Rosette kit, screw rod handle w/8 cast iron heads, Century, ca 1933 ....**25.00**

Scoop, candy; 1-pc molded glass, ca 1920s **28.00**

Shaker, flour; aluminum, paneled sides, Mirro, late 1920s, 2⅝x 2⅜" **4.50**

Salt and pepper shakers, Chalaine blue, 5", $100.00 for the pair.

Shredder/slaw cutter, tin, Wonder Grater, ca 1930s, 8½x 4½" ..**8.00**

Spice mill, painted cast iron, wall mount, Enterprise No 00, ca 1900 ....**40.00**

Spoon, basting; cast aluminum, Mueller & Co, 14" **8.00**

Spoon, pressed wood fiber, Sanispoon, American Container, ca 1920, 5" **4.00**

Spoon, stamped tin, grooved handle, 5¼" **3.00**

Strainer, curved wire, painted red handle, ca 1920s-30s, 5" ..**20.00**

Strawberry huller/chicken pin-feather puller, Spee-dee, 1" wide **5.00**

Teakettle, cast alumimum, hinged lid, Wear-Ever #330, 1903-15, 8" dia **45.00**

Thermometer, candy; metal w/green wood handle, Taylor, 1940s **15.00**

Thermometer & skewer set, Westinghouse Betty Furness, in original box **12.50**

Tongs, tan marbelized Catalin handles **6.00**

Vegetable parer, aluminum w/steel blade, De Vault, 1935 ....**6.00**

Water mellon plugger, iron ..**12.00**

Whip, New Dream Cream, Kohler Die & Specialty, 12" **30.00**

Whisk, wire spoon w/coiled spring bowl, wood handle, ca 1925-30 ....**10.00**

Knives

Collectors of pocketknives look for those with bone handles in mint, unsharpened condition, those with pearl handles, Case doctor's knives, and large display models. Refer to *The Standard Knife Collector's Guide, Second Edition,* by Ron Stewart and Roy Ritchie (Collector Books) and *Sargent's American Premium Guide to Knives and Razors, Identification and Values,* (Books Americana) for more information.

Browning, 2018F2, marked USA, pearl handle, 2-blade **36.00**

Browning, 2018F2, marked USA, wood handle, 2-blade **26.00**

Browning, 3318F2s, Germany, stag handle, 2-blade **42.00**

Browning, 504, Japan, stag handle, 3-blade **80.00**

Case, Muskrat, marked USA, bone handle, 2-blade, 1965-69, 3⅞" **50.00**

Case, 11011, marked XX, walnut handle, 1-blade, 1940-64, 4" **45.00**

Case, 2138LSS, 10 Dot, black composition handle, 1-blade, 1970, 5⅝" **40.00**

Case, 2229½, USA, slick black handle, 2-blade, 1965-69, rare, 2½" **125.00**

Case, 2345½, USA, slick black handle, 3-blade, 1960s, 3⅝" ..**125.00**

Case, 4100SS, 10 Dot, white composition handle, 1-blade, 1970, 5½" **75.00**

Case, 5172, marked USA, stag handle, 1-blade, 1960s, 5½"..**165.00**

Case, 5332, 10 Dot, stag handle, 3-blade, 1970, 3⅝" **65.00**

Case, 6111½L, marked XX, bone handle, 1-blade, 1940-64, 4⅜" **150.00**

Case, 620035EO, marked XX, black plastic handle, 2-blade, 1940-64, 3" **50.00**

Case, 62024½, Tested XX, green bone handle, 2-blade, 1920-40, 3" **150.00**

Case, 62131, marked XX, bone handle, 2-blade, 1964, 3⅝" ..**250.00**

Case, 6308, 10 Dot, bone handle, 3-blade, 1970, 3¼" **45.00**

Case, 6445R, marked USA, bone handle, 4-blade, 1960s, 3¾" ..**50.00**

Case, 661, sheath, Tested XX, green bone handle, 7½" ..**75.00**

Case, 92001T, Tested XX, cracked ice handle, 2-blade, 2⅝"..**110.00**

Case, 93047, marked XX, cracked ice handle, 3-blade, 1940-64, 3⅞" **250.00**

Case, 9333, marked XX, cracked ice handle, 3-blade, 1940-64, 2⅝" **40.00**

Keen Kutter, EC Simmons, Barlow, white celluloid handle, 2-blade, 3" **60.00**

Keen Kutter, EC Simmons, Congress, brown bone handle, 2-blade, 3¾" 85.00

Keen Kutter, EC Simmons, sleeveboard, pearl handle, 2-blade, 2⅞" 45.00

Keen Kutter, EC Simmons, trapper, brown bone handle, 1-blade 90.00

Keen Kutter, KS323, pen, ivory handle, 2-blade, 3" 40.00

Keen Kutter, K254, Barlow, brown bone handle, 2-blade, 3⅜" 60.00

Keen Kutter, 3315/CC, whittler, celluloid handle, 2-blade, 3⅝" 100.00

Keen Kutter, 366R, EC Simmons, whittler, ebony handle, 3-blade, 3⅝" 125.00

Keen Kutter, 801, Daddy Barlow, brown bone handle, 1-blade, 5" 125.00

Queen, 15, Congress, Rogers bone handle, 2-blade, 3½" 40.00

Queen, 22, Barlow, brown bone handle, 2-blade, 3½" 45.00

Queen, 57, pearl handle, 3-blade, 3⅜" 30.00

Queen, 60, Barlow, winterbottom bone handle, 1-blade, 3½" 35.00

Queen Steel, 11EO, winterbottom bone handle, 1-blade, 4"..25.00

Queen Steel, 48, whittler, winterbottom bone handle, 3-blade, 3½" 45.00

Remington, advertising, Kelly Tires, faux ivory handle, 2-blade, 3" 100.00

Remington, RC8, cocobolo handle, 2-blade, 3⅜" 70.00

Remington, R1103, brown bone handle, 2-blade, 3⅜" ...135.00

Remington, R2095, black & white composition handle, 2-blade, 3⅛" 90.00

Remington, R219, brass, long pull, 2-blade, 3⅝" 175.00

Remington, R3059, stockman's, metal, 3-blade, 4" 250.00

Remington, R378, cocobolo handle, 2-blade, acorn shield, 3¾" 150.00

Remington, R6063, Congress, brown bone handle, 2-blade, 4¼" 225.00

Remington, R6105, Congress, pyremite handle, 2-blade, 3" 125.00

Remington, R6423, bone handle, 3-blade, 3⅜" 125.00

Remington, R6625, sleeveboard, cracked ice handle, 2-blade, 3⅛" 90.00

Remington, R6723, whittler, brown bone handle, long pull, 3-blade, 3" 250.00

Remington, R6925, Congress, faux ivory handle, 2-blade, 3" ..125.00

Remington, R698, hawkbill, cocobolo handle, 1-blade, 4" ..110.00

Remington, R7425, sleeveboard, onyx handle, 2-blade, 3" ..95.00

Remington, R8034, bartender's, pearl handle, 2-blade, 3" 250.00

Western States, B249S, trapper, black composition handle, 2-blade, 4" 75.00

Western States, 06265C, bone handle, 2-blade, 3⅜" 30.00

Western States, 6111SP, Barlow, bone handle, 1-blade, 3⅜" 100.00

Western States, 643, whittler, cracked ice handle, 3-blade, 3¼" 35.00

Western States, 7372P, whittler, faux horn handle, 3-blade, 3¼" 125.00

Winchester, 1938, brown bone handle, 1-blade, 3⅜" ...125.00

Winchester, 2068, sleeveboard, celluloid handle, 1-blade, 3⅜" 180.00

Winchester, 2084, sleeveboard, blue celluloid handle, 1-blade, 3⅜" 160.00

Winchester, 2113, peanut, celluloid handle, 2-blade, 2¾" **125.00**
Winchester, 2641, trapper, cocobolo handle, 2-blade, 3⅞" **300.00**
Winchester, 2847, brown bone handle, 2-blade, 3¼" ...**125.00**
Winchester, 3959, stockman's, brown bone handle, 3-blade, 4" **250.00**

Labels

The colorful lithographed labels that were once used on wooden packing crates are being collected for their artwork and advertising. Clever association between company name or location and depicted themes are common; particularly good examples of this are usually most desirable. For instance, Santa Paula lemon labels show a jolly Santa Claus, and Red Cat oranges have a cat mascot.

Best Strike Apples, Pajaro Valley, 9x11", $35.00.

All Good Peaches, can, peaches on twig, EX **4.00**
Bare Foot Boy Tomatoes, can, barefoot boy by stream, M **4.00**
Beaver Cherries, lug box, beaver on pond, red background, M ...**2.50**

Best Reserve Succotash, can, corn, EX **12.00**
Butte Mountain Pears, mountain scene, red letters, 10½x7½", EX **7.50**
Cal-Fine Tomato Puree, can, WWII eagle, EX **2.00**
Camellia Oranges, spray of Camellias on white satin, 10x11", M **12.00**
Clipper Cranberries, ships at sea, 7x10", EX **5.00**
Cry Baby Grapes, lug box, baby crying on red background, M **3.00**
Del Monte Asparagus, can, red logo on green, 1-lb, M **3.00**
Del Monte Corn, can, red logo on green, 1-lb, M **2.00**
Del Monte Olives, can, red logo on green, 9-oz, M **2.00**
Ekco Tomatoes, lug box, boy shouting at cliff, M **2.00**
Elk Brand Prunes, can, elk's head on red background, M **6.00**
Elkhorn Peas, elk's head, 7x9", M **1.50**
Florida Cowboy Citrus, cowboy on horse, 7x7", EX **8.00**
Glen Ranch Lemons, 1920s house & citrus groves, 9x12", M **4.00**
Gold Band Pineapple, can, vista of Napa Valley, blue background, M **6.00**
Gold Dust Plums, can, black on orange, M **8.00**
Golden Eagle Oranges, eagle, 11x10", EX **5.50**
Hearts Delight Citrus, dancing couple, 9x9", EX **4.50**
Helena Grapes, lug box, view of Napa Valley, M **3.00**
Hi-Goal Asparagus, crate, polo player on horse, EX **5.00**
Holly Cherries, can, black cherries, red logo, M **10.00**
Honeysuckle Pears, can, yellow w/red trim, M **4.00**

Kiltie Grapefruit, plate w/grape-
fruit half on red plaid, M ..**4.00**
Lofty Lemons, glass of lemonade,
vista in center diamond,
9x12", M **3.00**
Mount Hamilton Plums, can, multicolored plums on red &
green, M **3.00**
Og-Na Sweet Corn, can, embossed
Indian Chief in profile, M .**3.00**
Red Star Apples, lg red star &
gold eagle, 9x11", M **5.00**
Rowley's Kidney Beans, can,
embossed bowl on blue, gold
logo, M **3.50**
Sea King Clams, can, bowl of
clams, EX **18.00**
Sierra Vista Oranges, orchard
scene, 11x10", EX **12.50**
Snow Crest Pears, lug box, snow-
covered mountain, dimen-
sional letters, M **2.50**
Summerland Lemons, ocean,
beach, cliffs & mountains,
9x12", M **15.00**
Sundown Grapefruit, desert &
mountains, 11x10", EX ..**40.00**
Sweet Briar Peaches, can, peaches
& pink flowers, M **6.00**
Universal Mixed Fruit, can, colorful
fruit vignette on red, M **5.00**
Ventura Maid Lemons, lady in maid's
uniform, 11x9", EX **13.50**
Waldorf Apples, bellhop carrying lg
apple on tray, 9x11", M **2.50**
Wayne Beets, can, portrait of
General Wayne, M **5.00**

Lace, Linens and Needlework

Crocheted and tatted lace
are varieties of handwork most
often encountered at flea markets today; and collectors can
still appreciate the tedium,
expertise, and eyestrain that
went into their making. If your
treasured laces are yellowed or
stained, an instant tea bath can
be used to obtain a natural ecru
look and is far less damaging to
the old threads than using bleach
to whiten them. Doilies are often
framed and hung in groupings on
bedroom walls or used to top
throw pillows. From remnants of
lace trims, you can create your
own Victorian 'waist.' Either trim
a ready-made or sew one up
using a basic pattern. The
newest use for lovely old crocheted pieces is to drape them
over one or both shoulders of a
man's vintage suit jacket (they're
made of wonderful fabrics).
Applique a long coordinating
man's tie around the neck and
down the front, and add a few
antique buttons for trim. Roll up
the sleeves so the lining will
show, and you have a 'boutique'
fashion of your own design!

Apron, chambray w/embroidered
flowers & scrolls, 1930s ..**35.00**
Bedspread, embroidered daisies,
blue ruffled trim w/lace, 45"
long **125.00**
Bloomers, white cotton, 4" eyelet
ruffles **120.00**
Boudoir cap, frothy crochet work
w/medallion & lg satin
bow **45.00**
Camisole, chemise, nainsook, &
lace w/pin tucks & feather
stitching **50.00**
Centerpiece, crocheted w/allover
diamond design, square ..**30.00**
Centerpiece, Flemish lace w/rose
& scroll design, ca 1900,
round **90.00**
Centerpiece, tatted linen w/scal-
loped edges **35.00**
Chair set, filet crochet w/holly &
bird design, 3-pc **80.00**

Collar, ecru linen w/embroidered flowers & machine-added lace, 1930s **40.00**
Collar, tatted ecru w/10 medallions, early 1900s, 21x4" **50.00**
Collar/cuff set, baby's, crocheted w/shamrock, rose, & thistle design **175.00**
Doily, ecru, crocheted, ca 1940, oval, 12x9" **25.00**
Dress, baby's, white nainsook w/ elaborate hand-embroidered design **40.00**
Handkerchief, blue chiffon w/ embroidered flowers, wide lace border **25.00**
Handkerchief, cotton batiste w/cutwork corners & tatted edging **40.00**
Hot pad, heavy crochet w/cardboard insert, 1915, oval ..**15.00**
Lingerie case, satin & lace w/handmade rosette, 14½x10" ...**45.00**
Luncheon cloth, linen, crocheted corners w/roses & leaves, 44x44" **45.00**
Pillow case, linen w/crocheted insert, pr **65.00**
Pillow sham, Battenberg design in center, attached ruffles ..**55.00**
Runner, linen, Swedish, stylized Christmas trees, 41" **45.00**
Tablecloth, linen, embroidered baskets of flowers, lace trim, 1930s **60.00**
Tea cloth, muslin, crocheted corners w/leaves & flowers, +6 napkins **65.00**
Towel, Can Can girl embroidered on stamped design, 1930s **12.50**

Law Enforcement

The field of law enforcement collectibles is very diverse and often highly specialized. This is a difficult field in which to establish values as the hobby is still basically in its infancy, and there are vast differences of opinion.

The most common law enforcement collectible is the badge. This symbol of authority first made its appearance in the late 1840s and gained widespread use during the late 1800s to the early 1900s. Made in a variety of materials, the most common is nickel-plated brass. There are some examples constructed of sterling silver or gold that are sometimes embellished with gems. The price of these badges usually begins with the current market price of the precious metal being used. Many badges will bear a hallmark or maker's name on the reverse. Beware! There are several companies and individuals who make reproduction badges! A good idea is to secure a copy of a reproduction catalog to protect yourself from individuals who try to sell these as originals.

Other popular law enforcement collectibles include photos, paper items such as posters, handcuffs, leg irons, uniforms, shoulder patches, and night sticks. Many collectors specialize in items from a specific era or location, which contributes to the wide diversity of values.

There are several books that offer information: *Badges of Law and Order* by George Virginies; the excellent work by Joe Goodson, *Old West Antiques and Collectibles*, and an outstanding new reference, *Badges of the U.S. Marshals*, by George Stumpf and Ray Sherrard. The field is also served well by the fine monthly newsletter, *Police Collector News*, published by Mike Bondarenko. Our advisor is Tony Perrin, who is listed in the Directory under Arkansas.

Badge, Chief of Police, Belmead TX, state seal, silver w/eagle atop **40.00**

Badge, Chief of Police, Washington DC **90.00**

Badge, Deputy Sheriff, Laramie, 5-point star, silver metal ...**20.00**

Badge, hat; Mexican police, enameled **16.00**

Badge, Naval Police, Seabees emblem, 1940s **85.00**

Badge, Safety Officer, Temple University, black enameling on silver **40.00**

Badge, Security Police, Indianapolis IN, 1950, NM ..**24.00**

Buckle, Police, Fargo ND, nickeled brass, ca 1900 ......**175.00**

Cabinet photo, policeman w/ badge, 1910s **25.00**

Club, hard rubber, Chicago maker's mark embossed on side **42.00**

Medal, San Francisco pistol tournament, 1933, silver w/ crossed pistols **25.00**

Pamphlet, Peter's Police Ammunition, 1930s **6.50**

Patrolman, Chicago, 5-point star, enameling on silver **80.00**

Reward postcard, $100 for Black Jack Hughes murderer, w/ photo, 1907 ....**65.00**

Reward postcard, $25 for return of stolen horse, 1907 .....**16.00**

Reward poster, $10 Reward for..., w/picture, 1911 ....**15.00**

Reward poster, FBI wanting man for auto theft, 1927 ....**6.00**

Reward poster, wanted man escaped from San Quentin, 1907, 8½x11" **45.00**

Lefton China

Since 1940 the Lefton China Co. has been importing and producing ceramic giftware which may be found in shops throughout the world. Because of the quality of the workmanship and the beauty of these items, they are sought after by collectors of today. Lefton pieces are usually marked by a fired-on trademark or a paper label found on the bottom of each piece. Our advisor is Loretta De Lozier, who is listed in the Directory under Iowa.

Bank, #01280 ....**8.00**
Birthday Girl, #1987J **8.00**
Creamer & sugar bowl, #5884 ..**10.00**
Lipstick holder **2.50**
Pin box, #217 ....**10.00**

Tea bag holder, #6672, $7.50.

Plate, Lord's Prayer **9.50**
Ring box, #207 ....**6.00**
Sparrow, #KW-864 ....**13.00**
Teapot, miniature **8.50**
Tumbler, #7685 ....**4.50**
Vase, #1102 ....**4.00**
Wall plaque, #057 ....**2.50**

Letter Openers

Made from wood, ivory, glass, and metals, letter openers are fun to collect without being expensive. Generally the most valuable are advertising openers and figurals made of brass, bronze, copper or iron.

Abalone, 5¼" **5.00**
Brass, dagger form, 9½", in red
    leather scabbard **15.00**
Brass, lion figural handle, Victo-
    rian **45.00**
Bronze, Prudential Has Strength
    of Gibralter, 1878-1948,
    6" **15.00**
Copper, Western Employer's Ser-
    vice, San Francisco/Oakland,
    6" **12.00**
Ivory, carved dagger form, Orien-
    tal, 12" **35.00**
Metal, arrowhead figural, Anaconda
    Copper & Brass, EX **15.00**

Metal, Gulf Oil **10.00**
Mother-of-pearl w/sterling handle,
    3" **7.50**
Plastic, Fuller Brush man figural,
    pink **8.00**
Silverplate, Protective Fire Insur-
    ance, EX **25.00**
Whalebone w/rosewood handle,
    7", EX **75.00**

License Plates

Early porcelain license plates are treasured by collectors, and often sell for more than $500 for the pair when found in excellent condition. The best examples are first-year plates from each state, but some of the more modern plates with special graphics are collectible too. Prices given below are for plates found in good or better condition. Our advisor is Richard Diehl, who is listed in the Directory under Colorado.

Alabama, 1985, Nat'l Guard ..**4.50**
Alaska, 1966, totem pole **25.00**
California, 1940 ....**20.00**
Colorado, 1975, Dealer **3.50**
Colorado, 1988, Nat'l Guard ..**25.00**
Delaware, 1974 ....**8.50**
Hawaii, 1978 ....**15.50**

Presidential Inauguration, Washington DC, 1981, $25.00.

Iowa, 1966 ....**3.50**
Kansas, 1915 ....**75.00**
Kansas, 1968, Disabled Vet-
    eran **7.50**
Kansas, 1984, Sunflower **5.50**
Louisiana, 1986, World's Fair ..**20.00**
Maryland, 1957 ....**12.50**
Minnesota, 1987, Explore **2.50**
Minnesota, 1988, Handicap ...**5.50**
Missouri, 1976, Bicentennial ..**7.00**
Montana, 1988, Centennial ..**19.50**
Nebraska, 1941 ....**25.00**
Nevada, 1987, Silver State **4.50**
New Jersey, 1934 ....**17.50**
North Dakota, 1986, Teddy ..**10.50**
Oklahoma, 1928 ....**18.50**
Oregon, 1991, Tree **4.00**
Pennsylvania, 1987, Friend ...**5.50**
South Carolina, 1989, National
    Guard **3.50**
South Carolina, 1989, Taxi **5.50**
South Dakota, 1988, Handicap ..**5.50**
Tennessee, 1959 ....**10.50**
Texas, 1958, pr **18.50**
Utah, 1979, Beehive **12.50**
Vermont, 1962 ....**6.00**

Liddle Kiddles

Produced by Mattel between 1966 and 1971, Liddle Kiddle dolls and accessories were designed to suggest the typical 'little kid' in the typical neighborhood. These dolls can be found in sizes ranging from ¾" to 4", all with posable bodies and rooted hair that can be restyled. Later, two more series were designed that represented storybook and nursery rhyme characters. The animal kingdom was represented by the Animiddles and Zoolery Jewelry Kiddles. There was even a set of extraterrestrials. And lastly, in 1979 Sweet Treets dolls were marketed.

Our values are for items that are mint on card or mint in box.

Deduct 25% for dolls complete with accessories but with the box or card missing, and 75% if no accessories are included but the doll itself is dressed. For further information we recommend *Liddle Kiddles Dolls and Accessories* by Tamela Storm and Debra Van Dyke (Collector Books).

Liddle Kiddles Club playset, 9", **$10.00.**

Lucy Locket Kiddles, 4 'magic' dolls, clothes that cling..**10.00**
Alice in Wonderliddle, 3½", w/rabbit, watch & booklet **45.00**
Baby Biddle, blue scarf, red jacket, 3", in convertible, M on card **25.00**
Baby Rockaway, Black, 2", w/green plastic bunny cradle **25.00**
Beddy-Bye Biddle, pink nightie, 3", w/yellow bed, pink bedspread **30.00**
Case, blue w/Howard Biff Boodle & Lola Liddle, 5" dia, M ..**7.00**
Chitty Chitty Bang Bang Kiddles, 4 dolls (2 2", 2 1") in book package **50.00**
Cookin' Hiddle, blue flocked dress, pink panties, 3½", doll only, M **20.00**
Cookin' Hiddle, 3½", w/7 pcs of yellow kitchen furniture **75.00**
Freezy Sliddle, in snow suit, 3½", on blue sled **25.00**

Greta Griddle, blue polka dotted dress, 3½", w/table & 2 chairs, M **30.00**

Harriet Heliddle, w/pusher mechanism, 4", pedals helicopter **25.00**

Heather Hiddlehorse, w/pusher mechanism, 4", rides pink horse w/wheels **35.00**

Ice Cream Sundae doll, Chocolottie, 2", in ice cream house ...**16.00**

Jewelry Kiddle, Flower Pin, 1" doll **12.00**

Jewelry Kiddle, Heart Necklace, 1" doll, blue heart w/pink stones **20.00**

Kiddle Collector's Case, pink w/8 Kiddles pictured, M (no insert) **8.00**

Kiddle Kolognes Paper Dolls, Whitman, #1992:59, 13x10" ...**10.00**

Kola Kiddles, Shirley Strawberry, 2", in bottle w/red cap & base, M **12.00**

Kones, Frosty Mint, 2", w/green cherry, ice cream & cone ..**12.00**

Kosmic Kiddle, Purple Glurple, 2½", in spaceship on rock base **25.00**

Liddle Biddle Peep, 3½", w/ staff, wooly sheep & storybook **45.00**

Liddle Kiddle Pop-Up Playhouse, 10x8½" closed, M **8.00**

Liddle Kiddle Town, pictures 9 Kiddles in town setting, 21" long, M **25.00**

Liddle Red Riding Hiddle, 3½", w/fuzzy wolf, basket, & storybook **45.00**

Lois Locket, Black, 2", gold locket w/green stones **25.00**

Lola Locket, shoulder-length hair, 2", gold locket, light green door **15.00**

Lolli-Grape, 2", w/purple lollipop, M **12.00**

Lucky Lion 2", w/safety pin on back **12.00**

Luvvy Duvvy Kiddle, 2", made for Valentine's Day, card is package **12.00**

Mini-Kiddle Pop-Up Soda Parlor w/¾" Kutie doll, soda parlor package **15.00**

Pop-Up Fairytale Castle w/¾" Princessa, package opens to castle **15.00**

Rapunzel & Prince, 2", in book-shaped box w/heart-shaped window **50.00**

Shelia Skediddle, 4", w/Skediddler pusher mechanism **15.00**

Sleeping Biddle w/Castle, w/eyelashes, 3½", w/castle & couch, M **65.00**

Snap Happy Patio Furniture, 4 chairs, picnic & end tables, chaise **10.00**

Surfy Skiddle, in pink & navy bikini, 3", on yellow surfboard, M **25.00**

Sweet Pea Kologne, 2", in pink bottle w/yellow cap & base **10.00**

Sweet Treats, Peachie Parfait, 2" doll in blue spoon **5.00**

Tea Party, Lady Lavender, 3½", w/flower-decaled cup & saucer **30.00**

Zoolery Mini Kiddle, ¾", in cage on gold-link bracelet or necklace **25.00**

Little Golden Books

Little Golden Books (a registered trademark of Western Publishing Company Inc.), introduced in October of 1942 were an overnight success. First published with a blue paper spine, the later spines were of gold foil. Parents and grandparents born in the '40s, '50s, and '60s are now trying to find the titles they had as children. From 1942 to the early

1970s, the books were numbered from 1 to 600, while books published later had no numerical order. Depending on where you find the book, prices can vary from 25¢ to $30 plus. The most expensive are those with dust jackets from the early '40s or books with paper dolls and activities. The three primary series of books are the Regular (1-600), Disney (1-140), and Activity (1-52).

Television's influence became apparent in the '50s with stories like the Lone Ranger, Howdy Doody, Hopalong Cassidy, Gene Autry, and Rootie Kazootie. The '60s brought us Yogi Bear, Huckleberry Hound, Magilla Gorilla, and Quick Draw McGraw, to name a few. A TV Western title from the '50s is worth around $12 to $18. A Disney from 1942 to the early '60s will go for $8 to $15 (reprinted titles would be lower). Cartoon titles from the '60s would range from $6 to $12. Books with the blue spine or gold paper spine (not foil) can bring from $8 to $15. If you are lucky enough to own a book with a dust jacket, the jacket alone is worth $20 and up. Paper doll books are worth around $30 to $36. These values are meant only to give an idea of value and are for 1st editions in mint condition. Condition is very important when purchasing a book. You normally don't want to purchase a book with large tears, crayon or ink marks, or missing pages.

As with any collectible book, a 1st edition is always going to bring the higher prices. To tell what edition you have on the 25¢ and 29¢ cover price books, look on the title page or the last page of the book. If it is not on the title page there will be a code of 1/ the alphabet on the bottom right corner of the last page. A is for a 1st edition, Z will refer to the twenty-sixth printing.

There isn't an easy way of determining the condition of a book. What is 'good' to one might be 'fair' to another. To find out more about Little Golden Books, we recommend *Collecting Little Golden Books* (published by Books Americana), a most informative book by our advisor, Steve Santi, who is listed in the Directory under California. See also Children's Books.

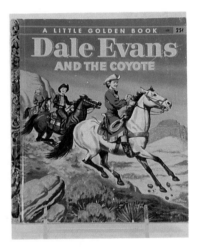

Dale Evans and the Coyote, #253, 1956, M, $12.00.

ABC Around the House, #176, 1978, M **4.00**
Albert's Stencil Zoo, #112, 1951, M **25.00**
Animals & Their Babies (wheel book), #A-29, 1959, M ...**10.00**
Animals of Farmer Jones, #11, 1942, M **20.00**
Best of All, A Story About the Farm; #170, 1978, M **4.00**
Captain Kangaroo & the Panda, #278, 1951, M **10.00**

Cars, #251, 1956, M **7.00**
Christmas Manger, #176, 1953,
  M **15.00**
Christmas Story, #158, '52, M ..**8.00**
Christopher & the Columbus,
  #103, 1951, M **8.00**
Come Play House, #44, 1948,
  M **20.00**
Corky, #482, 1962, M **10.00**
Fish, #5023, 1959, M **12.00**
Five Little Firemen, #64, 1948,
  M **15.00**
Frosty the Snowman, #142, 1951,
  M **8.00**
Gaston & Josephine, #65, 1949,
  M **15.00**

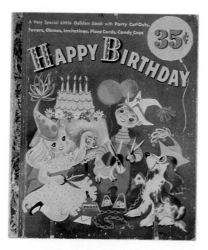

**Happy Birthday, Special Activity,
1st Edition, 1952, M, $12.00.**

Happy Family, #216, '55, M..**12.00**
Happy Man & His Dumptruck,
  #77, 1950, puzzle on back
  cover, M **20.00**
How Big, #83, 1949, M **10.00**
Huckleberry Hound Builds a
  House, #376, 1959, M ...**10.00**
Indian Stamps, #A13, '57, M ..**10.00**
Jack & the Beanstalk, #179, 1953,
  M **8.00**
Laddie & the Little Rabbit, #116,
  1952, M **8.00**

Little Boy w/a Big Horn, #100,
  1950, M **10.00**
Little Crow, #113, 1974, M **4.00**
Little Golden Book of Hymns,
  #34, 1947, M **10.00**
Little Golden Book of Poetry,
  #38, 1947, M **10.00**
Little Red Riding Hood, #42,
  1948, M **12.00**
Lively Little Rabbit, #15, 1943,
  M **18.00**
Magic Compass, #146, 1953,
  M **15.00**
My Baby Brother, #279, 1956,
  M **10.00**
My First Book of Bible Stories,
  #19, 1943 ....**15.00**
My Little Golden Book About
  God, #268, 1956, M **7.00**
My Little Golden Dictionary, #90,
  1949, M **10.00**
National Velvet, #431, '61, M ..**10.00**
Nurse Nancy, #346, '52, M ...**25.00**
Party Pig, #191, 1954, M **15.00**
Pat-a-Cake, #54, 1948, M **10.00**
Poky Little Puppy, #8, '42, M ..**20.00**
Prayers for Children, #5, 1942,
  M **20.00**
Rescuers, #D136, 1977, M **5.00**
Robin Hood, #D126, 1974, M ..**5.00**
Rusty Goes to School, #479, 1962,
  M **12.00**
Scamp, #D63, 1957, M **12.00**
Steve Canyon, #356, 1959, M ..**15.00**
Story of Jesus, #27, 1946, M ..**12.00**
Swiss Family Robinson, #D95,
  1961, M **12.00**
Tawney Scrawney Lion & the
  Clever Monkey, #128, 1974,
  M **5.00**
Tom & Jerry's Party, #235, 1955,
  M **5.00**
Tootle, #21, 1945, M **18.00**
Underdog & the Disappearing Ice
  Cream, #135, 1975, M ...**10.00**
Woodsy Owl & the Trail Bikers,
  #107, 1974, M **4.00**
Words (wheel book), #A-1, 1955,
  M **12.00**

Little Red Riding Hood

Little Red Riding Hood was produced from 1943 to 1957; some items were manufactured by the Hull Pottery of Crooksville, Ohio, who sent their whiteware to the Royal China and Novelty Company (a division of Regal China) of Chicago, Illinois, to be decorated. But a major part of the line was actually made by the Regal Company. For further information we recommend *Collecting Hull Pottery's Little Red Riding Hood* by Mark Supnick (L-W Book Sales). Watch for the announcement of another book on this subject by Joyce and Fred Roerig, authors of *The Collectors Encyclopedia of Cookie Jars* (Collector Books).

Butter dish **350.00**
Canister, salt **1,100.00**
Canister, sugar **650.00**
Cookie jar, open basket **300.00**

Cracker jar, skirt held wide, 8½" **550.00**
Creamer, tab handle **225.00**
Creamer & sugar bowl, head pour, w/lid **700.00**
Creamer & sugar bowl (open), side spout **300.00**
Match holder, wall hanging ..**900.00**
Pitcher, milk; ruffled skirt, w/apron, rare, 8½" **3,000.00**
Pitcher, milk; standing, 8" ..**265.00**
Planter, standing, wall hanging, rare **475.00**
Salt & pepper shakers, standing, 3¼", pr **50.00**
Salt & pepper shakers, standing, 4½", rare, pr **850.00**
Sugar bowl, crawling **250.00**
Teapot **350.00**

Lu Ray Pastels

Introduced in the 1940s by Taylor, Smith, and Taylor of East Liverpool, Ohio, Lu Ray Pastels is today a very sought-after line of collectible American dinnerware.

Salt and pepper shakers, 5¼", $150.00 for the pair.

Platter, 13½", $10.00.

It was made in solid colors: Windsor Blue, Gray, Persian Cream, and Sharon Pink.

Bowl, fruit; 5½"	**4.50**
Bowl, salad; lg	**35.00**
Bowl, vegetable; 9"	**10.00**
Casserole, w/lid	**60.00**
Chop plate, 14"	**18.00**
Creamer	**5.00**
Cup & saucer	**7.50**
Cup & saucer, demitasse; straight sides	**40.00**
Egg cup	**12.00**
Pitcher, juice; ovoid	**110.00**
Plate, 10"	**10.00**
Plate, 6"	**2.00**
Platter, 12" long	**9.00**
Salt & pepper shakers, pr	**8.50**
Sugar bowl, w/lid	**9.00**
Tidbit tray, 2-tier	**18.00**
Vase, bud; 2 styles, each	**150.00**

Lunch Boxes

In the early years of this century, tobacco companies often packaged their products in tins that could later be used for lunch boxes. By the 1930s oval lunch boxes designed to appeal to school children were produced. The rectangular shape that is now popular was preferred in the 1950s. Character lunch boxes decorated with the faces of TV personalities, super heroes, Disney and cartoon characters are especially sought after by collectors today. Our values are for excellent condition lunch boxes only (without the thermos unless one is mentioned in the line). Refer to *Pictorial Price Guide to Vinyl and Plastic Lunch Boxes and Thermoses* and *Pictorial Price Guide to Metal Lunch Boxes and Thermoses* by Larry Aikens (L-W Book Sales) for more information.

Metal

Betsy Clark, '77, w/thermos	**30.00**
Bozo, Aladdin, dome top, '63	**275.00**
Care Bear Cousins, Aladdin, w/ plastic thermos	**15.00**
Dark Crystal, King Seeley, 1982, w/plastic thermos	**30.00**

Dukes of Hazzard, 1980, $10.00.

Family Affair, King Seeley, 1969, w/plastic thermos **100.00**
Fireball XL5, 1960s **170.00**
Get Smart, '66, w/thermos ..**235.00**
Heathcliff, Aladdin, 1982, w/plastic thermos **30.00**
Holly Hobbie, Aladdin, 1975, w/plastic thermos **25.00**
Huckleberry Hound & Friends, Aladdin, 1961 ....**160.00**
James Bond, Aladdin, 1966 ..**170.00**
King Kong, American Thermos, 1977, w/plastic thermos ..**65.00**
Little Red Riding Hood, Ohio Art, 1982 ....**60.00**
Lone Ranger, 1980s **35.00**
Muppet Babies, King Seeley, 1985, w/plastic thermos **15.00**
Nancy Drew Mysteries, King Seeley, 1977 ....**35.00**
Partridge Family, 1971, w/thermos **70.00**
Peter Pan, Aladdin, 1969, w/plastic thermos **130.00**
Popples, Aladdin, 1986, w/plastic thermos **30.00**
Return of the Jedi, King Seeley, 1983, w/plastic thermos ..**15.00**
Sesame Street, Aladdin, 1979, w/plastic thermos **12.50**
Six Million Dollar Man, 1978, w/thermos **60.00**

Smurfs, King-Seeley, w/plastic thermos, NM **185.00**
Street Hawk, Aladdin, 1985 ..**125.00**
Transformers, Aladdin, 1986, w/plastic thermos **18.50**
US Mail, dome top, w/thermos **85.00**
Waltons, 1974 ....**35.00**
World of Dr Seuss, embossed steel, Aladdin, 1970, 7x8x4", EX **85.00**

Plastic

All Dogs Go To Heaven, unknown manufacturer, 1989, w/plastic thermos **40.00**
Astronauts, Thermos, 1986, w/plastic thermos **35.00**
Beach Bronto, Aladdin, 1984 ..**50.00**
Beetlejuice, Thermos, 1989, w/plastic thermos **20.00**
Care Bears, Aladdin, 1986, w/plastic thermos **14.00**
Cinderella, Aladdin, 1992, w/plastic thermos **15.00**
Dick Tracy, Aladdin, 1989, w/plastic thermos **15.00**
Dr Pepper, Taiwan, 1982, w/plastic thermos **50.00**
Dukes of Hazzard, Aladdin, 1981, w/plastic thermos **20.00**
Ewoks, Thermos, 1983, w/plastic thermos **30.00**
Flintstone Kids, Thermos, 1987, w/plastic thermos **40.00**
Garfield (Lunch), Thermos, 1977, w/plastic thermos **22.50**
GI Joe, Aladdin, 1986, w/plastic thermos **22.50**
Happy Meal, Fisher Price **15.00**
Hot Wheels, Thermos, 1984, w/plastic thermos **40.00**
Kool-Aid Man, Thermos, 1986, w/plastic thermos **30.00**
Lunch Man w/Radio, Fun Design, 1986 ....**25.00**
Mermaid, Thermos, 1989, w/thermos **22.50**

Mickey at City Zoo, Aladdin, 1985, w/thermos **17.50**
Popeye, King Seeley Thermos, 1964, w/thermos **300.00**
Rainbow Brite, Thermos, 1983, w/plastic thermos **15.00**
Smurfs, Thermos, England, 1973, w/plastic thermos **22.50**
Star Trek, Thermos, 1988, w/thermos **30.00**
Talespin, Aladdin, 1986, w/plastic thermos **25.00**
Tweety & Sylvester, Thermos, 1986, w/plastic thermos ..**65.00**
Wonder Woman Jr, Mexico, 1981 ....**65.00**

Vinyl

Annie, Aladdin, 1981, w/plastic thermos **75.00**
Barnum's Animals, Adco Liberty, 1978 ....**60.00**
Denim w/flowers, unknown manufacturer, 1984 ....**45.00**
Garfield, Mexico, 1978 ....**150.00**
Haunted House, Dart, 1979 ..**85.00**
Holly Hobbie, Aladdin, 1972, w/plastic thermos **60.00**
Little Ballerina, Bayville, 1975, w/Styrofoam thermos **90.00**
Pebbles & Bamm-Bamm, Gary, 1978, w/plastic thermos **225.00**

Pony Tail Tid-Bit-Kit, Thermos, 1960s **170.00**
Race Car (Puffy), unknown manufacturer **45.00**
School Bus (Puffy), unknown manufacturer, 1985 ....**45.00**
Sleeping Beauty, Aladdin, 1970, w/plastic thermos **300.00**
Washington Apple, unknown manufacturer **35.00**

Maddux of California

In operation since the late 1930s, Maddux made dinnerware accessories, figurines, TV lamps, cookie jars, etc., that are today becoming items of collector interest. The company is located in Los Angeles and continues today to produce and market their own products as well as contracted merchandise for various other companies.

Console set, pink 16" shell w/pr of Early Birds, #1067 ....**15.00**
Figurine, flamingo, #400 & #401, pr **47.50**
Figurine, horse, #982 ....**15.00**
Figurine, Siamese cat, Art Deco, black, 12¼", facing pr **55.00**

Ashtray, leaf shape, #797, 8", $7.50.

Planter, flamingo, pink, #515, 10½" **40.00**
TV lamp, Colonial ship, #892, 10½" **20.00**
TV lamp, covered wagon, #844, 11" **30.00**
TV lamp, double deer, running, natural, #829, 10½" **25.00**
TV lamp, mare & colt, Porcelain White, 11" **45.00**
TV lamp, nativity scene, 3-D planter, #846, 12" **25.00**
TV lamp, stallion, prancing, on base, #810, 12" **25.00**
TV lamp, swan planter, Porcelain White, #828, 12½" **20.00**

Magazines

Magazines are collected for both their contents and their covers, often signed by well-known illustrators or featuring well-known personalities from the sports or entertainment worlds. Their values hinge on the type and quality of the advertising they contain, their cover illustrations, genre, age, rarity, and condition. Values here reflect the worth of magazines in good average condition, unless otherwise described. See also Movie Memorabilia; National Geographics; TV Guides.

American Cookery Magazine, 1943, May-June, G **2.00**
American Home, 1937, April ..**2.50**
American Home Magazine, 1936, April **6.00**
American Junior Red Cross News, 1955, March **2.50**
American Rifleman, 1961, February **1.00**
Aviation Week & Space Technology, 1963, July 22, Manned Space Flight **20.00**

Better Homes & Garden, 1949, March **7.00**
Billboard, 1940, Sept 14, VG ..**18.00**
Boy's Life, 1959, December **4.00**
Car Classics, April 1976, 98 pages, 8x11" **4.50**
Children's Playmate, 1954, December **3.00**
Collier's, 1915, May 29, Civil War Veterans on cover, M **25.00**
Collier's, 1916, April 22, fashion couple on cover, M **25.00**
Collier's, 1955, November 11, Agatha Christie short stories, VG **10.50**
Cosmopolitan, 1934, June, Harrison Fisher cover, G **18.00**
Country Gentleman, 1928, December, Santa cover by Sundblom **6.00**
Country Gentleman, 1948, March, VG **5.50**
DISCoveries, 1989, September, Marty Robbins & Randy Travis **3.00**
Ebony, 1977, April **5.00**
Eerie, 1974, April, Ken Kelly cover, EX **4.00**
Etude, 1932, April, VG **3.00**
Family Circle, 1963, October ..**1.00**
Family Circle, 1968, June, Ann Landers cover, NM **4.50**
Goldmine, 1985, May 10, Record Value Guide, VG **3.50**
Good Housekeeping, 1969, February, Paul Newman cover ..**6.50**
Good Old Days, 1972, July **1.00**
Hobbies, 1946, November **2.00**
Home Arts, 1935, May, EX ..**15.00**
House & Garden, 1948, May, EX **6.00**
House Beautiful, 1940, March ..**4.50**
Jack & Jill, 1947, November ..**1.50**
Ladies' Home Journal, 1972, November **4.00**
Liberty, 1940, November 30, Sax Rohmer, G **12.50**
Life, 1937, Sept 6, Harpo Marx, VG **18.00**

Life, May 8, 1950, Jackie Robinson on cover, EX, $25.00.

Life, 1939, March 6, Tallulah Bankhead **18.00**

Life, 1946, February 4, Bob Hope & Bing Crosby cover **12.00**

Life, 1948, December 6, Montgomery Cliff **15.00**

Life, 1953, Audry Hepburn on cover, EX **20.00**

Life, 1958, December 1, Ricky Nelson **15.00**

Life, 1959, June 22, Next Decade in Space, Special Report on NASA **18.00**

Life, 1961, May 17, Alan B Shepart cover, EX **10.00**

Life, 1962, August 17, Marilyn Monroe cover **15.00**

Life, 1963, November 29, JFK memorial **12.00**

Life, 1963, September 27, stories of the 2nd 9 astronauts .**10.00**

Life, 1965, September 3, Anatomy of a Gemini Spacecraft cover ..**8.00**

Life, 1966, April 15, Louis Armstrong **7.00**

Life, 1966, Sophia Loren on cover, EX **7.50**

Life, 1967, November, Kennedy assassination, EX **12.00**

Life, 1969, July 4, Off to the Moon cover **9.00**

Life, 1969, November 21, Johnny Cash **10.00**

Literary Digest, 1931, February 14, VG **5.00**

Look, Honeymooners cover, November 5, 1966, NM ..**16.00**

Look, 1964, February 11, NY World's Fair preview **3.50**

Look, 1964, September 8 ....**4.00**

Mad Super Special, #14, Don Martin poster insert **4.00**

Manhunt, 1953, April, David Goodis, Evan Hunter, Mickey Spillane, G **10.00**

Marvel Science Stories, 1940, November, VG **25.00**

Modern Romances, 1944, February, EX **4.00**

National Lampoon, 1971, Back-to-School issue, VG **4.00**

National Lampoon, 1976, Gahan Wilson, VG **3.50**

Needlecraft, 1925, September ..**12.50**

New Yorker, 1963, December 21, EX **3.00**

Newsweek, 1941, September 8, Hitler on cover **10.00**

Old Car Illustrated, Fall 1976, 180 pages, 8½x11" **3.50**

Outdoor Adventures, 1957, John Steinbeck, Flight, VG ...**10.00**

Penthouse, 1977, Stephen King's Children of the Corn article, VG **20.00**

People, 1982, March 22, John Belushi on cover, EX **3.50**

Pic Entertainment, 1944, June 20, EX **5.50**

Playboy, 1953 December, Vol I, No 1, VG **1,500.00**

Playboy, 1954, October, VG ..**100.00**

Playboy, 1955, April, NM ...**100.00**

Playboy, 1957, December, VG ..**15.00**

Playboy, 1967, November, EX ..**4.00**

Playboy, 1970, January, NM ..**10.00**

Playboy, 1970, March, EX **3.00**

Playboy 1955, August, VG ...**45.00**

Popular Mechanics, 1965, November 1.50

Progressive Farmer, 1948, March, EX 5.00

Real Detective, 1937, December, VG 3.00

Redbook, 1935, VG 20.00

Redbook, 1989, December, Sally Field & Dolly Parton cover, VG 2.50

Rogue, 1960, Harlan Ellison, Deal from the Bottom, EX 14.00

Saturday Evening Post, 1907, November 23, Pilgrim hunting turkey, VG 10.00

Saturday Evening Post, 1912, December 7, Santa w/children, M 20.00

Saturday Evening Post, 1919, December 27, Santa in window, NM 12.00

Saturday Evening Post, 1924, October 24, Girl Scout w/dog, EX 10.00

Saturday Evening Post, 1931, March 14, lady at spinning wheel, EX 14.00

Saturday Evening Post, 1936, July 4, Captain America, NM ..14.00

Saturday Evening Post, 1938, August 20, cowboys & calfs, NM 12.00

Saturday Evening Post, 1942, January 3, GI baby, VG ..6.00

Saturday Evening Post, 1961, April 1, Rockwell cover, EX 10.00

Saturday Evening Post, 1963, December 14, JFK Memorial issue 8.00

Science Digest, 1968, November, VG 1.00

Sky & Telescope, 1982, October, 25 Years of Space Exploration, VG 4.00

Spinning Wheel, 1975, March ..2.50

Sports Illustrated, 1955, August 8, Cincinnati Reds, NM ..7.00

Sports Illustrated, 1958, September 29, World Series, NM 6.00

Sports Illustrated, 1962, November 19, Lions Football, NM 7.00

Sports Illustrated, 1970, October 19, World Series, M 10.00

Sunshine & Health, 1951, August, VG 3.00

Texas Highways, 1988, November, VG 1.00

Time, 1941, January 6, Winston Churchill, Man of the Year, EX 10.00

Time, 1942, December 21, Katharine Cornell, Judith Anderson, etc 5.00

Time, November 27, 1950, Hopalong Cassidy on cover, M, $20.00.

Time Weekly News, 1967, July 14, King Hussein cover 5.00

Town & Country, 1944, June ..5.00

True Confessions, 1936, Ginger Rogers on cover, EX 5.00

True Experiences, 1942, November 3.00

Twilight Zone, 1981, M 5.00

Vanity Fair, 1983, Thomas Wolfe's Last Poem, VG 4.00

War Cry (Salvation Army), 1937, December 5.00

Woman's Circle, 1967, May ...2.50

Woman's Day, 1950, July 4.50

Woman's Day, 1964, April **1.00**
Women's Household, 1969, September **2.50**
Youth Companion, 1922, May 4, VG **4.50**

Majolica

The type of majolica earthenware most often encountered was made during the 1880s and reached the height of its popularity in the Victorian period. It was produced abroad and in this country as well. It is usually vividly colored, and nature themes are the most common decorative devices. Animal and bird handles and finials and dimensional figures in high relief were used extensively. Refer to *The Collector's Encyclopedia of Majolica* by Mariann Katz-Marks (Collector Books) for more information.

Basket, floral pattern on turquoise, 6-sided, 6" long **285.00**
Bowl, florals on turquoise, scalloped top, 4x9" dia **200.00**
Bowl, mythological scene, lavender, Etruscan, 9¾" dia **175.00**
Bowl, shell shape, turquoise interior, shell feet, Holdcroft, 9" dia **225.00**
Bowl, strawberry blossom, on cobalt, unmarked, 5" dia **120.00**
Box, sardine; pineapple pattern, w/attached underplate, 9½" long **200.00**
Box, sardine; seaweed on cobalt, w/attached underplate, 7½" long **325.00**
Butter dish, floral pattern on cobalt, 7½" dia **250.00**
Butter pat, begonia leaf figural, Etruscan, 3¾" long **40.00**
Butter pat, begonia leaf on basketweave pattern, 3" dia ..**20.00**

Cake stand, leaf on plate design, turquoise, yellow trim, 9" dia **165.00**
Compote, Daisy pattern, pedestal foot, Etruscan, 5x9" **225.00**
Compote, grape & leaf pattern, pedestal foot, 4½x8½" ..**155.00**
Compote, wild rose & rope pattern on cobalt, 6x9¾" ..**225.00**
Creamer, Spaniel dog figural, 4½" **125.00**
Creamer, sunflower & classical urn pattern, Samuel Lear, 3½" **75.00**
Cup & saucer, bamboo & basketweave pattern **200.00**
Cuspidor, shell & seaweed pattern on cobalt, 6-sided top, 6" **225.00**
Dish, morning glory & picket fence pattern, mottled center, 7" dia **90.00**
Humidor, frog strumming a mandolin, 6¾" **185.00**
Mug, lily pattern, lavender interior, pedestal foot, Etruscan, 4" **165.00**
Mug, sunflower on dark blue, 3½" **135.00**
Pitcher, anchor & chain pattern, brown basketweave bottom, 8¼" **100.00**
Pitcher, bamboo & bow pattern, pewter top, 6" **160.00**
Pitcher, ivy on tree bark pattern, turquoise interior, 8" ...**160.00**
Pitcher, owl figural, marked Morley & Co, 8¼" **200.00**
Pitcher, parrot figural, pours through beak, French Faience, 11" **95.00**
Pitcher, stork w/fish in mouth in high relief, George Jones, 8¼" **500.00**
Pitcher, sunflower on brown bamboo background, 5" **80.00**
Pitcher, syrup; green leaf pattern, earth tones, pewter top, 4" **155.00**

Bread plate, Eat Thy Bread With Thankfulness, wheat pattern, 13" long, $150.00.

Pitcher, syrup; pineapple figural, pewter top, 5¼" **160.00**
Plate, bamboo & basketweave pattern, mottled center, unmarked, 8" **50.00**
Plate, bird in flight, turquoise, att to J Holdcroft, 8½" **155.00**
Plate, bow & basketweave pattern on turquoise, 6" **100.00**
Plate, classical scene in center, scalloped edge, Wedgwood, 8" **130.00**
Plate, mottled center, reticulated border, Wedgwood, 9" ..**100.00**
Plate, shell shape, mottled center, Wedgwood, 8½" **80.00**
Platter, begonia & floral on cobalt, handles, 11½" long **165.00**
Platter, flying crane & water lily on cobalt, 10½" dia **135.00**
Sugar bowl, leaf & bow pattern, handles, w/lid, 4" **125.00**
Sugar bowl, shell & seaweed pattern, Etruscan, handles, w/lid, 5" **225.00**
Vase, cobalt, figural lion feet, 9" **160.00**

Maps

There are literally thousands of road maps that have been issued from the early 1900s to the present. Hundreds of different oil companies offered maps at service stations as a service to their customers; for many years they were free! Official state highway departments as well as tourist information centers made maps available. Below is a general guide for the three categories mentioned. Prices apply to maps that are in excellent condition. For further information contact our advisor, Noel Levy; he is listed in the Directory under Texas.

American Oil, California, 1940s ..**4.00**
Amoco, Ohio, 1950s **3.00**
Amoco, Texas, 1920s **10.00**
APCo, Illinois, 1930s **5.00**
ARCO, Salem, 1960s **2.00**
Atlantic Oil, Philadelphia, 1940s **4.00**
Chevron, Arizona, 1970s **2.00**
Chevron, Idaho, 1965 ....**2.00**
Chevron, Los Angeles, 1977 ..**2.00**
Chevron, New Mexico, 1930s ..**5.00**
Citgo, Wisconsin, 1965 ....**2.00**
Cities Service, Minnesota, 1963 ....**2.00**
Co-Op, 1947, Missouri **4.00**
Conoco, Colorado, 1947 ....**4.00**
Conoco, Idaho, 1933 ....**5.00**
Conoco, Oklahoma, 1969 ....**2.00**
Deep Rock, Illinois, 1973 ....**2.00**
El Paso Oil, Arizona, 1961 .....**2.00**
Esso, Boston, 1958 ....**3.00**
Esso, New England, 1936 ......**5.00**
Exxon, New Jersey, 1973 ....**2.00**
Getty Oil, Pennsylvania, 1972 ..**2.00**
Gulf, Boston, 1947 ....**4.00**
Gulf, Illinois & Indiana, 1969 ..**2.00**
Humble Oil, Texas, 1952 ....**3.00**
Marathon, Tennessee, 1987 ...**1.00**
Mobilgas, North & South Dakota, 1949 ....**4.00**
Mobilgas, Pennsylvania, 1961 ..**2.00**
Phillips 55, Georgia, 1963 ......**2.00**
Phillips 66, Wyoming, 1938 ...**5.00**
Pure Oil, New York, 1930 ......**5.00**

Sohio, Ohio, 1936, $4.00.

Shell, Iowa, 1932	**5.00**
Shell, Los Angeles, 1942	**4.00**
Shell, Los Angeles, 1951	**3.00**
Shell, Ontario, 1938	**5.00**
Sinclair, New England, 1947	**4.00**
Sinclair, New York, 1934	**5.00**
Skelly, Missouri, 1955	**3.00**
Standard Oil, Chicago, 1956	**3.00**
Standard Oil, Michigan, 1971	**2.00**
Standard Oil, Wisconsin, 1936	**5.00**
Sunoco, Pennsylvania, 1946	**4.00**
Texaco, Mexico, 1941	**4.00**

Texaco, Montana, 1960	**2.00**
Texaco, New Jersey & Long Island, 1934	**5.00**
Texaco, New Mexico, 1938	**5.00**
Union 76, California, 1953	**3.00**
Vickers Oil, Montana, 1964	**2.00**
White Rose, Kansas, 1940	**4.00**

Marbles

Because there are so many kinds of marbles that interest today's collectors, we suggest you study a book on that specific subject such as one by Everett Grist, published by Collector Books. In addition to his earlier work on antique marbles, he has written a book on *Machine-Made and Contemporary Marbles* as well. His latest title is *Everett Grist's Big Book of Marbles*, which includes both antique and modern varieties. Remember that condition is extremely important. Naturally, chips occured; and though some may be ground down and polished, the values of badly-chipped and repolished marbles are low. Unless a size is given, values are for examples of average (⅝") size.

Akro Agate, box of 100 with patched and ribboned marbles, $200.00.

Akro Agate, carnelian **20.00**
Akro Agate, Imperial **15.00**
Akro Agate, ox-blood swirl on blue opaque **15.00**
Akro Agate, pumpkin half-&-half **1.00**
Bull's-eye china, 6 bull's eyes, red, green & black **30.00**
Clambroth, man-made, opaque w/thin lines of colored glass, sm **150.00**
Comic, Annie **80.00**
Comic, Bimbo **80.00**
Comic, Emma **60.00**
Corkscrew, Akro Agate, opaque white & transparent color ..**3.00**
Corkscrew, Akro Agate, tri-color **3.00**
Corkscrew, lemonade **20.00**
Corkscrew, limeade **15.00**
Corkscrew, Popeye, attributed to Akro Agate **15.00**
Flame, Christensen Agage, $45 up to **65.00**
Lutz, man-made, clear swirl, sm **100.00**
Mica, man-made, transparent glass w/flakes, blue **25.00**
Moonie, Akro Agate, opalescent **2.00**
Net core, white net core w/blue & green bands **25.00**
Peppermint Swirl, man-made, opaque, red, white & blue, sm **90.00**
Ribbon Swirl, white core w/ orange & purple bands ..**35.00**
Slag, amber, lg **6.00**
Slag, Christensen Agate **7.00**
Slag, purple onyx, lg **4.00**
Solid opaque, man-made, pink, 1 or 2 pontil marks, sm **50.00**
Sparkler, Akro Agate, multicolor w/glitter **7.00**
Sulfide, cow, 1⅛" **100.00**
Sulfide, dog, begging, 1¾" ..**125.00**
Sulfide, otter, 1½" **95.00**
Sulfide, squirrel on back legs, 1½", EX **75.00**

Swirl, unknown maker, 4-color **5.00**
Transparent Swirl, solid opaque core, sm **20.00**

Mar-Crest Stoneware

The Western Stoneware Company of Monmouth, Illinois, made products for Marshall Burns, Division of Technicolor, a distributor from Chicago, with the Marshall Burns trademark: 'Mar-Crest.' The most collectible of these wares was a line of old-fashioned oven-proof stoneware with a warm brown finish, including a candle-flame casserole, mugs, pitchers, plates, saucers, cereal bowl, mixing bowls, creamer and sugar, shakers, cookie jar, bean pot, candle holder, ramekins, 4" dessert, range set, divided vegetable bowl, and a coffee carafe or water jug. The spelling Marcrest or MarCrest may also be found.

Pitcher, 8", $9.00.

Bean pot, individual **3.50**
Bean pot, lg **22.00**
Bowl, cereal **4.50**
Bowl, divided vegetable; oval ..**10.00**

Bowl, mixing; size #1, 5" **5.00**
Bowl, mixing; size #2, 6" **5.00**
Bowl, mixing; size #3, 7" **6.00**
Bowl, mixing; size #4, 8¼" **7.50**
Bowl, mixing; size #5, 9½" **9.00**
Carafe **15.00**
Casserole, 8½", w/lid **15.00**
Casserole, 9" dia, w/lid & warming stand **25.00**
Casserole warmer **10.00**
Cookie jar **18.00**
Creamer **6.00**
Cup & saucer **6.00**
French soup, open, individual ..**6.00**
Mug **3.00**
Pitcher, 6" **7.00**
Pitcher, 8" **9.00**
Plate, dinner **4.00**
Salt & pepper shakers, pr **8.00**
Sugar bowl **7.00**

Match Safes

The popularity of match safes started around 1850 and peaked in the early 1900s. These small containers were designed to safely carry matches on one's person. They were made from numerous materials including tin, brass, sterling, gold, tortoise shell and aluminum. They became a popular advertising media at the turn of the century. Most safes can be distinguished from other smalls by a rough striking surface. Match safes have been and are still being reproduced; there are many sterling reproductions currently on the market. Our advisor is George Sparacio, who is listed in the Directory under New Jersey.

Advertising, celluloid wrapped, black printing, 2½x2½", EX **40.00**
Agate, cylindrical w/brass trim, 2⅝", EX **175.00**
Anheuser Busch w/trademark, plated brass, falling lid type, 2x1⅝" **45.00**
Art Nouveau, sterling, 2½x1⅜", EX **78.00**
Book figural w/2 painted matches, wood, 2x1½", VG **28.00**
Book shape w/bicycle motif, gutta percha, 2x1½", EX **135.00**
BPOE w/blue clock face, Pat Nov 11, 1899, 2⅝x1½", EX ..**175.00**
Brass w/allover design, Pat Sept 30, 1884, 3x1⅜", EX **42.00**
Celluloid wrapped, union label for cigar manufacturers, 2½x1½", EX **65.00**
Dog's head figural, floppy ears, glass eyes, plated brass, 2½", EX **225.00**
Domino, celluloid, cream w/black, 1¼x1¾", EX **85.00**
Enameled top w/people, spring lid, plated brass, 1⅜x1¾", French **345.00**
Flask figural, sterling, American, 2¼x1⅜", EX **130.00**
Horseshoe figural, plated brass, ⅞x1⅞", EX **125.00**
Ivory w/scrimshaw engraving on 1 side, 2⅜x1¾", EX **100.00**
Kate Greenaway motif, white metal, 2½x1½", EX **70.00**
Leather wrapped, pyrographic designs, cutter on bottom, 2½x1½" **38.00**
Masonic motif on plated brass inserts, 2½x1½", EX **65.00**
Pan American Expo, aluminum, 3x1½" **28.00**
Poodle begging, glass eyes, wood, 3", EX **235.00**
Rococo motif, sterling, 2¼x1¼", EX **55.00**
St Louis Expo, Palace of Arts, brass, 2⅞x1½", EX **55.00**
Unger, embossed Indian head, sterling, 2½x1½", EX ..**550.00**
Violin figural, plated metal, 2⅝x1", EX **95.00**

Matchcovers

The paper matchbook was patented on September 27, 1892, by Joshua Pussy. He sold his invention to Diamond Match Co., and after the turn of the century, matchbooks became the most popular form of commercial advertising for the next sixty years. No doubt the hobby of matchcover collecting started soon after the first matchcover was produced, but it formally got under way during the 1939 New York World's Fair for which colorful collector's sets were produced. Although all are not valuable, more matchcovers have been manufactured than any other collectible except coins and stamps. Ninety-eight out of every one hundred collectors 'shuck' the matchbook, removing the staple and matchsticks. They are then flattened and collected in special albums. In general, American matchcovers produced prior to the bicentennial had strikers on the front. Federal laws at that time mandated that the striker be moved to the back. Popular categories of collecting include restaurants, hotels, motels, girlies, sports, transportation, and beer/soda. Condition is king and prices will vary. Currently only one price guide is available with over 6,500 prices and descriptions. *The Matchcover Collector's Price Guide, 1st Edition,* ($16.95 + $3.25 shipping and handling) is available from The American Matchcover Collecting Club, P.O. Box 18481, Asheville, NC 28814. For club, collection, or estate sales information, we recommend our matchcover advisor, Bill Retskin. Call him at 704 254-4487 (no collect calls, please) or FAX: 704 254-1066. His newsletter, *The Front Striker Bulletin,* is listed in Clubs and Newsletters in the back of the book.

Note: Although 98% of collectible matchcovers are worth less than a nickel each, there are millions of different ones to collect. What follows are specific examples in popular categories from Bill's new book. All include the actual sale prices. This snapshot guide should be used only as a reference. A complete listing, including over 120 categories and a comprehensive matchcover glossary, is listed in Bill's price guide. Prices are for mint condition matchcovers only.

Key:
20S – 20 stick size
30S – 30 stick size
40S – 40 stick size
(B) – on the back
BE – blue
BS – striker on back
(B/W) – black and white
C – cover
CCC – Civilian Conservation Corps
DBE – dark blue
(F) – on the front
FB – full book
F/B– front and back
FL – full length
FS – front striker
G – Lion Match Co. Giant
GD – gold
HB – half back
HOF – Hall of Fame
(I) – inside
JL – jewel
LBE – light blue
OF – outfield
SR – silver
WE – white

1C,JL,FS,CAM Apollo 8, 1968, Type 1, Miami manumark **5.00**

1C,20S,BS,PAT The British War Relief Society, dated 1948, early (BS) **4.00**

1C,20S,FL Tic-Toc Lounge, photo of blond beauty **13.00**

1C,20S,FS Alt Heidelberg Beer, Columbia Breweries, Tacoma, USA **4.50**

1C,20S,FS CCC Camp, 220th Co, Camps 134, Canton NY ..**4.00**

1C,20S,FS Century of Progress 1933-34, I Will (F) (stock) **10.25**

1C,20S,FS Disney/Military from YW set, 133rd Field Artillery, bulldog **4.50**

1C,20S,FS Drink Bob's Cola, blond w/cola glass (F), slogan (B) **3.25**

1C,20S,FS Drink Dr X, The Tempting Beverage, same ad (F/B) **4.00**

1C,20S,FS Elect Ted Kantor for Sheriff, Primary April 12th, 1938 ....**2.50**

1C,20S,FS,FL Avoid Philadelphia Traffic, Chester/Bridgeport Ferry **3.00**

1C,20S,FS,FL Overnight Motor Transportation Co, truck & logo on side **4.25**

1C,20S,FS from Chez Paree Series, Red Buttons (B/W) photo (F) **5.50**

1C,20S,FS Group 1 Baseball, Melvin 'Mel' Ott, OF, NY Giants, HOF, 1951 ....**18.00**

1C,20S,FS Group 1 Hockey, Tan Set, Type VI, Louis Trudel, Black Hawks **3.00**

1C,20S,FS Hanley's Peerless Ale, Bull Dog, Providence RI (WE) **10.00**

1C,20S,FS hTs above aircraft, Truman Administration, Diamond Match Co **5.00**

1C,20S,FS New York World's Fair 1939-40, Belgian Pavilion Restaurant **6.50**

1C,20S,FS Play: The Egg & I starring Claudette Colbert & Fred MacMurray **7.75**

1C,20S,FS Roosevelt, 1936, United Behind the President **11.00**

1C,20S,FS Salesman's Blank, The Eddie Cantor Comedy Theatre, photo **15.00**

All marked Diamond Match Co., ca 1920: Boston & Albany R.R., $18.00; Camel cigarettes, $12.50; The Greenbrier, $10.00; Perkiomen Bridge Motor Co., $15.00.

1C,20S,FS Showalter Flying Service, Orlando FL, Go Air Taxi **5.50**

1C,20S,FS Texas Centennial, 1936, Dallas, Poultry Group (SR/BE) **7.50**

1C,20S,FS USS Harder, postwar US Navy ship **2.00**

1FB,20S California Zephyr Railroad, name only (F/B) (SR/BK) **5.00**

1FB,20S,FS Bessemer & Lake Erie RR Co, metallic, phone (F), map (I) **3.25**

1FB,20S,FS,FEA Burke's Seneca Restaurant, Canadiaiguq NY, Indians **7.50**

1FB,20S,FS Lindbergh Cover Lion Safety First Type 1 Hotel Astor, NYC **4,000.00**

1FB,20S Stork Club, New York City **3.25**

1FB,30S,BS 51st American Presidential Inauguration, 1989, seal (F) **3.00**

12B Commonwealth Games Set, numbered, contents 25, CBC Bank, 1982 ....**5.00**

12C,20S,FS Tums Wild Bird Set, 6 from series A, 6 from series C **11.50**

19C,20S,BS Playboy Club Set, HMH Pub (I), 1961, cities on footer **10.25**

2FB,G,FS French Casino in Chicago, nude on horse (B), Washington, DC **10.50**

24C,20S Ditados Populares, Portuguese Set, drawing (F), numbered **7.00**

5C,20S,FS Perkins Americana, Sketch 10, Mineral Tea Room, Mineral, VA **3.75**

5C,20S,FS Superior Americana Stock Design Set, 1966, Capitol, etc **2.00**

5C,20S,FS 12th Annual Central PA Stamp Get-Together, May 18th, 1957 ....**1.25**

60C,20S,FS Waverly Blankets Set, Made in South Africa **30.00**

Maytag Collectibles

Just one hundred years ago, F.L. Maytag started a farm equipment business in Newton, Iowa, with three partners and $3,000. Now in its centennial year, that modest start-up is the Maytag Company, the cornerstone of the Maytag Corporation and a giant in the home appliance industry, with projected sales of over a billion dollars for 1993. Long a household word – one of the top fifteen recognized brand names in America – Maytag is a distinguished pioneer in successful management concepts as well, a company with a 100-year reputation for quality and dependability second to none.

While archivists are delving through historical materials in celebration of Maytag's centennial, regular folk are rummaging through trunks in grandmother's attic in hopes of finding Maytag collectibles. Old Maytag appliances, instructional or promotional literature, song books, appliance parts, or accessories could be worth good money.

In addition to its well-known appliances, Maytag has manufactured other products that might surprise people. Before its entry into laundry products, Maytag was the largest manufacturer of feeder attachments for threshing machines. Then with the introduction in 1914 of Maytag's gas-powered Multi-Motor washer, the primary focus shifted from farm implements to easing the lives of farm wives with no access to electric power. Later ingenious attachments to these engine-driven washers created additional appliances such as butter churns, ice cream freezers, and meat-grinding equipment. Depending on whether they are gas or electric, these early washers are valued at $15 to $1,000 by collectors. Their accessories as collectibles range from $150 up.

Toy racers are among the most highly prized Maytag collectibles, selling for $2,000 to $5,000. The earliest of these miniature racing cars were made by Maytag dealers, who put Model 92 washing machines on wagons and used the Multi-Motor to power the vehicles. Approximately five hundred toy racers were manufactured by Maytag between 1934 and the beginning of World War II. They were sold to dealers for promotional use and also were bought by amusement parks to use as carnival rides.

Very early washing machine, minimum value $150.00. Photo courtesy of the Maytag Company.

Battery charger **1,000.00**
Engine caution plate, original ..**25.00**
Lawn mower, minimum **250.00**
Oil can, aluminum, from $15 up
   to **50.00**
Oil measuring cup, from $30 up
   to **75.00**
Square tub parts, ea **25.00**
Wrench, from $5 up to **100.00**

McCoy

A popular collectible with flea market goers, McCoy pottery has been made in Roseville, Ohio, since 1910. They are most famous for their extensive line of figural cookie jars, more than two hundred in all. They also made amusing figural planters, etc., as well as dinnerware, and vases and pots for the florist trade. Though some pieces are unmarked, most bear one of several McCoy trademarks. Beware of reproductions made by a company in Tennessee who is using a very close facsimile of the old McCoy mark. They are making several cookie jars once produced by McCoy as well as other now-defunct potteries. Some of these (but by no means all) are now being dated with a number, for example: '93,' below the mark. Refer to *The Collector's Encyclopedia of McCoy Pottery* by Sharon and Bob Huxford (Collector Books) for more information. See also Cookie Jars.

Ashtray, frothy white on rust, 4-
   part, square, 1964 ....**14.00**
Bank, keg form, Premium Metz
   Beer **45.00**
Bank, Seaman's Bank for Sav-
   ings **30.00**
Basket, Rustic, embossed pine
   cones, brown wash on light
   green **30.00**

Bean pot, hanging pea pods, brown, 1-handle, #22, 1943 ....**35.00**

Bean pot, Suburbia Ware, textured w/horizontal ridges, 2-qt **20.00**

Birdhouse, 1975, hanging **12.00**

Bowl, mixing; pink & blue stripes on yellow ware, early, med **18.00**

Cat feeder, late 1930s **30.00**

Condiment dish, made for the Heinz Co **4.00**

Grease jar, Cabbage, 1954 ...**40.00**

Miniature, deer, white matt, no mark **12.00**

Miniature, pouter pigeon, marked USA **12.00**

Mug, Robin Hood **20.00**

Novelty tray, shaped as cupped hands w/grapes at wrists, yellow **14.00**

Pitcher, allover relief designs, duck's neck handle, green, 1935 ....**45.00**

Pitcher, Antique Rose, 1959 ..**10.00**

Pitcher, Bucaneer, green, tankard form, 1926 ....**75.00**

Pitcher, embossed water lily at base, white matt, no mark, 1935 ....**18.00**

Pitcher, fanciful fish, mouth is pouring lip, blue gloss, 1949 ...**45.00**

Pitcher, tilt jug, yellow, lg **25.00**

Pitcher & bowl, 1967, 1-pc ...**20.00**

Planter, Arcature, 1951 ....**18.00**

Planter, frog with umbrella, 1954, $60.00.

Planter, bathtub, black gloss, 1967 ....**10.00**

Planter, black panther, 1950s ..**30.00**

Planter, Calypso, banana boat w/standing man, brown on ivory **50.00**

Planter, cat beside basket, yellow, USA, 1941 ....**15.00**

Planter, cradle **10.00**

Planter, gondola, 1955 ....**15.00**

Planter, green frog, 1950 .....**12.00**

Planter, Humpty Dumpty, marked USA **12.00**

Planter, Robin Hood **25.00**

Planter, rolling pin w/Blue Boy, no mark, 1952 ....**40.00**

Planter, snowman, 1947 ......**15.00**

Planter, stork by basket, pink gloss w/white & blue blanket, 1956 ....**15.00**

Planter, 3 fawns in woodland setting, 1954, lg **70.00**

Planter bookends, dogs w/fowl, 1955, pr **60.00**

Planting dish, butterfly motif, 1940 ....**18.00**

Stein, boot form, 1971 ....**20.00**

Strawberry jar, long-tailed bird atop, light green & brown, 1950 ....**25.00**

Tea set, Pine Cone, 1946, 3-pc ..**65.00**

Teapot, Sunburst Gold, 1957 ..**45.00**

Vase, double tulip, pink & white w/green leaves, 1955 ....**32.00**

Vase, embossed leaves & flowers, brown shading to green matt, 6" **20.00**

Vase, heart shape w/embossed roses, 4-footed, 1943 .....**18.00**

Vase, stylized spear point leaves, stepped neck w/handles, 1920s, 8" **65.00**

Vase, sunflower, 1954 ....**32.00**

Vase, Wild Rose, 2 pink roses in relief on yellow, 6x4" **15.00**

Wall pocket, apple, 1953 ......**30.00**

Wall pocket, birdbath, 1949 ..**30.00**

Wall pocket, orange on lg green leaf **35.00**

Wall pocket, 3 owls on trivet ..**32.00**
Window box, Grecian, white w/vein-
   ing & green swags **25.00**

Metlox

Since the 1940s, the Metlox
company of California has been
producing dinnerware lines,
cookie jars, and decorative items
which today have become popular
collectibles. Some of their most
popular patterns are California
Provincial (the dark green and
burgundy rooster), Red Rooster
(in red, orange, and brown),
Homestead Provincial (dark green
and burgundy farm scenes), and
Colonial Homestead (farm scenes
done in red, orange, and brown).
See also Cookie Jars.

**California Provincial, coffeepot,
11½", $40.00; tumbler, 5", $20.00;
juice, 3½", $9.00.**

California Ivy, bowl, 9" **25.00**
California Ivy, coaster **10.00**
California Ivy, cup & saucer ..**8.00**
California Ivy, gravy boat,
   w/underplate **25.00**
California Ivy, pitcher, ice lip ..**35.00**
California Ivy, plate, 15" **25.00**
California Ivy, plate, 6" **4.00**
California Ivy, salt & pepper
   shakers, pr **12.00**
California Ivy, sugar bowl &
   creamer **15.00**
California Provincial, bowl,
   fruit **8.00**
California Provincial, bowl, veg-
   etable; divided, handle ..**25.00**
California Provincial, bread
   tray **40.00**
California Provincial, coaster ..**12.00**
California Provincial, cup &
   saucer **10.00**
California Provincial, mug ...**25.00**
California Provincial, plate, bread
   & butter **4.00**
California Provincial, plate, chop;
   12" **25.00**

California Provincial, plate, din-
   ner **10.00**
California Provincial, plate, salad;
   7" **8.00**
California Provincial, platter,
   13½" **25.00**
California Provincial, salt &
   pepper shakers, pr **15.00**
Homestead Provincial, bowl,
   cereal; handle **10.00**
Homestead Provincial, bowl, veg-
   etable; lg **25.00**
Homestead Provincial, coffee-
   pot **60.00**
Homestead Provincial, creamer &
   sugar bowl, w/lid **25.00**
Homestead Provincial, cup **7.00**
Homestead Provincial, jewelry
   box **30.00**
Homestead Provincial, match
   holder **30.00**
Homestead Provincial, plate,
   chop; 12" **25.00**
Homestead Provincial, salt & pep-
   per shakers, pr **12.00**
Homestead Provincial, sprinkling
   can **25.00**
Navajo, bowl, deep, 13" **45.00**
Navajo, butter dish **30.00**
Navajo, chop plate, 12" **30.00**
Navajo, gravy boat, w/under-
   plate **30.00**
Navajo, platter, 12" **30.00**

Navajo, sugar bowl & creamer, w/lid **30.00**

Navajo, teapot **50.00**

Red Rooster Provincial, bowl, cereal; 6" **6.00**

Red Rooster Provincial, butter dish **30.00**

Red Rooster Provincial, creamer **10.00**

Red Rooster Provincial, plate, dinner; 10" **10.00**

Red Rooster Provincial, sugar bowl, w/lid **12.00**

Sculptured Daisy, bowl, vegetable; tab handles, 8" **20.00**

Sculptured Daisy, gravy boat ..**22.00**

Sculptured Daisy, plate, 10" ..**8.50**

Sculptured Daisy, teapot **40.00**

Sculptured Zinnia, plate, 7" ...**5.00**

Sculptured Zinnia, teapot **40.00**

Bowl, Blackberry, 5½" **12.00**

Bowl, Flared Lattice, footed, Fenton **25.00**

Candle holders, Daisy & Button, footed, 2½", pr **15.00**

Covered dish, Baseball **22.00**

Covered dish, Uncle Sam on battleship base **55.00**

Creamer, Paneled Wheat **50.00**

Fern bowl, fern fronds on sides, chain rim, oval, 10x8" ...**35.00**

Plate, Ancient Castle, 7" **40.00**

Plate, Heart Border **15.00**

Plate, Niagara Falls **30.00**

Plate, Woof Woof **50.00**

Salt cellar, master; Strawberry, footed **20.00**

Tray, Beaded Wheel **15.00**

Tray, dresser; flower-like handles, 9" **22.00**

Tumbler, Louisiana Purchase .**20.00**

Wine, Feather **25.00**

Milk Glass

Milk glass has been used since the 1700s to make tableware, lamps, and novelty items such as covered figural dishes and decorative wall plaques. Early examples were made with cryolite and ring with a clear bell tone when tapped.

Molds

The two most popular types of molds with collectors are chocolate molds and ice cream molds. Chocolate molds are often quite detailed and are usually made of tin or copper. While some are flat

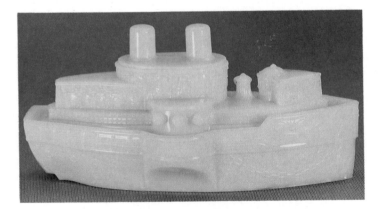

Covered dish, Battleship Maine, 4x8", $60.00.

backed, others make three-dimensional shapes. Baskets, Santas, rabbits, and those with holiday themes are abundant. Ice cream molds are usually made of pewter and come in a wide variety of shapes and styles.

Chocolate

Alphabet, tinned cast metal, marked Auerbach, 12x6" **50.00**
Baby, standing, steel alloy, marked Germany, ca 1910, 6x3⅛" **75.00**
Birds in flight, cast aluminum, ca 1945, 7" **30.00**
Bugle, stamped alloy, 9x4" ...**55.00**
Bulldog, marked Germany, 2-part, ca 1920s-40s, 5x5" **65.00**
Chicken, tin, marked w/dolphin stamp, ca 1900s, 4" **35.00**
Chimney sweep on roof w/ladder, alloy, no mark, 4½x2¾" ..**100.00**
Cigars, 5 tubes, 20th century, 2-part, 5x4½" **35.00**
Dutch boy, tinned nickel alloy, 1930s, 6" **65.00**

Father Christmas, 2-pc, 7" ...**95.00**
Horse, ca 1900s, 4x3" **50.00**
Jack & the Beanstalk, tinned copper, 8x5" **135.00**
Man in moon smoking pipe, metal alloy, 4¼x3" **55.00**
Nesting hen, stamped alloy, 2½x1¾" **45.00**
Owl on branch, tin-plated nickel alloy, marked France, 2" ..**90.00**
Rabbit sitting, basket on back, steel & copper alloy, ca '50s, 17½" **95.00**
Rabbit w/cart, cast aluminum, single hinge, 9" **32.50**
Rabbits on 4 eggs, white metal alloy, 20th century, 10½" **50.00**
Rocket w/boosters, ca 1965, 2-part, 9½x6" **42.50**
Santa Claus, solid nickel silver, 1900s-20s, 7¼" **115.00**

Food

Aluminim, heart form, marked Jell-O **12.50**
Aluminum, rabbit, sitting up, 10" **50.00**
Aluminum, Santa in chimney, ca 1960, 2-pc, 9" **7.00**

Elephant, 4", $20.00.

Maple sugar mold, reversible, dovetailed construction, 6x5½", $100.00.

247

Cast iron, Krum Kake, Minneapolis, MN, 1900s **50.00**

Cast iron, lamb, green enamel outside/white inside, 1900s, 9" **155.00**

Ceramic, glazed w/hand-painted apple, fluted sides, 4x5" ..**22.50**

Copper, tinned inside, pear form, 3½" **42.50**

Metal, 10 top hats in tray, 20th century, 14½x1¼" **27.50**

Nickel alloy, pr of hands, 20th century **37.50**

Plaster of Paris, simple shape, ca 1925, ½" to 4", each, from $3.00 to **10.00**

Redware, fluted tube, yellow glaze, marked John Bell, 19th century **275.00**

Redware, rabbit, sitting, ca 1850s, 2-pc **300.00**

Redware, Turk's head, 19th century, 7¾" dia **300.00**

Tin, fluted, tube center, ca 1890s-1900s, 7" dia **30.00**

Tin, heavy plate, hinged, 2-pc, for marzipan, 3x3" **30.00**

Wood, cow, EX carving, for cheese, ca 1910, 10" dia **50.00**

Wood, swan, 19th century, 2-pc, 3x4½" **195.00**

Ice Cream

Apple, E-239 ....**22.50**
Basket, 3-part, oval, E-305 ..**35.00**
Calla lily, 3-part, #210 ....**35.00**
Chick in egg, #600, 4" **35.00**
Cucumber, E-226 ....**25.00**
Easter egg, E-906 ....**22.50**
Football, #381, 3-pc **30.00**
Grape cluster, E-278 ....**20.00**
Rose, E-295 ....**30.00**
Snowman, #601, 5" **95.00**
Wedding ring, E-1142 ....**30.00**

Moon and Star

A reissue of Palace, an early pattern glass line, Moon and Star was developed for the market in the 1960s by Joseph Weishar of Island Mould and Machine Company (Wheeling, West Virginia). It was made by several companies. One of the largest producers was L.E. Smith of Mt. Pleasant, Pennsylvania; and L.G. Wright (who had their glassware made by Fostoria, Fenton, and Westmoreland) carried a wide assortment in their catalogs for many years. It is still

Syrup pitcher, 5", $28.00; cheese shaker, 5", $28.00.

being made on a very limited basis; but the most collectible pieces are those in red, blue, amber, and green – colors that are no longer in production. The values listed here are for pieces in red or blue. Amber and green prices (and crystal) should be 30% lower.

Ashtray, red or light blue, 10" ..**30.00**
Banana bowl, red or light blue, 12" long **45.00**
Banana bowl, red or light blue, 9" long **30.00**
Candle holder, red or light blue, 4½", pr **24.00**
Candy box, round body on short patterned foot, red or light blue, 6" **30.00**
Compote, scalloped rim, red or light blue, 7x10" **40.00**
Creamer & sugar bowl, red or light blue, 3" **25.00**
Cruet, red or light blue, 6¼" ..**32.00**
Nappy, 1-handle, red or light blue, 5½" **18.00**
Oil lamp, red or light blue, 12" ..**65.00**
Plate, red or light blue, 8" **25.00**
Salt & pepper shakers, straight sides, red or light blue, 4", pr **25.00**
Soap dish, oval, red or light blue, 2x6" **12.00**
Spoonholder, straight sides, red or light blue, 6" **30.00**
Toothpick holder, red or light blue **9.00**
Tumbler, red or light blue, 4" ..**12.00**
Water goblet, red or light blue, 11-oz **17.50**
Wine, red or light blue, 4½" ...**9.00**

Mortens Studios

Animal models sold by Mortens Studios of Arizona during the 1940s are some of today's most interesting collectibles, espe-

cially among animal lovers. Hundreds of breeds of dogs, cats, and horses were produced from a plaster-type composition material constructed over a wire framework. They range in size from 2" up to about 7", and most are marked.

Wire-Haired Terrier, $58.00; Cocker Spaniel, $55.00.

Beagle, standing, 6x6" **75.00**
Boston Terrier, ivory markings on black, standing, 6x6" **75.00**
Chihuahua, sitting, 3½x3" ...**75.00**
Collie, seated, 6" **90.00**
Doberman, standing, 7½x8" ..**90.00**
Horse, brown w/white blaze, tail & stockings, 9" long **120.00**
Pekingese, black details on tan, standing, 3½x4½" **80.00**
Pomeranian, standing, 4½" ..**70.00**
Siamese, seated, 5" **68.00**
St Bernard, 6½x8½" **95.00**

Motion Lamps

Though they were made as early as the '20s and as late as the '70s, the majority of these were made during the '50s, and strongly represent the tastes of that period. Made to sit on the radio or the TV, the theory in their design was that the heat of the bulb would set part of the lamp in motion (usually a cylinder would revolve), thereby creating the illusion of movement within a waterfall, a blazing fire, an underwater scene, etc. Refer to *Animated Motion Lamps, 1920s to the Present,* by Linda and Bill Montgomery (L-W Book Sales).

Bar Is Open, Visual Effects, plastic, 1970s, 13" **25.00**
Christmas Tree, LA Goodman, plastic, 1952, 17" **75.00**
Clock w/Fish, United Clock Corp, wood, 1950s, 11" **50.00**
Clock w/Mermaid, Dodge Inc, metal, 1950, 12" **90.00**
Disneyland, Econolite, plastic & tin litho, 1955, 11" **200.00**
Flames, Scene in Action, metal & plastic, 1931, 10" **80.00**
Forest Fire, Econolite (Roto-Vue Jr), plastic, 1949, 10" **40.00**
Forest Fire, LA Goodman, plastic, 1956, 11" **40.00**
Japanese Twilight, Scene in Action, glass & pot metal, 1931, 13" **100.00**
Merry-Go-Round, Econolite, plastic, 1948, 11" **50.00**

Niagara Falls, Econolite, Los Angeles, California, 1955, 11", $45.00.

On the Bayou, Econolite, picture, wood & glass, 1953, 10" ..**45.00**
Op-Lamp, Visual Effects Inc, plastic, 1970s, 13" **25.00**
Pennzoil Motor Oil, plastic, 1960s, 8" **40.00**
Serenader, Scene in Action, glass & metal, 1931, 13" **125.00**
Ships, Rev-o-Lite, bronze & plastic, 1930s, 10" **75.00**
Spirit of '76, Creative Light Products, plastic, 1973, 11" ..**20.00**
Story Book, LA Goodman, plastic, 1956, 11" **60.00**
Truck & Bus, Econolite, plastic, 1962, 11" **60.00**
White Christmas, Econolite, picture, plastic, 1953, 11" ..**50.00**

Movie Memorabilia

Anything connected with the silver screen and movie stars in general is collected by movie buffs today. Posters, lobby cards, movie magazines, promotional photos, souvenir booklets, and stills are their treasures. Especially valuable are items from the twenties and thirties that have to do with such popular stars as Jean Harlow, Bella Lugosi, Carol Lumbard, and Gary Cooper. See also Autographs; Beatles; Character Clocks and Watches; Dolls, Celebrity; Elvis Presley; Games; Rock 'n Roll; Shirley Temple; Three Stooges; Wizard of Oz; Western Heroes.

Ashtray, Charlie Chaplin, hand painted, 1960s, M **55.00**
Book, Our Gang, Romping Through the Hal Roach Comedies, Whitman, 1929 ......**55.00**
Calendar, Jayne Mansfield, 1957, original envelope, EX **60.00**

Book, A Day With Charlie McCarthy, paperback, $35.00.

Change purse, John Wayne, The Duke John Wayne 1907-79, 3", M **6.50**

Cigarette card, A Midsummer Night's Dream, cast photo, 4x2¾" **5.00**

Cigarette card, Follow the Fleet, Rogers & Astaire, 4x2¾" .**7.50**

Cigarette card, Gaslight, 3" ...**2.50**

Cigarette card, Goodbye Mr Chips, 1⅜x2⅝" **3.00**

Cigarette card, Mr Deeds Goes to Town, 3x2½" **5.00**

Cigarette card, Western Stars, Jaycee Tipped Cigarettes, set of 24 ....**27.50**

Coloring book, Betty Grable, dated 1951, EX **25.00**

Coloring book, Bing Crosby, unused, NM **20.00**

Coloring book, Bob Hope, Saalfield, 1954, EX **25.00**

Coloring book, Charlie Chaplin, Saalfield, 1941, 15x10"..**45.00**

Coloring book, Crossing the Country, EX **20.00**

Coloring book, Doris Day, 1958, EX **12.50**

Coloring book, Elizabeth Taylor, Whitman, 1950, M **30.00**

Coloring book, Eve Arden, 1953, EX **15.00**

Coloring book, Grace Kelly, 1956, EX **25.00**

Coloring book, Jackie Gleason, 1950s, NM **45.00**

Coloring book, Judy Garland, 1941, EX **40.00**

Coloring book, Lucille Ball & Desi Arnaz, 1950s, EX **25.00**

Coloring book, Rita Hayworth, 1940s, 18x12", EX **35.00**

Concert program, Judy Garland, 1960s, 20-pg, 8x12" **27.50**

Credit sheet, King David, Richard Gere, Universal, 1985 .....**1.00**

Figurine, Marilyn Monroe, 7-Year Itch pose, metal, ca '79, 2½", MIB **50.00**

Greeting card, Marilyn Monroe, 3-D, early '80s, 6½", M ...**4.00**

Lobby card, Bandits of Dark Canyon, ca 1948, 11x14", set of 5, VG **20.00**

Lobby card, Bonnie & Clyde, 1967, NM **3.00**

Lobby card, Bowery Boys, Mr Hex, 11x14", NM **25.00**

Lobby card, Coolhand Luke, Paul Newman, 1967, NM **4.50**

Lobby card, Devotion, Warner Brothers, 1946, 11x14", set of 7 ....**50.00**

Lobby card, Hope Lange, Love Is a Ball, 1963, EX **4.50**

Lobby card, Jane Mansfield, Promises Promises, black & white, EX **10.00**

Lobby card, Jubal, 1956, EX..**10.00**

Lobby card, Little Man Tate, Columbia, 1991, 11x14", set of 6 ....**10.00**

Lobby card, Night Crossing, color, 11x14", set of 8 ....**14.00**

Lobby card, The Glass Slipper, set of 8, NM **30.00**

Lobby card, The Music Man, 1962, EX **7.50**

Lobby card, The Seduction, Morgan Fairchild, 1981, 11x14", set of 5 ....**12.00**

Lobby card, Tumbleweed Trail, color, ca 1946, 11x14", EX ..**3.50**

Lobby card, Whispering Smith, color, ca 1935, 11x14" **3.50**

Magazine, Modern Screen, Carole Lombarde, May 1938 .....**25.00**

Magazine, Modern Screen, Lennon Sisters cover, April 1968, NM **10.00**

Magazine, Motion Picture, Ann Blyth cover, December 1954, EX **10.00**

Magazine, Movie Mirror, Ginger Rogers cover, June 1938 ..**17.50**

Magazine, Movie Story, Bette Davis cover, November 1938 ....**15.00**

Magazine, Photoplay, Jane Russell cover, December 1955 ......**8.00**

Magazine, Preview, Kim Basinger article, 1978, EX **15.00**

Magazine, Screen Album, Betty Grable cover, December 1946, EX **15.00**

Magazine, Screen Album, Janet Leigh cover, Spring 1951, EX **18.00**

Magazine, Screen Romances, Katharine Hepburn cover, July 1936, EX **25.00**

Magazine, Screen Romances, Loretta Young cover, June 1938 ....**15.00**

Magazine, Screenland, Linda Darnell cover, May 1941, EX **15.00**

Magazine, Silver Screen, Marilyn Monroe article, June 1954, VG **18.00**

Mask, Jimmy Durante, thin rubber, Topstone Toys, 1940s, EX **25.00**

Match book cover, Betty Grable, 1940s **10.00**

Music box, Charlie Chaplin, ceramic, 1973, M **30.00**

Note card, Marilyn Monroe, photo collage front, 5x7", set of 12, M **4.00**

Paint book, Margaret O'Brien, Whitman, 1943, NM **25.00**

Paperback, A Coal Miner's Daughter, 1980, NM **10.00**

Paperback, Marilyn Monroe, Diary of a Lover, Bantam, 1979 ....**7.50**

Photo, Groucho Marx, color portrait, 3x5" **7.50**

Pin-back button, Bing Crosby, On the Air for Kraft..., 2½" ..**20.00**

Pin-back button, Cape Fear ...**2.00**

Pin-back button, Douglas Fairbanks photo, Sampeck Triple-Service Suit **25.00**

Pin-back button, James Dean photo portrait, color, 2½" **20.00**

Pin-back button, Jane Mansfield, Now at Tropicana, sepia center, rare **65.00**

Pin-back button, Marilyn Monroe, 1956 Fan Club, 3" **5.00**

Pin-back button, Marilyn Monroe photo, cello, 1960s, 1¾" ...**20.00**

Pocket mirror, John Wayne color photo, promo item, 2x3" ..**6.00**

Poster, Bananas, Woody Allen, 1971, 1-sheet **45.00**

Poster, Bull Durham, Kevin Costner, 48x30" **8.00**

Poster, Desert Legion, Alan Ladd, 1-sheet **25.00**

Poster, Dr No, James Bond, 1980 reissue, 27x41", EX **32.50**

Poster, Girl of the Night, Anne Francis, 1960, 1-sheet ...**40.00**

Poster, Harry & the Hendersons, 1 sheet **5.00**

Poster, Pretty Woman, Gere & Roberts, 48x30" **10.00**

Poster, Regarding Henry, Harrison Ford, 30x48" **6.00**

Poster, Scanners, 27x41" **27.00**

Poster, Shock Treatment, Lauren Bacall, 1962, 27x40", EX ..**12.50**

Poster, Starman, 22x28" **8.50**

Poster, That's My Boy, Dean Martin & Jerry Lewis, 1951, 24x22", NM **35.00**

Poster, The Wild One, Marlon Brando, 1954, 1-sheet, linen backed, 41x27", M, $850.00.

Poster, The Old Frontier, Monte Hale photo, 22x28", EX ..**25.00**
Poster, Throw Mama From the Train, Danny De Vito, 60x 48" **7.00**
Poster, Where Vultures Fly, color, 1962, 22x28", EX **12.00**
Pressbook, Absent-Minded Professor **3.50**
Pressbook, Apple Dumpling Gang Rides Again **3.50**
Pressbook, Beyond the Poseidon Adventure, 28 pages **10.00**
Pressbook, Escape From the Planet of the Apes, Roddy, McDowell, 1971 ....**15.00**
Pressbook, Great Gatsby, 13x18", NM **5.00**
Pressbook, Jesus Christ Superstar, 8½x14" **5.00**
Pressbook, Man From Laramie, 12x18", EX **25.00**
Pressbook, Moonracker, James Bond **50.00**

Pressbook, Romeo & Juliet, 13x18" **6.00**
Presskit, Skin Deep, John Ritter, 5-still set **25.00**
Presskit, Tootsie, Dustin Hoffman, complete in folder, EX **17.50**
Program, Close Encounters of the Third Kind **4.00**
Sheet music, Mother Wore Tights, Betty Grable cover **8.00**
Sheet music, Shoo-Shoo Baby, Andrew Sisters, 1943, EX ..**7.50**
Sheet music, The Harvey Girls, Judy Garland, 1945, EX ..**35.00**
Slide viewer, Marilyn Monroe, Hong Kong, 1950s, 2x1½", NM **17.50**
Souvenir program, Raiders of the Lost Ark, 1984, photos, 64-pages **5.00**
Spoon, John Wayne, bust handle w/name, M **10.00**
Still, Benji, black & white, set of 8 ....**12.50**
Still, Doctor Zhivago, 1965, EX **15.00**
Still, Little Miss Marker, black & white, set of 8 ....**10.00**
Still, The Singing Nun, Debby Reynolds, 1966 ....**10.00**
Still, Walking My Baby Back Home, Donald O'Conner, 1953, EX **3.00**
Trailer, Indiana Jones & Temple of Doom, 35mm **35.00**
Trailer, Purple Rain, Prince, Warner Brothers, 1984, 35mm **20.00**
Valentine, Rudy Valee, ABC microphone & megaphone, 6" **20.00**

Napkin Rings

Figural silverplated napkin rings were popular in the late 1880s, and today's collectors enjoy finding hundreds of different designs. Among the companies best known for their manufacture are Meriden, Wm. Rogers, Reed and Barton, and Pairpoint (who made some of the finest). Kate Greenaway figurals, those with Kewpies or Brownies, and styles with wheels that turn are especially treasured.

Bird peering into nest, round base, Webster #178 .....**135.00**

Butterflies hold ring, fan forms base **100.00**

Camel on oval footed base, Meridan #269 ....**265.00**

Cat about to pounce, fly on ring, round base **175.00**

Cherries on side of ring, leafy base, Standard #732 ...**125.00**

Cherub in top hat kneels on round base, Meriden #222 .....**185.00**

Cherub plays w/bird under ring, octagonal base, Wilcox #4302 ....**125.00**

Cupid blowing horn, floral rectangular base, Simpson, Hall & Miller #051 ....**195.00**

Dog chases bird up ring, octagonal base **185.00**

Eagle holds shield, sits on rectangular base **115.00**

Foxes each side of ring, detailed base, Middletown #119 ..**200.00**

Goat on square base by ring, Knickerbocker #181 ....**165.00**

Grapes & leaves around ring, leafy base, Standard #701 ......**85.00**

Greenaway baby w/bonnet on chair, Middletown #98 ..**265.00**

Hummingbird on branch, leaf base, Toronto #1142 ....**135.00**

Lions resting on sawhorses on each side of ring **95.00**

Monkey dressed as man, rectangular base **130.00**

Owl w/violin, scrolled ring, ball-footed base **200.00**

Pig chasing mouse over ring ..**180.00**

Roses & leaves on oval ring, Rogers #4 ....**50.00**

Squirrel reading book, glass eyes, Meriden #282 ....**260.00**

Thistles on base hold ring, Meriden #664 ....**70.00**

Turkish dancer on each side of ring, Strictland #107 .....**75.00**

Napkin Rings, Catalin

For a less formal setting, Catalin (or Bakelite, if you prefer) napkin rings can add a cheerful bit of color to the table. Often found in delightful animal shapes and comic character forms, these accessories are becoming very collectible. Those with a contrasting inlaid eye or extra details (such as an animal with a ball on its head)

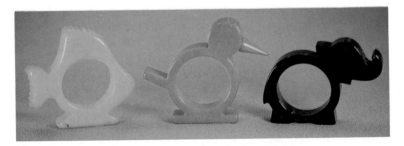

Fish, duck, or elephant, $25.00 each.

are a little more costly. As for color, red and orange rings are most often in demand, with blue a second favorite. Dark green, ivory, salmon pink, light green, yellow, and mottled butterscotch can also be found. Buyers beware! Many of these are being reproduced and sold for the 'old' prices.

Band, lathe turned, red, green or amber, 1¾" dia 8.00
Band, plain, colors, 2", set of 6, M in original box 40.00
Band, plain, red, green or amber, 2" dia 8.00
Chicken, no inlaid eye 25.00
Elephant w/ball on head 35.00
Mickey Mouse, w/decal 58.00
Rocking horse, w/inlaid eye ..66.00
Scotty, w/inlaid eye 38.00

National Geographics

The National Geographic Magazine was first introduced in October, 1888. There was only one issue that year and it together with the three published in 1889 make up Volume I, the most valuable group on the market. Volume I, No. 1, alone is worth about $12,000 in very good condition. A complete set of magazines from 1888 to the present is worth approximately $30,000 to $60,000, depending on condition, as condition and price are closely related. As time goes by, values of individual issues increase. The most sought-after years are pre-World War: 1888-1914. Still, some postwar recent issues command good prices. Be on the lookout for any in the following listing. Our advisor is Don Smith, who is listed in the Directory under Kentucky. Values are given for magazines in at least excellent condition.

1914, August, Grand Canyon ..20.00
1914, January, North Africa ..25.00
1914, Nov, Young Russia 20.00
1916, May, Land of the Incas ..12.00
1916, November, Larger North American Mammals 14.00
1917, October, Our Flag Number 18.00
1918, May, Smaller North American Mammals 12.00
1919, December, Military Insignias 15.00
1920, December, Falconry 11.50
1923, May, Tomb of King Tut ..13.00
1923, November, Horses 13.00
1923, October, Automobiles ..10.00
1926, January, Pigeons 9.50
1930, June, 1st World Airship Flight 9.00
1934, September, Flags of the World 8.50
1936, November, Trains 9.00
1937, April, Colonial Williamsburg 9.50
1937, January, Field Dogs 8.50
1937, October, Hounds 9.50
1938, November, Cats 10.00
1940, July, National Gallery of Art 8.00
1941, Dec, Working Dogs 9.50
1941, February, Dinosaurs 9.00
1941, October, Ancient Egypt ..12.50
1943, Dec, War Insignias 9.00
1943, June, Insignias 13.00
1943, October, Medals 11.00
1944, March, Greek Way 8.00
1946, November, Roman Way ..7.50
1947, September, Bird Dogs ..7.25
1948, December, Lascaux Paintings 6.75
1948, March, Circus 8.25
1949, July, Shells 10.75
1950, December, Gems 8.50
1953, September, Queen Elizabeth's Coronation 7.25
1961, April, Civil War 7.00

Nazi Collectibles

An area of militaria attracting a growing following today, Nazi collectibles are those things related to the Nazi rise and German participation in World War II. There are many facets to this field; among the items hunted most enthusiastically are daggers, medals, badges, patches, uniforms, and toys with a Nazi German theme.

Armband, WWII, Hitler Youth, complete w/RZM tag, M ..**15.00**
Badge, flak; Luftwaffe, nickel-plated silver, Juncker ..**175.00**
Badge, WWII, Luftwaffe Para-trooper, diving eagle on brass, EX **135.00**
Banner, WWII, swastika & cross, 15½-ft **100.00**
Book, Mein Kampf, soft bound, 1933, VG **48.00**
Cap, visor, Army Panzer officer, crush type w/pink & green trim, EX **335.00**
Chevron, WWII, Kriegsmarine Able Seaman, gold braid on blue **6.50**
Compass, WWII, Luftwaffe, wrist type, black Bakelite, EX **38.00**
Dagger, Kriegsmarine officer, Eickhorn, brass scabbard, EX **265.00**
Dog tag, WWII, Wehrmacht, blank, unissued **12.50**
Map, German streets, eagle & swastika, Hitler picture on back **32.50**

Newspapers

Earth-shaking news stories that make front-page headlines – war news, natural disasters, man-made catastrophes, etc. – are often the reason old newspapers were saved in the first place and are usually why they're being sought by collectors today. 'First reports' are the most valuable, and papers with large, visible headlines and good graphics on the front page are preferred. The Newspaper Society of America is listed in the Directory under Clubs and Newsletters. They will send you (for a $2.00 fee) a booklet with suggested prices and other valuable information.

1931, Knute Rockne killed in plane crash **8.00**
1931, Police Hunt for Capone, other titles, EX **7.50**
1932, Amelia Earhart Alone Over Atlantic **50.00**
1932, Lindbergh Offers Ransom, illustrations **20.00**
1933, FDR Inauguration Day, full-page photo **25.00**
1934, Police Shoot, Trail Pretty Boy Floyd, other titles ..**30.00**
1935, Will Rogers killed in plane crash **35.00**
1936, George V dies **10.00**
1937, Windsor & Wally Wed in Double Rites, illustration ..**7.00**

1948,'Dewey Elected' headline (prepared as an alternate issue before election results were in), $200.00.

1938, Judaism Is Criminal, other related titles **25.00**
1939, War begins **30.00**
1940, Hitler seizes Norway **6.00**
1941, Britain ready for Japanese attack on Singapore **7.50**
1945, Ernie Pyle Killed in Jap Ambush, photo, EX **8.00**
1945, First atomic bomb dropped, EX **30.00**
1945, Photo Story of the Sinking of the Andrea Dora **45.00**
1945, Russia Enters War **20.00**
1945, V-E Day or VJ-Day **32.50**
1951, MacArthur's homecoming in Washington, illustrations **10.00**
1963, JFK assassination, Nov 22, Dallas title **75.00**
1963, JFK assassination, Nov 22, other titles **25.00**
1963, JFK assassination, papers dated November 23 to November 26, each **5.00**
1963, Los Angeles Dam Disaster, EX **8.00**
1963, Pope John XXIII in State: First Pictures **10.00**
1964, McArthur Succumbs at 84 ....**10.00**
1969, Jayne Mansfield dies .**45.00**
1969, Liftoff From Moon-Now in Orbit, illustrations **25.00**
1969, Moon landing, illustrations, EX **18.00**
1972, Landslide Victory for Nixon, EX **15.00**
1972, Truman dies **12.50**
1973, Vietnam Peace Pact ...**10.00**
1974, Ford being sworn in, illustration **12.50**
1974, Nixon resigns **15.00**
1977, Bing Crosby dies **15.00**
1977, Elvis dies, Memphis paper, EX **35.00**
1977, Elvis dies, other titles ..**10.00**
1980, John Lennon Shot **22.50**
1984, Ansel Adams dies **10.00**
1984, Richard Burton dies ...**15.00**

Niloak

Produced in Arkansas by Charles Dean Hyten from the early 1900s until the mid-1940s, Niloak (the backward spelling of kaolin, a type of clay) takes many forms – figural planters, vases in both matt and glossy glazes, and novelty items of various types. The company's most famous product and the most collectible is their swirl or Mission Ware line. Clay in colors of brown, blue, cream, red, and buff were swirled within the mold, the finished product left unglazed on the outside to preserve the natural hues. Small vases are common; large pieces or unusual shapes and those with exceptional coloration are the most valuable. Refer to *The Collector's Encyclopedia of Niloak, A Reference and Value Guide,* by David Edwin Gifford (Collector Books) for more information.

Ashtray, Swirl, Mission Ware, second art mark, 1¼x3¼" **75.00**
Bowl, scalloped, Peacock Blue II, Hywood, 5½x2¾" **35.00**
Bowl, Swirl, Mission Ware, first art mark, 4" **90.00**
Creamer, Aladdin shape w/ ridges, honey brown glaze, 2½" **25.00**
Figurine, Scottie dog, black gloss, Hywood, 3¾" **45.00**
Figurine, Southern Belle, cast, medium blue matt, Hywood, 7" **90.00**
Pitcher, Lewis glaze, Hywood, 10" **50.00**
Planter, frog, medium blue gloss, 4¼" **30.00**
Planter, rooster, jade, 8½" **30.00**
Planter, swan, white satin, Hywood, 7½" **30.00**

Vase, Mission Ware, late 1930s, 3¼", $70.00.

Salad plate, petal design, Ozark Dawn II matt, 8" **35.00**
Shakers, letters S&P as handles, honey-colored glaze, Hywood, 3", pr **30.00**
Vase, applied handles, Stoin glaze, Hywood, 5" **90.00**
Vase, cornucopia shape, white satin, 7" **25.00**
Vase, Deco design, Ozark Dawn II matt, 6¼" **35.00**
Vase, Swirl, Mission Ware, ginger jar shape, second art mark, 5½" **80.00**
Wall pocket, Bouquet pattern, 5" **45.00**

Nippon

In compliance with American importation regulations, from 1891 to 1921 Japanese manufacturers marked their wares 'Nippon,' meaning Japan, to indicate country of origin. The term is today used to refer to the highly decorated porcelain vases, bowls, chocolate pots, etc., that bear this term within their trademark.

Many variations were used. Refer to *The Collector's Encyclopedia of Nippon Porcelain* (there are three volumes in the series) by Joan Van Patten (Collector Books) for more information.

Ashtray, moriage dragon, tri-cornered, 5½" **125.00**
Ashtray, windmill scene, 5" ..**135.00**
Butter dish, floral lid, Wedgwood trim, w/insert, 3¾x6" ...**225.00**
Cake plate, windmill scene, gold overlay on cobalt, handled, 10¾" **250.00**
Cake set, heavy gold overlay on cream, 7-pc **275.00**
Candlestick, palm trees, earth tones, 6¼" **120.00**
Candy dish, hunt scene, fluted, 4-footed, 7½" long **185.00**
Cheese dish, Wedgwood, slanted, 7¾" long **365.00**
Coffee set, heavy gold dragon motif on cream, 14-pc ..**425.00**
Compote, woodland scene, handled, 5" dia **100.00**
Creamer & sugar bowl, gold overlay swags on white **65.00**
Cup & saucer, demitasse; gold overlay on cobalt **70.00**
Decanter, heavily beaded, 7" ..**250.00**
Dish, serving; Indian in canoe, 2-tiered, 8½" dia **175.00**
Doll, policeman w/club, 3¾" ..**115.00**
Doll in bathtub, 2½x3" **125.00**
Dresser set, child's, roses on white w/gold overlay, 3-pc **200.00**
Feeding dish, child's, side view of girl holding doll, 7" **85.00**
Hanging pot, scene w/sailing ships, 5" **300.00**
Humidor, elk scene, geometric border, 5½" **525.00**
Inkwell, floral reserves on brown, 3" square **185.00**
Mug, Egyptian figures, geometric border, 5" **250.00**

Mug, man on camel, some moriage trim, 4¾" **225.00**

Nappy, American Indian decor, 5¼" dia **135.00**

Nut dish, Indian in canoe, handled, 5½" dia **145.00**

Nut dish, peanuts in relief, brown rim & handles, 7" **125.00**

Pitcher, floral reserve, gold overlay on cobalt, 7½" **425.00**

Plaque, bird on a tree branch, 9" dia **240.00**

Plaque, colorful basket of flowers, gold trim, 10" dia **200.00**

Plaque, doll face pattern, 6⅛" dia **85.00**

Plaque, floral scene w/man playing accordion, 7¾" dia ..**300.00**

Plate, gold overlay on cobalt, floral center, 7½" dia **70.00**

Powder box, light green w/doll face pattern, 3x4" dia ..**95.00**

Relish dish, florals w/Wedgwood trim, 7½" long **200.00**

Salt cellar, Washington Capitol Building, 2½" **35.00**

Sugar shaker, roses, pink on white w/gold overlay, 4" **125.00**

Tea set, child's, Sunbonnet Babies, gold trim, 23-pc **250.00**

Tea set, child's, white w/flowers & gold highlights, 17-pc ..**225.00**

Tea tile, windmill scene, octagonal, 5½" dia **65.00**

Toothpick holder, river scene, 3-handled, 2¼" **100.00**

Trinket box, stork w/baby, gold trim, 4" **150.00**

Trivet, river scene, canted corners, 5" **55.00**

Vase, bird on moriage branch, ornate handles, footed, 9¼" **350.00**

Vase, floral tapestry, bottle shape, 8½" **500.00**

Vase, florals w/Wedgwood trim, handled, 9" **375.00**

Vase, geishas in landscape, geometric border, handled, 8" ..**175.00**

Vase, stylized iris spray on textured background, heavy gold trim, green mark, 7½", $200.00.

Vase, gold on cream, house & stream in reserve, gold handles, 13½" **475.00**

Vase, gold overlay on cobalt, house & stream in reserve, 12" **375.00**

Vase, Indian in canoe, handled, 7" **295.00**

Vase, man on camel, gold overlay at top, gold handles, 7" ..**275.00**

Vase, river scene, handled, miniature, 2½" **50.00**

Noritake

Since the early 1900s the Noritake China Company has been producing fine dinnerware, occasional pieces, and figural items decorated by hand in delicate florals, scenics, and wildlife studies. One of their most popular dinnerware lines, Azalea, is listed in its own category. Refer to *The Collector's Encyclopedia of Noritake* by Joan Van Patten (Collector Books) for more information.

Ashtray, coastal scene w/blue bird, green mark, 5" **65.00**

Ashtray, horse heads, green rim, 3 red rests, red mark, 5" ..**100.00**

Basket, birds on perch, yellow, gold handle & trim, green mark , 6" **135.00**

Bowl, footed floral shape, looped handle, orange, red mark, 6" dia **100.00**

Bowl, lovebirds, black handles & trim, green mark, 7" dia ..**45.00**

Bowl, peacock center, decorative border, green mark, 7¼" dia...................................**45.00**

Cake plate, floral center, border, open handles, red mark, 11" dia **45.00**

Celery dish, goat head handles in relief, green mark, 12½" ..**95.00**

Chamberstick, pitcher shape, window pane design, red mark, 2¾" **80.00**

Cheese dish, floral, black handle & trim, slanted, green mark , 8" **100.00**

Condiment set on tray, landscape, gold trim, 7½" long **30.00**

Cookie/cracker jar, floral, gold finial & trim, footed, green mark **175.00**

Creamer & sugar bowl, cottage by tree & lake, 4½" **45.00**

Egg cup, fruit in compote design, gold trim, red mark, 3½" ..**30.00**

Honey jar, beehive form, applied bees, green mark, 5½" ...**75.00**

Humidor, humorous golfer, green mark, 6½" **350.00**

Jam jar, strawberries on honey-colored ground, green mark, 5½" **60.00**

Lemon dish, lemon in relief, green leaves, 6" dia **65.00**

Match holder, bell form, black knob & trim, 3¾" **85.00**

Mustard pot, gold lustre with floral finial, attached plate, 3½", $22.50.

Match holder, floral w/gold trim, wall mounted, green mark, 3½" **65.00**

Nappy, floral design, gold handle & trim, green mark, 5" dia ..**40.00**

Plaque, steamship & coastline, gold trim, 10" dia **200.00**

Playing card/cigarette holder, horse head, red mark, 3¾" **135.00**

Potpourri jar, blue & white, flower finial, red mark, 6" **85.00**

Powder puff box, southern belle from behind, green mark, 4" dia **160.00**

Ring tree, gold hand emerging from center, blue mark, square, 3" **55.00**

Sauce dish, tulip shape, floral interior, gold trim, red mark, 4" **45.00**

Sugar shaker, floral band on white, gold top & trim, 6½" **40.00**

Sweetmeat set, Deco fruit design, green mark **125.00**

Toothpick holder, flamenco dancer, 3 handles, green mark, 2¼" **65.00**

Tray, fruit border, gold handles & trim, red mark, 11" long ..**95.00**

Trinket box, Deco lady & dog, round on pedestal, 3" **65.00**

Vase, flared top, yellow to blue, gold trim, green mark, 7" **110.00**

Vase, urn shape, cottage by lake &
bridge, green mark, 8¾" ..**100.00**
Wall pocket, floral, flared rim,
gold trim, 8½" **110.00**

Nutcrackers

Of most interest to collectors
are nutcrackers marked with
patent information or those made
in the form of an animal or bird.
Many manufacturers chose the
squirrel as a model for their
nutcrackers; dogs were also
popular. Cast iron examples are
common, but brass, steel, and
even wood was also used. Refer
to *Ornamental and Figural
Nutcrackers* by Judith A. Ritten-
house (Collector Books) for more
information.

Alligator, cast brass, mounted to
base, ca 1890s, 7½" **100.00**
Antelope head, carved wood, glass
eyes, ca 1890s, 9" **130.00**
Anvil & blacksmith's hammer,
black painted cast iron,
Wright, 1960s, 4" **17.50**
Arcade, cast iron, lever action, ca
1920 ....**50.00**
Bearded man in skull cap, carved
wood, lever type **135.00**
Dragon, gold-painted cast iron,
sawtooth spine & tail, 13"
long **200.00**
Eagle head, cast iron, flat base,
1980s, 6" **12.50**
Eagle head, cast iron, 4-legged base,
American, ca 1890s, 7" **80.00**
Englishman, full figure, painted
carved wood, 8½" **275.00**
Enterprise, cast iron, clamp on,
lever action, ca 1914 .....**35.00**
Lady's legs, carved wood, late
1890s **50.00**
Lady's legs, cast brass, ca 1900s,
5½" **90.00**

**Wooden boxer dog with
glass eyes, probably Swiss,
early 1900s, 7", $150.00.**

Occupied Japan

Items with the 'Occupied
Japan' mark were made during
the period from the end of World
War II until April 1952. Porcelains, novelties, paper items,
lamps, silverplate, lacquer ware,
and dolls are some of the types of
exported goods that may bear this
stamp. Because the Japanese
were naturally resentful of the
occupation, it is felt that only a
small percentage of their wares
were thus marked. Although you
may find identical items marked
simply 'Japan,' only those with the
'Occupied Japan' stamp are being
collected. For more information we
recommend the series of three
books on Occupied Japan collectibles written by Gene Florence

for Collector Books. Items in our listings are ceramic unless another material is noted, and figurines are of average, small size.

Ashtray, frog figural **11.50**
Ashtray, knight w/shield, Lenwile China #6332 ....**7.50**
Ashtray, metal, embossed Statue of Liberty, Enco 2T388 ..**11.50**
Ashtray, metal, hand-shape ..**11.50**
Ashtray, metal, horse standing on side **16.50**
Ashtray, metal, leaf shape w/ embossed grapes **3.50**
Bell, Dutch girl **14.50**
Bookend, seated girl w/watering can, 3⅝", each **14.00**
Bowl, berry; Blue Willow **11.50**
Bowl, latticed fruit & flowers ..**11.50**
Bowl, leaf shape, brown w/flower in center, handled **12.50**
Cigarette box, dragon decor, w/2 ashtrays **30.00**
Cigarette box, metal, red w/sterling silver decor **22.50**
Creamer, cow figural, pale orange & cream, 8x4¾" **35.00**
Cup, white w/gold decor, ornate gold handle, 4-footed **9.50**
Cup & saucer, child's, white w/ royal blue border, gold highlights **15.00**
Cup & saucer, child's, yellow lusterware, shows house & picket fence **15.00**
Cup & saucer, dancing girls, gold highlights **22.50**
Cup & saucer, demitasse; floral decor w/orange luster rim **5.50**
Cup & saucer, demitasse; Oriental scene w/lady **9.50**
Cup & saucer, Florida souvenir ..**9.50**
Egg cup, chicken figurals, pr ..**20.00**
Figurine, angel on pink basket, 5" **38.00**
Figurine, angel sitting atop a shell **32.00**

Colonial couple, 7½", $40.00 for the pair.

Figurine, baby in green snowsuit, celluloid **27.50**
Figurine, boy w/accordion **8.50**
Figurine, cat w/red yarn **5.50**
Figurine, Colonial couple, man playing mandolin, 6⅛", pr ...**45.00**
Figurine, dancing couple, 3" ..**9.50**
Figurine, elf on caterpillar ..**14.00**
Figurine, frog on lily pad **16.50**
Figurine, girl holding doll, 4"..**13.50**
Figurine, girl holding songbook, 5¼" **22.50**
Figurine, hunter w/rifle & bag of game, bisque, 5" **40.00**
Figurine, lady bug w/bass fiddle & top hat, 3" **7.50**
Figurine, lady bug w/bat, 4" ..**14.00**
Figurine, lady in blue hat, bisque, 5" **16.50**
Figurine, man holding rake, bisque **13.50**
Figurine, old lady gnome, 3¾" ..**7.50**
Figurine, Oriental lady holding fan, blue skirt **16.50**
Figurine, pastoral couple by fence, bisque, 8⅛", pr **85.00**
Figurine, reclining cat **22.00**
Figurine, seated couple holding songbook, 3⅜" **11.50**
Lamp, Colonial couple, white w/gold highlights, 7⅜" ..**30.00**

Miniature, baby grand piano, 2⅛x2½x2" **15.00**

Mug, child's, Tom & Jerry in gold lettering, gold highlights ..**50.00**

Pencil holder, dog figural **8.50**

Pitcher, white w/embossed flowers, narrow neck **9.50**

Planter, accordion player w/dog, 4⅛" **11.50**

Planter, chicken w/egg **16.50**

Planter, donkey w/cart **9.50**

Planter, girl w/goose **5.50**

Planter, Oriental boy w/basket ..**8.50**

Planter, parrot looking down & left, 5¾" **20.00**

Planter, white dog w/blue spots, red bow around neck, 4⅝" **8.50**

Planter, zebra w/basket **7.50**

Plate, cabin scene w/5 chickens, sm **18.50**

Plate, Niagara Falls **8.50**

Platter, Blue Willow, 12" **28.50**

Powder jar, Colonial couple, bisque, oval, 7½x4¾" **16.50**

Ring box, heart shape, orange band top & bottom **14.50**

Salt & pepper shakers, clown crouching on drum, pr ..**32.50**

Shelf sitter, ballerina, porcelain, 6¼" **40.00**

Sugar bowl, Blue Willow **18.50**

Teapot, brown w/embossed gold flowers **32.50**

Teapot, white w/pink roses, gold trim **32.50**

Toby mug, winking left eye ..**18.50**

Toby pitcher, bartender holding 2 mugs, 4⅞" **32.50**

Toothpick holder, donkey pulling cart **3.50**

Toothpick holder, squirrel watching rooster **14.00**

Tumbler, stoneware, allover gray & green leaf design, 3½" **25.00**

Vase, matt white w/raised gold flowers & leaves, porcelain, 7¼" **40.00**

Old MacDonald's Farm

Made by the Regal China Co., items from this line of novelty ware designed around characters and animals from Old MacDonald's farm can often be found at flea markets and dinnerware shows. Values of some pieces are two to three times higher than a few years ago. The milk pitcher is especially hard to find.

Lacquered corner shelf with gold designs, 9½", $45.00.

Cookie jar, $275.00.

Canister, lg **350.00**

Canister, spice; sm **150.00**

Creamer, rooster **110.00**

Grease jar, pig **185.00**
Pitcher, milk **400.00**
Salt & pepper shakers, boy & girl,
  pr **80.00**
Salt & pepper shakers, churn,
  pr **80.00**
Salt & pepper shakers, feed sacks
  w/sheep, pr **165.00**
Sugar bowl, hen **125.00**
Teapot, duck's head **275.00**

Paper Dolls

Though the history of paper dolls can be traced even farther back, by the late 1700s they were being mass produced. A century later, paper dolls were being used as an advertising medium by retail companies wishing to promote sales. The type most often encountered are in book form – the dolls on the cardboard covers, their wardrobe on the inside pages – published since the 1920s. Celebrity and character-related dolls are most popular, and condition is very important. If they have been cut out, even when they are still in fine condition and have all their original accessories, they're worth only about half as much as an uncut doll. Refer to *The Collector's Guide to Paper Dolls* by Mary Young (Collector Books) for more information. See also Dolls, Betsy McCall.

Annette, Whitman #1953, 1964,
  uncut, M **75.00**
Baby Sparkle Plenty (Dick Tracy),
  Saalfield #1510, 1948, uncut,
  NM **100.00**
Betty Davis, Merrill, 1942, complete, M **60.00**
Buffy (Family Affair), Whitman
  #1995, 1968, uncut, M ..**40.00**

Donnie & Marie Osmond, Whitman, 1977, uncut, NM ..**20.00**
Doris Day, Whitman #1952, 1955,
  uncut, NM **55.00**
Gigi Perreau, Saalfield #2605-15,
  1951, uncut, NM **85.00**
Gloria Jean, Saalfield #1661,
  1940, uncut, M **95.00**
Green Acres, Whitman, Eva & Eddie
  on cover, 1967, NM **40.00**
Haley Mills Moon Spinners, Whitman, 1964, NM **40.00**
Jane Fonda Mod Fashions, Saalfield
  #1369, 1966, uncut, M **50.00**
Jane Powell, Whitman #118515,
  1951, uncut, M **85.00**
Janet Lennon, Whitman #1948,
  1961, uncut, M **45.00**
Lennon Sisters, Whitman #1991,
  1959, uncut, M **65.00**

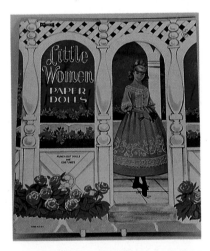

Little Women, Artcraft, original price 69¢, six uncut pages, $14.00.

Lucille Ball, Saalfield, 1945, complete, NM **65.00**
Marge's Little LuLu, Whitman,
  rectangular, 1970, M **18.00**
Marie Osmond Push-Out Dolls,
  Art, 1973, uncut, M **27.50**
Mrs Beasley, Whitman, 1972,
  uncut, M **30.00**

Munsters, birthday party scene cover, Whitman, 1966, uncut, M **125.00**

Pat Boone, Whitman #1968, 1959, uncut, NM **75.00**

Patience & Prudence, Abbot #1807, 1959, uncut, NM **75.00**

Patti Page, Bonnie Books #2739, 1959, uncut, NM **75.00**

Pebbles Flintstone, Whitman #1997, 1963, uncut, M ..**65.00**

Petticoat Junction, Whitman #1954, 1964, uncut, NM **60.00**

Rock Hudson, Whitman #2087, 1957, uncut, NM **60.00**

Rock Hudson, 2 cutouts, c 1957 by Whitman, EX **20.00**

Roy Rogers & Dale Evans, Whitman #1950, 1954, M ...**135.00**

That Girl, 3 Marlo Thomas punch-outs, Saalfield, 1967, NM **65.00**

Welcome Back Kotter, 14" die-cut doll, Toy Factory, 1976, sealed, M **25.00**

Wishnik (trolls), Whitman #1954, 1965, uncut, M **60.00**

Magazine Paper Dolls

American Dancer Magazine, Dancer Costumes, October 1933, complete **8.00**

Designer, Whole School of Children for You To Play With, November 1917 ....**8.00**

Instructor, A Doll of Long Ago, December 1936 ....**7.00**

Instructor, Paper Dolls, Dutch Children, March 1932 .....**8.00**

Jack & Jill, by Laura Sackett, November 1945, complete magazine **4.00**

McCall's, Betsy McCall Celebrates Lucia Day, December 1972 ....**2.00**

McCall's Needlework, Little Molly McCall & Her Pets, Fall 1924, NM **10.00**

Metropolitan, Mother Metropolitan's Healthy Boys & Girls, ca 1924-26 ....**12.00**

Parent's Magazine, Fall Washables Cut Outs for School, August 1939 ....**6.00**

People's Popular Monthly, Tommy Snooks & Bessie Brooks, June 1928 ....**7.00**

Pictorial Review, Adventures of Polly & Peter Perkins, December 1933 ....**10.00**

Pictorial Review, Dolly Dingle, Johnny, & the Story of Fido, June 1922 ....**15.00**

Pictorial Review, Dolly Dingle, July 1930 ....**14.00**

Pictorial Review, Dolly Dingle's Friend Douglas, May 1928, NM **14.00**

Pictorial Review, Dolly Dingle's Patriotic Party, February 1918 ....**16.00**

Pictorial Review, Dolly Dingle's Trip Around the World, April 1917 ....**18.00**

Pictorial Review, Dolly Dingle's World Flight, December 1932 ....**14.00**

Pictorial Review, Dolly Dingle's World Flight in Sweden, February 1933 ....**14.00**

Pictorial Review, Introducing Dolly Dingle's Father, July 1918 ....**16.00**

Pictorial Review, Kitty-Cutie of Dingle Dell, May 1913 ..**20.00**

Pictorial Review, Pin-a-Peep Show Hansel & Gretel, June 1925 ....**8.00**

Pictorial Review, Sammy Gets Ready for the Baseball Season, June 1920 ....**15.00**

Prairie Farmer, Our Junior Page Polly Peters, February 9, 1924 ....**6.00**

Primary Education-Popular Educator, Cut Outs for Columbus Day, 1928 ....**6.00**

Screen Life, Star Dolls #3, Bette Davis, April 1941 ....**40.00**

Simplicity Pattern Magazine, Simplicity Joan, ca 1950 ....**8.00**

The New Yorker, Soldier, by Alajalov, June 1945 ....**15.00**

The Woman's Magazine, Jean, Our Jointed Paper Doll; March 1913 ....**15.00**

The Woman's Magazine, Natascha of Russia, March 1918 ...**15.00**

The Woman's Magazine, Oh We're Three Famous Kittens, March 1920 ....**15.00**

Today's Magazine, The Polka Dots Learn To Fence, January 1915 ....**5.00**

Vanity Fair, The Grand Duchess Marie, February 1934 ...**20.00**

Vanity Fair, Vanity Fair's Own Paper Dolls, #3, Prince of Wales, 1934 ....**20.00**

Vogue, Dressmaker Doll, by Dorothy Cox, August 1933, 2-page **18.00**

Woman's Home Companion, Carl of California, April 1927 ....**10.00**

Woman's Home Companion, Little Assunta & Her Kewpie Doll, June 1913 ....**30.00**

Woman's Home Companion, Our Gang As Paper Dolls, October 1925 ....**18.00**

Woman's Home Companion, The Companion Paper Doll, February 1920 ....**16.00**

Woman's Home Companion, The Little Busybodies, November 1922 ....**14.00**

Paperback Books

Though published to some extent before the forties, most paperback book collectors prefer those printed from around 1940 until the late 1950s, and most organize their collections around a particular author, genre, publisher, or illustrator. Remember – (as is true with any type of ephemera) condition is extremely important. For more information, refer to 'Huxford's Paperbacks Value Guide' (Collector Books).

Aarons, Edward S; Assignment Madeleine, Fawcett 799, 1958, NM **12.50**

Albert, Marvin; Palm Springs Weekend, Dell 6813, 1963, movie tie-in, M **8.00**

Asch, Sholem; The Nazarene, Cardinal GC36, 1956, VG **2.50**

Asminov, Isaac; End of Eternity, Signet S1493, 1958, VG ..**4.00**

Avallone, Michael; Man From UNCLE, Ace G553, 1965, VG **3.00**

Barker, Wade; Vengeance Is His, Warner 30-032, 1981 ......**10.00**

Barrett, Michael; Escape from Zahrain, Fawcett 1206, '62, movie tie-in **8.00**

Bechdolt, Frederick R; Horse Thief Trail, Pennant P57, 1954, VG **5.00**

Bennett, Arnold; Jackie, Bobby & Manchester; Bee-Line 179, 1967, NM **12.00**

Bower, BM; Pirates of the Range, Pyramid F1018, 1964 ....**5.50**

Bronte, Emily; Wuthering Heights, Pocket 7, 1944, movie tie-in edition **3.00**

Brown, Harry; The Gathering, Ballantine 27386, 1977, movie tie-in, NM **10.00**

Buck, Pearl S; My Several Worlds, Cardinal GC35, 1956, VG ..**2.50**

Bulmer, Kenneth; Beyond the Stars, Ace M131, 1965, EX **4.00**

Burroughs, Edgar R; Moon Men, Ace 53752, VG **3.00**

Burroughs, Edgar R; Tarzan the Terrible, Ballantine F752, 1963, VG **5.00**

Burroughs, Edgar R; Tarzan Triumphant, Ace F194, 1962, VG **5.00**

Cerf, Bennet; Unexpected, Bantam 502, 1948, VG **6.00**

Charteris, Leslie; Saint Meets the Tiger, Avon 477, 1952 ....**12.00**

Christie, Agatha; Dead Man's Mirror, Dell 1699, 1971, M **2.00**

Christie, Agatha; Death Comes As the End, Pocket 465, 1947, VG **5.00**

Clarke, Arthur C; Islands in the Sky, Signet S1776, 1960, VG **4.00**

Clarke & Hyams, The Odyssey File, Ballantine 32108, 1985, NM **9.00**

Colette, S; Ecstacy, Popular Library G536, 1961, Hedy Lamar cover, NM **10.00**

Cooper, Saul; It Started in Naples, Gold Medal 1017, 1960, VG **7.00**

Curie, Eve; Madame Curie, Cardinal GC57, 1959, VG **2.50**

Daniels, Norman; Arrest & Trial, Lancer 72-696, 1963, TV tie-in, NM **12.00**

De Rosso, HA; End of the Gun, Perma M3014, 1955, VG **4.00**

Dos Passos, John; Manhattan Transfer, Penguin, 577, 1946, VG **4.00**

Doyle, Arthur Conan; Adventures of Sherlock Holmes, Popular G486, 1960 ....**7.50**

Evans, Evan; Rescue of Broken Arrow; Bantam 211, 1949, VG **2.50**

Farmer, Philip Jose; Tongues of the Moon, Pyramid F1055, 1964, VG **12.50**

Farrell, Henry; What Ever Happened to Baby Jane?, Avon G1146, 1960, VG **4.00**

Foreman, LL; Arrow in the Dust, Dell 11, 1954, VG **4.00**

Frazee, Steve; Alamo, Avon T446, 1960, movie tie-in, NM ..**15.00**

Frazee, Steve; The Outcasts, Popular Library 2345, 1968, TV tie-in, NM **7.50**

Friday, B; I Love You Alice B Toklas; Bantam 3919, Peter Sellers cover **10.00**

Gardner, Erle Stanley; Spurious Spinster, Pocket 4515, 1963, NM **4.00**

Haggard, H Rider; King Solomon's Mines, Dell 433, VG **12.50**

Hirschfeld, Burt; General Hospital, Lancer 72-917, 1965, TV tie-in, NM **12.50**

Ketchum, Philip; Woman in Armour, Avon G1164, 1963, NM **14.00**

Krepps, Robert; Diamond Fever, Dell F174, 1961, VG **2.50**

Krepps, Robert; El Cid, Gold Medal D1169, 1961, G **2.00**

Flames of Time, by Baynard Kendrick, Bantam, A-902, first paperback original, 1951, EX, $30.00.

L'Amour, Louis; First Fast Draw, Bantam 1905, 1959, EX ..**12.50**

L'Amour, Louis; Lando, Bantam 2494, 1962, Sackett novel, NM **12.00**

L'Amour, Louis; Taggart, Bantam 1977, 1959, VG **8.00**

Logan, Ford; Fire in the Desert, Ballantine 666, 1962, VG ..**3.50**

Loomis, Noel M; Cheyenne War Cry, Avon T368, 1959, NM **10.00**

MacRauch, Earl; New York, New York; Pocket 80850, 1977, movie tie-in **8.00**

Martin, Chuck; Bloody Kansas, Avon 654, 1950, NM **10.00**

Maugham, W Somerset; Of Human Bondage, Cardinal GC126, 1964, NM **3.00**

Moorcock, Michael; Lord of Spiders, Lancer 447-74, NM ..**7.50**

Morris, Wright; Love Among the Cannibals, Signet S1531, 1958, VG **3.50**

The Hellcats, by Robert F. Slatzer, Holloway House, #154, original 1967, scarce movie tie-in, VG, $38.50.

Nolan & Johnson, Logan's Run, Bantam 2517, 1976, movie tie-in, EX **10.00**

O'Rourke, Frank; Big Fifty, Dell 59, 1955, VG **4.00**

Panghorn, Edgar; West of the Sun, Dell 9442, '66, VG ...**3.00**

Powers, SR; Willing Flesh, Chariot 220, 1962, Mamie Van Doren cover, M **27.50**

Queen, Ellery; Adventures of Ellery Queen, Pocket 99, 1954, 22nd print **3.00**

Rhode, John; Dr Priestley Investigates, Avon 5, 1941, NM **42.50**

Rosenberg, Joel; The Sword & the Chain, Signet 2883, 1984, NM **10.00**

Sabatini, Rafael; Scaramouche, Bantam 5, 1945, VG **4.00**

Scott, Bradford; Gunsmoke Talk; Pyramid G865, 1963, VG **2.50**

Silverberg, Robert; Master of Life & Death, Ace D237, 1957, VG **5.00**

Smith, Cordwainer; Planet Buyer, Pyramid R1084, 1964, VG **4.50**

Spillane, Mickey; Kiss Me, Deadly; Signet 1007, 1953, NM **17.50**

Spillane, Mickey; The Big Kill, Signet 915, 1951, NM ...**17.50**

Steiger, Brad; Alien Meetings, Ace 01571, 1978, NM **6.00**

Thomas, Wayne; What's New in Hot Rodding; Gold Medal 1817, ca 1960s, M **8.50**

Tiger, John; I Spy, Popular Library SP400, 1965, TV tie-in, NM **10.00**

Trudeau, Gary; President Is a Lot Smarter...; Popular Library, 1973, M **7.50**

Vadim, Roger; Liaisons Dangereuses, Ballantine 586, 1962, movie tie-in **25.00**

Victor, Charles; The Whole Sky Burned, Avon S371, 1968, NM **6.00**
Weiss, Joe; Gang Girl, Beacon B372, 1961, NM **20.00**
Wells, HG; Time Machine, Berkley 380, 1957, VG **4.00**
Whipple, Chandler; Lt JFK Expendable, Nova N116F, 1964, EX **2.00**
Williams, Tennessee; Cat on a Hot Tin Roof, Signet S1590, 1958, NM **10.00**
Williams, Tennessee; Rose Tattoo, Signet 1236, 1955, VG **4.00**

Peach Lustre

Several dinnerware lines as well as baking dishes in white glassware with a lustrous gold fired-on finish sometimes called copper-tint was made by Fire-King from the early fifties through the mid-seventies. Refer to *Collectible Glassware of the '40s, '50s, and '60s* by Gene Florence (Collector Books) for more information.

Lustre Shell, bowl, soup; 6⅜" ..**5.00**
Lustre Shell, cup, 8-oz **3.00**
Lustre Shell, plate, dinner; 10" **5.00**
Lustre Shell, plate, salad; 7¼" .**3.00**
Lustre Shell, saucer, demitasse; 4¾" **1.50**
Lustre Shell, sugar bowl, w/lid ..**4.00**
Lustre Shell,cup, demitasse; 3½-oz **3.00**
Ovenware, casserole, knob cover, 1-qt **5.00**
Ovenware, pan, pie; 10" **5.00**
Peach Lustre, bowl, dessert; 5" ..**3.00**
Peach Lustre, bowl, soup plate; 7⅝" **5.00**
Peach Lustre, bowl, vegetable; 8¼" **7.50**

Peach Lustre, creamer, ftd **3.50**
Peach Lustre, cup, 8-oz **3.50**
Peach Lustre, plate, 11" **9.00**
Peach Lustre, saucer, 5¾" **75**
Peach Lustre, sugar bowl **3.50**
Royal Lustre, platter, oval, 9½x13" **6.00**

Pencil Sharpeners

The whittling process of sharpening pencils with pocket-knives was replaced by mechanical devices in the 1880s. By the turn of the century, many ingenious desk-type sharpeners had been developed. Small pencil sharpeners designed for the purse or pocket were produced in the 1890s. The typical design consisted of a small steel tube containing a cutting blade which could be adjusted by screws. Mass-produced novelty pencil sharpeners became popular in the late 1920s. The most detailed figurals were made in Germany. These German sharpeners originally sold for less than a dollar and are now considered highly collectible.

Disney and other character pencil sharpeners have been produced in Catalin, plastic, ceramic, and rubber. Novelty battery-operated pencil sharpeners can also be found. For over fifty years pencil sharpeners have been used as advertising giveaways – from Baker's Chocolate's and Coca-Cola's metal figural pencil sharpeners to the plastic 'Marshmallow Man' distributed by McDonald's©. As long as we have pencils, new pencil sharpeners will be produced and collected. Our advisor is Martha Hughes, who is listed in the Directory under California.

Bugs Bunny, battery operated, ca 1970, $35.00.

Alligator figural, twist type, plastic, ca 1960 ....**10.00**
Bathing beauty & dinosaur on base, twist to sharpen, plastic, 1980 ....**5.00**
Cylinder on base, hand crank, orange plastic, ca 1940 ..**25.00**
Goofy on sharpener, hand crank, green & white plastic, WDP, ca 1980 ....**20.00**
Ostrich figural, plastic, 1960 ..**10.00**
US Automation Pencil Sharpener, early hand crank, 1912 ..**75.00**
Woman holding up globe, twist type, metal, German, ca 1920, 3" **100.00**

Pennsbury

From the 1950s through the 1970s, dinnerware and novelty ware produced by the Pennsbury company was sold through tourist gift shops along the Pennsylvania turnpike. Much of their ware is decorated in an Amish theme. Barber shop singers were also popular, and a line of bird figures was made, very similar to Stangl's.

Ashtray, Doylestown Trust ..**18.00**
Ashtray, Hex, 5" dia **18.00**
Bowl, divided vegetable; Red Rooster **28.00**
Bowl, Dutch Talk, 9" **68.00**
Cup & saucer, Red Rooster ..**20.00**
Mug, beer; Amish couple **30.00**

Pitcher, Eagle, 6½", $32.00.

Pitcher, Folkart, 1-pt, 5" **25.00**
Plaque, What Giffs, 4" dia ...**32.00**
Plate, Black Rooster, 10" **22.00**
Salt & pepper shakers, Black Rooster, pitcher shape, pr **27.50**
Sugar bowl, Hex **20.00**

Peters and Reed

Peters and Reed founded a pottery in Zanesville, Ohio, around the turn of the century. By 1922 the firm became known as Zane Pottery. Several lines of artware were produced which are today attracting the interest of pottery collectors: High Glaze Brown Ware, decorated with in-mold relief; Moss Aztec, relief designs molded from red clay with a green-washed exterior; Chromal, with realistic or suggested scenics done in soft matt colors; Landsun; Shadow Ware; and Wilse Blue.

Ashtray, Landsun, blue & white, matt **38.00**
Bowl, Mirror Ware, green drip glaze on black iridescent, 2½x7" **45.00**
Bowl, Sheenware, blue & white swirls, flared top, #625 .**37.50**
Jug, Brown Ware, wreath sprigs, 5" **55.00**
Vase, Brown Ware, floral garlands, 5¾" **40.00**
Vase, Brown Ware, florals on 3 sides, tiny opening, 3-footed, 4½" **55.00**
Vase, Landsun, blue & brown, ball form, 3" **45.00**
Vase, Marbleized, blue, black, & yellow, 6" **50.00**
Vase, Moss Aztec, daisies, 8" .**70.00**
Vase, Moss Aztec, pansy, 6" .**42.00**
Vase, Pereco, green matt w/embossed grapes, #49, 12" ..**65.00**
Wall pocket, Egyptian, 9" ..**125.00**

Pez Collectibles

Although the history of Pez candy containers is very sketchy, collectors concentrate on the various character heads that have been a part of the Pez dispenser since the candy was introduced in the United States during the early 1950s. Some are very rare and already are being advertised with prices that exceed $100.00. Among them are the Alpine Man, Cowboy, Pineapple, Mary Poppins, Psychedelic Eye, Green Hornet, Bride, and Pear. Bear in mind that not all Pez containers are as valuable as those listed here. To learn more about this area of collecting, we recommend *A Pictorial Guide to Plastic Candy Dispensers* by David Welch. Our advisor, Jill Russell, is listed in the Directory under California.

Baseball glove **120.00**
Captain America **15.00**
Cat, black face **25.00**
Clown **25.00**

Vase, sprigged-on florals, handled, 5x9", $65.00.

Pirate, $20.00; Elephant, $30.00.

Cowboy **265.00**
Daniel Boone **95.00**
Doctor **40.00**
Donald Duck, original **10.00**
Fireman **18.00**
Giraffe **50.00**
Henry Hawk **20.00**
Indian Squaw **60.00**
Jiminy Cricket **35.00**
Lamb **10.00**
Lion **20.00**
Lion, w/crown **40.00**
Octopus, black **35.00**
Panther **45.00**
Penguin **50.00**
Peter Pan **50.00**
Pilot **35.00**
Pony, blue head **65.00**
Road Runner **20.00**
Rooster **25.00**
Rudolph **10.00**
Skull **10.00**
Snowman, original **10.00**
Spaceman **85.00**
Spiderman **8.00**
Sylvester Cat **8.00**
The Hulk, dark green **15.00**
Tweety Bird **10.00**
Zorro, w/logo **70.00**

Pfaltzgraff Pottery

Since early in the 17th century, pottery has been produced in York County, Pennsylvania. The Pfaltzgraff Company that operates there today is the outgrowth of several of these small potteries. A changeover made in 1940 redirected their efforts toward making the dinnerware lines for which they are now best known. Their earliest line was glossy brown with a white frothy drip glaze around the rim, called Gourmet Royal. Today collectors find an abundance of good examples and are working toward reassembling a set of their own. Village is another very successful line; it is tan with a stencilled Pennsylvania Dutch-type floral design in brown.

Giftware consisting of ashtrays, mugs, bottle stoppers, a cookie jar, etc., all with comic character faces were made in the 1940s as well. The line, called Muggsy, is also very collectible. Refer to *The Collector's Encyclopedia of American Dinnerware* by Jo Cunningham (Collector Books) for more information.

Gourmet Royale, bowl, cereal; 5½" **2.00**
Gourmet Royale, bowl, oval, #241, 7x10" **12.00**
Gourmet Royale, bowl, vegetable; divided **14.00**
Gourmet Royale, butter dish, ¼-lb, stick type **12.00**
Gourmet Royale, casserole, round, w/lid **16.00**
Gourmet Royale, creamer, #24 ..**5.00**
Gourmet Royale, cup **2.00**
Gourmet Royale, gravy boat, w/twin spout, #426, lg **12.00**
Gourmet Royale, mug #91 ....**3.00**

272

Gourmet Royal, see listings for specific values.

Gourmet Royale, pitcher, w/ice lip, #415 ....**16.00**
Gourmet Royale, plate, dinner; 10" **4.00**
Gourmet Royale, plate, salad; 6¾" **1.50**
Gourmet Royale, salt & pepper shakers, pr **4.50**
Gourmet Royale, saucer **1.50**
Gourmet Royale, sugar bowl, #22, w/lid **6.00**
Muggsy, canape holder, character (Carrie) face w/lift-off hat pierced for toothpicks **95.00**
Muggsy, cookie jar, character face, minimum value............**250.00**
Muggsy, mug, character face, any, from $35.00 up to **40.00**
Muggsy, mug, action-type figure (i.e. golfer, fisherman), any, from $65.00 up to **80.00**
Muggsy, mug, Black action-type figure **125.00**
Muggsy, shot mug, character face, from $45.00 up to **50.00**
Village, bowl, cereal; 6¼" **2.00**
Village, butter dish, ¼-lb, stick type **12.00**
Village, canister, w/lid, set of 4 ....**100.00**
Village, coffeepot, #550, 10"..**20.00**

Village, creamer **6.00**
Village, cup & saucer **3.00**
Village, custard cup **1.50**
Village, mug, #289, 4" **2.00**
Village, mug, footed, 5¼" **3.00**
Village, mustard jar **8.00**
Village, pitcher, water; #416, 2-qt **16.00**
Village, plate, dinner; 10½" ...**4.00**
Village, plate, salad; 7" **1.50**
Village, platter, oval, 14" **7.00**
Village, shakers, pr **4.00**
Village, sugar bowl, w/lid **6.00**

Photographica

Early cameras and the images they produced are today a popular area of collector interest. The earliest type of image was the daguerrotype, made with the use of a copper plate and silver salts; ambrotypes followed, produced by the wet-plate process on glass negatives. Tintypes were from the same era as the ambrotype but were developed on japanned iron and were much more durable. Size, subject matter, esthetics, and condition help determine value. Stereo cards, viewing devices, albums, photographs, and advertising memorabilia featuring camera equipment are included in this area of collecting. See also Cameras.

Albumen, Niagara Falls close-up, 16x19", in frame **115.00**
Albumen, Union soldiers w/flags, 3x3", EX **75.00**
Ambrotype, boy & girl w/dog on her lap, 9th plate **25.00**
Ambrotype, soldier, seated in uniform, some color, 6th plate, +case **45.00**
Bromide, War Weary Huns, German prisoners, 6½x8½"..**15.00**

Album, gold plush with applied metal stag and small mirror, stand-up type, 11x12", $80.00.

Cabinet photo, boy on high-wheeler bike, EX **30.00**

Cabinet photo, interior of Carpenter's Hall, Phila, VG **10.00**

Cabinet photo, Major Atom, Age 18 Years, midget in tux, Eisenmann, EX **12.50**

Cabinet photo, Veola Orsbon lady snake charmer, Kern Bros NY, VG **12.50**

Carte de visite, General Grant seated, stars on uniform ..**17.50**

Carte de visite, Henry W Longfellow, bust pose, EX **8.00**

Carte de visite, Libby Prison outdoor scene, Richmond VA, EX **1,750.00**

Carte de visite, Senorita Lucia Zarate the Mexican Liliputian, J Wood **20.00**

Carte de visite, Tom Thumb & his wife in later years, EX ..**10.00**

Carte de visite, 2 artillery soldiers clasping hands, Brown ..**30.00**

Case, thermoplastic, Accented Oval, 4th plate, VG **35.00**

Case, thermoplastic, floral cluster relief design, 6th plate, w/ ambrotype **50.00**

Case, thermoplastic, florals w/EX gold, oval, 3x1¼" **75.00**

Case, thermoplastic, scroll motif, 6th plate, w/daguerreotype, VG **60.00**

Daguerreotype, close-up portrait of lady w/hair in long curls, 4th plate **17.50**

Daguerreotype, couple w/3 children, 4th plate, VG **15.00**

Daguerreotype, lady & child w/ book beside table, 4th plate, +full case **48.00**

Daguerreotype, lady in white lace bonnet w/books, half plate, +case **85.00**

Daguerreotype, Quaker man seated in chair, top hat, 4th plate, EX **40.00**

Daguerreotype, sm boy in dress, 6th plate, EX **37.50**

Stanhope, pen/letter opener, souvenir of Niagara Falls ...**75.00**

Stereoview, Boston harbor from Bunker Hill **17.50**

Stereoview, German machine guns inspected by French, WWI era **3.00**

Stereoview, little girl & 4 dolls, VG **10.00**

Stereoview, San Francisco earthquake, Keystone, EX **27.50**

Stereoview, Sioux warrior on horseback w/children, Ingersoll, EX **15.00**

Stereoview, 1870s train wreck by DS Camp, Hartford CT .**12.00**

Tintype, farmhouse w/family outside, half plate, VG **27.50**

Tintype, fireman wearing leather fire belt, brimmed hat, 9th plate **35.00**

Tintype, GAR veteran w/GAR wreath & cord hat, 2¼x3¼", VG **20.00**

Tintype, hunter w/M1876 Winchester rifle, 6th plate **30.00**

Tintype, jockey wearing racing clothes w/gloves & whip, 2½x3½" **20.00**

Tintype, musician w/English horn, 4th plate, +case, EX **50.00**

Tintype, Union captain in full dress, 6th plate **40.00**

Tintype, 2-year-old baby in fancy carriage, 2½x3½" **12.50**

Pie Birds

What is a pie bird? It is a functional and decorative kitchen tool most commonly found in the shape of a bird. Other popular designs were elephants and black-faced bakers. More recently, figural pie vents were made as novelties. They were originally simple pie funnels used in England and Wales in the 1800s for meat pies. The basic functions of the pie bird (fent, funnel, chimney, safe, steamer) are to raise the crust to prevent sogginess and to allow the steam to escape to prevent bubbling over onto the oven floor. Pie birds are now at the peak of their appeal and collectibility; the new collector must be wary that there are new pie vents being sold by dealers (knowlingly in many instances) as old or rare and at double or triple the original cost (usually under $10.00). Our advisor for this category is Lillian M. Cole, who is listed in the Directory under New Jersey. Listed below are the most popular mass-produced pie birds found at US flea markets.

Alaskan Clay, new, white & brown marbled **25.00**
Baker man (or lady), Josef Originals, 2", either **18.00**
Benny the Baker, Cardinal China, 5¼", w/crimper & tester, 1950s **68.00**
Black chef, yellow, blue, or green suit, some marked JBP, old, 4½" **85.00**
Bluebird (speckled), heavy ceramic, 1941, 4½" **25.00**

Bluebird w/babies on yellow nest, circled C stamp, 1950, 5"..**60.00**
Canary w/puffed-out chest, pink or teal, 4½" **50.00**
Chick, white w/pink or blue base, Pillsbury Chick, Morton &/or Shawnee **20.00**
Chick, yellow w/pink beak, Josef Originals, 1950s-70s, 2" **18.00**
Chick w/bonnet, Josef Originals, 1950s-70s, 2" **18.00**
Duckling, long neck, blue, yellow, or pink airbrushed color, 1950s, 5" **20.00**
Elephant, grey on pink (or pink & white) drum, marked CCC, 1950s, 4" **60.00**
Fruit funnel (cherry, peach, apple), imported, w/sticker **20.00**
Nutbrown elephant, trunk twisted up, all white or all gray, stamped **60.00**
Owl, Josef Originals, 1950s-70s, 2" **18.00**
Rooster, long hooked neck, Pearl China, 5" (watch for Japanese repro) **45.00**

Rooster, $45.00.

275

Rooster, marked either Cb or
Cleminson, 1940s-60s, from
$15 to **25.00**
Songbird, gold painted beak &
feathers, US (LePere?) ..**45.00**
Songbird, pink, blue, or cinna-
mon **20.00**
Welsh pie dragon, gray or copper
lustre, 1970s **70.00**
White Dove Pottery, new, stamped
mark **16.00**

Pin-Back Buttons

Because most of the pin-backs
prior to the 1920s were made of
celluloid, collectors refer to them
as 'cellos.' Many were issued in
sets on related topics, Some
advertising buttons had paper
inserts on the back that identified
the company or the product they
were advertising. After the 1920s
lithographed metal buttons were
produced; they're now called
'lithos.' Some of the better examples are listed here; many common buttons are worth much less.
See also Advertising; Movie Memorabilia; Political.

**Black Student Union button
from the 1960s-'70s, scarce,
1½", $20.00.**

Al Smith, Cleveland Indians,
photo **25.00**
Auto race car & driver photo,
early **30.00**
Ben Franklin Club of Des Moines,
portrait, 2" **24.00**
Bob Hope photo, Beu James, James
J Walker for Mayor **28.00**
Bobby Baker for Secretary of
Treasury, M **2.00**
Brooklyn Dodgers, on baseball
ground **35.00**
California Junior Theatre Mati-
nee Club, color, VG **25.00**
Captain Charles A Lindbergh,
Price of USA, ⅞" **85.00**
Cassius Clay, early, 1½" **40.00**
Chico Carrasguel, Chicago White
Sox, photo, NM **35.00**
Corrigan, Gone Again **30.00**
Detroit, Where Life Is Worth Liv-
ing, lake scene, early **30.00**
Dodge Silver Anniversary 1914-
1939, blue & white **26.00**
Elk's 25th Anniversary, Las Vegas
NV, 1959 ....**32.00**
Ephrata Community Hospital,
ambulance scene, blue &
white, ca 1920s **20.00**
Everybody Loves Me, Little Miss
Move Me, image of doll on
blue ground **30.00**
George VI & Queen, 1910-1935,
1¼" **20.00**
Home-Coming M (Minnesota)
1919, color, NM **30.00**
I (eye pictured) Buy the Evening
Times, blue & yellow **25.00**
I Am for Wilson & 8-Hour Day,
white on blue, ⅝", EX **12.50**
I Go Pogo, Pogo portrait **20.00**
I Have Seen the Future, block let-
ters on solid ground **15.00**
If You Liked Hitler You'll Love
David Duke!, M **1.50**
Jungle Explorers, Order of the Ele-
phant, elephant, color **30.00**
Ken Maynard, Cole Bros Circus,
photo, rare, 1¼" **125.00**

Mail World's Fair 1904, black & white scenic center, lg ...**35.00**

Meet Me at the Big Store, Santa portrait **20.00**

Muhammad Ali Fight of the Century, March 8, 1971, 3" **46.00**

National Relief Assurance Co, Philadelphia, eagle & Liberty Bell **22.00**

Newark Bears, International League Champions 1932, early **36.00**

Pancho, photo & letters on yellow, 2" **48.00**

Patton's Rheumatic Remedy, York PA, red & blue **30.00**

Philco for '50...Quality First!, wreath border **20.00**

Plymouth, Four Years Better Than Before, red, white & blue, scarce **25.00**

RCA Victor Celebrates Tommy Dorsey Week **20.00**

Remember Kute Kris Kringle Club 1940, sm **20.00**

Service Award Dispatch (newspaper), Columbus portrait in center **20.00**

Souvenir of Kentucky Derby, horse head photo, 1940s **20.00**

Tom Corbett, flasher, 1¼" **22.50**

United We Shall Overcome, black & white hands clasped **1.75**

Universal's Great Chapter Play, Stanley in Africa, color ..**20.00**

Welcome to New Haven's 300th Birtday Party, color **20.00**

Pinup Art

This is a relatively new area of collector interest, and nice examples such as calendars, magazines, playing cards, etc., by the more collectible artists are still easy to come by. Collectors often center their attentions on the work of one or more of their favorite artists. Some of the better known are Petty, Vargas, Ballantyne, Armstrong, and Phillips. Pinup art was popular from the '30s into the '50s, inspired by Hollywood and its glamorous leading ladies.

Ashtray, Playmate holding key, painted glass, 1960s, M ..**25.00**

Blotter, Earl Moran girl, advertising w/3-month calendar, 4x9", NM **7.00**

Blotter, Vargas blond in tight dress, Call Anytime, 3⅜x6½", M **18.00**

Calendar, blond Petty girl, 1944, complete, 15x8", EX+ **55.00**

Calendar, Glamour Gal Proverbs, 1957, 13x8½", EX **110.00**

Calendar page, Petty girl, 1947, matted **7.00**

Card, Jayne Mansfield, full color, 1950s, full color **3.00**

Gatefold, Esquire, Vargas, Late Spring, EX **20.00**

Gatefold, Esquire, Vargas, Song for a Soldier, Feb 1943, EX ..**25.00**

Greeting card, Macpherson girl undressing, G **12.00**

Letter opener, Designed by Elvgren, die-cut plastic nude, 1950s, 8" **32.00**

LP record album, Petty, Music for the Boyfriend, G+ **25.00**

Magazine, Eyeful, Driben cover featuring farm girl, Dec 1952, EX **15.00**

Magazine, Motion Picture, Vargas cover featuring Mary Pickford, G+ **60.00**

Magazine ad, Esquire, Petty, Just Between Us, Darling, July 1937 ....**10.00**

Magazine pinup, Esquire, Petty, ... I Looked Under the Pillow &... ....**12.00**

Magazine pinup, Gallery, Van Gilder girl, nude, 1973 ......**5.00**

Magazine pinup, Playboy, Don Lewis art featuring topless Bunny, NM **4.00**

Magazine pinup, True, Petty, ... a Mink Coat Would Be Nice..., 1947 ....**20.00**

Mutoscope card, Rolf Armstrong, dancer, On the Beam, 3x5", EX **8.00**

Mutoscope card, Zoe Mozert, military blond being pursued, 1940s, NM **8.00**

Playing cards, Esquire, Al Moore girls, 1947, 2 decks, boxed, EX **12.00**

Print, artist signed, $30.00.

Print, D'Armaro, Danger!, cowgirl by fence, early 1950s, 12x17", NM **23.00**

Program, KO Munson girl on cover, Ice Follies, 1949, 11x9", EX **8.00**

Shot glass, Playmate w/key, painted, 1960s, 3", M **40.00**

Planters

The years from about 1930 until in the seventies was the era for figural ceramics. Planters were popular, especially those designed in the forms of animals, birds, and children. Though many were imported from Japan, companies here in the United States made them by the scores too. Those listed here are basically generic; see specific pottery companies such as McCoy, Shawnee, Cleminson, etc., for more descriptions and prices. Our advisor is Carol Silagyi, who is listed in the Directory under New Jersey.

Baby bottle, blue & white, 7½" long **5.00**

Baby pram, light blue **4.00**

Chicken, can be used as wall pocket or planter, 8½x6½", $20.00.

Chinese girl w/basket on each side of her **5.00**

Colonial couple, green top hat, yellow pants, green bonnet, pink dress **6.00**

Donkey w/lg cart, yellow, crazed, 5¼x7" **4.50**

Elephant, dark pink, 3x5½" ...**6.00**

Elephant, white, 5¼x7" **5.00**

Elf w/flower wheelbarrow **5.00**

Girl sitting at well, light blue ..**5.00**

Girl sitting at well, pink w/gold
trim **7.50**
Girl w/basket & duck, pink **5.00**
Oriental girl holding pot, pink &
blue tones **6.00**
Squirrel, light rose, 4" **4.50**
Stagecoach, gray, white &
maroon, 4⅛x6⅝" **10.00**
Tugboat **8.00**

Planters Peanuts

Since 1916 Mr. Peanut has
represented the Planters Peanuts
Company. Today he has his own
fan club of collectors who specialize in this area of advertising
memorabilia. More than fifteen
styles of the glass display jars
were made; the earliest was
issued in 1926 and is referred to
as the 'pennant' jar. The rarest of
them all is the 'football' jar from
the early thirties. Premiums
such as glass and metal paper-
weights, pens, and pencils were
distributed in the late 1930s;
after the war, plastic items were
offered.

**Plastic Mr. Peanut bank, 8½",
$15.00.**

Bank, Mr Peanut, hard plastic figu-
ral, 8½" on 3¼" dia base ..**15.00**
Beach towel, white w/Mr Peanut,
M **35.00**
Bowl, deep, flared rim, round
base, plastic, EX **20.00**
Buckle, gold-tone metal Mr
Peanut figural, M **10.00**
Cuff links, gold-tone metal ..**75.00**
Display, die-cut stand-up Mr
Peanut, 48" **18.00**
Doll, Mr Peanut, cloth, EX ..**15.00**
Frisbee, foam, 10" dia, M **12.00**
Jar, 6-sided, w/printed square
label **60.00**
Mechanical pencil, Mr Peanut
form, in wrapper, M **22.00**
Paint book, 1949, EX **30.00**

Peanut butter maker, Mr Peanut
figural, MIB **35.00**
Radio, Mr Peanut, MIB **75.00**
Refrigerator magnet, Mr Peanut
figural **12.00**
Sign, 1939 World's Fair, die-cut
cardboard, 7", VG **15.00**
Spoon, gold-tone metal w/enamel
Mr Peanut, demitasse ...**22.00**
Toothbrush, Mr Peanut handle
figural, M **10.00**
Tray, Mr Peanut Nut Tray, blue
plastic, 3-part, 5¼" dia ..**40.00**

Plastic Collectibles

While early plastic items
have long been a part of many
areas of collecting interest (for
instance, gutta percha photo cases
and jewelry), and over the past
several years we have seen a

tremendous acceleration in the values of Catalin and Bakelite items, there has been a recent surge of interest in mid-century and later kitchenware items, appliances, lamps, radios, etc., made of common plastic. Because the market is just starting to develop, an informed shopper should be able to find excellent examples at very low prices. See also Jewelry; Kitchen Collectibles.

Ashtray, marbelized Catalin, 4½" square **30.00**

Bottle opener, chrome plate, red handle **8.00**

Box, plain ivory celluloid, ½ x 2¾x1" **6.00**

Buttonhook, plain ivory celluloid, unmarked, 7¾" **6.00**

Carving set, knife & fork, steel w/Catalin handle **30.00**

Cigarette holder, orange w/mottled orange & black Catalin, 4½" **12.00**

Clock, alarm; Wesclox, Moonbeam Model S5J, ivory Catalin, ca 1937 ....**40.00**

Clock, shelf; Wilcox, ivory celluloid, Greek Temple facade, ca 1923 ....**42.50**

Dresser set, ivory & amber celluloid, marked Pyralin Mayflower, 6-pc **20.00**

Dresser set, ivory & faux tortoise shell w/embossed lady's head, 14-pc **75.00**

Figurine, bulldog, dark red celluloid, Putz type, Japan, 2⅜x3½" **10.00**

Figurine, polar bear, white celluloid, Putz type, Japan, 1⅞x3½" **10.00**

Figurine, ram, gray celluloid, Putz type, marked Made in USA, 1½x2" **6.00**

Hair receiver, ivory, unmarked, 4" dia **6.50**

Hairbrush, ivory, marked French Ivory, 8¾" **4.00**

Letter opener, black & amber Catalin, Art Deco stripes ..**20.00**

Nail buffer, ivory celluloid, marked French Ivory, 6" **4.50**

Nail file, ivory celluloid, unmarked, 7½" **3.50**

Picture frame, clear Lucite, Art Deco, 6" square **14.00**

Picture frame, easel back, marked Ivoroid, 2" dia **12.00**

Powder box, hand-painted florals on ivory, unmarked, 3x2½" dia **12.00**

Salad server, chrome w/green handle, pr **12.00**

Shaving brush, red Catalin ..**18.00**

Smoking set, 2 ashtrays, matchbox holder & humidor w/ Bakelite lids **20.00**

Kob-Knobs, Catalin, eight in original box, $40.00.

Political Collectibles

Pennants, posters, badges, phamplets – in general, anything related to a presidential campaign or politicians – are being sought by collectors who have an interest in the political history of our country. Most valued are items from a particularly eventful period or those things having to do with an especially colorful personality. See also Matchcovers.

Cigarette lighter, All the Way with LBJ, $45.00.

Arm band, white on blue felt, For Hoover & the GOP **40.00**
Balloon, Truman for President, M **28.00**
Banner, plastic, Nixon's the One!, 1968, 30x45", EX **12.00**
Book, souvenir; Republican 1972 National Convention, 288 pages, EX **20.00**
Book, Strategy of Peace, John Kennedy, 1st ed, 1960, 233 pages, G+ **25.00**
Can, Gold Water on gold over green, The Right Drink ..**14.00**
Candle, Elect Ford for 4 & portrait on frosted glass, 7x2½"dia **40.00**
Cane, Jimmy Carter for President 1976 on wooden shaft, peanut finial **40.00**
Cap, LBJ-USA, red, white & blue **30.00**
Car plate, Landon in red & gold on blue, tin, 4x13", 1936, EX **65.00**
Car plate, Nixon & Agnew, blue block letters on white ...**20.00**
Change purse, McKinley memorial **45.00**
Change purse, T Roosevelt, Give Every Man a Square Deal, scarce **150.00**
Charm bracelet, charms spelling NIXON w/Ohio map & elephant **35.00**

Clicker, Nixon portrait, Click w/Dick, blue & silver, 1960 ....**20.00**
Clock, presidents up through LBJ (featured at top), electric, round **75.00**
Coaster, cork, I Like Ike in red letters, round **5.00**
Donkey, LBJ, white w/red, white, & blue hat, plastic **25.00**
Earrings, metal elephant head w/Ike in ring hanging from trunk, EX **25.00**
Fan, hand-held type, Bush & Quayle, 1992 ....**7.00**
Fan, hand-held type, Freedom Fighers, King & Kennedy photos **30.00**
Fan, hand-held type, I'm a Taft Fan **50.00**
Fly swatter, plastic, Clinton & Gore **5.00**
Headband, cloth, Goldwater Next President, M in bag **17.00**
Inaugural medal, JFK-LBJ .**30.00**
Inaugural ticket, Kennedy & Johnson, 1961, complete, EX **20.00**
Inaugural ticket, Reagan & Bush, 1981, complete, EX **7.00**
Jugate card, Re-Elect Carter-Mondale, 9x12" **15.00**

Key chain, flasher type, I Like Ike & photo **30.00**

Knife, Regan-Bush, 1980 .....**14.00**

Light switch cover, pictures nude Nixon, Save Energy **20.00**

Lighter, Bic type, Bush caricature on Hot Seat **17.00**

Mask, Goldwater, cardboard ..**25.00**

Matchbook, Veterans for Nixon, EX **8.00**

Membership card, Truman & Barkley photo w/capital ..**85.00**

Memorial ribbon, William McKinley, woven **35.00**

Milk bottle top, cardboard, Buy War Bonds, Keep 'Em Flying **7.00**

Mug, Nixon face figural, white w/black eyebrows & brown handle **45.00**

Mug, The New Deal & portrait on shield in relief, glazed ceramic **25.00**

Nodders, JFK & Jackie kissing, pr **235.00**

Paper cup, I Like Ike, pictures Ike & elephants **18.00**

Paperweight, Goldwater bust, cast metal w/brass finish, 1964, EX **15.00**

Pencil, Goldwater-Miller, M ..**17.00**

Pennant, Alfred E Smith, blue felt w/white lettering, 1928, 29" **85.00**

Pennant, Goldwater portrait on blue, ...for President **35.00**

Pennant, Souvenir Washington DC, Hoover portrait **95.00**

Pennant, Willkie portrait & flags on blue, Win With Willkie ...**65.00**

Pillow, FDR & Washington portraits, capital building, fringed **65.00**

Plaque, Al Smith w/1928 on hat, bronze **160.00**

Plaque, die-cut tin profile portrait of McKinley **65.00**

Playing card, Hoover & Barbour, black on gold **40.00**

Pocket mirror, JFK portrait, black & white, oval **40.00**

Pocketknife, Nixon & Agnew jugate portrait, Vote Republican, round **30.00**

Poster, A Time for Greatness, Kennedy for President, 29x19", M **125.00**

Poster, America Needs Nixon & Lodge, black & white photos, 14x19" **35.00**

Poster, FDR, Here Is the Man We've Been Waiting For, 1932, sm **40.00**

Poster, FDR portrait, Man of Action, 9x12" **25.00**

Poster, The Adventures of Daffy Dick & Spiro T Pig, 22x29", NM **25.00**

Potholder, Eisenhower & Nixon, 1952 ....**35.00**

Program, Presidential 1953 Inauguration, 48-pages, 8½x11", NM **40.00**

Prohibition tag, The Home Vs the Saloon, w/child's photo ..**50.00**

Puppet, hand type, cloth w/ plastic head, Nixon & Agnew, pr **45.00**

Radio, Jimmy Carter caricature figural, transistor w/wrist strap **40.00**

Sheet music, Thank You Mr Hoover, That's the Best Day of the Year **25.00**

Stereoview card, Cleveland & Truman **12.00**

Sticker, Brooks, Willkie, & Green, red, white & blue **7.00**

Sticker, Vote For Nixon, Future You Save May Be Your Own, rectangular **4.00**

Tie, Vote for Landon & portrait on black **60.00**

Tie tac, brass, Carter photo w/3-color enameling, NM **15.00**

Tie tac, 3-D elephant w/black metal eyeglasses frames (Goldwater), 1" **40.00**

Tobacco canister, George Washington Cut Plug, red, white, & blue, 6" **75.00**
Tray, FDR portrait left of White House, rectangular **50.00**
Tumbler, JFK Memorial 1917-1967, clear glass, 6" **12.00**
Watch fob, Al Smith, metal w/ leather strap **50.00**
Watch fob, Taft & Sherman, metal w/leather strap **20.00**
Yo-Yo, Reagan portrait in sailor's hat, A Real Yo-Yo **15.00**

Pin-Back Buttons

Celluloid pin-back buttons ('cellos') were first used widely in the 1896 presidential campaign; before that time medals, ribbons, and badges of various kinds predominated. By the 1920s buttons with designs lithographed directly on metal ('lithos') became more common. The most attractive and interesting designs are found on 'classic' buttons made between 1900-15; and they (along with the plainer but very scarce buttons for presidental candidates of the 1920s) are also the most expensive.

Prices for political pin-back buttons have increased considerably in the last few years, more due to speculative buying and selling rather than inherent scarcity or unusual demand. It is still possible, however, to find quality collectible items at reasonable prices. In flea markets, recent buttons tend to be overpriced; the goal, as always, is to look for less familiar items that may be priced more reasonably.

Most collectors look for presidential items, but buttons for 'causes' (such as civil rights and peace) as well as 'locals' (governors, senators, etc.) are becoming increasingly popular as well. Picture buttons are the most desirable, especially the 'jugates' which show both presidential and vice-presidential candidates. Recently, 'coattail' items, featuring presidential and local candidates on the same button, have attracted a lot of interest. Most buttons issued since the 1964 campaign, with a few notable exceptions, should be in the range of $2.00 to $10.00. The listing here therefore concentrates on earlier items.

Condition is critical: cracks, scratches, spots, and brown stains ('foxing') seriously reduce the value of a button. Prices are for items in excellent condition. Reproductions are common; many are marked as such, but it takes some experience to tell the difference. The best reference book for political item collectors is Edmund Sullivan's *Collecting Political Americana*, the second edition of which has been recently published. Our advisor is Michael Engel, who is listed in the Directory under Massachusetts.

Abraham Lincoln, For President 1864, portrait, round brass shell **250.00**
Adlai Stevenson, All the Way ..., portrait w/hat, 1956, ⅞" ..**10.00**
Alton Parker & Henry Davis, jugate photo w/various designs, 1904 ....**150.00**
Bryan & Sewall, 16 to 1, jugate photo, 1896 ....**40.00**
Calvin Coolidge, Keep Coolidge, portrait in keystone, 1924, ⅞" **20.00**
Davis & Bryan (lettered), red, white & blue, 1924, ⅞" ..**100.00**
Debs & Stedman, Socialist 1912 Candidates, jugate photo, ⅞" **175.00**

Grover Cleveland, celluloid stud, 1884 ....**25.00**

Harrison & Morton (lettered), enamel stud, 1888 ....**30.00**

Harry S Truman, For President..., portrait, black & white, 1¼" **30.00**

Herbert Hoover, For President..., portrait, black & white, ⅞" **25.00**

James Blaine & John Logan, jugate photo w/eagle, brass shell, 1884 ....**200.00**

John F Kennedy, For President..., portrait, 1960, 3½" **15.00**

John F Kennedy, Man of the 60s, portrait, flasher, 1960, 2"....................................**10.00**

Theodore Roosevelt, portrait, red, white & blue, 1904, 1¼" **75.00**

Theodore Roosevelt, Roosevelt the American, portrait, 1912, ⅞" **50.00**

Warren G Harding, For President..., portrait, colored border, ⅝" **10.00**

William Henry Harrison, brass medal, 1840 ....**25.00**

William McKinley, portrait w/stars & stripes, 1896, ⅞" **15.00**

William McKinley & T Roosevelt, Full Dinner Bucket, jugate photo **100.00**

Postcards

The first postcards cards were printed in Austria in 1869, but it was the Columbian Exposition in 1893 that started the postcard craze that swept the country for years to come. Today's collectors tend to specialize in cards of a particular theme or by a favorite illustrator. Among the famous artists whose work you may find are Rose O'Neill, Philip Boileau, Alphonse Mucha, and John Winsch.

Advertising, Bromo-Seltzer, horse-drawn wagon, black & white, EX **30.00**

Advertising, Cherry Smash, Black servants on Mount Vernon lawn, EX **40.00**

Black theme, 2¢ stamp on reverse, $12.00.

284

Advertising, Hershey Chocolate Co, boating scene, 5½x2¾", VG **4.50**

Advertising, Shredded Wheat, #412, factory & Niagara Falls, NM **5.00**

Advertising, Trade Winds Restaurant & Lounge, linen, Art Deco, NM **4.50**

Advertising, Winchester Shells, shows 2 types, black & white, EX **40.00**

Al Lang Stadium, Home of St Louis Cards, Spring training, D Hanks **2.00**

Alice in Wonderland, Hallmark, 4x6" **125.00**

America Salutes Team USA, USPS for US Olympics, 4x6" **2.00**

Art Deco, lady in mink stole & muff, signed P Aranda ..**35.00**

Art Deco, man & woman standing at bar, signed G Meschini **30.00**

Art Nouveau, Raphael Kirchner, Geisha IV, Germany, 1901 ..**50.00**

Aviation, Army blimps at Lakehurst NJ, 1928, reprint ..**30.00**

Aviation, Curtis & His Biplane at the NY State Fair, 1910 ..**35.00**

Beautify America Get a Haircut, J Donnelly & Sons, 3x5¾" ..**1.00**

Beauty at Rest, reclining nude, black & white, 1950s reproduction **1.00**

Birthday Greeting, woven silk, Alpha series, London, EX **45.00**

Boston Braves Team of 1984, Tichnor, linen era **10.00**

Boy Scout National Jamboree, 1985, Smokey the Bear ...**2.00**

CA Honeymoon, couple in balloon (orange) gondola, Mitchell, 1910 ....**3.00**

Children dreaming, moving wheel shows toys, Merrimack reproduction **2.00**

Chimpanzee & nude, Mel Ramos, 4x6" **1.00**

Christmas, 2¢ stamp on reverse, $9.00.

Christmas Greetings, little girls carrying tree, silk **20.00**

Christmas Greetings, series #48/214, Father Christmas, 1910 ....**14.00**

Clapsaddle, A Merry Halloween, girl & black cat **28.00**

Clapsaddle, series #8, 4th Birthday, boy w/dog **12.00**

CM Russell, Indian Chief, Red Cloud **40.00**

Coors International Bicycle Classic, 1975 ....**2.00**

Desert Storm Airpower in Action, Air Force Assoc, 16 stickers, 4x6" **1.50**

Disney, It's a Small World, interior view, Florida **1.00**

Disney, tilt card & image changes, Goofy hands paint to Mickey, M **3.00**

Dolly Dingle Playtime, Dover, set of 24 ....**10.00**

Dustin Hoffman as Tootsie, Coral Lee, standard size **50**

Fire Co & Methodist Church Fredonia NY, linen era, Tichnor **1.50**

Fire-Fighting, Nichols Fire Dept 1919, sepia tone **35.00**

Flash Gordon, King Features, 1967, 3½x5½" **2.00**

Garfield, I'm Bored, Bored..., Jim Davis, Argus **50**

General Electric real record, cash contest, 1950s **8.00**

George Brett, The Quest 1980, Ted Watts, 1981 ....**3.00**

Girls of the South Seas (topless), Pacific Promotions, 4x6", set of 23 ....**20.00**

Golliwog, Still They Come, signed Attwell, published by Carlton **16.00**

Gone with the Wind, Classico, 4x6" **1.00**

Great American Smokeout, American Cancer Society, 1990, 4x6" **2.00**

Groundhog's Day, Merry Feb 2nd!, designed by Elsie, 1948 ...**35.00**

Halloween Greetings, series #26, E Nash, witch on pumpkin ..**50.00**

Hanukah candelabrum from Great Synagogue, Art Unlimited, Amsterdam **1.00**

Henry Kissinger caricature, Dervish, 4½x6½" **1.00**

Hold-to-light, Christmas & New Year Greetings, church, Germany 1905 ....**35.00**

Hold-to-light, Christmas Greetings, die-cut, angel praying **50.00**

Hold-to-light, Santa & reindeer, pub Meteor #531, Germany 1899 ....**75.00**

Hold-to-light, South Station Boston, MA, Koehler, EX **40.00**

Hold-to-light, Statue of Liberty, Avis Stamp Co, 1986 ....**7.00**

Hold-to-light, Whaleback Steamer Christopher Columbus ..**35.00**

HS Heinz, printed recipes & ketchup bottle, 3½x6" **1.00**

Jaguar XJ Sed, 2-door, 1970s ..**2.00**

John Davidson at Harrahs, Atlantic City NJ **2.00**

John F Kennedy, In Memoriam, AAA Novelty Co **1.50**

Johnny Carson & wife Joanna, Coral Lee, standard size **50**

Kawasaki 750, Turbo Art, Terry Pastor, Athena, 4x6" **1.00**

Knute Rocknee, Ted Watts **3.00**

Map showing division of Holy Land among 12 tribes, 4¾x6½" **1.25**

Marilyn Monroe, bright color, Lusterchrome 1950s **3.00**

Marilyn Monroe, Barcelona, F Cabanos **2.00**

New Year Greetings, from German travel magazine, Arab on camel **35.00**

New Year Greetings, girl in front of house, mechanical date changer **8.00**

Nixon w/printed autograph, Novco, Lusterchrome, M **2.00**

Pere Marguette Car Ferry, Kropp, 1930s **2.00**

Political, Presidential campaign for Democrats Bryan & Kern, 1908 ....**40.00**

Political, Progressive Party for Govenor of Massachusetts, 1914 ....**40.00**

Political, Roosevelt entering Yellowstone Park, Underwood, sepia, 1906 ....**35.00**

Puzzle card, Why Is a Married Man Like a Candle?, #240, 1906 ....**5.00**

RMS Queen Mary, Garboyle Marine Oils, ship's statistics & ad on back **25.00**

Romantic, series #V4, little boy & girl cupid under umbrella, 1911 ....**3.50**

Roy Knickman, bronze medalist 1984 Summer Olympics, black & white **2.00**

Royal Family, Dixon, 5x7" **1.00**

Save Our Rain Forests, frog, trees, etc, Athena, 4x6" ...**2.00**

Smurfs, Peyo, 4x6", pr **3.00**

Space Shuttle, Aircraft Designs, Martin Alton, Athena, 4x6" **1.00**

Stars of Tulsa...Music Festival, Oakridge Boys, Wynette, etc, 1978 ....**1.25**

Summer Olympics, 1984, Olympic torch close-up, M **1.00**

Sweet Nothings Whispered Overnight, Express Mail ad, 1986 ....**4.00**

Thanksgiving Greetings, HSV series #800, child praying **2.00**

Thanksgiving Greetings, Whitney, boy w/turkey's leg, 1916 ..**4.00**

Tinman & Scarecrow in Wizard Of Oz stage production, Windeatt, Chicago **50.00**

Tuck, Easter series #700, boy in sailor suit stands behind girl, 1910 ....**5.00**

Tuck, Happy Days series #521, little girl & boy hug, 1910 ..**6.00**

Tuck, Lindbergh & Ruth Elder standing, dark blue ground, unused, G **20.00**

Tuck, Little Boy Blue, series #9301, signed Barnes **10.00**

Tuck, Little Nemo, Good Morrow, Prithee..., G **12.00**

Tuck, Old Mother Hubbard, cat holding puppy, Barnes ..**10.00**

Whale Song, 3 whales, Athena, 4x6" **2.00**

Who Says You Can't Hurry Love, US Post Office, Valentine's Day 1987 ....**3.00**

Woodrow Wilson, That Belongs to Armenia, black & white, 1947, EX **30.00**

Yuri Gagarin 1st man in space, Kniga, 4x6" **1.50**

Precious Moments

Little figurines with inspirational messages called Precious Moments were created by Samuel J. Butcher and are produced by Enesco Inc. in the Orient. They're sold through almost every gift store in the country, and some of the earlier, discontinued models are becoming very collectible. Refer to *Precious Collectibles*, a magazine published by Rosie Wells Enterprizes Inc. for more information. Rosie is listed in our Directory under Illinois and again under Clubs and Newsletters.

He Careth for You, no mark, E-1377B, $95.00.

Angel Pushing Buggy, #16012, Flower mark, from $60.00 up to **65.00**

Boy & Girl Praying at Table, #E-5214, Hourglass mark, $85.00 up to **90.00**

Boy & Ink Spot, #100269, Flower mark **50.00**

Boy Jogger, #E-3112, Hourglass mark, from $60.00 up to ..**65.00**

Boy w/Wreath, #E-0506, Cross mark, from $55.00 up to ..**60.00**

Clown w/Books, #104396, Bow 'n Arrow mark **32.50**

Couple w/Gifts, #115290, Flower mark **60.00**

Dunce Boy, #E-9268, Flower mark, from $55.00 up to **60.00**

Girl & Frying Pan, #E-3118, Triangle mark **75.00**
Girl Holding Doll w/Dog, #105643, Flame mark **40.00**
Girl in Tree Swing, #524085, Vessel mark **55.00**
Girl Looking Into Manger, #E-0507, Dove mark, from $50.00 up to **55.00**
Girl Mailing Snowball, #112372, Flame mark **15.00**
Girl Sewing Boy's Pants, #106844, Vessel mark **55.00**
Girl Sweeping Dirt Under Rug, #521779, Vessel mark ...**40.00**
Girl w/Birds, #12092, Olive Branch mark **75.00**
Girl w/Goose in Lap, #E-5213, Cedar Tree mark **35.00**
Girl w/Present, #110930, Cedar Tree mark **30.00**
Girl w/Sick Bear, #100102, Flame mark, from $55.00 up to **60.00**
Girl w/Sick Bear, #100102, Olive Branch mark, from $65.00 up to **70.00**
Kneeling Girl, #522287, G-Clef mark **30.00**
Mouse w/Cheese, #E-2381, Cross mark **90.00**
Teacher w/Report Card, #12300, Cedar Tree mark **35.00**

Prints

Prints, as with any article of collectible ephemera, are susceptible to certain types of damage. Staining and foxing (brown spots caused by microscopic mold) are usually present to some extent and should be weighed against the desirability of the print. Margin tears may be acceptable if the print is a rare one, but avoid tears that affect the image itself. If margins have been trimmed to

less than ¾", the value is considerably lowered. For more information refer to *Those Wonderful Yard-Long Prints and More* and *More Wonderful Yard-Long Prints* by Keagy and Rhoden (self published) and *R. Atkinson Fox*, Vol 1 and 2, by Rita C. Mortenson (L-W Book Sales).

Bessie Pease Gutmann

Chuckles, #216, 1937, 11x14" ..**65.00**
In Port of Dreams, #214, 1937, 11x14" **75.00**
Love's Blossom, #223, 1927, 14x11" **65.00**
Mighty Like a Rose, #642, 1915, 11x15" **85.00**
Mischief, #122, 1924, round, 10½" dia **150.00**
Sunbeam, #730 ....**175.00**
Tasting, little child w/cup, sepia tone, #21, 1909, 12x9" ..**100.00**
Tommy, sepia tone, #788, 14x 21" **125.00**

Currier & Ives

Alnwick Castle, women & children by wooded stream, sm folio **80.00**
Bouquet of Roses, red, white, & pink, sm folio **95.00**
Catherine, full-length portrait, N Currier, sm folio **90.00**
Chappaqua Farm, West Chester County, NY, sm folio **185.00**
Father's Pride, mother & boy on sofa, N Currier, sm folio ..**70.00**
Fruit of Temperance, 1870, sm folio **450.00**
Harvest, men harvesting, others resting, sm folio **250.00**
Idlewild on the Hudson, couple on bridge, sm folio **195.00**
Indian Falls, 11x14" **165.00**
Inviting Dish, plate of fruit, 1870, sm folio **135.00**

Ladies Bouquet, flowers in glass vase, sm folio **60.00**
Life & Age of Man, sm **225.00**
Little Flower Girl, girl w/basket of flowers, sm folio **69.00**
Little May Blossom, girl w/bouquet, 1874, sm folio **80.00**
Little Sisters, girls holding hands, sm folio **45.00**
Lottie, portrait of a girl, vignette, sm folio **80.00**
Moonlight, The Ruins; man & woman in foreground, sm folio **90.00**
My Pet Bird, girl holding yellow bird, med folio **90.00**
My Three White Kitties, sm folio **125.00**
Old Blandford Church, Petersburg VA, Civil War hospital, sm folio **179.00**
Patriot of 1776, 1876, sm ...**165.00**
Popping the Question, N Currier, sm folio **50.00**
Queen of the South, girl, vignette, 17x13" **90.00**
Rose, rose & 5 buds, vignette, 11½x15½" **75.00**
Search the Scriptures, N Currier, sm folio **35.00**
Vase of Flowers, tulips, roses, & lilies, 1870, sm folio **129.00**
Virginia Water Windsor Park, boating scene, sm folio **150.00**
Washington Family, black & white, sm folio **70.00**
William Henry Harrison, portrait w/ green curtain, sm folio **60.00**
Young Chieftain, N Currier, 13½x17¾" **75.00**

Maxfield Parrish

Cassim in cave holding sword, 1909, original frame, 10x 12" **110.00**
Dreaming, nude near waterfall, 1928, original frame, 8x 12" **245.00**

Florentine Fete, 1920, original frame, 11x16" **145.00**
King Pompdebile, making grand entrance, 1925, original frame, 12x14" **95.00**
Knave in landscape, 1925, original frame, 12x14" **225.00**
Lady Ursula, lady before king, 1925, original frame, 12x14" **95.00**
Reveries, 2 maidens near garden fountain, 1927, original frame, 10x11" **185.00**
Six Ingredients, chefs holding platters, 1925, original frame, 12x14" **95.00**
Summer, nude by stream, 1911, original frame, 7x10" **75.00**

R. Atkinson Fox

English Garden, stone path, #57, 14x20" **75.00**
Land of Dreams, #14, 10x8" ..**65.00**
Mount Hood, pastels, #136, 8½x11" **65.00**
Spirit of Youth, signed, #4, in original frame, 18x10" **85.00**

R. Atkinson Fox, A Sheltering Bower, 15x11", $50.00.

Trusty Guardian, collie dog &
lamb, #11, 11x14" **175.00**
White Feather, Indian maid,
#309, 15x11" **250.00**

Wallace Nutting

Beech Borders, wooded stream,
10x12" **115.00**
Chair for John, girl writes letter
at fireside, 10x12" **195.00**
Coming Out of Rosa, w/Mother on
porch, 11x14" **195.00**
Double Border, Spring trees line
country road, 11x14" ...**145.00**
Granmother's Garden, English
scene, 13x16" **165.00**
Honeymoon Windings, orchard
reflects on country lane,
14x17" **150.00**
Many Happy Returns, country
orchard, 10x12" **125.00**
Memory of Childhood, country
house, 11x14" **150.00**
Prudence Drawing Tea, 14x
17" **235.00**
Swimming Pool, wooded stream,
14x17" **140.00**
Water Tracery, autumn stream,
11x14" **125.00**

Yard-Longs

American Girl, calendar, Pabst,
1912, CW Henning, ad on
back **225.00**
At the North Pole, otters, polar
bear, caribou, etc, Jos Hoover
& Son **250.00**

Home, Sweet Home, sheet music
& flowers, Paul DeLongpre,
1901 ....**150.00**
Lady, Selz Good Shoes, Haskell
Coffin, w/1920 calendar, ver-
tical **225.00**
Spring Is Here, Cambrill, copyright
1907 by Gray Litho **150.00**
Swallows over lily pads, copyright
1897 by J Hoover & Son ..**200.00**
The Favorites, roses in vase, A
Romes, vertical **150.00**
Yard of Chickens, CL VanVreden-
burgh, copyright 1905 by J
Ottmann, NY **150.00**
Yard of Pansies, Heinmuller ..**135.00**

Purinton

Popular among collectors due
to its 'country' look, Purinton Pottery's dinnerware and kitchen
items are easy to learn to recognize due to their bold yet simple
fruit and flower motifs created
with basic hand-applied colors on
a creamy gloss.

Bowl, dessert; Chartreuse **8.00**
Bowl, Normandy Plaid, clover
shape **18.00**
Bowl, spaghetti; Intaglio, 14½" ..**60.00**
Bowl, vegetable; Plaid **22.00**
Butter dish, Chartreuse, ¼-lb ..**35.00**
Canisters, Apple & Pear, 4-pc
set **145.00**
Canisters, Pennsylvania Dutch, 4-
pc set **160.00**

Yard of Roses, J. Ottmann Lithograph Co., 1901, $150.00.

Casserole, Apple, w/lid **35.00**
Child's set, plate, mug, & cereal
    bowl **100.00**
Cookie jar, Apple & Pear **50.00**
Creamer & sugar bowl, Apple &
    Pear, w/lid **25.00**
Creamer & sugar bowl, Plaid ..**18.00**
Cup & saucer, Apple **8.50**
Cup & saucer, Plaid **12.00**

Apple, oil cruet, 5", $14.00; vinegar cruet, 10", $20.00.

Honey jug, Ivy **12.00**
Jug, Apple, Kent, 1-pt **15.00**
Mug, juice; Rose, 6-oz **12.00**
Pickle dish, Intaglio, 6" **10.00**
Pitcher, Apple, water size **40.00**
Plate, Palm Tree, 9¾" **30.00**
Plate, Plaid, 9¾" **12.50**
Platter, Intaglio, 11" **25.00**
Relish, Apple, 3-section, center
    handle **25.00**
Salt & pepper shakers, Apple &
    Pear, range size, pr **20.00**
Salt & pepper shakers, Palm
    Tree, pr **45.00**
Snack plate, Apple **7.00**
Teapot, Apple, 2-cup **15.00**

Teapot, Intaglio, 6-cup **25.00**
Tumbler, Apple, 12-oz, 4¾" ..**12.00**
Tumbler, Apple & Pear, 2¾" ..**6.00**
Tumbler, Ivy, 10-oz **12.00**

Purses

From the late 1800s until well into the 1930s, beaded and metal mesh purses were popular fashion accessories. Flat envelope styles were favored in the twenties, and bags featuring tassels or fringe were in vogue. Enameled mesh bags were popular in the late twenties and into the thirties, decorated in Art Deco designs with stripes, birds, or flowers. Whiting and Davis and the Mandalian Manufacturing Company were two of the most important manufacturers.

The following are base values. Worth-assessing factors such as condition, age, manufacturer, country of origin, rarity, attractiveness, quality of workmanship and design, weight (when considering silver), size of beads, whether machine or handmade, must be taken into account. Listings are for purses in mint condition. Refer to *Antique Purses, A History, Identification, and Value Guide,* by Richard Holiner (Collector Books). Our advisor is Veronica Trainer; she is listed in the Directory under Ohio.

Chatelain purse, steel beads,
    4x4", M **120.00**
Cloth, metallic embroidery,
    France, 4x5", M **70.00**
Deco, enameled mesh, 3x6"..**175.00**
Finger ring purse, sterling silver,
    3x4", M **125.00**
Floral, fine glass beads, jeweled
    frame, 6½x10", M **475.00**

Floral, fine glass beads, sterling silver frame, 7x11", M ..**450.00**

Floral, fine glass beads, 7x11", M **300.00**

Floral, medium glass bead, celluloid frame, 6½x12", M ..**225.00**

Floral, steel beads in colors, jeweled frame, 7x12", M ...**350.00**

Geometrics, steel beads, 6x10", M **140.00**

Leather, hand tooled, 6x8" ..**150.00**

Lucite box purse, M, from $40 up to **60.00**

Mandalian Mfg Co, enameled mesh, fringe bottom, 3½x7", M **180.00**

Mandalian Mfg Co, enameled mesh, teardrop bottom, 4x7", M **225.00**

Miser's stockings purse, lightly beaded w/steel beads, 2x12", M **75.00**

Needlepoint, floral, jeweled frame, 7x6", M **275.00**

Petit point, floral, jeweled frame, 7x6", M **350.00**

Plastic beads, zipper, gate top, or flap closure, M, from $10 up to **50.00**

Reticule, crochet, 5x10", M ..**40.00**

Reticule, fine beads, floral pattern, 6x10", M **200.00**

Reticule, medium beads, floral pattern, 8x11", M **120.00**

Rhinestones, France, 4x5", M ..**80.00**

Rug pattern, fine glass beads, jeweled frame, 6½x11", M ..**400.00**

Scenic or figural pattern, medium beads, 8x11", M **300.00**

Scenic or figural pattern, steel beads, 7x12", M **375.00**

Tan O'-Shanter coin purse, lightly beaded, 2x2", M **75.00**

Tapestry, hand woven, sterling frame, 4x6", M **225.00**

Whiting & Davis, Dresden, enameled frame, fringe-cut bottom, 5x7", M **200.00**

Whiting & Davis, fringe-cut bottom, enameled frame, 5x7", M **225.00**

Puzzles

Of most interest to collectors of vintage puzzles are those made of wood or plywood, especially the early hand-cut examples. Character-related examples and those

Parker, fine beaded floral, $295.00; French beaded floral, $140.00.

representing a well-known personality or show from the early days of television are coming on strong right now and values are steadily climbing in these areas.

Archie, Jaymar, 1960s, frame tray, EX **8.00**
Banana Splits, Whitman, 1970, jigsaw type, NM **25.00**
Batman, Whitman, 1966, 150-pc, NM in box **28.00**
Beverly Hillbillies, 1960s, EX in box **7.50**
Bonanza, Milton Bradley, 1964, 100-pc, EX **40.00**
Bugs Bunny, Whitman, 1964, frame tray, 15x11", NM ..**15.00**
Cowboy on running horse, Saalfield, #7333, ca 1951, frame tray **8.50**
Dennis the Menace, frame tray, Whitman, 1960, M **10.00**
Dondi, swimming scene 'Water Fun,' Jamar, NM, in orig 7x10" box **20.00**
Eddie Cantor, Einson Freeman, 1933, EX **30.00**
Explorer's Clubhouse, Jaymar, 1959, 10x14", NM in box ..**10.00**
Favorite Funnies, Gasoline Alley & others, 1940, EX **15.00**
Felix the Cat, slide type, Rolex, 1960s, NM **32.50**
Felix the Cat, w/15 illustrated square tiles, M on card ..**30.00**
Flash Gordon, 1951, frame tray, M **85.00**
Flintstones, Warren, 1978, frame tray, EX **8.00**
Hopalong Cassidy, Milton Bradley, 1950s, MIB **25.00**
Hopalong Cassidy, 1950, set of 3, MIB **75.00**
Indian Chief, wood, 1930, EX ..**30.00**
Lassie, Whitman, 1957, frame tray, EX **15.00**
Little Lulu, Whitman, 1950s, M **35.00**

Skippy, marked Skippy, 1933, $14.00.

Puzzle Parties #1031, AC Gilbert Co, EX in original box ...**25.00**
Quick Draw McGraw, Whitman, 1960, frame tray, EX **12.50**
Road Runner characters, 1969, set of 4, EX **8.50**
Sleeping Beauty, frame tray, Whitman, 1959, M **10.00**
Superman, Saalfield, dated 1945, 500-pc, EX **160.00**
Terry & the Pirates, Jaymar, 1946, 7x10", EX **30.00**
Zorro, Whitman, 1957, frame tray, EX **17.50**

Quilts

The appreciation of quilting as an art form and the popularity of 'country' antiques have resulted in an increase in the sale of quilts, and the finer examples are often quite costly. There are several basic types of quilts: (1) appliqued

– having the decorative devices applied onto a solid top fabric; (2) pieced – having smaller pieces that have been cut out in a specific pattern, then stitched together to form the quilt top; (3) crazy quilts – made by stitching pieces of various sizes and shapes together following no orderly design; (4) trapunto – devised by stitching the outline of the design through two layers of fabric, one very loosely woven, and inserting padding into the design through openings made by separating the loose fibers of the underneath fabric.

Condition of a quilt is important; intricacy of pattern, good color composition, and craftsmanship contribute to its value. These factors are of prime concern whether evaluating vintage quilts or those by contemporary artists.

Appliqued

Butterfly Charm, 1930s, hand appliqued and quilted, 61x76", $345.00.

Applique Flowers, pastels on white w/orange frames, 1920s, 68x81" **140.00**

Autumn Leaves, tans, green, orange, & ivory, cotton batt, 1930, 74x83" **345.00**
Bouquets of Roses, pink, green, & yellow on light pink, 1985, 82x97" **345.00**
Centennial Lily, orange, yellow, & green, triple border, 1970, 104" sq **690.00**
Dogwood Blossoms, pink, green, brown, yellow, & white, 1940, 77x95" **400.00**
Hawaiian Orchid, navy & orchid print on orchid chintz, 1984, 90x108" **1,610.00**
Oak Leaf, solid red, green, & gold on white, cotton, ca 1930, 74x76" **445.00**
Ohio Rose, pink, green, & white, green sawtooth border, 1980, 64x80" **230.00**
Spring Bouquet, yellow, pink, & white, 1950s pattern, 1980, 80x100" **520.00**
Sunflower, abstract w/triple border, diagonal quilting, ca '45, 78x94" **490.00**
Tulip Basket, blue, red, pink, green, & white, 1930, PA, 65x83" **385.00**
Washington Cherry, ivory, peach, & green, embroidered, 1987, 90x108" **800.00**

Pieced

Amish Bars, blue w/black, feather-stitched border, 1987, 38x44" **155.00**
Basket, feedsack prints on periwinkle, EX stitching, ca 1930, 66x72" **310.00**
Bow Tie, blue & white, cotton, EX stitching, PA, ca 1915, 70x71", EX **375.00**
Cake Stand, yellow & white, feather wreaths, PA, ca 1920, 75x84" **335.00**

Cathedral Window, polyester & cotton, hand sewn, 1985, 86x104" **575.00**

Chimney Sweep, calicos & white, hand sewn, cotton batt, PA, 67x67", M **400.00**

Churn Dash, pink, blue, & white, hand sewn, KY 1974, 70x87" **18.00**

Clay's Choice, pink & white, pink lattices & hem binding, 1960, 74x88" **290.00**

Courthouse Steps, multi-pinks & black, hand sewn, IL, 1920s, 72x92" **230.00**

Crazy Quilt, satins & velvets, embroidery & painting, ca 1880, 62x83" **575.00**

Double Irish Chain, blues & browns, blue hand quilting, 1984, 50x50" **175.00**

Dresden Plate, blue & white, hand applique, MI, ca 1940, 74x84" **690.00**

Dresden Plate, calicos on rose, cotton, EX stitching, PA, 1930, 71x85" **275.00**

Evening Star, multicolor on white, WV, 1930, 64x81", G ...**276.00**

Fan, pastels & mixed prints, cotton, hand sewn, 1945, 64x84", NM **410.00**

Flower Garden, green & white w/prints & yellow center, 1955, 76x84" **200.00**

Flower Garden, multicolor prints & white, cotton, KY, 1950s, 57x72" **145.00**

Flower Garden, multicolor prints set in blue, 1920s, 64x79" ...**400.00**

Friendship, embroidered floral blocks set in blue, WV, 1930, 85x85" **460.00**

Friendship Album, embroidered white blocks, pink border, 1932, 66x71" **288.00**

Giant Dahlia, rust & cream, cross-hatched background, 1986, 80x95" **490.00**

Log Cabin, 1990s, machine pieced, hand quilted, 81x104", $345.00.

Irish Chain, multicolor on white, cotton, hand sewn, 1949, 78x84" **350.00**

Log Cabin, earth-tone diagonal stripes, hand sewn, 1979, 95x110" **518.00**

Lone Star, claret & white, double border, EX sewing, PA, 1910, 80x80" **335.00**

Lone Star, earth colors, hand sewn, cotton batt, PA, 1930s, 72x72", G **345.00**

Lovers Knot, pumpkin & white, cotton, hand sewn, TN, 1940s, 70x70" **145.00**

Nine Patch, red & white check w/gray polka dots, ca 1920, 66x78" **345.00**

Pansy, pink, yellow, & cream, 20 appliqued squares, 1930, 80x97", EX **375.00**

Peony Basket, pink, green, & tan, cotton, hand sewn, PA, 1925, 70x73" **400.00**

Pineapple, multicolor in gold w/red cornered frames, TN, 1955, 71x80" **375.00**

Postage Stamp, navy & red prints & solids, hand sewn, TN, 1935, 65x79" **525.00**

Puss in Corner, multicolor prints on white, cotton batt, '62, 86x86" **288.00**

Rambler, green & white cotton, hand sewn, PA, ca 1880, 73x83" **460.00**

Richmond, multicolor prints on white, cotton, PA, 1930, 73x92" **215.00**

Rose of Sharon, red, white, & green cotton, hand sewn, '30s, 80x93" **520.00**

Spider Webb, dark solids & prints, 1979, 82x99" **215.00**

State Bird, white & yellow blocks, multicolor embroidery, '70s, 80x97" **345.00**

Trip Around the World, solids w/wide purple border, 1970s, 85x108" **345.00**

Wedding Ring, pastels on white, green stitching, 1920s, 90x74", NM **328.00**

48 States Flowers, embroidered white blocks, green edge, 1957, 78x106" **328.00**

Radios

Collectors of vintage radios are especially interested in those made from the twenties through the fifties by companies such as RCA, Atwater Kent, Philco, and Crosley, though those produced by the smaller manufacturers are collectible as well, and even the modern transistors are catching on. Cathedral and breadboard styles are popular, so are Art Deco styles and those with a unique type of speaker, power source, or cabinet. Refer to *The Collector's Guide to Antique Radios* by Sue and Marty Bunis and *Collecting*

Transistor Novelty Radios, A Value Guide, by Robert F. Breed (L-W Book Sales) for more information. In our listings, all are table model radios unless otherwise described.

Admiral, #AM 786, wood, round dial, oval escutcheon, console, 1936, EX **110.00**

Admiral, #6A22, plastic, right round dial, 1950, EX **30.00**

Admiral, #6Y18, leatherette, inner dial, portable, 1949, EX **35.00**

Air Castle, #WEU-262, plastic, upper slide rule dial, 1950, EX **45.00**

Air King, #4706, painted plastic, AC, 1946, $40.00.

Airline, #04BR-397A, wood, center multiband dial, 4 knobs ..**55.00**

Airline, #74BR-1501B, plastic, lower slide rule dial, 1946 ....**80.00**

American Bosch, #460-R, wood, inner dial, fold-back top, console, 1934 ....**125.00**

Apex, #89, metal, center front window dial, 1929 ....**70.00**

Arvin, #240-P, plastic, center slide rule dial, portable, 1948, EX **40.00**

Arvin, #444, metal, right dial, rounded corners, 1946, EX **80.00**

Arvin, #850T, plastic, lg right round dial, 1955, EX **35.00**

Atwater Kent, #145, wood, lower round dial, tombstone style, 1934, EX **145.00**

Atwater Kent, #35, metal, low oblong case, right dial, 1926 ....**65.00**

Belmont, #401, 2-tone wood, airplane dial, upper grill, cathedral **195.00**

Bendix, #PAR-80A, luggage style, slide rule dial, portable, 1948 ....**35.00**

Bendix, #0526A, plastic, Deco case, upper slide rule dial, 1946 ....**65.00**

Brunswick, #22, wood, inner front dial, French doors, console, 1930 ....**150.00**

Capehart, #1P55, plastic, center round dial, handle, portable, 1955 ....**35.00**

Channel Master, #6509, plastic, transistor, portable, 1960, EX **35.00**

Coronado, #15RA33-43-8246A, plastic, round dial, 1952, EX **30.00**

Crosley, #E-20-MN, plastic, square dial, 1953 ....**75.00**

Crosley, #F-110BK, plastic, w/ handle, battery operated, portable, 1953 ....**35.00**

Crosley, #11-101U, plastic, lg louvered dial, 1951, EX **115.00**

Crown, #TR-670, diamond-shaped window dial, transistor, portable, 1960 ....**25.00**

Delco, #R-1228, plastic, slanted slide rule dial, 1947 ......**55.00**

Dewald, #901, wood, lower round dial, 4 knobs, tombstone **115.00**

Emerson, #AX-238, wood, inner right dial, chest-type table model, 1939 ....**250.00**

Emerson, #32, walnut, right dial, rounded top, 1934, EX ..**100.00**

Emerson, #336, plastic, right dial, top handle, 1940, EX **45.00**

Fada, #263W, plastic, sm right dial, rounded corners, 1936 ....**85.00**

GE, #P-796A, blue leatherette, side dial, transistor, portable, 1958 ....**35.00**

GE, #T-129C, turquoise plastic, round dial, footed, 1959 ....**25.00**

GE, #517F, red plastic, thumbwheel dial, alarm clock, 1951, EX **45.00**

Grunow, #570, 2-tone wood, lower round dial, 3 knobs, tombstone, EX **120.00**

Magnavox, #AM-22, plastic, right window dial, battery, portable, 1960 ....**15.00**

Mitchell, #1251, white plastic, radio/bed lamp, round dial knob, 1949 ....**70.00**

Motorola, #45P2, plastic, metal dial plate, Pixie portable, 1956, EX **40.00**

Olympic, #FM-15, plastic, trapezoid case, slide rule dial, 1960, EX **25.00**

Philco, #38, 2-tone wood, window dial, cathedral, 1930, EX **110.00**

Philco, #46-420, plastic, curved dial & 2 knobs on top, 1946 ....**60.00**

Philco, #51-631, red plastic, upper slide rule dial, portable, 1951 ....**25.00**

Philco, #54, wood, 1933, $70.00.

RCA, #1X56, red plastic, half-moon dial, side knob, 1952, EX **40.00**

RCA, #15X, plastic, slanted dial, red dot pointer, 1940, EX **40.00**

Silvertone, #2, metal, contrasting round dial & knob, 1950, EX **75.00**

Silvertone, #7204, brown plastic, AM/FM slide rule dial, 1957 ....**25.00**

Sparton, #132, plastic, oval case, half-moon dial, 1950, EX ..**60.00**

Truetone, #D1117, wood, slide rule dial, footed, chest-type table **60.00**

Truetone, #D2810, plastic, upper slanted dial, 2 knobs, 1948 ....**40.00**

Zenith, #A-600, leatherette, multiband dial, antenna, portable, 1957 ....**80.00**

Zenith, #705, wood, window dial, flared footed base, 1933, EX **115.00**

Zenith, #750L, leather case, top handle, transistor, portable, 1959 ....**40.00**

Novelty

A Team (BA Baracus), Mr T in muscleman's pose, 1983, 5x4¾" **25.00**

Big Bird, decaled 2-D shape of Big Bird's head, #1720, 1985, 5x4" **15.00**

Blabber Mouth, red smiling lips on white square, 1985 Nasta, 5" **40.00**

Donald Duck, decaled 2-D shape of Donald's head, 7½x5" **35.00**

Dukes of Hazard, decaled 2-D shape of boys & their car, 1981, 4x7½" **20.00**

Fonz, jukebox form featuring the Fonz, 1977, 6x4½" **25.00**

Gumby, figural, AM/FM model #7015, 1985 by Perma Toy, 12x6" **40.00**

Jimmy Carter Peanut, smiling president atop peanut shell, 1977, 7½" **45.00**

Michael Jackson, AM/FM pocket size w/decal of Michael, 1984, M **20.00**

Mork from Ork Eggship, model #4461, 1979, 7x4¼" dia ..**30.00**

Mustang Fastback, marked Philco/Ford model P22, ca 1966, 7½x2¾" **40.00**

My Little Pony, pony & rainbow, figural, 1973, 3½x4" **15.00**

Pacman, figural, 1982, 4¼" ..**30.00**

Raggedy Ann & Andy, heart-shaped 2-D w/paper decal, 1974, 4x4¾" **25.00**

Scooby Doo, decaled 2-D head of Scooby, 1972, 7½x4" **35.00**

Snoopy Outline, 2-D, black trim, 1974, United Features, 6½x 5" **15.00**

Tony the Tiger, registration #993394, made in Hong Kong by PRI, 7x4", $35.00.

Spiderman Head, 3-D, 1978 Marvel Comics/Amico Inc, 5¼x3¼" **40.00**

Stanley Tape Measure, thumbwheel controls on top, life-size PRI mold **40.00**

Tom & Jerry, the 2 molded together in 3-D, 1972, MGM by Marx, 4¾x6" **50.00**

Tune-A-Cow, cross-eyed black & white cow, 1 of series, 5½x3½" **15.00**

Cup and saucer, CB&Q, Violets and Daisies, $68.00.

Railroadiana

Memorabilia relating to the more than 175 different railway companies that once transversed this great country of ours represents one of the largest and most popular areas of collecting today. Because the field is so varied, many collectors prefer to specialize. Lanterns, badges, advertising, dinnerware, silver, locks, and tools are only a sampling of the many types of relics they treasure. Some enjoy toy trains, prints showing old locomotives, or old timetables – in short, virtually anything that in any way represents the rapidly disappearing railway system is of value. Refer to *Railroad Collectibles, Third Revised Edition,* by Stanley L. Baker (Collector Books) for more information.

Dinnerware

Bowl, Missouri Pacific, footed, flared rim, 1926, 2¼x6¼" dia **40.00**

Bowl, soup; Amtrak, National pattern **12.00**

Bowl, vegetable; Milwaukee, Traveler pattern, pink, 4½" **45.00**

Cup, bouillon; Great Northern **65.00**

Cup & saucer, demitasse; Southern, Piedmont pattern ..**95.00**

Cup & saucer, Southern Pacific, Prairie Mountain Wildflower pattern **95.00**

Cup & saucer, Union Pacific, Winged Streamliner **65.00**

Fork, ice cream; CCC&ST, Commonwealth pattern, 3 lg tines **20.00**

Glass, iced tea; Santa Fe in white script, 6" **14.00**

Glass, old-fashioned; Illinois Central, Main Line America, 4½" **25.00**

Glass, water; Pennsylvania RR, gold logo w/Madison Square history **5.00**

Knife, dinner; Southern, Century pattern **12.00**

Plate, dinner; Atlantic Coast Line, Carolina pattern, 9" **40.00**

Plate, dinner; Spokane, Portland, & Seattle, Red Leaves pattern, 9" **40.00**

Plate, salad; Southern, Peach Blossom pattern, 1920s, 7½" **45.00**

Platter, Burlington Northern, Gold Key pattern, 7" **17.00**

Sauce dish, Union Pacific, The Challenger, 4½" **16.00**

Teapot, Amtrak, National pattern, w/lid **17.00**

Tongs, sugar; Union Pacific, Sierra, claw feet **50.00**

Miscellaneous

Ashtray, Rock Island, red logo on round bottom, 4¼" square top, M **12.00**

Badge, for assistant conductor, Long Island RR, lg logo in blue, M **40.00**

Badge, for conductor's hat, Denver & Rio Grande, embossed metal, M **85.00**

Blotter, Chicago Great Western, dated March 1931, 3¾x8½" **16.00**

Brochure, Northern Pacific, Yellowstone Park, 1913 ......**25.00**

Brochure, Southern Pacific, The Shasta Route, ca 1915, NM **45.00**

Change tray, ...Stockton & Darlington 1825-1925, bronze **17.00**

Cuff links, Monon, Engine #9 logo, pr **12.00**

Flare box, from Rio Grande yards, red-painted metal **15.00**

Hat, blue & black w/2 white bands, 2 silver buttons, G **40.00**

Key, berth; T-shape, 2-color brass, unmarked, 3x4" **25.00**

Key, caboose; NYO&W, 13760 Adlake **35.00**

Key, switch; C&A RR – S (serifs), tapered barrel w/ring **50.00**

Key, switch; C&EI, 906 1 Adlake, unused **20.00**

Lantern, Texas & Pacific, Adlake Kero, short red globe, complete **85.00**

Lock, Pennsylvania RR, heart-shaped brass, w/chain & key, M **150.00**

Mechanical pencil, Frisco, gold print on black, gold ends **12.00**

Menu, dinner; Welcome Aboard the Southwest Limited, June '76 ....**6.00**

Menu, Great Northern Railroad, colorful, 1944, EX **12.50**

Menu holder, Great Northern, pierced sides w/2 pencil holders, 1946 ....**95.00**

Pass, Pullman Co, blue, 1902, G **15.00**

Pass, Wabash Railroad Co, gray paper, 1911, 3x4¾" **10.00**

Placemat, Southern Pacific, striped cloth, logo in 2 corners ...**19.00**

Lighters, M&StL, Zippo, $30.00; A&S, Rolex, $22.00.

Playing cards, Great Northern, double deck, 1951, original box **90.00**

Pocket calendar, Union Pacific, 1970 ....**4.00**

Sign, REA Express, for baggage cart, cardboard, diamond shape, 8x8" **45.00**

Sign, SOO Line, heavy metal, white embossed vertical letters, 22x4" **85.00**

Tallow pot, CB&QRR embossed on bottom, teapot style, 5" ..**30.00**

Ticket punch, Great Northern, punches '2d,' Poole Bros, Chicago **25.00**

Timetable, Illinois Central, 1952, NM **12.00**

Timetable, New York Central, Adirondack mountains, 1906, NM **12.00**

Torch, B&O RR embossed on 5" hollow handle, teapot style, 4½" **35.00**

Waiter's cap, Union Pacific, paper, opens to fit, 5½x11" **6.00**

Watch fob, Northern Pacific, enamel on bronze, Monad logo **85.00**

Water can, NP RY embossed on side, pour spout, hinged lid, bail, 14" **25.00**

Window lifter, marked CB&Q RR, oak w/leather & metal end, 14" long **50.00**

Razors

Straight razors are prized for their beautifully decorated blades and handles, often portraying nudes, animals, scenes, or slogans popular at the time of their manufacture. Values are determined by assessing the blade style, pattern of the handle, and manufacturer's mark. Corn razors, used to remove corns from the feet, are also collectible. An approximate manufacture date may be arrived at through study of various types of blades. Those made before the 19th century were crude wedge-shaped affairs that evolved through many improvements in form as well as material to the fully hollow ground blades of the 1880s. Refer to *The Standard Knife Collector's Guide, 2nd Edition,* by Roy Ritchie and Ron Stewart (Collector Books) for more information. In our listings, values are given for razors in mint condition (blades unground and retaining their original sheen) with composition handles.

Ace, Kinfolks Inc, Little Valley, NY **125.00**

Adoration Hand-Forged, Solingen, Germany **25.00**

American Razor Works, NY ..**35.00**

Banty, Union Cut Co, Olean, New York **125.00**

Barbers Extra Special, Indianapolis, Indiana **40.00**

Ben Hur Cut Co, New York & Germany **15.00**

Bengal **15.00**

Brilliant Cutlery Co, Germany ..**20.00**

Charmer, Kohen Companies, St Louis, Missouri **25.00**

Clauss, Fremont, Ohio **60.00**

Dixie Blue Steel, Union City, Georgia **40.00**

Double Dollar Razor, Keith, Simmons Co, Tennessee **45.00**

Echo Razor Co, Germany **15.00**

Ed Wusthof, Solingen **25.00**

Elliot & Sons Celebrated **30.00**

Fredrick Reynolds, Sheffield, England **20.00**

Genco Army & Navy, Geneva, New York **35.00**

Gun Metal, Dayton, Ohio **20.00**

Hollinger Hand-Made, Fremont, Ohio **40.00**

Hudders Best **25.00**
James Johnson Silver Steel ..**50.00**
Lee Gold Imports, Roe, NY **15.00**
Mon Cadillac, Michels Inc, New
    York & Germany **25.00**
New Comfort, Cranford, New Jer-
    sey **18.00**
Peter & Michels, New York &
    Germany **25.00**
Ran-Tan-Ka-Rus **35.00**
Smith Brothers, Boston **30.00**
Tonsorial Gem, New York & Ger-
    many **20.00**
Tramp, Made in Germany ...**25.00**
Wade & Butcher, Sheffield, Eng-
    land **125.00**

Reamers

Though made for the simple task of extracting citrus juices, reamers may be found in fanciful figurals as well as the simple utilitarian styles. You may find wood, ceramic, or metal examples, but the most popular with collectors are those made of glass. Fry, Hazel Atlas, Hocking, Jeannette, and McKee are among the largest producers of the glass reamer, some of which (depending on color and rarity) may bring prices well into the hundreds of dollars. Refer to *Kitchen Glassware of the Depression Years* by Gene Florence (Collector Books) for more information.

Cambridge, crystal, tab handle,
    sm **15.00**
Cambridge, jadite, spout, loop
    handle **135.00**
Cambridge, Seville yellow, loop
    handle **210.00**
Federal Glass, pink, ribbed, loop
    handle **20.00**
Fry, emerald green, straight
    sides **30.00**

Hazel Atlas, decorated pitcher
    w/reamer **35.00**
Hazel Atlas, green, 4-cup pitcher
    w/reamer, marked A&J ..**35.00**
Hazel Atlas, white, pitcher, stip-
    pled, tab handle **40.00**
Hocking, fired-on black, tab han-
    dle **13.00**
Hocking, green, 4-cup pitcher
    w/reamer, flat **25.00**
Indiana Glass, pink, loop handle,
    spout **50.00**
Jeannette, pink, Hex Optic,
    bucket **45.00**
Jeannette, ultramarine, loop han-
    dle **90.00**
McKee, custard w/red trim, em-
    bossed McK, loop handle ..**40.00**
Sunkist, vaseline green, embossed
    letters, loop handle **35.00**
Sunkist, white, embossed, loop
    handle **75.00**
US Glass, decorated crystal, 2-cup
    pitcher, loop handle **25.00**
US Glass, light pink, 2-cup
    pitcher, loop handle **40.00**
Valencia, white, embossed letters,
    loop handle **110.00**
Westmoreland, decorated crystal,
    flattened loop handle **90.00**

Records

Records that made it to the 'Top Ten' in their day are not always the records that are prized the highest by today's collectors, though they treasure those which best represent specific types of music: jazz, rhythm and blues, country and western, rock and roll, etc. Many search for those cut very early in the career of artists who later became super stars, records cut on rare or interesting labels, or those aimed at ethnic groups. A fast-growing area of related interest is picture sleeves for 45s. These are often worth more than the record itself, especially if they feature superstars from the fifties or early sixties. Condition is very important.

Refer to *The American Premium Record Guide* by Les Docks for more information. Values for 78 rpm records are given for records in like-new conditon; 45s are assumed to be at least excellent, unless another condition is noted. Record collectors tend to be very critical, so learn to watch for loss of gloss; holes, labels, or writing on the label; warping; and scratches.

Extended Play

Anthony, Ray; Drive In/Panama/etc, Capitol 1-678, VG **5.00**

Beatles, Roll Over Beethoven/This Boy (etc), Capitol 1-2121, VG **50.00**

Bellafonte, Harry; Take My Mother Home/Noah (etc), RCA 9130, VG **4.00**

Cole, Nat King; Forgive My Heart/That's All (etc), Capitol 1-696, VG **8.00**

Como, Perry; Joy to the World/Frosty the Snowman (etc), RCA 497, EX **7.50**

Crosby, Bing; First Noel/God Rest Ye Merry... (etc), Decca 38274, EX **12.00**

Deep Purple, Smoke on the Water/Highway, Warner 2701, VG **4.00**

Fisher, Eddie; Cheek to Cheek/All By Muself (etc), RCA 426, EX **3.00**

Garner, Erroll; Time on My Hands/Passing... (etc), Columbia 9391, VG **13.50**

Gorme, Eydie; Chicago/Tip Toe Through... (etc), ABCP 218, VG **4.50**

Griffin, Andy; Make Yourself Comfortable/Swan Lake, Capitol 1-630, VG **15.00**

Helms, Bobby; My Special Angel/Borrowed Dreams, Decca 2629, VG **6.00**

Ink Spots, Bless You/Gypsy (etc), Decca 2008, VG **10.00**

Ives, Burl; Yesterday/Scarlet Ribbons (etc), Decca 34554, EX **15.00**

Kenton, Stan; Painted Rhythm/Peanut Vendor, Capitol 4-724, VG **6.00**

Locklin, Hank; Please Help Me I'm Falling/Livin' Alone, RCA 4366, VG **2.00**

Mantovani, Ah! Sweet Mystery of Life (+3 more), London 6075, EX **6.00**

Miller, Glenn; I Guess I'll Change.../Sleepy Town Train, RCA 0125, VG **4.00**

Presley, Elvis; King Creole/As Long As I Have You, RCA EPA 4319, VG **35.00**

Presley, Elvis; Loving You/Teddy Bear (etc), RCA EPA 1-1515, VG **45.00**

Presley, Elvis; Rip It Up/When My Blue Moon..., RCA EPA 992, G **8.00**

Seeburg, Java/I've Got a Crush on You (etc), Seeburg 105, VG.....................................**3.00**

Three Suns, I Don't Stand a Ghost of.../Cumana (etc), RCA 1333, VG **4.00**

Picture Sleeves

Air Supply, Even the Nights Are Better, Arista 0692, M **2.00**

Alman Brothers Band, Straight From the Heart, Arista 0618, M **5.00**

Annette, Mister Piano Man, Buena Vista 405, EX **27.50**

Armstrong, Louis; Ten Feet Off the Ground, Buena Vista 465, M **6.00**

Autry, Gene; Be Honest w/Me (7 others), Columbia H-1663, VG **10.00**

Bare, Bobby; I Don't Believe I'll Fall in Love Today, RCA 8083, VG **8.50**

Belafonte, Harry; Pretty As a Rainbow, RCA 5722, VG ..**8.00**

Blue Swede, Never My Love, EMI 3938, VG **1.50**

Boone, Pat; Walking the Floor Over You, Dot 16073, VG **5.00**

Bowie, David; Let's Dance, EMI 8158, VG+ **3.50**

Boyd, Jimmy; I Saw Mommy Kissing Santa Claus, Columbia 4-152, VG **18.00**

Bread, If, Atlantic 89868, VG ..**1.50**

Brothers Johnson, I'll Be Good to You, A&M 1806, VG **3.50**

Buckinghams, Hey Baby, Columbia 44254, EX **15.00**

California Raisins, Rudolph the Red Nosed Reindeer, Atlantic 89008, EX **2.00**

Carpenters, Rainy Days & Mondays, A&M 1260, VG **5.00**

Chubby Checker, Birdland, Parkway 873, M **12.00**

Cole, Nat King; Ramblin' Rose, Capitol 4804, VG **5.00**

Collins, Phil; Two Hearts, Atlantic 88980, VG **1.50**

Culture Club, Karma Chameleon, Virgin 04221, VG **1.50**

Darin, Bobby; You're the Reason I'm Living, Capitol 4897, EX **14.00**

Dean, Jimmy; Dear Ivan, Columbia 42259, VG **6.00**

Diamond, Neil; Heartlight, Columbia 03219, M **2.50**

Donovan, Mellow Yellow, Epic 10098, VG **8.00**

Duran Duran, Save a Prayer, Capitol 5338, VG **1.50**

Eddy, Duane; Forty Miles of Bad Road, Jamie 1126, VG ..**14.00**

Everly Brothers, Crying in the Rain, Warner 5250, VG ..**15.00**

Four Seasons, Patch of Blue, Philips 40662, VG **12.00**

Francis, Connie; Breakin' in a Brand New Broken Heart, MGM 12995, VG **10.00**

George, Harrison; You, Apple 1884, EX **8.00**

Gibb, Andy; I Just Want To Be Your Everything, RSO 872, VG **2.00**

Grand Funk, Shinin' On, Capitol 3917, VG **4.00**

Haggard, Merle; I Take a Lot of Pride in What I Am, Capitol 2289, EX **5.00**

Houston, David; With One Exception, Epic 10154, VG **4.00**

Jackson, Michael; Wanna Be Startin' Somethin', Epic 03914, VG **4.00**

Jagger, Mick; Let's Work, Columbia 07306, EX **2.00**

James, Sonny; I'll Never Find Another You, Capitol 5914, VG **4.00**

Joel, Billy; Back in the USSR, Columbia 07626, EX **2.50**

Journey, Still They Ride, Columbia 02883, VG **1.50**

Laine, Frankie; Moonlight Gambler, Columbia 10780, VG **10.00**

Liberace, Rosary, Columbia 48007, VG **10.00**

Madonna, Live To Tell, Sire 28717, VG **1.50**

March, Little Peggy; My Teenage Castle, RCA 8189, VG ...**11.00**

McCartney, Paul; Take It Away, Columbia 03018, VG **3.00**

Mellencamp, John Cougar; Small Town, Riva 884, M **3.00**

Milli Vanilli, Blame It on the Rain, Arista 19904, M **2.50**

Monkees, DW Washburn, Colgems 1023, VG **11.00**

O'Toole, Peter; Where Did My Childhood Go, MGM 14087, M **11.00**

Pointer Sisters, Dare Me, RCA 14126, VG **1.50**

Presely, Elvis; Puppet on a String, RCA 447-0650, VG **18.00**

Presley, Elvis; Suspicious Minds, RCA 47-9764, VG **9.00**

REO Speedwagon, Don't Let Him Go, Epic 02127, VG **1.50**

Rodgers, Jimmie; Are You Really Mine, Roulette 4090, VG ..**8.00**

Springsteen, Bruce; Born in the USA, Columbia 04680, VG **1.50**

Travolta, John; Grease (You're the One That I Want), RSO 891, VG **4.00**

Valli, Frankie; To Give, Philips 40510, VG **8.00**

45 rpms

Albert, Morris; Feelings, RCA 10279 ....**1.50**

Andrew Sisters, Rum & Coca Cola, Capitol 3658 ....**2.00**

Anka, Paul; Hurry Up & Tell Me, RCA 47-8237 ....**3.50**

Berry, Chuck; Sweet Little Rock & Roll, Chess 1709 ....**3.00**

Boone, Pat; Gee Whittakers, Dot 15435 ....**1.50**

Bowie, David; Changes, RCA 74-0605 ....**3.50**

Captain & Tennille, Love Will Keep Us ..., A&M 1672 ...**3.50**

Carpenters, Rainy Days & Mondays, A&M 1260 ....**3.50**

Cash, Johnny; Train of Love, Sun 258 ....**2.00**

Chubby Checker, Slow Twistin', Parkway 835 ....**1.50**

Cline, Patsy; Your Kinda Love, Decca 31588 ....**2.00**

Creedence Clearwater Revival, Suzie Q, Fanta 616 ....**3.50**

Diamond, Neil; Shilo, Bang 575 ....**3.25**

Drifters, Save the Last Dance for Me, Atlantic 2071 ....**5.00**

Earth, Wind & Fire, Saturday Nite, Columbia 3-10439 ..**3.50**

Everly Brothers, Bye Bye Love, Barnaby 502 ....**3.00**

Fantastics, There Goes My Love, RCA 7572 ....**5.00**

Fats Domino, Blueberry Hill, Imperial 5407 ....**3.00**

Four Tops, Walk Away Renee, Motown 1119 ....**4.00**

Greene, Jack; It's Time To Cross That Bridge, MCA 40179 ..**4.00**

Humperdinck, Engelbert; Release Me, Parrot 40011 ....**4.00**

Intruders, Cowboys To Girls, Gamble 214 ....**4.00**

Joel, Billy; Just the Way You Are, Columbia 10646 ....**1.50**

Jones; Tom; Say You'll Stay Until Tomorrow, Epic 8-50308 ..**4.00**

King, Teddy; Mr Wonderful, RCA 6392 ....**2.00**

Lee, Brenda; My Whole World Is Falling Down, Decca 31510 ....**5.50**

Lewis, Jerry Lee; Great Balls of Fire, Sun 281 ....**3.00**

Marmalade, Rainbow, London 20059 ....**4.00**

Nelson, Willie; Pretty Paper, RCA 47-9029 ....**4.00**

O'Jays, I've Cried My Last Tear, Imperial 66121 ....**3.50**

Peaches & Herb, When He Touches Me, Date 2-1637 ....**2.50**

Perkins, Carl; Blue Suede Shoes, Sun 234 ....**3.00**

Rainwater, Marvin; Whole Lotta Woman, MGM 12625 ......**3.00**

Reddy, Helen; Delta Dawn, Capitol 3645 ....**4.00**

Rivers, Johnny; Memphis, Imperial 66032 ....**3.50**

Ronstadt, Linda; When Will I Be Loved, Capitol 4050 ....**2.00**

Simon, Paul; Mother & Child Reunion, Columbia 4-45547 ...**4.00**

Sinatra, Frank; My Funny Valentine, Capitol 488 ....**3.50**

Sonny & Cher, I Got You Babe, MCA 60112 ....**3.00**

Stafford, Jim; Spiders & Snakes, MGM K-14648 ....**3.50**

Statler Brothers, Thank You World, Mercury 73485 ....**3.50**

Temptations, My Girl, Gordy 7010 ....**3.50**

Temptations, You're My Everything, Gordy 7063 ....**3.00**

Three Dog Night, Never Been To Spain, Dunhi 4299 ....**3.50**

Valli, Frankie; My Eyes Adored You, PS 003 ....**3.00**

Vinton, Bobby; Roses Are Red, Epic 5-9509 ....**4.00**

Warnes, Jennifer; Right Time of the Night, Arista 0223 ....**3.00**

Williams, Hank; Ramblin' Man, MGM 11120 ....**6.00**

Wonder, Stevie; Heaven Help Us, Tamla 54200 ....**3.50**

78 rpms

Al Hopkins & His Buckle Busters, Black Eyed Susie, Brunswick 175 ....**7.50**

Alabama Creole Band, Choo Choo, Claxtonola 40397 ....**12.50**

Allen, Jules; Home on the Range, Victor 21627 ....**6.50**

Alomo Garden Band, St Louis Hop, Champion 15132 ..**10.00**

Ames, Tessie; Rider Blues, Silvertone 3565 ....**40.00**

Baby Benbow, Down Home Gal, Okeh 8098 ....**25.00**

Banta, Frank; My Sugar, Victor 19705 ....**7.50**

Birmingham Five, No Man's Mama, Champion 15047 ....**12.50**

California Vagabonds, Waitin' for Katy, Gennett 6126 ....**15.00**

Calloway, Ermine; Do Something, Edison 52570 ....**18.50**

Casa Loma Orchestra, Shadows of Love, Brunswick 6738 ....**8.50**

Cleighton, Peter; Love Is Gone, Okeh 06375 ....**8.50**

Crowder Brothers, Got No Use for Women, Vocalion 03030 ..**12.50**

Dixie Jazz Hounds, Hula Lou, Domino 306 ....**12.50**

English, Peggy; Charleston Baby O'Mine, Vocalion 15093 ..**8.50**

Fats Domino, Brand New Baby, Imperial 5085 ....**18.50**

Glenn Miller & His Orchestra, Wistful & Blue, Decca 1284 ....**10.00**

Glinn, Lillian; Best Friend Blues, Columbia 14330-D **50.00**

Golden Gate Orchestra, I Miss My Swiss, Banner 1569 ....**6.50**

Greene, Amos; I'm Lonely & Blue, Supertone 9707 ....**14.50**

Hall, Wendell; Headin' Home, Columbia 1028-D **6.50**

Hutchens, John; Hard Luck Jim, Champion 15751 ....**12.50**

Intervals, Here's That Rainy Day, Class 304 ....**6.50**

Kincaid, Bradley; Sweet Betsy From Pike, Bluebird 5321 ....**8.50**

La Veeda Dance Orchestra, Strut Yo' Stuff, Columbia 1549-D ...**25.00**

Langford, Frances; When Mother Played the Organ, Victor 24191 ....**12.50**

Lewis Bronzeville 5, Cotton Blossom Blues, Bluebird 8433 ....**12.50**

Mack, Bill; Forever I'll Wait for You, Imperial 8192 ....**7.50**

Martin, Sara; Last Go Round Blues, Okeh 8045 ....**16.50**

Master Melody Makers, Keep Your Kisses, National Music Lovers 1161 ....**7.50**

New Orleans Owls, West End Romp, Columbia 688-D .**25.00**

Oak Mountain Four, Medley, Champion 15874 ....**8.50**

Original Dixieland Five, Tiger Rag, Victor 25524 ....**8.50**

Potter & James, Down on the Farm, Supertone 9541 ..**10.00**

Ray Miller & His Orchestra, Red Hot Mama, Brunswick 2681 ....**7.50**

Rhythm Wreckers, Sugar Blues, Vocalion 3341 ....**7.50**

Richards, Chuck; Blue Interlude, Vocalion 2877 ....**12.50**

Ritter, Tex; Lady Killin' Cowboy, Decca 5076 ....**12.50**

Roye, Ruth; Big-Hearted Bennie, Columbia 63-D **10.50**

Scottsdale String Band, Down Yonder, Okeh 45188 ......**12.50**

Six Jumping Jacks, Football Freddy, Brunswick 4946..**8.50**

Slim Green, Tricky Woman Blues, Murray 501 ....**16.50**

Smith, Bessie; Weeping Willow Blues, Columbia 14042-D **18.50**

Stone, Jimmy; Midnight Boogie, Imperial 8137 ....**8.50**

Turner, Dave; That Old Covered Bridge, Supertone 9318 ..**8.50**

University Six, My Baby Knows How, Harmony 296-H **8.50**

Washboard Wonders, Feather Your Nest, Bluebird 6495 ....**7.50**

Watkins, Viola; Jelly & Bread, Jubilee 5007 ....**8.50**

Watson, Harvey; Weeping Willow Tree, Challenge 330 ......**10.00**

Young, Jackson; I Know My Name Is There, Champion 15333 .....**8.50**

Red Wing

Taking their name from the location in Minnesota where they located in the late 1870s, the Red Wing Company produced a variety of wares, all of which are today considered noteworthy by pottery and dinnerware collectors. Their early stoneware lines, Cherry Band, and Sponge Band (Gray Line), are especially valuable and often fetch prices of several hundred dollars on today's market. Production of dinnerware began in the thirties and continued until the pottery closed in 1967. Some of their more popular lines – all of which were hand painted – were Bob White, Lexington, Tampico, Normandie, Capistrano, and Random Harvest. Commercial artware was also produced. Perhaps the ware most easily associated with Red Wing is their Brushware line, unique in its appearance and decoration. Cattails, rushes, florals, and similar nature subjects are 'carved' in relief on a stoneware-type body with a matt green wash its only finish. Refer to *Red Wing Stoneware, An Identification and Value Guide,* and *Red Wing Collectibles*, both by Dan and Gail de Pasquale and Larry Peterson (Collector Books) for more information.

Dinnerware

Bob White, bowl, cereal **10.00**

Bob White, bowl, tab handles, 5¾" **14.00**

Bob White, bowl, tab handles, 8¼" **20.00**

Bob White, bowl, vegetable; w/ lid **25.00**

Bob White, cookie jar **140.00**

Bob White, cup & saucer **8.00**

Bob White, hors d'oeuvres bird ..**30.00**

Bob White, pitcher, water; 60-oz **35.00**

Bob White, plate, 11¾" **9.00**

Bob White, plate, 6½" **3.50**

Bob White, trivet **125.00**

Capistrano, bowl, soup; 8" **8.00**

Capistrano, cup & saucer **8.00**

Capistrano, plate, 5" **5.00**

Capistrano, plate, 8" **8.00**

Iroquois, casserole, 2-qt **40.00**

Iroquois, gumbo **25.00**

Iroquois, plate, 10" **10.00**

**Magnolia, coffee server,
$32.50; dinner plate, $10.00;
cup and saucer, $8.00.**

Iroquois, plate, 7" **7.00**
Tampico, bowl, deep, 12" **40.00**
Tampico, bowl, 5½" **8.00**
Tampico, bowl, 8" or 9", each ..**25.00**
Tampico, creamer & sugar bowl,
   w/lid **30.00**
Tampico, cup & saucer **12.00**
Tampico, gravy boat, w/under-
   plate **25.00**
Tampico, pitcher, water; sm ..**25.00**
Tampico, plate, dinner; 10½" ..**10.00**
Tampico, platter, 13" **25.00**
Tampico, relish, divided **25.00**
Tampico, sugar bowl & creamer,
   w/lid **30.00**
Tampico, tray, 2-tier **25.00**

Stoneware

Beater jar, advertising grocery
   store, blue stripes on salt
   glaze **85.00**
Beater jar, Holiday Greeting, salt
   glaze, dated 1924 ....**75.00**
Beater jar, Red Wing...Eggs,
   Cream Salad Dressing, salt
   glaze **65.00**
Bowl, Christmas Greetings, 1938,
   Protovin, IA; Saffron spatter-
   ware **60.00**
Bowl, mixing; blue, rust & cream
   sponging, 6" dia **55.00**
Bowl, mixing; blue & red sponged
   Saffron wide band, panels
   below, 7" **65.00**

Bowl, mixing; Rock Dell, blue & red
   stripes, 8½" dia **40.00**
Bowl, mixing; sponged, 1900s, 11"
   dia **140.00**
Bowl, mixing; yellow & white mar-
   bleized, 9½" dia **40.00**
Butter jar, Albany slip, low style,
   5-lb **35.00**
Churn, dasher type, dated 1915,
   2-gal, w/wood lid **150.00**
Jug, white, molded seam, wide
   mouth, 1-qt **40.00**
Milk pan, white, North Star mark
   on bottom **75.00**

Riviera

Made by the Homer Laughlin
China Company, Riviera was a
line of colored dinnerware that
was sold through Murphy's dime
stores from 1938 until sometime
in the late 1940s. A sister line to
Fiesta, Riviera was lighter in
weight, unmarked, and inexpensive. Refer to *The Collector's
Encyclopedia of Fiesta* by Sharon
and Bob Huxford (Collector Books)
for more information.

Bowl, baker; 9" **18.00**
Bowl, cream soup; w/underplate,
   ivory **65.00**

**Syrup pitcher, red, $110.00; jug
with lid, red (very rare color),
$200.00; platter, 11¼", red,
$18.00.**

Bowl, nappy; 9¼" **18.00**
Butter dish, ½-lb **85.00**
Pitcher, juice; mauve blue ..**175.00**
Plate, 10" **30.00**
Plate, 7" **8.00**
Plate, 9" **13.00**
Platter, w/closed handles, 11¼" ..**18.00**
Platter, 11½" **15.00**
Sauce boat **18.00**
Saucer **3.00**
Sugar bowl, w/lid **16.00**
Teacup **8.50**
Teapot **90.00**
Tidbit, 2-tier, ivory **70.00**
Tumbler, handled **60.00**
Tumbler, juice **40.00**

Rock 'n Roll

Concert posters, tour books, magazines, sheet music, and other items featuring Rock 'n Roll stars from the '50s up to the present are today being sought out by collectors who appreciate this type of music and like having these mementos of their favorite preformers around to enjoy. See also Beatles; Elvis Presley.

Aerosmith, ballpoint pen, X-rated scene, M **8.00**
Alice Cooper, concert ticket, 1973 ....**7.50**
Allman Brothers, lg metal mushroom, 1970s tour **15.00**
Bill Haley & His Comets, sheet music, Rock Around the Clock **15.00**
Bruce Springsteen, backstage pass, 1980s **5.00**
Chubby Checker, poster, Twist Around the Clock, 1-sheet **30.00**
Dave Clark 5, poster, Get Yourself a College Girl, 1-sheet ..**20.00**
Davey Jones, photo hanger, cardboard, 1967, VG **120.00**

Dick Clark, notebook binder, photo & teen graphics on pink, 11x14" **78.00**
Dick Clark, patch, iron-on, 1950s **8.00**
Donny & Marie Osmond, colorforms, MIB **8.50**
Donny & Marie Osmond, playset, TV show stage, Mattel, 1976, NM in box **85.00**
Donny Osmond, doll, MIB ...**15.00**
Everly Brothers, sheet music, Like Strangers **5.00**
Fabian, patch, iron-on, 1950s ..**3.00**
Genesis, program **2.50**
Gerry & the Pacemakers, insert card, Ferry Cross the Mersey **20.00**
Grateful Dead, backstage pass ..**4.00**
Grateful Dead, tour program, gold cover, English & Egyptian, 1978, EX **85.00**
Herman's Hermits, poster, 1965, 24x26", in original mailing tube, NM **25.00**

Ink Spots, record brush, 3½", $15.00.

Jimi Hendrix & Janis Joplin, 2-sided coin, '70, sealed in orig package **12.00**
Kiss, Gene Simmons Halloween costume, Ben Cooper, 1977, MIB **80.00**

Kiss dolls, Mego, 1977, 12½", $75.00 each.

Kiss, Kiss on Tour board game, 1978, NM in box **36.00**

Kiss, pencil, color portrait of Gene Simmons or Paul Stanley, 1978, M **5.00**

Kiss, viewmaster set, 1979, NM in envelope w/color photo of group **35.00**

Led Zeppelin, button, 1977 Summerfest, 3" **15.00**

Marie Osmond, doll, Mattel, 1970s, 12", MIB **25.00**

Michael Jackson, doll, Grammy Awards, LJN, MIB **35.00**

Michael Jackson, radio, AM, Ertl, 1984, MIB **20.00**

Mick Jagger, poster, Performance, 1960s, 9x7", NM **30.00**

Monkees, bracelet, gold logo charm, M on card **22.00**

Monkees, clothes hanger, Reybert, 1967, 16x13½", NM **50.00**

Monkees, finger puppet, Remco, 1968, 3", set of 4, NM **40.00**

Monkees, guitar, plastic w/photos, Mattel, 1967, EX **40.00**

Monkees, Mike Nesmith finger puppet, w/boots, Remco, 1970, 5", M **35.00**

Monkees, newspaper supplement, August 1967, EX **2.50**

Monkees, paperback, The Monkees Tale, by Eric Lefcowitz, EX **3.50**

Monkees, pin-back button, logo in red on yellow, NM **20.00**

Monkees, tambourine, pictures all 4, 1967, EX **75.00**

Paul Anka, sheet music, Diana **6.00**

Ricky Nelson, magazine, Life, 1958, EX **12.00**

Rolling Stones, concert ticket, 1976 ....**7.50**

Rolling Stones, Pixerana fold book, 12 fold-out photos, English, 1964 ....**20.00**

Rolling Stones, 3-D flicker button, tongue logo, lg **10.00**

Tommy Sands, poster, Sing Boy Sing, 1-sheet **10.00**

Rockingham

A type of utilitarian ware favored in America from the early 1800s until after the 1920s, Rockingham is easily identified by its mottled brown sponged-on glaze. While some items are simple and unadorned, many are molded with high-relief designs of animals, vines, leaves, cherubs, and human forms. Figural hound handles are often found on pitchers. Some of the finest examples of Rockingham was made at the Vermont potteries of Norton and Fenton, and you may find ill-informed dealers and collectors that mistakenly refer to this ware as 'Bennington.' However, hundreds of potteries produced goods of a very similar appearance, and proper identification of the manufacturer is often difficult, if not impossible.

Bank, church figural, 3¼" **75.00**
Bank, man clutching pitcher, inscribed on back, repaired, 4½" **170.00**
Bowl, shallow, 3¾x13" **60.00**
Flask, morning-glories embossed, ovoid, repaired, 7½" **85.00**
Flowerpot, acanthus leaves, 2-pc, hairline, 10" **65.00**
Mug, straight sides, 3½" **100.00**
Pie plate, 11" **135.00**

**Pitcher, embossed cherubs, 9",
$150.00.**

Pitcher, batter; flintware, yellow & brown glaze **140.00**
Pitcher, berries relief, 8½" **150.00**
Pitcher, hunt scenes & vintage, sm chips, 8½" **175.00**
Pitcher, plain, 11", EX **125.00**
Pitcher, squat, minor hairlines, 3½" **45.00**
Plate, bear's paw mottle, leaf border, sq, 8x9" **80.00**
Soap dish, oval, 4¾" **85.00**
Teapot, paneled, embossed leaves, chips, 5" **125.00**

Roselane Sparklers

A line of small figures with a soft shaded finish and luminous jewel eyes was produced during the late 1950s by the Roselane Pottery Company who operated in Pasadena, California, from the late 1930s until possibly into the 1970s. The line was a huge success. Twenty-nine different models were made including elephants, burros, raccoons, fawns, dogs, cats, and fish. Not all pieces are marked, but some carry an incised 'Roselane Pasadena, Calif.' or 'Calif. U.S.A'; others may have a paper label. Our advisor for this category, Lee Garmon, is listed in the Directory under Illinois.

Stylized owl, $15.00.

Angelfish, pink jeweled eyes, California USA, 4½" **7.00**
Cat, slanted aqua jeweled eyes, sitting, C in circle USA mark, 4½" **4.00**
Deer, pink jeweled eyes, standing, unmarked, 5½" **5.00**
Deer, upturned head, satin-matt brown on white, plastic eyes, 4x3½" **12.00**

Deer w/antlers, jeweled eyes & collar, standing, unmarked, 4½" **6.00**

Elephant, jeweled eyes & headpiece, 6" **12.00**

Kitten, aqua jeweled eyes, sitting position, 1¾" **2.00**

Modern owl, black w/gold trim, lg plastic eyes, 1960-70s, 5¼" **10.00**

Siamese cat, jeweled eyes & collar, sitting, unmarked, 7" **10.00**

Spaniel dog, blue jeweled eyes, C in circle USA mark, 4½" .**5.00**

Rosemeade

Novelty items made by the Wapheton Pottery Company of North Dakota from 1941 to 1960 are finding an interested following among collectors of American pottery. Though smaller items (salt and pepper shakers, figurines, trays, etc.) are readily found, the larger examples represent a challenge to collectors who prize them highly. The name of the novelty ware, 'Rosemeade,' is indicated on the paper labels (many of which are still intact) or by the ink stamp. Our advisor for this category, Bryce L. Farnsworth, is listed in the Directory under North Dakota.

Ashtray, pheasant figurine ..**125.00**

Bank, buffalo, Jamestown, North Dakota **350.00**

Basket, molded rose handle ..**75.00**

Figurine, goose, 2", pr **110.00**

Figurine, prairie dog, 1¾", pr ..**22.50**

Figurine, seals, mini, set of 3 ..**40.00**

Flower frog, bird **35.00**

Planter, bird on log **25.00**

Planter, boot, lg **45.00**

Planter, pony **75.00**

Salt cellar, dove **100.00**

Flower frog, pheasant, 4¾", $75.00.

Shakers, dog head, Chow Chow, pr **35.00**

Shakers, elephant, pr **60.00**

Shakers, leaping deer, pr ...**160.00**

Shakers, pelican, lg, pr **65.00**

Shakers, pig, pr **40.00**

Shakers, tulip, pr **35.00**

Shakers, turkey, lg, pr **45.00**

Spoon rest, pheasant **60.00**

Sugar bowl & creamer, corn design **35.00**

Tray, sitting bear, marked Teddy Roosevelt Memorial Park **175.00**

Vase, koala bear on stump, figural 8½" **375.00**

Vase, turquoise matt, flared top, bulbous, 5½" **50.00**

Roseville

Founded by George Young in 1892, the Roseville Pottery Company produced quality artware, utility ware, and commercial lines of the finest quality until they closed in the 1950s. Of the major American potteries, Roseville's production pieces are among the finest, and it is a rare flea market that will not yield several excellent examples from the 'middle period.' Some of the early artware lines require perseverance to acquire, while others such as their standard brown-glazed 'Rozane' is easy to locate. During the twenties and thirties, they produced several lines of children's serving dishes decorated with Santa Claus, chicks, rabbits in jackets, Sunbonnet Babies, and various other characters, which are today treasured by their own band of devotees. While many pieces of Roseville are signed with some form of the company name, others that originally had only paper labels may now be unmarked. Careful study of Roseville lines may result in your finding one of the few bargains left at the flea markets today. Refer to *The Collector's Encyclopedia of Roseville Pottery* by Sharon and Bob Huxford (Collector Books) for more information.

Apple Blossom, bud vase, #379, 7" **40.00**
Apple Blossom, ewer, 8" **85.00**
Artwood, vase, 8" **65.00**
Aztec, lamp, 11" **280.00**
Baneda, vase, 5½" **175.00**
Bank, Uncle Sam **115.00**
Bittersweet, candlestick, 3" .**30.00**
Blackberry, console bowl, 13" ..**225.00**
Bleeding Heart, vase, #138, 4" ...**45.00**
Bushberry, cornucopia, #3 ...**50.00**
Capri, bowl, 9" **20.00**
Carnelian, loving cup vase, 5"..**45.00**
Cherry Blossom, lamp base ..**415.00**

Cherry Blossom, vase, 5" ...**165.00**
Clematis, basket, #387, 7" ...**75.00**
Clematis, candle holder, #11, 4½", pr **60.00**
Clematis, flowerpot, 5½" **65.00**
Columbine, vase, #20, 8" **60.00**
Corinthian, ashtray, 2" **65.00**
Corinthian, candlestick, 8" ..**55.00**
Cosmos, vase, 3" **45.00**
Dahlrose, pillow vase, 5" **85.00**
Dahlrose, triple bud vase, 6" ..**85.00**
Dawn, #827, 6" **75.00**
Dogwood II, bowl, 2" **45.00**
Donatello, candlestick, 8", pr ..**150.00**
Donatello, compote, 5" **88.00**
Donatello, double bud vase, 5"..**55.00**
Dutch, mug, 5" **77.00**
Earlam, vase, 6" **75.00**
Egypto, pitcher, 5" **275.00**
Elsie the Cow, mug, #B1 ....**115.00**
Florane, bud vase, 8" **50.00**
Florentine, bowl, 9" **50.00**
Florentine, wall pocket, 7" ...**90.00**
Foxglove, conch shell, #426, 6"..**55.00**
Freesia, pitcher, #20, 10" ...**165.00**
Futura, bowl, 3½" high **150.00**
Gardenia, tray, 15" **90.00**

Holland mug, $45.00.

Imperial I, vase, 10" **125.00**
Iris, bowl, #359, 5" **140.00**
Ivory II, candelabra, 5½", pr ..**125.00**
Ivory II, hanging basket, 7"..**85.00**
Ixia, bowl, #387, 6" **55.00**

La Rose wall pocket, 7¼", $75.00.

Jonquil, bowl, 4" **55.00**
La Rose, bowl, 9" **60.00**
Landscape, planter, 4½" **70.00**
Laurel, vase, 6" **105.00**
Lotus, vase, #L3, 10" **120.00**
Lustre, candle holder, 8", pr ...**55.00**
Magnolia, mug, #3, 3" **55.00**
Matt Color, bowl, 3" **30.00**
Mayfair, tankard, #1107, 12" ..**70.00**
Ming Tree, console bowl, #528,
    10" **60.00**
Mock Orange, basket, #909,
    8" **90.00**
Moderne, lamp, #799, 9" **225.00**
Mongol, bowl vase, 3" **275.00**
Monticello, vase, 4" **65.00**
Morning Glory, vase, 8" **240.00**
Mostique, jardiniere, 10" ...**150.00**
Orian, bowl, 6" **85.00**
Panel, candlestick, 8", pr ...**165.00**
Panel, pillow vase, 6" **85.00**
Pasadena, ashtray, 8½" **30.00**
Peony, double cornucopia,
    #172 ....**50.00**
Peony, vase, #57, 4" **35.00**
Persian, bowl, 3½" **90.00**
Pine Cone, bowl, #632, 3" **58.00**
Poppy, bowl, 12" **115.00**
Primrose, vase, 6½" **85.00**

Raymor, cup & saucer, #151 ..**20.00**
Raymor, gravy, 9½" **15.00**
Rosecraft, vase, 8" **90.00**
Rosecraft Vintage, bowl, 5" ..**95.00**
Rozane Light, pitcher, flowers,
    4" **160.00**
Rozane Light, vase, leaves, 5" ..**140.00**
Rozane Royal, vase, 7" **165.00**
Russco, vase, 7" **60.00**
Silhouette, cigarette box **45.00**
Silhouette, vase, #785, 9" **75.00**
Snowberry, ashtray **40.00**
Sunflower, candlestick, 4" ..**150.00**
Teasel, bowl, #342, 4" **40.00**
Thornapple, basket, #342, 10" ..**200.00**
Thornapple, candle holder, 2½",
    pr **65.00**
Topeo, bowl, 2½" **115.00**
Tourmaline, planter, 12½" ...**95.00**
Utility Ware, pitcher, decorated,
    4" **45.00**
Velmoss II, double cornucopia,
    8½" **75.00**
Velmoss Scroll, vase, 6" **85.00**
Water Lily, ewer, #10, 6" **45.00**
Water Lily, vase, #81, 12" ..**110.00**
White Rose, cornucopia, #143,
    6" **30.00**
White Rose, vase, 6" **77.00**
Wincraft, planter, #231, 10" ..**55.00**
Wisteria, vase, 6" **200.00**
Zephyr Lily, cookie jar, 10" ..**200.00**

Rowland and Marsellus

Souvenir and commemorative plates marked Rowland and Marsellus or with an R & M within a diamond were manufactured by various Staffordshire potteries for these American importers who added their own backstamp to the blue-printed wares that were popular in gift shops from the 1890s until 1920. Plates are encountered most often, though cups and saucers, pitchers, etc., were also made.

Plate, General View of the Falls (Niagara), rolled edge, 10", $55.00.

Cup & saucer, Souvenir of Yale **65.00**
Plate, Alaska-Yukon-Pacific Exposition, Seattle 1909, coupe, 10" **50.00**
Plate, Biltmore House, Asheville NC, pink, fruit & flower border **50.00**
Plate, Horseshoe Curve, fruit & flower border **50.00**
Plate, Jamestown & Norfolk VA, state seal, coupe, 6" **30.00**
Plate, National Monument to the Forefathers **50.00**
Plate, Plymouth, Return of the Mayflower, coupe, 10" ...**50.00**
Plate, Providence RI, State House, rolled edge, 10" ..**50.00**
Plate, World's Fair St Louis MO, Jefferson portrait **75.00**
Plate, Yale, university seal, coupe, 6" **30.00**
Tumbler, Souvenir of Seattle ..**65.00**
Tumbler, Views of Washington DC **65.00**

Royal China

Several lines of the dinnerware made by Royal China (Sebring, Ohio) are becoming very collectible, especially their Blue

Willow ware and Currier and Ives, decorated with scenes of early American life in blue on a white background.

Colonial Homestead

Bowl, 5½" **3.00**
Bowl, 6¼" **5.00**
Casserole, w/lid **30.00**
Cup & saucer **4.00**
Gravy boat, w/underplate **18.00**
Plate, dinner **3.50**
Plate, 7" **2.50**
Salt & pepper shakers, pr **10.00**
Teapot, w/lid **35.00**

Currier & Ives

Ashtray **10.00**
Bowl, berry; 5¾" **3.00**
Bowl, cereal **7.00**
Bowl, soup; flat, 8½" **8.00**
Bowl, vegetable; 10" **20.00**
Bowl, 9" **18.00**
Butter dish, w/lid, ¼-lb **25.00**
Casserole, w/lid **60.00**
Creamer **5.00**
Cup & saucer **4.50**
Gravy boat **13.00**
Gravy boat, w/underplate **25.00**
Pie plate, 10" **15.00**
Plate, bread & butter; 6" **3.00**
Plate, calendar; 1975 ....**12.00**
Plate, chop; 11" **20.00**
Plate, dinner; 10½" **5.00**
Plate, salad; 7¼" **7.00**
Platter, handled, 10" dia **15.00**
Platter, 13" **22.00**
Salt & pepper shakers, pr **15.00**
Sugar bowl, w/lid **12.00**
Tumbler, juice **10.00**
Tumbler, milk glass **7.00**
Tumbler, 13-oz, 5½" **12.00**
Tumbler, 9-oz, 4¾" **12.00**

Memory Lane

Ashtray **10.00**

Currier and Ives, soup bowl, $8.00; gravy boat, $13.00; cup and saucer, $4.50.

Bowl, berry; sm 3.00
Bowl, soup; flat 5.50
Bowl, vegetable, rnd 8.50
Butter dish 16.00
Butter dish, ¼-lb 25.00
Creamer 5.00
Cup & saucer 4.00
Pie plate 9.50
Plate, dinner 4.00
Platter 12.50
Salt & pepper shakers, pr 10.00
Sugar bowl 5.00
Teapot 30.00
Tumbler, lg 11.00

Old Curiosity Shop

Ashtray 5.00
Bowl, fruit; 5½" 3.00
Bowl, soup; flat, 8½" 6.00
Bowl, 10" dia 12.50
Cake plate, handled, 10" 13.00
Creamer 3.00
Cup & saucer 4.00
Gravy boat 10.00
Plate, bread & butter 2.50

Plate, dinner 4.00
Salt & pepper shakers, pr 12.50
Sugar bowl, w/lid 6.00
Teapot 35.00

Willow

Bowl, blue, 5½" 4.50
Bowl, cereal; pink 7.00
Bowl, soup; blue, flat 10.00
Bowl, vegetable; blue, 9" 15.00
Cake plate, blue, tab handles, 10" 11.00
Casserole, pink, w/lid 35.00
Creamer, blue 5.00
Creamer & sugar bowl, pink ..12.00
Cup & saucer, blue, angular handle 7.50
Plate, blue, 10" 10.00
Plate, blue, 6" 4.00
Plate, dinner; blue, 9" 8.00
Plate, salad; pink 5.00
Salt & pepper shakers, pk, pr ..13.50
Saucer, blue 1.50
Tidbit, blue, 2-tier 26.00
Tidbit, pink, 3-tier 50.00

Royal Copley

Produced by the Spaulding China Company of Sebring, Ohio, Royal Copley is a line of novelty planters, vases, ashtrays, and wall pockets modeled after appealing puppy dogs, lovely birds, innocent-eyed children, etc. The decoration is airbrushed and underglazed; the line is of good quality and is well received by today's pottery collectors. We recommend *Royal Copley* by Leslie Wolfe, edited by Joe Devine (Collector Books). The book has been brought back by popular demand and includes updated 1992 values. Our advisor, Joe Devine, is listed in the Directory under Iowa.

Ashtray, heart w/birds, 5½"..**15.00**
Ashtray, leaf w/bird, 5½" **7.50**
Bank, rooster, Chicken Feed in raised letters, 7½" **37.00**
Bank, teddy bear, paper label, rare, 7½" **42.00**
Bud vase, parrot on stump, yellow, 5" **10.00**
Figurine, black cat, 8" **28.00**
Figurine, cockatoo, multicolor, 8¼" **25.00**
Figurine, dancing lady, 8" **35.00**

Full-bodied deer by Copley stump planter, 8", $20.00.

Figurine, grouse, 4¾" **20.00**
Pitcher, daffodil, pink & yellow, 8" **24.00**
Pitcher, pome fruit, blue background, 8" **24.00**
Planter, apple, 5½" **10.00**
Planter, cat & cello, 7½" **40.00**
Planter, coach, teal blue, 3¼x 6" **14.00**
Planter, cocker head, 5" **12.00**
Planter, dog & mailbox, paper label, 7¾" **17.00**
Planter, dog w/string base, 7"..**50.00**
Planter, duck & mailbox **40.00**
Planter, duck & wheelbarrow, paper label, 3¾" **13.00**
Planter, erect white poodle, 7" .**22.00**
Planter, finch & apple, paper label only, 6½" **13.50**
Planter, fruit plate plaque, 7" ..**12.00**
Planter, gazelle, 9" **24.00**
Planter, girl bust, blue wide brim hat, hand under chin, 7½" **24.00**
Planter, ivy, window box, paper label only, 4x7" **8.00**
Planter, kitten & book, 6½" ..**20.00**
Planter, mature wood duck, 7¼" **18.00**
Planter, pirate head, pink head covering, 8" **27.00**
Planter, kitten & boot, 7½" ...**30.00**
Planter, pup w/suitcase, 7" ...**25.00**
Planter, rooster, 7¼" **15.00**
Planter, teddy bear, 8" **35.00**
Planter, teddy bear on tree stump, 5½" **20.00**
Planter, woodpecker, floral design on stump, 6¼" **13.50**

Royal Haeger, Haeger

Manufactured in Dundee, Illinois, Haeger pottery has recently become the focus of much collector interest, especially the artware line and animal figures designed by Royal Hickman. These were produced from 1938 through the 1950s and are recognized by their strong lines and distinctive glazes. For further information consult *Collecting Royal Haegar* by Lee Garmon and Doris Frizzell (Collector Books). Ms. Garmon is listed in the Directory under Illinois.

Gazelle vase, R-225, $25.00 each.

Bookends, ram w/lg horns, R-132, 9", pr **32.00**
Bowl, leaf figural, oval, applied fruit handle, R-821, 19" long **25.00**
Candle holders, swan on pedestal, blue, R-516, 8", pr **24.00**
Cookie jar, Cookie Barrel, R-1657, 12" **35.00**
Dish, candy; applied calla lily finial, blue, 7½" dia **25.00**
Dish, polar bear figural on lid, blue, oval, R-644, 7½" wide **25.00**
Figurine, dachshund, Ebony, R-736, 14½" long **22.00**
Figurine, matador, red, #6343, 11¼" **50.00**
Lamp, TV; comedy & tragedy masks, Ebony, 9" **35.00**
Pitcher, Ebony Cascade, R-1619S, 16" **10.00**

Planter, Madonna, white, #374, 6" **6.00**
Planter, Scottie dog, white, #3377, 6" long **8.00**
Planter, wren house, 9½" **25.00**
Plate, leaf figural, R-126, 15"..**8.00**
Urn, 2-handled, Black Cascade, RG-150 ....**8.00**
Vase, Peter Pan, R-917, 10" ..**30.00**

Russel Wright Dinnerware

Dinnerware designed by one of America's top industrial engineers is today attracting the interest of many. Some of his more popular lines are American Modern, manufactured by the Steubenville Pottery Company (1939-'59), and Iroquois, introduced in 1944. Refer to *The Collector's Encyclopedia of Russel Wright Designs* by Ann Kerr (Collector Books). Mrs. Kerr is listed in the Directory under Ohio.

Ashtray, Harker White Clover, decorated **28.00**
Bowl, cereal; Meladur, 9-oz **8.00**
Bowl, fruit; Casual, restyled, 5¾" **6.00**
Bowl, fruit; Casual, 9½-oz, 5½" ..**6.00**
Bowl, fruit; Knowles, 5½" **7.50**
Bowl, soup; Sterling, 6½" **10.00**
Casserole, American Modern, w/lid, 12" **40.00**
Cup, American Modern **10.00**
Cup, Highlight **18.00**
Cup, tea; Harker White Clover ..**8.00**
Cup & saucer, Casual, restyled, set **10.00**
Cup & saucer, Home Decorator, plastic **7.00**
Dish, vegetable; Harker White Clover, 7½" **18.00**
Mug, Highlight **30.00**

Home Decorator (plastic), dogwood pattern, cup and saucer, $7.00; dinner plate, $4.50; fruit bowl, $6.00.

Plate, bread & butter; American Modern, 6¼" **3.50**
Plate, dinner; Casual, 10" **8.00**
Plate, dinner; Highlight **25.00**
Platter, serving; Residential ..**15.00**
Platter, Sterling, oval, 7½" ...**12.50**
Salt & pepper shakers, American Modern, pr **14.00**
Salt & pepper shakers, Casual, stacking, pr **10.00**
Sauce boat, Knowles **25.00**
Saucer, tea; Harker White Cover, decorated **3.00**
Sugar bowl, Knowles, w/lid .**18.00**
Tumbler, iced tea; American Modern, 13-oz, 5" **25.00**

Salt Shakers

You'll probably see more salt and pepper shakers during your flea market forays than T-shirts! Since the 1920s they've been popular souvenir items, and considerable amounts have been issued by companies to advertise their products. These advertising shakers are always good, and along with miniature shakers (1½" or under) are some of the more valuable. Of course, crossover categories (Black Americana, Disney, Rosemeade, Shawnee, Ceramic Arts Studios, etc.) are expensive as well. There are many good books on the market; among them are *Salt & Pepper Shakers, Identification & Values, Books I, II, and III,* by Helene Guarnaccia and *The Collector's Encyclopedia of Salt & Pepper Shakers* (there are two in the series) by Melva Davern (all published by Collector Books).

Amish couple on bench, red & black metal, tall, 3-pc ...**18.00**
Anniversary hearts, footed, gold-trimmed bone china, pr ..**10.00**
Asparagus spears, ceramic, pr **5.00**
Barred Plymouth Rock chickens, ceramic, pr **12.00**
Baseball player condiments on tray, shakers & mustard, ceramic, 4-pc **40.00**
Bear & beehive nesters, ceramic, 1940s-50s, Japan, 2-pc ..**10.00**
Bears in white pants & green waistcoats, ceramic, Germany, pr **25.00**
Bellhop w/luggage, red & yellow suit, ceramic, 1-pc **25.00**
Black cat, long stylized body, red clay, 1-pc (not Shafford) ..**12.00**
Bowling ball & pin, ceramic, miniature, pr **30.00**
Bumper cars, red & yellow, ceramic, Vandor, pr **15.00**
Cabbage girls, blonds' faces in cabbage hats & bodies, ceramic, pr **10.00**
Car & stop sign, ceramic, miniature, pr **20.00**
Cardinals perched on snowy leaves, ceramic, pr **12.00**
Celery people, celery heads on sitting human bodies, ceramic, pr **12.00**
Chocolate candies, w/paper wrappers, miniature, pr **24.00**

Christmas mice, white w/red Santa hats, ceramic, pr **10.00**

Christmas pigs, white w/red & green accents, pr **8.00**

Circus tigers perched on red, white, & blue balls, ceramic, pr **10.00**

Clowns, white w/blue & red accents, American Pottery, pr **12.00**

Corn people, ceramic, Napco, 1938, pr **12.00**

Cow condiment, resting cow divides into shakers & mustard, 3-pc **45.00**

Cowboy & cowgirl, he in black, she in red, ceramic, Japan, pr **8.00**

Cupcakes, brown & white w/confetti colors & cherry on top, pr **8.00**

Donkeys, animated, smiling, wearing hats, ceramic, pr **10.00**

Dumbo, hand-painted white pottery, Walt Disney, 1940s, pr **20.00**

Dustpan & wisk broom, gold trim, miniature, pr **22.00**

Dutch couple, Ceramic Art Studio, pr **25.00**

Dutch couple on bench, ceramic w/wood bench, 3-pc **12.00**

Dutch girl w/buckets, ceramic, 1930s-40s, Japan, pr ..**15.00**

Egg cup couple, 'egg head' shakers rest in egg cup bodies, 4-pc **15.00**

Elephants, black w/red, sitting, droopy ears, red clay, pr **9.00**

Fish, animated, 1 green & 1 yellow, ceramic, pr **8.00**

Football & head w/helmet, ceramic, pr **8.00**

Frogs, sitting piggyback, Fitz & Floyd, ceramic, 2-pc **18.00**

Gatepost shakers attached to gate, ceramic, Japan, 1-pc **8.00**

Goofy, sitting, hand-painted white pottery, Walt Disney, 1940s, pr **20.00**

Grapes, hand-painted ceramic, 1940s-50s, Japan, pr **10.00**

Greyhounds, running, porcelain, pr **18.00**

Hippos, animated, ceramic w/blue-gray glaze, pr **10.00**

Huggers, pink bears, $30.00 for the pair.

Humpty Dumpty, white w/blue & black accents, ceramic, pr **15.00**

Ice cream cones, bone china, pr ..**9.00**

Indian chief & tepee, chief is seated, ceramic, pr **18.00**

Irons, sitting upright, plastic, pr **8.00**

Kangaroo w/twins, mother is holder, ceramic, 3-pc **18.00**

Lawnmower, shakers rest on top, movable parts, plastic, 3-pc **25.00**

Lighthouse & sailboat, ceramic, miniature, pr **35.00**

Lions, toy-type which appear to have movable parts, pr ..**15.00**

Little Red Riding Hood, ceramic, Hull, ca 1943, pr **35.00**

Log cabins, chalkware, 1920s-50s, pr **8.00**

Maracas, handles upright, wood, Occupied Japan, pr **15.00**

Mice, black w/lg ears & red bows, red clay, pr **8.00**

Milk bottles, Mitchell's Dairy ..**20.00**

Monkey in car, green hat & car, ceramic, 2-pc **15.00**

Monkeys sitting on bananas, ceramic, pr **12.00**

Mr & Mrs Santa Claus, dressed in western fashion, ceramic, pr **18.00**

Octopuses, animated, red-glazed ceramic, pr **10.00**

Old Milwaukee beer cans, pr ..**10.00**

Old woman & shoe, ceramic, pr **30.00**

Owls, dressed as doctors & wearing glasses, ceramic, pr ..**12.00**

Palm trees, attached at base, ceramic, 1-pc **12.00**

Peanut people, peanut heads, seated gold-trimmed bodies, ceramic, pr **14.00**

Pearl shakers resting in blue oyster shell, plastic, 3-pc **15.00**

Pelicans, stylized, ceramic, Occupied Japan, pr **12.00**

Penguins, Peppy & Salty in top hats, enamel on wood, pr ..**8.00**

Piano, push keys & shakers pop up, plastic, 3-pc **15.00**

Pilgrim couple, stylized, ceramic, pr **12.00**

Pilgrim hats, white w/black bands & gold buckles, ceramic, pr **10.00**

Pineapples, metal, pr **5.00**

Pocket watch & coin purse, ceramic w/gold trim, miniature, pr **22.00**

**Poodles, red clay, Japan, 4½",
$10.00 for the pair.**

Poodles, shaker heads rest on sugar & creamer bodies, red clay, 4-pc **25.00**

Rabbits, white, 1 holds a flower, ceramic, Avon, pr **15.00**

Raggedy Ann & Andy, ceramic, 1970s, pr **22.00**

Rainbow trout, ceramic, pr ..**10.00**

Red pepper heads, bow tie bases, ceramic, pr **10.00**

Red peppers, ceramic, 1940s-50s, Japan, pr **5.00**

Rocking horses, chalkware, 1920s-50s, pr **9.00**

Rocking horses, 1 black & 1 white painted pot metal, pr **15.00**

Rooster & hen, shaker heads rest on sugar & creamer bodies, 4-pc **25.00**

Rudolph the Red Nosed Reindeer, heads, ceramic, Lefton, pr **12.00**

Shaving mug & brush, ceramic, miniature, pr **20.00**

Silos, advertising AO Smith Harvestore, royal blue, ceramic, pr **35.00**

Skillets, w/lids, black knobs & handles, plastic, 1950s **6.00**

Slot machines, plastic, 1950s, pr **7.00**

Soda bottles, green glass w/Squirt logo, 1940s, pr **12.00**

Squirrel & acorn huggers, ceramic, 1950s-60s, Japan, pr **8.00**

Squirrels, long stylized bodies, sometimes called 'Longfellows,' pr **10.00**

Steamship, wood boat is holder for blue & red smokestack shakers, 3-pc **10.00**

Strawberries resting on leaf plate, ceramic, 3-pc **12.00**

Thunderbird totems, wood w/painted accents, pr **12.00**

Turtles in vests & hats looking up, ceramic, Japan, pr **12.00**

Violin & accordion, ceramic, miniature, pr **22.00**

Walrus, 1 w/white tusks, ceramic, brown glaze, pr **15.00**
Washington Monument, Bakelite, 1930s, pr **30.00**
Washington Monument, Japanese lustre, pr **18.00**
Watermelon slices, ceramic, Japan, pr **8.00**
Windmill condiments on tray, shakers & mustard, ceramic, 4-pc **25.00**
Windmills, natural wood, Denmark, pr **8.00**
Winking cowboy & hat, bust pose w/cigarette, ceramic, 2-pc **12.00**
Yellow birds on a branch, ceramic, 1930s-50s, 1-pc **12.00**
Zebras, stylized, ceramic, pr ..**10.00**

Schoop, Hedi

During the 1940s and '50s, Hedi Schoop managed a small operation in North Hollywood, California, where she produced novelty wares such as figurines, lamps, and other decorative items. Refer to *The Collector's Encyclopedia of California Pottery* by Jack Chipman (Collector Books) for more information.

Candle holder, mermaid, ca 1950, 13½" **125.00**
Figurine, Conchita, Mexican lady w/2 baskets, 12½" **45.00**
Figurine, flower girl w/applied flowers, 9" **35.00**
Figurine, peasant woman dancing, holds bowl above her head, 13" **40.00**
Figurine, seated cat, bow w/ applied bell **32.00**
Flower holder, 2 girls w/joined hands, rare, 8" **90.00**
Lamp, TV; jazz combo, #375, rare **175.00**

Lady with baskets, 12½", $55.00.

Planter, hobby horse, 5" **30.00**
Tray, King of Diamonds **35.00**
Vase, crowing rooster, ca 1949, 12" **40.00**

Scottie Dogs

Scottie dog collectibles are available for every budget. From inexpensive greeting cards to rare porcelains there is a vast array of items to be found. Though some art work dates to the early 1920s, the majority comes from the 1930s and '40s. Many of these items are dimestore novelties; others were designed for major advertising campaigns. Today thousands of collectors search for these treasures, making this field of collecting one of the hottest in the marketplace. For further information we recommend contacting Donna and Jim Newton, who are listed in the Directory under Indiana. In 1983 the Newtons began publishing the *Scottie Sampler*, a quarterly newspaper offering historical data, current market prices, features, photos, and ads.

Advertising, Avon President's
  Award Figurine, 1983 ...**85.00**
Advertising, bookmark, Cracker
  Jack, tin litho **28.00**
Advertising, figurine, President's
  Award, Avon, 1983 ....**85.00**
Advertising, soda bottle, Scotty,
  painted label **10.00**
Advertising, tin, Mrs Stevens'
  Candy, 9" dia **30.00**

Ashtray/match holder, black amethyst glass, $50.00.

Book, Mr M'Tavish, Marion
  Bullard, 1933 ....**20.00**
Book, Portrait of a Dog, Mazo
  Dela Roche, illustrated by
  Dennis, 1930 ....**30.00**
Bookends, figurals, Cambridge,
  clear, 6½x5", pr **125.00**
Clock, Playful Scottie, Lux,
  3¾x4¼" **225.00**
Door knocker, Scottish Terrier,
  brass, 4x2" **15.00**
Figurine, Begging His Share,
  Hummel, ca 1956 ....**185.00**

Figurine, full figure, Sabino,
  glass, 4" long **55.00**
Ice bucket, black Scottie, Cambridge **85.00**
Inkwell, head, glass eyes, hinged,
  glass, 3" **150.00**
Mold, chocolate; full body,
  standing, #28842, Anton
  Reiche **150.00**
Pin, Scottie head w/cap & pipe,
  celluloid **40.00**
Planter, Niloak, 4x3½" **15.00**
Plate, Scottie against mountain
  background, Royal Doulton,
  10" **155.00**
Powder jar, Akro Agate, pink,
  6" **85.00**
Punchboard, Gone With the Wind
  Girl & Scottie, 9x9" **45.00**
Purse, crochet, Scottie cutouts in
  plastic handles **35.00**
Shakers, black Scottie heads,
  Rosemeade, pr **25.00**
Tea set, child's, ceramic w/decal of
  girl & dog, 13-pc, MIB ...**25.00**
Toy, xylophone, Scottie pictures
  on ends, tin, +mallets & orig-
  inal box **20.00**
Wall hanging, Scottie watching
  2 playing dogs, tapestry,
  38x20", M **35.00**
Wall pocket, Scottie head, Japan,
  round, 7" **25.00**

Scouting Collectibles

Founded in England in 1907 by Major General Lord Baden-Powell, scouting remains an important institution in the life of young boys and girls everywhere. Recently scouting-related memorabilia has attracted a following, and values of many items have escalated dramatically in the last few years. Early 1st edition handbooks often bring prices of $100.00 and more. Vintage uniforms are scarce and highly valued, and one of the rarer medals, the Life Saving Honor Medal, is worth several hundred dollars to collectors. Refer to *A Complete Guide to Scouting Collectibles* by Rolland J. Sayers for more information. Mr. Sayers is listed in the Directory under North Carolina.

Arm band, Boy Scout, National Jamboree Staff, red on white felt, '57 ....**25.00**

Arm band, National Jamboree Health Services, 1977 ...**15.00**

Ashtray, National Jamboree, 1977 ....**3.00**

Badge, Senior Girl Scout, Mariner, 1953 ....**20.00**

Bank, Cub Scout figural, composition **30.00**

Binoculars, Official BSA, plastic, 1950s, in vinyl case **20.00**

Blotter, Boy Scout, National Jamboree, NY Council, 1937...............................**10.00**

Book, Ernest Thompson Seton's America, Selections From Works, 1954 ....**30.00**

Book, The Girl Scouts Rally, Saalfield, 1921, VG **6.00**

Book, The Scout in Aviation, by Hyman, 1982 ....**10.00**

Button, I'm Going (to the 1937 Jamboree), multicolor, ⅞", EX **75.00**

Calendar, Girl Scout, 1920 ..**100.00**

Calendar, Pointing the Way, by Rockwell, 1962, 22x46", complete **15.00**

Calendar, Scouting Outing, by Rockwell, 1968, 16x32", complete **25.00**

Camera, Official Boy Scout, Seneca #2, box type, 1940s.........**20.00**

Cigarette card, Players & Sons, Baden-Powell profile, 1950 ..**3.00**

Cigarette lighter, National Jamboree, Staff, 1969 ....**7.50**

Coin, National Jamboree, brass, 1953 ....**8.50**

Collapsible cup, Girl Scout, aluminum, 1950 ....**5.00**

Compass, Boy Scout, Sylva Pathfinder, plastic, 1950, square **6.00**

Decal, Exploring Is the Program, black **1.00**

Decal, National Jamboree, 1957 ....**3.00**

Decal, Order of the Arrow, Indian Head w/blue border **3.00**

Doll, Girl Scout, hard plastic, Terri Lee, 1949-53, 16" ..**20.00**

Figurine, Boy Scout, McKinzie, bronze-like finish, 5½" **7.50**

First Aid kit, Boy Scout, Johnson & Johnson, rectangular, 1938 ....**12.00**

Game, The Boy Scout Progress Game, 1926, complete in box **50.00**

Game, Trupe, 1939, complete in box **30.00**

Handbook, Girl Scout, 1933, G ..**6.00**

Handbook, Order of the Arrow Brotherhood Ceremony, 1948 ....**20.00**

Key chain, National Jamboree, 1953 ....**3.00**

Knife, BSA #1046, 5-blade, bone-like handle, Tenderfoot shield, '70s **5.00**

Knife, BSA #1371, 1-blade, plastic handles, brass bolsters, 4¾" **8.50**

Knife, BSA #1392, Young Hunter, 9-in-1 tool & padlock, 1982 ....**5.00**

Knife, Cattaraugus #D-2589, 4-blade, no bail, 1931-42 ..**20.00**

Knife, Sea Scout, w/marlin spike, belt shackle, bone handle, ca 1935 ....**17.50**

Knife, 3-blade, can opener end w/shackle, 1936 ....**50.00**

Lantern slide, Baden-Powell in full uniform, 1930 ....**30.00**

Lapel pin, Explorer Silver Award, sterling silver, 1958-68 ..**35.00**

Magazine, Boy's Life, 1933, EX **10.00**

Medal, Scout's Key, gold logo w/key on green & white ribbon, boxed **25.00**

Membership card, Order of the Arrow, 1930 ....**5.00**

Merit badge, Emergency Preparedness **3.00**

Merit badge, Wilderness Management **2.00**

Model kit, wood with white plastic sails, complete, #1698, $30.00.

Money clip, Boy Scouts, National Jamboree, gold w/logo, 1969 ....**3.00**

Neckerchief, Boy Scout, full square, 1930-50 ....**3.50**

Pamphlet, Cub Scout Helps, BSA issue **2.00**

Pamphlet, What Scouts Can Do, 1921 ....**10.00**

Paper dolls, Girl Scout, 1958, complete in box **20.00**

Paperweight, Boy Scout, World Jamboree, clear plastic w/ logo, 1967 ....**8.00**

Patch, Comanche Trail Council, hat type **9.00**

Patch, Explorer Scout Apprentice, red & blue twill, ca 1948-58 ....**5.00**

Patch, National Jamboree, solid emblem, 1981 ....**4.50**

Patch, National Jamboree Sea Scout, 1973, square **20.00**

Patch, Old Hickory Council, round, sm **3.00**

Photo, scouts at campfire, black & white, dated 1932, 5x7", EX **10.00**

Photo, uniformed girl w/badges, black & white, 1921, 6x8", EX **15.00**

Pin, Girl Scout First Class, tri-foil w/clover leaf **6.00**

Pin, WWI award, Service in Agriculture..., metal, 1917, ¾x1" ..**80.00**

Plate, Scoutmaster, Rockwell & Gorham, ceramic, limited edition **75.00**

Playing cards, Boy Scouts, Official issue, 52 cards in box **10.00**

Postcard, Baden-Powell & Lady Baden-Powell's grave markers, 1970s **3.00**

Postcard, Brownie, The Holden Hand, 1930s **10.00**

Poster, Boy Scout, For God & Country, recruiting **6.00**

Record, Boy Scout, Bugle Calls, 1950-60, 78rpm **10.00**

Ring, Cub Scout, sterling w/ logo **6.00**

Sheet music, Baden-Powell March, by Read, bust portrait on front **15.00**

Souvenir book, National Jamboree, 1960 ....**5.00**

Tie bar, Camp Ranger, clip-on style **5.00**

Tie bar, Eagle Scout Leader, sterling, 1940-60s, w/kit **5.00**

Trade card, Fisher Candy Co, bust view of Baden-Powell, ca 1900 ....**6.00**

Uniform, Girl Scout Official Dress, 1936-39, complete **30.00**

Watch, Official Boy Scout, Elgin, #1735, 1944 ....**20.00**

Watch fob, Boy Scout Signaling, silver, 1915 ....**50.00**

Wings, Brownie, 1935, lg **5.00**

Sewing Items

Sewing notions from the 1800s and early 20th century, such as whimsical figural tape measures, beaded satin pincushions, blown glass darning eggs, and silver and gold thimbles are pleasant reminders of a bygone era – ladies' sewing circles, quilting bees, and beautifully hand-stitched finery.

**Child's machine, Singer, 7",
$110.00.**

Button, lapel; Knitting Arts Exhibition Award, brass, sm ..**7.50**
Buttonhole cutter, slides to expose blade, 3" **45.00**
Darner, black egg w/repousse sterling handle **35.00**
Emery, strawberry, red taffeta w/ red velvet cap, 2½", EX ...**48.00**
Knitting gauge, Good Shepard Yarns advertising, celluloid, 6½" **15.00**
Lace bobbin, celluloid **1.50**
Pin box, celluloid w/applied flowers, cushion w/drawer below, 4x4½" **55.00**
Pin box, colorful cardboard lid, 1940s, 2x2½", EX **6.50**
Pin holder, Puritan label, mahogany, 2" dia **10.00**
Scissors, folding type w/celluloid handles, 2", EX **45.00**

Scissors, stork figural, base metal, 3½" **20.00**
Tape measure, Hoover vacuum figural, EX **40.00**
Tape measure, house, celluloid, multicolor, 2", EX **60.00**
Tape measure, Lydia Pinkham both sides, 1½" disk **65.00**
Tape measure, turtle, Pull My Head, Not My Leg, metal, EX **40.00**
Tatting shuttle, brass finish, 3¼" **25.00**
Tatting shuttle, Tartanware, EX **65.00**
Thimble box, plexiglas, 6 shelves inside, sliding door, 8½x12" **37.50**
Thimble case, embossed bucket shape w/brass gilt, blue lining, 1¾" **65.00**
Thimble stand, Deco lady figural, base metal, 2½" **48.00**
Thimble stand, elephant w/trunk up, base metal, 2x3" **68.00**

Thimbles

Sterling, chased roses & leaves, unmarked **55.00**
Sterling, chased scroll, Waite-Thresher **26.00**
Sterling, heavy applied chased border, unmarked **45.00**
Sterling, house & farm scene w/bridge, scrolled rim, unmarked **37.50**
Sterling, overlapping daisies, Webster **48.00**
Sterling, plain band, Louis XV rim, unmarked **35.00**
Sterling, plain band, scroll rim, Simons **24.00**
Sterling, plain panels w/diamond indentations, unmarked ..**35.00**
Sterling, wide Delft enamel border, Gabler **40.00**
Sterling, 10 panels, alternately engraved, unmarked **25.00**

Shaving Mugs

The first character shaving mugs made about 1840 were decorated in relief. These are mugs that have an embossed image that projects out of the side of the mug. It may be in the form of a person, an animal, or a fish, for instance. Around 1880 the character mug became a full-form figural taking in the entire mug. Mugs have been made of china, bisque, glass, or metal and may have a matching figural brush handle. Our advisor is David C. Giese, who is listed in the Directory under Virginia.

Character Shaving Mugs

Devil, bisque, signed, w/matching
    brush handle **650.00**
Elk head, Royal Bayreuth, w/soap
    dish **280.00**
Fish, upsidedown, china scuttle
    type **160.00**
Fish, walking, scuttle type, w/
    soap dish **65.00**

Flower, scuttle type **165.00**
Hippo, china scuttle type, w/soap
    dish **150.00**
Indian, w/feather handle ...**150.00**
Indian brave, scuttle type ..**170.00**
Monkey, scuttle type **150.00**
Monkey, w/dish in hands **95.00**
Whale, scuttle type **80.00**

Relief-Molded Shaving Mugs

Buffalo, bisque, ca 1880, maker's
    mark on bottom **200.00**
Elk, bisque, signed, w/matching
    brush handle **225.00**
Man smoking pipe, ca 1850,
    signed **80.00**
Swan, milk glass **150.00**
Viking face, milk glass, ca 1870 ..**85.00**
Woman barber, bisque, 1840 ..**200.00**
Woman's face, matching brush
    handle **175.00**

Shawnee

The novelty planters, vases, cookie jars, salt and pepper shakers, and 'Corn' dinnerware made

Lady's face, pink bisque, matching brush handle, $550.00.

by the Shawnee Pottery of Ohio are attractive, fun to collect, and are still available at reasonable prices. The company operated from 1937 until 1961, marking their wares with 'Shawnee, U.S.A.,' and a number series, or 'Kenwood.' Refer to *The Collector's Guide to Shawnee Pottery* by Janice and Duane Vanderbilt (Collector Books) and *Collecting Shawnee Pottery* by Mark Supnick (L-W Book Sales) for more information. See also Cookie Jars.

Butter dish, Lobster **65.00**
Cookie jar, King Corn, #66, minimum value **135.00**
Creamer, elephant, USA **12.00**
Creamer, Smiley, blue & yellow, #86 ....**50.00**
Cup, King Corn, #90 ....**30.00**
Figurine, resting gazelle, black w/white horns, #614 ...**45.00**
Figurine, squirrel **40.00**
Mug, Queen Corn, #69 ....**35.00**
Nappy, Valencia, 9½" **10.00**
Pie bird, white w/pink (or white w/blue) **20.00**
Pitcher, Charlie Chicken, marked Chanticleer **70.00**
Pitcher, Fruit, ball jug, #80 ..**70.00**

Pitcher, Sunflowers, ball jug, marked USA **80.00**
Pitcher, Valencia, green, ball jug, USA **17.00**
Planter, gristmill, green, #769..**15.00**
Planter, highchair, USA #727 ..**45.00**
Planter, stagecoach, #733 ....**28.00**
Plate, Valencia, yellow, 10" **7.00**
Platter, Queen Corn, #96, 12"..**45.00**
Relish dish, King Corn, #79..**17.00**
Salt & pepper shakers, Charlie Chickens, lg, pr **30.00**
Salt & pepper shakers, Fruit, USA, lg, pr **30.00**
Salt & pepper shakers, King Indian Corn, pr **65.00**
Salt & pepper shakers, Lobster, red claws on white bases, pr **20.00**
Salt & pepper shakers, Muggsy, sm, pr **40.00**
Salt & pepper shakers, Puss 'n Boots, sm, pr **60.00**
Salt & pepper shakers, Queen Corn, sm, pr **17.00**
Salt & pepper shakers, Smileys, red bib, lg, pr **60.00**
Sock darner, girl figural **30.00**
Sugar bowl, Clover Bud, USA ..**40.00**
Sugar bowl, fruit design, #83 ..**35.00**
Teapot, Clover Bud, USA **70.00**
Teapot, Queen Corn, #75 .....**70.00**
Teapot, Rose, USA **40.00**
Utility jar, white basketweave design w/green trim, marked USA **60.00**
Vase, doe in shadow box, #850 ..**22.00**
Wall pocket, girl w/rag doll, USA #810 ....**18.00**

Salt and pepper shakers, Charlie Chicken, gold trim, $60.00 for the pair.

Sheet Music

The most valuable examples of sheet music are those related to early transportation, ethnic themes, Disney characters, a particularly popular actor, singer, or composer, or with a cover illustration done by a well-known artist. Production of sheet music peaked during the 'Tin Pan Alley Days,' from the 1880s until the 1930s. Covers were made as attractive as possible to lure potential buyers, and today's collectors sometimes frame and hang them as they would a print. Flea markets are a good source for sheet music, and prices are usually very reasonable. Most are available for under $5.00. Some of the more valuable examples are listed here. Refer to *The Sheet Music Reference and Price Guide* (Collector Books) by Anna Marie Guiheen and Marie-Reine A. Pafik and *Collector's Guide to Sheet Music* by Debbie Dillon (L-W Book Sales) for more information.

Last Night on the Back Porch, $5.00.

After the Cake Walk, Nathaniel Dett, Black cover, 1900..**15.00**

Ain't She Sweet? photo of Sophie Tucker, 1927 ....**20.00**

Baby Mine, Disney cover, 1941..**15.00**

Barking Dog, The; photo of Crew Cuts, 1954 ....**5.00**

Beyond the Blue Horizon, photo of Jeannette MacDonald, 1930 ....**10.00**

Black & Blue Rag, Hal G Nichols, Black face on cover, 1914 ..**20.00**

Blue Is the Night, photo of Norma Shearer, 1930 ....**8.00**

Carolina, Lew Brown & Jay Gorney, photo of Janet Gaynor, 1939 ....**5.00**

Debutante Waltz, photo of Arthur Murray, 1934 ....**5.00**

Dream, Johnny Mercer, photo of The Pied Pipers, 1945 .....**3.00**

Embraceable You, photo of Judy Garland & Mickey Rooney, 1942 ....**10.00**

Everybody's Doin' It Now, Irving Berlin, photo of Betty Bond, 1911 ....**10.00**

Fight Is On, The; WWI cover, 1918 ....**20.00**

For You a Rose, cover artist Harrison Fisher, 1917 ....**35.00**

Four Little Blackberries, Black cover, 1907 ....**50.00**

Graduation Day, photo of The Four Freshman, 1956 .....**5.00**

Grieving for You, photo of Al Jolson, 1920 ....**15.00**

He's on a Boat That Sailed Last Wednesday, 1913 ....**35.00**

Heigh-Ho, cover from movie Snow White, 1938 ....**10.00**

Hiawatha's Melody of Love, Indian girl cover, 1920 ..**35.00**

Hickory Dickory Dock, Edward G Nelson & Fred Rose, 1936.................................**5.00**

I Dug a Ditch, photo of Judy Garland & Kathryn Grayson, 1943 ....**10.00**

I Love You Truly, Carrie Jacobs Bond, 1920 ....**15.00**

Johnny Doughboy Found a Rose in Ireland, photo of Kate Smith, 1942 ....**10.00**

Lady Bird, Cha, Cha, Cha; cover by Rockwell, 1968 ....**25.00**

Little Curly Hair in a High Chair, photo of Eddie Cantor, 1940 ....**5.00**

Little Orphan Annie, advertising for Ovaltine, 1931 ....**40.00**

Lone Star Moon, photo of Harry James, 1947 ....**3.00**

Marshmallow World, photo of Arthur Godfrey, 1949 ......**5.00**

Moonlight Waltz, Victor LaSalle, Indian cover, 1912 ....**20.00**

My Funny Valentine, photo of Jane Russell & Jeanne Crain, 1937 ....**10.00**

Oh! Mother I'm Wild, Deco cover by LS Reiss, 1920 ....**10.00**

Oui, Oui Marie; WWI cover, 1918 ....**15.00**

Pleasant Dreams, Deco cover, 1919 ....**10.00**

Poor Me, cover by James Montgomery Flagg, 1921 ....**35.00**

Right Somebody To Love, Shirley Temple photo cover, 1936..**10.00**

Shine On, Harvest Moon; photo of Nora Bayes & Jack Norworth, 1918 ....**10.00**

Sipping Cider Thru a Straw, photo of Fatty Arbuckle **10.00**

Someday, I'll Meet You Again; photo of Humphrey Bogart, 1944 ....**5.00**

St Louis Blues, photo of Nat King Cole, 1942 ....**5.00**

Ten Baby Fingers, mother & child on cover, 1920 ....**15.00**

Thousand Violins, A; photo of Bob Hope & Rhonda Fleming, 1949 ....**5.00**

Three Little Words, photo of Amos & Andy, 1930 ....**60.00**

Ugly Duckling, The; photo of Danny Kaye, 1951 ....**5.00**

We are Ready, Uncle Sam cover, 1917 ....**25.00**

Wedding Bells Rag, AB Coney, 1910 ....**10.00**

Who's Afraid of the Big Bad Wolf?, Mickey Mouse cover, 1934 ....**10.00**

You're Just in Love, Irving Berlin, 1950 ....**8.00**

Zip-A-Dee-Doo-Dah, Disney cover, 1946 ....**10.00**

Shell Pink Milk Glass

Made by the Jeanette Glass Company from 1957 until 1959, this line is made up of a variety of their best-selling shapes and patterns. The glassware has a satiny finish, and the color is the palest of peachbloom. Refer to *Collectible Glassware of the '40s, '50s, and '60s* by Gene Florence (Collector Books.)

We'll Make Hay While the Sun Shines, Arthur Freed and Nacio Herb Brown, 1933, Crosby and Davies on front, $10.00.

Ashtray, butterfly shape **15.00**
Bowl, Pheasant, footed, 8" ...**35.00**
Bowl, wedding; w/lid, 6½" **22.50**
Bowl, wedding; w/lid, 8" **25.00**

Candle holder, 2-light, pr **35.00**
Candy dish, w/lid, square, 6½" .**30.00**
Celery & relish, 2-part, 12½" ..**45.00**
Cigarette box, butterfly finial ..**90.00**
Cookie jar, w/lid, 6½" **80.00**
Honey jar, beehive shape, notched
    cover **35.00**
Powder jar, w/lid, 4¾" **30.00**
Punch base,tall, 3½" **25.00**
Punch bowl, 7½-qt **50.00**
Punch cup, also fits snack tray, 5-
    oz **6.00**
Punch ladle, pk plastic **8.00**
Punch set, 15-pc **155.00**
Tray, Lazy Susan, complete
    w/base **125.00**
Tray, Lazy Susan, 5-part **40.00**
Tray, snack; w/cup indent,
    7¾x10" **9.00**
Tray, 5-part, 2-handle, 15¾" ..**40.00**
Vase, cornucopia, 5" **15.00**
Vase, heavy bottom, 9" **65.00**
Vase, 7" **35.00**

Shirley Temple Collectibles

Shirley Temple's impish charm has allured movie-goers from the very beginning of the early 1930s. This admiration felt by many has followed her through her many adult accomplishments as well. Please consult *Shirley Temple Dolls and Collectibles* by Patricia R. Smith (Collector Books) for more information. Our advisor, Gen Jones, is listed in the Directory under Massachusetts. See also Directory, Clubs and Newsletters; Dolls, Shirley Temple.

Ad, Little Princess, full color, full
    page from magazine **4.00**
Ad, Wheaties, for cobalt glass
    bowl giveaway **10.00**
Book, Hollywood Lolitas, paper-
    back, M **15.00**
Book, How I Raised Shirley Tem-
    ple, Saalfield, 1935, G ...**40.00**
Book, Little Colonel, Anne Fel-
    lows Johnston **36.00**
Book, Shirley Through the Day,
    Saalfield, 10x10", EX **30.00**
Cereal bowl, white portrait on
    cobalt blue glass, 1930s, origi-
    nal **50.00**
Christmas card, Hallmark, 1935,
    M **30.00**
Coloring set, Saalfield, 1930s, EX
    in box **95.00**
Doll, baby, composition, rubber, &
    cloth, swivel head, M original,
    16" **700.00**

Creamer, cobalt blue with white portrait, 4¼", $37.50; mug, 3¾", $40.00.

Doll, composition, all original for Now & Forever, Ideal, 1934, 18" **850.00**

Doll, composition, dressed as Our Little Girl, 1935, 18" ...**850.00**

Doll, composition, organdy dress for Curly Top, 1935, 13" **650.00**

Doll, composition & cloth, swivel head, hazel eyes, marked 20/#2, 22" **900.00**

Doll, vinyl, all original, 1959, 15" **265.00**

Figurine, Blue Bird, Danbury Mint **30.00**

Figurine, salt glaze, riding outfit, 4½", VG **25.00**

Lobby card, Kiss For Corliss, EX **15.00**

Lobby card, The Blue Bird, set of 5 ....**75.00**

Magazine, Home Movies, April 1939, black & white, EX ..**25.00**

Magazine, Life, 1942, G **10.00**

Magazine, Look, February 15, 1949, EX **7.50**

Magazine, Motion Picture, November 1950, EX **15.00**

Magazine, Movie Stars, August 1942, NM **10.00**

Mirror, School Days, 1937 .....**5.00**

Pamphlet, Story of My Life, give-away in 1935, M **25.00**

Paper dolls, Saalfield, #2112, ca 1930, EX **65.00**

Paper dolls, 1988 reproduction .**3.50**

Paperweight, picture under plastic, 1930s **10.00**

Photo, signed, black & white, 1930s, 8x10" **60.00**

Plate, Nostalgia, Captain January, MIB **35.00**

Playing cards, 1930s, MIB ...**65.00**

Program, Tournament of Roses, 1939, 38-pg, 11x8½" **20.00**

School tablet, 1930s, 9x6", EX **20.00**

School tablet, 1935, M **40.00**

Sheet music, Animal Crackers in My Soup, 1935, EX **20.00**

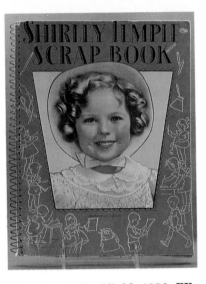

Scrapbook, Saalfield, 1936, EX, $45.00.

Sheet music, Bright Eyes on the Good Ship Lollipop, 1937, EX **25.00**

Sheet music, Goodnight My Love, Stowaway, EX **18.00**

Sheet music, Rebecca of Sunny-brook Farm, The Toy Trumpet, 1938, EX **20.00**

Song album, Sam Fox Publishing, 1937 ....**25.00**

Song album, Sing With Shirley Temple, 1935, VG **32.00**

Spoon, likeness in bowl & on handle **10.00**

Tea set, Ideal, pink plastic, original box **235.00**

Video, Kiss & Tell, EX **25.00**

Shot Glasses

Shot glasses, old and new, represent a new area of interest to today's collectors and are relatively easy to find. Basic values are given for general categories of shot glasses in mint condition.

Glasses that are in less-than-mint condition will obviously be worth less than the price given here. Very rare and unique items will be worth more. Sample glasses and other individual one-of-a-kind oddities are a bit harder to classify and really need to be evaluated on an individual basis. For more information we recommend *Shot Glasses: An American Tradition* by our advisor for this category, Mark Pickvet. He is listed in the Directory under Michigan, and information about a newsletter is given in our Clubs and Newsletters section.

Aluminum **3.00**
Glass, barrel form **6.00**
Glass, coated inside & out w/ black enamel to look like porcelain **4.00**
Glass, Culver 22k gold **8.00**
Glass, cut, whiskey tumbler ..**100.00**
Glass, Depression, in colors ...**8.00**
Glass, Depression, clear, tall ..**6.00**
Glass, European, gold trim, round, sm **3.00**
Glass, general **3.00**
Glass, general, etched **7.50**
Glass, general, frosted **3.00**

Glass, general, frosted, w/gold trim **6.00**
Glass, general, w/gold trim **5.00**
Glass, iridized carnival-type ..**50.00**
Glass, plain advertising **2.00**
Glass, pressed design, whiskey tumbler **75.00**
Glass, soda advertising **12.50**
Glass, square, w/design **7.50**
Glass, square, w/etching **10.00**
Glass, square, w/2-tone pewter design **13.00**
Glass, tourist, Taiwan **3.00**
Glass, tourist, turquoise & gold design **4.00**
Glass, w/pewter design, lg ...**10.00**
Glass, w/shield design in pewter **10.00**
Porcelain, general **7.50**
Porcelain, tourist **4.00**
Pre-prohibition whiskey sample glass **20.00**

Silhouette Collectibles

These pictures with the subject matter reverse painted on the glass (which is usually curved) were popular dimestore items from the '20s until the '50s, and you'll often see them at flea mar-

Cobalt blue, $10.00 to $15.00; dark yellow Depression Glass, $3.00 to $4.50; souvenir, ruby stained, $20.00 to $25.00.

kets and antique malls. Subjects range from animals and trees to children and courting couples, and some may incorporate advertising or perhaps a thermometer. Refer to *The Encyclopedia of Silhouette Collectibles on Glass* (Shadow Enterprises) by Shirley Mace for more information. She is listed in the Directory under Minnesota.

Pictures

Baby portrait, This Little Piggy, convex, Benton, 8x6" **30.00**
Campfire scene, advertising on reverse, flat, Newton Co, 8x10" **15.00**
Colonial couple in a landscape, convex, Benton, 5x4" **18.00**
Colonial girl, flat, Reliance, 4x4" **15.00**
Elegant couple in a landscape, flat, West Coast Corp, 9x7" ...**20.00**
Elegant woman seated at vanity, flat, NRA stamp, Reliance, 9x12" **35.00**

Benton Glass Co, #198, 6x8", $35.00.

Fishing scene, flat, attached calendar, Newton Co, 7½x 5½" **25.00**
George Black Grain Co, advertising, snow scene, convex, Baco, 5x4" **18.00**
Girl in garden, Happy in Her Garden, flat, West Coast Co, 8x5½" **20.00**
Girl mailing letter, The Answer, flat, Buckbee-Brehm, 6x 4" **18.00**
Girl w/parasol, convex, Bilderback's Inc, 9" dia **15.00**
Girls frolicking above water, flat, Volland PF Co, 9x6½" ...**45.00**
Kitten by a stream, convex, Benton, 5x4" **20.00**
Little boy w/his dog, titled Garden Romp, flat, Reliance, 5x7" **20.00**
Little Red Riding Hood, flat, Reliance, 8x10" **25.00**
Romantic couple on bridge, flat, Flowercraft, 10x4" **20.00**
Romantic scene, At the Gate, flat, Deltex Co, 5x4" **18.00**
Ship on choppy sea, convex, Peter Watson, 5" dia **20.00**
Ship on rough sea, Homeward Bound, flat, NRA stamp, Reliance, 5x4" **12.00**
Waseca Processing Co, convex, thermometer at side, Erickson Co, 5x4" **50.00**
Windmill scene, flat, Art Publishing Co, dated Feb 21, 1934, 3½x5" **15.00**
Women knitting & spinning thread, At The Gate, flat, Newton, 6x8" **17.00**

Snowdomes

The term snowdome refers broadly to any water-filled paperweight, but there are several distinctly different styles. Round glass globes which sit on a separate base have been made in a variety of shapes and materials and were first designed in the middle of the 19th century. Flea markets offer this type (which were made in America and Italy in the '30s and '40s) as well as newer ones which are produced today in Austria and the Orient.

Small plastic half-moons with blue backs often serve as souvenirs or Christmas toys. This style originated in West Germany in the 1950s. Dozens of other shapes followed, including round and square bottles, short and tall rectangles, cubes, and other simple shapes.

Figurals made of plastic were especially popular in the 1970s. Either the entire object was an unusual shape, or a figure of an animal, mermaid, etc., was draped over a large plastic dome. Today snowdomes of this type are made of glass, ceramic, or artplas (very heavy plastic) in elaborate shapes. Some collectors buy all three styles while others specialize in only one.

For further information we recommend contacting Nancy McMichael, author of *Snowdomes*, the first illustrated book on this subject, and editor of *Snow Biz*, the first newsletter and collector club. She is listed in the Directory under the District of Columbia. See also Clubs and Newsletters.

Advertising, Co name on base, oily liquid, 1950s, 2¾" glass globe **50.00**
Ashtray, Bakelite, glass globe w/scene, decaled base, 1930s **55.00**
Award, oily liquid, black or brown base, ca 1950s, 2¾" glass globe **60.00**
Bank, all plastic, souvenir scene, square base, slit at back ..**8.00**
Black subjects in glass globe, ceramic base **100.00**
Calendar, perpetual; all plastic, 2 knobs either side of square base....................................**8.00**
Cartoon character, plastic, sm ..**10.00**
Christmas theme, plastic half-moon, sm **5.00**
Commemorative (moon landing, etc), plastic bottle shape..........**15.00**

Empire State, New York, $40.00; Apple, souvenir of New York City, $15.00.

Disney character, plastic dome, marked Monogram, 1960s **30.00**

Disney character, styles other than above listing **12.00**

Figural, animal draped across lg plastic dome **10.00**

Figural, animal or character w/ water ball 'tummy,' '70s ..**15.00**

Figural cartoon character, plastic, 1970s **50.00**

Fraternal, oily liquid, glass globe on black base, flat sides, 1950s **60.00**

Marx, copyrighted plastic half-moon, 1960s, set of 6, MIB **50.00**

Religious theme, saint in glass globe, decal on plastic base, 1930s **40.00**

Roly-poly, Santa or snowman on top half of water compartment, 1970s **14.00**

Saint or souvenir scene in glass atop shell base, Italy, 1940s **12.00**

Shakers, souvenir scene or place plaque inside, plastic, 1950s, each **8.00**

Snowman, glass globe on plastic or ceramic base, 1940s ..**30.00**

Souvenir, glass w/bisque figure, Bakelite base, decal, 1940s **40.00**

Souvenir, glass w/bisque figure, ceramic base, decal, ca 1940-50 ....**40.00**

Souvenir, plastic, city, any shape **7.00**

Souvenir, plastic, sm tourist attraction, any shape **8.00**

Souvenir, plastic, state, any shape **6.00**

Souvenir, plastic, television shape **7.00**

Souvenir, plastic, treasure chest shape **8.00**

World War II general or serviceman, glass globe on ceramic base **50.00**

World's Fair, glass bisque Trilon & Perisphere, 1939 ....**75.00**

World's Fair, plastic ball on red calendar base **20.00**

World's Fair, plastic half-moon shape **15.00**

Soda Fountain Collectibles

The days of the neighborhood ice cream parlor are gone; the soda jerk, the mouth-watering confections he concocted, the high counter and bar stools now a thing of the past. But memories live on through the soda glasses, ice cream scoops, milk shake machines, and soda fountain signs that those reluctant to forget treasure today.

Container, Borden's Malted Milk, aluminum **50.00**

Container, milk shake; glass ..**10.00**

Dipper, Beatrice **5.00**

Dipper, Gem City **10.00**

Dipper, Marvel, 1937 ....**12.00**

Dipper, Myer's Deluxe **15.00**

Dipper, Safe-T-Cone **10.00**

Dish, banana split; clear glassware, footed **15.00**

Dish, banana split; frosted glassware, flat **5.00**

Dish, sundae; Burt, metal **3.00**

Dish, sundae; double dip, pebbled finish **25.00**

Dish, sundae; Lily, metal **3.00**

Dish, sundae; triple dip **40.00**

Dispenser, Grapola, porcelain base, 1918, EX **100.00**

Dispenser, Johnson's Fudge ..**15.00**

Dispenser, Middleby **200.00**

Dispenser, Mission Orange, glass barrel, black lid & base ..**200.00**

Dispenser, Mission Real Fruit Juice, green **175.00**

Flavor board, Hawthorne Mellody Ice Cream, 10x20" **25.00**

Fountain glass, Green River, syrup line **20.00**

Fountain glass, Howell's Root Beer, short, heavy **25.00**

Fountain glass, Nestles, syrup line, 6¼" **10.00**

Fountain glass, 7-Up, green ..**15.00**

Ice cream holder, glass, embossed cones, 3" **30.00**

Ice cream paddle, metal, lg ..**11.00**

Ice cream paddle, sm **8.00**

Mixer, Hamilton Beach, #10 ..**50.00**

Photo, interior view, front counter service, after 1905 ....**10.00**

Poster, Surecrest Soda, cardboard **12.00**

Sign, Meadow Gold Ice Cream..**15.00**

Sign, 7-Up, tin, flange **20.00**

Straw holder, Sani-Straw, w/lid & rod **200.00**

Syrup bottle, Grenadine Syrup, Lyons Magnus, 9½" **15.00**

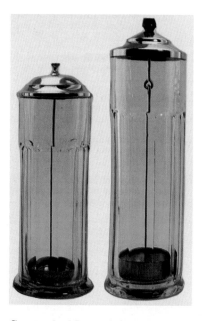

Straw holders, lift lid, 11½", $140.00; tilt top, 13½", $150.00.

Syrup bottle, Lemon-Blend, cork top **35.00**

Trade card, Brunswick Ice Cream, roses, 2¼x6¼" **3.00**

Trade card, White Mountain Freezers, young lady, 3¼x 4¼" **3.00**

Tray, Cherry Blossom, narrow rectangle **150.00**

Tray, Justrite Ice Cream, 10½x 15½" **30.00**

Wafer holder, Reliance **100.00**

Spoons

Since the 1890s, spoons have been issued as souvenirs, to commemorate an event, in honor of a famous person, or on the occasion of a holiday. Today's collectors prefer those with high-relief designs on handle as well as bowl, Indian or other full-figure handles, enameled or gold-washed trim, and examples that are dated or from a limited edition. While the design is more important than the material, silver is, of course, preferred over silverplate. Spoons described below are standard size and sterling unless noted otherwise.

Alamo etched in bowl, scrolls on handle **12.50**

Ann Arbor MI in bowl, sheaves of wheat on handle, demitasse **12.00**

Antioch IL in bowl, heavy floral design on handle **14.50**

Atlantic City in bowl, twisted handle, demitasse **12.50**

Battleship Maine in bowl, scrolls on handle, demitasse **12.50**

Bermuda, enameled sea horse on handle, demitasse **8.00**

Birmingham AL in bowl, embossed flowers & leaves in bowl, demitasse **16.00**

Charlie Chaplin bust on handle, plain bowl, silverplate ..**15.00**

Chicago in fancy script on handle, embossed Ft Dearborn in bowl **20.00**

Christmas 1914 in gold-washed bowl, beaded edge on handle, demitasse **12.00**

Columbian Expo & bust on handle, plain bowl, silver-plate **18.00**

Crater Lake cutout on handle, plain bowl, demitasse **7.50**

Denver CO & US Mint in bowl, mule, state seal & miner on handle **16.50**

Duluth in bowl, scrolls & 1900 on handle **14.50**

Eastside OR & embossed Turn-around on handle, plain bowl, ca 1950 ....**12.50**

Easter in bowl, embossed flowers & scrolls on handle **16.50**

Empire State Building on handle, plain bowl, demitasse **7.50**

England in bowl, enameled floral handle, hallmarked, demi-tasse **7.50**

Gladys in bowl, florals & scrolls on handle, demitasse **7.50**

Golden Gate Bridge embossed on handle, plain bowl **12.50**

Hollywood CA & porcelain shield on handle, marked Germany, demitasse **7.50**

Honolulu & cut-out pineapples on handle, plain bowl, demi-tasse **6.00**

Hot Springs AR in bowl, ornate scrolls on handle **14.00**

Idaho state seal on handle, plain bowl, demitasse **7.50**

Jamestown ND in bowl, embossed flower & 'C' on handle ...**14.50**

Knotts Berry Farm on handle, plain bowl, demitasse **7.50**

Las Vegas & Indian head on handle, plain bowl, ca 1960, demitasse **9.50**

Liberty Bell & house on handle, plain bowl, demitasse **9.50**

Longfellow's monument engraved in bowl **8.00**

Los Angeles etched in bowl, etched & enameled floral handle **16.50**

Masonic emblems on handle, plain bowl **14.50**

Mayville WS in bowl, embossed floral handle **14.50**

Medford OR in bowl, embossed flo-ral handle, demitasse **12.50**

MGM Grand Hotel & lion head logo on handle, plain bowl, ca 1975 ....**9.50**

Minneapolis in bowl, pioneers at top of handle, demitasse .**7.50**

Montana & cut-out florals on handle, plain bowl, demitasse **7.50**

Mt Pleasant IA in bowl, ornate poppy on handle, initial M on back **15.00**

Mt Rainier National Park on han-dle, plain bowl **14.50**

Mt Vernon VA on handle, Wash-ington's home in bowl, demi-tasse **7.50**

Nashville TN in bowl, cut-out florals on handle, demitasse **11.50**

New Orleans & St Louis Cathedral on handle, plain bowl, demi-tasse **7.50**

Niagara Falls in bowl, enameled seal & maple leaf handle ..**15.00**

Old Faithful Inn cutout in handle, plain bowl **14.50**

Santa Paula CA & floral in bowl, ornate scrolls on handle ..**14.50**

Scottsbluff NE & etched mountains on handle, plain bowl **12.50**

Seattle & Space Needle on handle, plain bowl, demi-tasse **7.50**

Spokane & state seal on handle, plain bowl, demitasse **7.00**

St Louis MO & etched fair build-ing in bowl, fancy scrolled handle **18.50**

Statue of Liberty engraved in
bowl, city skyline on handle,
demitasse **40.00**
Towle's Log Cabin Maple Syrup
on handle, silverplate, demi-
tasse **17.50**
Waco & Cotton Palace embossed
in bowl, scrolls on handle, silverplate **7.50**
Washington & bust on handle,
plain bowl **12.50**
Whist 1904 in bowl, raised scrolls
on handle **22.50**

Sports Collectibles

Memorabilia related to sports
of any kind is attracting a following of collectors, many of whom
specialize in the particular sport
that best holds their interests.
See also Baseball Cards; Pin-Back
Buttons; Sports Pins.

Bank, Miami Dolphins, Super
Bowl Champs, 3" square,
EX **15.00**
Beer stein, Super Bowl 21, heavy
glass, 1987, 7" **20.00**

Bobbin' head, St Louis Cardinals,
on gold base, EX **65.00**
Book, Time Life's History of Base-
ball, Aaron, Mays & Clemente
cover, M **30.00**
Booklet, Bob Mathias, Union Oil
Co, ca 1958, NM **6.00**
Booklet, How To Play Baseball,
by Rogers Hornsby, 1956,
NM **35.00**
Booklet, Want To Be a Tennis
Champion?, 1945, 29 pages,
7x5", EX **6.50**
Bumper sticker, Yankees Ready
for the '80s, M **5.00**
Cup, plastic, St Louis Cardinals,
5½", M **3.00**
Cup, plastic, Yankee Stadium,
Pride & Power, 1988, M ..**5.00**
Display box, Fleer baseball
card, shows players, 1983,
empty **7.50**
Game, Big Sneeze, Ideal, 1968,
EX **22.50**
Game, Ernie Banks' Instruc-
tional Batting & Record,
1970s, M **40.00**
Game, Mickey Mantle's Back-
yard Baseball, '50s, M in
bag **150.00**

Bob Feller's Wheaties magazine advertisement, ca 1950s, $6.00.

Game, Pro Soccer, Milton Bradley, 1968, EX **15.00**

Game, Varsity Football, Cadaco, 1950, complete, EX **15.00**

Handbook, Kessler Football, 1983, EX **5.00**

Magazine, Football Illustrated, 1938, EX **30.00**

Magazine, Life, Kickoff of Colts, 1960, EX **8.00**

Magazine, Sports Illustrated, Alex Karras cover, 1964, NM **7.50**

Magazine, Sports World, 1971, EX **20.00**

Newspaper, The Los Angeles Major League Baseball News, 1962, EX **30.00**

Paperweight, Chicago Cubs, white metal player figural, 1920s, 6¾" **225.00**

Pass, National Assn Professional Baseball Leagues, '69 ...**10.00**

Patch, red & white embroidered cloth, Chicago White Sox, 1969, M **17.50**

Pennant, Detroit Tigers in white on red felt, 1950s, 12x29½", EX **20.00**

Pennant, New York Black Yankees, 1940s, 22", NM **90.00**

Photo, Los Angeles Raiders, color, 1982, 9x14", NM **8.50**

Photo, Sammy White, Roston Red Sox, 1950s, 8x10" **8.00**

Photo, Women's Tennis Champ of 1922, black & white, 7x9"..**15.00**

Playing cards, New York Yankees, 1950s, NM **10.00**

Postcard, New York Mets, 1983, M **6.00**

Postcard foldout, Chicago Today, 1930s, NM **20.00**

Poster, advertising, Adidas, World Cup Soccer, 1982, 17x24", NM **5.00**

Poster, advertising, Chicago Bears & Coors, '85 schedule, 18x24" **4.00**

Poster, advertising, Jackie Robinson & Coca-Cola, 18x24", M **25.00**

Poster, advertising, Michael Jordon & Sports Illustrated, 23x35", NM **10.00**

Poster, advertising, Pete Rose, Ty Cobb & Wheaties, 18x24", NM **15.00**

Poster, boxing, George Foreman, Taking a Punch, EX **10.00**

Poster, Dennis Conner w/America's Cup trophy, The Thrill of Victory **5.00**

Poster, Jack Nicklaus, 1986 Sports Highlights, M **20.00**

Poster, New York Mets 25th Anniversary, 1986, 22x32", NM **15.00**

Program, Hershey Figure Skating Club, 1937, 10 pages, VG ..**25.00**

Program, Red Smith Sports Award Dinner, 1969, EX **5.00**

Program, Tennesse vs Alabama, football, Oct 1939, 70 pages, G **16.00**

1931 World Series program from St. Louis, VG, $135.00.

Score book, Cleveland Indians vs Boston Red Sox, 1948 ...**10.00**

Sheet music, There Goes the Ball Game, 1977, EX **25.00**

Sign, advertising, Lou Gehrig/ Ken-Wel Gloves, cardboard, '30s, 10x13" **45.00**

Ticket, 32nd International Bowling Tournament, 1932, 5x3", M **5.00**

Ticket stub, Joe Louis & Lee Ramage, Feb 1935, NM **20.00**

Ticket stub, Minnesota at Oakland, 1977 ....**6.00**

Tumbler, National Football Championship, TX U, 1969, 6¾", M **25.00**

Yearbook, baseball, Mays, Mantle, & Drysdale cover, 1963, EX **10.00**

Yearbook, Brooklyn Dodgers, W Mullin cover, 1952, 8½x11", EX **80.00**

Sports Pins

Sports pins are given away by major league baseball sponsors at ballparks. Some sponsors such as Unocal and Chevron have a specific game night when a pin is given away to fans at the gate. The pin is then sold at participating stations while supplies last. Our advisor is Tony George, who is listed in the Directory under California.

Angels, 1986, California Egg Commission **10.00**

Angels, 1987, California Egg Commission **10.00**

Angels, 1989, California Egg Commission, All Star **13.00**

Angels, 1992, Sport Mart, Nolan Ryan, set of 4 ....**40.00**

Athletics, 1986, California Egg Commission **6.00**

Athletics, 1987, California Egg Commission **6.00**

Athletics, 1988, Unocal, set of 4 ....**35.00**

Athletics, 1989, The Equitable, Old Timers Game **5.00**

Athletics, 1989, Unocal, set of 5 ....**12.00**

Athletics, 1990, Examiner-Dot Racing Champ, 1990 .....**20.00**

Athletics, 1990, Pre-season Bay Bridge Series **12.00**

Athletics, 1990, Rickey Henderson Night, California Raisins **15.00**

Athletics, 1990, The Equitable, Old Timers Game **5.00**

Athletics, 1990, Unocal, World Champs, set of 5 ....**12.00**

Athletics, 1991, Unocal, Uniform history, set of 5 ....**10.00**

Athletics, 1992, Unocal, Record Setters, set of 5 ....**10.00**

Blue Jays, 1989-92, Labatts Beer (4 styles), 1 each year **4.00**

Blue Jays, 1991, Coca-Cola All Star Fan Fest **7.00**

Braves, 1992, Chevron, set of 3 ....**12.00**

Brewers, 1988, Unocal, assorted logos, set of 4 ....**16.00**

Brewers, 1991, US Oil, set of 4 ....**25.00**

Cardinals, 1987, Levi Strause..**15.00**

Cardinals, 1988, Levi Strause..**10.00**

Cardinals, 1989, Levi Strause..**12.00**

Cardinals, 1990, Levi Strause..**10.00**

Cardinals, 1991, Coca-Cola ..**12.00**

Cardinals, 1992, Coca-Cola, set of 10 ....**55.00**

Cubs, 1988, Unocal, set of 4 ..**12.00**

Cubs, 1989, Unocal, set of 4 ..**12.00**

Cubs, 1990, Unocal, set of 4 ..**12.00**

Dodgers, 1987, Unocal, 25th Anniversary Dodger Stadium, set of 6 ....**18.00**

Dodgers, 1988, Coca-Cola Caravan **10.00**

Dodgers, 1988, Unocal, Award Winners, set of 6 ....**12.00**

Dodgers, 1989, Unocal, World Series Championships, set of 6 ....**12.00**

Dodgers, 1990, United Way, Unocal Centennial **10.00**

Dodgers, 1990, Unocal, 100-Year
Anniversary, set of 6 .....**10.00**

Dodgers, 1991, Unocal, Record
Setters, set of 6 ....**10.00**

Dodgers, 1992, Unocal, 30-Year
Anniversary, set of 6 .....**10.00**

Giants, 1989, Chevron, set of
3 ....**30.00**

Giants, 1989, The Equitable, Old
Timers Game **6.00**

Giants, 1990, Chevron, set of 4 ..**20.00**

Giants, 1991, Chevron, Hall
of Fame inductees, set of
3 ....**15.00**

Indians, 1986, Opening Day ..**20.00**

Indians, 1987, Opening Day ..**15.00**

Indians, 1988, Opening Day ..**15.00**

Indians, 1988, Unocal-Wahoo
logo, set of 3 ....**10.00**

Indians, 1989, Group Leader .**25.00**

Indians, 1989, Unocal-Wahoo
logo, set of 3 ....**10.00**

Indians, 1990, Group Leader ..**25.00**

Indians, 1991, Group Leader ..**25.00**

Indians, 1991, Sunoco (display box
at stations), set of 5 ....**25.00**

Indians, 1992, Sunoco, 60-Year
Anniversary, set of 4 .....**16.00**

Mariners, 1988, Unocal, set of
4 ....**12.00**

Mariners, 1990, Red Apple Farms,
w/cards, set of 5 ....**50.00**

Mariners, 1992, Chevron-Seattle
Power Co, set of 5 ....**20.00**

Mets, 1990, Sharp, World Series
Championship, set of 4 ..**20.00**

Orioles, 1989, Toyota World Series
Titles, set of 3 ....**30.00**

Orioles, 1991, Toyota-Memorial
Stadium Commission, set of
2 ....**20.00**

Padres, 1986, Great American
Bank, Colbert, w/card **8.00**

Padres, 1986, Great American
Bank, McCovey, w/card ..**12.00**

Padres, 1987, California Egg
Commission **12.00**

Padres, 1988, Kay's Jewelers-Eric
Show, w/card **12.00**

Padres, 1989, San Diego Sports
Network, set of 3 ....**30.00**

Padres, 1990, San Diego Sports
Network, set of 3 ....**25.00**

Padres, 1990, Vons/Coca-Cola,
Templeton, w/card **10.00**

Padres, 1991, San Diego Cable
Sports Network, set of 3 ..**25.00**

Padres, 1991, Vons/Coca-Cola,
Coleman, w/card **8.00**

Padres, 1992, Vons/Coca-Cola, All
Star logo, w/card **8.00**

Pirates, 1990, TCBY World Series
Championships, set of 5 ..**35.00**

Pirates, 1991, Block Buster Video,
record setters, set of 5 ...**30.00**

Pirates, 1992, Block Buster Video,
player jerseys, set of 5 ..**30.00**

Rangers, 1990, Chevron, Nolan
Ryan, w/card, set of 4 ...**18.00**

Reds, 1989, Pizza Hut, player
numbers, set of 5 ....**25.00**

Royals, 1990, Phillips 66, Brett,
White & logo, set of 3 ....**35.00**

Royals, 1991, Phillips 66, Saberhagen & logo, set of 2 ....**30.00**

Royals, 1992, Phillips 66, Brett &
logo, set of 2 ....**25.00**

Tigers, 1989, Unocal, set of 4 ..**16.00**

Tigers, 1990, Unocal, set of 4 ..**12.00**

Tigers, 1992, Unical, World Series
Championships, w/cards, set
of 3 ....**25.00**

Twins, 1985, All-Star Warm Up
Day **10.00**

Twins, 1987, Star Tribune, Homer
Hankey **8.00**

Twins, 1989, Unocal, set of 4 ..**14.00**

Twins, 1992, Gatorade, Tony
Oliva **10.00**

White Sox, 1989, Coca-Cola, history, set of 6 ....**30.00**

White Sox, 1990, Coca-Cola, logos,
set of 5 ....**25.00**

White Sox, 1991, Scott Peterson
Ballpark Franks, hats, set of
4 ....**16.00**

White Sox, 1991, Scott Peterson Ballpark Franks, logos, set of 4 ....**16.00**

White Sox, 1991, Unocal, Inaugural Season **5.00**

Yankees, 1990, Kodak, logo, w/subscription **6.00**

Stangl

Originally known as the Fulper Pottery, the Stangl Company was founded in 1913 and until its closing in 1972 produced many lines of dinnerware as well as various types of artware. Birds modeled after the prints of Audubon were introduced in the early 1940s. More than one hundred different birds were produced, most of which are marked with 'Stangl' and a four-digit number to identify the species. Though a limited few continue to be produced, since 1976 they have been marked with the date of their production.

Birds

Bluebird, #3276 ....**85.00**

Cardinal, #3444, pink, revised male **75.00**

Chestnut-Backed Chickadee, #3811 ....**100.00**

Cock Pheasant, #3492, antique gold **125.00**

Cockatoos, #3405D **175.00**

Hummingbirds, #3599D **275.00**

Key West Quail Dove, #3453, single wing up **275.00**

Lovebird, #3400 ....**55.00**

Oriole, #3402, 3¼" **60.00**

Painted Bunting, #3452, 5"..**100.00**

Rivoli Hummingbird, #3627, w/ pink flower **120.00**

Rufous Hummingbird, #3585, 3" **55.00**

Yellow-Headed Verdin, #3921 ..**400.00**

Yellow-Throated Warbler, #3924 ....**150.00**

Dinnerware

Bowl, divided vegetable; Country Garden **35.00**

Bowl, Fruit, 8½" **22.50**

Bowl, Thistle, 10" **30.00**

Butter dish, Wild Rose **35.00**

Candlesticks, Antique Gold, #5138, pr **25.00**

Coaster, Star Flower, 5" **10.00**

Cup & saucer, Country Garden ..**15.00**

Cup & saucer, Orchard Song ..**12.00**

Cup & saucer, Thistle **10.00**

Gravy boat, Fruit & Flowers ..**18.00**

Pitcher, Amberglo, ½-pt **15.00**

Plate, dinner; Bittersweet **8.00**

Plate, Fruit, 10" **15.00**

Plate, Orchard Song, 8" **10.00**

Platter, Wild Rose, 14x10½" ..**30.00**

Salt & pepper shakers, Blueberry, pr **15.00**

Sugar bowl, Wild Rose **15.00**

Vase, Antique Gold, #5144, 4½x 5" **15.00**

Star Trek Collectibles

'Star Trek' has influenced American culture like no other show in the history of television. Gene Roddenberry first created the Star Trek concept in 1964, and it has been gaining fans ever since. The longevity of the television show in syndication, the release of six major motion pictures, and the success of 'Star Trek, The Next Generation' television show, have literally bridged two generations of loyal fans. This success has spawned thousands of clothing, ceramic, household, jewelry, and promotional items; calendars; plates;

comics; coins; costumes; films; games; greeting and gum cards; party goods; magazines; models; posters; props; puzzles; records and tapes; school supplies; and a wide assortment of toys. Most of these still turn up at flea markets around the country, and all are very collectible. Double the value for an excellent condition item when the original box or packaging is present.

Belt, child's, Kirk's profile on buckle, Lee Belts, 1976 ...**7.00**

Binoculars, white plastic w/ orange eyepieces, Larami Corp, 1968, M **12.00**

Book, Mission to Horatios, Whitman, 1968, hardcover, EX **8.00**

Book, Star Trek the Motion Picture, by Gene Roddenberry, signed, EX **50.00**

Buckle, Space the Final Frontier, Indiana Metal Co, 1982, 2½" dia **16.00**

Calendar, A Calendar for Crew of Starship Enterprise, 1975, 23x35" **6.00**

Calendar, Star Trek Animated Calendar, Lincoln Enterprises, #0104, 1975 ....**10.00**

Calendar, Star Trek 6, 1993 ..**10.00**

Calendar, Stardate Calendar 1978, Ballantine Books, August 1977 ....**16.00**

Charm, Enterprise profile, Lincoln Enterprises, 1970, 1¾" **10.00**

Check book cover, Star Fleet Academy, T-K Graphics, 3¼x 6¼" **4.00**

Clock, wall; Enterprise, ASA Inc, electric, 1974, 8" dia **35.00**

Colorforms, Star Trek Action Set, 1975, M **15.00**

Coloring book, 20th Anniversary, set of 4 ....**15.00**

Cup, Star Trek The Motion Picture & Coca-Cola, plastic, 1979, 32-oz **4.00**

Decal sheet, insignias, Lincoln Enterprises, #1801, 1980, 1-sheet **3.00**

Decanter, Spock figural, marked Grenadier on bottom **40.00**

Doll, Decker, cloth & painted vinyl, Mego Corp, 1980, 12", MIB **35.00**

Doll, Mr Spock, painted vinyl, Mego Corp, 1974, 8", M in package **20.00**

Dreeble (tribble that purrs), M **22.00**

Earrings, starship outlined on clear Lucite block, Aviva, pr **4.00**

Eraser, McCoy head figural, yellow, Deiner Ent, 1984 .....**1.00**

Flashlight, Light Beam, blue plastic, General Mills, 1979, 3¾" **4.00**

Flashlight, Ray Gun, Larami Corp, 1968, 7½x10¾", M on card **15.00**

Greeting card, Starlog Magazine, 1976, 24-card set **30.00**

Gum card wrapper, Kirk & Spock, Topps, 1976, EX **7.50**

Iron-on transfer, Klingon cruiser w/Klingon Power, AMT Corp, 1974-76 ....**5.00**

Key chain, Star Trek The Motion Picture, Aviva, 1980, 1x1" square **5.00**

Magnet, tribble figural, Lincoln Enterprises, 1975 ....**2.00**

Movie viewer, hand held, w/2 films, M on card **40.00**

Mug, 20th Anniversary, gold on white porcelain, 1986 ....**12.00**

Paint-by-Number kit, Enterprise w/Saturn, Hasbro, 1972, 8x11", M **25.00**

Paperback, Making of Star Trek, 1st edition, 1968, 64 pages photos **7.50**

Patch, Enterprise USS, starboard profile on black, 3x4" **3.00**

Patch, medical insignia on gold leatherette, 1980 ....**3.00**

Patch, Romulan Bird of Prey on shield, 1976, 3x3" **4.00**

Patch, Welcome Committee, 1976, 3x4" oval **4.00**

Pendant, gold starship orbiting planet, American Miss, 1974, M **6.00**

Photo, Star Trek the Motion Picture, James Doohan, black & white, 8x10" **5.00**

Photo, Uhura, black & white, signed, 8x10" **25.00**

Pin, Klingon **6.00**

Pin, Romulan Scout **8.00**

Pinback, Beam Me Up Scotty!, Button-Up, 1986, 1½" **1.00**

Pinback, crew photo, Paramount Pictures, 1974, 3½x2¼" ...**4.00**

Pinback, Search for Spock, Kirk photo, Button-Up Company, 1984, 1½" **2.00**

Playing cards, Star Trek Wrath of Kahn, Movie Players, 1982, M **7.50**

Playset, Telescreen Console, Mego, battery, 1977, MIB **95.00**

Postcard, Enterprise, Trotter Photo, 1977, 3x5" **2.00**

Poster, Enterprise & crew, black & white, Fantasy House, 1975, 18x23" **8.00**

Poster, Gamesters of Triskelion, Paramount Pictures, 1984, 19x23" **6.00**

Poster, Search for Spock, Paramount Pictures, 1984, 12x36" **7.50**

Poster, Space The Final Frontier, Monster Times Magazine, 1972, 16x23" **8.00**

Pressbook, Star Trek The Wrath of Kahn, 66-pg **6.00**

Program, International Convention, 1976, 24-pg, 8½x11" **25.00**

Collector plate, Spock, Ernst/Paramount Pictures, 8½", $40.00.

Putty, Larami Corp, 1979, M on Star Trek The Motion Picture card **3.00**

Puzzle, Enterprise, Aviva, 1979, 551-pc, MIB **10.00**

Puzzle, Planet Klingon, dated 1974, frame tray, 10x14", EX **12.50**

Record, Leonard Nimoy...Music From Outer Space, Dot Records, 1968 ....**30.00**

Spock's ears, painted plastic, 1976, M on card **12.50**

Squirt gun, gray plastic phaser, Aviva, 1979 ....**8.00**

Stein, Wrath of Kahn Series, ceramic, Image Products, 1982, set of 3 ....**85.00**

Sticker, Beam Me Up Scotty, T-K Graphics, 2¼x11" **2.00**

Sticker, Save Star Trek-Write NBC, Star Trek Enterprises, 1968, 4x13" **10.00**

Stickpin, I Am a Trekkie, Lincoln Enterpises, 1976 ....**5.00**

Toy, Tribble, battery-operated purr **20.00**

Wallet, brown vinyl w/circle decal, Larimi, 1977 ....**6.00**

Writing tablet, Spock, ruled, coarse-grain paper on gum pad, 1970 ....**4.00**

Star Wars Collectibles

Capitalizing on the ever-popular space travel theme, the movie 'Star Wars' with its fantastic special effects was a mega box office hit of the late 1970s. A sequel called 'Empire Strikes Back' (1980) and a third hit called 'Return of the Jedi' (1983) did just as well, and as a result, licensed merchandise flooded the market, much of it produced by the Kenner Company. Refer to *Modern Toys, American Toys 1930 to 1980,* by Linda Baker (Collector Books) for more information.

Action set, Play-Doh, 3 cans & 3 hinged molds, 1978-79, MIB **10.00**

Activity book, Luke Skywalker cover, Random House, M ..**10.00**

Baking pan, R2-D2 form, Wilton, early 1980s, NM in box ..**17.50**

Bookmark, Boba Fett, Random House, 1983 ....**3.00**

Bubble bath container, refueling station, Omni, NM **15.00**

Buckle, logo on leather, 1977 ..**15.00**

Calendar, May the Force Be With You All Through the Year, 1978, EX **7.50**

Candle, figural Chewie, Wilton Enterprises, M in package ..**8.00**

Decal, Yoda, fan club premium, 4x5" **3.50**

Doll, Chewbacca, painted vinyl, Kenner, 1978-80, complete, 15", EX **75.00**

Doll, C3-PO, jointed metallic plastic, Kenner, 1979-80, 12", EX **45.00**

Doll, Luke Skywalker, cloth & painted vinyl, Kenner, 1978-80, 12", M **150.00**

Earrings, R2-D2, metal, Weingeroff Enterprises, 1977, pr **20.00**

Game, Escape From Death Star, Kenner, 1978-79 ....**15.00**

Key ring, C-3PO figural, Weingeroff Enterprises, 1977 ..**8.00**

Light saber, inflatable vinyl tube on flashlight handle, Kenner, 1978 ....**20.00**

Lobby card, Empire Strikes Back, 1980, 12x14", set of 8, NM **50.00**

Lobby card, Return of the Jedi, 1983, 12x14", set of 8, NM **50.00**

Lobby card, 1977, 1st edition, full color, 12x14", set of 8, NM **75.00**

Notebook, Chewie on cover, Letraset, pocket size **10.00**

Paint set, Wicket, Craft Master, MIB **10.00**

Paperback, Star Wars, by George Lucas, Ballantine, #26061, 1st edition **25.00**

Patch, logo & blue stars on yellow background **6.00**

Patch, Star Wars A New Hope embroidered on triangle, M **6.00**

Darth Vader picture frame, black plastic, 11", $28.00.

Pin-back button, Leia, 1½" **3.00**

Playset, Bespin Freeze Chamber, Kenner, ca 1978, boxed, minimum value **150.00**

Playset, Creature Cantina, molded plastic, Kenner, 1979-80, 14x8" **25.00**

Playset, Ewok Village, Kenner, early 1980s, EX **55.00**

Playset, Ewoks' Tree House, Kenner, ca early 80s, complete **45.00**

Playset, Imperial Attack Base, molded plastic, Kenner, 1980-81, EX **25.00**

Puzzle, Hans Solo & Chewbacca photo, 1978, Kenner, 140-pc **7.50**

Robot, IG-88, gray molded plastic, Kenner, 1980, 15", w/accessories **125.00**

Robot, R2-D2, Kenner, battery, 1978-80, 8", M **60.00**

Salt & pepper shakers, Yoda figural, Sigma, ca 1977, pr **175.00**

Sewing pattern, Return of Jedi costumes, McCall's, #772 ......**6.00**

Sheet music, Star Wars Theme, 20th-Century Fox **25.00**

Spaceship, Darth Vader's Star Destroyer, diecast, Kenner, 1980, 3½" **35.00**

Spaceship, Imperial Trooper Transporter, Kenner, ca 1979, 10½", M **30.00**

Spaceship, Land Speeder, molded plastic, Kenner, 1978-80, 9½x6", M **20.00**

Spaceship, Rebel Armored Snowspeeder, Kenner, 1980-82, 12½", M **30.00**

Spaceship, Twin Ion Engine Fighter, Kenner, 1978-81, MIB **45.00**

Spaceship, Twin Pod Cloud Car, Kenner, 1980-81, 10x9x3½", M **25.00**

Spaceship, X-Wing Fighter, Kenner, battery operated, ca 1978, EX **25.00**

Standee, C3-PO, color diecut, 20th-Century Fox, 65x42" **175.00**

Statue of Liberty Collectibles

For over one hundred years the Statue of Liberty has been the single object universally identified with our country. Hundreds of companies have adopted the name and symbol to represent their products, and Ms. Liberty's second century began with an outpouring of new high quality representations which accompanied her 1986 restoration. These included items such as ceramic pins, American-made Liberty statues, watches, knives, medals, prints, and scores of other objects adorned with Liberty's likeness.

Because of her wide appeal, so many varied products were made that flea market hunts result in exciting finds. Few collecting fields offer the opportunity for such diversity; some Liberty collectors have chosen to limit their searches to specific areas, such as postcards, medals, or ephemera. Our advisor is Mike Brooks, who is listed in the Directory under California.

Bank, Liberty bust, 1986, 6" ..**10.00**

Biscuit tin, Loose-Wiles, octagonal, EX **40.00**

Candle holder, frosted glass, 10" **35.00**

Cardboard box & contents, Liberty Baking Cups **14.00**

Certificate, donor; Liberty restoration, 1986 ....**5.00**

Clock, Ingraham, Liberty on case, 1885 ....**225.00**

Doorknob, embossed, ca 1890 ..**45.00**

Fob, WWI **17.00**
Game box, Home History, Milton
   Bradley, 1909 ....**15.00**
Handkerchief, silk, w/Allied
   nations' flags, WWI **12.00**
Jar, Liberty Maraschino Cher-
   ries **7.00**
Knife, silver, Woolworth building
   on reverse, 3" **22.00**
Lithograph, Root & Tinker,
   1883 ....**130.00**
Medal, World Liberty Penny,
   Woodrow Wilson on reverse,
   1918, 3" dia **32.00**

Figural lamp with clock face in base, marked Warrtenburg, 14½", $45.00.

Medals, Liberty Centennial, various
   ones, from $5.00 up to **10.00**
Paperweight, round, hand
   painted, The Bartholdi
   Statue, 1880s **125.00**
Penny pipe, clay, w/Liberty trans-
   fer **30.00**
Pin-back button, Liberty Centen-
   nial, ceramic, from $2.00 up
   to **5.00**
Pin-back button, Liberty Loan of
   1917 ....**7.00**
Pin-back button, No Beer, No
   Work **15.00**
Plate, rolled edge, Rowland &
   Marsellus **70.00**
Postcard, hold-to-light, 1903 ..**35.00**
Poster, Lest I Perish, WWI era ..**105.00**
Razor, straight blade, etched Lib-
   erty, Sheffield, ca 1885 ..**75.00**
Ribbon, silk, Paris Exposition,
   1878 ....**80.00**
Stanhope viewer, 1980s **30.00**
Statue, American Committee,
   1886, 6" **100.00**
Statue, gas lamp, 1886, 36" ..**400.00**
Statue, papier-mache, 39½"..**75.00**
Stereo card, Liberty Arm &
   Torch, Centennial Exposi-
   tion, 1876 ....**62.00**
Trade card, Bartholdi Central
   Draft Burner **10.00**
Trade card, mechanical, Eagle
   Pencil Co **50.00**
Tramp art wood carving, 14x
   10" **85.00**
Vase, pressed glass, Liberty sup-
   ports sm bowl & flower holder,
   1900 ....**250.00**
View book, SR Stoddard, 1891 ..**25.00**

Stoneware

   From about 1840 and throughout the next hundred years,
stoneware clay was used to pot
utility wares such as jugs, jars,
churns, and pitchers. Though a

brown Albany slip was applied to some, by far the vast majority was glazed by common salt that was thrown into the kiln and vaporized. Decorations of cobalt were either slip trailed, brushed on, or stenciled; sgraffito (incising) was used on rare occasions. The complexity of the decoration has a great deal of bearing on value, and examples carrying the mark of a short-lived company are often at a premium. Refer to *Collector's Guide to Country Stoneware and Pottery* by Don and Carol Raycraft (Collector Books) for more information.

Jar, flowers brushed on in cobalt, New York state, 1850s, $300.00.

Churn, brushed cobalt fish, ovoid, 16", EX **950.00**

Crock, brushed flower & capacity mark, 1870s, 6-gal **175.00**

Crock, cobalt dragonfly, Lyons Cooperative Pottery Co, 1870s, 3-gal **165.00**

Crock, cobalt floral, 1870s, 4-gal **155.00**

Crock, slip-trailed capacity mark, ca 1880, 2-gal **85.00**

Crock, stenciled Macomb Pottery Co..., molded, Bristol glaze, 3-gal **80.00**

Crock, stenciled maker's mark, Monmouth, molded, Bristol glaze, 3-gal **55.00**

Jar, canning; Hamilton & Jones in cobalt stencil, 9", NM ..**125.00**

Jar, cobalt flower, impressed Peach, handles, ovoid, 12½", EX **500.00**

Jar, cobalt foliage around shoulder, tooling, ovoid, 14", EX ..**450.00**

Jug, brushed cobalt #2, J&S Hart, ovoid, 13" **250.00**

Jug, brushed cobalt waves, 1870s-1880s, 2-gal **185.00**

Jug, cobalt floral & leaves, New York Stoneware Co, 1870s, 2-gal **165.00**

Jug, cobalt flower basket, Ft Edward, repaired, 18" ..**300.00**

Jug, deep cobalt flower, mid-1800s, 2-gal **200.00**

Jug, Ferrand, Williams & Co Wholesale Druggist stencil, 1880s, 2-gal **135.00**

Jug, incised Compliments of WG Ginder..., Albany slip, ca 1900, 5½" **135.00**

Jug, J Dearborn & Co, hairline in handle, 11" **35.00**

Jug, smoked gray salt glaze, minor flakes, 6" **75.00**

Jug, 2-handled, alkaline glaze, 1860s-70s, 3-gal **265.00**

Pitcher, brushed cobalt flower, marked Sipe Nichols & Co, 13", EX **1,000.00**

Pitcher, brushed cobalt highlights at handle, #4, ovoid, 17" **115.00**

Strawberry Shortcake Collectibles

Strawberry Shortcake came onto the market around 1980 with a bang. The line included everything to attract small girls – swimsuits, bed linens, blankets, anklets, underclothing, coats, shoes, sleeping bags, dolls and accessories, games, toys, and delightful items to decorate their rooms. It was short lived, though, lasting only until near the middle of the decade. Our advisor is Geneva Addy; she is listed in the Directory under Iowa.

Blanket	**15.00**
Clock, alarm; Big Ben type	**30.00**
Doll, rag type, 18"	**30.00**
Figurine, Strawberry Shortcake or friends, mini, each	**6.00**
Lamp, figural base, w/printed shade, each	**40.00**
Lamp, plain metal w/Strawberry Shortcake printed shade	**40.00**
Picnic set, snail & lg cart, forms table when upside down, w/ dishes	**20.00**
Pony & cart	**8.00**
Purple Pie Man, plastic, skinny, about 7"	**22.00**
Sheets, regular or twin	**10.00**
Telephone, figural Strawberry Shortcake w/messages, 15"	**35.00**

String Holders

Until the middle of this century, spools of string contained in devices designed for that purpose were a common sight in country stores as well as many other businesses. Early examples of cast iron or wire and those with advertising are the most desirable and valuable, but later figurals of chalkware or ceramics are also quite collectible.

Apple & berries, chalkware ..**22.50**

Ball, nickled brass w/foot, ca 1908	**115.00**
Beehive, cast iron, counter style, 5½x6½", EX	**65.00**
Bird, yellow on green string nest, ceramic	**25.00**
Cat's face, ceramic	**17.50**
Court jester, plaster	**40.00**

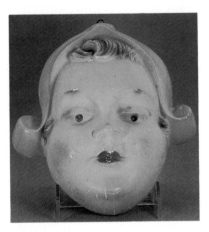

Dutch girl, chalkware, 8", VG paint, $35.00.

Mammy face, chalkware, marked Canada, NM paint	**265.00**
Sailor, eyes to side, w/pipe, chalkware	**35.00**
Strawberry w/face, chalkware, EX	**30.00**
3 Nuns in prayer, chalkware, string through hands	**55.00**

Sunday Funnies

Sunday funnies in color have been issued continuously since 1896. Early comics included The Yellow Kid, Katzenjammer Kids, and Little Nemo. The '30s spawned Buck Rogers, Flash Gordon, Dick Tracy, and Superman. The pages of these and comic book through the '80s are actively collected by a growing number of fans. Our advisor is David H. Begin, who is listed in the Directory under California.

Archie, 1946 ....**8.00**
Betty Boop, 1930s **5.00**
Bringing Up Father, 1918-25 ..**6.00**
Bringing Up Father, 1930s **3.00**
Buck Rogers, #1, 1930 ....**250.00**
Buck Rogers, Fulls, 1930-35 ..**7.00**
Dick Tracy, 1950s **1.00**
Flash Gordon, #1, 1934 ......**300.00**
Flash Gordon, 1934, w/paper
    dolls **25.00**
Flash Gordon, 1935-38 ....**8.00**
Katzenjammer Kids, 1900 ...**10.00**
Katzenjammer Kids, 1920 .....**4.00**
Little Nemo, Fulls, 1905-14 ..**20.00**
Little Orphan Annie, 1920s ...**4.00**
Prince Valiant, Fulls, 1937 ..**100.00**

Prince Valiant, late 1930s, full page, $6.00.

Tarzan, #1, 1930 ....**100.00**
Tarzan, Foster, 1931-37 ....**6.00**
Yellow Kid, 1890s **100.00**

Swanky Swigs

During the 1930s through the 1950s, Kraft cheese products were sometimes packed in glassware tumblers decorated with various animals, flowers, stripes, etc., ranging in size from about 3½" to 4½". Some of the more valuable are the Texas Centennial tumblers; they're usually priced at $20 to $25.

Bird & elephant, red, 3¾" **3.50**
'Bustling Betsy, blue, 3¼" **8.50**
Carnival, yellow, red, green, or
    blue, 3½", each **5.00**
Cat & rabbit, green, 4½" **14.50**
Cornflower, dark blue flowers
    w/green leaves, 3½" **3.00**
Cornflower, red, 3½" **3.00**
Duck & horse, black, 3¾" **3.50**
Forget-Me-Nots, yellow, w/label,
    3½" **8.50**
Jonquil, yellow flowers w/green
    leaves, 3½" **4.50**
Tulips, light blue flowers w/green
    leaves, 3¾" **3.00**
Tulips, red flowers w/green leaves,
    4½" **14.50**
Tulips in pots, green, w/paper
    label, 3½" **8.50**
Tulips in pots, red, 3½" **3.50**
Violets, green leaves, 3¼" **8.50**

Swatch Watches

Swatch watches, one of the hottest new collectibles in the United States, have been around since 1983 when a few nondescript watches were produced. Along the way something happened. They began to show up in unusual colors and original designs and became a sensation in Europe as fashion watches. Recently a Swatch watch brought over $25,000.00 at auction. While this is not typical of Swatch values, it does add to the aura of Swatch, and it seems everyone must own one. Rare Swatches can still be found at garage sales and flea markets. Even the early models are now highly desirable.

Condition is extremely important. To bring the highest price, a watch must be brand new and never worn. While there is some interest in used Swatches, this market is better left to advanced collectors and experienced dealers. All Swatches are dated on the back. The first number is usually the year of manufacture. Example: 5123; the 5 indicates 1985, the 12 the twelfth week of the year, and the 3 the third day of the week. Most Swatches are assigned a model number by the factory. These numbers do not appear on the watch.

Collector's clubs have been organized in many countries; some have as many as 20,000 members. In 1991 the first monthly Swatch magazine hit the stands in Italy, only to be completely sold out in less than one week. Our advisor is Timesavers; see Directory under Illinois. Refer to *Collector's Guide for Swatch Watches* (W.B.S. Marketing) for more information (see California). Values are given for watches mint in box with guarantee papers. Used watches are worth about 50% less.

Antibes, LW 102, 1987 ....**90.00**
Asetra, GK 137, 1991 ....**125.00**
Blue Matic (automatic), SAN 100, 1991 ....**145.00**
Boss, GR 109, 1991 ....**65.00**

Commander, Maxi Swatch, GB 115, 1987 ....**160.00**
Cosmesis, GM 103, 1990 ....**125.00**
Cosmic Encounters, GS 102, 1986 ....**350.00**
Don't Be Too Late, GA 100, 1984 ....**800.00**
Eclipses, BG 128, 1989 ......**175.00**
Engineer, GB 139, 1991 ....**80.00**
First Designer Watch, GB 103, 1983 ....**1,000.00**
Golden Jelly (Swatch collectors special), GZ 115, 1991..**100.00**
Gulp, GG 139, 1991 ....**50.00**
Happy Fish (scuba model), SDN 101, 1991 ....**150.00**
Heartbreak, GX 101, 1988 ...**70.00**
Hollywood Dreams (Christmas special), GZ 116, 1990 ....**1,500.00**
Jelly Fish, GK 100, 1990 .....**75.00**
Kailua Diver, GB 712, 1988 ..**190.00**
Lionheart, LK 102, 1986 ......**40.00**
Mc Intosh, GB 116, 1987 ...**325.00**
Medici's, GB 127, 1989 ....**450.00**
Model Avec Personnages (Keith Haring), GZ 100, 1986 ......**1,600.00**
Nicholette, LB 105, 1985 ...**150.00**
Rave, Elvis Presley illustrated on band, GK 134, 1991 ......**50.00**
Rollerball (quartz chronograph), SCB 107, 1991 ....**125.00**
Ruffled Feathers, GF 100, 1986 ....**100.00**
Sir Limelight (w/diamonds), GB 106, 1987 ....**750.00**
Swatchtable set, 3 pieces (cucumber, pepper, bacon & eggs), 1991 ....**1,250.00**
The Globe, GB 137, 1991 ...**125.00**
Tutti Frutti, GW 109, 1987 ..**70.00**
Valkyrie, LP 101, 1986.........**50.00**
White Night, GW 110, 1989 ..**80.00**

Bondi Beach, Wipeout, GB 714, 1989, Spring/Summer, $310.00 MIB.

Tea Leaf Ironstone

Ironstone decorated with a copper lustre design of bands and leaves became popular in the 1880s. It was produced by potters in both England and America until the early 1900s. See the introduction to Ironstone for information concerning items marked 'Red Cliff.'

Baker, rectangular, Meakin, 8¾x6½" **30.00**

Bone dish, crescent, Meakin, 9⅝x3⅛" **75.00**

Bowl, pie crust edge, 2½x7½" ..**65.00**

Bowl, soup; Lily of the Valley ..**45.00**

Bowl, vegetable; Sunburst, 6-sided, w/lid, Shaw **175.00**

Butter pat, square, Meakin, 2¾" **15.00**

Butter pat, unmarked, English, 2⅞" **12.00**

Creamer, Fish Hook, Meakin, 5x5½" **140.00**

Cup & saucer, straight-sided, Meakin **75.00**

Gravy boat, Adams Microtex, attached underplate, EX ..**95.00**

Mug, Chinese, Shaw **165.00**

Nappy, rectangular, Wilkinson, 5⅝x3⅞" **22.00**

Pitcher, Square Ridged, Wedgwood, 7¾" **145.00**

Plate, Grindley, 9" **22.00**

Platter, rectangular, Meakin, 11x8", EX **37.50**

Sugar bowl, Bamboo, w/lid, Meakin, 6¾" **65.00**

Teapot, Fish Hook, Meakin, 8½" **195.00**

Teapot, Red Cliff **80.00**

Teapots

Tea drinking and the serving of 'afternoon tea' has gained a renewed popularity in recent years, sparking the ever-growing interest in teapots. While the first teapots were manufactured in the late 16th century, early examples (including those from the 1700s and 1800s) are often found in museums or large auction houses.

Almost every pottery and porcelain manufacturer in Europe, Asia, and America has produced teapots. Most collectors start with a general collection of many different teapots until they decide on the specific category that appeals to them. These might include miniatures, doll or toy sets, those made by a certain manufacturer, figurals, or a particular style or type of decoration. Figural teapots are very popular. Many were made in the '50s and '60s in Japan during their reconstruction period for the export market.

Books on teapots in general are not comprehensive. *An Anthology of British Teapots* by Miller and Berthoud is available for $24.95 from John Ives Bookseller, 5 Normanhurst Drive, Twickenham, Middlesex, TW1 1NA, England. This is a coffee table-style book; because of the rate of exchange it's best ordered by charge card. Also available at local bookstores is *The Eccentric Teapot* by Garth Clark for $29.95. Refer to Index for various manufacturer names. For further information our advisor, Tina M. Carter, is listed in the Directory under California. See also Clubs and Newsletters for *Tea Talk*.

British Royal Navy, brown, coralene, rope mark, NM **25.00**

Brown Betty, Ridgeway England, paper label, 2-cup **12.00**

Brass with hand decoration, marked India, 2-cup, $10.00; 1-cup, $7.00.

China, rough surface w/scenes of people, unmarked **10.00**

Cube, Hall, British patent numbers, color other than red or cobalt **18.00**

Cube, Hall, British patent numbers, red or cobalt, each ..**22.00**

Cube, marked Staffordshire England, florals or scrolls, new **16.00**

Ellgreave, marked Div of Wood & Sons England, w/florals ..**22.00**

Ironstone, marked w/wreath, Poland, 6-cup **8.00**

Japan, coralene, gold decor, marked, 6-cup, NM **11.00**

Japan, coralene, raised enamel dots & flowers, 2-cup **8.00**

Japan, majolica, half-circle form, marked **12.00**

Japan, majolica, men at table w/ale, marked **14.00**

Milk glass, unmarked, w/lid, 1¼", +2 cups & saucers **6.00**

Milk glass, unmarked, w/lid, 1¼", NM **4.00**

Moss Rose, electric, marked Japan, 2-cup **14.00**

Moss Rose, marked Made in Japan, w/music box **30.00**

Occupied Japan, floral design, miniature, 1", NM **4.00**

Pottery, gray w/ribbed section, unmarked, 2-cup **8.00**

Ridgeway, brown w/stripes, no mark **9.00**

Souvenir, china w/gold trim, marked Made in Germany, NM **15.00**

Souvenir, marked Made in Japan, miniature, 2" **5.00**

Souvenir, marked Made in Japan, miniature, 2", +cup, saucer & stand **10.00**

Wade, spatter, octagonal, marked, VG **15.00**

Ceramic Figurals

Airplane, SS Tea on side, gold trim, Fitz & Floyd **48.00**

Cat, paw spout, tail handle, marked CMI, Japan **29.00**

Cat, white china, marked China, 2-cup **10.00**

Chef w/bee on nose, Japan ...**35.00**

Cottage Ware, Price Brothers, England, 6½" **50.00**

Duck w/frog on lid **25.00**

Elephant w/howdah, lustreware, Japan **40.00**

Friar, marked w/number, not Goebel **15.00**

Girl, Red Wing **45.00**

German ceramic figural pig, #722 AK on bottom, 7½", $65.00.

quite collectible. The 'classic' bear is one made of mohair, straw stuffed, fully jointed, with long curving arms tapering at the paw and extending to the knees. He has very long skinny feet, felt pads on all paws, embroidered claws, a triangular, proportionately small head, a long pointed snout, embroidered nose and mouth, and a hump at the back of his neck. Refer to *Teddy Bears and Steiff Animals* by Margaret Fox Mandel (Collector Books) for more information.

Kilban Cat, white tuxedo, Sigma **85.00**
Lady's head, w/black hat lid, marked Japan **15.00**
Mickey Mouse, Donald Duck, Treasure Craft, 6-cup **18.00**
Miss Cutie Pie, blue, pink, or yellow, A3506/B1-Japan, Napco, each **35.00**
Orange w/face, Florida, no mark, 2-cup **10.00**
Santa, holding cup, marked Taiwan, 6-cup **12.00**
Tom cat w/tie, Takahashi, Japan **45.00**
Tomato w/face, marked Hand-Painted Japan **17.00**
Witch on broom **35.00**

Teddy Bears and Related Collectibles

Only teddies made before the 1940s can be considered bona fide antiques, though character bears from more recent years are also

English (possibly Chiltern), mohair with excelsior and kapok stuffing, four claws stitched to velveteen pads, ca 1940s, 16", $225.00.

Bear, beige mohair, brown floss nose/mouth, jointed, 1960s, Steiff, 6" **200.00**
Bear, blue mohair, red open mouth, jointed, growler, Fechter, 13½" **200.00**
Bear, cotton plush, mohair pads & ears, waste cotton stuffed, 1950s, 13" **25.00**
Bear, long curly mohair, 1950s, Zotty, 6½" **250.00**
Bear, mohair, kapok body, unjointed, lg feet, 1960s, Chiltern, 26" **150.00**

Bear, mohair, scoop shovel snout, long toes, 1950s, Steiff, 5½" **200.00**

Bear, pink mohair, fully jointed, squeaker, Grisly logo, 1960s, 15" **140.00**

Bear, white mohair, fully jointed, growler, 1940s, Farnell, 19", EX **250.00**

Bear, white sheepskin, red leather pads, 1950s, Schenker, Austria, 13" **125.00**

Bear, white woolly plush, floss nose & mouth, fully jointed, 1920s, 12" **135.00**

Bear, wooly mohair, kapok stuffed, glass eyes, 1940s, 9½" **80.00**

Book, Paddington's Garden, 1st US ed, 1973, 32-pg, EX ..**15.00**

Book, The Friendly Bear, Robert Bright, 1st edition, 1957, VG **20.00**

Christmas ornament, German glass, figural, early 1900s, 3" **100.00**

Hankie, cotton, lg bear in 1 corner, sm bear in other 3, 1930s-40s **10.00**

Plate, ABC; dressed-up bears in center, semiporcelain, Smith-Phillips, 7" **50.00**

Postcard, bear in nightgown w/candle, Good Night, copyright 1907, M **18.00**

Reamer, milk glass, enamel bear w/balloons, Fenton Glass Co, sm **190.00**

Snow baby, black reclining bear, Made in Japan, 3½" long ..**65.00**

Tea set, child's, Sports Minded Bears decals, Japan, set for 6 ....**325.00**

The Three Stooges

A wide range of Three Stooges merchandise has been produced honoring the comedy trio of Moe, Larry, and Curly over the last six decades. Starting with a set of beautifully crafted hand puppets in 1935 through a set of PVC Christmas ornaments in 1991, the Stooges' likenesses can be found on a wide array of products. Such items include bubble gum cards, finger puppets, comic books, records, beanies, school bags, flicker rings, vinyl punching bags, coloring books, 8mm films, and toys. For further information we recommend contacting Soitenly Stooges Inc.; they are listed in the Directory under Illinois.

Coloring book, 1985, M **6.00**

Comic book, Gold Key, #14, EX **10.00**

Comic book, Gold Key, #18, EX **6.00**

Doll, plush, Collins Co, 1982, 12", M on card, set of 3 ....**09**

Film, 16mm, 1940s or 50s, EX in original box **40.00**

Film, 8mm, 1960s, EX in original box **35.00**

Flicker sheet, portrait w/name, 4 per sheet, uncut **20.00**

Hand puppet, Larry, ca 1950, EX **15.00**

Insert card, Snow White & Stooges, 1961, 14x36" ...**50.00**

Lobby card, Outlaws Is Coming, color, 1965, set of 8 ....**20.00**

Poster, cereal premium, 1977, 11x14" **5.00**

Poster, Go Around the World in a Daze, 1964, 41x27" **55.00**

Punch-out book, 1962, M ...**150.00**

Record, ...Come to Your House To..., original sleeve **25.00**

Record, Sing Happy Yuletide Songs, EX in picture sleeve **20.00**

Sticker, cartoon art, 1980, M in original package **1.50**

Toy watch, non-mechanical, Occupied Japan, 1947 ....**35.00**

Tiffin Glass

Founded in 1887 in Tiffin, Ohio, the Tiffin Glass Company was one of several companies comprising the U.S. Glass Company. They made tablewares and decorative items. They are most famous for their black satin glass, which they made during the 1920s. U.S. Glass was sold in 1959; in 1962 the plant closed for a short time but soon reopened as the Tiffin Art Glass Company. Their main products were tableware, stemware, and various types of decorative items.

Byzantine, cordial **35.00**
Byzantine, goblet, water **25.00**
Byzantine, tumbler, iced tea ..**22.50**
Cadena, plate, yellow, 9¼" ...**37.50**
Camelot, sherbet **7.50**
Cerice, bud vase, 10½" **45.00**
Cerice, creamer, footed **25.00**
Cerice, plate, 12" **45.00**
Cherokee Rose, bud vase, 11"..**45.00**
Cherokee Rose, candlesticks, #5902, 2-light, pr **70.00**
Cherokee Rose, centerpiece bowl, 13" **65.00**
Cherokee Rose, cocktail **20.00**
Cherokee Rose, creamer **22.50**
Cherokee Rose, sherbet, tall ..**17.50**
Classic, champagne **24.00**
Classic, cocktail **35.00**
Classic, goblet, water **25.00**
Classic, parfait **45.00**
Elyse, wine **35.00**
Empress, vase, smoke & crystal, 11¾" **150.00**
Fairfax, goblet, iced tea; platinum trim **15.00**
Fairfax, plate, platinum trim, 8" **10.00**

Fairfax, sherbet, platinum trim, tall **12.00**
Flanders, claret, pink **75.00**
Flanders, plate, pink, 8" **20.00**
Flanders, tumbler, iced tea ..**26.00**
Flanders, wine **28.00**
Flying Nun, champagne **34.00**
Fuchsia, cocktail **25.00**
Fuchsia, cordial **45.00**
Fuchsia, cup **37.50**
Fuchsia, goblet, water **28.00**
Fuchsia, mayonnaise, w/liner ..**40.00**
Heirloom, goblet, water **10.00**
Huntington, sherbet, tall **12.50**
Julia, plate, amber, 10¼" **18.00**
June Beau, champagne **12.00**
June Beau, goblet, water; 8" ..**17.00**
June Night, bowl, salad; 7" ..**30.00**
June Night, tumbler, iced tea; footed **30.00**
June Night, tumbler, juice; 5-oz **20.00**
Juno, goblet, water; green pastel **20.00**
Midnight Mist, wine **20.00**
Persian Pheasant, cocktail ..**20.00**
Persian Pheasant, cordial **40.00**
Persian Pheasant, wine **35.00**
Princess, vase, 4" **22.50**
Rambler Rose, goblet, water ..**23.00**
Rambler Rose, sherbet **20.00**
Rambler Rose, tumbler, iced tea **23.00**
Riviera, goblet, water **20.00**
Riviera, wine **24.00**
Roselyn, plate, yellow, 8" **10.00**
Sylvan, cup & saucer, pink ..**35.00**
Twilight, bonbon, heart shape, 7" **60.00**
Twilight, flower arranger **95.00**
Wisteria, champagne **15.00**
Wisteria, plate, 8" **15.00**
Wisteria, tumbler, juice **25.00**

Tobacciana

Now gone the way of the barber shop and the ice cream parlor, the cigar store with its carved wooden Indian at the door and the aroma of fine tobacco in the air is no more. But the clever figural cigar cutters, the hand-carved Meerschaum pipes, the cigar molds, and humidors are still enjoyed as reminders of our country's younger days and for the workmanship of long-ago craftsmen.

Cigar holder, meerschaum, figural rabbit atop, amber stem, 3¼" **150.00**
Cutter, cigar; antler handle, German manufacturer, 9" ...**65.00**
Cutter, cigar; brass, Patented March 28, 1916, 1½" **25.00**
Cutter, plug; Prize Cutter by S Lee, w/cork former **60.00**
Match safe, Climax Cut Plug, tin, EX **48.50**
Match safe, San Felice Cigars, M **125.00**
Paperweight, Honest Cut Plug Tobacco, glass, EX **75.00**
Pipe, meerschaum, carved horse, in leather case, EX **110.00**
Pipe, meerschaum, nude lady, EX, +case **225.00**

Pipe, wolf's head, detailed carving, amber stem, 7" **300.00**

Tools

When considering the construction of early tools, one must admire the hand-shaped wood, the smithy-wrought iron, and the tooled leather. Even factory-made tools from the late 1800s required a good deal of hand finishing. Most desirable to tool collectors are those with the touch mark of the craftsman or early examples marked by the manufacturer. Value is determined by scarcity, condition, usefullness, and workmanship.

Auger, double twist bit, wood T-handle, 20½" **10.00**
Awl, leather; Myers Famous Lock Stitch, 1936, NM in box ..**15.00**
Axe, hewing; marked Wm Beatty & S/Cast Steel/Chester, 9x9", G **16.00**
Bunion stretcher, pliers type, marked Lightning, Fulton IL, 16½" **20.00**

Meerschaum pipe with face of bearded man, NM in original case, $125.00.

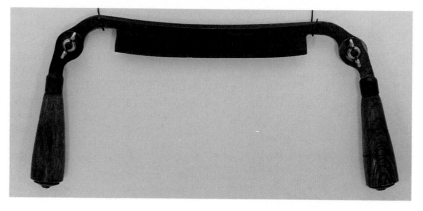

Draw knife, folding handles, 8" blade, $26.00.

Cornhusking peg, hand-forged steel, old leather strap, 4½" **5.00**

Divider, marked GWS, curly maple, age crack, 34" ..**185.00**

Drill, hand; cast iron, wood handles, Miller Falls Co #980, 15", G **14.00**

Gauge, marking; maple, oak thumbscrew, uncalibrated, unmarked, 10½" **4.50**

Hammer, tack; CS Osborne & Co #4, rosewood handle, 11", EX **25.00**

Hook, butcher's; stirrup-type handle, 6¼" **6.00**

Ice tongs, double-hinged wrought iron, 13", EX **26.00**

Knife, farrier's; wood handle, marked Burdizzo, Made in Italy **8.50**

Pincers, blacksmith's; hand-wrought, 10¾" **10.00**

Plane, beading; Bleson & Wood, Watertown NY, VG **25.00**

Rule, Lufkin #2072, 3-fold w/level, NM **145.00**

Slide rule, brass-framed indicator w/plastic viewer, Peru IN, VG **7.50**

Soldering iron, hand-forged iron rod holds 4-sided copper head, 12" **22.50**

Sprayer, brass & copper, Blizzard, Made by DB Smith, wood handle, G **25.00**

Wrench, auto; marked Ford in script & M in circle, 10", VG **5.00**

Wrench, pipe; Stillson & Walworth Mfg Co, ca 1920, 7", VG **6.50**

Toothpick Holders

Toothpick holders have been made in hundreds of patterns, in art glass, pattern glass, opalescent, and translucent glass of many colors, in novelty designs and figural forms. Today they are all popular collectibles, many relatively easy to find and usually affordable.

Bassettown **45.00**

Box-in-Box, green w/gold **30.00**

Bulging Loops, green **35.00**

Bulging Loops, green opaque ..**55.00**

Champion **28.00**

Chrysanthemum Leaf Swirl, clear w/gold **95.00**

Chute & Ladders **22.00**

Colorado, green w/gold **45.00**

Cordova, green **27.50**

Scalloped Panel, green **35.00**
Scalloped Swirl, ruby stained ..**55.00**
Scroll w/Cane Band, clear w/ruby
 stain **85.00**
Star in Bull's Eye, gold trim ..**30.00**
States **45.00**
Sunflower Patch **55.00**
Swirl & Panel **32.50**
Texas Star **55.00**
Thousand Eye, amber **25.00**
Tiny Thumbprint, custard ...**55.00**
West Virginia Optic, green ..**35.00**
Wisconsin, pink opalescent ..**55.00**
Wreath & Shell, vaseline opales-
 cent **200.00**
X-Ray, green w/gold **45.00**

Daisy and Button, amber, silverplated rim, 2½", $25.00.

Cornell, green **45.00**
Creased Bale, pink **50.00**
Daisy & Button w/V Ornament,
 blue **45.00**
Dolphin, amber **90.00**
Double Ring Panel, rose **40.00**
Flower & Pleat, amber stain-
 ed **110.00**
Gaelic, clear w/gold **32.00**
Geneva, custard **135.00**
Georgia Gem **22.00**
Horseshoe & Clover, milk glass ..**20.00**
Iris w/Meander, green opales-
 cent **45.00**
Jefferson Optic, blue, souvenir ..**55.00**
Ladders w/Diamonds **30.00**
Mardi Gras **45.00**
Michigan **32.00**
Minnesota **32.00**
New Jersey **45.00**
Palm Leaf, green opaque **95.00**
Pansy, blue **45.00**
Pleating, ruby stained **30.00**
Punty Band, custard, souvenir ..**45.00**
Quartered Block **45.00**
Reverse Swirl, vaseline opales-
 cent **75.00**
Rising Sun **35.00**

Toys

Toy collecting is a very popular hobby, and if purchases are wisely made, there is good potential for investment. Toys from the 1800s are rarely if ever found in mint condition but should at least be working and have all their original parts. Toys manufactured in the 20th century are evaluated more critically. Compared to one in excellent condition, original box intact, even a slightly damaged toy may be worth only about half price. Character-related toys, space toys, toy trains, and toys from the sixties are among the more desirable. Several good books are available, if you want more information: *Modern Toys, American Toys 1930 to 1980,* by Linda Baker (Collector Books); *Collectible Male Action Figures* by Paris and Susan Manos (Collector book), *Collector's Guide to Tootsietoys* by David E. Richter (Collector Books); *Toys, Antique and Collectible,* and *Character Toys and Collectibles* by David Longest (Collector Books); *Collecting Toys*

Soldiers, Collecting Toy Trains, and *Collecting Toys,* by Richard O'Brien (Books Americana). See also Character Collectibles; Star Trek; Star Wars.

Battery Operated

Most of the battery-operated toys made from the forties through the sixties were made in Japan, even though some were distributed by American companies such as Linemar and Cragstan, who often sold them under their own names. Because of their complex mechanisms, few survive. Condition is very important in evaluating a battery-op, and the more complex their movements, the more they're worth.

Acro, Chimp Porter, plush & vinyl, MIB **125.00**
Alps, Bubble Blowing Monkey, 10½", MIB **180.00**
Alps, Busy Housekeeper Bear, plush, 1950s, 9", MIB ..**320.00**
Alps, Fishing Polar Bear, EX **180.00**
Alps, Frankie Roller Skating Monkey, remote control, 12", MIB **250.00**
Alps, Happy Fiddler Clown, tin w/fabric clothes, 10", EX **315.00**
Alps, Happy Santa, plays trap drum set, 9", MIB **250.00**
Alps, Hooty the Happy Owl, hoots & flaps, remote control, 9", EX **100.00**
Cragstan, DC-7, 19", MIB ..**350.00**
Japan, Barney Bear Drummer, tin & plastic, remote control, 11", EX **180.00**
Japan, Cockadoodledoo Rooster, walks & crows, 7", EX ..**120.00**
Japan, Jolly Pianist, plush dog in red vest, 8", EX **150.00**

Japan, Peppy Puppy, plush, remote control, 9", MIB **125.00**
Linemar, Crawling Baby, celluloid, fabric clothing, 10", MIB **125.00**
Linemar, Sleeping Baby Bear, 8", EX **300.00**
Linemar, Spanking Bear, mama spanks baby bear, 1950s, 9", MIB **435.00**
Mego, Chee Chee Chihuahua, plush, remote control, 8", EX **45.00**
Sunrise, Golden Locomotive, tin, bump & go, EX **45.00**

Breyer Animals

Breyer collecting has grown in popularity throughout the years. The beautiful and strikingly detailed models remain as well crafted and as lifelike as ever; they've been produced since the early 1950s and are still being made today. The horse models dominate the Breyer collection, however cattle, dogs, cats, farm animals, and wildlife are also included. Condition and rarity are the most important factors to consider when evaluating the models, but supply and demand are very important as well. A common model's price does not come close to the price of a rare model. Our advisor is Terri Mardis-Ivers, who is listed in the Directory under Oklahoma.

Adbullah Famous Takehner, 1989 Limited Edition #817, MIB **34.00**
American Indian Pony #710, 1989, MIB **34.00**
Appaloosa Running Stallion #210, NM **19.00**
Appaloosa Stock Horse #232, EX **16.00**

Breyer, Palomino, 9½", $15.00; fighting white stallion, 5", $20.00.

Balking Mule, dark brown w/halter, EX **75.00**
Bassett Hound, EX **15.00**
Black Angus Bull, 5½x10", EX **26.00**
Black Tennessee Walker Stallion #60, EX **23.00**
Buckskin Quarter Horse Gelding, G **15.00**
Cinnamon Baby Bear, EX **10.00**
Clydesdale Dapple Gray #82 Glossy Stallion, EX **50.00**
Elk Bull, 1987, MIB **34.00**
Family Arabian Mare, woodgrain, NM **35.00**
Family Stallion #4, glossy white, EX **20.00**
Fighting Stallion, woodgrain, NM **50.00**
Poodle, silver, EX **35.00**
Red Roan Running Stallion, EX **75.00**
Smokey the Cow Horse #69, EX **36.00**
Spanish Fighting Bull, EX ..**43.00**
Texas Longhorn Steer, EX ...**40.00**
Western horse, black w/snap-on saddle, lg, EX **50.00**
Western horse clock, battery operated, NM **50.00**
Western pony, black or white, w/saddle, sm, EX **25.00**
Western pony, Dodge City KS on sticker on rump, w/saddle, sm, EX **35.00**

Dakin

Dakin produced both plush and vinyl figures from the '60s to the '70s; in the '80s they came out with a line of Warner Brothers characters made of plush. These are the collectible ones, though they are still producing plush animals. Some of the harder-to-find characters are pricey, but you can usually get a common one for under $40.00, mint in the package. Unpackaged examples in excellent condition will be worth half as much at best. Our figures are vinyl unless noted plush.

Dakin, Speedy Gonzales, vinyl with cloth and felt clothing, 1968, 7½", M, $30.00.

Bambi, EX **22.00**
Bugs Bunny, in Uncle Sam outfit, 1975, EX **28.00**
Bugs Bunny, jointed, 10½", EX ..**25.00**
Cool Cat, EX **32.50**
Daffy Duck, 1975, 7", EX.......**10.00**
Deputy Dawg, 1976, MIB **50.00**
Fred Flintstone, complete clothes, EX **28.00**

Fred Flintstone, M in NM package **45.00**
Goofy Grams (Houston Astros mascot), 1971, w/tag, EX, scarce **135.00**
Merlin the Magic Mouse, 1970, 8", NM **25.00**
Olive Oyl, 10", w/tag, M **35.00**
Pebbles, w/original tag, VG ..**22.50**
Pink Panther, 1971, MIB **42.00**
Porky Pig, 1968, w/tag, NM..**25.00**
Road Runner, 1968, w/original tag, 7", M **25.00**
Smokey Bear, 1983, w/tags, MIB **60.00**
Sylvester the Cat, 1969, w/ whiskers, EX **20.00**
Tweety, 1969, 7½", EX **20.00**
Wile E Coyote, finger puppet, 1970s, M in package **22.50**
Wile E Coyote, jointed, 1968, 7", M **25.00**
Wile E Coyote, 1968, w/tag, 12", EX **22.50**
Wile E Coyote, 1969, 10", M in bag **45.00**
Woodsey Owl, w/painted eyes, MIB **65.00**
Yogi Bear, 1968, 8", M in bag ..**50.00**
Yosemite Sam, vinyl w/fuzzy beard & removable hat, 1968, 7", M **30.00**

Diecast

Probably the three most collected diecasts are the Lesneys (Matchbox), Corgi, and Dinky. Matchbox toys are still readily available at flea markets and garage sales. Corgi toys can still be found occassionally while Dinky toys are not often seen but certainly well worth the search! Of the three mentioned, Dinky toys are the oldest. Production started in 1933 and ceased, at least in Great Britain, in 1979. Corgi toys are the newcomers, having been made since 1956. Of these three companies, they are the only one still producing toys in Great Britain. Lesney Toys started the Matchbox series in 1953. In 1969 the Matchbox Superfast line of toys was introduced. It was Lesney's attempt to compete with a new market entry – the Hot Wheels line by Mattel. Superfast models had wider tires and much thinner axles. At this time Lesney also stared to put dates on the baseplates of their toy cars. Superfast vehicles are commonly found and much more readily available than the 'regular wheels' preceeding them. Some of the models known as regular wheels have been reissued as Superfast editions.

In 1968 Mattel introduced the Hot Wheels line to the market. Most of its early issues were 'muscle cars' such as Camaros, Firebirds, Barracudas, Chargers, Mustangs, etc. The first few years were known as 'redlines' because the sidewalls of the tires had a red line around them similar to a whitewall tire. These are highly collectible at present but hard to find in good condition – being most often found with missing hoods and bent axles.

Another popular collectible diecast is the Tootsietoy. The Tootsietoy name was first used in the 1920s by Dowst & Company of Chicago. The majority of the models issued from the 1940s through the 1960s were in either a 3", 4", or 6" series. The detailing on most Tootsietoys is not as good as that of the Matchbox, Corgi, or Dinky toys, but they are affordable and very popular among collectors.

Years of production are approximate. Values listed are for

examples in very good or better
condition. Our advisor is Mark
Giles, who is listed in the Directory under Nebraska.

Corgi, #229, Chevrolet Corvair,
1961-1966 ....**58.00**
Corgi, #263, Rambler Marlin,
1966-1969 ....**58.00**
Corgi, #266, Chitty Chitty Bang
Bang, 1968-1972 ....**220.00**
Corgi, #276, Oldsmobile Toronado,
1968-1970 ....**60.00**
Corgi, #320, The Saints Jaguar,
1978-1981 ....**30.00**
Corgi, #356, VW Army Bus, 1964-
1966 ....**74.00**
Corgi, #416, Buick Police Car,
1977-1978 ....**31.00**
Corgi, #445, Plymouth Station-
wagon, 1963-1965 ....**57.00**

**Dinky baggage hauler, 4½", EX,
$50.00.**

Dinky, #114, Triumph Spitfire
Convertible, 1963-1970..**70.00**
Dinky, #131, Cadillac Eldorado
Convertible, 1956-1962 ..**82.00**
Dinky, #170, 1949 Ford 4-Door,
1954-1959 ....**66.00**
Dinky, #191, 1958 Dodge 4-Door,
1959-1964 ....**100.00**
Dinky, #212, Ford Cortina Rally
Car, 1967-1969 ....**49.00**
Dinky, #449, 1960 Chevy El
Camino, 1961-1968 ....**60.00**
Dinky, #532, 1958 Lincoln Pre-
miere, 1959-1965 ....**82.00**
Matchbox, Regular Wheels, #1-E,
Mercedes Truck, 1968 ...**10.00**

**Matchbox #8 caterpillar tractor,
1955, NM, $35.00.**

Matchbox, Regular Wheels, #16-
C, Scammel Dump Truck/
Snowplow, 1961 ....**22.00**
Matchbox, Regular Wheels, #17-D,
Horse Box Truck, 1969 ....**7.00**
Matchbox, Regular Wheels, #19-D,
Lotus Racing Car, 1965 ..**17.00**
Matchbox, Regular Wheels, #21-
D, Foden Concrete Truck,
1969 ....**9.00**
Matchbox, Regular Wheels, #23-
C, House Trailer Caravan,
1967 ....**17.00**
Matchbox, Regular Wheels, #36-C,
Opel Diplomat, 1966 .....**13.00**
Matchbox, Regular Wheels, #40-B,
Leyland Royal Tiger Coach,
1961 ....**18.00**
Matchbox, Regular Wheels, #41-
C, Ford GT 40, 1965 ......**13.00**
Matchbox, Regular Wheels, #57-
C, Land Rover Fire Truck,
1966 ....**20.00**
Matchbox, Regular Wheels, #6-D,
Ford Pickup, 1969 ....**8.00**
Matchbox, Regular Wheels,
#62-C, Mercury Cougar,
1969 ....**13.00**
Matchbox, Regular Wheels, #70-
B, Atkinson Grit Spreader,
1965 ....**12.00**
Matchbox, Regular Wheels, #71-
B, Jeep Gladiator Pickup,
1964 ....**16.00**
Matchbox, Regular Wheels, #8-E,
Ford Mustang, 1966 ......**10.00**
Matchbox, Superfast, #1-H, Dodge
Challenger, 1976 ....**8.00**

Matchbox, Superfast, #12-G, Citroen GX, 1979 ....**6.00**

Matchbox, Superfast, #13-F, Baja Dune Buggy, 1971 ....**8.00**

Matchbox, Superfast, #2-G, Hovercraft, 1976 ....**9.00**

Matchbox, Superfast, #22-E, Blaze Buster, 1975 ....**7.00**

Matchbox, Superfast, #34-F, Vantastic, 1975 ....**9.00**

Matchbox, Superfast, #46-E, Stretcha Fetcha, 1972 .....**7.00**

Matchbox, Superfast, #5-E, Lotus Europa, 1969 ....**10.00**

Matchbox, Superfast, #5-F, Seafire Boat, 1975 ....**6.00**

Matchbox, Superfast, #6-F, Mercedes 350 SL, 1973 ....**6.00**

Matchbox, Superfast, #7-F, VW Golf, 1976 ....**6.00**

Mattel, Hot Wheels, Classic Nomad, 1970 ....**37.00**

Mattel, Hot Wheels, Custom AMX, 1969 ....**33.00**

Mattel, Hot Wheels, Custom Barracuda, 1968 ....**42.00**

Mattel, Hot Wheels, Custom Cougar, 1968 ....**35.00**

Mattel, Hot Wheels, Custom Firebird, 1968 ....**34.00**

Mattel, Hot Wheels, Custom VW, 1968 ....**27.00**

Tootsietoy, 3", American LaFrance Pumper, 1954 ....**14.00**

Tootsietoy, 3", Ford Country Sedan Station Wagon, 1960 ....**13.00**

Tootsietoy, 3", Ford Custom 4-Door Sedan, 1949 ....**14.00**

Tootsietoy, 3", Plymouth Belvedere, 1957 ....**11.00**

Tootsietoy, 3", Volkswagon Bug, 1960 ....**6.00**

Tootsietoy, 4", Chevrolet Cameo Pickup, 1956 ....**20.00**

Tootsietoy, 4", Ford Ranch Wagon, 1954 ....**20.00**

Tootsietoy, 6", International K-5 Stake Truck, 1940 ....**18.00**

Tootsietoy, 6", Mack L-Line Tow Truck, 1947 ....**14.00**

Fisher-Price

Allie Gator, #653, VG **45.00**

Bouncing Bunny Cart, #307, VG **20.00**

Buzzy Bee, #325, pull toy, has plastic wings, 1950-56, VG **18.00**

Chick Basket Cart, #302, VG ..**20.00**

Ducky Cart, #11, EX **50.00**

Looky Chug-Chug, #161, w/tender, VG **75.00**

Molly Moo Coo, #132, VG **10.00**

Mother Goose, #164, VG **25.00**

Musical Sweeper, #100, metal top, wooden wheels & handle, 1950-52, VG **75.00**

Nifty Station Wagon, #234, w/roof & 4 figures, VG **100.00**

Nosey Pup, #445, VG **20.00**

Picnic Basket, #677, 1975-79, complete **12.50**

Fisher Price, #739 Poodle Zilo, 8½x7¾", VG, $90.00.

Pony Chime, #132, VG **30.00**

Pop-Up Pluto, Pluto on paddle, WD Enterprises **135.00**

Pudgy Pig, #478, VG **20.00**

Puffy Engine, #444, EX **40.00**

Smokie Engine, #642, VG **20.00**

Tailspin Tabby, #455, VG **85.00**

Toy Wagon, #131, VG **125.00**

Friction

Animal Satellite, Japan, Sputnik
   type, dog inside, 1950s, 4",
   EX **60.00**
B-29 Bomber, Japan, tin, 1950s,
   19", EX **150.00**
Cadillac Police Car, Japan, tin,
   1950s, 5" long, EX **35.00**
Car & Trailer, Japan, blue & silver,
   tin, 1950s, 16", EX **125.00**
Garage Truck, Japan, tin, 5" lever
   action, 1950s, EX **25.00**
Greyhound Bus, metal, 1960s, 10"
   long, M **60.00**
Jeep, Japan, 1960s, 9", EX ..**15.00**
Passenger Ship, Japan, tin,
   1950s, 6", MIB **135.00**
Playtime Airlines, airplane,
   Linemar, tin, 7" w/4 props,
   EX **70.00**
Power Shovel Truck, Linemar, tin,
   1950s, 11", EX **60.00**

Guns

Airborne Commando Burp Gun,
   plastic, Marx, 1950s, 14"
   long, EX **40.00**
Bull Dog cap pistol, Hubley, cast
   iron, 1935, 6¼" long, EX .**40.00**
Cap pistol, Hubley, 2 guns in 1,
   diecast, twist-off barrels,
   MIB **95.00**
Cork-popper pistol, Wyandotte,
   spur trigger, EX **25.00**
Daisy Targeteer air pistol, ca
   1947, M **40.00**
Detective Snub-Nose Special, die-
   cast, Marx, 1950s, EX ...**75.00**
Dyna-Mite derringer, diecast,
   Nichols, 3½", M on card ..**50.00**
G-Man, Linemar, mechanical, tin,
   4" long, MIB **75.00**
Lone Ranger cap pistol, Kilgore,
   cast iron, 1938, 8½", VG ..**75.00**
Pirate Pistol, Hubley, MIB ...**90.00**
Scout cap pistol, Stevens, cast
   iron, 1940, 6⅛", VG **45.00**

Six Shooter cap pistol, Kilgore,
   cast iron, 1935, 6½", EX ..**55.00**
Stallion, diecast, 1950s, 7", w/tag
   & box of caps, M **75.00**

Hartland Figures

Hartland Plastics Inc. was
formed in Hartland, Wisconsin, in
the 1950s. The durable material
used to make the figures was virgin acetate. Figures were hand
painted with an eye for detail.
The Western and Historic Horse-
men, Miniature Western Series,
Authentic Scale Model Horses,
Famous Gunfighter Series, and
the Harland Sports Series of
Famous Baseball Stars were a
symbol of the fine workmanship
that was a fact of life in the
1950s. Football and bowling figures and religious statues were
also made. Our advisor is Terri
Mardis-Ivers, who is listed in the
Directory under Oklahoma.

Annie Oakley & Palomino, w/sad-
   dle, hat & gun, EX **175.00**
Babe Ruth, bat missing, yellowed,
   EX **175.00**
Bret Maverick, w/hat & guns,
   EX **170.00**
Bret Maverick & horse, w/saddle,
   hat & guns, EX **300.00**
Buffalo Bill & horse, w/US Mail
   saddle, hat & guns, EX ..**245.00**
Champ Cowboy & black horse, w/
   red saddle & hat, EX **160.00**
Champ Cowgirl, w/red shirt &
   white pantskirt, missing hat
   & gun, NM **40.00**
Cochise & semirearing black &
   white paint horse, w/saddle,
   NM **100.00**
Dale Evans & Buttermilk, com-
   plete, EX **150.00**
Dick Groat (baseball figure),
   M **900.00**

Hartland, Tonto on Scout, large size, EX, $70.00. (With accessories, NM, $115.00.)

General Custer & Palomino, w/ flag, hat, saddle & sword, complete, EX **185.00**

Horse, w/molded-on saddle & bridle, 6¼", EX **15.00**

Lawman Gunfighter, w/hat & guns, complete, EX **140.00**

Little League bat boy, 4", M ..**230.00**

Mickey Mantle, New York Yankees, EX **250.00**

Rebel & horse, complete, EX ..**350.00**

Swissco Musical Shrine w/Rosary & Glowing Light, wind-up, incomplete **50.00**

Willie Mays, NM **240.00**

Wyatt Earp & horse, w/saddle, hat, & guns, NM **95.00**

Hasbro

Digger the Dog, pull toy, plastic, 1974-80, M **4.00**

Popeye Gum Machine Bank, plastic w/glued-on paper eye, 1968-75, M **10.00**

Ricochet Racers, cars release when trigger is pulled, ca 1974, M **20.00**

Scooter the Tooter, plastic clown w/vinyl arms, 1980-present, M **4.00**

Squirt the Animals, water target game, 1978-present, M ...**4.00**

Weebles Ghost Van, ghost & labels glow in the dark, ca 1977, M **5.00**

Weebles Haunted House, hinged, ca 1976, complete, M **15.00**

Weebles Treasure Island, ca 1975, complete, M **20.00**

Weebles Tumblin' Funhouse, complete, M **12.00**

Weebles Wigwam, ca 1975, complete, M **8.00**

Ideal

Carpet Sweeper, brittle plastic, roller underneath, early 1950s, M **12.00**

Delivery Van, brittle plastic, rubber wheels marked, 1950, M ..**15.00**

Dishwasher, wind-up, plastic hose, lift-out basket, & dishes, 1950, EX **20.00**

Mr Machine, plastic wind-up, bellows-operated whistling tune, 1977, M **10.00**

Mr Rogers Neighborhood Hand Puppets, stuffed cloth, 1977, M, each **5.00**

Pecking Chicken, brittle plastic, chicken pecks food from pan, 1950, M **15.00**

Phantom Raider, plastic, battery operated, ca 1964, complete, M **85.00**

Powermite Workbench, battery operated, ca 1969, complete, M **30.00**

Scoop Loader, plastic w/rubber tires, working scoop, 1950, M **15.00**

Super City Skyscraper Building set, ca 1968, complete ...**20.00**

Tea set, red marbled plastic, ca 1950, complete, set of 4 .**25.00**

United States Ship, inflatable vinyl, smokestacks squeak, 1950, M **12.00**

US Marine Air Sea Rescue Plane, plastic wind-up, 1960s, 10" long, EX **35.00**

Male Action Figures and Accessories

Accessories, Action Man Bunk Bed, 1970s, M in package, minimum value **25.00**

Accessories, Astronaut Suit, 1960s, M in package **30.00**

Accessories, Combat Field Pack, #7502, 1960s, M in package **50.00**

Accessories, Communications Flag Set, #7704, 1960s, minimum value **90.00**

Accessories, Field Pack, 1960s, M in package **60.00**

Adventure Team Membership Kit, 1970-76, complete, M **35.00**

Book & record set, Secret of Mummy's Tomb, '70s, sm, minimum value **10.00**

Canteen, 1960s, child size, minimum value **15.00**

Doll, GI Joe Man of Action, 1970-76, M **125.00**

Doll, Russian Infantry Man, 1966, M in package **75.00**

Doll, Super Joe, 1977, 8¼", M ..**35.00**

GI Joe Electric Drawing Set, #8266, 1960s, minimum value **25.00**

Helicopter, Adventure Team Search for Stolen Idol, '70s, minimum value **250.00**

Official Membership Pack, complete, ca 1966, M **40.00**

Outfit, Action Man British Infantryman, 1970s, M, minimum value **50.00**

Outfit, Action Man Palitory Frogman, 1970s, M, minimum value **90.00**

Six Million Dollar Man, bionic arm, Kenner, 1975, 13", VG, $8.00.

Outfit, Adventure Team Hidden Treasure, '70s, M on card ..**8.00**

Outfit, Super Joe Emergency Rescue, 1977, M on card **15.00**

Pencil box, Hasbro, color label on plastic **30.00**

Playset, Adventures of GI Joe Jungle Explorer, '60s, MIB ..**250.00**

Playset, Adventures of GI Joe Underwater Diver, 1960s, M in package **175.00**

Playset, Air Adventure Fantastic Freefall, ca 1960s, M in package **175.00**

Playset, Demolition Set, w/ dressed figure, 1960s, minimum value **150.00**

Playset, Super Joe Magna Tools, 1977, M on card **20.00**

Poncho, 1970s, child size, M in package, minimum value **25.00**

Sticker Fun Book, Whitman, 1960s, minimum value ..**15.00**

Tank, Action Man Palitory German Armoured Car, 1970s, M, minimum value **150.00**

Marx

Acrobat Marvel, tin wind-up monkey, 1930s, EX **150.00**

Auto Road Racer set, #9530, $\frac{1}{32}$ scale, complete, EX **100.00**

B-24 Bomber, tin wind-up, 1940, 18" wingspan, EX **300.00**

Battleship USS Washington, tin friction, 1950s, 14", EX................**185.00**

Benjali Tiger, plastic head, battery operated, 12", EX ...**60.00**

Brewster the Rooster, plush, battery operated, 10", EX ...**60.00**

Buttons, plush dog, battery operated, 12", EX **165.00**

Carry All Fighting Knights playset, 1968, NM in EX tin litho case **80.00**

Climbing Bulldozer, tin wind-up, adjustable shovel, 11", EX in box **200.00**

Crazy Corkie Corn Hopper, tin litho, vinyl nose, 1967, 4", MIB **100.00**

Donald Duck, plastic bobbin' head figure, 1950s, EX **20.00**

Gobbling Goose, plastic wind-up, lays golden eggs, 1950s, 9", NM **110.00**

Gold Star Moving Van, tin, 14 plastic animals, 1950s, 21", MIB **200.00**

Hi-Test Gas Pump, vinyl, wind-up walker, D Dean, 1960s, 4½", NM **75.00**

Huckleberry Hound Car, tin friction, Hanna Barbera, 1962, 4", NM **200.00**

Marxie Saxaphone Scooter, plastic, figure & motorcycle, 1969, MIB **45.00**

Mighty Kong Gorilla, tin & plush, battery operated, remote control, EX **225.00**

Presidents, painted plastic figures, 3", 1970s, set of 36, NM **45.00**

Running Scottie, tin litho wind-up, 1939, 5", MIB **165.00**

Sand & Gravel truck, tin litho, wooden wheels, 1940s, 10", EX **85.00**

Target Range, 1950s, 11", M ..**35.00**

Train, plastic wind-up locomotive, tin cars, 1950s, 6" long, M **65.00**

Tricky Taxi, tin wind-up, 1940s, 4", NM in torn box **95.00**

Trix-A-Ball, ball balancing game, battery operated, EX **20.00**

Marx, Yellow Cab, friction, 7" long, NM, $160.00.

Mattel

Bugs Bunny Talking Hand Puppet, gray & white plush, vinyl face, ca '68 ....**12.00**

Bugs Bunny Talking Puppet, plush, vinyl face, pull string, 1968, EX **8.00**

Build-A-Train, painted wood blocks, ca 1971, 8x5½" assembled, VG **5.00**

Calliope, pumper rod inflates balloon & keys play, '80, M ..**12.00**

Cowboy Ge-Tar/Music Box, black plastic w/western decals, 1952, M **20.00**

Crackfire Firecracker, metal firing mechanism, ca '75, 5½x2" dia **14.00**

Mother Goose-in-the-Box, plastic head & cloth body, metal box, ca 1971 ....**9.00**

Preschool Bus Playset, snap-on figures, ca 1978, complete, VG **15.00**

Mattel, Giraffe-in-the-Music-Box, 1967, VG, $15.00.

Putt-Putt All Aboard Motor Railroad, ca 1976, complete, VG **12.00**

Tog'l Toy Chest, colored plastic blocks, VG in box **5.00**

Tool Box, plastic, ca 1978, complete, 12x8x7", M **12.00**

Tuff-Stuff Movie Camera, turning crank shows pictures, ca 1975, VG **4.50**

Tuff-Stuff Vacuum, rotating cylinder, cloth bag, ca 1974-present, 19" **4.50**

Model Kits

Figure-type model kits have increased in price and popularity greatly in just the last five to eight years. Those of us who built these kits in the late '50s to mid '70s want to recapture our lost collections. But those days of 98¢ kits are gone. Prices for plastic figure kits can vary, depending on who is buying and selling and in what part of the country, and most importantly, the condition of the model. The prices listed here represent unassembled kits in their original boxes, in very fine to mint condition. As a rule of thumb, assembled kits (built-ups) are priced at about half the value of the lower end of the price range for a boxed kit. (Note: this does not always hold true on 'higher' priced kits.) Remember, an item is only worth as much as a person is willing to pay for it.

With the rapid growth of this segment of collecting, it is very easy to become confused or disenchanted with your dealings. Educate yourself on the type of kits you want and then hit the flea markets and garage sales. Or find an established kit dealer – this way if you have a question or complaint you'll know that they'll still be there to help. Our advisors are Bill Bruegman (Aurora models), author of *Aurora History and Price Guide*, and Gordy Dutt (kits other than Aurora), who are both listed under Ohio in the Directory.

Addar, General Ursus (Planet of the Apes), #103, 1973, EX **30.00**

Aluminum Model Toy Co, Mr Spock, #5956, 1970s, $25 up to **50.00**

Aurora, Alfred E Neuman, Humorous Series, NM **249.00**

Aurora, American Astronaut, MIB **98.00**

Aurora, Archie's Car, TV-Related Series, MIB **289.00**

Aurora, Batman, Superhero Series, MIB **389.00**

Aurora, Blue Knight of Milan, 1956-62, MIB **89.00**

Aurora, Captain Kidd, Knights & Warriors Series, MIB ..**149.00**

Aurora, Creature of Black Lagoon, Monsters of the Movie Series, MIB **229.00**

Aurora, Cro-Magnon Man, MIB **59.00**

Aurora, Dick Tracy's Space Coupe, Superhero Series, MIB **179.00**

Aurora, Dr Jekyll, Monsters of the Movies Series, MIB **119.00**

Aurora, Frankenstein, Glow-in-the-Dark Series, 1969, MIB ..**189.00**

Aurora, Frankenstein, Original Monster Series, MIB ...**459.00**

Aurora, Godzilla, Original Monster Series, MIB **1,500.00**

Aurora, Green Beret, Knights & Warriors Series, MIB ..**189.00**

Aurora, Illya Kuryakin, Spy Series, M **229.00**

Aurora, James Bond 007, Spy Series, MIB **449.00**

Aurora, John F Kennedy, MIB ....:**179.00**

Aurora, Johnny Unitas, Sports Series, MIB **229.00**

Aurora, Mod Squad Station Wagon, TV-Related Series, NM ..**159.00**

Aurora, Nutty Nose Nipper, Humorous Monster Series, 1965, MIB **350.00**

Aurora, Phantom of the Opera, Glow-in-the-Dark Series, NM in box **219.00**

Aurora, Sir Galahad of Camelot, Knights & Warriors Series, MIB **98.00**

Aurora, Superman, #462, comic-style box, 1963-68, MIB ..**349.00**

Aurora, Susie Whoozis, #201, 1968, MIB **98.00**

Aurora, The Lone Ranger, Superhero Series, MIB **249.00**

Aurora, The Mummy, Glow-in-the-Dark Series, MIB ..**129.00**

Aurora, Vampirella, Monster Scene Series, EX **195.00**

Aurora, Willie Mays, Sports Series, MIB **329.00**

Aurora Viking Ship #320, MIB, $45.00.

Aurora, Zorro, #801, 1965-66, MIB **398.00**

Bachman, Bluejay, #9008, 1960s, $7 up to **12.00**

Hawk, Davey the Psycho Cyclist, #531, 1963, $50 up to **75.00**

Ideal, Rhinocerous, #3853, Marvel Metal Series, 1960, $15 up to **25.00**

Lindberg, Satan's Crate, #279, 1965, $100 up to **125.00**

Marusan, Jupiter II Spaceship (Lost in Space), #809, 1966, $500 up to **1,000.00**

Monogram, Cylon Raider (Battlestar Galactica), #6026, 1978, $25 up to **40.00**

Monogram, UFO, #6012, 1979, $25 up to **35.00**

MPC, Alien, #1-1961, 1979, $50 up to **75.00**

MPC, Barnabas (Dark Shadows), #1-1550, 1969, $150 up to ...**200.00**

MPC, C-3PO (Star Wars), #1-1913, 1978-79, $25 up to **35.00**

MPC, Strange Change Time Machine, #1-0903, 1974-76, $50 up to **75.00**

MPC, Yellow Submarine, w/4 Beatles figures, #617, 1968, $200 up to **300.00**

Multiple Products Inc, Automatic Baby Feeder, #955, '65, minimum value **20.00**

Precision Plastics, US Navy Frogman, #M-401, 1959, $50 up to **100.00**

Pryo, Dimetrodon Dinosaur, #D278, 1960s, $15 up to **25.00**

Pryo, Wyatt Earp US Marshal, #278, 1960s, $20 up to ..**30.00**

Remco, Flintstones Motorized Paddywagon, #452, 1961, $75 up to **150.00**

Renwal, Visible Trout, #817, 1959, $15 up to **20.00**

Revell, Bonanza (Ben, Hoss, & Little Joe), #H-1931, 1966, $50 up to **100.00**

Revell, Cat in the Hat (Dr Seuss character), #Z-2000, 1960, $30 up to **60.00**

Revell, John Lennon (Beatles), #H-1352, 1964, $100 up to **200.00**

Revell, Rat Fink, #H-1305, 1963, $50 up to **75.00**

Revell, Robbin' Hood Fink, #H-1270, 1965, $300 up to ..**400.00**

Monsters

Create a Monster Kit, Colorforms, 1960s, EX **27.50**

Dracula, doll, 19", M in coffin box **70.00**

Frankenstein, doll, Remco, 1979, 9", NM **30.00**

Frankenstein, tin, battery operated, drops his pants, Japan, 13", M **160.00**

Great Garloo, Marx, 1961, battery operated, remote control, EX in box **400.00**

Monster Lab, Ideal, 1963, battery operated, VG in box **80.00**

Monster Print Putty, Colorforms, 1965, M on card **60.00**

Muffy, figure, Imperial, 1986, M **10.00**

Voodoo Doll Game, Schaper, 1967, NM in 12x12" box **40.00**

Wolfman, notebook binder, 1963, EX **30.00**

Wolfman, tumbler, frosted decal glass, Anchor-Hocking, 1963, 7" **27.50**

Playskool

Bear Wagon, 4-pc plastic stacking bear on blue wagon, M **4.00**

Chiming School Bell, plastic w/chiming mechanism, 7½", M **5.00**

Col-O-Rol Wagon, wood, wagon holds cubes, blocks, & cylinders, 1951, M **20.00**

Lacing Shoe Shape Sorter, wood and fibreboard with plastic wheels, 8½" long, EX, $20.00.

Color Glow Copter, plastic w/ paper lithographed windshield, 1977, M **3.50**

Cook N' Serve Grill, plastic, ca 1977, complete, M **15.00**

Milk Carrier, painted wood, ca 1963, complete, EX **30.00**

Peas in a Pod, green vinyl pod holds 3 plastic peas, 1973, M **3.00**

Pounding Bench, wood, complete, EX **3.00**

Rattle, push toy, wood & plastic, 23½" long, M **7.00**

Shape Sorter, plastic base holds flat wooden shapes, complete, M **8.00**

Stacking Rings, bell rings as wooden disks are put on post, EX **20.00**

Traveling Pet Hospital, plastic, complete, M **18.00**

Work bench, wood, ca 1951, 5¾x 11½", complete, EX **20.00**

Ramp Walking Figures

Ramp walkers date back to at least 1873 when Ives produced a a cast iron elephant walker. Wood and composite ramp walkers were made in Czechoslovakia and the USA in the 1920s through the 1940s. The most common were made by John Wilson of Watsontown, Pennsylvania. These sold worldwide and became known as 'Wilson Walkies.' Most are two-legged and stand approximately 4½" tall.

Plastic ramp walkers were manufactured primarily by the Louis Marx Co. from the 1950s through the early 1960s. The majority were produced in Hong Kong, but some were made in the USA and sold under the Marx logo or by Charmore Co., which was a subsidiary of the Marx Co.

The three common sizes are: (1) small premiums about 1½" x 2"; (2) the more common medium size, 2¾" x 3", and (3) large, approximately 4" x 5". Most of the smaller walkers were unpainted, while the medium and large sizes were hand or spray painted. Several of the walking types were sold with wooden or colorful tin lithographed ramps. Randy Welch is our advisor for ramp walkers; he is listed in the Directory under Maryland.

Baby Teeny Toddler, walking baby girl, plastic, Dolls Inc, lg **50.00**

Baby Walk-a-Way, plastic, Marx, lg **40.00**

Baby walking, w/moving eyes, cloth dress, plastic, lg **40.00**

Baby walking in Canadian Mountie uniform, plastic, lg ..**50.00**

Baseball player w/bat & ball ..**30.00**

Bear **15.00**

Big Bad Wolf & 3 Little Pigs ..**90.00**

Boy & girl, dancing **40.00**

Bull **15.00**

Bunny pushing cart **45.00**

Bunnies carrying lg carrot **30.00**

Camel w/2 humps, head bobs up & down **20.00**

Chicks carrying lg decorated Easter egg **30.00**
Chilly Willy penguin on sled pulled by parent **25.00**
Chinamen carrying duck in basket **30.00**
Chipmunks in marching band, playing drum & horn **30.00**
Chipmunks w/acorns **30.00**
Cow, plastic w/metal legs, sm ..**15.00**
Cow, Wiz Walker Milking Cow, plastic, Charmore, plastic, lg ..**50.00**
Cowboy on horse, plastic w/metal legs, sm **20.00**
Czechoslovakian, dog on 4 legs, wood & composite **20.00**
Czechoslovakian, man w/carved wood hat, wood & composite **25.00**
Czechoslovakian, monkey, wood & composite **30.00**
Czechoslovakian, pig, wood & composite **20.00**
Czechoslovakian, policeman, wood & composite **35.00**
Dachshund **15.00**
Dairy cow **15.00**
Disney, Big Bad Wolf & Mason Pig **40.00**

Disney characters: Donald Duck pulling nephews in a cart, $35.00; Donald and Goofy riding a co-cart, $40.00; Goofy on a hippo, $40.00; Minnie pushing a baby stroller, $35.00.

Disney, Donald w/wheelbarrow **25.00**
Disney, Jiminy Cricket w/bass violin **20.00**
Disney, Mad Hatter & March Hare **40.00**
Disney, Mickey & Donald riding gator **40.00**
Disney, Mickey & Minnie carrying basket of food **40.00**
Disney, Mickey & Pluto, hunting **40.00**
Disney, Mickey pushing lawn roller **35.00**
Disney, Pluto **20.00**
Disney, 2 of 3 Little Pigs **40.00**
Dog (Pluto-like), plastic w/metal legs, sm **15.00**
Donald Duck w/wheelbarrow, plastic w/metal legs, sm **30.00**
Double walking doll, boy behind girl, plastic, lg **45.00**
Duck **15.00**
Duck (mama) w/3 ducklings ..**25.00**
Dutch boy & girl **30.00**
Elephant, plastic w/metal legs, sm **20.00**
Farmer pushing wheelbarrow ..**20.00**
Figaro the cat w/ball **25.00**
Firemen **25.00**
Fred & Wilma on dinosaur, Marx, 1960s, NM **120.00**
Frontiersman w/dog **75.00**
Funny Face Kool-Aid, Choo-Choo Cherry, w/plastic coin weight **60.00**
Funny Face Kool-Aid, Goofy Grape, w/plastic coin weight **60.00**
Funny Face Kool-Aid, Root'n Toot'n Raspberry, w/plastic coin weight **60.00**
Goat **20.00**
Hanna-Barbera, Astro **80.00**
Hanna-Barbera, Astro & George Jetson **80.00**
Hanna-Barbera, Fred & Wilma on dinosaur **60.00**
Hanna-Barbera, Fred Flintstone & Barney **40.00**

Hanna-Barbera, Fred on green Dino **60.00**
Hanna-Barbera, Pebbles on purple Dino **60.00**
Hanna-Barbera, Top Cat & Benny **65.00**
Hanna-Barbera, Yogi Bear & Huckleberry Hound **50.00**
Hap & Hop soldiers **20.00**
Horse, plastic, lg **30.00**
Horse, yellow plastic w/rubber ears & string tail, lg **30.00**
Horse w/English rider, plastic, Marx, lg **40.00**
Indian woman w/baby on travois **75.00**
Kangaroo w/baby in pouch ..**25.00**
King Features, Little King & guard **60.00**
King Features, Popeye w/spinach can wheelbarrow **25.00**
Long John Silver, Captain Flint, green, 1989, w/plastic coin weight **15.00**
Long John Silver, Flash turtle, green & yellow, w/plastic coin weight **15.00**
Long John Silver, Quinn penguin, black & white, w/plastic coin weight **15.00**
Long John Silver, Sydney dinosaur, yellow & purple, 1989, w/coin weight **15.00**
Long John Silver, Sylvia dinosaur, lavender & pink, '89, w/coin weight **15.00**
Marty's Market lady w/shopping cart **35.00**
Marx Animals w/Riders Series, Ankylosaurus w/clown ..**25.00**
Marx Animals w/Riders Series, Bison w/native **25.00**
Marx Animals w/Riders Series, Hippo w/native **25.00**
Marx Animals w/Riders Series, Lion w/clown **25.00**
Marx Animals w/Riders Series, Stegosaurus w/Black caveman **25.00**

Marx Animals w/Riders Series, Triceratops w/native **25.00**
Marx Animals w/Riders Series, Zebra w/native **25.00**
Mexican cowboy on horse, plastic w/metal legs, sm **20.00**
Mickey & Minnie Mouse, plastic w/metal legs, sm **40.00**
Milking cow, plastic, Marx, lg ..**40.00**
Monkeys w/bananas **50.00**
Mother Goose w/goose **50.00**
Nursemaid w/baby stroller ..**15.00**
Pig **15.00**
Pluto, plastic w/metal legs, sm **25.00**
Popeye, celluloid, Erwin, lg ..**60.00**
Popeye & Whimpy, heads on springs, plastic, Marx, lg **65.00**
Pumpkin head man & woman, faces on both sides **45.00**
Reindeer **25.00**
Sailors SS Shoreleave **20.00**
Santa & Mrs Claus (faces on both sides) **40.00**
Santa & Snowman (faces on both sides) **40.00**
Santa w/open gold sack **45.00**
Santa w/white sack **40.00**
Sheriff facing outlaw **50.00**
Spark Plug the horse **125.00**
Tin man robot w/cart **100.00**
Wilson, Black Mammy, wood & composite **35.00**
Wilson, clown, wood & composite **30.00**
Wilson, elephant on 4 legs, wood & composite **30.00**
Wilson, Eskimo, wood & composite **60.00**
Wilson, Indian chief, wood & composite **45.00**
Wilson, Little Red Riding Hood, wood & composite **35.00**
Wilson, nurse, wood & composite **30.00**
Wilson, Olive Oyl, wood & composite **150.00**
Wilson, penguin, wood & composite **25.00**

Wilson, Pinocchio, wood & composite **150.00**
Wilson, Popeye, wood & composite **150.00**
Wilson, rabbit, wood & composite **40.00**
Wilson, sailor, wood & composite **30.00**
Wilson, Santa Claus, wood & composite **60.00**
Wilson, soldier, wood & composite **25.00**
Wilson, Whimpy, wood & composite **150.00**
2 Pigs w/pig in basket **35.00**

Slot Race Cars

Slot car racing was very big in the '70s. You could race on your own track at home or go 'downtown' to a multi-course commercial track, where prizes were sometimes awarded to the grand winner. The cars were made in various sizes, from the small HO scale models up to some that were 10" or so in length. Electric transformers were the source of the power that was transmitted along the track to the motors of the cars themselves. Our advisor is Gary Pollastro, who is listed in the Directory under Washington. Values are given for mint-condition cars (not MIB).

AMT (Authentic Model Turnpike), most cars, 1/24 scale **40.00**
Aurora AFX, Dodge Charger Daytona, #1753, HO scale ...**25.00**
Aurora AFX, Peace Tank, #1782, HO scale **40.00**
Aurora Hop-up Kit, HO scale, boxed **100.00**
Aurora Thunderjet, Batmobile, #1385, HO scale **150.00**
Aurora Thunderjet, Cobra GT, white, #1375, HO scale..**30.00**

Aurora Thunderjet, Dino Ferrari, red, #1381, HO scale **30.00**
Aurora Thunderjet, Ferrari, #1368, HO scale **40.00**
Aurora Thunderjet, Ford GT, #1374, HO scale **30.00**
Aurora Thunderjet, Green Hornet, #1384, HO scale ...**150.00**
Aurora Thunderjet, Mustang hardtop, white, #1372, HO scale **60.00**
Aurora Truck, Ryder Rental, yellow, #8001, HO scale **20.00**
Aurora Vibrator, Hot Rod coupe, #1554, HO scale **50.00**
Aurora Vibrator, Jaguar convertible, white, #1541, HO scale **50.00**
Aurora Vibrator, Mercedes Benz convertible, gray, #1542, HO scale **50.00**
Aurora Xcellerator, Vega (#3), #2746, HO scale **40.00**
Eldon, Mustang Fastback, 1/32 scale **30.00**
Eldon, Station Wagon, 1/32 scale **35.00**
Strombecker, Cheetah, 1/32 scale **35.00**
Strombecker, Ford GT, 1/32 scale **30.00**

Space Toys and Robots

Apollo II Eagle Lunar Module, tin, battery operated, 9", NM **125.00**
Apollo Lunar Module kit, Revell, unassembled, 1969, MIB .**65.00**
Buck Rogers Flash Blast Attack Ship, Tootsietoy, cast metal, 1930s, M **165.00**
Dino Robot, Japan, tin, battery operated, 11", NM in box ..**900.00**
Friendship 7 Space Capsule, tin friction, w/astronaut, 7" long, EX **80.00**
Game, Rocket Race to Saturn, 1950s, complete, EX **25.00**

Milky Way Swirl Mixer Space Ship, blue plastic, Rocher, 1950s, 13", NM **65.00**

Moon Creature, Marx, tin wind-up, 5½", EX **175.00**

Moon Map Puzzle, Selchow & Righter, 1970, 10x14", MIB **30.00**

Planet Patrol Target Set, litho tin, 4 alien darts, Marx, 1950s, 15x15" **25.00**

Playmates of the Clouds Hi-Flyer Kite, Little Boy, 1950s, NM **22.50**

Record, Little Space Girl, 1950s, M in color picture sleeve **12.50**

Rocket Ship Space Pistol, Irwin, ca late 1940s, EX **35.00**

Rocket ship, Sparkling Space Ranger, friction type, 1950s, 7", MIB **60.00**

Space Crawler, Mattel, battery operated, 1966-70, complete, EX **50.00**

Space Ranger X-200 spaceship, Pyro, silver plastic, 1950s, 7¼", EX **65.00**

Space-O-Phone, futuristic phone set, blue & yellow plastic, MIB **125.00**

Sparky Robot, Japan, tin wind-up, sparks in eyes, 8", EX ..**185.00**

Sparky Robot, Japan, tin wind-up, 2 square gold robots on horse, 6", M **200.00**

Tattoo sheet, space graphics, AJW & Son, 1953, 8½x7½", 1 sheet **15.00**

Video Robot, Japan, battery operated, screen in chest, 10", EX **75.00**

Tonka Toys

This company is noted for its assortment of all types of trucks and heavy equipment, farm trucks, tractors, and vans. Since the mid-forties they have produced quality painted metal toys. Our advisor is Doug Dezso, who is listed in the Directory under New Jersey.

Allied Van Semi, #400, 1951, 23½" long, M **350.00**

Boat Transport Semi, #41, 1959, 28" long, 5-pc, EX **550.00**

Camper, #70, 1964, 9½" long, M **175.00**

Carnation Milk Delivery Van, #750, 1955, EX **375.00**

Cement Mixer Truck, #120, 1960, 15½" long, M **200.00**

Elastolin soldiers, from $15.00 to $30.00 each.

Dragline & Semi Trailer, #44, 1959, 26¼" long, 3-pc, G **175.00**

Dump Truck & Sand Loader, #116, 1961, 23¼" long, M **140.00**

Fisherman Pickup, #110, 1960, 14" long, M **100.00**

Green Giant Transport Semi, #650, 1953, 22¼" long, EX **200.00**

Jeep Pumper, #425, 1963, 10¾" long, EX **140.00**

Jeep Universal, #249, 1962, 9¾" long, EX **60.00**

Jet Delivery, #410, 1962, 14" long, M **275.00**

Lumber Truck, #998, 1956, 18¾" long, M **185.00**

Military Jeep, #251, 1963, 10½" long, M **65.00**

Minute Maid Delivery Van, #725, 1954, 14½" long, G **300.00**

Nationwide Moving Semi, 1958, 24¼" long, M **240.00**

Parcel Delivery Van, 1957, 12" long, EX **300.00**

Stake Truck, #56, 1964, 9½" long, EX **65.00**

Steam Shovel, #50, 1947, 20¾" long, M **125.00**

Suburban Pumper, #990, 1956, 17" long, M **300.00**

Terminal Train, #720, 33⅜" long, 4-pc, EX **175.00**

Thunderbird Express Semi, 1957, 24" long, G **125.00**

Tractor-Carry-All Trailer, #130, 1949, 30½" long, G **90.00**

Utility Dump Scooter, #301, 1962, 12½" long, M **100.00**

Wrecker Truck, #250, 1949, 12½" long, EX **200.00**

Toy Soldiers

Ajax, AJ7, charging rifleman, M **5.00**

All-Nu, 112, General MacArthur, M **12.00**

All-Nu, 116, soldier w/wireless radio, M **6.00**

All-Nu, 119, ski trooper, M **6.00**

Auburn, A17, wounded soldier, M **35.00**

Auburn, A20, sniper, crawling w/rifle on shoulder, M ...**72.00**

Auburn, A27, marching soldier, VG **14.00**

Auburn, A3, Infantry bugler, VG **14.00**

Barclay, B54, Naval officer, short stride, tin cap, G **45.00**

Barclay, B81, Navy doctor, in white, flat underbase, M **18.00**

Barclay, B85, sitting w/arm in a sling, VG **14.00**

Barclay, EB17, Indian w/bow, VG **9.50**

Barclay, EB18, flagbearer, EX **12.50**

Barclay, EB9, cadet marching at slope, EX **12.50**

Barclay, 2B1, cowboy firing pistol, right arm high, M **12.00**

Barclay, 2B15, sailor at attention, M **14.00**

Barclay, 2B21, cowboy firing pistol, right arm at waist, M **12.00**

Beton, BT102, Indian w/bow on running horse, M **7.00**

Beton, BT105, Indian warrior holding lasso, 4", M **8.00**

Beton, BT108, Infantry w/walkie-talkie, M **5.00**

Beton, BT118, machine gunner, kneeling, M **5.00**

Crescent, CR16, US Marine, saluting, M **10.00**

Crescent, CR22, Indian kneeling w/bow, M **7.50**

Crescent, CR47, nurse holding towel, M **10.00**

Grey Iron, G13, US Infantry officer, M **15.00**

Grey Iron, G40, US Marine, VG **12.00**

Grey Iron, G42, Royal Canadian Police, VG **24.00**

Grey Iron, G47, Indian brave, shielding eyes, M **22.00**

Grey Iron, G72, Boy Scout saluting, VG **14.00**

Grey Iron, G78, pirate w/sword, VG **14.00**

Grey Iron, G94, Red Cross Doctor, M **30.00**

Jones, J27, nurse w/bag, VG ..**60.00**

Jones, J34, Indian on rearing horse, VG **75.00**

Jones, MA21, American Engineer Bomber of 1918, throwing grenade, VG **60.00**

Manoil, M13, drummer, hollow base version, VG **40.00**

Manoil, M206, wounded soldier lying down, VG **85.00**

Manoil, M41, machine gunner, sitting, marked near right leg, M **22.00**

Manoil, M50, tommy gunner, 2nd version, VG **15.00**

Manoil, M55, bomb thrower, 3 grenades in pouch, VG ..**12.00**

Manoil, M60, aviator, M **20.00**

Manoil, M93, soldier w/gas mask & gun, VG **15.00**

Marx, 18MA, Infantry Private w/ automatic rifle, brown uniform, VG **6.00**

Marx, 42MA, wounded soldier, M **8.00**

Marx, 50MA, General, M **12.00**

Marx, 7MA, American cowboy, standing, M **8.00**

Timpo, 7010, officer marching w/sword, M **18.00**

Timpo, 7019, officer at ease, M ..**18.00**

Trains

Alps, battery operated, 1950s, 7" locomotive, MIB **140.00**

American Flyer, #2333 Santa Fe ABA passenger 4-car set, EX **1,000.00**

American Flyer, #2338 Milwaukee Road freight set, '56, EX ..**495.00**

American Flyer, #2355 NYC AA diesel freight set, '53, EX ...**695.00**

American Flyer, #312 NYC steam freight set, 1953, EX ...**250.00**

American Flyer, #345K NYC steam freight set, 1956, EX **395.00**

American Flyer, #50 royal blue freight set, 1951, complete, VG **275.00**

American Flyer, #736 Berkshire steam train, 4 aluminum cars, EX **800.00**

American Flyer, Franklin, 6-car set, 1958, EX **350.00**

American Flyer, GG-1 Tuscan Congressional Passenger, 1955, EX **2,000.00**

American Flyer, Mid-Atlantic freight set, MIB **375.00**

American Flyer, NYC AA F-3 Diesel freight set, 1950, EX **595.00**

American Flyer, Rock Island General engine, MIB **150.00**

American Flyer AF AA Diesel Aluminum Passenger Set, 1950, EX **295.00**

Cragstan, electric shuttle, engine, & 5 cars, MIB **150.00**

Hornby, #3, 0 gauge, tin litho, 14", EX **55.00**

Lionel, #145 Operating Gateman, MIB **50.00**

Lionel, #1615 steam switcher work train, EX **395.00**

Lionel, #18402 operating burro crane, MIB **95.00**

Lionel, #18405 operating Santa Fe burro crane, MIB **95.00**

Lionel, #18406 operating track maintenance car, MIB ..**95.00**

Lionel, #2035 steam freight train, smoke & whistle, 1951, EX **350.00**

Lionel, #229 steam passenger train, 1940, EX **395.00**

Lionel, #2332 GG-1, green 1-motor engine & 4 freight cars, 1948, EX **795.00**

Lionel, #253 electric passenger set, green, 1925, EX in box **495.00**

Lionel, #3656 operating cattle car set, 1951, EX **75.00**

Lionel, #50 operating gang car, EX **50.00**

Lionel, #623 Santa Fe diesel switcher freight set, 1953, EX **295.00**

Lionel, #9224 operating horse car set, EX **95.00**

Transformers

It was in 1984 that the Transformer toy line arrived on the toy shelves in the United States. The original line was made up of only twenty-eight figures. Eighteen were cars that were known as the Autobots, the heroic warriors determined to put an end to the evil Deceptions. There were only ten Deceptions (evil robots) who could turn into such things as a jet or a handgun. From these twenty-eight figures soon came many more. To date, there are over two hundred different Transformers in the United States, not counting the many Transformers in Japan that were never imported here.

From this simple beginning started a craze which continues to this day. Immediately stores were flooded with children and collectors of all ages desperate to own one of these complex, attractively boxed, futuristic warriors. A transformer was a wonderful thing to have, not only for itself but for the world of excitement and wonder which came with it. The story of the Transformers was told through several different comic books as well as a series of animations and a highly successful movie.

The popularity of the Transformers, which were products of Japan, was reflected by the Japanese when the American Transformer show came to Japan. Immediately Japanese Transformer shows appeared as well. In all there were five separate television series and two original video animation series produced in Japan.

Hasbro decided to discontinue their Transformer line in the fall of 1990. While calling Transformers 'an exciting and integral line of toys,' Hasbro service representatives claimed that there was not enough interest expressed in the toys to continue to produce them in this country. Still, Transformers have lived on in the hearts of many and have become sought-after collectibles. There are a number of successful Transformer fan clubs, such as TransAction (which has a huge list of members from all over the world). The popularity of Transformers is far from dead as even in Europe new Transformers are coming into stores all the time. A new limited edition series of Transformers is just being introduced in the United States. It is most likely that Transformer popularity will grow even more in the future.

There is an extremely wide range of prices on Transformers due to the fact that they came in many different sizes. Prices given here are for Transformers in unopened original boxes. One that has been opened or used is worth much less (about 25% to 75%), depending on whether it has all its parts (weapons, instruction book, tech specks, etc.) and what kind of condition it is in. Our advisor is David Kolodny-Nagy, who is listed in the Directory under District of Columbia. See also Clubs and Newsletters.

1984, Bumblebee, Minibot, from $3.00 up to **7.00**

1984, Megatron, Decepticon leader, from $20.00 up to **85.00**

1984, Omega Supreme, Autobot defense base, from $40.00 up to **95.00**

1984, Optimus Prime, Autobot leader (original), from $25.00 up to **100.00**

1984, Prowl, Autobot, from $10.00 up to **25.00**

1984, Soundwave, Decepticon communications, from $20.00 up to **35.00**

1985, Grimlock, Dinobot, from $20.00 up to **30.00**

1985, Shockwave, Decepticon operations, from $30.00 up to **45.00**

1986, Galvatron, Decepticon City Commander, from $20.00 up to **30.00**

1986, Ultra Magnus, Autobot City Commander, from $25.00 up to **30.00**

1987, Goldbug, Throttlebot, from $2.00 up to **5.00**

1987, Punch/Counterpunch, from $15.00 up to **20.00**

1987, Sixshot, Six Charger Decepticon, from $25.00 up to....................................**30.00**

1988, Double Dealer, Powermaster Mercenary, from $25.00 up to **35.00**

1988, Hori-bull, from $10.00 up to **20.00**

1989, Airwave, Micromaster, from $8.00 up to **10.00**

1989, Deathsaurus (available only in Japan), from $47.00 up to **50.00**

1989, Flat Top, Micromaster Transport, from $5.00 up to **6.00**

1989, Star Saber (available only in Japan), from $65.00 up to **85.00**

1990, Jazz, Action Master, from $4.00 up to **5.00**

1990, Optimus Prime, Action Master armored convoy, from $25.00 up to **27.00**

1990, Sprocket, Action Master attack cruiser, from $12.00 up to **15.00**

Wind-Ups

Japanese wind-up toys are a fun and exciting field of toy collecting. The fascination with Japanese toys stems from their simplistic but exciting actions and bright and attractive colors. Many of the boxes that these toys came in are almost as attractive as the toys themselves! Best of all, they can still be found at flea markets and antique shows in mint condition. Our advisor, Phil Helley, is listed in the Directory under Wisconsin.

Atomic Robot Man, Occupied Japan, 5" **350.00**

Baby Tortoise, Occupied Japan, 5¼" **45.00**

Barnacle Bill, Chein, Popeye look-alike, waddles, 1940, EX..**125.00**

Bear on Reindeer, MM Co, 5½" ..**140.00**

Bell Ringing Santa, Alps Co, 7" ..**60.00**

Busy Squirrel, Alps Co, 3" ...**65.00**

Chevrolet, w/back motion, SKK Co, 5" **95.00**

Circus Bear, Occupied Japan, TM Co, 6½" **135.00**

Circus Parade, 12" long **155.00**

Clippity Clop Car, Yone Co, 3"..**65.00**

Combat Soldier, TN Co, 6"..**125.00**

Dancing Sam, AHI Co, 9" ..**250.00**

Donald Duck Drummer, Line Mar, 6" **250.00**

Drinking Bear, Line Mar Toys, 5" **85.00**

Egg Head Man, Echo Co, 6" .**75.00**

Fishing Bear, TN Co, 6" **85.00**

Cragstan Performing Seal with monkey and fish, TPS Co, 8", MIB, $150.00.

Hopping Cary the Crow, 4" ..**125.00**
Jumping Donkey w/Cowboy, MM Co, 5" **85.00**
Log Rolling Bear, TM Co, 6½" ..**135.00**
Mama Kangaroo w/Baby, Japan, tin, baby bounces in pouch, 8", EX **100.00**
Mighty Robot, N Co, 5½" ...**165.00**
Moon Creature, Marx, 6"....**150.00**
Musical Monkey, w/cymbal & drum, MM Co, 8" **85.00**
News Cub-Bear, TN Co, 6" ..**155.00**
Scuba Diver, Chein, flippers move, tin & plastic, 12", EX ...**75.00**
Skip Rope Animals, Cragston Co, 4½" **165.00**
Spin Cart, Spinaroo Alps Co, 5½" **225.00**

Yo-Yos

Alox Manufacturing, Flying Disc, 2⅛", wood, ca 1950s, M ..**35.00**
Buster Brown, multicolor lithographed tin, EX **30.00**
Duncan, Cattle Brand, brand on simulated wood, ca 1965, NM **22.50**
Duncan, Glow Imperial, red letters on cream w/logo, ca 1965, EX **20.00**
Duncan, Satellite Lighted, battery operated, ca mid-1960s, M on card **25.00**

Duncan, Strings, Official Egyptian Fibre Strings, M in package **10.00**
Freddy Krueger, 1989, M on card **10.00**
Hasbro, Glow-Action, dated 1968, M on card **45.00**
Mickey Mouse Club, logo on white, M in bubble pack **15.00**
Whirl King, Standard Model, 3", red & blue w/gold logo, 1950s, M **35.00**

Trading Cards

Baseball cards represent a collectible field that virtually everyone is aware of, but non-sports cards are collectible as well, and a newly released book, *Collector's Guide to Trading Cards* by Robert Reed (Collector Books) thoroughly covers the subject from Disney to Desert Storm. Most are very inexpensive, but some are already pricey. For instance, from 1933 a Goudey Indian Chewing Gum card is valued at from $10.00 to $50.00, and a 1966 Topps Flipper card up to $70.00. If you were to accumulate the whole Flipper set (there are 30 in the series), they would be worth from $1,400.00 to $1,800.00!

Comic Images, Incredible Hulk, 1991, set of 40, minimum value **10.00**
Dart Flipcards, Beetle Juice, 1990, set of 100 w/20 stickers, complete **15.00**
Donruss, Elvis, 1978, set of 66, $25 up to **35.00**
Donruss, Fiends & Machines, 1970, set of 66, minimum value **20.00**
Donruss, Knight Rider, 1983, set of 55, minimum value ...**10.00**

Donruss, Addams Family, 1964, set of 66, each, minimum value **5.00**

Dynamic, Barbie & Ken, 1962, set of 35, each, minimum value ..**5.00**

Eclipse, True Crime, 1992, set of 110, minimum value **15.00**

Ed-U-Cards, Lone Ranger, 1950, set of 120, each, minimum value **7.00**

Ed-U-Cards, US Presidents, 1976, set of 35, minimum value ..**40.00**

Fleer, Believe It or Not, 1970, set of 84, minimum value ..**100.00**

Fleer, Casper, 1960, set of 66, per card, minimum value **4.00**

Fleer, Hogan's Heroes, 1966, set of 66, each, minimum value ..**5.00**

Fleer, Race USA, 1972, set of 72, each, minimum value **2.00**

Gard, Wild West, 1979, set of 25, minimum value **12.00**

Goudey, Histories of Aviation, 1936, set of 10, each, minimum value **35.00**

Film Funnies, Gum Inc., 1930s, $36.00 to $55.00 each.

Leaf, Munsters, 1964, set of 72 w/16 stickers, minimum value **250.00**

Manor, Star Trek, 1979, set of 33, minimum value **8.00**

Mattel, Barbie, 1990, set of 300, $25 up to **35.00**

National Chicle, Tom Mix, set of 48, each, minimum value **22.00**

Pacific, Leave It to Beaver, set of 60, minimum value **25.00**

Pacific, Wizard of Oz, 1990, set of 110, minimum value **10.00**

Philadelphia Gum, Green Berets, 1966, set of 66, minimum value **80.00**

Philadelphia Gum, Robert F Kennedy, 1968, set of 55, minimum value **75.00**

Post, Roy Rogers Pop-Ups, 1952, set of 30, each, minimum value **15.00**

Pro Set, Dinosaurs, 1992, set of 65, minimum value **10.00**

Topps, A Team, 1983, set of 66, minimum value **6.00**

Topps, Addams Family, 1991, set of 99 w/11 stickers, minimum value **16.00**

Topps, Alf, Series I, 1987, set of 69 w/11 stickers, minimum value **12.00**

Topps, Alien, 1979, set of 84 w/22 stickers, minimum value ..**18.00**

Topps, Astronauts, 1963, set of 55, each, minimum value **2.50**

Topps, Brady Bunch, 1969, set of 88, each, minimum value ..**3.00**

Topps, Buck Rogers, 1979, set of 88 w/22 stickers, minimum value **12.00**

Topps, Buck Rogers, 1979, set of 88 w/22 stickers, minimum value **12.00**

Topps, Close Encounters, 1978, set of 66 w/11 stickers, minimum value **8.00**

Topps, Dallas Cowboy Cheerleaders, 1981, set of 30, minimum value **15.00**

Topps, Dick Tracy, 1990, set of 88 w/11 stickers, minimum value **5.00**

Topps, Elvis Presley, 1956, set of 66, each, minimum value ..**9.00**

Topps, ET, 1982, set of 87 w/ 12 stickers, minimum value **12.00**

Topps, Evel Knievel, 1974, set of 60 w/22 stickers, each, minimum value **1.50**

Topps, Garbage Pail Kids Stickers I, set of 88, minimum value **120.00**

Topps, Ghostbusters II, 1989, set of 88 w/11 stickers, minimum value **5.00**

Topps, Mork & Mindy, 1978, set of 99 w/22 stickers, minimum value **15.00**

Topps, New Kids Series I, 1990, set of 88 w/11 stickers, minimum value **8.00**

Topps, Planet of the Apes, 1969, set of 44, minimum value **75.00**

Topps, Simpsons, 1990, set of 88 w/22 stickers, minimum value **8.00**

Topps, Wanted Posters, 1967, set of 24, minimum value ...**50.00**

Topps, Zorro, 1958, set of 88, minimum value **200.00**

Turkish Trophies, Actresses, 1902, set of 25, minimum value **225.00**

Wonder Bread, Star Wars, 1977, set of 16 ....**12.00**

Ziegler, Adventures at Giant Bar/Space, 1951, set of 26, each **5.50**

Trolls

The first trolls to be mass produced in America were molded from wood carvings made by Thomas Dam of Denmark. As the demand for these trolls increased, several US manufacturers were licensed to produce them. The most noteworthy of these were Uneeda doll company's Wishnick line and Scandia House Enterprise's True Trolls. Thomas Dam continued to import his Dam Things line from Scandinavia.

Today trolls are enjoying a renaissance as baby boomers try to recapture their childhood; as a result, values are rising. The trolls described below are rare and hard-to-find examples from the '60s. Remember, trolls that receive top dollar must be in mint condition. Our advisor is Roger Inouye, who is listed in the Directory under California.

Alligator, Dam Things, 5½", from $250 up to **375.00**

Bat Cave, Ideal, w/molded furnishings, from $100 up to **200.00**

Black Santa, Dam Things, 11½", from $200 up to **350.00**

Book, Wishnik Color & Play, Whitman, Uneeda, 1966, from $75 up to **100.00**

British Guard, Dam Things, 8½", rare, from $200 up to ..**350.00**

Cookie cutter, troll form, Mills, 3½", from $35 up to **50.00**

Dam clown, yellow eyes, red nose, painted clothes, marked Dam Things, 1965, 5½", $175.00 to $250.00.

Cow, brown w/black bell, Dam Things, lg, from $175 up to **250.00**

Elephant, gray w/red bell, Dam Things, lg, from $175 up to **250.00**

Girl Monkey, red & white outfit, Dam Things, 8½", from $200 up to **250.00**

Halloween costume, Wishnik, complete, MIB, from $55 up to **100.00**

Handle bar grips, figural, plastic, pr, from $85 up to **100.00**

Horse, Dam Things, 9", from $200 up to **250.00**

Lamp, Wishnik troll, 18", complete, rare, from $175 up to **250.00**

Love Bug, original clothes, Regal, 4½", rare, from $75 up to **150.00**

Monkey, blue & white outfit, Dam Things, 3½", from $100 up to **135.00**

Pencil topper, figural, Dam Things, 1965, 1½", from $20 up to **45.00**

Playset, Troll Party, Marx, MIB, from $150 up to **200.00**

Reindeer, red bell, brown hair, Dam Things, 3½", from 100 up to **135.00**

Shakers, boy & girl figurals, ceramic, 3½", pr, rare, from $100 to **150.00**

Troll, stuffed body, Scandia House, 5", from $45 up to **65.00**

Turtle with green shell, Dam Things, 10½", from $300 up to **375.00**

Two-Headed Troll, 8", from $150 up to **200.00**

Vehicle, Troll Log Car, plastic, Irwin, for 3" trolls, from $75 up to **100.00**

Viking, molded helmet & sword, Dam Things, 3½", from $100 up to **135.00**

TV Guides

For most people, their *TV Guide* spends a week on top of their TV set or by the remote and then is discarded. But to collectors this weekly chronicle of TV history is highly revered. For many people, vintage *TV Guides* evoke happy feelings of the simpler days of youth. They also hunger for information on televisions shows not to be found in reference books. As with any type of ephemera, condition is very important. Some collectors prefer issues without address labels on their covers. Our advisor is Jeffrey M. Kadet, *TV Guide* Specialist, who is listed in the Directory under Illinois.

1954, May 14-20, Frank Sinatra on cover **16.50**

1955, December 10-16, Lucille Ball on cover **30.00**

1955, January 22-28, Ed Sullivan on cover **10.00**

1956, February 11-17, Perry Como on cover **9.50**

1957, March 23-29, Ernie Ford on cover **15.00**

1958, March 1-7, Lassie on cover **12.00**

1959, January 10-16, Milton Berle on cover **10.00**

1960, October 22-28, Debbie Reynolds on cover **8.00**

1960, September 10-16, Dick Clark on cover **12.50**

1961, February 4-10, Clint Eastwood on cover **35.00**

1961, July 1-7, Flintstones on cover **32.00**

1962, May 12-18, Don Knotts on cover **10.00**

1963, June 8-14, Johnny Carson on cover **7.50**

1964, June 6-12, Amanda Blake on cover **10.00**

1964, November 21-27, Jim Neighbors as Gomer Pyle on cover **10.00**

1965, April 24-30, Andy Griffith on cover **15.00**

1966, April 16-22, Petticoat Junction girls on cover **12.00**

1967, May 13-19, Elizabeth Montgomery on cover **10.00**

1968, August 24-30, cast of Star Trek on cover **50.00**

1968, March 9-15, Jackie Gleason on cover **5.00**

1969, February 15-21, Raymond Burr on cover **6.00**

1969, November 29-December 5, cast of Bonanza on cover ..**15.00**

1970, April 4-10, cast of Brady Bunch on cover **20.00**

1970, October 17-23, Partridge Family on cover **10.00**

1971, April 17-23, Paul Newman on cover **5.00**

1972, November 18-24, Bea Arthur as Maude on cover **5.00**

1973, July 14-20, Sonny & Cher on cover **7.00**

1974, October 12-18, Valerie Harper on cover **4.00**

1975, April 26-May 2, cast of McCloud on cover **4.00**

1975, September 6-12, Fall preview issue **12.00**

1976, September 25-October 1, Charlie's Angels on cover ..**14.00**

1978, November 19-25, Frank Sinatra on cover **5.00**

1978, October 21-27, cast of WKRP on cover **7.50**

1979, December 1-7, Barbara Walters on cover **4.00**

1980, July 12-18, cast of Dukes of Hazzard on cover **5.00**

1981, January 17-23, Ronald Reagan on cover **3.00**

1982, October 23-29, Linda Evans & Joan Collins on cover ..**5.00**

1983, March 5-11, Valerie Bertinelli on cover **3.00**

1984, March 3-9, Ann Margaret & Treat Williams on cover ..**4.00**

1985, April 27-May 3, cast of Family Ties on cover **5.00**

1986, March 22-28, Bill Cosby on cover **3.00**

1987, October 24-30, Bruce Willis & Cybil Shepherd on cover ...**5.00**

1988, February 6-12, Jaclyn Smith & Robert Wagner on cover **4.00**

1989, March 4-10, Vanna White on cover **3.00**

1990, April 21-27, Arnold Schwarzenegger on cover **4.00**

Typewriter Ribbon Tins

Typewriter ribbon containers made of tin have been produced from shortly before 1900 through the 1970s. They are a delightful collectible because they are small and easily displayed, they can be found at most flea markets or through advertising, and they are still reasonably priced for the average collector. Value depends primarily on the graphics of each tin and the rarity of each brand. Over 1,000 different ribbon tins are known to exist, and most are found in good condition. Generally, the more graphically pleasing a tin is, the more valuable it is. Tins with animals, flowers, pretty women, typewriters, airplanes, ships, etc., are worth between $5.00 to $15.00. Others that simply state a brand name are valued under $5.00. Some examples follow. Our advisor is Hobart D. Van Deusen, who is listed in the Directory under Connecticut.

Advocate, lg lion **12.00**

Allied, sea gull **6.00**
Black Hawk, Indian **8.00**
Carter's Guardian, airplanes ..**12.00**
Carter's Midnight **4.00**
Codo Super-Fiber, round **6.00**
Columbia Twins, 2 girls, orange **8.00**
Ditto, plain **4.00**
Elk, round, yellow & blue **5.00**
Fine Service, sm airplane **7.00**
Herald Square, plain **6.00**
Hub, square **6.00**
Kee Lox, square, red **4.00**
MBP, round, yellow & green ..**4.00**
Park Avenue Roytype, round, blue **4.00**
Secretarial, round, silver **4.00**
Silver Brand, plain **3.00**
Star, Webster's **4.00**
Tagger, round, maroon **4.00**

Universal

Located in Cambridge, Ohio, Universal Potteries Incorporated produced various lines of dinnerware from 1934 to the late 1950s, several of which are especially popular with collectors today. Refer to *The Collector's Encyclopedia of American Dinnerware* by Jo Cunningham (Collector Books) for more information.

Mixed Fruit pattern, 4", $15.00 for the pair.

Ballerina, egg cup **15.00**
Ballerina, sugar bowl, w/lid ..**12.00**
Calico Fruit, custard **4.00**
Calico Fruit, pitcher, milk ...**22.00**
Calico Fruit, plate, 9" **6.00**
Cat-tail, bowl, cereal **6.00**
Cat-tail, plate, dinner **10.00**
Cat-tail, sugar bowl, handles ..**6.00**
Circus, spoon **25.00**
Holland Rose, plate, 6" **4.00**
Hollyhocks, salad bowl **17.50**
Iris, pie plate **15.00**
Iris, plate, dinner **6.00**
Kitchenware, bean pot, red & white **30.00**
Largo, salt & pepper shakers, pr **6.00**
Rambler Rose, gravy boat **7.50**
Red Poppy, plate, utility; 11½"..**10.00**
Windmill, bowl, utility; w/lid, sm **6.00**
Windmill, salt & pepper shakers, pr **12.00**
Woodvine, creamer **7.00**
Woodvine, cup & saucer, set ..**8.00**

Valentines

One of the fastest-growing time frames of interest in valentine cards today would be from the 1940s through the 1960s. Cards from this era include mechanical, penny, and boxed valentines. Valentines can also cross over into many other collections, such as Black memorabilia, advertising, transportation, cartoon characters, folk art, and so on.

Please keep these factors in mind when determining the value of your valentines: age, condition, size, category, and whether or not there is an artist's signature present. All of these were taken into consideration when the following valentines were priced. Also, it is important to remember that the

East Coast tends to have a higher market value for them than the West Coast, due primarily to higher demand in the East. Our advisor for this category is Katherine Kreider, who is listed in the Directory under California.

In the listings that follow, HCPP stands for honeycomb paper puff, and MIG indicates valentines marked Made In Germany.

American Greeting, Black child on open-out, 1945-50s, 5¾x 4½", NM **10.00**

American Greeting, open-up w/ elephant & plastic light bulb, 1950s **10.00**

Car, litho w/children & dog inside, MIG, 1920s, 8½x6½", EX ..**30.00**

Comic valentine, signed by Hugh Chennoweth, 1934, VG..**10.00**

G Carrington & Co, Chicago IL, goat, mechanical, 5½x4", NM **10.00**

G Carrington & Co, native American, mechanical, 1950s, VG.....................................**5.00**

H Fishlove & Co, plastic, wind-up heart, #522, 1958, NM ..**45.00**

Hall Bros, stand-up dog w/felt ears, 1940s, 8½x6¾", VG ..**5.00**

Hallmark, Cinderella's coach, 1960, 9x7", VG **1.00**

Hallmark, musical, 1959, 9x7½", VG **15.00**

Hallmark, valentine booklet, 3-D, 4 pages, 1961, 9x7", NM ..**8.00**

HCPP, gazebo w/children playing instruments, MIG, 1920s, 10½x8", NM **125.00**

HCPP, Wheel of Love, USA, 1920s, 9x5", NM **75.00**

Heart w/hand-painted wood clothespin, 1940s, 4½x3", EX **15.00**

Little Boy Blue, mechanical litho, USA, 1930s, 10¾x7¾", NM **75.00**

Little Jack Horner, mechanical, Louis Kautz, USA, 1926, 6x3¾", NM **40.00**

Little Lulu, 1950s, 4x4½", EX **15.00**

Louis Kautz, cat, mechanical, stands w/tab, USA, 6¾x4", EX **15.00**

Mechanical, big-eyed children on teeter totter held in bulldog's mouth, MIG, 6¾x4", NM, $150.00.

Louis Kautz, girl cooking heart at stove, litho, USA, 7½x6", EX **15.00**

Mastiff w/child on back, litho, stands w/tab, MIG, 3¼x4⅛", NM **10.00**

Mechanical, ballerina w/plastic eyes that roll, MIG, early 1920s, EX **20.00**

Mechanical, bulldog, neck moves up & down, MIG, 8½x3½", EX **20.00**

Mechanical, dragonfly w/angel on back, stands w/tab, 7x5½", NM **15.00**

Mechanical, Dutch lady, children pop in & out of wooden shoe, MIG, VG **20.00**

Mechanical, fan w/kitten in center opens & closes, expands to 7", NM **10.00**

Mechanical, stockbroker, stands w/tab, MIG, 1940s, 4¼x3¼", NM **10.00**

Norcross, elephant, stands w/tab, 1940s, 11x7½", VG **5.00**

Rolling pin, I'm Rolling in Dough, 4x1½", VG **5.00**

Rose, long stem, full bloom, 7½x 5", EX **10.00**

Rust Craft, dog w/felt ears, stands w/tab, 1946, 9½x7½", NM **6.00**

Rust Craft, girl dressed for winter w/puppy, 1929, 4x4½", VG..**4.00**

Rust Craft, parasol, USA, 7x5", VG **6.00**

Snow White & dwarfs baking pie, WD Enterprises, 1938, 5x4½", VG **25.00**

Wiley Fox, mechanical, WDP, USA, 1938, 5x4½", VG ..**25.00**

Wizard of Oz, Lion, Loew's Inc, NM **35.00**

3-D children w/sailboat & puppy, 1940s, 5½x4", EX **20.00**

3-D tennis court w/2 children playing tennis, 1920s, 7½x6", VG **25.00**

3-D train, Ambassador Cards, 1959, 7x9½", NM **25.00**

Van Briggle

Van Briggle pottery has been made in Colorado Springs since 1901. Fine art pottery was made until about 1920 when commercial wares and novelties became more profitable products. The early artware was usually marked with the date of production and a number indicating the shape. After 1920 'Colorado Springs' in script letters was used; after 1922 'U.S.A.' was added. Van Briggle is most famous for his Art Nouveau styling and flat matt glazes. Refer to *Collector's Encyclopedia of Van Briggle Art Pottery* by Richard Sasicki and Josie Fania (Collector Books) for more information.

Bookends, dog, Persian Rose, AA mark only, pr **185.00**

Bowl, heart-shaped leaves, Persian Rose & blue, #858, USA, 6" **100.00**

Bowl, turquoise, boat shape, scalloped, 5" long **60.00**

Creamer, Persian Rose, paper label, 2½" **40.00**

Cup, turquoise, 6 incised panel lines, 1917, 3½" dia **50.00**

Figurine, elephant, turquoise, trunk raised, 4¼x3¼" **95.00**

Figurine, seated nude holding lg shell, light blue, 7" **150.00**

Lamp, Grecian urn, turquoise, original shade, 11½" **75.00**

Lamp, nude, right arm overhead, drape behind her, blue, 1920s, 17" **400.00**

Mug, bisque, buff clay, 1908-11, 4¾" **165.00**

Paperweight, sombrero, turquoise, 2½x5¼x4⅜" **75.00**

Plaque, peacock, turquoise w/ red shading on tail, #807, 1908-11, 7" **285.00**
Vase, bowl; acorns & oak leaves, light green, #670, ca 1908, 4x5½" **360.00**
Vase, bowl; leaves, Persian Rose, #733, 3¾x6" **110.00**
Vase, flowers & roots (3 each side), Persian Rose & blue, 5x4" **125.00**
Vase, leaves swirled around top, Persian Rose & dark blue, 4½" **80.00**
Vase, luna moths, Persian Rose & blue, #684, 2¾" **65.00**
Vase, robin's egg blue, classic form, #313, dated 1918, 8x4" **235.00**
Vase, upright arrow leaves, dark blue on light blue, ca 1920, 10x6" **285.00**

Vernon Kilns

From 1931 until 1958, Vernon Kilns produced hundreds of lines of fine dinnerware, which today's collectors enjoy reassembling. They retained the services of famous artists and designers such as Rockwell Kent and Walt Disney, who designed both dinnerware lines and novelty items as well, examples of which are at a premium.

Anytime, platter, 13¼" **12.00**
Bel-Air, gravy boat **16.00**
California Shadows, coffee cup, jumbo **15.00**
Chatelaine Jade, cup & saucer, pedestal foot **18.00**
Chatelaine Jade, plate, 7½" .**10.00**
Chintz, bowl, 5½" **2.50**
Fantasia, figurine, Baby Pegasus, #19 ....**300.00**
Fantasia, figurine, Satyr, #2 ..**225.00**

Fantasia, shakers, Mushroom, pr **120.00**
Gingham, pitcher, bulbous, 1-pt **17.50**
Homespun, cup & saucer **10.00**
Homespun, salt & pepper shakers, pr **16.00**
Lei Lani, demitasse cup **20.00**
Lei Lani, tumbler **18.00**
Lollipop Tree, cup **4.00**
Mayflower, plate, 10½" **15.00**
Monterey, pitcher, 2-qt **25.00**
Monterey, sugar bowl, w/lid ..**10.00**
Organdie, divided vegetable, oval, 11½" **15.00**
Organdie, platter, 12" **10.00**
Philodendron, vegetable bowl, oval **15.00**
Plate, Baker's Chocolate, 10" ..**45.00**
Plate, Bits of the Old South, Southern Mansion **15.00**
Plate, Carlsbad Caverns **10.00**
Raffia, chop plate, 12¾" **15.00**
Raffia, syrup, drip-cut top ...**30.00**
Rose-a-Day, dinner plate, 10" ..**8.00**

Salamina dinner plate, Rockwell Kent design, 9½", $95.00.

Salamina, plate, 14" **150.00**
Salamina, sugar bowl, w/lid, regular **95.00**
Tam O'Shanter, carafe **30.00**
Tam O'Shanter, dinner plate, 10" **8.00**

Tam O'Shanter, salt & pepper
   shakers, pr **10.00**
Tickled Pink, butter dish **12.50**
Tickled Pink, salt & pepper
   shakers, pr **6.00**
Ultra California, creamer, pink ..**8.00**
Ultra California, tumbler **15.00**

View-Master and Tru-Vue

View-Master, the invention of William Gruber, was first introduced to the public at the 1939-1940 New York World's Fair and at the same time at the Golden Gate Exposition in California. Since then, thousands of reels and packets have been produced on subjects as diverse as life itself. Sawyers View-Master even made two different stereo cameras for the general public, enabling people to make their own personal reels, and then offered a stereo projector, to project the pictures they took on a silver screen in full color 3-D.

View-Master has been owned by five different companies: the original Sawyers Company, G.A.F. (in the October 1966), View-Master International (in 1981), Ideal Toy Company, and Tyco Toy Company (the present owners).

Unfortunately, after G.A.F. sold View-Master in 1981, neither View-Master International, Ideal, nor Tyco Toy Company have had any intention of making the products anything but a toy items, selling mostly cartoons. This, of course, has made the early non-cartoon single reels and the three-reel packets desirable items.

The earliest single reels from 1939-1945 were not white in color, but were originally dark blue with a gold sticker in the center and came in attractive gold-colored envelopes. Then they were made in a blue and tan combination. These early reels are more desirable as the print runs were low.

Most white single reels are very common, as they were produced from 1946 through 1957 by the millions. There are exceptions, however, such as commercial reels promoting a product, and reels of obscure scenic attractions, as these would have had smaller print runs. In 1952 a European division of View-Master was established in Belgium. Many reels and items made there are more valuable to a collector since they are hard to find in this country.

In 1955 View-Master came up with the novel idea of selling packets of three reels in one colorful envelope with a picture or photo on the front. Many times a story booklet was included. These became very popular and sales of single reels were slowly discontinued. Most three-reel packets are desirable, whether Sawyers or G.A.F., as long as they are in nice condition. Nearly all viewers are common and have little value, except the very early ones, such as the Model A and Model B. These viewers had to be opened to insert the reels. The blue and brown versions of the Model B are rare. Another desirable viewer is the Model D, which is the only focusing viewer that View-Master made. Condition is very important to the value of all View-Master items, as it is with most collectibles. Our advisor is Mr. Walter Sigg, who is listed in the Directory under New Jersey.

Camera, Focusing Model D ..**30.00**
Camera, Mark III, M in case ..**100.00**
Camera, View-Master Personal
    Stereo, M, original case ..**100.00**
Close-Up lens, for Personal cam-
    era **100.00**
Film cutter, for View-Master cam-
    era **100.00**
Packet, Addams Family, 3-reel
    set, M in package **50.00**
Packet, Belgium made, 3-reel set, M
    in package, from $4 up to ..**35.00**
Packet, miscellaneous subject, 3-
    reel set, M in package, from
    $3 up to **50.00**
Packet, Munsters, 3-reel set, M in
    package **50.00**
Packet, scenic, 3-reel set, M in
    package, from $1 up to ..**25.00**
Packet, TV or movie, 3-reel set, M
    in packet, from $2 up to ..**50.00**
Projector, Stereo-Matic 500 ..**200.00**
Reel, Belgium made, from $1 up
    to **10.00**
Reel, blue-backed, $2.50 up to ..**10.00**
Reel, commercial, brand-name
    product, from $5 up to ..**50.00**
Reel, gold center, gold-colored
    package **10.00**
Reel, Sawyer, white, early, from
    25¢ up to **5.00**
Reel, 3-D movie preview **50.00**
Sleeping Beauty, Sawyers, ca
    1950s, 3-reel set, EX in enve-
    lope **25.00**
Viewer, any rare model, minimum
    value **100.00**
Viewer, Model B, blue or brown,
    each **100.00**

Tru-Vue

Tru-Vue, a subsidiary of the Rock Island Bridge and Iron Works in Rock Island, Illinois, was first introduced to the public at the 1933 Century of Progress Exposition in Chicago. With their popular black and white 3-D film-strips and viewers, Tru-Vue quickly became the successor to the Stereoscope and stereocards of the 1800s and early 1900s. They made many stereo views of cities, national parks, scenic attractions and even some foreign countries. They produced children's stories, some that featured personalities and nightclubs, and many commercial and instructional film-strips.

By the late 1940s, Sawyers View-Master had become a very strong competitor. Their full-color 7-scene stereo reels were very popular with the public and had cut into Tru-Vue's sales considerably. So it was a tempting offer when Sawyers made a bid to buy out the company in 1951. Sawyers needed Tru-Vue, not only to eliminate competition, but because Tru-Vue owned the rights to photograph Disney characters and the Disney-land theme park in California.

After the take-over, Sawyers View-Master continued to carry Tru-Vue products but stopped production of the 3-D filmstrips and viewers. Instead they adopted a new format with 7-scene 3-D cards and a new 3-D viewer. These were sold mainly in toy stores. All of the pictures were on a cheaper 'East-mancolor' slide film, and most of them have today faded into a magenta color. Many cards came apart, as the glue that was used tends to separate quite easily. The value of these, therefore, is low. (Many cards were later remade as View-Master reels using the superior 'Kodachrome' film.) On the other hand, advertising literature, dealer displays, and items that were not meant to be sold to the public often have considerable collector value.

When G.A.F. bought View-Master in 1966, they gradually phased out the Tru-Vue format.

Viewer, Tru-Vue, toy-size, in original box, $15.00.

Card, Tru-Vue, from $1.00 up to......................................**3.00**
Filmstrip, children's story, from $1.00 up to........................**3.00**
Filmstrip, commercial (promoting products), from $20.00 up to **50.00**
Filmstrip, instructional, from $5.00 up to......................**15.00**
Filmstrip, ocean liners..........**15.00**
Filmstrip, personality (Sally Rand, Gypsy Rose Lee, etc), from $15.00 up to **20.00**
Filmstrip, scenic, from $1.00 up to **5.00**
Filmstrip, World's Fair **7.50**
Viewer.....................................**5.00**

Wade

Wade porcelain is probably best known for the small, machine-made figurines packed in boxes of Red Rose Tea. The Wade Group of Potteries, however, has produced an enormous range of wares throughout its years of operation, from beautiful figurines through general lines of tableware. The Wade Group of Potteries originated in 1810 with a small, single-oven pottery near Chesterton, just west of Burselm, England. This pottery owned by Henry Hallen was eventually taken over by George Wade who had opened his own pottery, also in Burslem, in 1867.

Both the Hallen pottery and the original George Wade pottery specialized in ceramic and pottery items for the textile industry then booming in northern England. By the early 20th century, the two potteries merged, taking the name of George Wade Pottery, which in 1919 became George Wade & Son Ltd. George Wade's brother, Albert, had interests in two potteries, A.J. Wade Ltd. and Wade Heath & Co. Ltd., which manufactured decorative tiles, teapots and other related dinnerware. In 1938 Wade Heath took over the Royal Victoria Pottery, also in Burslem, and began producing a wide range of figurines and other decorative items. In 1947 a new pottery was opened in Portadown, Northern Ireland, to produce both industrial ceramics and Irish porcelain giftware. Originally known as Wade (Ulster) Ltd., the pottery soon changed its name to Wade (Ireland) Ltd.

In 1958 all the Wade potteries were amalgamated, becoming the Wade Group of Potteries. The most recent addition to the group is Wade (PDM) Ltd., incorporated in 1969, a marketing arm for the advertising ware made by Wade Heath. In 1989 the Wade Group of Potteries was bought out by Beauford Engineering. With this takeover Wade Heath and George

Wade & Son Ltd., along with their subsidiaries, were combined to form Wade Ceramics Ltd. In 1990 Wade (Ireland) Ltd. changed its name to Seagoe Ceramics Limited. If you'd like to learn more about Wade ceramics, we recommend *The World of Wade* by Ian Warner and Mike Posgay; Mr. Warner is listed in the Directory under Canada.

Advertising Items

Bell's Whiskey, decanter, Prince William's birth, empty, unboxed **60.00**
Bell's Whiskey, decanter, Prince William's birth, w/contents, boxed **200.00**
Bell's Whiskey, decanter, Queen's 60th birthday, empty, unboxed **50.00**
Bell's Whiskey, decanter, Queen's 60th birthday, w/contents, boxed **160.00**

KP Friars

Brother Angelo **20.00**
Brother Benjamin **10.00**
Brother Crispin **20.00**
Brother Francis **20.00**
Brother Peter **10.00**
Father Abbot **12.00**

Large Nursery Favourites

Bo Peep **45.00**
Boy Blue **25.00**
Cat & the Fiddle **30.00**
Goosey Gander, original 1976 issue **100.00**
Goosey Gander, 1991 reissue ..**25.00**
Humpty Dumpty **20.00**
Jack **20.00**
Jack Horner **20.00**
Jill **20.00**
Little Miss Muffet **20.00**
Mary Mary, original 1974 issue ..**36.00**

Mary Mary, 1990 reissue **20.00**
Old Woman in the Shoe, original 1976 issue **25.00**
Old Woman in the Shoe, 1991, reissue **25.00**
Polly Kettle, original 1973 issue **25.00**
Polly Kettle, 1990 reissue **20.00**
Puss-in-Boots **40.00**
Queen of Hearts **40.00**
Three Bears **45.00**
Tom Piper, original 1973 issue ..**32.00**
Tom Piper, 1990 reissue **20.00**
Tommy Tucker **25.00**
Wee Willie Winkie **20.00**

Miscellaneous Dishes

Bonbon dish, pattern No. 228, late 1930s, rare, $60.00.

Everlasting candles, pr, MIB ..**125.00**
Everlasting candles, unboxed, pr **100.00**
Gothic covered dish **55.00**
Gothic vase **60.00**
Scottie teapot, lg **200.00**
Scottie teapot, sm **175.00**

Wall Pockets

If you've been interested enough to notice, wall pockets are everywhere – easily found, relatively inexpensive, and very diversified. They were made in Germany, Japan, Czechoslovakia, and by many, many companies in the United States. Those made by companies best known for their art pottery (Weller, Roseville, etc.) are in a class of their own, but the novelty, just-for-fun wall pockets stand on their own merits. Examples with large, colorful birds or those with unusual modeling are usually the more desirable. See also McCoy.

Colorful parrot on flowering tree, marked Czechoslovakia, 10", $25.00.

Bird on blue cornucopia, 7" **8.00**
Flying duck on brown cornu-
   copia **10.00**
Grapes on bark-like texture,
   Japan, 7" **8.50**
Hanging sock, blue & green ..**12.00**
Owl figural, Japan, 6" **17.50**
3 bananas, Treasure Craft, South
   Gate CA **8.00**

Warwick

From 1887 until 1951, the Warwick China Company operated in Wheeling, West Virginia, producing both dinnerware and art ware vases. Many of their vases utilized Victorian shapes and featured lovely ladies, monks, or flowers. Refer to *Warwick, A to W,* and *Why Not Warwick* (self published) by Donald Hoffman, whose address is listed in the Directory under Illinois.

Vase, A Beauty, roses on brown,
   15" **265.00**
Vase, Bonnie, matt tan, portrait,
   10¼" **310.00**
Vase, Bouquet #2, matt tan, pine
   cones, 10½" **265.00**
Vase, Carnation, pink, Hilda type
   w/boa, 9" **220.00**
Vase, Clematis, roses on green,
   10½" **285.00**
Vase, Clytie, pink, Hilda type
   holding violets, 6½" **325.00**
Vase, Dahlia, red, Countess Anna
   Potaka, 8½" **300.00**
Vase, Dainty, florals on brown,
   4½" **280.00**
Vase, Gem, florals on brown, #A-
   16, 12" **220.00**
Vase, Henrietta, florals on brown,
   #A-27, 10" **220.00**
Vase, Lemonade, florals on red,
   6½" **145.00**
Vase, Lily, florals on brown,
   9½" **200.00**
Vase, Magnolia, florals on red, #E-
   2, 10½" **255.00**
Vase, Narcis #1, florals on brown,
   #A-27, 8½" **220.00**
Vase, Orchid, portrait on pink,
   #H-1, 10¼" **265.00**
Vase, Pansy, florals on brown,
   4" **90.00**
Vase, Queen, birds on white, #D-
   1, 12" **325.00**
Vase, Royal #1, lady in lg hat on
   brown, #A-17, 10" **300.00**
Vase, Tobio Jug #1, fisherman on
   red, #E-3, 7¾" **195.00**
Vase, Verona, charcoal gray, #C-6,
   11¾" **185.00**

Vase, Violet, brown, #A-40, 4" ..**110.00**
Vase, Warwick, portrait on pink,
10" **310.00**

Watch Fobs

The accumulation of watches
and their related jewelry has
been of interest to men since the
invention of the pocket watch in
the early 1500s. This jewelry in
the form of pins, chains, and
fancy links was the forerunner of
the present-day fob. The collecting boom of the past ten years
has stimulated interest in fobs;
however, fobs have been popular
for the past 100 years in some
form. The leather strap-type (ca
1870s to present) has long been
preferred by working men; a
pocket watch with a fob was a
practical timepiece as it wasn't
attached to the working wrist.
Fobs have been a means for companies to advertise their products. Since most men who work
with heavy equipment or farm
machinery wore them, it was natural for companies to promote
new products and equipment
through advertising fobs. Men
would also go to conventions
where they were often issued a
ribbon with a medal attached to
it. After the convention the medal
would be taken off and worn as a
fob. For further information contact our advisor Margaret
Kaduck, author of several books,
who is listed in the Directory
under Ohio.

Allis-Chalmers, #460B, equipment,
bronze, recent issue **5.00**
Allis-Chalmers, 19 diesel, diamond w/initials, bronze,
1950s **20.00**

American Federation of Labor,
Bastian Bros, Rochester,
bronze, 1932 ....**8.00**
Austin-Western Construction
Equipment, Aurora IL, bronze,
recent issue **8.00**
Bantam & equipment on shield,
Schield-Bantam, bronze, recent
issue **5.00**
Battle Axe Shoes, shoe & axe on
shield, silver, 1908 ....**25.00**
BPOE, Arkansas Elks, enameled
bronze, 1912 ....**12.00**
Broom Sewing Machine, emboss-
ed machine on silvered metal,
1½" **40.00**
Caterpillar, Ohio Machinery
Co, Cleveland, silver,
1970s **6.00**
Chicago 1934 World's Fair, SD
Childs, blue enamel on
bronze, 1934 ....**20.00**
City of Troy NY, Police 3000, Bastian Bros, silver, 1940s ..**15.00**
Columbian Stoves, 'C' around
shield, red on silvered brass,
1½" **40.00**
DeLavel, We use the Cream Sep-
arator, blue on bronze, 1910,
G **25.00**
Detroit Diesel in center of
engine's flywheel, bronze,
recent issue **8.00**
Dillion Electric Co, Canton OH,
machine in wreath, silver,
1908 ....**40.00**
Dr Pepper Co, Waco USA, shows
factory, silver, 1910 ....**50.00**
Euclid Earth Moving Equipment,
truck, silver, 1950s **12.00**
Firemen's Association of PA,
Heeren Bros, Pittsburgh PA,
silver, 1907 ....**25.00**
Frank G Hough Co, Libertyville
IL, Greenduck Co, bronze,
recent issue **8.00**
Gold Medal Flour, white enamel
& gold paint on leather,
bronze, 1905 ....**20.00**

45th Great Council of Indiana, marked O.R.M., $15.00.

Goodyear, flying foot & tire embossed on brass, 1½" ..**40.00**

Grit Family Newspaper Selling Agent, multicolor, 1920s **15.00**

Heinz '57,' '57' embossed on silvered brass, 1½" **50.00**

Heinz Products, Greenduck Co, Chicago, girl w/bottle, silver, 1910 ....**40.00**

Highway Equipment Co, Leavens, Attleboro MA, silver, 1960s **8.00**

International Harvester, multicolor enameled metal, imported issue **6.00**

Jersey Spreader, Hasbrouck Heights NJ, equipment, silver, 1960s **12.00**

John Deere, deer, mother-of-pearl on bronze, 1920s **60.00**

Joy Ram Track Drill, Leavens, Atteboro MA, bronze, 1960s **6.00**

Lauson Frostking, enameling on bronze, 1¼x2", EX **65.00**

Lima Shovels, Lima OH, shovel against globe, bronze, 1950s **25.00**

Melroe Bobcat, Gwinner ND, equipment, bronze, 1970 ..**6.00**

National Cash Registers, cash register, silvered brass, 1½" **40.00**

National Sportsman Magazine, CD Lyons Co, Mansfield MA, bronze, 1920 ....**20.00**

Old Reliable Coffee, Dayton OH, product, silver, 1907 ......**35.00**

P (letter) in solid brass, 1925 ..**8.00**

Pattersonville NJ Centennial, 1792-1892, silver, 1892 ..**15.00**

Pettibone, muscular man holds machine, bronze, 1960s ..**10.00**

PH Co, Cranes & Elevators, Milwaukee WI, silver, recent issue **6.00**

Rhode Island state seal, red & blue enamel on silver, 1915 ...**10.00**

State Automobile Insurance Association, bronze, 1920 .....**20.00**

Stevens Detroit, Whitehead & Hoag Co, elephant form, bronze, 1912 ....**25.00**

Two-Republic Life Insurance Co, Greenduck Co, enameled metal, 1920 ....**20.00**

WS Tyler Company, Cleveland OH, bronze, 1912 ....**20.00**

Yale Trojan, Batavia NY/San Leandro CA, equipment, bronze, 1967 ....**6.00**

Watt

Since making an appearance a few years ago in a leading magazine on country decorating, Watt Pottery has become highly collectible. Easily recognized by its primary red and green brushstroke patterns on glossy buff-colored backgrounds, these items often carry a stenciled advertising message in addition to designs of apples, tulips, starflowers, and roosters. It was made in Crooksville, Ohio, from about 1935 until the plant was destroyed by fire in 1965. Refer to *Watt Pottery, An Identification and Price Guide,* by Sue and Dave Morris (Collector Books) for more information.

Bean server, Apple, #75, individual **75.00**
Bowl, Apple, #602, ribbed, 1¾x 4¾" **45.00**
Bowl, Apple, #8, advertising **60.00**
Bowl, Autumn Foliage, #9, ribbed, 9" **30.00**
Bowl, cereal; Apple, #94 ......**35.00**
Bowl, cereal; Cherry, #23 .....**35.00**
Bowl, mixing; Apple, #07, ribbed, 3¼x7" **50.00**
Bowl, mixing; Dutch Tulip, #63, 4x6½" **65.00**
Bowl, mixing; Green-On-Brown Starflower, #5, 2¾x5" **30.00**
Bowl, mixing; Rooster, #5, 2¾x5" **55.00**
Bowl, mixing; Tulip, #63, 4x6½" **60.00**
Bowl, Rooster, #58, 3¼x10½" ..**90.00**
Bowl, spaghetti; Apple, #39, 3x13" **150.00**
Casserole, Cherry, #3/19 ......**90.00**
Casserole, Old Pansy, #3/19 ..**65.00**
Cookie jar, Apple, #21 ....**300.00**
Cookie jar, Kitch-N-Queen, #503 ....**125.00**
Cookie jar, Starflower, #21 ..**160.00**
Creamer, Rooster, #62 ....**85.00**
Creamer, Starflower, #62 .....**75.00**
Cup & saucer, Cut-Leaf Pansy ..**75.00**
Cup & saucer, Pink-on-Black Starflower **85.00**
Cup & saucer, Pink-on-Green Starflower **65.00**
Dutch oven, Cut-Leaf Pansy, 7x10½" **150.00**
Grease jar, Apple, #01 ....**250.00**

**Pitcher, Dutch Tulip, #15, 5½",
$85.00.**

Pie plate, Cut-Leaf Pansy, 9" ..**80.00**
Pitcher, Blue & White Banded, 7" **45.00**
Pitcher, Dutch Tulip, #16, 6½" ..**125.00**
Pitcher, Old Pansy, #15, 15½" ...**55.00**
Platter, Cherry, #31, 15" dia ..**145.00**
Platter, Pink-on-Green Starflower, #31, 15" dia **110.00**
Salt & pepper shakers, Apple, barrel form, pr **245.00**
Salt & pepper shakers, Autumn Foliage, hourglass form, pr **155.00**
Tumbler, Apple, #56, 4½" ...**325.00**

Weil Ware

The figurines, wall pockets, and other decorative novelties made from the 1940s through the mid-1950s by Max Weil are among several similar types of California-made pottery that has today become the focus of much collector attention. Refer to *The Collector's Encyclopedia of California Pottery* by Jack Chipman (Collector Books) for more information.

Bowl, salad; Rose, sm **4.00**
Butter dish, Blossom, ¼-lb ..**25.00**
Coffee server, Bamboo **20.00**
Cup & saucer, Rose **5.00**

Vase, girl by square post, 10½", $32.50.

Dish, Dogwood, divided, square, 10½" **12.00**
Figurine, boy w/wheelbarrow..**22.00**
Figurine, girl w/bowl, 11" **25.00**
Planter, girl figural, artist signed, #1899, 11" **30.00**
Plate, Rose, 10" **6.00**
Vase, Ming Tree, w/coralene, 8½" **35.00**

Weller

Sam Weller's company made pottery in the Zanesville, Ohio, area from before the turn of the century until 1948. They made lovely hand-decorated artware, commercial lines, garden pottery, dinnerware, and kitchenware. Most examples are marked with the company name, either in block letters or script. Refer to *The Collector's Encyclopedia of Weller Pottery* by Sharon and Bob Huxford (Collector Books).

Arcadia, bud vase, bud shape, white, 7½" **20.00**
Ardsley, corner vase, embossed iris design, paper label, 7" **85.00**
Baldin, bowl, embossed apples, no mark, 4" **100.00**
Barcelona, candle holders, stylized flowers, ink stamp, 2x5" dia, pr **75.00**
Blossom, wall vase, 2 blossoms on single branch, 7½" **70.00**
Blue Drapery, bowl, embossed flowers over embossed folds, 4" **35.00**
Blue Ware, comport, fruit motif, impressed mark, 5½" ..**175.00**
Cameo, hanging basket, white embossed flowers on blue, no mark, 5" **70.00**
Chase, vase, fan shape, white-on-blue hunt scene, 8½" ...**250.00**
Classic, window box, green, 4" high **70.00**
Darsie, vase, embossed swags-&-tassel motif, fluted rim, pink, 7½" **30.00**
Fairfield, vase, cherubs embossed around top band, no mark, 8" **75.00**
Florala, candle holders, embossed flowers, impressed mark, 5", pr **65.00**
Glendale, vase, urn shape, embossed bird motif, impressed mark, 5" **165.00**

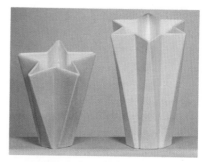

Atlas vases, 10½", $65.00; #C-10, 13", $85.00.

Ivoris, powder box, w/lid, plain, round, 4" **45.00**
Ivory, wall pocket, stag, 9"..**250.00**
Klyro, planter, embossed flowers, square, 4" **55.00**
Knifewood, bowl, embossed daisies, impressed mark, 3" **75.00**
Lido, planter, leaf shape, 2x 9" **25.00**
Loru, cornucopia, blue, footed, script mark, 4" **20.00**
Lustre, basket, blue, no mark, 6½" **60.00**
Manhattan, vase, green, flowers & leaves at random, handles, 8" **70.00**
Marbleized, bowl, impressed mark, 1½x5½" dia **45.00**
Melrose, basket, grape decoration, impressed mark, 10" ...**175.00**
Mirror Black, bud vase, flared top, 5½" **40.00**
Neiska, vase, golden color w/ filigree handles, script mark, 6½" **30.00**
Novel, comport, apple handles, black trim, tall pedestal, 5½" **60.00**
Oak Leaf, planter, oak leaves on blue, script mark, 6" **35.00**
Paragon, bowl, incised stylized flowers on blue, script mark, 4½" **55.00**
Pearl, bowl, embossed swags & jewels, impressed mark, 3" **80.00**
Pierre, sugar bowl, embossed basketweave, pink, script mark, 2" **15.00**
Roma, console bowl, w/liner, embossed grape design, 4½x16" **175.00**
Roma, jardiniere, embossed swags-&-roses design, no mark, 5" **60.00**
Roma, vase, embossed swags & roses below row of perforated ovals, 9" **70.00**

Rosemont, jardiniere, apples on checked ground, impressed mark, 5" **85.00**
Rudlor, console bowl, embossed blossoms, beaded handles, 4½x17½" **50.00**
Velvetone, vase, blended pastels on horizontal ridges, fluted rim, 10" **100.00**
Wild Rose, vase, embossed flower & stem on green, footed, 7½" **30.00**
Woodcraft, fan vase, embossed fruit tree design, no mark, 8" **65.00**
Woodcraft, vase, embossed branch w/apple, no mark, 13" **125.00**
Zona, comport, incised flowers on plain pedestal, 5½" **60.00**
Zona, dinner plate, embossed apple design, no mark, 10" **25.00**
Zona, pitcher, apples on branch, branch handle, impressed mark, 6" **50.00**

Western Collectibles

Items such as chaps, spurs, saddles, and lariats represent possibly the most colorful genre in the history of our country, and collectors, especially from the western states, find them fascinating. The romance of the Old West lives on through relics related to those bygone days of cowboys, Wild West shows, frontier sheriffs, and boom-town saloons.

Ashtray, Boots & Saddle pattern, Wallace China, 5½", M ..**65.00**
Autograph, Bvt Major-General CC Augur, Indian fighter, ca late 1860s **24.00**
Book, Buskskin & Blanket Days, 1st edition, Doubleday, 1957, w/jacket **30.00**

Book, Crazy Horse & Custer, 1975, 486 pages, EX **20.00**

Book, Drifting Cowboy, by Will James, Grosset & Dunlap, w/dust jacket **25.00**

Branding iron, iron, 48", G ..**28.00**

Buffalo skull, lg horns **180.00**

Catalog, HR Miller Saddle Co, Kansas City, MO, 60 pages, dated 1962, M **40.00**

Catalog, tack & equipment, Montgomery Ward, 1920s, NM..................................**28.00**

Check, mining vignette, WA Clarke & Brother, Bankers, 1893, NM **18.00**

Coin, Texas Centennial, Heads You Win Tails You Lose, 1936 ....**22.50**

Collar, cowboy's, tooled leather, M **125.00**

Cuffs, tooled leather w/snap closure, Gopher Brand, 6", pr **90.00**

Envelope, Wells Fargo Express logo w/CA coastal routes, 1870s, NM **18.50**

Handcuffs, marked Mattarick Manufacturing, VG **50.00**

Handcuffs, screw type, marked Hiatt, replaced key **120.00**

Hat, boy's, brown w/white graphics & cord, JC Penney, 1950s, EX **90.00**

Hat, light tan beaver Stetson, ca 1950s, missing hat band, EX **180.00**

Holster, plain leather, marked SJ Barton, single belt loop cut in back **95.00**

Inkwell, steer hoof w/brass fittings, glass bowl, EX **35.00**

Long horns, 32" across, VG ..**67.50**

Map, California gold-bearing regions, hand colored, dated 1853, VG **45.00**

Milk bottle, Cheyenne Frontier Days, The Daddy of Them All, 1-qt **47.50**

Newspaper, Detroit Free Press, July 22, 1876, Custer's Massacre, EX **55.00**

Newspaper, Leslie's Weekly, Capture of Fort Hindman, 1863, VG **35.00**

Photo, lawman holds his gun on man w/upraised arms, G **45.00**

Photo, 9 mounted cowboys w/cattle in background, ca 1915, 6½x8½" **40.00**

Pin-back button, RT Frazier's Famous Pueblo Saddles, 2¼", M **150.00**

Postcard, JH Wilson Saddlery Co, color photo, 1910, EX **42.50**

Print, Chief of Blackfoot Nation, by Catlin, 1903, 11x14", NM **50.00**

Program, Buffalo Bill's Wild West Show, dated 1908, EX..............................**140.00**

Scabbard, for Winchester '73 rifle, marked Royal, w/rawhide laces **50.00**

Sleeve cuffs, tooled leather w/lacing & snap, old, EX **65.00**

Spurs, bull rider's, leather, ¾" rowels, VG **70.00**

Spurs, very plain, 1½" shank w/ ⅝" band, 1½" rowell, new straps **75.00**

Stereoview, Blackfoot Indian village at Glacier Park, Keystone View Co **20.00**

Stereoview, Great San Francisco Earthquake & Fire, ca 1906, VG **20.00**

Stock certificate, WI & CO Silver Mining Co, 3 vignettes, unissued **5.00**

Tin, Orcico Cigars, Indian portrait, slip lid, 5x6x4", VG **250.00**

Trade card, Dr WF Carver Evil Spirit, Scout, Wild West, 4½x 7" **50.00**

Western Heroes

Interest is very strong right now in western memorabilia – not only that, but the kids that listened so intently to those after-school radio episodes featuring one of the many cowboy stars that sparked the airways in the '50s are now some of today's more affluent collectors, able and wanting to search out and buy toys they had in their youth. Put those two factors together, and it's easy to see why these items are so popular. *Character Toys and Collectibles* by David Longest (Collector Books) has lots of good information on Western heroes. See also Character Watches; Movie Memorabilia.

Gene Autry songbook, Western Music Publishing, 8x12", NM, $35.00.

Cisco Kid, comic album, 1953, M **20.00**

Cisco Kid, mask, Tip Top Bread premium, EX **16.50**

Cisco Kid & Pancho, cereal bowl, milk glass, black lettering, 1950s, M **25.00**

Cisco Kid & Pancho, coloring book, Saalfield, EX **15.00**

Dale Evans, costume w/hat, 1950s, complete, MIB ...**55.00**

Davy Crockett, book bag, 1950s, EX **15.00**

Davy Crockett, canteen, 1950s, EX **25.00**

Davy Crockett, coonskin cap, vinyl & plush, gold portrait, 1950s, EX **25.00**

Davy Crockett, doll, 1950s, MIB **125.00**

Davy Crockett, holster set, leather, 1950s, MIB **55.00**

Davy Crockett, lamp, ceramic, 1955, EX **50.00**

Davy Crockett, mug, milk glass, 1950, EX **15.00**

Davy Crockett, sheet music, 1954 ....**16.50**

Davy Crockett, wallet, vinyl, 1950s, EX **10.00**

Gene Autry, bicycle horn, ca 1950, M **40.00**

Gene Autry, coloring book, ca 1950, 8x11", VG **12.50**

Gene Autry, comic book, Dell, 1950s, M **12.00**

Gene Autry, Cowboy Paint Book, 1940, 15x10", M **65.00**

Gene Autry, guitar, Silvertone, ca 1950, EX **65.00**

Gene Autry, pin-back button, Sunbeam Bread premium ...**15.00**

Gene Autry, rain boots, red & black w/logo, 8", EX **35.00**

Gene Autry, toy pistol, signed, M **40.00**

Hopalong Cassidy, alarm clock, metal, 1950s, EX **100.00**

Hopalong Cassidy, bath rug, ca 1950s, EX **15.00**

Hopalong Cassidy, bicycle horn, 1950s, MIB **95.00**

Hopalong Cassidy, binoculars, Hoppy logo, 1950s, EX ..**20.00**

Hopalong Cassidy, birthday card, Now You're 6, Buzza, 1950, EX **7.50**

Hopalong Cassidy, cereal bowl, marked WS George, EX ..**15.00**

Hopalong Cassidy, coasters, 1950s, set of 4, EX **20.00**

Hopalong Cassidy, fan club card, paper, 1950s, EX **7.50**

Hopalong Cassidy, flashlight pistol, 1950s, EX **40.00**

Hopalong Cassidy, jigsaw puzzle, Milton Bradley, 1950s, MIB **25.00**

Hopalong Cassidy, mug, marked WS George, M **15.00**

Hopalong Cassidy, neckerchief, black satin, 1950s, EX ..**20.00**

Hopalong Cassidy, night light, Hoppy riding Topper **7.50**

Hopalong Cassidy, party invitation, Buzza, 1950s, M ...**12.00**

Hopalong Cassidy, pencil case, ca 1950, EX **15.00**

Hopalong Cassidy, pin-back button, in the Daily News, portrait center **40.00**

Hopalong Cassidy, plate, ceramic, shows Hoppy on Topper, 9" dia, M **35.00**

Hopalong Cassidy, pocketknife, M **35.00**

Hopalong Cassidy, postcard, Savings Club, EX **12.50**

Hopalong Cassidy tin wind-up toy by Marx, 9½", EX, $95.00.

Hopalong Cassidy, scrapbook, simulated leather cover, 1950s, 14", NM **55.00**

Hopalong Cassidy, wallet, leather, 1950s, EX **25.00**

Hopalong Cassidy & Topper, pin-back button, red, white & black, EX **20.00**

Lone Ranger, badge, Bond Bread premium, EX **25.00**

Lone Ranger, blotter, Bond Bread premium, EX **15.00**

Lone Ranger, figure, molded plaster, dated 1938, 4", M **40.00**

Lone Ranger, hairbrush, wooden handle, 1939, VG **20.00**

Lone Ranger, paint book, Whitman, 1941, M **25.00**

Lone Ranger, pedometer, metal, M **45.00**

Lone Ranger, pencil sharpener, silver bullet type, EX **25.00**

Lone Ranger, scrapbook, Whitman, ca 1950, M **45.00**

Red Ryder, child's chaps, dyed leather, ca 1950s, NM..**130.00**

Red Ryder, comic book, Dell, 1950, EX **7.50**

Rin Tin Tin, compass, 1950s ..**60.00**

Rin Tin Tin, View Master set, complete, M **15.00**

Roy Rogers, belt, child's, 1950s, EX **25.00**

Roy Rogers, harmonica, 1950s, EX **16.00**

Roy Rogers, lamp, painted figural plaster, 1950s, 11", EX ..**85.00**

Roy Rogers, mug, plastic figural, 4", EX **15.00**

Roy Rogers, plate & mug set, ceramic, 1950s, M **40.00**

Roy Rogers, playing cards, 1950s, MIB **25.00**

Roy Rogers, souvenir book, dated 1950, EX **25.00**

Roy Rogers, trading card, bubble gum, 1955, set of 24 ......**25.00**

Roy Rogers, wallet, vinyl, 1950s, EX **20.00**

Roy Rogers & Dale Evans, record, 78 rpm, 1950s, w/ sleeve, M ..**10.00**

Roy Rogers & Trigger, camera, 1950s, EX **30.00**

Roy Rogers & Trigger, horseshoe, hard red rubber, ca 1950s, 5½" **7.50**

Roy Rogers & Trigger, pin-back button, photo & letters on yellow, 2" **25.00**

Tom Mix, arrowhead compass, plastic, EX **25.00**

Tom Mix, coloring book, 1950s, 11x8½", NM **40.00**

Tom Mix, draw & paint book, Whitman, 1930s, NM **35.00**

Tom Mix, glow-in-the-dark spurs, EX **35.00**

Tom Mix, musical bird call ..**12.00**

Tom Mix, periscope, Ralston Straight Shooters premium, EX **40.00**

Tom Mix, pin-back button, Yanki-boy Play Clothes, photo on yellow, 2" **55.00**

Tom Mix, telescope, 1930s ...**60.00**

Wyatt Earp, coloring book, 1950s, EX **15.00**

Wyatt Earp, Marshall's badge, 1950s, M on card **18.00**

Wyatt Earp, mug, milk glass, 1950s, M **10.00**

Zorro, charm bracelet, child's, 1960s, EX **25.00**

Zorro, costume, child's, M **35.00**

Zorro, hand puppet, cloth & vinyl, 1960s, EX **10.00**

Zorro, target game, w/dart gun, Knickerbocker, 1950s, complete, M **95.00**

Zorro, water pistol, Knickerbocker, NM **35.00**

Westmoreland

Originally an Ohio company, Westmoreland relocated in Grapeville, Pennsylvania, where by the 1920s they had became known as one of the country's largest manufacturers of carnival glass. They are best known today for the high quality milk glass which accounted for 90% of their production.

Ashtray, Beaded Grape, square, 4" **8.00**

Basket, Paneled Grape, milk glass, ruffled, 5½" **52.50**

Bonbon, Paneled Grape, milk glass, ruffled, w/metal handle, 8" **50.00**

Bottle, toilet; Paneled Grape, milk glass, 5-oz **62.50**

Bowl, Beaded Grape, flared top, footed, 8" **55.00**

Bowl, Paneled Grape, milk glass, lipped, 9" **100.00**

Bowl, Paneled Grape, milk glass, shallow, 8½" **55.00**

Bowl, Sawtooth, milk glass, flared top, footed, 12" **38.00**

Bud vase, Paneled Grape, milk glass, 9" **10.00**

Wedding bowl, milk glass with hand-painted ribbons and roses, 8", $65.00.

Cake salver, Paneled Grape 1881, milk glass, 11½" **50.00**

Candleabra, Lotus 1921, milk glass, 3-lite, pr **60.00**

Candle holder, Old Quilt 500, milk glass, 4", pr **22.00**

Candy jar, Paneled Grape, milk glass, w/lid, 3-footed **32.50**

Canister, Paneled Grape, milk glass, 7" **110.00**

Celery or spooner, Paneled Glass, milk glass, 6" **40.00**

Chocolate box, Paneled Grape, milk glass, w/lid, 6½" **52.50**

Cigarette box, English Hobnail, milk glass, w/lid **22.00**

Cordial, 1000 Eye, crystal ...**12.00**

Creamer, Old Quilt 500, milk glass, 3¾" **10.00**

Creamer, Panelled Grape, ruby red **14.00**

Cruet, Paneled Grape 1881, milk glass, w/stopper **22.50**

Cup & saucer, American Hobnail, milk glass **10.00**

Cup & saucer, English Hobnail, milk glass **15.00**

Dish, hand form, milk glass ..**17.00**

Egg plate, Paneled Grape, milk glass, 12" **75.00**

Figurine, bird in flight, amber marigold, wings out, 5" wide **25.00**

Figurine, Porky Pig, milk glass, hollow, 3" long **15.00**

Figurine, pouter pigeon, 1" ..**20.00**

Figurine, turtle paperweight, Green Mist, no holes, 4" long **22.00**

Goblet, water; Della Robia, milk glass **20.00**

Ladle, Paneled Grape, milk glass, sm **10.00**

Marmalade, Paneled Grape, milk glass, w/ladle **57.50**

Nappy, Paneled Grape, milk glass, bell shape, 5" **22.00**

Parfait, Paneled Grape, milk glass, 6" **23.00**

Pitcher, Paneled Grape, milk glass, 32-oz **37.50**

Plate, Beaded Edge, milk glass, coupe, 8¼" **10.00**

Plate, Beaded Edge, milk glass, 6" **3.00**

Plate, Beaded Edge, milk glass w/hand-painted peaches, 7½" **15.00**

Plate, bread; Paneled Grape, milk glass, 6" **14.00**

Relish, Paneled Grape, milk glass, 3-part, 9" **39.50**

Rose bowl, Doric #3, milk glass, 6½" **45.00**

Salt & pepper shakers, American Hobnail, pr **16.00**

Sauce boat, Paneled Grape, milk glass **30.00**

Sherbet, English Hobnail, milk glass, square w/foot **6.00**

Soap dish, Paneled Grape, milk glass **77.50**

Sugar bowl, Beaded Grape, milk glass **12.50**

Toothpick, Paneled Grape, milk glass **24.00**

Tumbler, iced tea; Della Robia, milk glass, footed **8.00**

Tumbler, iced tea; Princess Feather, amber, 5½" **12.00**

Vase, Paneled Grape, milk glass, bell shape, 11½" **47.50**

Wheaton Bottles

Though the Wheaton Company of Millville, New Jersey, made several series of bottles, those with portraits of our country's presidents are the most collectible. Many colors have been used, including some iridescents.

Andrew Jackson, from $30.00 up to **35.00**

Calvin Coolidge, from $20.00 up to **25.00**

FDR (Franklin Delano Roosevelt),
from $20.00 up to **25.00**
Franklin Pierce, second or corrected version, from $30.00
up to **35.00**
Gerald R Ford, from $10.00 up
to **15.00**
Herbert Hoover, from $10.00 up
to **15.00**
James K Polk, from $30.00 up
to **35.00**
John Adams, from $20.00 up
to **25.00**
John Tyler, from $15.00 up to ..**25.00**
Rutherford B Hayes, from $35.00
up to **40.00**
Rutherford B Hayes, second or
corrected version, from $30.00
up to **35.00**
Ulysses S Grant, from $15.00
up to **20.00**
William Howard Taft, from $20.00
up to **25.00**
Zachary Taylor, second or cor-
rected version, from $30.00
up to **35.00**

Wicker

Wicker became a popular
medium for furniture construction
as early as the mid-1800s. Early
styles were closely woven and
very ornate; frames were of heavy
wood. By the turn of the century
the weaving was looser and styles
were simple. Today's collectors
prefer tables with wicker tops as
opposed to wooden tops, matching
ensembles, and pieces that have
not been painted.

Baby scales, lg open weave top on
metal scale base **190.00**
Basket, funerary type, open weave
w/twist handle, 27" **50.00**
Basket, picnic; suitcase type,
w/original utensils, EX ..**45.00**

Chair, arm; open weave, flat arm-
rests, ball feet, Bar Harbor
style **320.00**
Chair, side; fancy scroll back, ball
finials, cane seat, wrapped
legs................................**190.00**
Chair, side; scrollwork, cabriole
legs, Whitney, EX **335.00**
Chair, side; tight weave apron,
diamond design, fabric seat,
37" **185.00**
Lamp, tight weave, bottle form,
lg foot base, Lloyd Mfg, ca
1910s **260.00**
Log carrier, lg tight weave
round base, wicker handle,
ca 1930 ....**90.00**
Ottoman, circular tight weave w/
beadwork on skirt, Heywood-
Wakefield **280.00**
Pedestal, square top, tapered column, Heywood-Wakefield,
35", EX **200.00**
Plant stand, circular top w/braid
trim, 4 wrapped legs w/cross
bars **110.00**
Plant stand, machine-woven
fiber w/shelf, turned legs,
1920s **150.00**
Plant stand, tight weave box, 4
turned legs, ca 1925 ....**160.00**
Rocker, child's; close weave w/
diamond on skirt, Lloyd Mfg,
ca 1920s **185.00**
Rocker, close weave, cathedral
back, innerspring seat, wood
rockers **320.00**
Rocker, open weave, rounded
back, caned seat, stuffed
cushion, ca 1915 ....**360.00**
Rocker, sewing; curliques & beadwork, natural finish, 1890s,
sm **355.00**
Sewing table, close weave, ball
feet, gallery shelf, handle,
1920s **190.00**
Table, occasional; fine-weave skirt
under wood top, 1 shelf, ca
1930s **260.00**

Table, occasional; tight weave, braid trim, wood top & shelf, ca 1920 ....**190.00**

Table, occasional; tight weave, gallery tray top & shelf, ball feet **260.00**

Whatnot shelf, elaborate curliques & beadwork, 3 wood shelves **290.00**

Willow Ware

Inspired by the lovely blue and white Chinese exports, the Willow pattern has been made by many English, American, and Japanese firms from 1750 to the present. Many variations of the pattern have been noted; pink, black, green, and multicolor Willow ware can be found in limited amounts. The design has been applied to tinware, linens, glassware, and paper goods, all of which are treasured by today's collectors. Refer to *Blue Willow* by Mary Frank Gaston (Collector Books) for more information. See also Royal China.

Ashtray, advertising, English, unmarked, 4" dia **30.00**

Baking dish, oven proof, Japan, 2½x5" dia **30.00**

Bowl, cereal; Shenango China ..**20.00**

Bowl, salad; square, Ridgway, 9" **80.00**

Bowl, vegetable; divided, Allerton, 7¼" **85.00**

Bowl, vegetable; pink, Japan 9¾" **25.00**

Butter dish, Josiah Wedgwood, covered, 8" dia **175.00**

Canister set, barrel shape, graduated sizes, Japan **250.00**

Coffeepot, granite ware, 6" ..**80.00**

Creamer, hotel ware, Shenango China, 2½" **30.00**

Creamer, Scroll & Flower border, Royal Worcester Crown Willow, 2" **60.00**

Cup & saucer, demitasse; Two Temples II, Copeland **45.00**

Dresser box, porcelain, late 1880s, English, 3" dia **90.00**

Flatware, plastic & stainless steel, 4-pc place setting, Japan..**50.00**

Ginger jar, Scroll & Flower border, pink, English, unmarked, 9" **85.00**

Gravy dish, stick handle, 2 spouts, Lean & Gravy printed inside **70.00**

Honey dish, Midwinter, 4"....**35.00**

Horseradish dish, Doulton, 5½" dia **55.00**

Humidor, brown w/gold trim, Doulton, 6½" **225.00**

Humidor, flow blue, ca 1900, Wiltshaw & Robinson, 5" ...**275.00**

Ladle, 7", unmarked **125.00**

Leaf dish, English, unmarked, 5½" **140.00**

Mug, milk glass, silk-screened pattern, Anchor Hocking, 3" **10.00**

Mug, Two Temples II pattern, hotel ware, Sebring Pottery, 3½" **15.00**

Pitcher, Red Willow, marked Japan, 6", $45.00.

Mustard pot, barrel shape, unmarked, 2½" **70.00**

Mustard pot, cylinder shape, flared rim, Shenango China, 2½" **50.00**

Pie server, Japan, 10" **35.00**

Pitcher, carnival-type glass, 1940s, Jeannette Glass, 10" **100.00**

Pitcher, cylindrical, Butterfly border, rope handle, 9¾" ..**150.00**

Pitcher, Schweppes advertising, English, 4" **135.00**

Pitcher, triangular shape, Doulton, 6" **175.00**

Plate, cake; handles, English ..**90.00**

Plate, Mandarin center, Dagger border, pink, English, unmarked, 6" **18.00**

Salt shaker, triangular shape, Japan, 2" **15.00**

Shaving mug, scuttle style, Gibson & Sons, 3¼" **250.00**

Snack dish, long figural dog, 5 sections, Japan **40.00**

Spoon rest, double style, Japan, 9" **40.00**

Teapot, ball shape, Red Willow, 6-cup capacity, Johnson Bros **90.00**

Tumbler, juice; ceramic, Japan, unmarked **20.00**

Tumbler, juice; clear glass, Libbey Glass, 3½" **15.00**

Winchester

Originally manufacturing only guns and ammunition, after 1920 the Winchester Company produced a vast array of sporting goods and hardware items (more than 7,500) which they marked 'Winchester Trademark, USA.' The name of the firm changed in 1931, and the use of the trademark was discontinued. Examples with this mark have become collectors' items.

Brochure, featuring M-65, 218 Bee **35.00**

Can opener, VG **45.00**

Catalog, 1914, EX **85.00**

Chisel, ¾", G **25.00**

Flashlight, marked USA, 6¾", EX, $30.00.

Grease gun, red & green box, very early, NM **25.00**

Handsaw, #W8, 24", NM **85.00**

Ice pick, #9501, wood handle, 8½" **65.00**

Knife, #1761, steel, wood handle, 17", NM **95.00**

Letter opener, dated 1922, NM ..**90.00**

Meat grinder, #W31, EX+ **75.00**

Padlock, brass & iron, EX ..**135.00**

Pliers, snap ring; #2184, 5", EX+ **70.00**

Rake, garden; VG **85.00**

Razor strop, EX **90.00**

Reel, #2242, NM **125.00**

Scissors, #9016, lg, EX **35.00**

Screwdriver, #7360, w/brass, 3¼", EX **35.00**

Screwdriver, very thin shaft, 14", EX **65.00**

Thermometer, EX **135.00**

Thermos, 1-qt, EX **135.00**

Token, brass, eagle under company name, Keep an Opened Mind, ⅞" **65.00**

Wirecutters, #2166, 6", NM ..**65.00**

Wrench, #1837, 8½" **50.00**

Wireware

Before the turn of the century, wire was twisted together

for strength and fashioned into items that ranged from large garden benches to small household items, both utilitarian and decorative in nature. Some of the more common items available today include egg baskets, soap savers, and dish drainers.

Basket, convertible type, nickled iron, Rayment Supply, ca 1910-20s **20.00**
Birdcage, enameled iron & perforated sheet metal, 1910, 18x11x7¾" **90.00**
Bottle carrier, tinned w/twisted center handle, footed, holds 6 bottles............................**40.00**
Castor holder, 3 cups w/twisted center handle, footed, Pat 1874 ....**50.00**
Comb holder, twisted wire w/ loop **85.00**
Cooling rack, mesh bottom, footed, 2x18x11" **60.00**
Country store bag & string holder, folding, heavy wire **150.00**
Dish towel holder, twisted wire, slip-ring prongs, 13½" ...**17.50**
Egg basket, bail handle, 5¼x7½" dia top **45.00**
Egg basket, looped wire top, footed, 10" **55.00**
Egg basket, retinned wastebasket style, ca 1909, 15x 12" dia **35.00**
Fly screen, close-knit oval shape, ca 1910, 10" **25.00**
Ladle, oyster-straining; heavy wire **20.00**
Lamp chimney cleaner, heavy wire w/moveable parts, 16½" **25.00**
Pie holder & cooler, tinned 4-plate style, ca 1915 ....**20.00**
Pie plate lifter, fork shape w/wood handle **42.00**
Pie plate lifter, spring action, finger & thumb loops, 14¾" **35.00**

Rug beater, looped design w/wood handle **22.00**
Sieve, oblong, slides to fit bowl, ca 1890 ....**25.00**
Soap saver, wire mesh box, wood handle on twisted shaft, ca 1920-40s **15.00**
Toaster, 2" between racks, 2 feet at front, 1 at handle, ca 1860, 8x8" **110.00**

Wizard of Oz

Frank L. Baum's famous series of Oz stories inspired the award-winning 1939 movie, staring Judy Garland and a star-studded cast. A short-lived radio program sponsored by Jell-O was broadcast in the early 1930s. And with the Golden Anniversary of the film's debute, renewed interest has spured many new items as well as reproductions onto the market. *Wizard of Oz Collector Guide* by Jay Scarfone and William Stillman is recommended for further information. Our advisor is Lori Landgrebe, listed in the Directory under Illinois. See also Clubs and Newsletters.

Calendar, Denslow illustrations, 1982, M **8.00**
Collector plate, Lion, Knowles, no box **25.00**
Coloring book, Great Fun Time, Creative Child Press, 1987 ......**2.50**
Dolls, cloth, toilet tissue premium, 1970s, set of 4 ....**30.00**
Figure, Scarecrow, PVC, Presents, 1987-88, EX **4.00**
Figure, Wicked Witch, PVC, Presents, 1987-88, NM **5.00**
Figurine, Dorothy, PVC, Presents, 1987, M **4.50**
Figurines, Pewter Fancy, 1970s, set of 4 ....**25.00**

409

Game, Cadaco, MIB **8.00**

Game, Wonderful Game of Oz, Parker Bros, 1921, NM in box **225.00**

Magazine ad, Collier's, color, 1939, full page, EX **12.50**

Peanut butter tin, Swift, pyramid style, 2-lb **45.00**

Postcard, ruby slipper **2.00**

Puppet, Tinman, Proctor & Gamble **15.00**

Puzzle, Dorothy & Glenda, Golden, 1988, frame tray, M in shrink-wrap **6.00**

Puzzle, in canister, Storyland, complete **10.00**

Recipe booklet, Jell-O, 1930s, EX **45.00**

Record, Disney, w/11-page book, EX **17.50**

Scarecrow-in-the-Box, Off to See the Wizard, Mattel, 1967 ..**20.00**

Sheet music, Over the Rainbow, 1939 ....**25.00**

Sweeper, New Oz, Bissel, 1939, adult or child size **80.00**

Tin, Swift's Peanut Butter, colorful tin, bail handle **35.00**

Toy watch, Tinman & Scarecrow, tin, Occupied Japan, 1940s-1950s **15.00**

Trash can, metal, marked Cheinco Made in USA, 1975 ....**40.00**

Tumbler, Emerald City, Swift, green, fluted **25.00**

Tumbler, Scarecrow, Kentucky Fried Chicken **45.00**

Valentines, Cleo, MIB **7.50**

Woodenware

Most of the primitive hand-crafted wooden bowls and utensils on today's market can be attributed to a period from late in the 1700s until about 1870. They were designed on a strictly utilitarian basis, and only rarely was any attempt made toward decoration. The most desirable are those items made from burl wood – the knuckle or knot of the tree having a grain that appears mottled when it is carved – or utensils with an effigy-head handle. Very old examples are light in weight due to the deterioration of the wood; expect age cracks that develop as the wood dries.

Bowl, butter; burl, refinished ..**825.00**

Bowl, turned poplar, red painted exterior, repaired crack, 24" dia **200.00**

Butter worker, maple, paddle w/grooves, 2" wide **28.00**

Cheese box, bentwood, 11½x15" dia **58.00**

Compote, burl, heavy foot, 5x6", EX **250.00**

Dipper, figured maple, bird's-eye bowl, 11½", EX **85.00**

Drying rack, child's **20.00**

Flour scoop, 11" **60.00**

Lemon squeezer, tiger maple ..**65.00**

Match holder, hand-carved maple, fancy design, ca 1850s ..**110.00**

Peg rack, pine, 3 hand-whittled hooks **55.00**

Pie crimper, 3¼" **28.00**

Plate, poplar, 10", EX **300.00**

Spoon, hand carved, 4½x5½" flat bowl, 20" handle **36.00**

Spoon rack, holds 6, fancy back, 16¾x10" **145.00**

Toddy stick, rounded 4-point star stirrer pegged to handle, 15" **45.00**

World's Fairs and Expositions

Souvenir items have been distributed from every fair and exposition since the mid-1850s.

Examples from before the turn of the century are challenging to collect, but even those issued for much later events are desirable.

1893 Columbian, Chicago

Book, Official Guide, Hand Book, Anderson, 192 pages **20.00**
Box, Jewel of Virginia Tobacco, litho tin, 4x3x2" **55.00**
Paperweight, Horticulture Building, boats on water, multicolor, 4x2" **50.00**
Plate, Art Palace, black on white, gold trim, marked England, 6" **45.00**
Stereoview, The Great Cactus, Horticulture Building, BW Kilburn **5.00**
Ticket, Manhattan Day, M ...**20.00**
Trade card, Fisheries Building photo-lithograph, Jersey Coffee, 3x5" **10.00**
Tray, World's Fair 1893 engraved, openwork border, metal, 4½" dia **25.00**
Watch case opener, pocket watch figural, globe design, Souvenir...1893 ....**25.00**

1901 Pan American

Advertising card, 2 ladies on blue globe, much expo information, 3x5" **10.00**
Clock, real frying pan w/works, 17" **350.00**
Doll, kewpie type, celluloid, arms move, Pan-Am on feet, 3"..**50.00**
Envelope, buffalo on globe, Electric Tower, blue on white, 6x3½" **15.00**
Letter opener, made from flattened nail, globe design, 5½" **22.50**
Napkin ring, buffalo design, engraved floral, beaded border, aluminum **20.00**

Paperweight, sea shells enclosed in glass, Souvenir...1901, 3" dia **25.00**
Penny, 1901 Indian head, aluminum holder marked Good Luck Souvenir... ....**17.50**
Shot glass, When You Drink Do of Me Think, frosted buffalo design **30.00**
Spoon, US Gov't Building, Indian & falls on handle, 4½" ...**15.00**

1904 St. Louis

Cigar label, Temple of Fraternity, Temple Cigar Co, 6x8½" ..**7.00**
Coin purse, Festival Hall, 100 Years 1903, paper litho over cloth **15.00**
Cup & saucer, Ceylon Court, Pure Ceylon Tea, colors on white porcelain **75.00**
Letter opener, Cupid, cornucopia & scrolls, nickel-plated brass, 6" **65.00**
Pincushion, seashell w/cushion in center, 5½" **25.00**

St. Louis, 1904, postcard, hold-to-light, unused, M, $20.00.

Scarf, St Louis 1803-1904 Purchase Monument, multicolor cotton, 16" **77.00**
Sheet music, Exposition March & 2-Step, McKinley Music Co, VG **12.00**
Tip tray, It's a Shame To Take the Money, lithographed aluminum, 3x5" **29.00**

1915 Panama Pacific

Handkerchief, Exposition San Francisco 1915, lace trim, 12" **5.00**

Mirror, Independent Order of Foresters, Tower of Jewels, 2½" dia **55.00**

Pin-back button, multicolored logo, 1", w/Liberty Bell charm **45.00**

1933 Chicago

Ashtray, Firestone Tires, rubber tire figural w/amber glass insert **50.00**

Bank, American Can Co, lithographed tin, 1934 date, w/ closure, 3" **20.00**

Bracelet, comet logo & 1933 center, 6 other designs, metal, 1" wide **15.00**

Candle holder, Hall of Science & Federal Building, metal, 4x2" pr **45.00**

Cap, Fort Dearborn, Science & Administration Buildings, red felt **50.00**

Cent, elongated, A Century of Progress Sky Ride Chicago 1933 ....**10.00**

Fan, wood spokes, oriental scene, 10x15" (open) **45.00**

Handbook, Athletic Institute's Badminton, 1940s, set of 4, EX in box **15.00**

Mug, nude female handle, molded designs & dates, green, 6½" **45.00**

Napkin ring, comet logo, 3 buildings, gold on red, 1½" dia **15.00**

Plate, Federal Building Court of States, floral border, 8¼" **40.00**

Postcard, Paul Desmuke the Armless Wonder, Ripley's Believe It or Not **7.50**

Program, Wings of a Century, illustrated, 12 pages + covers, 8x11" **15.00**

Tea ball, teapot shape, attached medallion w/comet design, metal **17.50**

Tie clip, sky ride design, 1934 date, bar type **12.50**

Umbrella, Chicago 1933, blue & red paper, bamboo spokes, 28" dia **35.00**

Watch fob, Leonard Refrigeration, overview of fair, brass, 1¼" dia **25.00**

1939 New York

Bank, lithographed buildings & Trylon & Perisphere on tin, 3x2" dia **30.00**

Belt buckle, blue & orange logo on silverplate, 1½x1½" **22.00**

Bookmark, Christian Science Building, red tassel, bronze-color metal **15.00**

New York, 1939, card of six 'trylon' and 'perisphere' plastic buttons, M, $15.00.

Bookmark, Westinghouse... woven in black on orange cloth, 12" **12.50**

Cent, elongated, Trylon & Perisphere design & 1939 ...**10.00**

Cigarette box, Syroco Wood, raised Trylon & Perisphere, 6x4x2" **25.00**

Doily, Trylon & Perisphere/1939, floral edge, 5x8" **20.00**

Folder, Routes to World's Fair, map of city, schedule of special days **5.00**

Guide book, First Edition 1939, well illustrated, 256 pages, 5x8" **20.00**

Hot pad, Administration Building embossed on silver cloth, 8x6", NM **15.00**

Jam jar, glass, grape clusters, fair symbols, w/lid, 3¼" **40.00**

Match cover, Wrigley's Spearmint Gum, EX **5.00**

Pencil sharpener, Trylon & Perisphere figural, orange & black, 5x2" **35.00**

Pendant, RCA Building/Trylon & Perisphere in color on blue felt, 3x8" **15.00**

Pin, brass, cut-out design of Westinghouse Robot, 1" **30.00**

Plate, blue Shelter Building, floral border, Copeland, 10½" **85.00**

Postcard, Belgium Exhibits Building, Underwood black & white series **4.00**

Spoon, Aviation Building, Trylon & Perisphere, Wm Rogers, 6" **10.00**

Swizzle stick, Turf Trylon Cafe, cobalt blue glass, 6" **5.00**

1962 Seattle

Brochure, Standard Oil Co, Space Needle cover, map of fair & Seattle **3.00**

Certificate, from One Million Silver Dollar Display **3.00**

Cup & saucer, US Science Pavilion, 5 multicolor scenes, pr **12.50**

Dish, multicolor Space Needle center, openwork border, heart shape, 5" **10.00**

Key chain, attached viewer shows Space Needle, original mailing tag **10.00**

Tumbler, Boulevards of the World, dark blue & white, gold rim, 5½" **12.50**

1964 New York

Coaster set, multicolor views on wood, 6 in original package, 4" dia **14.00**

Jacket, Greyhound arm patch, blue w/gold-tone Expo buttons **75.00**

Milk lid, Vatican Pavilion, VG .. **.50**

Photo album, brown w/gold logo, vinyl, 12 unused pages, 3½" **2.00**

Poster, Official Postcard Sales Promotional, multicolor, 17x18", VG **10.00**

Puzzle, Milton Bradley, frame tray, set of 3, NM in box **17.50**

Tray, Peace Through Understanding, multicolor image on tin, VG **9.00**

Yellowware

Utility ware made from buff-burning clays took on a yellow hue when covered with a clear glaze, hence the name 'yellow ware.' It is a type of 'country' pottery that is becoming quite popular due to today's emphasis on the 'country' look in home decorating. It was made to a large extent by the Ohio potters, though some was made in the eastern states as well. Very seldom do you find a marked piece.

Bowls, pitchers, and pie plates are common; mugs, rolling pins and lidded jars are more unusual and demand higher prices; so do items with in-mold or mocha-like decoration. Refer to *Collecting Yellow Ware, An Identification and Value Guide,* by John Michel and Lisa S. McAllister (Collector Books).

Bank, frog; green overglaze, 1890-1930 ....**175.00**
Batter bowl, embossed leaf design, Ohio or England, late 1800s **175.00**
Beater jar, advertising, original beater, tin lid, 1910-30 ..**125.00**
Beater jar, Foremost Dairies, 1900s **50.00**
Bowl, blue banded rim & body, American, thru mid-20th century **175.00**
Bowl, mixing; brown bands, 20th C, 9" dia **40.00**
Bowl, mixing; brown mocha on cream band, 11⅜" **185.00**
Bowl, mixing; green sponging, 1890s, 5¼" **50.00**
Bowl, white band oversponged w/ Rockingham, late 1800s ..**175.00**
Butter crock, slip-dot flower design between white rings, w/lid **150.00**

Cookie jar, barrel shaped w/ embossed design top & bottom, 1900-40 ....**135.00**
Cuspidor, embossed design w/ black, 1850-1910 ....**125.00**
Custard cup, Rockingham glaze, 1890-1930 ....**20.00**
Egg cup, plain, 1850-1900 ..**200.00**
Jar, plain octagonal shape, from mid-1800s **200.00**
Jug, plain, labeled Pearl China & Pottery, Ohio, 1930s, miniature **150.00**
Mold, dark yellow, sm fruit design in center, late 1800s, round, 8" **200.00**
Mold, grapes, octagonal shape w/fluted sides, 1840-1890, 7" **165.00**
Mold, plain, Turk's cap form, fluted, 1860-1900, 12" dia **225.00**
Mug, 3 white slip, straight-sided, 1890-30 ....**200.00**
Pie bird, plain, Nutbrown, England, 1880-1920 ....**125.00**
Pipkin, Rockingham glaze, steam vent in lid & handle, short, round **250.00**
Pitcher, clear glaze, Bennington form, 1900-30, 7" **150.00**
Pitcher, 3-banded Gothic design, Midwest, early 1900s ..**160.00**
Tumbler, Rockingham glaze, probably Ohio, 1880-1920 ..**150.00**

Pitchers, Midwest, first half of the 20th century, left to right: $95.00; $110.00; $175.00.

DIRECTORY

The editors and staff take this opportunity to express our sincere gratitude and appreciation to each person who has in any way contributed to the preparation of this guide. We believe the credibility of our book is greatly enhanced through their efforts. Check these listings for information concerning their specific areas of expertise.

You will notice that at the conclusion of some of the narratives, the advisor's name is given. This is optional and up to the discretion of each individual. We hope to add more advisors with each new edition to provide further resources to you, our readers. If you care to correspond with anyone listed in our Directory, you must send a SASE with your letter.

Arizona
Lund, O.B.
13009 S. 42nd St.
Phoenix, 85044
602-893-3567
Specializing in milk bottles

Arkansas
Antiques of Law and Order
Tony Perrin
H.C. 7, Box 53A
Mena, 71953
501-394-2863 after 5 p.m.
Specializing in law enforcement and crime-related antiques and memorabilia

California
Begin, David H.
138 Lansberry Ct.
Los Gatos, 95032
Specializing in the buying and selling of comic strip art

Brooks, Mike
7335 Skyline Boulevard
Oakland, 94611
510-339-1751
Specializing in typewriters, early televisions, Statue of Liberty

Carter, Tina
882 S Mollison
El Cajon, 92020
619-440-5043
Specializing in tea-related items, teapots, tea tins, children's and toy tea sets, coffeepots, etc.

Escoe, Adrienne
P.O. Box 342
Los Alamitos, 90720
Specializing in glass knives; editor of

Cutting Edge, newsletter; SASE required for information concerning club or newsletter

George, Tony
22366 El Toro Rd. #242
Lake Forest, 92630
714-583-7530
Specializing in sports pins, watch fobs

Hughes, Martha
4128 Ingalls St.
San Diego, 92103
619-296-1866
Specializing in advertising and figural pencil sharpeners

Inouye, Roger
2622 Valewood Ave.
Carlsbad, 92008
619-729-8739
Specializing in Trolls

Kingsbury Productions & Antiques
Katherine Kreider
4555 N Pershing Ave., Ste. 33-138
Stockton, 95207
209-467-8438
Specializing in valentines

Mallette, Leo A.
2309 S Santa Anita Ave.
Arcadia, 91006-5154
Specializing in Betty Boop

Manochio, Dennis C.
4th of July Americana &
Fireworks Museum
P.O. Box 2010
Saratoga, 95070
408-996-1963 or 800-456-5732
Specializing in 4th of July and fire-

works memorabilia, old fireworks items, Chinese firecrackers, labels, books, etc.

Mantz, John
ABWCS
American Barb Wire Collectors Society
1023 Baldwin Rd.
Bakersfield, 93304
805-397-9572
Specializing in antique barb wires

Russell, Jill
3103 Lincoln Ave.
Alameda, 94501
Specializing in Pez

Santi, Steve
19626 Ricardo Ave.
Hayward, 94541
510-481-2586
Specializing in Little Golden Books and look-alikes; author of *Collecting Little Golden Books,* published by Books Americana and available from author for $10.95 plus $2 postage and handling; information requires SASE

Stroller, Nate
960 Reynolds Ave.
Ripon, 95366
209-599-5933
Specializing in Maytag collectibles and pedal cars

Utley, Bill
P.O. Box 3572
Downey, 90242
310-861-6247
Specializing in flashlights and related material such as catalogs and advertising

Van Ausdall, Marci
666-840 Spring Creek Dr.
Westwood, 96137
916-256-3041
Specializing in Betsy McCall dolls and accessories

W.B.S. Marketing
P.O. Box 3280
Visalia, 93278-3280
209-564-0409 or FAX 209-564-0113
Author of *W.B.S. Collector's Guide for Swatch Watches.* Specializing in Swatch watches

Colorado
Diehl, Richard
5965 W. Colgate Pl.
Denver, 80227
303-985-7481
Specializing in license plates

Connecticut
Van Deusen, Hobart D.
28 the Green
Watertown, 06795
203-945-3456
Specializing in typewriter ribbon tins

District of Columbia
Kolodny-Nagy, David
3701 Connecticut Ave. NW #500
Washington, 20008
202-364-8753
Specializing in Transformers, Robotech, and any other robots or Japanese animated items

McMichael, Nancy
P.O. Box 53262
Washington, 20009
Author of the first illustrated book on the subject, *Snowdomes*, published by Abbeville Press; editor of *Snow Biz,* a quarterly newsletter on snowdomes

Florida
Cohen Books and Collectibles
Joel J. Cohen
P.O. Box 810310
Boca Raton, 33481
407-487-7888 or FAX 407-487-3117
Specializing in Disneyana, Disney books, and animation art

Poe-Pourri
Bill and Pat Poe
220 Dominica Circle E
Niceville, 32578-4068
904-897-4163
Specializing in buy-sell-trade fast-food collectibles, cartoon glasses, and other character collectibles; send $2 for current catalog

Seiderman, Jack
1631 NW 114 Ave.
Pembroke Pines, 33026-2539
305-438-0928 or FAX 305-438-0932
Specializing in buying and selling of cigarette lighters. A year's subscription of illustrated catalogs with prices

is available for $8.50 (or $12.50 overseas 1st class)

Georgia
Rogers, Thomas M., Jr.
1466 W Wesley Rd.
Atlanta, 30327
Specializing in mechanical, dexterity-type puzzles

Illinois
Courter, J.W.
R.R. 1
Simpson, 62985
Phone or FAX 618-949-3884
Author of *Aladdin – The Magic Name in Lamps, Aladdin Collectors Manual & Price Guide #14, Aladdin Electric Lamps,* and *Aladdin Electric Lamps Price Guide #1;* information requires SASE

Garmon, Lee
Glass Animals
1529 Whittier St.
Springfield, 62704
217-789-9574
Co-author of *Glass Animals & Figural Flower Frogs of the Depression Era.* Specializing in glass animals, Royal Haeger, Royal Hickman, and Roselane Sparklers

Hoffman, Pat and Don, Sr.
1291 N Elmwood Dr.
Aurora, 60506
708-859-3435
Specializing in Warwick; authors of *Warwick, A to Z,* and *Why Not Warwick.*

Landgrebe, Lori
2331 E Main St.
Decatur, 62521
217-423-2254
Specializing in buying and selling of Wizard of Oz and ladies' compacts.

Rosie Wells Enterprises Inc.
R.R. #1
Canton, 61520
309-668-2565
Author of *The Ornament Collector's Price Guide to Hallmark's Ornaments and Merry Miniatures* and *Precious Moments® Collectibles.* Specializing in Enesco ornaments, David Winter, Carlton ornaments, Lowell Davis Collection 'All God's Children,' and Coca-Cola ornaments

Rodrick, Tammy
R.R. 2, Box 163
Sumner, 62466
618-947-2240
Specializing in Avon, antiques, and collectibles

Soitenly Stooges Inc.
Harry S. Ross
P.O. Box 72
Skokie, 60076
708-432-9270
Specializing in Three Stooges memorabilia

Timesavers
Steve Berger
Box 400
Algonquin, 60102
708-658-2266 or FAX 708-658-9033
Specializing in Swatch watches

TV Guide Specialists
Jeff Kadet
P.O. Box 20
Macomb, 61455
309-833-1809
Specializing in buying and selling of *TV Guide* from 1948 through 1993

Wallin, Richard R.
Box 1784,
Springfield, 62705
217-498-9279
Specializing in airline memorabilia

Indiana
Steve G. Gabany, Ph.D.
The Clock Doctor
585 Woodbine
Terre Haute, 47803-1759
Specializing in cameras and clocks

Wee Scots Inc.
Donna Newton
P.O. Box 1512
Columbus, 47202
Specializing in Scottie dog collectibles

Iowa
Addy, Geneva D.
P.O. Box 124
Winterset, 50273
515-462-3027
Specializing in Imperial Porcelain, Pink Pigs, and Strawberry Shortcake collectibles

De Lozier, Loretta
1101 Polk St.
Bedford, 50833
712-523-2289
Specializing in Lefton China

Devine, Joe
D&D Antique Mall
1411 3rd St.
Council Bluffs, 51503
712-232-5233 or 712-328-7305
Specializing in Royal Copley

Kansas
Anthony, Dorothy Malone
World of Bells Publications
802 S Eddy
Ft. Scott, 66701
Specializing in bell research and publication; author of *World of Bells*, #5 ($8.95); *Bell Tidings* ($9.95); *Lure of Bells* ($9.95); *Collectible Bells* ($10.95); *More Bell Lore* ($11.95); autographed copies available from the author; please enclose $2.00 for postage

Kentucky
Betty's Antiques
Betty Hornback
707 Sunrise Lane
Elizabethtown, 42701
502-765-2441
Specializing in Kentucky Derby and horse racing memorabilia

Books Are Everything
R.C. and Elwanda Holland
302 Martin Dr.
Richmond, 40475
606-624-9176
Specializing in vintage and collectible paperback books

Don Smith's National Geographic Magazine
3930 Rankin St.
Louisville, 40214
502-366-7504
Specializing in *National Geographic* magazines and related material, with price guide available for $12 postpaid; mail order only

Maryland
Losonsky, Joyce and Terry
7506 Summer Leave Lane
Columbia, 21046-2455
Their book, *The Illustrated Collector's Guide to McDonald's® Happy Meal®*

Boxes, Premiums, and Promotions©, is available from the authors for $6.95 plus $2 postage and handling

The Shoe Lady
Libby Yalom
P.O. Box 7146,
Adelphi, 20783
301-422-2026
Specializing in glass and china shoes and boots. Author of *Shoes of Glass* (with updated values) available from the author by sending $15.95 plus $2 for postage to above address

Welch, Randy
1100 Hambrooks Blvd.
Cambridge, 21613
410-228-5390
Specializing in walkers, ramp-walking figures, and tin wind-up toys

Massachusetts
Bruce, Scott; Mr. Cereal Box
P.O. Box 481
Cambridge, 02140
617-492-5004
Publisher of *Flake* magazine; author of *Complete Cereal Boxography*. Specializing in buying, selling, trading cereal boxes, cereal displays, and cereal premiums; free appraisals given

Engel, Michael
29 Groveland St.
Easthampton, 01027
413-527-8733
Specializing in political Americana prior to 1960

Jones, Gen
294 Park St.
Medford, 02155
617-395-8598
Specializing in Shirley Temple memorabilia

Michigan
Bruner, Mike
6980 Walnut Lake Rd.
W Bloomfield, 48323
313-661-2359
Specializing in telegraph and express memorabilia, insulators, exit globes, railroad lanterns, lightning rod balls, target balls, and porcelain advertising

Pickvet, Mark
P.O. Box 90404
Flint, 48509
Specializing in shot glasses (SASE required for information); author of *Shot Glasses: An American Tradition* and *The Definitive Guide to Shot Glasses;* available from Antique Publications, P.O. Box 553, Marietta, OH 45750

Minnesota
Mace, Shirley
Shadow Enterprises
Box 61
Cedar, 55011
612-434-6416
Author of *Encyclopedia of Silhouette Collectibles on Glass* (available from the author), and specializing in silhouette collectibles

Missouri
Aunt Sadie's Antiques
Don Komlos
P.O. Box 621
107 S Central
Eureka, 63025
314-938-9212
Dealer in general line of antiques and collectibles

Nebraska
Giles, Mark
P.O. Box 821
Ogallala, 69153-0821
308-284-4360
Specializing in English-made die-cast toy vehicles from the 1950s and 1960s

New Jersey
Cole, Lillian M.
14 Harmony School Rd.
Flemington, 08822
908-782-3198
Specializing in collecting pie birds, pie vents, pie funnels; also pie bird research

Dezso, Doug
864 Paterson Ave.
Maywood, 07607
Specializing in candy containers, nodders, Pep pins, Shafford cats, Tonka toys

Sigg, Walter
3-D Entertainment
P.O. Box 208
Smartswood, 07877
Specializing in View-Master and Tru-View

Silagyi, Carol and Richard
C.S. Antiques & Jewelry
P.O. Box 151
Wyckoff, 07430
201-934-6528 (leave message)
Specializing in figural ceramics: cookie jars, sprinklers, egg cups, banks, teapots, napkin holders, toothbrush holders, salt and pepper shakers, canisters, grease jars, etc.

Sparacio, George
P.O. Box 791
Malaga, 08328
609-694-4167
Specializing in match safes

Vintage Cocktail Shakers
Stephen Visakay
P.O. Box 1517
W Caldwell, 07007-1517
Specializing in vintage cocktail shakers; by mail and appointment only

New York
Arlene Lederman Antiques
150 Main St.
Nyack, 10960
914-358-8616
Specializing in vintage cocktail shakers, 18th through 20th-century antiques, American, European, furniture, glass, decorative accessories, and collectibles

Brenner, Howard S.
106 Woodgate Terrace
Rochester, 14625
716-482-3641
Author of *Comic Character Clocks and Watches* published by Books Americana. Specializing in character and comic timepieces

Doucet, Larry
Dick Tracy Collectibles
2351 Sultana Dr.
Yorktown Heights, 10598
Specializing in Dick Tracy memorabilia

Eisenstadt, Robert
P.O. Box 020767
Brooklyn, 11202-0017
718-625-3553 or FAX 718-522-1087
Specializing in gambling chips and other gambling-related items

Gerson, Roselyn
P.O. Box Letter S

419

Lynbrook, 11563
516-593-8746
Author of *Ladies' Compacts of the 19th & 20th Centuries,* a 240-page, 8½" x 11" hardcover book, available from the author for $34.95 plus $2 postage and handling

Luchsinger, Paul P.
104 Deer Run
Williamsville, 14221
716-689-6580.
Specializing in antique and unusual corkscrews

Margolin, Freddi
P.O. Box 5124P
Bay Shore, 11706
Author of *The Official Price Guide to Peanuts Collectibles.* Specializing in *Peanuts* collectibles

Sternfeld, Sue
90-60 Union Turnpike
Glendale, 11385
718-847-6883
Specializing in Pez and Soakies

North Carolina
Kaifer, Carole S.
P.O. Box 232
Bethania, 27010
Specializing in novelty animated and non-animated clocks

Retskin, Bill
P.O. Box 18481
Asheville, 28814
704-254-4487 or FAX 704-254-1066
Author of *The Matchcover Collector's Price Guide, 1st Edition* (available for $16.95 plus $3.25 shipping and handling), and editor of *The Front Striker Bulletin.* Specializing in matchcovers

Sayers, Rolland J.
Southwestern Antiques & Appraisals
P.O. Box 629
Brevard, 28712
Specializing in Boy Scout Collectibles.
Author of *Guide to Scouting Collectibles,* available from the author for $19.95 plus $3.50 postage

North Dakota
Farnsworth, Bryce L.
1334 14½ St. South
Fargo, 58103
Specializing in Rosemeade

Ohio
Bruegman, Bill
137 Casterton Ave.
Akron, 44303
216-836-0668 or FAX 216-869-8668
Author of *Toys of the Sixties; Aurora History and Price Guide*; and *Cartoon Friends of the Baby Boom Era.* Write for information about his magazine and mail order catalogs. Specializing in Aurora figure kits and toys from the baby boom era

Dutt, Gordy
Box 201
Sharon Center, 42274-0201
216-239-1657 or FAX 216-239-2991
Specializing in models other than Aurora, also Weirdos & Rat Finks

Kaduck, Margaret
P.O. Box 26076
Cleveland, 44126
216-333-2958
Specializing in watch fobs, postcards, and advertising items. For more information on her many books or monthly mail auctions call or send SASE.

Kerr, Ann
P.O. Box 437
Sidney, 45365
513-492-6369
Author of *Collector's Encyclopedia of Russel Wright Designs.* Specializing in work of Wright, interested in 20th-century decorative arts

Marsh, Thomas
914 Franklin Ave.
Youngstown, 44502
216-743-8600 or 800-845-7930
Publisher of *The Official Guide to Collecting Applied Color Label Soda Bottles.* Specializing in applied colored label soda bottles and related items

Trainer, Veronica
P.O. Box 40443
Cleveland, 44140
216-871-8584
Specializing in beaded and mesh purses

Oklahoma
Terri's Toys & Nostalgia
Terri Mardis-Ivers
1104 Shirlee

Ponca City, 74601
405-762-TOYS or 405-762-5174
No collect calls please. Specializing in buying and selling character collectibles, advertising items, Breyer and Hartland figures, lunch boxes, etc.

Oregon
Morris, Tom
Prize Publishers
P.O. Box 8307
Medford, 97504
503-779-3164
Author of *The Carnival Chalk Prize*, a pictorial price guide on carnival chalkware figures with brief histories and values for each

Pennsylvania
Foley, Edward
227 Union Ave.
Pittsburgh, 15202
412-761-0685
Specializing in advertising porcelain door push plates

Greenfield, Jeannie
310 Parker Rd.
Stoneboro, 16153
412-376-2584 (evenings)
Specializing in egg timers, cake toppers, and Jasco bells

Hain, Henry F., III
Antiques & Collectibles
2623 N Second St.
Harrisburg, 17110
717-238-0534
Lists available of items for sale

Homestead Collectibles
Art and Judy Turner
P.O. Box 173
Mill Hall, 17751
717-726-3597
Specializing in Jim Beam decanters and Ertl die-cast metal banks

Huegel, Joan L.
1002 W 25th St.
Erie, 16502
Specializing in bookmarks

McEntee, Phil
Where the Toys Are
45 W Pike St.
Canonsburg, 15317

412-745-4599
Open 7 days 10:30 a.m. - 5:00 p.m.
Specializing in antique and collectible toys and games

Posner, Judy
R.D. 1, Box 273
Effort, 18330
717-629-6583
Specializing in figural pottery, cookie jars, salt and pepper shakers, Black memorabilia, Disneyana; lists available

South Carolina
Roerig, Fred and Joyce
R.R. 2, Box 504
Walterboro, 29488
Specializing in cookie jars

Tennessee
McCarver, Patrick
5453 N Rolling Oaks Dr.
Memphis, 38119
901-682-6761
Author of *Gone With the Wind Collector's Guide*; buys and sells Gone With the Wind memorabilia

Texas
Levy, Noel
Last Chance Gas
P.O. Box 595699
Dallas, 75359-5699
214-987-3513
Specializing in oil company and official state highway road maps

Nossaman, Darlene
5419 Lake Charles
Waco, 76710
817-772-3969
Author of *Homer Laughlin China Identification Guide*. Available from the author for $8.50 plus $1.50 postage.

Norris, Kenn
P.O. Box 483
Sanderson, 79848-4830
915-345-2640
Specializing in schoolhouse collectibles, barbed wire literature and Li'l Abner

Pringle, Joyce
Chip & Dale Collectibles
3500 S Cooper
Arlington, 76015
817-467-7030
Specializing in Boyd art glass, Summit, and Moser

Woodard, Dannie
P.O. Box 1346
Weatherford, 76086
Author of *Hammered Aluminum, Hand Wrought Collectibles,* and publisher of *The Aluminist* newsletter

Virginia
Cranor, Rosalind
P.O. Box 859
Blacksburg, 24063
Author of *Elvis Collectibles, Second Edition* (Overmountain Press)

De Angelo, Larry
516 King Arthur Dr.
Virginia Beach, 23464
804-424-1691
Specializing in California Raisin collectibles

Giese, David
1410 Aquia Dr.
Stafford, 22554
703-569-5984
Specializing in character shaving mugs

Reynolds, Charlie
Reynolds Toys
2836 Monroe St.
Falls Church, 22042
703-533-1322
Specializing in banks, figural bottle openers, toys, etc.

Washington
Pollastro, Gary T.
4156 Beach Dr. SW
Seattle, 98116
Specializing in toy slot race cars from 1960s and 1970s

Thompson, Walt
Box 2541,
Yakima, 98907-2541
509-452-4016
Specializing in charge cards and credit-related items

Wisconsin
Helley, Phil
Old Kilbourn Antiques
629 Indiana Ave.
Wisconsin Dells, 53965
608-254-8659
Specializing in Cracker Jack items, radio premiums, toys (especially Japanese wind-ups), banks, and old Dells souvenir items marked Kilbourn

Phoneco
207 E Mill Rd.
P.O. Box 70
Galesville, 54630
Specializing in antique to modern telephones and parts

Rowe, Rick Jr.
Childhood, The Sequel
HC1, Box 788
Saxon, 54559
715-893-2257
Specializing in '50s and '60s toys

Canada
Warner, Ian
P.O. Box 93022
499 Main St.
S Brampton
Ontario L6Y 4V8
905-453-9074 or FAX 905-453-2931
Specializing in Wade pottery

CLUBS & NEWSLETTERS

ABWCS
American Barb Wire Collectors Society
John Mantz
1023 Baldwin Rd.
Bakersfield, CA 93304
805-397-9572
Bi-monthly newsletter, $10.00 per year, includes membership for entire family and discount buying privileges. Sample copy free. Inquiries invited

American Matchcover
Collecting Club
P.O. Box 18481
Asheville, NC 28814
704-254-4487 or FAX 704-254-1066

American Pottery Journal
P.O. Box 14255
Parkville, MO 64152
816-587-9179
Subscription: $30 for 12 isssues

American Quilter's Society
P.O. Box 3290
Paducah, KY 42002-3290
$15 annual membership includes 4 issues of *American Quilter* magazine

The Antique Trader Weekly
P.O. Box 1050
Dubuque, IA 52004
Subscription: $28 (52 issues) per year, sample: 50¢

The Bell Tower
P.O. Box 19443
Indianapolis, IN 46219
Official publication of the American Bell Association International, Inc.

Beyond the Rainbow
Collector's Exchange
P.O. Box 31672
St. Louis, MO 63131

Bookmark Collector
Joan L. Huegel
1002 W 25th St.
Erie, PA 16502
Quarterly newsletter, $5.50 per year ($6.50 in Canada), sample copy: $1 plus stamp or LSASE

Compact Collectors
P.O. Box Letter S
Lynbrook, NY 11563
516-593-8746

Cookie Jarrin'
The Cookie Jar Newsletter
R.R #2, Box 504
Walterboro, SC 29488
803-538-2487
Subscription: $19.95 per year

Cowboy Museum & Gallery
Jack Glover (author *Bobbed Wire VIII*)
209 Alamo Plaza
San Antonio, TX 78025
512-229-1257

Cutting Edge
Adrienne S. Escoe, Editor
P.O. Box 342
Los Alamitos CA 90720
Newsletter of glass knife collectors, published quarterly. Subscription: $2.50 per year, sample: 50¢

The Daze
Teri Steel, Editor/Publisher
Box 57
Otisville, MI 48463
313-631-4593.
The nation's market place for glass, china, and pottery

Docks, L.R. 'Les'
Shellac Shack
Box 691035
San Antonio, TX
78269-1035.
Send $2 for a 72-page catalog of thousands of 78 rpm records that Dock wants to buy, the prices he will pay, and shipping instructions

Doorstop Collectors of America
The Doorstopper Newsletter
Jeanne Bertoia
2413 Madison Ave.
Vineland, NJ 08630
Send $1 for sample copy of newsletter; $20 per year dues for club or $25 per year for family

Fiesta Collector's Quarterly
China Specialties Inc.
19238 Dorchester Circle
Strongville, OH 44136.
$12 (four issues) per year

FBOC (Figural Bottle Opener Collectors)
c/o Craig Diner
Box 251
Townsend, VT 05353
Please include SASE

FLAKE
The Breakfast Nostalgia Magazine
P.O. Box 481
Cambridge, MA 02140
617-492-5004
Bimonthly illustrated issue devoted to
one hot collecting area such as Disney,
etc.; plus letters, discoveries, new
releases, and ads; single issue: $4 ($6
foreign), annual: $20 ($28 foreign);
free 25-word ad with new subscription

Flashlight Collectors of America
Newsletter
Bill Utley
P.O. Box 3572
Downey, CA 90242
310-861-6247 (evenings)
$12 for four issues per year

The Front Striker Bulletin
Bill Retskin
P.O. Box 18481
Asheville, NC 28814
704-254-4487 or FAX 704-254-1066
Quarterly newsletter for matchcover
collectors, $17.50 per year for 1st
class mailing plus $2 for new member
registration

The Hall China Collector Club
Newsletter
P.O. Box 360488
Cleveland, OH 44136
Subscription: $9.00 per year for 4
issues

H.C. Fry Glass Society
P.O. Box 41
Beaver, PA 15009

Headquarters Quarterly
G.I. Joe Collectors
Joe Bodnarchuk
62 McKinley Ave.
Kenmore, NY 14217-2414

Holiday Happenings Collector Club
Susan Holland
6151 Main St.
Springfield, OR 97478
503-726-0740
Members share an interest in boxed
Christmas ornaments (especially in Hallmark Keepsakes). Dues are $10 a year
and a monthly newsletter is published

The Laughlin Eagle
c/o Richard G. Racheter
1270 63rd Terrace South
St. Petersburg, FL 33706
Subscription: $18.00 per year for 4
issues

Maytag Collectors Club
Nate Stoller
960 Reynolds Ave.
Ripon, CA 95366
209-599-5933

McDonald's Collecting Tips Newsletter
Meredith Williams
Box 633
Joplin, MO 64802
Send SASE for information

McDonald's Collector Club
Joyce and Terry Losonsky
7506 Summer Leave Lane
Columbia, MD 21046-2455
301-381-3358

Mystic Light of the Aladdin Knights
J.W. Courter
R.R. 1, Box 256
Simpson, IL 62985
Phone or FAX: 618-949-3884
Subscription: $20 per year for bi-
monthly issues with current buy-
sell-trade information; postpaid first
class

Our McCoy Matters
Kathy Lynch, Editor
P.O. Box 14255
Parkville, MO 64152-7255
816-587-9179 or FAX 816-746-6924
Bi-monthly publication includes classi-
fied ads. Subscription: $24.00 per year

Peanuts Collector Club
Andrea Podley
539 Sudden Valley
Bellingham, WA 98226
$16 a year or SASE for more details

Pen Fancier's Club
1169 Overcash Dr.
Dunedin, FL 34698
Publishes bimonthly magazine of pens and mechanical pencils. Subscription: $45 per year, sample: $6.00

Pie Birds Unlimited Newsletter
Lillian M. Cole
14 Harmony School Rd.
Flemington, NJ 08822
908-782-3198

Police Collector News
Mike Bondarenko, Publisher
R.R. 1, Box 14
Baldwin, WI 54002

Powder Puff, newsletter
P.O. Box Letter S
Lynbrook, NY 11563
Contains information covering all aspects of compact collecting, restoration, vintage ads, patents, history, and articles by members and prominent guest writers. A 'Seekers and Sellers' column and dealer listing is offered free to members

Roseville's of the Past
P.O. Box 681117
Orlando, FL 32868-1117
407-294-3980
Subscription: $19.95 per year

Scottie Sampler and fellowship group
Wee Scotts
P.O. Box 1512
Columbus, IN 47202

Shawnee Pottery Collectors' Club
Box 713
New Smyrna Beach, FL 32169
SASE required when requesting information

The Shirley Temple Collectors News
8811 Colonial Rd.
Brooklyn, NY 11209
718-745-7532 or FAX 718-921-6444
Dues: $20 per year; checks payable to Rita Dubas

Shirley Temple Collectors by the Sea
P.O. Box 6203
Oxnard, CA 93031
Dues: $14 per year

The Shot Glass Club of America
Mark Pickvet, Editor
P.O. Box 90404
Flint, MI 48509
$6 yearly membership includes a monthly 3-page newsletter

Smurf Collectors' Club
24 Cabot Road West, Dept. P
Massapequa, NY 11758
Specializing in Smurf memorabilia, 1957-1990

Snow Biz
c/o Nancy McMichael
P.O. Box 53262
Washington, D.C. 20009
Quarterly newsletter (subscription: $10 per year) and collector's club, annual meeting/swap meet

Tea Talk
419 N Larchmont Blvd. #225
Los Angeles, CA 90004
310-659-9650 or FAX 310-828-2444
Quarterly newsletter (subscription: $17.95 per year).

Transformer Club
Liane Elliot
6202 34th St. NW
Gig Harbor, WA 98335

View-Master Reel Collector
Roger Nazeley
4921 Castor Ave.
Philadelphia, 19124;
215-743-8999

Watcher (Swatch)
Collector Newsletter
P.O. Box 3280
Visalia, CA 93278-3280

The Willamette Valley Collectors Club
For further information contact:
S. Holland
6151 Main St.
Springfield, OR 97478
503-726-0740
Members share an interest in both old and newer collectibles of all kinds

World Airline Historical Society
3381 Apple Tree Lane
Erlanger, KY 41018
Membership: $15 per year

World's Fair Collectors' Society Inc.
P.O. Box 20806
Sarasota, FL 34238
813-923-2590

The Yellow Brick Road
Fantasy Museum & Gift Shop
Rt. 49 & Yellow Brick Rd.
Chesterton, IN 46304
219-926-7048

INDEX

430

Schroeder's
ANTIQUES
Price Guide

. . . is the #1 best-selling
antiques & collectibles value guide on the market today,
and here's why . . .

Schroeder's
ANTIQUES
Price Guide

OUR #1 BEST SELLER!

Identification & Values Of Over 50,000 Antiques & Collectibles

8½ X 11 • 608 Pgs. • PB • $12.95

• *More than 300 advisors, well-known dealers, and top-notch collectors work together with our editors to bring you accurate information regarding pricing and identification.*

• *More than 45,000 items in almost 500 categories are listed along with hundreds of sharp original photos that illustrate not only the rare and unusual, but the common, popular collectibles as well.*

• *Each large close-up shot shows important details clearly. Every subject is represented with histories and background information, a feature not found in any of our competitors' publications.*

• *Our editors keep abreast of newly-developing trends, often adding several new categories a year as the need arises.*

If it merits the interest of today's collector, you'll find it in *Schroeder's*. And you can feel confident that the information we publish is up to date and accurate. Our advisors thoroughly check each category to spot inconsistencies, listings that may not be entirely reflective of market dealings, and lines too vague to be of merit. Only the best of the lot remains for publication.

Without doubt, you'll find
SCHROEDER'S ANTIQUES
PRICE GUIDE
the only one to buy for
reliable information and values.

COLLECTOR BOOKS
A Division of Schroeder Publishing Co., Inc.